A PRACTICAL APPROACH TO

PLANNING LAW

A PRACTICAL APPROACH TO PLANNING LAW

NINTH EDITION

Victor Moore
LLM, BARRISTER
Professor of Law Emeritus,
University of Reading

OXFORD
UNIVERSITY PRESS

Great Clarendon Street, Oxford OX2 6DP

Oxford University Press is a department of the University of Oxford.
It furthers the University's objective of excellence in research, scholarship,
and education by publishing worldwide in

Oxford New York

Auckland Cape Town Dar es Salaam Hong Kong Karachi
Kuala Lumpur Madrid Melbourne Mexico City Nairobi
New Delhi Shanghai Taipei Toronto

With offices in

Argentina Austria Brazil Chile Czech Republic France Greece
Guatemala Hungary Italy Japan Poland Portugal Singapore
South Korea Switzerland Thailand Turkey Ukraine Vietnam

Published in the United States
by Oxford University Press Inc., New York

Ninth edition published 2005

British Library Cataloguing in Publication Data
Data available

Library of Congress Cataloging in Publication Data
Data available

ISBN 0-19-927279-4

3 5 7 9 10 8 6 4

Typeset by RefineCatch Limited, Bungay, Suffolk
Printed in Great Britain by
on acid-free paper by
Ashford Colour Press Ltd, Gosport, Hants.

The Town Clerk's Views

'In a few years this country will be looking
As uniform and tasty as its cooking.
Hamlets which fail to pass the planners' test
Will be demolished. We'll rebuild the rest
To look like Welwyn mixed with Middle West.
All fields we'll turn to sports grounds, lit at night
From concrete standards by fluorescent light:
And over all the land, instead of trees,
Clean poles and wire will whisper in the breeze.
We'll keep one ancient village just to show
What England once was when the times were slow—
Broadway for me. But here I know I must
Ask the opinion of our National Trust.
And ev'ry old cathedral that you enter
By then will be an Area Culture Centre.
Instead of nonsense about Death and Heaven
Lectures on civic duty will be given;
Eurhythmic classes dancing round the spire,
And economics courses in the choir.
So don't encourage tourists. Stay your hand
Until we've really got the country plann'd.'

John Betjeman, 1948*

PREFACE

The Planning and Compulsory Purchase Act 2004 is arguably the most significant planning legislation to have been introduced since the present system of planning control was created by the Town and Country Planning Act 1947. Without doubt the death sentence now given by the Act to the current development plan system and its replacement by Regional Spatial Strategies and Development Plan Documents, represents a sea-change in the way in which decisions about land use are to be determined. Henceforth, local planning authorities will be denied the opportunity they may have once had to avoid complying with central government targets, particularly those being directed at new house building in their area.

These changes will require that all those engaged in land use matters will need to become familiar with new terms and new concepts. So out go SPs, LPs, and UDPs. In comes a new development plan system aptly described by one Parliamentary critique (Baroness Hanham) using the Government's own acronyms, as follows: 'the LDF shall be set out in an LDS, comprising LDDs, some of which are DPDs, namely the CS, AAPs and a proposals map. Other documents will be LDDs but not DPDs, namely SPDs, and the SCI, although the SCI will be treated as a DPD—sometimes. These documents will require SA and may need SEA. The DP will be the DPDs plus the RSS or SDS.'

New and developing concepts introduced by the Act include 'community involvement' and 'sustainable development'. A sceptic in this area of law may well consider that the former means no more than a commitment to consult at every successive stage of the development process until planning permission has inevitably been granted. And as for sustainable development, its ephemeral nature suggests that like the term 'brotherhood of man' it will come to mean all things to all people. Why else can examples not have been given of development which would not be permitted now had the concept of sustainable development been introduced into the system earlier.

Lastly, a warning and an apology. Apart from the provisions dealing with the development plan system, many of the other changes made by the new Act have, at the time of writing, not yet been fully implemented. Although I have endeavoured to flag those areas affected, readers should take note.

The work of integrating the provisions of the new Act into this edition have proved to be the proverbial nightmare. I have tried to interpret accurately the complexity of the new provisions with the continuous stream of material published by the Office of the Deputy Prime Minister during the passage of the Bill and subsequently. But, as has been said to have been a failure of the Greek poet Homer, I too may have nodded.

Victor Moore
February 2005

PREFACE TO THE FIRST EDITION

Given the large number of excellent books available on the subject of planning law, some excuse is obviously needed to justify this new addition to existing literature.

The invitation to write a book of no more than 350 pages, including appendices, on the subject and without the use of footnotes, proved to be a challenge impossible to resist.

In the pages that follow therefore, I have tried to prune what is an extremely difficult and complex subject down to its basic principles. I have attempted to describe planning law and its administration in both simple and practical terms, and resisted the temptation to stray too far into technical details or to refer to judicial decisions which have made occasional departures from those basic principles.

Two aspects, however, must be drawn to the reader's attention. First, limitations of space has meant this book does not deal with the law and practice in Scotland, which, although substantially similar to that for England and Wales, has a number of significant differences. Secondly, the book has anticipated the bringing into force of the changes made to the law by the planning provisions of the Housing and Planning Act 1986. It is expected, however, that the provisions of the Act not yet in force will be brought into force by commencement order before the year has run its course.

Lastly, after years of promise, a new General Development Order is expected to be promulgated shortly. But as anyone interested in the use and development of land will know, if a publication in this subject were to await the translation of all proposals into reality, no books on planning law would be published at all.

October 1987

CONTENTS — SUMMARY

CONTENTS

TABLE OF CASES

NOOKS and CORNERS

POOR old Liverpool is getting ready to be European City of Culture next year – a Eurotitle second only to the Olympic Games for bringing cultural, economic and social catastrophe to any city.

Liverpool city council has used the accolade to encourage an orgy of commercial redevelopment (*Eyes passim ad nauseam*) which has little or nothing to do with the title's intended purpose. And, like Ken Livingstone, this once left-wing city thinks high buildings are cool (for the full horror of what is proposed see www.skyscrapercity.com/showthread.php?t=218577). The principal development, originally called the Paradise Project but now given the catchy title of "Liverpool One", is a £920m scheme by Grosvenor Estates under construction on the land between the Crown Court and Lord Street and the Albert Dock. This is claimed as Europe's biggest retail scheme. There will also be hotels and luxury flats in the largest gated community in Europe. Lucky Liverpool.

What used to stand here was the Neo-Classical Custom House designed by John Foster. This noble landmark was gutted in the Second World War and subsequently demolished to relieve unemployment – did it not occur to the bone-headed authorities that restoration might have relieved unemployment? Never mind: that is past history. On its site was laid out Chavasse Park. And now, between a new and improved and smaller five-acre park and the Strand, the road by the docks and Pierhead, a 17-storey block with 326 "high specification apartments" is rising. Needless to say, a fashionable foreign firm has been wheeled in to design it – that of Cesar Pelli, the Argentinian-American commercial architect who gave London the Canary Wharf tower. Mr Pelli has designed a "dramatic raking corner feature" and his team of architects "say they have designed an intricate, iconic, curved and glazed building, aimed to be sympathetic to its place among Liverpool's famous waterfront buildings". Well, they would, wouldn't they?

All this is depressing enough, but its name, "One Park West", is a vapid American-style appellation which tells us more than we need to know about Grosvenor Estates and Liverpool. Grosvenor chose the name because the building will overlook Chavasse Park – so why not call it "One Chavasse Park" or "the Chavasse Tower", or whatever? This matters, as Chavasse Park was named after Noel Chavasse, who was not just a local hero but one of the most admirable heroes of the First World War. The son of Bishop Chavasse of Liverpool, Captain Chavasse was in the Royal Army Medical Corps and won the VC and Bar, not for fighting but for tending and rescuing the wounded on the battlefield under fire and regardless of his own safety. He died of his wounds in 1917. If Liverpool, in its Year of Culture, cannot continue to honour Chavasse then it should be ashamed.

AS IT happens, Bishop Chavasse was the man who got the project for a cathedral in Liverpool going, which resulted in Sir Giles Gilbert Scott's stupendous masterpiece. Naturally, this last great Gothic Revival building has to be brought into the 21st century and revamped by 2008 – at a cost of £3m – to attract more visitors. One initiative is "the Great Space", a film theatre providing an interactive and exciting display about the cathedral. Even more essential in a modern religious building is somewhere to eat, and a Mezzanine Café Bar has been created in the north-west transept above the bookshop, on a new steel and glass mezzanine floor designed by the local architects Brock Carmichael, with Mather & Co. as consultants.

Oh dear: it is all a bit reminiscent of the crass new restaurant in the Victoria & Albert Museum (Eye 1178). Liverpool Cathedral now proudly advertises "our newly opened contemporary 'lite bite' café bar where you can meet and eat, and enjoy a brand new view of the cathedral". And, what's more, both visitors and worshippers in the body of the cathedral can enjoy a brand new view of the exciting bright Café Bar. They can also enjoy its noise. Diners on the mezzanine merely have to look over the glass parapet to enjoy the view, for the tall space overhead in the transept flows (with architects space always "flows") into the Great Space beyond. The result is that anyone trying to hear Evensong, say, or pray can have their thoughts concentrated by the cheerful secular sound of rattling cutlery, plates being dropped, diners chatting and children screaming, which echoes all around Sir Giles's great church. It is the same fatuous mistake that that supreme genius Milord Foster made in the new Law Library in Cambridge (Eye 888), forgetting that, unless space is enclosed, sound travels. And modern cafés with their bright, clean hard surfaces are very noisy indeed.

So much for the Great Space being a sacred space. Of course, cathedrals and churches need an income for maintenance and repairs, especially in the absence of serious state funding and with Tessa Jowell squeezing English Heritage to death. Some initiatives, however, seem to defeat their aim by ruining the building or betraying its purpose. But in the 21st century perhaps it is a mistake to think that cathedrals are for religion. They are for the tourist industry and making money, just as – in Liverpool – the European City of Culture accolade is really for commercial development and making money.

'Piloti'

●THE THINGS THEY SAY: "Frankly, there is not much ideological difference to the way Conservative Westminster is run from Labour Newham." – Sir Simon Milton, leader of Westminster city council, *Guardian*, 7 March.

STAY AWHILE

TORY Bedfordshire county councillors are at each others' throats over the toxic "Citizen Service Partnership" affair (*Eye* 1179), which has now claimed its first casualty.

Cllr David Lawrence's mistake was to embarrass deputy leader Richard Stay, who chaired BCC's aptly-named "CSP oversight committee" and should have spotted problems with the multi-million IT project that put internet access in, er, a few phone boxes in Dunstable.

Stay's predecessor as deputy – CSP portfolio-holder Paul "Where's" Walley – has vanished while Knacker looks into £8m in accounting "anomalies".

The *Eye* has seen a series of emails exchanged between BCC's near-hysterical Tory councillors. In one Lawrence writes to Stay: "As the portfolio holder the buck stopped with you. I would expect therefore in due course a full statement from you." Stay huffily replies: "Are you expecting me to resign?" prompting a third councillor, Stephen Male, to interject in the style of one of Harry Enfield's Scousers that everyone should "CALM DOWN!"

Questioned about the emails, Stay declared: "I will not be resigning. I sat on the CSP joint committee but the very nature of fraud is that you don't know it is happening…" Pause. "If any fraud occurred, that is."

The day after the email exchange, Cllr Lawrence was told he would be deselected as candidate for the Mid Beds district council division he has served since 2003. Stay, er, stays. For now.

●ONE of the most hotly contested nominations in the annual Rotten Boroughs awards is that of "Tory Bigot of the Year". Staking an early claim for 2007 is 79-year-old Cllr Ted Pateman, who has had to resign from South Cambridgeshire district council after breezily informing colleagues last month that "there are all sorts of wogs here – I don't differentiate between them but treat them all as if they were English". Cllr Pateman explained that he was not being racist. In fact his remark was meant to show what a tolerant sort of place South Cambs is.

KELLY ZEROES

THE government's target of getting all "social" housing up to its own "decent homes standard" by 2010 looks remoter by the day.

At present councils whose tenants vote in favour of keeping the local authority as their landlord are not eligible for the shedloads of money available to those who opt for privatisation.

Despite this, in recent weeks tenants in Brighton, Taunton Deane and Gravesham have all overwhelmingly voted No to having their homes transferred. Crawley council called off its ballot and decided to retain its housing stock after the strength of opposition became clear. In total 124 councils have opted to retain ownership of their housing stock and are calling on the government to make the "fourth option" – of making funds equally available to those who vote against privatisation – a reality.

Local government secretary Ruth Kelly, who patronises council tenants as "in need of help" and "vulnerable", has announced a scheme that would allow tenants to buy as little as a 10 per cent stake in the value of their homes. The current minimum stake under shared-ownership rules is 25 percent. Kelly failed to mention that tenants who opt for 10 per cent "ownership" would be responsible for, er, 100 per cent of any repair bills.

This would help the government achieve its "decent homes" target without having to cough up much more for improvements, because the homes of those buying 10 per cent stakes will be taken out of the reckoning. Brilliant!

PS: Under the existing council housing finance system more than £1.5bn is siphoned out of tenants' rents each year by government to spend as it pleases. Since 1990 a total of £24bn has been trousered in this manner, more than enough to bring the entire stock of council properties up to the decent homes standard – twice.

● IT'S GOOD to see that the Lib-Dem party remains a broad church under the Emperor Ming. In Liverpool it has welcomed as a council candidate one Phil Moffat, who not long ago was acting as unofficial mainland spokesman for Ian Paisley's Democratic Unionist Party – just the ticket for a city which has seen its share of sectarian tension over the years. Meanwhile in Lewes, Sussex, Lib-Dem district councillor Marina Pepper, former Page Three girl, white witch and currently the *New Statesman*'s agony aunt, has been giving a local freesheet her views on global warming. It is a Very Bad Thing, concludes Marina, although it does have one advantage. In the unseasonably mild weather, she writes, "I wear no underwear beneath my short cotton skirt." Steady, Ming, steady!

"We've got lots of opportunities in caring for 12-year-olds"

LEVELLING THE PLAYING FIELDS

THE sale of school playing fields may be

TABLE OF STATUTES

Paragraph references in **bold** indicate that the text is reproduced in full

EC Secondary Legislation

European Convention of Human Rights and Fundamental Freedoms (ECHR)

TABLE OF RULES AND REGULATIONS

Paragraph references in **bold** indicate that the text is reproduced in full

1

HISTORICAL INTRODUCTION

Before there existed any public control over the use and development of land, landowners 1.01
were free to use their land in any way they wished, subject only to any limitations in the grant under which they held it and to obligations placed upon them at common law. In essence, therefore, provided an owner acted within the limitation of his estate or interest and committed no nuisance or trespass against his neighbour's property, he was free to use [illegible] for the purpose for which it was economically best suited. Today, most societies [illegible] this freedom be restricted for the public good, but also that the use to [illegible] determined by the long-term interests of the community as a [illegible] uence of the incidence and spread of individual land [illegible]

[illegible] of the 19th century, public health legislation in Great Britain 1.02
[illegible] he worst effects of insanitary housing conditions, it was not [illegible] vas made to deal with more general land use problems such as [illegible] ible uses or the lack of amenity land. The Housing, Town Plan- [illegible] narily concerned with housing in that it gave wide powers to local [illegible] ouses and to clear existing substandard housing. Section 54 of that [illegible] authorities the power to prepare schemes:

> [illegible] nich is in course of development or appears likely to be used for building [illegible] neral object of securing proper sanitary conditions, amenity, and conveni- [illegible] with the laying out and use of the land, and of any neighbouring lands.

H[illegible] ning of planning law. Yet from the start it was plagued by a number of p[illegible] which have recurred and remained unresolved to the present day.

Se[illegible] 1909 Act was discretionary in that local authorities were not required to 1.03
pre[illegible] s, merely empowered to do so. The Housing, Town Planning etc. Act 1919, atte[illegible] emedy that defect by requiring the council of every borough or urban district with [illegible] tion of over 20,000 to prepare schemes for land in the course of development or lik[illegible] e used for building purposes. Despite the fact that in 1919 Parliament set a time limit f[illegible] preparation of these schemes, the time-limit had to be extended on a number of occasio[illegible] as authorities found that the formidable task of preparing schemes could not be accomp[illegible] shed within the time set for doing so.

Although in 1919 the time taken to prepare schemes may have been exacerbated by the 1.04
shortage of people possessing the necessary technical skills, the problem of delay has never been satisfactorily resolved. Under the Town and Country Planning Act 1947, local planning authorities were required within three years to submit to the Minister a development plan

for their area. Most authorities found they were unable to do so within that period. Then, under the Town and Country Planning Act 1968, although no time-limit was laid down for the submission of structure plans to the Secretary of State, it took some 14 years before the last structure plan was submitted to him for approval. Similar delay problems have applied with regard to the preparation, alteration or replacement of all subsequent types of development plan.

1.05 Unfortunately for the planning process, development pressures often build up faster than planners can plan. Hence the more outdated a development plan may be, the less relevant it becomes to making decisions about the use and development of land and the greater the pressure on authorities to rely on other material considerations than the development plan and to make land use decisions on an individual and *ad hoc* basis.

1.06 Another problem with the 1909 Act was that before a scheme could be implemented it had to be approved by central government and an opportunity given to people to object to its provisions. The difficulty in this area is that democracy and speed do not always go hand in hand, and if the public are to be given the right to influence the content of the scheme or plan, the preparation and approval or adoption process is by that much delayed. Later legislation has perpetuated the right of the public to object to proposals in any development plan submitted for approval or adoption. Under the Town and Country Planning Act 1947, the Minister was required to consider any objections made to a development plan submitted to him for approval. Under the Town and Country Planning Act 1968, he was required to consider any objections made to a structure plan submitted to him for approval. Under the Town and Country Planning Act 1990 every local planning authority was required to consider objections made to the content of any development plan prepared by the authority. Now, under the Planning and Compensation Act 2004, the local planning authority must consider any objections made to a development plan document.

1.07 The third problem to arise under early planning legislation came to be known as the compensation/betterment problem. Planning control can affect property values for better or worse, and the problem that needed to be solved was how to treat those whose land had either decreased in value (the compensation aspect), or increased in value (the betterment aspect) due to a scheme. The early legislation allowed local authorities to recover from owners 50 per cent of any increase in the value of land due to the making of a scheme. At the same time, it gave owners a right to receive compensation from the authority for any decrease in the value of their land. Under the Town and Country Planning Act 1932, the amount of betterment which a local authority could recover from owners was increased from 50 to 75 per cent. In addition, however, the owner was given the right to require payment to be deferred until he had actually realised the increased value through the sale of the land or its development. If this did not happen within five years as regards land zoned for industrial or commercial purposes, or 14 years in any other case, no betterment at all was payable.

1.08 The operation of these provisions proved disastrous. A local authority wishing to control the development of land in their area might find themselves faced with a heavy liability for compensation which they would have difficulty in meeting unless they were also prepared to allow some development in the area. On the other hand, a local authority not wishing to restrict development in their area might hope to obtain a considerable sum by way of betterment from owners, without any liability to pay compensation. As it turned out, however, the collection of betterment proved to be almost impossible, mainly because of the lapsing provisions previously referred to.

The failure to deal satisfactorily with the financial consequences of land use planning meant the failure of land use planning itself. It has been estimated that after more than a quarter of a century of effort the number of schemes which were prepared and approved under the 1909 Act and subsequent legislation could be counted on the fingers of one hand! **1.09**

The advent of the Second World War presented an opportunity to consider whether a more effective system for the control of land use could be found. The opportunity had been taken to set up a number of bodies charged with investigating particular facets of the land-use system. The three main reports produced by this exercise were the Barlow Report, the Scott Report and the Uthwatt Report. **1.10**

The Barlow Report This was the report of the Royal Commission on the Distribution of Industrial Population (Cmd 6153). Set up in 1937, it enquired into the causes of the geographical distribution of the industrial population, and considered the social, economic and strategic disadvantages resulting from the concentration of industry and industrial population in cities and regions and to consider what methods should be taken to counteract them. The report advocated the dispersal of industry from congested urban areas and the progressive redevelopment of those areas wherever necessary.

The Scott Report This was a report of a Committee on Land Utilisation in Rural Areas (Cmd 6378). The Committee was asked to consider the problems of piecemeal development of agricultural land and the unrestricted development of the coastline.

The Uthwatt Report This report, perhaps the most influential of the three, was by the Expert Committee on Compensation and Betterment (Cmd 6386) under the chairmanship of Uthwatt J. The main feature of this report was an examination of the problem of compensation and betterment. In so doing it identified the twin concepts of shifting value and floating value.

The idea behind the concept of shifting value was that planning control did not reduce the total sum of land values, but merely redistributes them by increasing the value of some land whilst decreasing the value of other land. Because of this it was possible for one authority to find themselves paying compensation for restrictions on development, whilst a neighbouring authority could recover betterment because of those same restrictions. The lesson to be learnt, therefore, was that financial arrangements to deal with the compensation/betterment problem could not be dealt with at a local level. **1.11**

The idea behind the concept of floating values was that potential value is by nature speculative. Development may take place on parcel A or parcel B. The prospect floats over both parcels. The value of any parcel of land is obtained by estimating whether the development is likely to take place on one parcel of land or on some other. Where planning restrictions are imposed on land and owners are given the right to claim compensation for any loss so caused, they will tend to assume that but for those restrictions the floating value would settle on their land, rather than on the land of their neighbours. The result was that owners claiming compensation would tend to overestimate the prospect of the development taking **1.12** place on their land, so that in total, all claims for compensation over an area could far exceed the actual loss of development value suffered.

Town and Country Planning Act 1947 All three reports contributed significantly to the system of land use control established by the Town and Country Planning Act 1947. The Act came into effect on 1 July 1948. The essential features of that Act were as follows:

(a) It created local planning authorities and required each authority to prepare a development plan for their area indicating the manner in which they proposed land in their area should be used, whether by development or otherwise, and the ways by which any such development should be carried out.
(b) All land was made subject to planning control, not just land within a scheme prepared by the authority. As a result, apart from minor development, any person wishing to develop land had first to obtain express planning permission to do so from the local planning authority. In deciding whether to grant or refuse permission, the authority were to be guided by the provisions of the development plan.
(c) Wide powers were given to local planning authorities to deal with development carried out without planning permission.
(d) Wide powers were given to local planning authorities to secure the preservation of trees and buildings of architectural or historic interest and to control the display of advertisements.
(e) If a person was granted planning permission for any development falling outside the existing use of his land, he had to pay a development charge to the State equal to the value of that permission.
(f) If a person was refused planning permission for such development, no compensation was paid for that refusal.
(g) To compensate landowners affected by (e) and (f) above who may perhaps have purchased their land before the Act came into force at a price reflecting its value for development, the Act set up a fund of £300 million. Any owner who could prove that his land had depreciated as a result of the 1947 Act could make a claim against the fund for the difference between the value of the land for existing use purposes and its value on the assumption the Act had not been passed. Payments from the fund were to be made in 1954.

1.13 It will be seen that the financial provisions of the Act ((e) to (g) above), effectively dealt with the problems examined by the Uthwatt Committee. The sum of £300 million was an estimate of the total development value of land nationally, and claims against the fund were, if necessary, to be scaled down, so that in total they added up to that sum. Furthermore, since the fund was administered by central government, local planning authorities were now free to make planning decisions without any regard to the economic or financial consequences of so doing.

1.14 Most of the financial provisions of the 1947 Act have now been dismantled. In particular, the Town and Country Planning Act 1953 abolished the development charge. Although further attempts were made by the Land Commission Act 1967 and the Development Land Tax Act 1976 to recoup for the community part of the development value of land which would otherwise accrue to the owner, no special tax on development value now exists, although an owner may be liable to pay capital gains tax on such value if he realises a capital gain on the disposal of his land. One further point should be noted. Today, developers may be required to contribute to some of the external costs borne by the community as a result of their proposals, through the use of what is known as planning obligations or contributions.

It will be remembered that the 1947 legislation contained no provision for the payment of compensation to a landowner refused planning permission for development which fell outside the existing use of his land. When the development charge was abolished in 1953, it was decided to maintain that rule, so that in general since the 1947 Act no compensation has been payable for any loss incurred by the refusal of planning permission for such development, or indeed for the grant of planning permission made subject to conditions. **1.15**

This general rule, however, was subject to one exception. An owner could claim compensation if he or his successors in title could show the existence of a claim made under the 1947 Act against the £300 million fund in respect of loss suffered as a result of the Act. In such rare cases, the compensation was limited to the amount of the claim or the amount of the loss due to the planning decision, whichever was less. Even this exception however, has now been abolished. The Planning and Compensation Act 1991 repealed almost all existing statutory provisions providing for the payment of compensation for adverse planning decisions. **1.16**

With regard to the non-financial provisions of the 1947 Act however, the elements of the system established at that time have withstood the passage of time. Although numerous changes and improvements have been made to the statutory provisions since that date, the basic scheme of the legislation remains the same. **1.17**

Changes since 1947 Among the many changes made since 1947 mention might be made of:

(a) A number of major reorganisations of local government, which have led to changes in the number and size of local planning authorities and their respective functions.
(b) Changes to the development of the plan system.
(c) The progressive strengthening of the provisions for enforcing planning control, and of the provisions relating to the preservation of buildings of special architectural or historic interest.
(d) The introduction of environmental impact considerations in making decisions about land use.

Yet despite the continued reverence of the law to the basic elements of the system as introduced in 1947, the law has become not only more complex, but also considerably more disparate in its application. Today, quite apart from the normal technicalities of the law and its procedures, a landowner wishing to develop his land may have additionally to consider such matters as: whether his land is within a simplified planning zone, a national park, an area of outstanding natural beauty, a conservation area or a site of special scientific interest; what plan or plans constitute the development plan for the area; whether the development proposed is permitted under the Town and Country Planning (General Permitted Development) Order 1995 or some special development order; whether the proposed development is subject to environmental impact assessment; and whether there is a building on the land of special, architectural or historic interest, or a tree protected by a tree preservation order; or the land contains a scheduled monument.

The Town and Country Planning Act 1990 Town and country planning legislation had been consolidated previously in the Town and Country Planning Act 1962, and again in the Town and Country Planning Act 1971. Since that date, planning legislation has been amended frequently. So much so, that in 1989, the Government decided to ask the Law Commission to consolidate the legislation yet again. It was decided that the consolidation should involve four separate Acts of Parliament. Consolidation of legislation does not involve changes in the substance of the law. In this case, however, the opportunity was taken to correct a number of anomalies and inconsistencies of a technical nature. Subject to these changes however, the Acts restated existing law. The four Acts, which all received the Royal Assent on 24 May 1990, were:

Town and Country Planning Act 1990
This Act consolidated certain enactments relating to town and country planning but excludes special controls in respect of buildings and areas of special architectural and historic interest and in respect of hazardous substances.

Planning (Listed Buildings and Conservation Areas) Act 1990
This Act consolidated certain enactments in relation to special controls in respect of buildings and areas of special architectural or historic interest.

Planning (Hazardous Substances) Act 1990
This Act consolidated certain enactments relating to special controls in respect of hazardous substances.

Planning (Consequential Provisions) Act 1990
This Act made provision for repeals, consequential amendments, transitional and transitory matters and savings in connection with the consolidation of enactments in the Acts mentioned above, including provisions to give effect to the recommendations of the Law Commission. This Act was largely concerned with ensuring continuity. Thus, for example, it provided that any document made, served or issued after the coming into force of the consolidating Acts which refer to an enactment repealed by the consolidation was to be construed as referring to the corresponding provision of the relevant new Act. In addition, for the most part, statutory instruments made under the old legislation were to continue to have effect as though made under the new consolidating Acts.

1.18 With the exception of the Planning (Hazardous Substances) Act 1990, most of the provisions of the Acts came into force on 24 August 1990. Hereinafter, the main Act, the Town and Country Planning Act 1990, will be referred to simply as 'the 1990 Act'.

The Planning and Compensation Act 1991 Because it is not possible to make substantial changes to legislation in a consolidation Act, the need to make a number of important changes to planning law had to await separate amending legislation. The Planning and Compensation Act 1991 received the Royal Assent on 25 July 1991. As its name implies, it amended the law relating to both planning and to compulsory acquisition procedure and to the assessment of compensation for the compulsory acquisition of land. With regard to planning, the Act made important changes to the law relating to development plans, the definition of development, appeals, enforcement notices, listed buildings and other specific matters. Those changes have been incorporated in the text that follows.

The Environment Act 1995 This Act contained provisions for the establishment of an Environment Agency for England and Wales and a Scottish Environment Protection Agency, and other measures to improve the protection and management of the environment. In the land use field, the Act made provision for the existing National Park Boards to be wound up and replaced by new National Park Authorities, who would be the local planning authority for the area of the Park. In addition, the Act provided for an initial review and updating of mineral planning permissions granted in the 1950s, 60s and 70s, and the periodic review of all mineral planning permissions thereafter.

The Scotland Act 1998 and the Government of Wales Act 1998 These Acts devolved many of the planning powers exercised by the Parliament of the United Kingdom on a national basis to the Scottish Parliament and to the National Assembly for Wales.

The Human Rights Act 1990 This Act, which came into force on 2 October 2000, incorporated into domestic law the provisions of the European Convention on Human Rights. Its provisions are dealt with in Chapter 20.

The Greater London Authority Act 1999 This Act established a Mayor and a Greater London Assembly for the Greater London Area, and contained a power to enable the Mayor to direct local planning authorities to refuse planning permission in specified cases where on strategic grounds it was necessary to do so.

The Planning and Compulsory Purchase Act 2004 This Act received the Royal Assent on 13 May 2004. Its provisions are based on a consultation paper issued by the Government in December 2001 entitled 'Delivering a Fundamental Change'. The Act introduces important changes to many areas of planning law, including changes both to the development plan system and to planning control. Changes to the development plan system include the creation of spatial development strategies and local development schemes to replace existing development plans. Changes to the planning control system embrace the introduction of 'business zones' wherein planning permission would not need to be sought for certain kinds of development; the abolition of crown immunity; changes in the basis of planning obligations; the ending of the practice of twin tracking; requiring development to be commenced within three years; a strengthening of enforcement provisions end the provision of providing a new process for the handling of decisions on major infrastructure projects.

Many of the provisions of the Act are "free-standing", in the sense that they contain provisions additional to those found in the Town and Country Planning Act 1990. Other provisions of the 2004 Act however, operate by repealing or amending, or by the substitution of existing provisions in the 1990 Act. **1.19**

The Act is being brought into effect by commencement orders, with contemporaneous changes being made to related rules and regulations. It is likely, however, to be protracted, that the provisions, on Crown Immunity will not be fully implemented until the end of 2005, and the regulations on planning contributions not until the end of 2006. **1.20**

2

PLANNING ORGANISATION

From its very beginning in 1909, planning legislation has given to local authorities direct power and responsibility for carrying on the day-to-day administration of land use control. Central Government's role in the administration of planning began as, and has since remained, the supervision and co-ordination of the way in which those powers and responsibilities are exercised. **2.01**

There are, of course, many bodies with a role to play in the field of town and country planning. Basically, however, planning organisation has two main tiers, a Central Government tier under the mantle of the Secretary of State, and a Local Government tier in the shape of local planning authorities. **2.02**

A. THE SECRETARIES OF STATE

Nowhere in the law is there to be found any general statement of the responsibilities of the Secretary of State. The duty imposed on a predecessor, the Minister of Town and Country Planning, which was set out in the Minister of Town and Country Planning Act 1943, 'of securing consistency and continuity in the framing and execution of a national policy with **2.03** respect to the use and development of land throughout England and Wales', was repealed in 1970. One should shed no tears. The duty imposed was too vague and too wide to be legally enforceable. It did represent, however, a statement of the political responsibility of that Minister to Parliament; and in that same sense, the statement, though now unwritten, describes the political responsibility of the Secretary of State.

2.04 Under our governmental system there is more than one Secretary of State. Yet in law his office is one and indivisible, so that any Secretary of State may exercise the powers of any other. The functions of any particular Secretary of State, however, are normally allocated to him by Order in Council made under the Ministers of the Crown Act 1975. In this way, in the field of planning law, the First Secretary of State, exercises powers in relation to England. This is an office held by the Deputy Prime Minister. In Scotland, the powers were until 1999 exercised by the Secretary of State for Scotland and in Wales, by the Secretary of State for Wales.

2.05 The position with regard to both Scotland and Wales changed dramatically following the passing of the Scotland Act 1998 and the Government of Wales Act 1998. Under the Scotland Act 1998, Scotland now has a separate Parliament and its own executive. Under the Act the Scottish Parliament is given power to make primary legislation within its own area of competence, an area which includes both town and country planning and the environment. The Scottish Parliament is also able to decide policy so that, over a period of time, Scottish planning law and practice may diverge substantially from the traditionally unified approach which has characterised United Kingdom planning law since its inception.

2.06 The position in Wales is somewhat different. The Government of Wales Act 1998 established not a Welsh Parliament, but a National Assembly of Wales. Unlike the Scottish Parliament, the National Assembly has no power to amend primary legislation. As with Scotland, however, the Assembly has the power to make and amend subordinate or secondary legislation, but limited of course to those Westminster Acts for which the Assembly is made responsible. Here, as in Scotland, these areas include town and country planning and the environment. In essence, therefore, the decisions which were previously made by the Secretary of State for Wales in relation to those areas are now made by the National Assembly of Wales. These decisions will, of course, not only include the making of policy, but such matters as the determination of appeals under the Town and Country Planning Act 1990.

2.07 As far as England is concerned, the First Secretary of State is presently assisted in the exercise of his powers and functions by three Ministers of State. They are the Minister for Local and Regional Government, the Minister for Housing and Planning and the Minister for Regeneration and Regional Development. There are also two Parliamentary Under-Secretaries of State, each with special responsibilities.

2.08 These arrangements, however, are political arrangements allowing for the sharing of departmental responsibilities between a number of Ministers in the same Department of State. They in no way affect the particular powers and functions which in law are placed exclusively upon the Secretary of State.

2.09 Following the creation of a new Department of National Heritage in 1992, responsibility for the listing of historic buildings in England passed to another Secretary of State, the Secretary of State for National Heritage. In 1997, his title was changed to the Secretary of State for Culture, Media and Sport. Controls over works to historic buildings, however, remain the responsibility of the First Secretary of State. The Secretary of State for Culture, Media and Sport is responsible for scheduling ancient monuments and granting scheduled monuent consents; repair notices and associated compulsory purchase orders; and policy, procedures and reserve powers in respect of the designation of conservation areas.

The organisation of planning administration places the First Secretary of State at the apex of a pyramid of power. Despite many attempts made over the years to shift more of the responsibility for planning decisions from central to local government, planning organisation remains a hierarchy of centralised pontification, with the Secretary of State the supreme central pontiff. So it is that, however small a parcel of land may be, the final say in determining the use to which that land can be put is given, in law, to the Secretary of State. **2.10**

Governmental powers and duties are broadly analysed as being of three kinds, namely legislative, administrative and judicial. So too, may the powers and duties of the Secretary of State under planning legislation be analysed. **2.11**

Legislative powers

Despite the length of the 1990 Act, many of its provisions are no more than general statements of principle. The Secretary of State, however, is given power by the Act to fill in the detail by making regulations or orders. Under s 333 of the 1990 Act, the power to make regulations and many of the more important orders are exercisable by statutory instrument. The use of this power is subject to varying degrees of parliamentary control or scrutiny. Statutory instruments are normally required to be laid before Parliament for a period of 40 days. The more important statutory instruments also require an 'affirmative resolution' of both Houses of Parliament during that period before they come into effect. With others, the statutory instrument comes into effect automatically, unless during that period either House of Parliament passes a 'negative resolution' preventing it from doing so. Finally, some statutory instruments have merely to be laid before Parliament, thus avoiding any more formal parliamentary control. **2.12**

Under the 1990 Act, most statutory instruments containing *regulations* are subject to the negative resolution procedure. So too are most statutory instruments containing a *development order*. Most other statutory instruments containing orders, however, including the important Town and Country Planning (Use Classes) Order, have merely to be laid before Parliament. Three of the main statutory instruments made by the Secretary of State are: **2.13**

(a) *Town and Country Planning (Use Classes) Order 1987.* This Order (see Appendix B) specifies 11 'use classes' for the purpose of s 55(2)(f) of the 1990 Act. Its significance is that where buildings or other land are used for a purpose within any of the classes specified in the Order, the use of the buildings or other land for any purpose within the same class is not to be taken to involve development.

(b) *Town and Country Planning (General Permitted Development) Order 1995 (GPDO).* The main purpose of this Order (see Appendix C) is to grant planning permission for certain classes of development without the need to make an application to the local planning authority for an express grant of planning permission. In many cases, the permission given by the Order is subject to extensive conditions and limitations. Development specified in the Order is commonly referred to as 'permitted development'. This Order is hereafter referred to as the General Permitted Development Order or the GPDO.

(c) *Town and Country Planning (General Development Procedure) Order 1995 (GDPO).* This Order (see Appendix D) specifies the procedures connected with planning applications, appeals to the Secretary of State and related matters so far as these are not laid down in the 1990 Act and the Town and Country Planning (Applications) Regulations 1988. It also deals with the maintenance of registers of planning applications, applications for certificates of lawful use or development and other related matters. This Order is hereafter referred to as the General Development Procedure Order or the GDPO.

2.14 Proposals to amend all the above orders have been made, but have not yet been implemented. The power of the Secretary of State to make these orders, though subject to varying degrees of parliamentary control, shows the extent of his legislative power. By reducing the number of 'classes' in the Use Classes Order, or by extending the content of a class, he can reduce the number of activities which constitute development and therefore require planning permission. By widening the scope of the development permitted by the GDPO, he can remove activities which constitute development from the general control of local planning authorities. It is significant that when the last major amendment to the Order was made in 1981, it was estimated that its effect was to reduce the number of applications for planning permission made to local planning authorities by some 15 to 20 per cent.

2.15 The Secretary of State also has power under s 59 of the 1990 Act to make a special development order. Unlike a general development order which will normally apply to all land, a special development order grants planning permission only for the development of the land specified in the order. Although the power has been used sparingly, its scope can be illustrated by the case of *Essex CC v Ministry of Housing and Local Government* (1967) 18 P & CR 531. An inquiry had been held into objections to the possible choice of Stansted as the site of the third London airport. After the inquiry the Government announced its intention to grant planning permission for the development of the site to the British Airports Authority by means of an order made under what is now s 59 of the 1990 Act. Since the public inquiry, the Minister had taken into account further questions of fact, and the county council claimed that in accordance with the rules of natural justice the Minister was not entitled to make an order until he had received and considered representations made to him on the new facts. In an action against the Minister the council asked, *inter alia*, for a declaration that the action of the Minister in purporting to decide to grant planning permission for the development was *ultra vires*, void and of no effect. In an application to have the writ and statement of claim struck out, the Minister claimed that they disclosed no reasonable cause of action, were frivolous and vexatious and an abuse of the process of the court. In granting the application to strike out, the Court held that the power of the Minister to make a special development order under the section was a purely *administrative legislative power*, for the exercise of which he is responsible to nobody except Parliament, and that no duty was imposed on him to act judicially before making an order under the section.

2.16 What the Court was here recognising was that the decision to grant planning permission by a special development order was an administrative act, but one exercised by the Minister in a legislative form.

Another example of the use made of a special development order is the *Town and Country Planning (Telecommunication Networks) (Railway Operational Land) Special Development Order 1982, SI 1982/817*. This order granted planning permission to lay cables (to be used for the carrying of cable television) along the route of railway lines. The grant of planning permission in this way thus relieved cable television operators from having to make an express application for planning permission to every local planning authority through whose land a cable was to run. **2.17**

Mention should also be made of the following bizarre, but perfectly legal, use of the Secretary of State's power to grant planning permission by special development order. **2.18**

In 1977 an application for planning permission was made to construct an oxide fuel reprocessing plant at Windscale (now known as Sellafield) in Cumbria. Because of the public concern over the proposed development, the Secretary of State 'called in' the application for his own decision rather than leave the decision to be made by the local planning authority. Then, following a public local inquiry into the application and objections made to it, the Inspector recommended that, subject to conditions, the application should be granted. Normally, the Secretary of State would have done no more than decide whether or not to accept his Inspector's recommendation. In this instance, however, he considered that Parliament should be able to express a view on the proposed development. He decided, therefore, to refuse the application for planning permission. In so doing, he avoided any objections which might arise as a result of his quasi-judicial role in the planning process. The parliamentary debate was then able to take place without giving rise to an obligation on the Secretary of State to reopen the inquiry if fresh evidence was forthcoming during the course of the debate. The Secretary of State then granted, by special development order (Town and Country Planning (Windscale and Calder Works) Special Development Order 1978, SI 1978/523), planning permission for the very same development which he had earlier refused, with the parliamentary debate taking place on a 'prayer' against the order. **2.19**

A somewhat different procedure was followed, however, with regard to the decision on an application by the Central Electricity Generating Board to build a nuclear power station at Sizewell, in Essex. After receiving the report of the Inspector, both Houses of Parliament were given an opportunity to debate the report and the issues involved. In the debate in the House of Commons, the Secretary of State made it clear that he was there to listen to the views which would be expressed and that he had no intention of commenting or making observations on the report. Shortly after the debate had been held the Secretary of State proceeded to grant planning permission for the development proposed in the application. **2.20**

Administrative powers

Although local planning authorities are the primary bodies responsible for the day-to-day administration of planning, the Secretary of State has wide power to ensure that they act in accordance with his general policy. He also has wide power to enable him to supervise and co-ordinate their individual activities. In addition, he provides general guidance and advice to local planning authorities on how they should exercise their powers. **2.21**

2.22 One of the basic documents through which the Secretary of State exercises general policy control is the development plan for an area. Under the 1947 legislation he was required to approve all development plans prepared by local planning authorities. When the 'two part' development plans prepared under Part II of the 1990 Act were introduced in 1968, he was required to approve only the structure plan part, which he could do in whole or in part and with or without modifications or reservations. Then, following the Planning and Compensation Act 1991, planning authorities were given the power to *adopt* all types of development plan. The Secretary of State's policy control over a structure plan's content, however, was secured by the requirement in s 31(6)(a) of the 1990 Act, that in formulating the general policies to be included in a structure plan, the authority must have regard to specified matters including 'any regional or strategic planning guidance given by the Secretary of State to assist them in the preparation of the plan'. The Secretary of State's powers over the content of the development plan for an area would, it was thought, be secured in many other ways. Whether the plan be a structure plan, a local plan or a unitary development plan, he had the power to object formally to proposals to be contained in the plan (ss 13(5), 33(5) and 40(6)) and he may call in the plan for his own approval (ss 18(1), 35A(1) and 44(1)). Finally, he had the power to direct a local planning authority to modify proposals contained in a plan (ss 17(1), 35(2) and 43(4)). The power given to local planning authorities to adopt their own development plans, leaving the Secretary of State with selective powers to secure compliance with his policies did not produce the effect intended. In particular, the system failed to make provision for the large increase in residential development which the Secretary of State wished to see. Accordingly, the Planning and Compulsory Purchase Act 2004 ended the earlier relaxation of the Secretary of State's general power of control by giving him the power to prescribe the contents of a draft revision of the Regional Spatial Strategy for a Region, as well as to require its revision. He also has the power to direct changes to a local planning authority's local development scheme and to approve the authority's local development documents.

2.23 The powers of the Secretary of State also extend to determining appeals made under s 78 of the 1990 Act against the refusal by a local planning authority to grant planning permission, or against a decision to grant planning permission subject to conditions. In the year 2003/4, the Secretary of State (or an Inspector acting on his behalf), determined 22,550 appeals (about 3 per cent of the total number of applications made) under the provisions of s 78 of the 1990 Act, of which 33 per cent were allowed. This is in marked contrast to the 25 per cent success rate which was common in the mid-1970s, and the 41 per cent success rate reached in the mid-1980s. Now, the proportion of appeals allowed is fairly constant and has been between 33 and 36 per cent over the last few years.

2.24 There is no doubt that since 1991 onwards until quite recently, the legal presumption in favour of the development plan contained in section 54A of the 1990 Act has had the effect of reducing the number of appeals made. The present position, however, is that, perhaps because of economic growth, there has been since 2001/2 a continuous rise in the number of planning applications made to local authorities. As the number of planning applications has increased, so too has the number of appeals made to the Secretary of State. These have risen by 50 per cent over the same period. In fact the percentage rise in the number of appeals made is greater than the corresponding increase in the number of applications made, no doubt because the refusal dates are also rising. A recent report, has also examined the rise in the number of appeals made since 2001/2. The facts that have led to this rise appear to include a wish of both authorities and developers to test the parameters of new and revised policies that have been introduced and the pressure on local authorities to meet Best Value Performance Indicators for decision-taking, so reducing the opportunities to resolve issues through pre-application discussions and negotiations.

The Secretary of State is also required under s 174 of the 1990 Act, to determine appeals made against enforcement notices served by local planning authorities; and in doing so, he may uphold, quash or vary the enforcement notice, and may, in appropriate circumstances, grant planning permission for the development to which the notice relates. In the year 2003/4, the Secretary of State for the Environment (or an Inspector acting on his behalf), determined 3,210 appeals against enforcement notices, of which 75 per cent were upheld or varied, with the remainder being allowed. **2.25**

Under the 1990 Act, the Secretary of State determines appeals against decisions of local planning authorities in many other areas, including decisions relating to certificates of lawfulness of existing use or development (s 191), certificates of lawfulness of proposed use or development (s 192), the display of advertisements (s 220), and the cutting down, topping or lopping of trees the subject of a tree preservation order (s 208). He may also be required to confirm orders made by local planning authorities revoking or modifying a planning permission previously granted (s 97), orders requiring a use of land to be discontinued or the alteration or removal of buildings or works (s 102) and notices requiring that development begun but not completed should be completed (s 94). **2.26**

Under s 77 of the 1990 Act, the Secretary of State may by a direction which he has power to withdraw 'call in' applications for planning permission for his own determination, rather than allow them to be determined by the local planning authority. The power is used very selectively, the Secretary of State exercising the power only if planning issues of more than local importance are involved. **2.27**

The guidelines for the exercise of the Secretary of State's call-in power were restated by a junior Minister on behalf of the Secretary of State in the House of Commons on 12 December 2000. According to that statement, his policy is to be very selective about calling in planning applications. He will, in general, only take this step if planning issues of more than local significance are involved. Each case is considered on its merits, but they could include, for example, cases which: **2.28**

— may conflict with national policies on important matters;
— could have significant effects beyond their immediate locality;
— give rise to substantial regional or national controversy;
— raise significant architectural or urban design issues; or
— may involve the interests of national security or of foreign Governments.

In the year 2003/4, the Secretary of State called in 110 applications for his own determination. Of these, most were in respect of housing or retail development.

The power of the Secretary of State to call in a planning application under s 77 is unfettered, subject, of course, to its being exercised having regard to all material considerations and not being perverse. In *Lakin v Secretary of State for Scotland* 1988 SLT 780, the Secretary of State **2.29** decided not to call in one of two competing applications for the development of a superstore in Stirling. It was recognised that only one of the two would succeed; and in the other an appeal to the Secretary of State was pending. The Scottish courts considered that in not calling in the application for his own decision the Secretary of State was effectively determining its planning merits and this was both improper and unfair. However, in *R v Secretary of State for the Environment, Transport and the Regions, ex p Carter Commercial Developments Ltd* [1999] PLCR 125, the Secretary of State decided to call in just one of two competing planning applications. In an action seeking judicial review of that decision the High Court held that the Secretary of State could so proceed so long as he had regard to the implications for the consideration of any other proposals, as one of the relevant considerations in his decision. The application was refused.

2.30 In *South Northamptonshire Council v Secretary of State for the Environment* (1995) 70 P & CR 224, the Court of Appeal held that the Secretary of State did not have to give reasons for *not* calling in an application, though in practice he normally would do so.

2.31 In *R (on the application of) Hadfield v Secretary of State for Transport, Local Government and the Regions* (CD/3295/01, 12 June 2002) Sullivan J refused an application for judicial review of a decision by the Secretary of State to call in an application for planning permission to use buildings as a dwelling house. The land was within the Green Belt and the planning officer had recommended refusal. The Council however did not accept that recommendation and resolved that permission be granted. As a result, the application was referred to the Secretry of State as a 'departure application'; who then decided to call it in.

2.32 In *R (on the application of Adlard and others) v Secretary of State for Environment, Transport and Regions* [2002] JPL 1379, the Court of Appeal refused to grant an application for judicial review of a decision of the Secretary of State to refuse to call in an application for the redevelopment of Fulham Football Ground. It had been unsuccessfully argued that under the Human Rights Act 1998 objectors to the development were entitled as of right to an oral hearing given the very major development with important consequences for local people. Since then, a number of other legal challenges to the decision of the Secretary of State not to call in an application for planning permission based upon human rights grounds have also failed.

2.33 Specific instances where the Secretary of State has exercised his call-in power have included proposals for development at Windscale (mentioned above), the redevelopment of Spitalfields Market, Stamford Bridge football stadium, extensions to airport capacity at Stansted and London (Heathrow), proposals for the construction of an aerodrome for use by short take-off and landing (STOL) aircraft on land in the London Docklands and later, proposals to extend the runway and to install runway approach lighting. More recently, he called in for his own decision the application by the British Airports Authority to build a fifth terminal at London (Heathrow) Airport.

2.34 In addition to the power to call in applications for planning permission for his own decision, the Secretary of State also has power under the Planning (Listed Buildings and Conservation Areas) Act 1990 to call in for his own decision applications made to the local planning authority for listed building consent.

2.35 Associated with the Secretary of State's power to call in applications for his own determination, is his power under the General Development Procedure Order, Art 14, to give a direction to local planning authorities restricting their power to grant planning permission for development, either indefinitely or for a specified period of time. Such directions are made with regard either to a class of application or to an application for a specific site. The Act contains no requirement that reasons be given. The purpose of the power appears to be to protect the Secretary of State's right to call in the application by giving him time to consider whether or not he should in fact exercise that power. A direction so given, however, does not take away the power of the local planning authority to refuse to grant planning permission for the development proposed. Occasionally too, the power is used to safeguard land from development, where the land is needed for further public works such as roads or other transport facilities. In England between May 1997 and December 1998, some 536 directions were issued by the Secretary of State under this power.

In addition, under the General Development Procedure Order, Art 10(3), the Secretary of State may give directions to a local planning authority requiring the authority to consult with any person or body named in the direction before granting planning permission. The authority named in the direction may well be the Secretary of State. In this way the body consulted is formally made aware of particular planning applications. In cases where the Secretary of State is required to be consulted, he may decide to use his powers either to give a direction to the local planning authority under Art 14, or decide without more to call in the application for his own decision under s 77. **2.36**

An example of the exercise by the Secretary of State of his powers under Arts 10 and 14 is the requirement that local planning authorities consult him on any applications for development comprising gross shopping floor space of 20,000 square metres or more and prohibiting the grant of planning permission for such development until at least 21 days after the consultation. Consultation is not required, however, where the local planning authority decides to refuse the application. The relevant direction, the Town and Country Planning (Shopping Development) (England and Wales) (No 2) Direction 1993 is contained as an Annex to Circular 15/93. Other examples are the Town and Country Planning (Playing Fields) (England) Direction 1998 (proposals for the development of playing fields against the advice of the Sports Council) and the Town and Country Planning (Residential Development on Greenfield Land) (England) Direction 2000 (proposals for the development of land comprising the provision of 150 houses or flats or of houses or flats on five hectares or more on land not previously developed). **2.37**

Yet another direction issued by the Secretary of State under articles 10 and 14 of the General Permitted Development Order is the Town and Country Planning (Residential Density) (London and South East England) Direction 2002. The Direction which is contained in an Annex to Circular 01/02, requires local planning authorities in those areas to consult the Secretary of State on any application for housing development which the authority does not propose to refuse, where the application comprises or includes the provision of houses or flats on sites of one hectare or more, and where the residential density is either not provided in the application or will be less than 30 dwellings per hectare. **2.38**

In the year 1998/99 170 applications were referred to the Secretary of State under such directions. A further 1,146 applications were referred to him under the directions relating to development not in accordance with the development plan. **2.39**

2.40 Mention should also be made of the Secretary of State's wide default powers (e.g., under s 51 of the 1990 Act in relation to development plans, and ss 100 and 104 in connection with the revocation of planning permission and the discontinuance of a use). Although default powers have been rarely exercised, the powers under sections 100 and 104 allow him to impose a particular course of action on a local planning authority. According to statistics given to Parliament, default powers to revoke the grant of planning permission by local planning authorities were exercised by the Secretary of State on 18 occasions between 1955 and 1973. In 1991, he was reported as having given notice to the Borough of Poole that he was considering whether or not to revoke the deemed planning permission granted by the Borough to itself for residential development on land which formed part of a site of special scientific interest. In the same year, the Secretary of State issued a direction that planning permission granted by Wealden District Council for a dwelling house be revoked after two previous applications for similar developments on the same site had been refused by the council and, on appeal, by the Secretary of State.

2.41 More recently in the autumn of 1992, the Secretary of State decided to hold an administrative inquiry into the operation of the planning system by North Cornwall District Council. The terms of reference of the inquiry were 'to consider the issues which have been raised about the administration of the planning system in North Cornwall and to make recommendations on any desirable changes in the formulation of policy or in procedures'. Quite separately from the setting up of this inquiry, the Secretary of State also announced he was considering whether it would be expedient for him to exercise his powers under ss 100 and 104 of the 1990 Act to make orders revoking two planning permissions previously granted by the Council and/or requiring the discontinuance of use or the removal of buildings or works. The action arose because of a number of complaints made about the lack of consistency in planning decisions made by North Cornwall District Council. The Council had been criticised by the Local Government Ombudsman over particular planning decisions, and the District Auditor had also made criticisms in a public interest report. Such criticisms had been the subject of wider public comment with the showing of a Channel 4 TV programme 'Cream Teas and Concrete' in December 1991, which had featured specific cases.

2.42 The report of the inquiry set up by the Secretary of State in 1992 and published towards the end of 1993, found that the North Cornwall District Council had granted planning permission for sporadic development in the open countryside on an inconsistent basis and contrary to national planning guidance and approved policies in the county structure plan. The report also criticised inappropriate decisions by the Council and its committees, the lack of formally adopted policies, inadequate publicity arrangements and a number of procedural problems. Following this concern and the resulting inquiry, the Secretary of State in August 1993 exercised his power to revoke a planning permission granted for a farmer's retirement house in North Cornwall as being contrary to planning policy,and in another case took steps to require the carrying out of landscaping and further works to the exterior of an agricultural dwelling in order to minimise its effect on an Area of Outstanding Natural Beauty.

2.43 It appeared, however, that the grant of planning permission for development contrary to planning policy guidance may have occurred in areas other than North Cornwall. Following criticism by the Commission for Local Administration in Wales and the Welsh Affairs Select Committee of the House of Commons of similar practices by local planning authorities in the principality, the Secretary of State for Wales thought it appropriate to write to all Welsh local planning authorities to remind them of the need to be fair and consistent in the treatment of planning applications.

Some local planning authorities have been able to recognise their own shortcomings. One local planning authority recognised its own shortcomings. In 1995, Bassetlaw District Council appointed an independent expert to investigate concerns relating to a number of planning matters which centred on planning permissions granted by the Council against officer advice, almost all of which appeared to involve a single developer. His report (the Phelps report), which was accepted by the Council, contained recommendations which included a call for the Planning Committee to resign *en bloc* to restore confidence in the planning system and programmed training for Committee Members into how the planning system works and the implications for them of national, regional and county guidance. **2.44**

The Bassetlaw report had an interesting sequel. In December 1996, the High Court in *R v Bassetlaw DC, ex p G. A. N. Oxby* [1997] JPL 576, rejected an application to quash two decisions of the District Council to grant planning permission for the development of two sites identified in the report, made on the alleged basis that the decisions were affected by fraud and/or bias. The application had been brought by the Leader of the Council in conjunction with the respondent Council, following the Council's consideration of the Phelps report. **2.45**

At the outset of the case, three preliminary points had been taken, namely whether the Leader of the Council had a sufficient interest; whether there was an alternative remedy available to the Council; and whether the application had been made out of time. **2.46**

With regard to the first point, Popplewell J, after reviewing the case law and relevant literature on standing, held that the law had moved on since the well known case of *Inland Revenue Commissioners v National Federation of Self Employed and Small Business* [1981] 2 WLR 722 (the 'Mickey Mouse' case), and he was, therefore, prepared to accept that the applicant, as a ratepayer, had sufficient standing to bring the proceedings. **2.47**

With regard to the last point, Popplewell J held that although it was not incumbent upon the Council to start judicial review proceedings until 14 March 1996 when they had received the report of the Phelps inquiry, in not submitting the application for judicial review until 21 June 1996 and having regard to the length of time since planning permission has been granted, the application had not been made promptly. **2.48**

It is on the second preliminary point however, that the judgment raised issues of greater importance. After referring to the powers available to the District Council under ss 97 and 107 of the 1990 Act to revoke planning permission, Popplewell J held that the effect of the application for judicial review was to circumvent those statutory provisions, and he felt it would be quite wrong in this instance to allow the matter to proceed in that way given that there was an alternative remedy which the Council could pursue. One of the many factors which may have influenced this decision was that the landowners themselves were innocent of any fraud or bias that may have been present in the decision to grant planning permission. **2.49**

The Court of Appeal ([1999] PLCR 283), however, took a somewhat different view. Whilst **2.50** upholding the decision of Popplewell J that the leader of the Council had sufficient *locus* to bring the proceedings, the Court of Appeal found that there had been no undue delay and that what delay there was was marginal. More importantly, the Court reversed his finding that judicial review should not lie to quash the Council's decisions. In the Court's view it was legitimate and proper for the Council to seek to have the planning permissions set aside without the payment of compensation. According to the Court, it was not just that they (the landowners) should enjoy the benefit if they should not have received it in the first place. They had no legitimate grievance in being deprived of what they should never have had.

2.51 Two of the most recent and significant examples of the use made by the Secretary of State of his power to revoke or modify a planning permission which resulted in a legal challenge occurred in the cases of *Alnwick District Council* and *Restormel District Council*. In *Alnwick DC v Secretary of State for the Environment, Transport and the Regions* [2000] JPL 473 the High Court refused an application by the District Council to quash the Secretary of State's decision, made on the recommendations of his Inspector, to make an order modifying a grant of planning permission which the Council had given for development contrary to the provisions of the development plan, by the deletion from it of Class A1 retail use.

2.52 The District Council's main argument was that in deciding to make the order, the Secretary of State had misdirected himself in law in holding that the obligation on the Council to pay compensation was a factor he was obliged to ignore in deciding whether it was expedient to modify the permission.

2.53 In dismissing the argument, Richards J held that in so far as the financial consequences of modification did not relate to the use and development of land, they were not capable of amounting to a material consideration. He also considered that the Council's argument that the payment of compensation would jeopardise proposed leisure facilities was a consideration that was too remote, and that the Council had not elaborated or supported it by any detailed evidence.

2.54 It will be recalled that where the Secretary of State exercises his power to revoke or modify, it is in the nature of a default power. The Secretary of State's policy with regard to the exercise of that power was set out on his behalf in the House of Commons on 20 December 1989 where it was said:

> . . . My Rt. Hon. Friend's practice has been to use this power only rarely. He has taken the view that the power should be used only if the original decision is judged to be grossly wrong, so that damage is likely to be done to the wider public interest . . .

2.55 The District Council had argued that the Secretary of State had mis-applied that policy by failing to look at the consequences of the grossly wrong decision for the wider public interest. Dismissing that argument also, Richards J held that the words 'so that' were words of explanation rather than consequence. Accordingly, the finding that the damage to the wider public interest lay in the harm to Alnwick's vitality and viability as a shopping centre was a proper application of the Secretary of State's policy.

2.56 As a result the District Council became liable to pay compensation to Safeway Stores plc, who had purchased the site subsequent to the grant of the permission. The sum was thought likely to be substantial; probably in excess of £4m. It is understood, however, that through an agreement whereby the landowner who had sold the land to Safeway Stores agreed to buy the land back at the same price that it had been sold for and the meeting by the Council's insurers of Safeway's legal costs, the liability of the District Council was minimal.

The other recent and significant example of the use by the Secretary of State of his powers under s 100 of the 1990 Act to revoke or modify a planning permission occurred in March 2000, where he modified a planning permission for B1, B2, B8 and non-food retail use granted by Restormel Borough Council, by deleting from the planning permission the reference to the non-food retail use. It had been the intention of the developers to use the land for a 'factory outlet centre'. The Inspector appointed to hold an inquiry into the proposed order had found that the grant of planning permission made in May 1997 was in conflict with both the relevant policies and provisions of the development plan and with national policy guidance in PPG 6 and PPG 13. In addition, she found that the development would materially harm the vitality and viability of nearby established shopping centres. These findings and the Inspector's conclusion that the decision to grant permission was grossly wrong, were accepted by the Secretary of State.There then followed a challenge not to the Secretary of State's decision, but to the original grant of planning permission which had been made in May 1997. Although the Council had twice been advised before the modification proceedings had commenced that judicial challenge to the grant of permission by the Council would not succeed, the Council now sought to challenge the grant subsequent to the making of the order. The action, *R v Restormel BC ex p Parkyn and Corbett*, was brought by the Chairman of the Council's Planning and Building Control Committee on behalf of the Council, and by another councillor acting in his capacity as elector and council taxpayer. The grounds of challenge were that the Council had failed to apply s 54A of the 1990 Act and had left out of account material considerations;and had also failed to refer the application to the Secretary of State as a 'departure application', that is, an application for development not in accordance with the development plan. In the High Court [2000] JPL 1211, the challenge to the grant of permission was rejected on the grounds, inter alia, of the long delay in applying for judicial review and bearing in mind that any challenge brought by the Council before the decision on the modification order would have been so lacking in merit that it would have failed. Both councillors then sought and obtained leave to appeal from the Court of Appeal. However, the Council, acting through the Chairman of the Planning and Building Control Committee, withdrew its appeal. The other councillor proceeded with his appeal, but the Court of Appeal ([2001] JPL 1415) upheld the High Court decision. The developers then sought compensation from the Council for the loss resulting from the modification of the permission. In August 2004, compensation of £1,586,000 was awarded to the developers by the Lands Tribunal. **2.57**

In order to inform local planning authorities and others about his policies and to lessen the need for him to use the powers he possesses (e.g., by keeping to a minimum the number of appeals made to him from decisions of local planning authorities), the Secretary of State issues Planning Policy Guidance Notes (PPGs), Planning Policy Statements (PPSs), Circulars, White Papers and other minor policy statements. The importance to local planning authorities and others who are concerned with the use and development of land of Planning Policy Guidance and Planning Policy Statements containing the Secretary of State's policy on major planning policies cannot be overestimated. **2.58**

2.59 In 1988, the Secretary of State first began to issue PPGs to provide guidance on general and specific aspects of planning policy and Minerals Planning Guidance notes (MPGs) to provide advice on the control of minerals development. The aim of PPGs and MPGs was intended to provide concise and practical guidance on planning policies, in a clear and accessible form. Since 1988, the role of Departmental Circulars has been restricted to giving advice on legislation and procedures. In addition, the Secretary of State began to issue Regional Planning Guidance (RPGs) to provide guidance to local planning authorities on regional planning policies.

2.60 The following are the PPSs, PPGs, MPGs and RPGs now issued and in force:

Planning Policy Statements

PPS7 **Sustainable Development in Rural Areas (2004)**
This Statement sets out the Government's planning policies for rural areas.

PPS11 **Regional Spatial Strategies (2004)**
This Statement sets out the procedural policy on the nature of Regional Spatial Strategies and on the preparation of revisions to them.

PPS12 **Local Development Frameworks (2004)**
This Statement focuses on procedural policy and to process of preparing local development documents.

PPS22 **Renewable Energy (2004)**
This Statement sets out the Government's planning policies for renewable energy.

PPS23 **Planning and Pollution Control (2004)**
Contains guidance on the relevance of pollution controls to the exercise of planning junctions. It is intended to complement the new pollution control framework under the Pollution Prevention and Control Act 1999 and the PPC Regulations 2000. It contains two Annexes.
Annex 1: Pollution Control, Air and Water Quality
Annex 2: Development on Land Affected by Contamination

2.61 **Planning Policy Guidance Notes**

PPG1 **General Policy and Principles (February 1997)**
This revision of an earlier PPG1 (published in 1992) now provides a more strategic commentary on the Government's planning policies.

PPG2 **Green Belts (January 1995)**
States the general intentions of Green Belt policy, including its contribution to sustainable development objectives. Explains the purposes of including land in Green Belts and the general presumption against inappropriate development within Green Belts.

PPG3 **Housing (March 2000)**
Sets out the Government's policies on the provision of housing land and emphasises the key role of the planning system in meeting the demand for housing.

PPG4 **Industrial and Commercial Development and Small Firms (November 1992)**
Emphasises the importance of a positive approach towards development which contributes to national and local economic activity.

PPG5 **Simplified Planning Zones (November 1992)**
Explains the working of this special procedure for facilitating development or redevelopment in designated areas by removing the need for a planning application for certain types of development proposals.

PPG6 **Town Centres and Retail Development (June 1996)**
Emphasises the sequential approach to selecting sites for development, for retail, employment and leisure and other key town centre uses; and clarifies the three key tests for assessing retail developments.

PPG8 **Telecommunications (August 2001)**
Gives comprehensive advice on planning aspects of telecommunications development, including radio masts and towers, antennas, radio equipment housing, public call boxes, cabinets, poles and overhead wires. This recent guidance takes into account changes to the GDPO rights that apply to the telecommunications industry and to health considerations in making decisions about telecommunications development.

PPG9 **Nature Conservation (October 1994)**
Gives advice on the relationship between planning control and nature conservation.

PPG10 **Planning and Waste Management (October 1999)**
Brings policies in respect of waste management in PPG23 (July 1994) up to date with developments in waste policy and the setting up of the Environment Agency.

PPG12 **Development Plans (December 1999)**
Provides a strategic review of the role and importance of development plans.

PPG13 **Transport (March 2001)**
Contains policy advice on how local authorities should integrate transport and planning at national, regional, strategic and local level to promote more sustainable transport choices for both people and the movement of freight; to promote accessibility to jobs, shopping, leisure facilities and services by public transport, walking and cycling; and to reduce the need to travel, especially by car.

PPG14 **Development on Unstable Land (April 1990)**
Explains the effects of instability on development and land use. Emphasises the need for instability to be taken into account in plan preparation and development control decisions, together with the self-standing Annex (March 1996) Landslides and Planning.

PPG15 **Planning and the Historic Environment (September 1994)**
Explains the role of the planning system in the protection of historic buildings, conservation areas and other elements of the historic environment.

PPG16 **Archaeology and Planning (November 1990)**
Sets out policy on preservation of any archaeological remains.

PPG17 **Planning for Open Space, Sport and Recreation (July 2002)**
Describes the role of the planning system in assessing opportunities and need for open spaces, sports and recreation facilities and safeguarding open space with recreational value.

PPG18 **Enforcing Planning Control (December 1991)**
Describes the comprehensive range of planning enforcement powers available to

local planning authorities in Part VII of the Town and Country Planning Act 1990 (as amended by the Planning and Compensation Act 1991); and gives policy guidance about how these discretionary powers should be used to remedy the most commonly experienced breaches of planning control.

PPG19 Outdoor Advertisement Control (March 1992)
Covers legislation, the operation of the advertisement control system, criteria for determining advertisement applications and appeals.

PPG20 Coastal Planning (September 1992)
Sets out policy for coastal areas and advice on developments that require a coastal location, as well as guidance on the Heritage Coast.

PPG21 Tourism (November 1992)
Outlines the economic significance of tourism and its environmental impact, explains how the needs of tourism should be dealt with in development plans and the use of planning powers to regulate and facilitate tourist-related development.

PPG24 Planning and Noise (September 1994)
Advises on the use of planning powers to minimise the adverse impact of noise; outlines the main considerations in determining applications for both noise-sensitive development and for activities which generate noise; introduces the concept of noise exposure categories for residential development.

PPG25 Development and Flood Risk (July 2001)
Gives guidance on how flood risk should be considered at all stages of the development process in order to reduce damage to property and life.

2.62 Minerals Planning Guidance Notes

MPG1 General Considerations and the Development Plan System (June 1996)
Sets out the principles and key planning objectives for minerals planning and advises on the preparation of minerals development plans and the determination of minerals planning applications.

MPG2 Applications, Permissions and Conditions (July 1998)
Provides guidance on planning applications for minerals development, planning permissions and the imposition of planning conditions.

MPG3 Coal Mining and Colliery Spoil Disposal (March 1999)
Provides advice to mineral planning authorities and to the coal industry in England on how to ensure that the development of coal resources and the disposals of colliery spoil only take place in accordance with the full and proper protection of the environment and the principles of sustainable development.

MPG4 Revocation, Modification, Discontinuance, Prohibition and Suspension Orders etc. (August 1997)
Provides guidance on the review of mineral working sites, including the compensation implications.

MPG5 Stability in Surface Mineral Workings and Tips (January 2000)
Gives guidance with respect to stability in surface mining workings and on good practice in the design, assesment and inspection of excavated slopes and tips.

MPG6 **Guidelines or Aggregates Provisions in England (April 1994)**
Provides advice on how to ensure that the construction industry continues to receive an adequate and steady supply of minerals at the best balance of social, environmental and economic costs.

MPG7 **The Reclamation of Mineral Workings (November 1996)**
Gives advice on policies and conditions necessary to ensure that land worked for minerals is returned to a beneficial after-use at the earliest opportunity.

MPG8 **Planning and Compensation Act 1991: Interim Development Order Permissions (IDOs) — Statutory Provisions and Procedures (September 1991)**

MPG9 **Planning and Compensation Act 1991: Interim Development Order Permissions (IDOs) — Conditions (March 1992)**

MPG10 **Provision of Raw Material for the Cement Industry (November 1991)**
Gives guidance on ensuring that the quarrying of raw materials for the cement industry has full regard to the environment.

MPG11 **The Control of Noise at Surface Mineral Workings (1993)**
Guidelines on how both planning controls and good environmental practice can be used to keep noise emissions to environmentally acceptable levels.

MPG12 **Treatment of Disused Mine Openings and Availability of Information on Mined Ground (March 1994)**
Covers problems associated with and methods of dealing with disused mine openings and information on mined ground.

MPG13 **Guidelines for Peat Provision in England (July 1995)**
Provides advice on the exercise of planning control over the extraction of peat.

MPG15 **Provision of Silica Sand in England (September 1996)**
Explains how the supply of silica sand can be maintained at the best balance of social, environmental and economic cost.

Note too, that the Government has also issued a Martine Mineral Guidance Note (MMG1) giving guidance on the extraction of wedging of sand, ground and other minerals from the English seabed.

Regional Planning Guidance Notes **2.63**

RPG1 **Strategic Guidance for the North East (June 1989)**
RPG6 **Regional Planning Guidance for East Anglia (November 2000)**
RPG8 **Regional Planning Guidance for the East Midlands (January 2002)**
RPG9 **Regional Planning Guidance for the South East (March 2001)**
RPG10 **Regional Planning Guidance for the South West (September 2001)**
RPG11 **Regional Planning Guidance for the West Midlands (September 1995)**
RPG12 **Regional Planning Guidance for Yorkshire and the Humber (October 2001)**
RPG13 **Regional Planning Guidance for the North West (March 2003)**

Wales has its own planning policy and minerals policy guidance notes, such as Planning Policy (Wales) (2002) and Minerals Planning Policy (Wales) (2000). **2.64**

The policy contained in Policy Statements and Guidance Notes constitutes a material consideration which local planning authorities, and indeed the Secretary of State himself, must take into account in exercising their planning powers. This aspect is dealt with in Chapter 11. Occasionally, significant planning policy changes may be announced through **2.65** statements made by the Secretary of State in Parliament. This method is generally used when urgent policy modifications need to be made to an already published PPG or PPS or to resolve differences that have occurred in a policy's interpretation.

2.66 As previously indicated, the Secretary of State also issues Circulars. Those often contain the Secretary of State's views on the meaning and effect of new legislation. Although they are helpful to an understanding of the law, they are not authoritative interpretations of the law, the courts being the only body with power to do this.

2.67 In 2001, the Government considered that there was too great a volume of national planning policy guidance because of its extent (852 pages) and the fact that the degree of detail contained in them stifled regional and local flexibility. The Government considered that national planning policy should concentrate on policy issues that needed to be resolved at national level. Accordingly, it intended to review all PPGs and MPGs and to concentrate on delivery of national planning objectives. It would focus particularly on PPG1, PPG4, PPG6, PPG15 and PPG16. It is expected that as the review proceeds, Planning Policy Guidance (PPGs) will be updated and reissued as Planning Policy Statements (PPSs)

Judicial powers

2.68 Although as stated above, the interpretation of the law is a matter for the courts, the Secretary of State has power in specific situations to make preliminary determinations of law. In dealing with an appeal against an enforcement notice, for example, he may have to decide whether the activity enforced against is development and thus a breach of planning control. He also has power to determine whether or not a particular activity constitutes development in dealing with an appeal made to him against a determination made by a local planning authority as to whether or not a proposed activity would be lawful. These matters are essentially matters of law, which the person affected and the local planning authority may either decide to accept or to challenge in the courts.

2.69 Although the occasions when the Secretary of State acts judicially may be few, he frequently has to act in a quasi-judicial capacity. It is now established law that in dealing with such matters as appeals from the decisions of local planning authorities, the Secretary of State is acting in a quasi-judicial capacity and thus bound to observe the rules of natural justice. These rules provide considerable procedural safeguards for the parties involved in the appeal and ensure that the parties are given what has been described by the House of Lords as a 'fair crack of the whip'. The matter is dealt with more fully in Chapter 17.

B. LOCAL PLANNING AUTHORITIES

County planning authorities and district planning authorities

2.70 In parts of England the powers conferred by the 1990 Act on the local planning authority are exercisable by two local authorities, namely by the county council as the county planning authority for their area and by the district council as the district planning authority for their area.

This dual responsibility for the exercise of planning powers, however, is absent in many parts of the country including Greater London and the metropolitan areas. Following the abolition of the Greater London Council and the metropolitan county councils on 1 April 1986, the only local authorities with power to act as the local planning authority in those areas are the London boroughs and the metropolitan districts respectively. **2.71**

Furthermore, the dual responsibility which previously existed in many parts of England has been curtailed further as a result of changes to the structure of local government brought about by the Local Government Act 1992. That Act has now led to the dismemberment of much of the two-tier system of local government in England and the replacement of many authorities by newly created 'unitary authorities', each exercising within their own area the planning powers previously exercised separately by the county council as county planning authority and the district council as district planning authority for the area. **2.72**

Outside London and the metropolitan areas there are now a further 45 unitary authorities. In the remainder of the country there are 34 county councils; and within those counties 238 district councils. **2.73**

The division of responsibility between the county planning authority and the district planning authority where a two-tier system of local government still exists is discussed later. **2.74**

Joint planning boards

In order to provide cohesion in the administration of planning functions over a wider area than that administered by a single county or district planning authority, s 2 of the 1990 Act allows the Secretary of State to constitute a joint board as the county planning authority for the areas or parts of the areas of any two or more counties, or as the district planning authority for the areas or parts of the areas of any two or more districts. Under the section, such boards are bodies corporate, with perpetual succession and a common seal. It is believed that joint boards have been established on only two occasions. In 1973, the Lake District Special Planning Board and the Peak Park Joint Planning Board were created to administer planning functions in the areas of the respective national parks. Both Boards were wound up on 1 April 1997. **2.75**

National Park authorities

The Environment Act 1995, s 63, gives the Secretary of State power to establish, for any National Park, a 'National Park authority' to carry out, in relation to the Park, the functions conferred on such an authority by or under the Act. Section 67 amends the 1990 Act by inserting a new s 4A which has the effect that, for most purposes, the National Park authority for a Park shall be the sole planning authority for the area of the Park. Accordingly, functions conferred by or under the planning Acts on a planning authority (including the preparation and maintenance of structure plans, local plans, minerals and waste local plans and development control) will in relation to the Park, become functions of the National Park authority and not of any other authority. **2.76**

Acting under these powers, the Secretary of State established in 1996, National Park Authorities for the following National Parks: Dartmoor, Exmoor, Lake District, Northumberland, **2.77**

North Yorkshire Moors, Peak District and Yorkshire Dales. The new National Park Authorities assumed their full planning functions on 1 April 1997. In Wales, National Park Authorities have been established for National Parks at Brecon Beacons, the Pembrokeshire Coast and Snowdonia, and those authorities assumed full planning functions on 1 April 1996.

2.78 In September 1999 it was announced that the relevant administrative steps were to be taken to create further National Parks for the New Forest and for the South Downs.

Urban development corporations

2.79 Under Part XVI of the Local Government, Planning and Land Act 1980, the Secretary of State was empowered, subject to approval by both Houses of Parliament, to make orders designating urban development areas and to set up urban development corporations (UDCs) to secure the regeneration of those areas. The criteria adopted for the selection of such areas were the level of unemployment, the amount of derelict and vacant land and the extent to which public sector funds would be likely to lever private sector investment to regenerate the area. Under the Act, UDCs had general powers to acquire, hold, manage, reclaim and dispose of land, to carry out building and other operations and to provide services and infrastructure.

2.80 Under s 149 of the 1980 Act, the Secretary of State could, by order, provide that a UDC should be the local planning authority for the whole or any portion of its area, for such purposes of Part III of the 1971 Act (now Part III of the 1990 Act) (i.e., development control functions), and in relation to such kinds of development, as may be prescribed. Once such an order had been made, the UDC became for the purposes of Part III of the 1990 Act the local planning authority for the area in place of any authority who would otherwise be the local planning authority for that area, in relation to such kinds of development as are specified in the order.

2.81 The Planning and Compulsory Purchase Act 2004 has amended the 1980 Act to allow any member of the Board of the UDC, a committee or sub-committee of members, or a member of the Board's staff, to exercise planning functions conferred on the UDC by section 149 of the 1980 Act. Accordingly, a UDC can now delegate planning functions in the same way as any other local planning authority is able to do. This amendment recognises that given the Government's commitment to regeneration, a growing number of UDCs will be created in the future. UDCs recently established are at Thurrock; Milton Keynes; and Thames Gateway. It should also be noted that the Act of 2004 allows the Secretary of State to direct that Part 2 of that Act (local development schemes and local development orders) shall not apply to the area of a UDC.

2.82 In the past, UDCs were set up in many areas, including London; Liverpool; the Black Country; Greater Manchester (Trafford Park); Tyne and Wear; Teesside; Cardiff Bay; Central Manchester; Leeds; Sheffield; Wolverhampton; Bristol; Birmingham Heartlands and Plymouth. Unlike enterprise zones, no fixed life was set for UDCs, and in the last few years all have been progressively wound up, so that planning powers have now been returned to the appropriate local authority for each area.

The Urban Regeneration Agency

Part III of the Leasehold Reform, Housing and Urban Development Act 1993 establishes, as a body corporate, the Urban Regeneration Agency. The Agency's main object is to secure the regeneration of land in England which is suitable for regeneration and which is vacant or unused; in an urban area and underused or ineffectively used; or is contaminated, derelict, neglected or unsightly. The Agency is given wide powers, which include a power to acquire, hold, manage, reclaim, improve, develop, redevelop and dispose of land. Under s 170 of the 1993 Act, the Secretary of State is given power to designate urban regeneration areas, which are intended to be similar to urban development areas designated under the Local Government, Planning and Land Act 1980 (see 2.79), save that the regeneration of the area will be carried out by the Urban Regeneration Agency rather than a specially created Urban Development Corporation. Where the Secretary of State has exercised his powers to make a designation order, the order may provide that the Agency shall be the local planning authority for the whole or any part of the designated area for such purposes of Part III of the 1990 Act and ss 57 and 73 of the Planning (Listed Buildings and Conservation Areas) Act 1990 as may be specified in the order; and in relation to such kinds of development as may be so specified. Under a new s 8A of the 1990 Act, where a designation order transfers any of the planning functions mentioned above to the Agency, the body which would otherwise be the local planning authority for the area in question may no longer exercise those functions. In practice, the Agency prefers to be known as English Partnerships. **2.83**

In exercising functions as a local planning authority, the Agency must act objectively in carrying them out. In a case involving an urban development corporation, *R v Teesside Development Corporation, ex p William Morrison plc and Redcar and Cleveland BC* [1998] JPL 23, a grant of planning permission by the Corporation was quashed because it had allowed its functions as a regeneration agency to dominate if not dictate the performance of its planning functions, to the extent that it failed to make any objective judgment on the planning merits in breach of policies in the structure plan for the area. The same considerations, it seems, would apply to the carrying out of planning functions by the Urban Regeneration Agency. **2.84**

Enterprise zone authorities

Under s 179 of and Sch 32 to the Local Goverment, Planning and Land Act 1980, the Secretary of State is given power to designate, by order, an area of land as an enterprise zone. Enterprise zones were originally conceived as experimental. The hope was that by removing certain tax burdens and by relaxing or speeding up a number of administrative controls, private sector industrial and commercial activity within the zones would be encouraged. **2.85**

Schedule 32 provides that each enterprise zone should be administered by an enterprise zone authority. Furthermore, s 6(1) of the 1990 Act provides that an order made under Sch 32 may provide that the enterprise zone authority shall be the local planning authority for the area for such purposes of the Planning Acts, and in relation to such kinds of development as may be prescribed by the order. The order may also provide that the enterprise zone authority shall be the local planning authority for the area covered by the scheme to the extent mentioned in the order, to the exclusion of the body which would otherwise be the local **2.86** planning authority for the area. As far as planning control is concerned, s 82 of the 1990 Act provides that the adoption or approval of a simplified planning scheme has effect to grant in relation to the zone, planning permission for development specified in the scheme or for development of any class so specified. Hence an express application for planning permission is not necessary for such development.

2.87 The schedule also provides that the designation order should specify the period for which the area is to remain an enterprise zone. So far all the designation orders have limited the life of the zone to ten years from the date of the order. It is believed that only four enterprise zones now remain, and that all their designations will have ended by 2006. In 2003, the Government announced that it had no plans to extend or replace enterprise zones.

Housing action trusts (HATs)

2.88 Under s 62 of the Housing Act 1988, the Secretary of State is given power to establish housing action trusts. The purpose of these trusts is to secure the improvement of local authority housing stock which may be transferred to them in their area, and then hand them over to other owners and managers. Most HATs have been given a life span of ten years. Under s 67 of that Act, the Secretary of State may by order, provide that for such purposes of Part III of the 1990 Act (development control) and ss 67 and 73 of the Planning (Listed Buildings and Conservation Areas) Act 1990 (publicity for applications for planning permission affecting the settings of listed buildings or conservation areas), and in relation to such kinds of development as may be specified in the order, a housing action trust shall be the local planning authority for the whole or part of its area.

2.89 Under s 8 of the 1990 Act, where such an order is made, the trust shall be the local planning authority for such area, in place of any authority who would otherwise be the local planning authority for that area in relation to the development, as may be specified in the order.

2.90 So far as is known, few HATs have been established since 1988.

Broads Authority

2.91 Under the Norfolk and Suffolk Broads Act 1988, a Broads Authority was established with a general duty to manage the Broads for the purposes of conserving and enhancing the natural beauty of the Broads; to promote the enjoyment of the Broads by the public; and to protect the interests of navigation. Under s 5 of the 1990 Act, the Broads Authority is made a local planning authority for the Broads for certain limited purposes (mainly with regard to trees and rights of entry) and the sole district planning authority in relation to many other provisions of the Act such as those relating to the preparation of local plans and development control.

Division of planning powers between the county planning authority and the district planning authority

2.92 Bodies that may be a local planning authority within an area are thus county councils, district councils, joint planning boards, National Park authorities, Urban Development

Corporations the Urban Regeneration Agency, enterprise zone authorities, housing action trusts and the Broads Authority. The main functions of local planning authorities are two-fold; namely the preparation and maintenance of a development plan or a local development scheme and local development documents for their area and development control, which includes such matters as the determination of applications for planning permission and the service of enforcement notices.

In those parts of the country where there is both a county planning authority and a district planning authority for an area, the basic scheme of the 1990 legislation is to distribute planning powers and functions in the area between the two main authorities in the following way. **2.93**

Development plans and local development schemes

(a) The county planning authority was required under the 1990 Act to prepare and maintain a structure plan for their area. In addition, the county planning authority, as the mineral planning authority for the county, was required to prepare a minerals local plan for their area. Furthermore, under a provision introduced by the Planning and Compensation Act 1991, the county planning authority was required to prepare a waste local plan, either separately or as part of a joint waste and minerals local plan. **2.94**

Now, under the Planning and Compulsory Purchase Act 2004, structure plans are to be phased out and replaced by a Regional Spatial Strategies prepared by the Regional Planning Boards; waste and mineral local plans are also to be phased out and replaced by a waste and minerals local development scheme prepared by county planning authorities, together with local development documents prepared in accordance with the scheme.

(b) Under the 1990 Act, a district planning authority was required to prepare a local plan where there was a structure plan covering their area. Where the district planning authority is a unitary authority, it had to prepare a unitary development plan. In such cases that authority was also responsible for preparing waste and minerals plans. Under the Planning and Compulsory Purchase Act 2004 all local plans are to be phased out and replaced by a local development scheme prepared by the district planning authority, together with local development documents prepared in accordance with the scheme.

Development control

(a) The county planning authority are mainly responsible for development control functions within their area in respect of 'county matters'. County matters are defined in para 1 of Sch 1 to the 1990 Act and include the winning and working of minerals. Within England, the development of land relating to the use of land; the carrying out of operational development; or the erection of plant or machinery used or proposed to be used, wholly or mainly, for the purposes of recovery, treating, storing, processing, sorting, transferring, or disposing of waste, is also a county matter (see the Town and Country Planning (Prescription of County Matters) Regulations 2003, SI 2033/1033). **2.95**

A problem has arisen in relation to applications for planning permission which include both a county matter and a non-county matter. Which tier of local planning authority has the jurisdiction to determine such an application? In *R v Berkshire CC, ex p Woking-* **2.96** *ham DC* [1997] JPL 461, Beldam LJ (in the Court of Appeal) held that the test to be applied was whether in substance an application for permission to develop land was a county matter, whilst Potter LJ held the test to be whether the content of the application was such that, having regard to the proposed overall user of the site in question, that part of the application which related to a county matter forms a substantial element of it. Accordingly, the Court refused to rule that Berkshire County Council had no jurisdiction to determine an application for planning permission for a waste recycling and transfer station together with buildings for light industrial use. It was also held, obiter, that the words of the statute did not permit an application to be treated as two or more separate applications to be determined by different authorities, because to sever could cause an administrative nightmare.

(b) The district planning authority will normally be responsible for all other development control functions within their area. Development control includes not only the determination of applications for planning permission and related matters, but also the enforcement of planning control.

2.97 Recent statistics show that 675,000 applications for planning permission and related consents were made to district planning authorities in England in 2003/4, as against 1,858 applications made to county planning authorities. Most of that latter number related to applications for mineral development and the deposit of waste. Not surprisingly, only about 23 per cent of applications determined by counties are done so within the statutory eight-week period.

C. GREATER LONDON

2.98 The Greater London Authority Act 1999 established a Greater London Assembly for the Greater London Area with the purpose of promoting economic and social development in Greater London and the improvement of the environment in the area. The Act also provides that Greater London should have a directly elected Mayor, with the power to exercise any of the important functions of the Authority on its behalf. In effect therefore the decision-making power of the Assembly is confined to the approval of the budget and the making of certain key appointments. In particular, the Act requires that the Mayor should prepare and keep under review a 'spatial development strategy' for the Greater London Area. The spatial development strategy which is to contain the Mayor's general policies for the use and development of land in Greater London will, when adopted, be similar to the Regional Spatial Strategies prepared for the rest of the country under the Planning and Compulsory Purchase Act 2004. Under s.38 of the 2004 Act, the Mayor's spatial development strategy is to become part of the development plan for the Greater London Area along with development plan documents which have been adopted or approved by the London Boroughs or the City of London Corporation. Neither the Mayor nor the Greater London Assembly are the local planning authority for their area. The London Boroughs and the City of London Corporation remain the sole planning authorities for their areas, though in preparing their development plan documents they are required to have regard to the Mayor's spatial development strategy.

The Mayor is also a statutory consultee for a specific range of applications for planning permission having potential strategic importance and, in such cases, he has the power to direct the refusal of planning permission. That power is available to the Mayor if he believes that to grant the application would be contrary to his spatial development strategy or prejudicial to its implementation, or otherwise contrary to good strategic planning in Greater London. If the Mayor should direct the refusal of such an application, and the developer is dissatisfied with the decision, the developer may have no choice but to appeal against the refusal to the Secretary of State. However, the Secretary of State has the power to issue a direction prohibiting a local planning authority from implementing a direction from the Mayor in prescribed circumstances or during prescribed periods. Development considered to have potential strategic importance is defined in the Town and Country Planning (Mayor of London) Order 2000, SI 2000/1493. The type of development there defined includes: **2.99**

Large Scale Development **2.100**

Category 1A

1. Development which—
   (a) comprises or includes the provision of more than 500 houses, flats or houses and flats; or
   (b) comprises or includes the provision of flats or houses and the development occupies more than ten hectares.

Category 1B

1. Development which comprises or includes the erection of a building or buildings—
   (a) in the City of London and with a total floorspace of more than 30,000 square metres; or
   (b) in Central London (other than the City of London) and with a total floorspace of more than 20,000 square metres; or
   (c) outside Central London and with a total floorspace of more than 15,000 square metres.

Category 1C

1. Development which comprises or includes the erection of a building in respect of which one or more of the following conditions is met:
   (a) the building is more than 25 metres high and is adjacent to the River Thames;
   (b) the building is more than 75 metres high and in the City of London; or
   (c) the building is more than 30 metres high and outside the City of London.

Category 1D

1. Development which comprises or includes the alteration of an existing building where:
   (a) the development would increase the height of the building by more than 15 metres; and
   (b) the building would, when the development were completed, be higher than a relevant threshold set out in paragraph 1 of Category 1C.

Major Infrastructure **2.101**

Category 2A

1. Development which comprises or includes mining operations where the development occupies more than ten hectares.

Category 2B

1. Waste development to provide an installation to handle more than 50,000 tonnes per annum of waste produced outside the land in respect of which planning permission is sought.

Category 2C

1. Development to provide:
   (a) an aircraft runway;
   (b) a heliport (including a floating heliport or a helipad on a building);
   (c) an air passenger terminal at an airport;
   (d) a railway station;
   (e) a tramway, an underground, surface or elevated railway, or a cable car;
   (f) a bus or coach station;
   (g) an installation for a use within Class B8 (storage or distribution) of the Use Classes Order where the development would occupy more than 4 hectares;
   (h) a crossing over or under the River Thames; or
   (i) a passenger pier on the River Thames.
2. Development to alter an air passenger terminal to increase its capacity by more than 500,000 passengers per year.

2.102 **Development which may affect strategic policies**

Category 3A

1. Development which would be likely to:
   (a) result in the loss of more than 200 houses, flats, or houses and flats (irrespective of whether the development would entail also the provision of new houses or flats); or
   (b) prejudice the use for residential use of more than four hectares of land which is used for residential use.

Category 3B

1. Development—
   (a) which occupies more than four hectares of land which is used for a use in class B1 (business), B2 (general industrial) or B8 (storage or distribution) of the Use Classes Order; and
   (b) which would prejudice the use of that land for any such use.

Category 3C

1. Development which would prejudice the use as a playing field of more than two hectares of land which is used as a playing field.

Category 3D

1. Development—
   (a) on land allocated as Green Belt or Metropolitan Open Land in the development plan, in proposals for such a plan, or in proposals for the alteration or replacement of such a plan; and
   (b) which would involve the construction of a building with a floorspace of more than 1,000 square metres or a material change in the use of such a building.

Category 3E

1. Development which does not accord with the development plan and—
   (a) comprises or includes the provision of more than 2,500 square metres of floorspace for a use or uses falling within one of the following classes Use Classes Order—
      (i) class A1 (retail);
      (ii) class A2 (financial and professional);
      (iii) class A3 (food and drink);
      (iv) class B1 (business);
      (v) class B2 (general industrial);
      (vi) class B8 (storage and distribution);
      (vii) class C1 (hotels);
      (viii) class C2 (residential institutions);
      (ix) class D1 (non-residential institutions);
      (x) class D2 (assembly & leisure);

or

   (b) comprises or includes the provision of more than 150 houses or flats, or houses and flats.

Category 3F

1. Development for a use other than residential use and which includes the provision of more than 200 car parking spaces in connection with that non-residential use.

Development on which the Mayor must be consulted by virtue of a direction of the Secretary of State **2.103**

Category 4

1. Development in respect of which the local planning authority is required to consult the Mayor by virtue of a direction given by the Secretary of State.

3

SIMPLIFIED PLANNING ZONES

A. THE CONCEPT

The Housing and Planning Act 1986 gave local planning authorities power to designate simplified planning zones in their area. The power is now to be found in ss 82 to 87 of the 1990 Act. **3.01**

Simplified planning zones (SPZs) are an extension of the planning regime which had been pioneered in enterprise zones. By granting planning permission for development specified in the SPZ scheme, developers know with certainty the precise type of development that can be carried out within the zone without having to make (and pay for) a planning application. This secures that the work, expense and delay associated with the preparation, making, processing and determination of applications for planning permission are thereby saved. **3.02**

SPZs cannot be set up in national parks, conservation areas, the Broads, areas of outstanding natural beauty, land identified in a development plan as part of a green belt or land forming part of an area of special scientific interest under s 28 or 29 of the Wildlife and Countryside Act 1981. **3.03**

Under s 82 of the 1990 Act, an SPZ is an area in respect of which an SPZ scheme is in force. The adoption or approval of an SPZ scheme operates to grant in relation to the zone, or to any part of it specified in the scheme, planning permission for the development specified in the scheme or for the development of any class so specified. The section also provides that any planning permission granted under an SPZ scheme may be unconditional, or subject to such conditions, limitations or exceptions as may be specified in the scheme. **3.04**

Schemes prepared under these provisions may be either general or specific. A general scheme will grant a general or wide permission for almost all types of development, but list exceptions where an application for planning permission will be required. A specific scheme will **3.05** identify the specific type or types of development permitted and any limitations imposed. An application for planning permission would then have to be made for any development not specified in the scheme.

3.06 Planning permission cannot be granted by an SPZ scheme for development for which an environmental impact assessment is required under the Town and Country Planning (Environmental Impact Assessment) (England and Wales) Regulations 1999. There is nothing to prevent schedule 2 development being included within a SPZ, but such development can only be granted permission by the SPZ provided the development has been the subject of a 'screening opinion' or a direction by the Secretary of State, that is not development requiring environmental impact assessment (see Chapter 12).

3.07 As with enterprise zone schemes, an SPZ scheme may include subzones, where the full range of planning permission available elsewhere in the zone may be curtailed. Examples of subzones might include health and safety subzones around hazardous installations or contaminated land, or where an SPZ adjoins a residential or other environmentally sensitive area. Most SPZs are likely to be designated in older urban areas where a stimulus is needed to promote regeneration of the area and to encourage economic activity.

B. USE OF SPZ SCHEMES

3.08 According to advice given in 1986 by the Secretary of State, SPZs could be used in the following diverse circumstances:

(a) Where a development plan makes provision for development in an area for the first time — for example, a new 'industrial park' — the development plan will establish the allocation of the land for development, leaving an SPZ scheme to grant planning permission to allow the development to take place.

(b) Where an old industrial estate has become obsolete and needs to be replaced, an SPZ scheme can be drafted to permit a wide range of extensions, changes of use and redevelopment.

(c) Where a large disused site, such as former railway sidings in a central location, can be used for mixed industrial, warehousing, commercial and retailing development, a general SPZ scheme could grant planning permission for the widest possible range of development.

(d) Where a large tract of land in a single ownership is awaiting redevelopment, an SPZ scheme can be used to grant planning permission for one predominant use such as housing with local shops and community amenities or for mixed commercial development.

(e) Where an area has been selected for large-scale residential development, an SPZ scheme can lay down broad objectives and essential design criteria, leaving freedom to the developer to decide such things as the exact mix of dwelling types, the layout, landscaping, elevation and choice of materials.

(f) Where an authority have prepared a development brief for a particular site, setting out the kinds of development the authority would like to see take place, an SPZ scheme can be prepared granting planning permission for that development.

These examples apart, the Secretary of State envisaged SPZs as also being used to provide better co-ordination between development and the provision of supporting infrastructure, to assist in the refurbishment of old industrial areas, to enhance sales of underused publicly owned land and assist in the redevelopment and rehabilitation of inner city housing areas. **3.09**

Guidance to local planning authorities and others on SPZs is set currently out in PPG5: Simplified Planning Zones. In addition, the primary statutory framework for SPZs is supplemented by the Town and Country Planning (Simplified Planning Zones) Regulations 1992. **3.10**

Despite the fact that little use appears to have been made of the concept of simplified planning zones since they were first introduced in 1985, the Government considered amendments to the 1990 Act should be made where necessary in order to reflect the new development plan system introduced by Part I of the Planning and Compulsory Purchase Act 2004. The amendments made to s.83 of the 1990 Act now provide that henceforth a simplified planning zone should only be made in England where a Regional Spatial Strategy identifies the need for such a zone in the area of a local planning authority. The section also provides for the scheme to be in conformity with the regional spatial strategy. **3.11**

C. DURATION OF AN SPZ SCHEME

Section 85 of the 1990 Acts as amended by the Planning and Compulsory Purchase Act 1990 and the 2004 Act provides that an SPZ scheme shall take effect on the date of its adoption or approval or the date specified in the scheme, and be for the period specified by the scheme but no longer than ten years. At the end of that specified period the scheme, and the planning permission it grants, will cease to have effect. If, however, at the end of that period, development authorised by the permission has been begun, it may be completed. If it has been begun but completion is unreasonably delayed, the authority may serve a completion notice under the provisions of s 94 of the 1990 Act. The provisions of s 56 of the 1990 Act apply in determining when development authorised by an SPZ scheme has been begun. (These provisions are dealt with later in Chapter 15.) **3.12**

D. EARLY EXAMPLES OF SPZs

The first SPZ adopted was in Derby and covered 18 acres of derelict land one mile south of the city centre and adjacent to Derby County Football ground to provide over 300,000 sq. ft. of industrial and office space accommodating several hundred jobs. The scheme granted planning permission for the erection of buildings and use of land for Business, General Industrial and Storage or Distribution uses (covered respectively by Classes B1, B2 and B8 of the Use Classes Order). The permission granted was made subject to a number of conditions. Within the zone there were a number of subzones, where the full range of permission granted elsewhere in the zone was restricted. **3.13**

3.14 The second simplified planning zone adopted was designated for Willowbrook, Corby, by the Corby District Council. The scheme granted planning permission for General Industrial and Storage and Distribution uses (covered respectively by Classes B2 and B8 of the Use Classes Order). As with the Derby zone scheme, the permission granted was made subject to conditions (e.g., vehicular access and height of buildings) and contained a subzone where permission was granted for business use and for no other purpose.

The present position

3.15 Under amendments made to the 1990 Act by the Planning and Compulsory Purchase Act 2004, the local planning authority must make an SPZ if they decide it is desirable to do so. The Act also repeals the provision whereby any person may request the local planning authority to prepare an SPZ. The procedure for the preparation and adoption of SPZ schemes is somewhat similar to that required for the preparation of pre-2004 development plans. The procedure is dealt with in Sch 7 to the 1990 Act as amended by the 2004 Act and the regulations made thereunder.

4

DEVELOPMENT PLANS: BEFORE THE PLANNING AND COMPULSORY PURCHASE ACT 2004

PREFACE

This Chapter provides an outline of the various forms of development plan prepared since the introduction of the Town and Country Planning Act 1947.

Following the passing of the Planning and Compulsory Purchase Act 2004, most of the material in this Chapter dealing with the creation and operation of the system of structure plans, local plans and unitary development plans contained in the Town and Country Planning Act 1990 will be of limited relevance. Nevertheless, this Chapter may continue to be relevant with regard to general legal principles established during the currency of this system, as well as having a lingering significance with regard to the transitional provisions as the changes to the new system established by the 2004 Act are gradually introduced. For these reasons, after describing the general principles of the development plan system first introduced by the 1968 Act, Sections F to N of this Chapter set out in detail (albeit in the present tense), the statutory provisions which governed the creation and operation of that system under the 1990 Act.

A. HISTORICAL INTRODUCTION TO DEVELOPMENT PLANS

4.01 Development plans play a vital part in the system for the control of development. They constitute the main backcloth against which applications for planning permission are determined and decisions are made on whether or not to issue an enforcement notice to terminate unauthorised development. The strength of the development plan system is that it ensures that there is both a rational and a consistent basis for making those decisions.

4.02 It should be emphasised that although there is a presumption in favour of development plans they are not entirely prescriptive. They do not, for example, guarantee that an application for planning permission for development which conforms with the provisions of the development plan for an area will necessarily be granted, or that development which does not accord with the development plan will not be granted.

4.03 Development plans have a further purpose, namely the co-ordination of those factors which influence the scale, location and timing of the development or redevelopment of land, particularly with regard to the extent and availability of the necessary infrastructure.

4.04 Although the primary purpose of development plans has remained fairly constant from the first moment an obligation was placed on all local planning authorities to prepare them following the Town and Country Planning Act 1947, the form and content of development plans has undergone considerable change. Between 1948 and 2004 there have been three different types of development plan system, each of has able to influence the way in which development control functions under the planning Acts were exercised. The three types have been:

(a) Development plans prepared under provisions contained originally in the Town and Country Planning Act 1947.
(b) Development plans prepared under provisions contained originally in the Town and Country Planning Act 1968, comprising structure plans and local plans.
(c) Unitary development plans prepared under the provisions contained originally in the Local Government Act 1985 following the dissolution of the Greater London Council and the Metropolitan County Councils in April 1986. In many areas of the country where further unitary authorities have been created following the reorganisation of local government under the Local Government Act 1992, authorities have been required to prepare unitary development plans in preference to maintaining a structure and local plan.

B. DEVELOPMENT PLANS PREPARED UNDER THE 1947 ACT

The Town and Country Planning Act 1947 provided that as soon as may be after the appointed day (1 July 1948), each local planning authority should carry out a survey of their area and, within three years, or such extended period as the Minister might allow, submit to him a report of the survey together with a development plan for their area. The purpose of the survey was to assemble and collate information about the area to form the basis for the preparation of the authority's plan for that area. **4.05**

The purpose of the old-style development plan was to indicate the manner in which the local planning authority proposed that land in their area should be used, whether by the carrying out thereon of development or otherwise, and the stages by which such development should be carried out. In addition, the Act provided that a plan might in particular define the sites of proposed roads, public and other buildings and works, airfields, parks, pleasure grounds, nature reserves and open spaces, or allocate areas of land for use for agricultural, residential, industrial or other purposes of any class specified in the plan. The development plan could also define as an area of comprehensive development, an area which in the opinion of the authority should be developed as a whole for the purposes of dealing with extensive war damage, bad lay-out, or obsolete development, or for the purpose of relocating population or industry or replacing open space in the course of the development or redevelopment of an area. The statutory basis for the old-style development plans as now been removed and such plans are now part of history. **4.06**

The 1947 Act recognised the ever-changing nature of land use planning by imposing on each local planning authority a duty, once in every five years, to carry out a fresh survey of their area, and to submit to the Minister a report of the survey, together with proposals for any alterations or additions to the plan which appeared to them to be required. After 1968, these plans could not be amended without the Secretary of State's approval. **4.07**

Defects of the 1947 development plans system

4.08 By the mid-1960s, it had become clear that the development plan system established under the 1947 Act was failing to meet current needs. One of the main difficulties was that the content of the old-style development plans had been based on the two assumptions: that the population would remain stable and that there would be little growth in the volume of motor traffic. In fact, both these assumptions proved to be false. An increase in the population which followed the end of the Second World War had led to an increase in the demand for hospitals, schools and housing. An increase in the standard of living in the same period had led to an increase in the number of motor vehicles using the roads, to a need for investment in a new road programme to accommodate those vehicles, and thus to the growth of development pressure on land where it had never previously existed. In theory at least, it should have been possible for the old-style development plans to be amended to accommodate the changes that were then taking place. In practice, however, this proved to be impossible because of the rapid pace of change and the law's requirement that the same administrative procedures be followed for proposals to amend development plans as were required for their original preparation.

4.09 In addition, however, the old-style development plans had a further and more fundamental defect. The plans concentrated on land use, and did so in excessive detail. The concentration took place at the expense of many other factors which help to shape the environment but also require to be integrated into land use planning, such as national investment programmes and social and economic objectives. Indeed, in retrospect it seems unlikely that a single statutory document would ever be able to perform both functions adequately.

4.10 Against this background, in 1964 the Government set up a Planning Advisory Group comprising officers of local government, the professions and departments concerned to advise it on the future of the development plan system. Its report, *The Future of Development Plans,* published in 1965, recommended the gradual adoption of a new 'two-tier' development plan system. Most of the report's recommendations were given effect in the Town and Country Planning Act 1968; and later consolidated, first in the Town and Country Planning Act 1971, and now in the 1990 Act.

C. DEVELOPMENT PLANS PREPARED UNDER THE 1968 ACT

4.11 The statutory provisions relating to the two-tier development plan system which was introduced into the law by the Town and Country Planning Act 1968 are now to be found in Part II of the 1990 Act and the associated Town and Country Planning (Development Plan) (England) Regulations 1999, SI 1999/3280 (the Development Plan Regulations). The essence of the system was the creation of a single development plan for an area but one having two tiers, namely, a structure plan tier and a local plan tier, with each tier performing a different but related function.

4.12 The purpose of the structure plan tier of the development plan was that it should sketch general lines of development in an area with a broad brush. Basically, structure plans were concerned with land use, but dealt with it in terms of policies applicable to the major land uses such as employment, housing, education and recreation, and, in particular, transport policy and lines of communication within the area and in relation to neighbouring areas. Structure plans set out policies and proposals of structural or strategic importance for an area. They also provided important links between national economic and social planning and local land use planning. Because structure plans dealt with policies and proposals for a wide area in very general terms, they did not deal with individual properties or show the precise boundaries of areas where particular policies apply.

Local plans, on the other hand, were much more detailed than their parent structure plan. **4.13**
They dealt with local issues, but within the context of the policies set out in the structure plan. They developed and applied the policies of the structure plan in force for the area, and showed how these policies related to precisely defined areas of land. Local plans also provided the basis for the exercise of a local planning authority's development control functions. In addition, by allocating sites for particular purposes, they formed the basis on which the development or redevelopment of an area could proceed.

D. DEFECTS OF THE 1968 DEVELOPMENT PLANS SYSTEM

Although work had begun in 1971 on the preparation of the first structure plans, it was not **4.14**
until 1985, some 14 years later, that all the 82 'first-generation' structure plans which were to cover England and Wales had been approved. Subsequently, local (county) planning authorities were engaged in preparing alterations to structure plans; and in some cases, their complete replacement.

According to the Department of the Environment in 1986, one of the main reasons for **4.15**
the slowness in preparing and approving structure plan proposals was that many of the written statements and explanatory memoranda were much longer than they actually needed to be.

In the first round of approved structure plans, it was found that several contained more than **4.16**
100,000 words of policies and explanatory material. Many of them were also found to contain an inordinately large number of 'policies'; typically more than 100, but in one case 250. Overall, most of the structure plans submitted for approval contained development control policies of excessive length, leading to many modifications having to be made by the Secretary of State.

A second difficulty causing delay in the preparation and approval of structure plans was a **4.17**
widespread tendency for some local planning authorities to include policies in them that had little or nothing to do with land use planning or the physical environment. Examples of irrelevant policies in structure plans submitted for approval included those relating to building design standards, storage of cycles, the development of co-operatives, racial or sexual disadvantage, standards of highway maintenance, parking charges, the location of picnic sites and so-called 'nuclear-free zones'. In all these cases, approval by the Secretary of State was delayed by the need to delete or modify these proposals from the submitted structure plan.

4.18 As far as local plans were concerned, by 1986 only 474 local plans had been adopted and the average time taken between the deposit and the adoption of local plans was about 20 months. Although the Secretary of State regarded many local plans as too detailed and containing policies unrelated to the purposes of development plans, the main reason for delay in the adoption of local plans was seen as the length and complexity of the procedures for preparing them and the relationship between local plans and structure plans.

4.19 The defects of the 1968 development plan system led local planning authorities to begin to rely on non-statutory plans and policies to guide development in their areas, rather than take the formal steps of altering an existing development plan or preparing a new one. The result was that the public were denied the right to object to these plans and policies as they were not subject to the rigours of an independent examination in public, or to a public local inquiry.

4.20 Yet another difficulty was that there was little regional input into the content of plans particularly structure plans. To deal with this problem, the Government introduced Regional Planning Guidance (RPGs). For a number of years the first stage in the transmission of a national land use policy to local land use decision taking has been this guidance. According to Planning Policy Guidance Note 11 (PPG11) (now replaced by Regional Spatial Strategics PPS11) the function of regional planning guidance was expressed in the following terms:

> RPG sets out broad strategic policies at the regional level where there are matters which, though not of national scope, apply across regions or parts of regions and need to be considered on a scale wider than the area of a single strategic planning authority.

4.21 The main purpose of an RPG was to provide a regional spatial strategy within which local authority development plans and local transport plans could be prepared. They were intended to provide a broad development strategy for the region over a fifteen- to twenty-year period and identify the scale and distribution of provision for new housing and priorities for the environment, transport, infrastructure, economic development, agriculture, minerals and waste treatment and disposal. Their task was not to provide a regional checklist of everything that should be covered in a development plan. By virtue of being a spatial strategy they also informed other strategies and programmes.

4.22 The importance of RPGs in guiding and informing local planning authorities in the preparation of development plans was underpinned by statute. By s.31 (6) of the Town and Country Planning Act 1990, authorities were required to have regard to RPGs in formulating the general policies contained in structure plans. Corresponding duties were imposed in relation to unitary development plans and local plans by s.12(6) of the 1990 Act and regulation 20 of the Town and Country Planning (Development Plan) (England) Regulations 1999. The guidance in an RPG could also be a material consideration in the consideration of individual planning decisions.

4.23 It is important to note, however, that the preparation and formulation of RPGs was not governed by statutory provisions. The procedures followed were in fact non-statutory and are contained in PPG11. This non-statutory procedure mirrored to a great extent the statutory procedures land down by the 1990 Act and regulations made thereunder for the preparation of structure plans. The procedure involved the preparation of draft regional planning guidance by the Regional Planning Body in consultation with the relevant Government

Offices and major stakeholders. Then follows its publication; the consideration of written representations; the holding of an examination in public before an independent panel, and a report by the panel to the Secretary of State; publication of a further version of the RPG; further consultation, and eventually the issue of the RPG in its final form.

From the above, it should be clear that the translation of national planning policies into policies that determine local land use decisions, were synthesised from Central Government through regional planning, then structure or strategic planning, to local and unitary development plans. **4.24**

E. CHANGES TO THE 1968 DEVELOPMENT PLANS SYSTEM

The Government eventually decided upon the major legislative changes needed to the development plan system, which it introduced in the Planning and Compensation Act 1991. The legislative basis of the 1968 development plans system now found in Part II of the 1990 Act, has been amended by the 1991 Act. The key features of the system thereafter were as follows. **4.25**

Structure plans

(a) County councils were required to prepare (where they had not already done so) a *single* structure plan to cover the whole of their area. **4.26**

(b) County councils could adopt their own structure plans and so longer send them to the Secretary of State for his approval.

(c) The Secretary of State could by regulation prescribe the particular land use matters with which the general policies in a structure plan are to be exclusively concerned (s 31(4)). Such regulations could make different provisions for different cases and could be subject to any direction given in a particular case by the Secretary of State (s.31(9)).

(d) In formulating the general policies to be included in a structure plan, the relevant authority was required to have regard to specified matters including 'any regional or strategic planning guidance given by the Secretary of State to assist them in their preparation of their plan' (s 31(6)(a)).

(e) An authority wishing to prepare proposals in respect of a structure plan which the Secretary of State has previously called in and approved, in whole or in part, had first obtain the consent of the Secretary of State to do so (s 32(3)).

(f) A statutory duty was imposed on authorities to undertake pre-plan consultations with the public and other parties regarding matters to be included in the plan.

(g) The Secretary of State had an express right to object to such proposals, so long as he does so in accordance with the relevant regulations (s 33(5)).

(h) The Secretary of State was given power at any time during the period between the sending to him of a copy of the authority's proposals and their adoption, to direct the local planning authority to modify its proposals in such respects as are indicated in the direction (s 35(2)). A direction would normally indicate the nature of the change required to be made to the plan, but did not otherwise specify the amendment to be made.

(i) The Secretary of State had power at any time during the period between the sending to him of a copy of the authority's proposals and their adoption, to direct that all or any part of the proposals shall be submitted to him for his approval (s 35A(l)). The effect of such a direction was to prevent the local planning authority taking any further steps for the adoption of any of the proposals until the Secretary of State has given his decision on the proposals or the relevant part of the proposals (s 35A(2)(a)). Furthermore, once called in, the proposals or the relevant part of the proposals were not to have effect unless approved by the Secretary of State (s 35A(2)(b)). Having called in the proposals for his own decision, the Secretary of State could reject the proposals or approve them in whole or in part and with or without modifications or reservations (s 35A(4)). It is believed that the power to call in a development plan for the Secretary of State's own determination had not been exercised since May 1997.

(j) A local planning authority was required to hold an examination in public into any matter affecting their consideration of proposals to alter or replace a structure plan which they consider 'ought to be examined'. Similarly, if the Secretary of State calls in structure plan proposals for his own decision, he was given the power to hold an examination in public into such matters as he specifies (s 35B(2)). Any examination in public, whether held at the behest of the Secretary of State or the local planning authority, was to be conducted by a person or persons appointed by the Secretary of State (s 35B(3)). Where the local planning authority held an examination in public into matters affecting their proposals, the person or persons conducting the examination made a report to the authority, who had then to consider the report and decide what action to take, if any, on the report's recommendations. No one had a right to be heard at an examination in public. Attendance was by invitation. However, the local planning authority has the power to invite any person to take part in the examination, subject, of course, to the overriding right of the person conducting the examination to invite additional participants to take part. Where, however, the examination in public followed the call-in of structure plan proposals by the Secretary of State the power to invite any person to take part in the examination in public lay with the Secretary of State, not with the local planning authority (s 35B(5)).

(k) The Secretary of State had the power, exercisable after consultation with the Lord Chancellor, to make regulations with respect to the procedure to be followed at any examination in public (s.35B(6)). This power had never been exercised.

Local plans

4.27 Every local planning authority in a non-metropolitan area was required to prepare a single local plan covering the whole of its administration area (s 36(1)).

4.28 The Act emphasised the basic relationship between a structure plan and a local plan. The statute provided that 'a local plan shall be in general conformity with the structure plan' (s 36(4)). The county planning authority is required to supply the district planning authority with either a statement that the local plan or the proposals are in general conformity with the structure plan, or a statement that they are not in such conformity (s 46(2)). Where a statement of non-conformity is given, the 1990 Act now provided that it shall be treated by the district planning authority as an objection made to the provisions of the local plan (s 46(4)).

The 1990 Act provided that the local plan may designate any part of the authority's area as an action area. If an action area was so designated, the local plan had to contain a description of the treatment proposed by the authority for that area (s 36(7) and (8)). **4.29**

At one time, policies for the winning and working of minerals were contained within local plans or in a specific type of local plan called a subject plan. Under the 1990 Act it became the duty of the mineral planning authority to prepare a plan, to be known as a 'minerals local plan' for its area, formulating the authority's detailed policies for its area in respect of the winning and working of minerals or the deposit of mineral waste (s 37(1) and (2) of the 1990 Act). Since the mineral planning authority in a non-metropolitan area would, unless there was a unitary authority for the area, be a county planning authority, minerals local plans in those areas covered the whole of the administrative area of the county. **4.30**

As with the procedure for the alteration or replacement of a structure plan, a local planning authority, in preparing a local plan, is required to take steps to ensure that adequate publicity is given to its proposals. The remainder of this Chapter is, as indicated in the Preface to it, expressed in the present tense. **4.31**

F. STRUCTURE PLANS — PREPARATION AND ADOPTION

The survey

As with the 1947 style development plans, the development plans prepared under the 1968 scheme are based upon a survey. Section 30 of the 1990 Act provides that a local planning authority shall keep under review the matters which may be expected to affect the development of their area or the planning of its development; and may, if they think fit, at any time institute a fresh survey of their area examining those matters. Section 30 indicates a number of particular matters the authority are required to examine and keep under review. These include: **4.32**

(a) The principal physical and economic characteristics of the area of the authority and, so far as they may be expected to affect that area, of any neighbouring areas.
(b) The size, composition and distribution of the population of that area.
(c) The communications, transport system and traffic of that area and, so far as may be expected to affect that area, of any neighbouring area.
(d) Such other matters as may be prescribed or as the Secretary of State may in a particular case direct.

The survey is intended to provide information relating to the existing characteristics of the area covered by the proposed plan in order to assist in the formulation of the policies to be contained in the plan. **4.33**

Continuity, form and content

Since the whole of the country is covered by approved structure plans, the provisions that follow apply to proposals made to alter an approved plan, or to proposals for replacement of a plan. Section 32 of the 1990 Act provides that a local planning authority may at **4.34** any time prepare proposals for the alteration to the structure plan for their area, or for its replacement. An authority may not, however, without the consent of the Secretary of State, prepare proposals in respect of a structure plan if the plan or any part of the plan has been approved by the Secretary of State following a direction from him (under s 35A of the 1990 Act) that the proposals be submitted to him for approval. In addition, the Secretary of State is given power to direct an authority to prepare proposals for the alteration or replacement of a structure plan within a specified period.

4.35 Note that s 31(7) provides that where there is a structure plan relating to part of the area of the local planning authority, the authority shall prepare proposals for replacing those structure plans with a single structure plan relating to the whole of their area.

4.36 The form and content of a structure plan are determined by its function, and broad policies and proposals are best described in words. Hence s 31(2) of the 1990 Act provides that:

> A structure plan shall contain a written statement formulating the authority's general policies in respect of the development and use of land in their area.

4.37 In addition s 31(3) of the 1990 Act requires a structure plan to include policies and proposals in respect of:

(a) the conservation of the natural beauty and amenity of the land;
(b) the improvement of the physical environment; and
(c) the management of traffic.

4.38 In formulating their general policies for inclusion in the plan, s 31(6) requires authorities to have regard to;

(a) any regional or strategic guidance given by the Secretary of State . . .;
(b) current national policies;
(c) the resources likely to be available; and
(d) such other matters as the Secretary of State may prescribe or . . . direct.

4.39 In addition, in formulating their general policies, the Town and Country Planning (Development Plan) (England) Regulations 1999 (the 'Development Plan Regulations') require authorities to have regard to such matters as:

(a) economic, environmental and social considerations;
(b) the national waste strategy;
(c) the objectives of preventing major accidents and limiting the consequences of such accidents; and;
(d) the need;
  (i) in the long term, to maintain appropriate distances between establishments and residential areas, areas of public use and areas of particular sensitivity or interest; and
  (ii) in the case of existing establishments, for additional technical measures in accordance with Article 5 of the Directive so as not to increase the risks to people.

4.40 The requirement that a structure plan should formulate the authority's 'general policies' for its area (s 31(2)) is in marked contrast to the requirement that a local plan should contain 'detailed policies' for the development and use of land in the authority's area (s 36(2)). In *JS*

Bloor Ltd v Swindon BC [2001] EWHC Admin 966 an unsuccessful attempt was made to challenge a policy in a structure plan as outside the Act on the ground that it was not a 'general policy', but one requiring too detailed a level of consideration to be included in the structure plan. The policy sought to give directional guidance as to the location of major housing development, which, it was contended, was a matter of detail to be dealt with through the local plan process. The High Court held that the scope of the phrase 'general policy' was a matter of law for the courts to determine, but the question of whether a particular policy was within its scope was a matter for the decision-maker.

Although the form of the structure plan is a written statement, s 31(5) of the 1990 Act provides that the structure plan should also contain such diagrams, illustrations or other descriptive or explanatory matter in respect of the general policies and proposals as may be prescribed; and such other matters as the Secretary of State may, in any particular case, direct. The Development Plan Regulations provide that a structure plan shall contain a diagram, called a key diagram, illustrating the general policies formulated in the plan's written statement. The Development Plan Regulations go on to provide that a structure plan may also contain an inset diagram, drawn to a larger scale than the key diagram, illustrating the application of the general policies to part of the area covered by the structure plan. It is significant that the regulations go on to provide that no key diagram or inset diagram contained in a structure plan 'shall be on a map base'. This provision thus helps to prevent the identification on a structure plan of any particular parcel of land. **4.41**

Under s 32(5) of the 1990 Act, any proposals for the alteration or replacement of a structure plan must be accompanied by an explanatory memorandum. This explanatory memorandum must summarise the reasons which in the opinion of the local planning authority justify each of their proposals; any information on which the proposals are based; the relationship of the proposals to general policies for the development and use of neighbouring land which may be expected to affect the area to which the proposals relate; and may contain such illustrative material as the authority think appropriate. **4.42**

The explanatory memorandum is not a part of the structure plan though a copy has to be made available for inspection by the public along with the authority's proposals for the alteration or replacement of a structure plan; and a copy has to be sent to the Secretary of State along with the authority's proposals. Moreover, it was held in *Holden v Secretary of State for the Environment* [1994] JPL B1 that the explanatory memorandum does not form part of the relevant development plan for the purposes of s 54A of the 1990 Act (see later). **4.43**

Preparation and approval

Pre-deposit consultation

Since 1968, however, it was thought that the public and others should be able to influence the content of the development plan before the authority had become committed to any specific solution to the planning problems of their area, and before they took formal action to secure the plan's approval. The provisions relating to the preparation of the new-style development plans reflect this approach. **4.44**

4.45 Section 33(1) of the 1990 Act provides:

> When preparing proposals for the alteration or replacement of a structure plan for their area and before finally determining their contents the local planning authority shall—
>
> (a) comply with—
> (i) any requirements imposed by regulations made under section 53; and
> (ii) any particular direction given to them by the Secretary of State with respect to a matter falling within any of paragraphs (a) to (c) or (e) of sub-section (2) of that section; and
>
> (b) consider any representations made in accordance with those regulations.

4.46 Regulation 10 of the Development Plan Regulations provides that:

(1) When preparing proposals for a statutory plan or for the alteration or replacement of such a plan, . . . and before finally determining the contents of the proposals, the local planning authority shall consult—
(a) the Secretary of State for the Environment, Transport and the Regions;
(b) any local authority (except the council of any parish) for an area covered by the proposals;
(c) any local planning authority for an area adjacent to the area covered by the proposals;
(d) the Environment Agency;
(e) the Countryside Agency and the Nature Conservancy Council for England, in England;
(f) the Historic Buildings and Monuments Commission for England.

(2) The local planning authority shall consider any representations made by the consultees before finally determining the contents of the proposals.

(3) The local planning authority shall prepare a statement of any other persons they have consulted when preparing their proposals, in addition to those listed in paragraph (1), and of any steps they have taken to publicise their proposals and to provide persons with an opportunity of making representations in respect of those proposals.

4.47 It will be seen that in addition to the list of prescribed consultees in Regulation 10(1), local planning authorities are also given a discretion to consult others. The view taken by the Government is that authorities should use their judgment to determine what degree of publicity and consultation is appropriate, so allowing them flexibility to tailor their approach according to circumstances. Clearly proposals for a replacement structure plan may warrant wider publicity and consultation than proposals for a relatively minor alteration to an existing plan. Nevertheless, local planning authorities are expected to consult organisations with a particular interest in the proposals, including conservation and amenity groups and businesses, development and infrastructural interests.

The deposit of proposals

4.48 Section 33(2) of the 1990 Act provides that where an authority have prepared proposals for the alteration or replacement of a structure plan, they shall:

(a) make copies of the proposals and the explanatory memorandum available for inspection at such places as may be prescribed by . . . regulations;

(b) send a copy of the proposals and the explanatory memorandum to the Secretary of State; and
(c) comply with any requirements imposed by those regulations.

Regulation 11 of the Development Plan Regulations provides that an authority shall make the proposals available for inspection at the authority's principal office and such other places within their area as they consider appropriate; give notice of the fact by advertisement in the prescribed form; and give notice in similar form to any consultee under Regulation 10(1). The proposals made available for inspection must be accompanied by the explanatory memorandum, and a statement prepared by the local planning authority of persons consulted (other than those specifically identified in the regulations) together with steps taken by the authority to publish their proposals and to provide persons with an opportunity to make representations in respect of those proposals. **4.49**

Each copy of the proposals made available for inspection or sent to the Secretary of State in accordance with s 33(2) must state the prescribed period within which objections may be made to the authority. Regulation 12 of the Development Plan Regulations provides that: **4.50**

> The period within which objections and representations may be made to the local planning authority with respect to proposals for the alteration or replacement of a structure plan, made available for inspection under section 33(2)(a) shall be six weeks beginning with the date on which a notice given pursuant to Regulation 11(1)(b) is first published in a local newspaper.

The regulation also provides that objections and representations shall be made in writing and addressed to the local planning authority in accordance with the details given in the published notice. **4.51**

Section 33(5) of the 1990 Act provides that persons who may make objections in accordance with the regulations include, in particular, the Secretary of State. **4.52**

The authority must, of course, consider objections made in accordance with the Act and Regulations. Accordingly, s 33(6) of the 1990 Act provides that the proposals shall not be adopted by the authority until after they have considered any objection made in accordance with the regulations or, if no objections are made, after the expiry of the prescribed six-week period. **4.53**

It will be seen that the regulations allow 'representations' as well as objections to be made with respect to proposals for the alteration or replacement of a structure plan. Regulation 12(3) requires the local planning authority to consider in addition to any objections made, any representations made in accordance with the regulation. **4.54**

Adoption of proposals

Section 35(1) of the 1990 Act provides that: **4.55**

> . . . the local planning authority may by resolution adopt proposals for the alteration or replacement of a structure plan, either as originally prepared or as modified so as to take account of—
>
> (a) any objections to the proposals; or
> (b) any other considerations which appear to them to be material.

4.56 Section 35B(1) of the Act, however, provides that before adopting proposals for the alteration or replacement of a structure plan:

> . . . the local planning authority shall, unless the Secretary of State otherwise directs, cause an examination in public to be held of such matters affecting the consideration of the proposals as—
>
> (a) they consider ought to be so examined; or
> (b) the Secretary of State directs.

4.57 Two other matters should be noted. First, s 35B(3) provides that an examination in public shall be conducted by a person or persons appointed by the Secretary of State for that purpose. This provision is intended to ensure that the person or persons appointed should be independent of the local planning authority. Secondly, s 35B(4) provides that no person shall have a right to be heard at an examination in public. Under s 35B(5), however, the right of the local planning authority to take part is recognised, as is the overriding power of the person or persons holding the examination in public to invite any person to take part.

4.58 It is for the local planning authority responsible for the preparation of the structure plan, however, to make the initial decision as to the matters with which the examination in public will be concerned; and also the persons invited to take part in it. Under Regulation 14 of the Development Plan Regulations, the local planning authority must give notice of this information by advertisement at least six weeks before the opening of the examination in public; and the notice must invite representations to be made to the local planning authority on both the list of matters selected and the persons invited to take part.

4.59 As regards the selection of matters chosen for examination and the participants invited to take part in the examination in public, the Code of Practice on Structural Plans, issued by the Secretary of State in December 1999 says:

> 32 The authority should select only those issues arising on the deposited proposals on which they need to be more fully informed by means of public discussion in order to reach their decisions. All objections and representations will be looked at to see whether they give rise to issues which should be selected for examination. Responsibility for the selection of matters for examination lies with the authority unless the Secretary of State has used his reserve powers to direct the authority to examine a particular matter. The authority will, however, consult with the panel before finalising the list of matters to be examined.
>
> 33 Objection and representations will also help to identify those authorities, organisations and individuals whom the authority should consider inviting to take part in the EIP. The basic criterion in selecting participants will be the significance of the contribution which they can be expected to make to the discussion of the matters to be examined, either from their knowledge or from the views they have expressed. The authority and the panel have joint responsibility for the selection of participants to appear at an EIP.
>
> 34 As the purpose of an EIP is to discuss the selected issues, rather than to hear objections, it is not intended that all those who have objected should be invited to the examination. It is also unlikely that all those whose objections or representations relate to issues selected for discussion will be invited to take part. The aim will be to select participants (whether statutory bodies, interest groups or individuals) who between them represent a broad range of viewpoints and have a relevant contribution to make. Participants will not necessarily be just those who made objections or representations. As noted . . . the authority should make the list of issues and those who have been invited to participte available for inspection when the EIP is advertised.

> 35 There will be an opportunity for those who wish to send written comments about the selection of matters and participants to do so. The notice will state that comments made within this period will be considered and the authority, after consulting the Chair, may add or make changes to the list. However, since the published selection will have been made on the basis of the additional information considered necessary to enable the authority to take a decision on the deposited proposals, it is not normally likely that many changes will be necessary.

It has always been the intention and the form, that the person or persons (colloquially referred to as the panel) holding the examination in public should be as independent as possible, which explains the overriding power of the panel to invite persons to take part in the examination in public who have not been invited to do so by the local planning authority. **4.60**

The examination in public was a new kind of forum created by the Town and Country Planning Act 1972 as a result of the unique and special character of structure plans. Under the old-style development plan system, objectors to the plan were given an unfettered right to attend a local inquiry held into it by the Secretary of State. Had that right been made available for the new-style structure plans, the length of each inquiry might have been considerably prolonged by the duplication of evidence given by individuals making similar objections. In addition, it was feared that the nature of the structure plan might itself lead to an increase in the number of objectors, and therefore to an increase in the number who might wish to attend the subsequent local (public) inquiry. Hence the traditional forum for considering the authority's plan and objections to it was redesigned and given the new name of examination in public to distinguish it from the more traditional form of a local inquiry; and along with it the introduction of a process of selection for objectors and others wishing to attend. **4.61**

The panel

In the early days when the Secretary of State had decided to hold an examination in public, he normally proceeded to appoint three persons to conduct the examination, one of whom he appointed as chairman. The chairman was normally an independent person with a wide range of relevant experience in central or local government or in the professions concerned with land use. **4.62**

One of the other two members of the panel was likely to be a senior official from the appropriate regional office of the Department of the Environment, and the third member a senior Inspector from the Planning Inspectorate of the Department. Exceptionally, the Secretary of State could appoint assessors to assist the panel in cases where expert knowledge in a specialist field was essential. **4.63**

The role of the panel was to examine the matters selected for discussion to ensure that all information needed to reach a decision on the proposals had been made available. The Code of Practice now says that the EIP will take place before an independent chair, appointed by the Secretary of State, supported by one or more experts to form a panel. The panel will normally have only one other member but exceptionally it may be necessary to appoint a third. Unlike the traditional public local inquiry, the examination in public does not proceed by way of an examination-in-chief where the proposals are presented, followed by cross-examination of those presenting them and then possibly their re-examination. For **4.64** this reason, although it is open to participants to be accompanied or be represented by professional advisers, the practice has not been encouraged.

4.65 According to the Code of Practice:

> 43 The aim will be to secure a satisfactory examination of those issues selected for discussion, so that the authority can obtain the additional information needed to reach decisions on the plan. Particular attention will be paid to issues on which it seems likely that changes may need to be made before the plan is adopted. Such issues should, where appropriate, be investigated in such depth that there will be no need to re-open the examination later in relation to modifications which the authority propose to make.
>
> 44 The examination will take the form of a probing discussion involving the authority and other participants, led by the Chair or another member of the panel. As a general rule, the Chair will draw attention to those issues on which information and clarification are required, taking into account any statements submitted by participants. Participants may be invited to enlarge on their objections or statements or to question other participants, but the ordering of the discussion will be a matter for the Chair.
>
> 45 The Chair will ensure that the selected issues are examined in appropriate depth to enable the panel to make recommendations. Although the Chair may sometimes consider it necessary to discuss the detailed implications of the plan's general policies and proposals, the panel will, in reporting to the planning authority, confine their recommendations to the level of detail appropriate for a structure plan.
>
> 46 The panel will not have Counsel to assist them. It is not necessary for participants to be professionally represented. Participants should not feel that their contribution will be ineffective without such representation. The panel will take an active part in the discussion: if they consider that participants (whether a group or an individual) have a relevant point or argument which has not been developed sufficiently, the panel may take it up and pursue it.
>
> 47 It will be open to participants to be accompanied at the examination by professional or other advisers; to have their contributions made on their behalf; and to arrange for persons with special knowledge of a subject to take part in the discussion on their behalf. If a participant's place at the table is to be taken at any point by an adviser acting on behalf of the individual or group, this should be arranged in advance with the Panel Secretary.
>
> 48 An issue to be discussed may involve the interests of a government department (including the Department of the Environment, Transport and the Regions). Where it is considered that the department concerned can make a useful contribution to the discussion, it will be invited to send a participant. He or she will be there to explain the department's views about the plan which concern them, and to give appropriate information; the representative may explain departmental policies and their relevance, but will not be required to discuss their merits.

At the end of the examination in public, the report of the panel, together with its recommendations, is sent to the local planning authority. The authority must then give consideration to them before deciding whether or not to adopt the proposals, either as originally prepared or with modifications.

Ministerial intervention

4.66 As well as having the power to object to proposals for the alteration or replacement of a structure plan, the Secretary of State has power under s 35 of the 1990 Act, if it appears to him that the proposals are unsatisfactory, to direct the authority to modify the proposals in such respects as are indicated in the direction. An example of the use of this power occurred in early 1994, when the Secretary of State directed the Peak Park Joint Planning Board to include in its revised structure plan a requirement that the Board should 'have regard to the need to maintain a stock of permitted reserves [i.e., an aggregates land bank] appropriate for the National Park area . . . unless exceptional circumstances prevail'. Since then, the Secretary of State has used the power on at least six occasions including directing the modification of plans for Suffolk, Surrey, Berkshire, Kent, Bedfordshire and West Sussex. In the case of the last four of these, the directions related to the failure of the plans to propose adequate housing provision.

The wide extent of the Secretary of State's power under s 35 was seen in *R v West Sussex CC Secretary of State for the Environment, Transport and the Regions* [1999] PLCR 365, where the County Council unsuccessfully sought judicial review of a direction made by the Secretary of State which required the Council to modify proposals made in its structure plan so as to increase the number of new houses for which provision was to be made in the plan until the year 2011. According to the Court of Appeal, the Secretary of State is entitled under this power to direct the modification of proposals whether or not the planning authority has adopted them after proper consideration and testing, and whether or not they have received or are consistent with the approval of the panel which conducted the examination in public into the plan. Furthermore, the exercise of the power by him was not inhibited or limited by the terms of any planning guidance issued under the Act. Indeed, the judgment confirms the pre-eminence of the Secretary of State when arguments occur between central and local government as to the content of a development plan. The exercise of that power by the Secretary of State can only be challenged therefore, on the well-known *Wednesbury* principles. **4.67**

In addition to this power, under s 35A of the 1990 Act, the Secretary of State may, at any time before the local planning authority have adopted their proposals, direct that all or any part of the proposals shall be submitted to him for approval. Where the Secretary of State uses this power, he may approve the proposals in whole or in part and with or without modifications or reject them. **4.68**

Consideration of Panel's report

Regulation 15 of the Development Plan Regulations provides that following an examination in public and after considering the report of the panel holding the examination, the local planning authority must prepare a statement of the decisions they have reached in the light of the report and any recommendations contained in it, together with the reasons for those decisions. **4.69**

The failure to give reasons which are proper and adequate and deal with the substantial points that have been raised has given rise to much litigation, particularly with regard to the preparation and approval of local plans. Many of the cases are referred to in 4.7.2.6. In one recent case, *Test Valley BC v Hampshire CC* [2002] PLCR16, the High Court quashed part of a structure plan for breach of Regulation 16 where the local planning authority had failed, except by inference, to deal with an issue which the panel had described as a 'principal issue'. **4.70**

Modification of proposals

4.71 Regulation 17 of the Development Plan Regulations provides that where:

> . . . a local planning authority proposing to modify proposals . . . for the alteration or replacement of a structure plan (whether to comply with a direction given by the Secretary of State or on their own initiative) shall, unless they are satisfied that the modifications they intend to make will not materially affect the content of the proposals—
>
> (a) prepare a list of the modifications with their reasons for proposing them;
> (b) make copies of that list available for inspection at any place at which the plan proposals have been made available for inspection;
> (c) give notice by local advertisement [in the prescribed form]; and
> (d) serve a notice in similar form on any person who has objected to, or made a representation in respect of, the plan proposals in accordance with these regulations and not withdrawn the objection or representation, and such other persons as the authority think fit.

4.72 The need to advertise proposed modifications to a structure plan is regarded by the courts as important. In October 1990, in an unreported decision, the High Court quashed by consent, two policies in the Lancashire Structure Plan on the ground that there had been a failure to advertise the proposed modifications as required by the then Structure and Local Plan Regulations.

4.73 The period within which objections and representations may be made to the local planning authority in respect of proposed modifications is six weeks from the date notice was first published in a local newspaper. The regulations require the objections and representations to be made in writing.

4.74 In dealing with the consideration of objections to proposed modifications proposed by the local planning authority, the Guide to Procedures says:

> 59 When the six-week period for objections to modifications or to a decision not to accept a recommendation in the panel report has expired, the authority must consider all the objections made and decide whether it is necessary to re-open the EIP. If they decide to propose further modifications, either directly in response to objections or following receipt of panel recommendations (if the EIP is re-opened), these must be advertised in accordance with the procedure described above. However, if the authority decide that no further modifications materially affecting the content of the plan need to be contemplated, they will give another notice of their intention to adopt the plan after 28 days.
>
> 60 The authority have discretion whether to re-open the EIP in connection with all or any of the objections made to its proposed modifications, or to any decision not to accept EIP panel's recommendation. A re-opened EIP to consider matters raised by proposed modifications will not normally be necessary where the matters raised have already been considered, or where there are objections to the decision by the authority not to accept recommendations in the panel report. The Secretary of State advises authorities to re-open an EIP only where the modifications raise issues that were not examined at the earlier stage but need further consideration. This may arise, for example, if it is proposed to substitute an entirely different proposal for one which was in the plan as considered earlier, so that the objections made to the proposed modification include new evidence which needs further public examination.
>
> 61 If the authority re-open the EIP, they must carry out the same procedure for giving public notice as they did for the original EIP. At the end of the process the EIP Chair reports to the authority who then decide what action to take on each of the recommendations. The authority

must prepare a statement of their decisions to each recommendation and give their reasons for reaching them, paying particular attention to any recommendation they do not accept.

Where, after the holding of an examination in public into a structure plan, or a public local inquiry into a local plan, the panel or the Inspector (as the case may be) recommends modifications to the authority's draft proposals, the way in which the modifications are dealt with has given rise to some difficulty. There are a number of reasons for this: **4.75**

(a) the continuing issue by government departments of Planning Guidance Notes and draft planning guidance notes;
(b) the acceptance by planning authorities of modifications proposed by objectors during the adoption process;
(c) the fact that many local plans are prepared in tandem with alterations to structure plans, and any change in the draft structure plan may have a domino effect on the content of the local plan;
(d) the pressure on local authorities to complete development plan preparation and adoption as soon as possible.

With regard to the issue of new guidance during the course of an examination in public or public local inquiry, the Panel or Inspector would be expected to take this into account in making recommendations; and the local planning authority will have to decide whether formal modifications need to be made to the proposed plan. **4.76**

If new guidance is issued after the Panel or Inspector has reported, the local planning authority will again have to decide whether any formal modifications are needed to the plan to reflect the new guidance. However, if new information becomes available at a late stage in the adoption process, and the modification of the plan would only delay implementation of proposals not affected by the new information, it may be preferable to adopt the plan and start an early review of the adopted plan. **4.77**

The adoption

Under Regulation 19 of the Development Plan Regulations, when a local planning authority resolve to adopt proposals for the alteration or replacement of a structure plan, the authority must: **4.78**

(a) publish a notice once in the *London Gazette* and for two successive weeks in at least one local newspaper stating the date on which the plan was adopted, and the date when it became operative (copies of this notice, together with copies of the plan as adopted and copies of the reports and other relevant documents, must be made available for inspection at the authority's office); and
(b) send an individual notice to anyone who asked to be notified of the adoption of the plan and to the Secretary of State.

G. LOCAL PLANS — PREPARATION AND ADOPTION

As indicated earlier, local plans set out, within the general context of the structure plan, detailed policies and specific proposals for the development and use of land. The content of a **4.79** local plan is an important guide in the making of planning control decisions. Local plans also enable local communities to participate in decisions about where development should be accommodated in their area.

Form and content

4.80 Section 36(1) of the 1990 Act provides that the local planning authority shall, within such period (if any) as the Secretary of State may direct, prepare for their area a plan to be known as a local plan.

4.81 In addition, s 39 provides that a local planning authority may at any time prepare proposals for alterations to the local plan for their area, or for its replacement. Any proposals for the alteration of a local plan may relate to the whole or part of the area to which the plan relates. By s 36(2) of the 1990 Act, a local plan shall contain a written statement formulating the authority's detailed policies for the development and use of land in their area.

4.82 Section 36(3) provides that the policies in the local plan shall include policies in respect of:

(a) the conservation of the natural beauty and amenity of the land;
(b) the improvement of the physical environment; and
(c) the management of traffic.

4.83 In formulating their detailed policies the authority is required to have regard to such information and other considerations as the Secretary of State may prescribe or, in a particular case, direct; and the provisions of any enterprise zone scheme designated under the Local Government, Planning and Land Act 1980 (s 36(9)).

4.84 The section expressly excludes from inclusion in a local plan, policies in respect of the winning and working of minerals or the depositing of mineral waste and policies in respect of the depositing of refuse or waste materials other than mineral waste. This is because the 1990 Act requires the preparation of separate minerals local plans and waste local plans (see below).

4.85 In addition, a local plan may designate any part of the authority's area as an action area, i.e., an area which is to be treated comprehensively by development, redevelopment or improvement (or partly by one and partly by another method) commencing during a prescribed period. If an area is so designated, the plan must contain a description of the treatment proposed by the authority. Under the Development Plan Regulations the prescribed period is 10 years from the date the plan was first made available for inspection (Regulation 8).

4.86 Although it is provided that a local plan should contain a written statement etc., s 36 provides that it must also contain:

(a) a map illustrating each of the detailed policies, and
(b) such diagrams, illustrations or descriptive matter in respect of policies as may be prescribed,

and may contain such descriptive or explanatory matter as the authority think appropriate. For the purposes of s 36, 'policies' include 'proposals'.

The Development Plan Regulations specify that the map included in a local plan shall be called the proposals map and shall be a map of the authority's area reproduced from, or based upon, an Ordnance Survey map and shall show national grid lines and reference numbers. Furthermore, the regulations provide that policies for any part of the authority's area may be illustrated instead on a separate map on a larger scale than the proposed map, to be called an inset map (Regulation 6). **4.87**

Under Regulation 7, a local plan must contain a reasoned justification of the policies formulated in the plan. The reasoned justification should contain a statement of the regard which the local planning authority have had in formulating their policies to any enterprise zone scheme in their area. **4.88**

Deposit of proposed plan

Pre-deposit consultation

The 1999 Regulations no longer prescribe a list of pre-deposit statutory consultees. Although the view is taken that it is for local planning authorities to decide for themselves those whom they need to consult on particular issues relating to the plan, Annex C of PPG 12 Development Plans (December 1999) gives details of organisations which local planning authorities may wish to consult on specific issues. This new procedure envisages consultation to be based on a 'key issue' approach which identifies the main issues and choices which need to be resolved by the plan. **4.89**

The deposit of proposals

As with the provisions in the 1990 Act relating to pre-deposit consultation, the provisions relating to the deposit of proposals contained in a local plan in s 40(2) to (7) of the Act replicate almost in their entirety the provisions found in s 33(2) relating to the deposit of proposals for the alteration or replacement of a structure plan (see 4.6.3.2). However, as with pre-deposit consultation, the regulations relating to local plans dealing with the deposit of the proposals, differ somewhat from those relating to structure plans. **4.90**

The regulations introduced in December 1999 provide for a two-stage deposit for local plans. **4.91**

The first stage

Once the authority has prepared their local plan for deposit, they must advertise the fact by publishing a notice in two successive weeks in at least one local newspaper circulating in the area covered by the plan and also once in the *London Gazette*. The notice must specify where copies of the plan and other relevant documents (including the authority's statement of pre-deposit consultation and publicity) have been deposited and when they are available for inspection. The advertisement must also specify the objections and representations in support of the plan may be made within six weeks of the plan being placed on deposit. **4.92**

Objections and representations made after the six week period may often be 'taken on board' by the authority along with those made within the six weeks period, though there is no requirement that an authorities must do so. In *R v Hinkley and Bosworth Borough Council, ex p F. L. Fitchett and J. S. Bloor (Services) Ltd* [1997] JPL754 the High Court granted judicial review of the decision made by the authority not to entertain objections received by the Council **4.93** after the six-week period had expired. In this case, the relevant regulation had required objections to be made to the Council by midnight on 12 November. The Council had indicated to objectors that objections received by 5 p.m. on Monday 13 November would nevertheless be treated as 'duly made'. The applicants had delivered their objections to the Council's offices at 5.04 p.m. on that day. The Court held that the Council's decision not to entertain the applicant's objections *Wednesbury* unreasonable given that they had accepted objections made earlier that day.

4.94 The local planning authority may after considering objections made to and representations on the deposited plan at the first stage, decide to enter into discussions with a view to negotiating revised proposals which meet objections. Should these be resolved, the objector will then be invited to withdraw the objection at the second (revised) deposit stage. If objections are, however, unresolved at this stage, they will be automatically carried forward to be dealt with by the Inspector at the inquiry stage.

The second stage (revised deposit)

4.95 At this stage the authority will produce a revised plan indicating the changes that have been made from the initially deposited plan. It will also include changes which the authority wishes to make to the initially deposited plan.

4.96 Having produced a revised plan, the local planning authority must then advertise the fact that the plan is to be placed on revised deposit by a notice including the same details as given in the notice of deposit stage, including notice that objections may be made to the revised deposit within a period of six weeks. It should be noted however, that objections or representations at the revised deposit stage are limited to those proposals which the authority has changed between the deposit and the revised deposit stages.

Adoption of proposals

4.97 Section 43 of the 1990 Act provides that:

> (1) . . . the local planning authority may by resolution adopt proposals for a local plan or for its alteration or replacement, either as originally prepared or as modified so as to take account of—
>
> (a) any objections to the plan; or
>
> (b) any other considerations which appear to them to be material.

4.98 As stated, however, s 40(7) provides that a local plan or proposal for its alteration or replacement shall not be adopted by the authority under s 43 until:

(a) after they have considered any objections made in accordance with the regulations; or
(b) if no such objections are made, after the expiry of the prescribed period.

4.99 Unlike proposals for the alteration or replacement of a structure plan where the local planning authority must normally cause an examination in public to be held, s 42 of the Act provides:

> (1) Where any objections have been made, in accordance with the regulations, to proposals for a local plan or for its alteration or replacement copies of which have been made available for inspection under section 40(2), the local planning authority shall cause a local inquiry or other hearing to be held for the purpose of considering the objections.

(2) The local planning authority may cause a local inquiry or other hearing to be held for the purpose of considering any other objections to the proposals.

(2A) No local inquiry or other hearing need be held under this section if all persons who have made objections have indicated in writing that they do not wish to appear.

By Regulation 26 of the Development Plan Regulations a local planning authority must: **4.100**

> . . . at least six weeks before the opening of any local inquiry or other hearing which they cause to be held to consider objections to a plan or proposals to which Regulation 22 refers—
>
> (a) give any person who has objected to, or made a representation in respect of, the plan or proposals in accordance with these Regulations and not withdrawn the objection or representation, notice of the time and place at which the inquiry or other hearing is to be held, the name of the person appointed to hold it, and its purpose; and
>
> (b) in the case of a local inquiry, give notice of that information by local advertisement.

Where an inquiry is held, it is conducted by an Inspector appointed by the Secretary of State. **4.101**
Although the Act provides for regulations to be made to allow the local planning authority to nominate the person appointed to hold the inquiry, no regulations to permit this have yet been made. The reason for this is that there is little public confidence in the ability of a local planning authority to appoint a person having the kind of independence which is associated with those now appointed by the Secretary of State, most of whom are members of the Department's Planning Inspectorate.

No regulations have ever been made prescribing the procedure to be followed at any public **4.102**
local inquiry or hearing. The procedure is to a great extent governed by the Code of Practice on Local Plans and Unitary Development Plans issued by the Secretry of State in December 1999. Although the code has no statutory force, compliance with it reduces the prospect of a subsequent legal challenge being made to a plan based upon an allegation that objections have not been fairly considered or that there had been a breach of natural justice. The code is not exhaustive, however, and situations may sometimes arise which the code does not cover.

Adoption procedure

At the close of the local inquiry, the Inspector conducting the inquiry will report to the local **4.103**
planning authority. Regulation 26(2) of the Development Plan Regulations provides that:

> A local planning authority shall, within eight weeks of receiving the report of the person holding an inquiry or other hearing . . . make that report available for inspection . . .

Under Regulation 27, the local planning authority is required to consider the Inspectors' report and recommendations and afterwards to prepare a statement of the decisions they have reached in the light of the report and any recommendations contained in the report; and the reasons for these decisions which do not follow a recommendation contained in the report.

The duty upon a local planning authority to consider the report of the person holding the **4.104**
inquiry and to prepare a statement of the decisions reached in the light of the report and recommendations and to give reasons for those decisions is a heavy one. In *Miller v Wycombe DC* [1997] JPL 951 the Court dismissed an appeal against a decision of the High Court to quash part of the authority's local plan where there had been a deficiency of reasons given for the decision made. According to Pill LJ:

> It was incumbent upon the Council . . . to demonstrate that minds had been applied to the Inspector's report, the recommendations and the findings which had led to it. Specific consideration of his findings was required.

4.105 In his Lordship's view the council:

> failed to deal with the substantial points raised by the independent Inspector. They [did] not either express reasons for disagreeing with his findings or give a reasoned explanation for ignoring them in favour of other considerations which they consider[ed] important.

4.106 In *Welsh Development Agency v Carmarthenshire CC* [2000] JPL 692, the Court of Appeal summarised the case law relevant to this duty and the approach that should be made to it. First, according to the Court, the local planning authority must consider the recommendations of the Inspector in accordance with normal public law principles, that is, with an open mind and fairly grappling with the substantial points raised. Secondly, the reasons which are to be given can, in appropriate circumstances, be brief and terse. If no new point is raised by the Inspector which requires consideration, the reasons of the authority can constitute a repetition of its case as seen in *Westminster City Council v Great Portland Estates plc* [1985] AC 661. Thirdly, where a point is raised by the Local Plan Inspector, the planning authority must deal with it. Mere repetition of its previous stance is not in such cases adequate. Fourthly, where the question is essentially one of planning judgment, the reasons may need little elaboration as stated by Lord Bridge in *Save Britain's Heritage v No 1 Poultry Ltd* [1991] 1WLR153. Fifthly, in examining the adequacy of reasons, a Regulation 27(1) statement is not to be looked at *in vacuo* but in the context of the documentation in which it arises.

4.107 As with proposals for the alteration or replacement of a structure plan, a local planning authority may propose, after considering the report of the Inspector, to modify their proposals for the alteration or replacement of a local plan.

4.108 In doing so, the authority must comply with the provisions of Regulation 29 of the Development Plan Regulations. The period within which objections and representations may be made to the local planning authority in respect of the proposed modification is six weeks from the date notice was first placed in a local newspaper. The regulations require objections and representations to be made in writing. The authority have a discretion as to whether or not to hold a further public local inquiry. The courts have taken the view that a decision not to hold a further inquiry can only be challenged on *Wednesday* unreasonable grounds. The Secretary of State has taken the view that a decision to hold a fresh inquiry should only be taken in exceptional circumstances. The exercise by a local planning authority of this discretion has given use to much litigation. It includes the following cases.

4.109 In *British Railways Board v Slough BC* [1993] JPL 678, the High Court quashed part of the authority's local plan on the ground that the refusal of the authority to hold a fresh inquiry had been unreasonable, given that after the Inspector conducting the inquiry into the plan had proposed modifications to the authority's proposals for the use of a particular piece of land, the authority had proposed yet another modification to the proposals for the use of the land. In that case the proposed modification was a completely different proposal from that considered at the inquiry. There had, in effect, been a volte-face by the Council on the appropriate use of the land after the holding of the inquiry.

However, in *Pelham Homes Ltd v Secretary of State for the Environment* [1995] JPL 816, the High Court found that it was not unreasonable of Runnymede Borough Council not to hold a further inquiry before adopting a first alteration to its local plan after receiving the Inspector's report and recommendation on the proposed alterations. The authority's case was the same in all material particulars as it had been at the original inquiry and the new material taken into account was limited in amount and significance. **4.110**

Despite the language of the relevant statutory provisions, it seems that an obligation to hold a further inquiry may also exist in cases where the authority are minded to adopt the plan as originally proposed and without modifications where objections remain to the original proposals. **4.111**

An extreme example of a local planning authority closing its mind to all arguments is seen in *Stirk v Bridgnorth DC* (1996) EGCS 159. There the applicants had made objections to a proposal in the local plan that their land be included in the Green Belt, their objections being based upon modifications which had been made to the 'parent' structure plan by the Secretary of State, shortly before the local plan had been placed on deposit. The objections were subsequently upheld by the local plan Inspector, who recommended that modifications be made to the local plan to exclude the applicant's land from the Green Belt. Despite this the authority decided not to accept the recommendation, maintaining that the matter had been adequately debated at the local plan inquiry. In granting the application to quash that part of the local plan which defined the Green Belt to include the applicant's property, the High Court held that the authority had failed to give proper consideration to the Inspector's report and recommendation, so that the decision to adhere to the plan without modification was perverse and irrational. Furthermore, the High Court held that even if the authority's consideration of the Inspector's report had been adequate, the decision not to hold a further inquiry was still flawed because the applicants had no opportunity to comment at the inquiry on the points made by the Inspector in his report, nor did they have an opportunity to comment upon new material which formed part of the authority's case for rejecting the Inspector's reasoning. The decision to quash was subsequently upheld by the Court of Appeal 73 PCR 439. **4.112**

It should not be forgotten that although there are no Inquiry Procedure Rules for structure or local plan inquiries analogous to those which govern s 78 appeals, there is, nevertheless, an obligation on those who both propose and decide on the content of the plan to act fairly in considering objections to it. Part of this process involves the scrutiny and consideration of objections by an independent Inspector. **4.113**

In *Housebuilders Federation Ltd v Stockport MBC and Secretary of State for the Environment, Transport and the Regions* [2000] JPL 616, the Court accepted counsel's formulation of the obligations placed upon a local planning authority by Regulation 16(1) as requiring the authority (1) to deal with the substantial points raised by the Inspector and (2) to demonstrate that its mind had been applied 'thoroughly conscientiously and fairly' to the Inspector's report. **4.114**

A further example of the need to act fairly is seen in the case of *Harlowby Estates Ltd v Harlow DC* (1997) JPL 541 where the local plan Inspector had recommended that a plan be modified to exclude the applicant's land from the Green Belt and that it be allocated for housing. Contrary to that recommendation, the authority proposed to retain the applicant's land in **4.115** the Green Belt, but in order to meet any housing shortfall to modify the plan to allocate other land for housing in place of the applicant's land. The applicant then objected to the proposed modification, seeking to substitute his own land in place of the other land selected for housing. Then, despite the applicant's objections, the Council proceeded to adapt the local plan with the modifications the authority had proposed.

4.116 The applicant then successfully sought an order under s 287 of the 1990 Act to quash the relevant provisions in the plan. The High Court held that the Inquiry had at no point considered the possibility of allocating the other land for housing. It had never addressed the site-specific objections to it which had been raised by the applicant, nor had any comparison been made between the alternative proposals. The facts clearly indicated that a further inquiry should have been held.

4.117 Almost the final word in this area is the case of *Warren v Uttlesford DC* [1997] JPL 562. In order to provide for new housing consequent upon the expansion of facilities at Stansted Airport to accommodate an increase in passenger numbers from 8 to 15 million per year, the Council had proposed in a consultation draft of a local plan for the area the provision of 2,500 new housing units to be constructed at two separate sites. The applicants and others had objected to that proposal at the consultation draft stage and were no doubt relieved to find that when the plan was formally placed on deposit, the proposal for two separate sites had been abandoned and replaced by a proposal for a single unified settlement of 2,500 units closer to the airport.

4.118 Objections were then raised by *others* to the proposal as a result of which a local plan inquiry was held and the Inspector, after considering the issues, recommended that the new housing be allocated to four separate sites rather than the one proposed in the plan.

4.119 The applicants, who sought to quash the relevant parts of the local plan, had not appeared at the Inquiry. They had asked to do so to present their case as counter-objectors to those who supported a dispersed site strategy being put forward by other objectors. The Inspector had declined the applicants' request for them to appear, but had indicated he would take into account written representations, be they objections to or in support of proposals in the plan.

4.120 In due course the Council decided to accept the Inspector's recommendation and advertised a proposed modification to the plan to provide for a housing allocation to the four dispersed sites. The applicants then objected to the proposed modifications, but subsequently claimed that before adopting the local plan with these modifications the Council should have given them the opportunity to present their objections at a further inquiry. In dismissing this application, Mr George Bartlett QC sitting as a Deputy Judge in the High Court, held that the decision not to hold a further inquiry had not been unreasonable, since no new point of substance had been made by the applicants in their objections to the modifications and there were no new issues to be argued at another inquiry. In the Deputy Judge's view in deciding whether or not to hold a further inquiry, one had to look at the totality of the local plan procedure. One also had to consider the interests of other parties who had participated in the earlier stages of the local plan adoption process, notably those who had argued in favour of the modifications being made and the extent to which they might be prejudiced or burdened by a further inquiry. Also of importance was the public interest in having an up-to-date operative local plan without delay. In his judgment, the most important single consideration in any decision as to whether to hold a further inquiry was whether the proposed modification raised any new issue not before the Inspector.

The applicants then appealed against the decision of the Deputy Judge to the Court of Appeal. In dismissing the appeal ([1999] JPL 1130), the Court held that one of the matters to be considered when deciding whether or not to hold an inquiry to consider objections to proposed modifications, is whether or not the decision would be unfair to counter-objectors. If the authority failed to consider the point or came to an adverse conclusion, the decision was liable to be struck down. In deciding whether the authority's decision not to hold an inquiry was procedurally unfair, the Court had to bear in mind not merely the position of the parties before the Court, but also all others who might be affected by any order the Court might make quashing the decision. The Court also had to give weight to the authority's 'view of the general situation' in deciding not to hold an inquiry. There had been no unfairness in the authority's decision. **4.121**

At the end of the day, however, one cannot help feeling considerable sympathy for the objectors. They were forced, at the inquiry stage, to sit on the sidelines as mere observers of a contest that was to decide the future of their area; and they would have been better off had the proposal in the consultation draft been carried through into the draft plan when placed on deposit — when they would have appeared, as of right, at the local plan inquiry as objectors to proposals in the plan. **4.122**

The judgments in both the *Stirk* and *Warren* cases were quoted with approval in *Doncaster MBC v Rossington Hall Investments Ltd* [2001] PLCR 242. The respondents had wished to develop land part of which was in the approved green belt in the current development plan. The local planning authority was in the course of preparing a Unitary Development Plan for the area and, being in favour of the development, provided for it in the new plan. The respondents did not appear at the UDP inquiry, but provided witnesses to support the council's case. In his report, the Inspector found insufficient justification for the development and recommended that it be deleted from the plan and that the land should be retained within the green belt. After considering the Inspector's report the Council accepted his recommendations and proceeded to publish lhe required modifications to the plan. The Council then rejected the respondent's objections to the proposed modifications and refused to hold a second inquiry. The respondent successfully applied to the High Court to quash the relevant part of the plan. On appeal however, the decision of the High Court was overturned by the Court of Appeal [2001] PLCR 242, who held that the Council was entitled to consider that the respondent's proposals were not new and that the issues they raised had in substance been addressed by the Inspector. There had been nothing perverse or unfair in the Council refusing to hold a second inquiry. **4.123**

Other recent authorities on this issue include *Drexfine Holdings Ltd v Cherwell DC* [1998] JPL 361 where the High Court considered that the following matters should be included in considering whether a further public inquiry should be held: **4.124**

(a) whether the issue raised had been previously subject to independent scrutiny by an Inspector;
(b) the advice in para 69 of Annex A to PPG 12 (now cancelled);
(c) whether a second inquiry would be of material benefit to the decision-making process;

(d) delay and the desirability of securing an up-to-date adopted development plan; and
(e) fairness to the objector and other parties.

4.125 In *Berridge v Doncaster MBC* [2000] JPL 531, the High Court followed the criteria laid down in the *Warren* and *Drexfine* decisions.

4.126 In *Alfred McAlpine Homes Northumbria Ltd v Darlington BC* [1999] JPL 53, a failure by the authority properly to take into account matters (a), (b), (c) and (e) above in deciding not to hold a further inquiry, led the High Court to quash the material parts of the authority's local plan.

4.127 Lastly, in *Bainbridge v Hambledon DC* (7 December 1999), Sullivan J in a wide-ranging review of previous authorities concerning decisions by local planning authorities not to hold a further inquiry, said:

> There is no rule that the local planning authority is unable to disagree with an Inspector's findings of 'primary fact' and adhere to views earlier expressed. The underlying rule which emerges from all of the authorities cited above is that the reasons must demonstrate that the local planning authority has grappled with the reasoning underlying the Inspector's recommendation. That rule accurately reflects the different functions of the Inspector and the local planning authority in the Local Plan System: the former inquires and recommends, the latter decides in the light of the inquiry and recommendations.

4.128 In considering all the above cases, it should be noted that the relevant regulations were those issued in 1991 which did not include a provision for a two-stage deposit for local plans now contained in the 1999 regulations. Indeed, the 1999 regulations may have been introduced in part in an attempt to reduce the likelihood of a need for a modifications inquiry and thus resolve many of the problems which gave rise to the litigation.

The adoption

4.129 As with proposals relating to structure plans, Regulation 31 of the Development Plan Regulations provides that when a local planning authority resolves to adopt proposals for a local plan or for the alteration or replacement of a local plan, the authority should publish a notice once in the *London Gazette* and for two successive weeks in at least one local newspaper stating the date on which the plan was adopted, and the date when it became operative (copies of this notice, together with copies of the plan as adopted and copies of the reports and other relevant documents, must be made available for inspection at the authority's office), and send an individual notice to anyone who asked to be notified of the adoption of the plan.

Certificate of conformity

4.130 The 1990 Act contains a number of provisions designed to protect the integrity of the two-tier development plan system.

4.131 Section 36(4) of the 1990 Act boldly states:

> A local plan shall be in general conformity with the structure plan.

To be doubly sure of the effectiveness of this provision, however, s 46 of the Act provides that an authority responsible for the local plan shall not proceed to the pre-deposit consultation process required by s 40 unless the county planning authority have issued a certificate that the proposals conform generally to the structure plan. The procedure involves the district planning authority serving on the county planning authority a copy of the plan or proposals. The county planning authority must then issue a statement that the plan or proposals are in general conformity; or that they are not in such conformity. In the case of the latter, the statement must specify the respects in which the plan or proposals are not in such conformity; and that statement must then be treated by the local planning authority as a statutory objection to the plan or proposals.

Although the requirements that a local plan should be in general conformity with the structure plan will normally prevent any conflict arising between the two, s 46(10) of the 1990 Act provides that if a conflict does arise, the provisions of the local plan shall prevail over the structure plan. The provision does not apply, however, where a structure plan has been altered or replaced, and the planning authority have notified the district planning authority under s 35C of that fact and that, in their opinion, the local plan does not so conform. **4.132**

Secretary of State's power to call in

As with applications for planning permission where the Secretary of State has a right to call in the application for his own determination, the Secretary of State has the right to call in a local plan proposal for his approval. Section 44(1) of the 1990 Act provides: **4.133**

> After copies of proposals have been sent to the Secretary of State and before they have been adopted by the local planning authority, the Secretary of State may direct that the proposals or any part of them shall be submitted to him for his approval.

With regard to that sub-section, s 44(2) of the 1990 Act further provides that if the Secretary of State issues a direction in accordance with s 44(1): **4.134**

(a) the authority shall not take any further steps for the adoption of any of the proposals until the Secretary of State has given his decision on the proposals or the relevant part of the proposals; and
(b) the proposals or the relevant part of the proposals shall not have effect unless approved by him and shall not require adoption by the authority under section 43.

The power to call in a local plan proposal is only likely to be used in a limited range of circumstances. It is likely that the Secretary of State would only consider it appropriate to do so: **4.135**

(a) where the plan (i.e. local plan proposals) raises issues of national or regional importance; or
(b) where the plan (i.e. local plan proposals) gives rise to substantial controversy, for example, having an impact beyond the area of the plan-making authority.

The Secretary of State may also call in local plan proposals for his consideration where the local planning authority have failed to modify them to take into account an objection made by the Ministry of Agriculture, Fisheries and Food (s 44(3)). **4.136**

Once local plan proposals have been called in by the Secretary of State, he may, under s 45 either approve them or reject them. **4.137**

4.138 The power to call in local plan proposals under this provision and then to reject them has only been used on a limited number of occasions. In January 1986 the Secretary of State gave a direction to the London Borough of Southwark that the North Southwark Local Plan should not have effect unless approved by him. According to the Secretary of State, he took the action because of conflict between the local plan and national policies on industrial development. He also considered that as proposed to be adopted, the local plan was inconsistent with the objects and general powers of the London Docklands Urban Development Corporation to secure regeneration of its area.

4.139 After considering the plan, the Inspector's report of the public local inquiry and the council's decision on that report, he decided to use his power under the section to reject the plan. In doing so, the Secretary of State said he considered the plan conflicted both with government policies spelt out in Circulars and the approved Greater London Development Plan. He also noted that the plan was opposed in general to private investment in the area and was critical and hostile to the objectives of the development corporation. He considered that these defects, which the council were not prepared to rectify, were of such a nature as to flaw fundamentally the plan as a whole.

4.140 Another example occurred in 1987. Then, at the same time as Merton London Borough Council were considering proposals for a Wimbledon Town Centre Local Plan, the Secretary of State had to consider two competing applications for planning permission for the development of the town centre, only one of which was favoured by the council. One of the applications he was considering on appeal following the refusal of the application by the council. The other he was considering following his decision to call-in the application for his own determination. As things stood there was thus a danger of inconsistency between his decision on the applications and the council's decision on the local plan.

4.141 The Secretary of State decided, therefore, to call-in the local plan in order that he could consider it at the same time as he was considering the Inspector's report following the public inquiry into the appeal and called-in application. His reason for so doing was to consider whether any action was necessary to bring about consistency as between the local plan and the specific decisions on the applications; and, if so, what steps should be taken to achieve that consistency.

4.142 In addition to the two cases mentioned above, the Secretary of State has also called in for environmental and highway reasons a local plan for Berwick-upon-Tweed and a local plan for the London Borough of Lewisham. A further eight local plans prepared by former metropolitan county councils were called in by the Secretary of State in 1986 but there the power was used to enable them to be carried forward to approval following the abolition of those councils.

4.143 The 1990 Act also gives a reserve power to the Secretary of State to enable him to direct a local planning authority to modify one or more of its local plan proposals (s 43(4)). This power allows the Secretary of State to direct an authority to alter part of its plan and might be appropriate where the part appears to be seriously at variance with national policy. In 1998, the Secretary of State issue a direction under s 43(4) requiring the Cotswold District Council to modify 13 policies, proposed in its emerging district-wide local plan so that the policies would be consistent with national land use policies. The Secretary of State had earlier made formal objections to the plan at the deposit stage and also subsequently when proposed modifications were published.

In 1999, the Secretary of State issued a direction under s 43(4) requiring the Stratford-on-Avon District Council to modify proposals in the District local plan, because he believed the policies conflicted with national policies on Green Belts set out in PPG2. **4.144**

In *R (on the application of Spelthorne LBC) v Secretary of State for the Environment, Transport and the Regions* [2001] PLCR 326, the High Court, in refusing to quash a direction by the Secretary of State to modify a policy in the authority's development plan relating to affordable housing, considered that the Secretary of State was entitled to take into account broader planning issues than were individual local authorities. **4.145**

H. MINERALS LOCAL PLANS AND WASTE LOCAL PLANS

In addition to structure and local plans, local planning authorities may also be required to prepare minerals local plans and waste local plans. **4.146**

Minerals local plans

Until the Planning and Compensation Act 1991, policies for the winning and working of minerals were contained either within local plans or in a specific type of local plan called a subject plan. Now under amendments made by the 1991 Act, a duty is placed on mineral planning authorities (see Chapter 21) to prepare a plan, to be knownas a 'minerals local plan' for their area, formulating the authority's detailed policies for their area in respect of the winning and working of minerals or the deposit of mineral waste. Since the mineral planning authority for areas where a two-tier system of local government is in operation is the county planning authority, minerals local plans will, in those areas be 'county-wide' plans covering the whole of the administrative area of the county. Outside those areas policies for the winning and working of minerals or the deposit of mineral waste will be contained in the unitary development plans for those areas. **4.147**

Under s 37 of the 1990 Act substituted by the Planning and Compensation Act 1991, a minerals local plan 'shall contain a written statement formulating the authority's detailed policies for their area in respect of development consisting of the winning and working of minerals or involving the depositing of mineral waste'. A minerals local plan must also contain a map illustrating each of the detailed policies in the plan and such diagrams, illustrations or other descriptive matter in respect of the policies as may be prescribed. It may also include such descriptive or explanatory matter as the authority think appropriate. The new section also requires a minerals local plan to be in general conformity with the structure plan. In most other respects, the same procedures apply to the adoption of minerals local plans, as apply to the adoption of local plans generally. **4.148**

Waste local plans

4.149 The Planning and Compensation Act 1991 introduced a new statutory requirement for local plan coverage of development involving the depositing of refuse or waste materials (other than mineral waste). Where there is a unitary development plan for an area, policies in respect of development involving the deposit of refuse or waste materials are contained in the plan. Elsewhere, applications for planning permission for development involving the deposit, treatment, storage, processing and disposal of refuse or waste materials, other than mineral waste, are decided by county planning authorities. A new s 38 of the 1990 Act, inserted into the Act by the 1991 Act, now requires county planning authorities either to prepare a separate waste local plan, or to combine it with their minerals local plan.

4.150 The purpose of a waste local plan is to address the land-use implications of the authorities' waste policies, including, for example, the need for sites and facilities in particular areas and suitable locations for such sites having regard to geological and hydrological considerations.

4.151 Waste local plans should be distinguished from waste management plans, which are plans drawn up by waste regulation authorities under the Environmental Protection Act 1990. Waste management plans are concerned with the types and quantities of waste circulating in an area and the facilities available in the area for its disposal. Waste local plans must have regard to waste management plans and any inconsistencies between them justified in the reasoned justification for the waste local plan.

4.152 As with minerals local plans, the same procedures apply to the adoption of waste local plans as apply to local plans.

I. UNITARY DEVELOPMENT PLANS

4.153 Following the abolition of the Greater London Council and the metropolitan county councils by the Local Government Act 1985, the existing two-tier system of local planning authorities in Greater London and the metropolitan area of England was reduced to one. From 1 April 1986, the London boroughs and the metropolitan districts began to exercise all the functions of the local planning authority in their areas.

4.154 The Local Government Act 1985 also made provision for the introduction in the Greater London and metropolitan areas of new 'unitary development plans' (UDPs). The authority for these plans is now contained in Part II of the 1990 Act. Each local planning authority in these areas was required to prepare a UDP for their area. It should be noted that the Secretary of State may direct a local planning authority to prepare a UDP within a specified period. That power could be used to ensure the preparation at the same time of a cluster of UDPs which, together, will cover a much larger area than that covered by a plan prepared by any individual local planning authority.

4.155 Following the reorganisation of local government structure under the Local Government Act 1992, the Secretary of State may direct a unitary authority to prepare a unitary development plan for its area. If no order is made, the unitary authority will have a responsibility to maintain both the structure and local plan for its area.

The essence of the new UDP is that it is prepared in two parts. Part I contains the authority's general policies for their area, whilst Part II formulates those policies in detail. 4.156

In 1989, the Government stated its intention to harmonise the terminology and detailed procedures for plan-making in the metropolitan areas and London with what was proposed for the rest of England and Wales. The aim would be to provide, so far as it was possible to do so, 'uniform, or closely comparable procedures, for the preparation and adoption of development plans throughout England and Wales, so as to assist public understanding of the system and its effective operation'. This was done in the Act of 1991. 4.157

The significant features of the UDP procedures are as follows: 4.158

(a) The Secretary of State has power to make regulations prescribing the particular aspects of development and land use with which the general policies in Part I of the UDP are to be exclusively concerned (s 12(3B)). This provision is similar to one that covers structure plans and, as in that case, is designed to help the local authority to concentrate on key strategic issues in formulating general policies to be included in the plan.
(b) A local planning authority is required in formulating their general policies in Part I of the UDP to have regard specific matters. In particular, the Secretary of State may prescribe additional matters that local planning authorities are required to take into account (s 12(6)).
(c) The provisions relating to UDPs in the 1990 Act were modified as regards the pre-plan public participation process, and the procedures to be followed on deposit of the plan.

The position is as follows: 4.159

Section 12(3) of the 1990 Act now provides:

> Part I of a unitary development plan shall consist of a written statement formulating the authority's general policies in respect of the development and other use of land in their area.

Under s 12(3A), those policies must include policies in respect of: 4.160

(a) the conservation of the natural beauty and amenity of the land;
(b) the improvement of the physical environment; and
(c) the management of traffic.

Section 12(3B), however, provides that regulations may prescribe: 4.161

> the aspects of such development and use with which the general policies in Part I of a unitary development plan are to be concerned, in which case the policies shall be concerned with those aspects and no others.

Section 12(6) further provides: 4.162

> In formulating the general policies in Part I of a unitary development plan the authority shall have regard to—
>
> (a) any regional or strategic planning guidance given by the Secretary of State to assist them in the preparation of the plan;
> (b) current national policies;

(c) the resources likely to be available; and
(d) such other matters as the Secretary of State may prescribe or, in a particular case, direct.

4.163 Section 12(4) of the 1990 Act provides:

Part II of a unitary development plan shall consist of—

(a) a written statement formulating in such detail as the authority think appropriate . . . their proposals for the development and use of land in their area;
(b) a map showing those proposals on a geographical basis;
(c) a reasoned justification of the general policies in Part I of the plan and of the proposals in Part II of it; and
(d) such diagrams, illustrations or other descriptive or explanatory matter in respect of the general policies in Part I of the plan or the proposals in Part II of it as the authority think appropriate or as may be prescribed.

4.164 Provision is also made for the local planning authority to designate in Part II of the UDP any Part of the authority's area as an action area. They must also take into account in preparing the plan the provisions of any scheme under Sch 32 to the Local Government, Planning and Land Act 1980 relating to land in their area which has been designated as an enterprise zone.

4.165 Paragraph 4(1) of Part I of Sch 2 to the 1990 Act further provides that Part II of the plan shall include any local plans in force at the time when the UDP is prepared, but subject to any alterations which may be set out in Part II of the plan.

4.166 As might be expected, the Act requires that the proposals in Part II of a UDP shall be in general conformity with Part I; and that a UDP shall not be adopted unless Part II of the plan is in general conformity with Part I.

4.167 The procedures for the preparation of UDPs have always been based closely upon the procedures for the preparation of local plans. Thus s 11 gives a discretion to the authority to institute a survey of their area. A duty is also placed on an authority preparing a UDP, and before finally determining its contents, to carry out pre-deposit consultations.

4.168 As with local plan preparation, the procedure involves the local planning authority having to consider any objections made to a UDP and to hold a local inquiry or other hearing for that purpose, to which the Tribunal and Inquiries Act 1992 is to apply (ss 15(1) and 16).

4.169 As with the procedure for the preparation and adoption of local plans, the Secretary of State has a power to call in the UDP for his approval (s 18). He may do this for the whole or a Part of the UDP, at any time between it being placed on deposit and a copy being sent to the Secretary of State, and its adoption by the local planning authority. If the Secretary of State exercises his power of call-in, the local planning authority must not take any further steps in connection with the adoption of the plan until he has given his decision on the plan or the relevant Part of it; and the plan or relevant Part of it will have no effect unless it is approved by him. It seems that the power of call-in extends not only to the whole or Part of the UDP, but to part of any of the two Parts of the UDP. So the Secretary of State may, for example, call in only the transport policies contained in Part I of the UDP in order to ensure that they are compatible with national transport policies. He may then proceed to approve that part of Part I which contains the transport policies, leaving the remainder of Part I and Part II of the UDP to be adopted by the local planning authority. If, however, the Secretary of State has approved the whole or part of Part I of the UDP with modifications, the local planning authority may be required to make modifications to Part II of the UDP in order to make Part II conform generally to Part I. It should also be noted that under the Development Plan Regulations 1999, the procedures for the preparation and adoption of local plans described earlier in this chapter apply for the most part equally to UDPs.

J. TRUNK AND OTHER ROADS AND DEVELOPMENT PLANS

Sections 24 and 49 of the 1990 Act provide an important limitation on the ability of the public to influence the content of structure and local plans at the preparation stage. The sections provide that neither the Secretary of State nor the local planning authority shall be required to consider representations or objections made to development plans if in their view the representations or objections are in substance related to things done or proposed to be done in pursuance of orders or schemes made under various provisions of the Highways Acts. **4.170**

Under existing provisions of the Highways Acts, the provision of trunk roads (which includes motorways) was, until May 1997, the responsibility of the Secretary of State for Transport. The consequence of these arrangements was that although the trunk road construction programme was promoted and funded by central government, it was superimposed upon and remained outside the normal land use planning system. Since there can be no greater influence on the location of development than that provided by the trunk road network, it was remarkable that the system for authorising trunk roads was distinct and separate from that determining the grant of planning permission for other development. **4.171**

The fact that procedures for the planning of development has no choice but to accept the existence of the Government's trunk road programme has given rise to much criticism. Accordingly, the Government decided to involve the Highways Agency in the preparation of the content of Regional Planning Guidance which itself influences the content of development plans, and the preparation of local transport plans to complement development plans. The changes recognise that transport strategies have implications for land development and for development plans. Also, that planning decisions on land use can impact on transport strategies. Ideally then, development plans and transport plans should be prepared in parallel. This is unlikely to be possible, however, since local transport plans are not subject to any statutory procedures and can be prepared more quickly. The hope is that, despite this, planning strategies and transport strategies will be consistent with each other. **4.172**

K. JUDGE IN THEIR OWN CAUSE

It is sometimes claimed that in allowing a local planning authority to adopt their own plans, the legislature has made the authority a judge in their own cause. To some extent there may be truth in this claim, but it should be noted that there are a number of restraints in the preparation and adoption process which inhibit the way in which the discretion given to a **4.173** local planning authority is exercised. First, there is the safeguard of publicity for the authority's proposals required by the 1990 Act (ss 13, 33 and 40), for UDPs, and structure and local plans respectively. Secondly, proposals in a local plan must be in general conformity with the structure plan (ss 36(4) and 46) and proposals in Part II of a UDP with Part I of the plan (s 12(7)). Thirdly, if objections are duly made and not withdrawn, the local planning authority must hold an examination in public or a public local inquiry or other hearing to consider them (ss 13, 35B and 42(2)). Fourthly, the examination in public or local inquiry or hearing is conducted by an independent panel or Inspector and the procedure made subject to the Tribunals and Inquiries Act 1992 (ss 16(3), 35(8) and 42(6)). Fifthly, the report of the panel or Inspector has to be considered by the authority and a statement made of the decisions reached in the light of the report, together with reasons for reaching those decisions. Sixthly, the Secretary of State is given power to call in development plan proposals for his own approval (ss 18(1), 35A and 44) or direct the authority to modify proposals in the plan (ss 17(1), 35(3) and 43(4)).

4.174 Despite these restraints, however, it is still possible for a local planning authority to adopt policies in the face of sustained and prolonged opposition from local objectors. This is seen in the case of *R v Hammersmith & Fulham LBC, ex p People before Profit Ltd* [1981] JPL 869.

4.175 The applicants were an association of persons who had objected to proposals in a local plan for the redevelopment of part of Hammersmith Broadway. A public local inquiry had been held into their objections, and the Inspector conducting the inquiry had found almost entirely in their favour. After considering the Inspector's report and his recommendations, however, the local planning authority resolved to reject them. The authority also resolved to grant planning permission for the development of the site in accordance with the proposals in the plan that the Inspector had criticised.

4.176 The Divisional Court refused the applicants leave to apply for judicial review to quash the resolutions to reject the Inspector's recommendations and to grant planning permission for the development on the ground that the authority had kept throughout within the law, and that the applicants had no reasonable case which would entitle the court to quash the decision. In giving judgment, Comyn J said that one consequence of this unhappy case was to lead him to believe that public inquiries very often had no useful purpose at all. He went on to say that he was slightly perturbed to think that a public inquiry of up to a month's length would take place and its findings be so favourable and yet the authority could dismiss it virtually out of hand.

4.177 In this case the local planning authority had the law on their side. In the absence of any call-in by the Secretary of State, the authority were the political monarch in their own area and were taking what had become a political decision. Research in this area shows that 90 per cent of the recommendations made by Inspectors following inquiries into local plans are accepted by the local planning authority. Where they have not done so, the issues have usually been minor and have related to the application of policy to specific sites. In considering this aspect, however, it should be remembered that the Secretary of State, in determining applications for planning permission (either after call-in or on an appeal against an adverse decision by the local planning authority), may well take into account any recommendations made by an Inspector following an inquiry into a local plan which the local planning authority have decided to reject unless, that is, the new s 54A prevents such a course.

L. MEANING OF THE TERM 'DEVELOPMENT PLAN'

The development plan is rarely a single document. Following the implementation of the changes to the development plan system introduced by the Planning and Compensation Act 1991, the development plan for an area comprises: 4.178

(a) In non-metropolitan areas:
   (i) the structure plan;
   (ii) the local plan;
   (iii) the minerals local plan; and
   (iv) the waste local plan; or
   where there is a unitary authority and the Secretary of State has so prescribed the unitary development plan.
(b) In metropolitan areas: the unitary development plan.

Note that following the coming into effect of the new development plan provisions of the Planning and Compulsory Purchase Act 2004, the above plans will continue to be part of the development plan for the area, along with the Regional Spatial Strategy for the region, during the transition period.

M. LEGAL EFFECT OF A DEVELOPMENT PLAN

The end-product of the plan-making process is to provide, as far as possible, a concise statement of the policy framework within which development in any area is to be controlled or allowed. This aim is reflected in a number of statutory provisions found in the 1990 Act and elsewhere. The main provisions are: 4.179

(a) In dealing with applications for planning permission, s 70(2) of the 1990 Act requires that the local planning authority 'shall have regard to the provisions of the development plan, so far as material to the application, and to any other material considerations'.

The precise meaning of the phrase 'shall have regard to the provisions of the development plan' has been judicially considered on a number of occasions. In *Simpson v Edinburgh Corporation* 1961 SLT 17, Lord Guest said that the expression 'shall have regard to' did not in his view mean 'slavishly adhere to'. According to his Lordship, the phrase requires the local planning authority to consider the development plan, but it does not oblige them to follow it. He went on: 4.180

> In view of the nature and purpose of a development plan . . . I should have been surprised to find an injunction on the planning authority to follow it implicitly, and I do not find anything in the Act to suggest that this was intended. . . . It was also pointed out that if the phrase was mandatory, then the addition of the words 'to any other material considerations' . . . would, if the development plan and other material considerations were inconsistent, face the planning authority with an impossible task of reconciling the two. . . . The [local] planning authority are to consider all the material considerations, of which the development plan is one.

Following the commencement of the relevant provisions of the Planning and Compulsory 4.181

Purchase Act 2004, the extent to which these plans will continue to be part of the development plan for an area will be subject to the conditional arrangements in schedule 8 to the Act.

4.182 The view expressed by Lord Guest in *Simpson v Edinburgh Corporation* was considered and followed in *Enfield London Borough Council v Secretary of State for the Environment* [1975] JPL 155, where Melford Stevenson J refused to quash a grant of planning permission given by the Secretary of State for industrial development in the green belt contrary to the provisions of the development plan which he had approved. The court held that the words 'have regard to' did not make adherence to the plan mandatory.

4.183 The Planning and Compensation Act 1991 altered the significance of this provision. Section 26 of the 1991 Act provided that the following provision should be added at the end of Part II of the 1990 Act:

> **54A.** Where, in making any determination under the planning Acts, regard is to be had to the development plan, the determination shall be made in accordance with the plan unless material considerations indicate otherwise.

4.184 The effect of this new provision is discussed further in Chapter 12. It should be noted, however, that s.54A was repealed by the Planning and Compulsory Purchase Act 2004, and replaced by s.38(6) of that Act which states: '. . . the determination must be made in accordance with the plan unless material considerations indicate otherwise'.

(b) Where planning permission for development is necessary and has not been obtained, s 172(1) of the 1990 Act requires the local planning authority, in considering whether to issue an enforcement notice requiring the breach to be remedied, to have 'regard to the provisions of the development plan and to any other material considerations'.

(c) In considering whether to revoke or modify a permission granted for development on an application made under Part III of the 1990 Act, s 97 of the Act requires the local planning authority to have regard 'to the development plan and to any other material considerations'.

(d) In considering whether to make an order requiring discontinuance of the use of land or the removal or alteration of buildings or works, s 102 of the 1990 Act requires the local planning authority to have regard 'to the development plan and to any other material considerations'.

(e) In exercising powers under s 226 of the 1990 Act to compulsorily acquire land in connection with development and for other planning purposes, a local authority is required, in considering whether land is suitable for development, redevelopment or improvement, to have regard, *inter alia*, 'to the provisions of the development plan, so far as material' and 'to any other considerations which would be material for the purpose of determining an application for planning permission for development on the land'.

(f) The interests of owner-occupiers of land may be 'blighted' where an indication has been given in a development plan that land may be required for some public purpose. In such cases, Part VI of the 1990 Act allows the owners of certain interests in land so affected to serve 'blight notices' on the appropriate authority requiring the authority to purchase their interests.

(g) Where land is being acquired by a public authority for some public purpose, the compensation paid for the interest acquired is normally based on its market value. In order to assist in the determination of that value, the Land Compensation Act 1961 provides that the parties may assume that, were it not for the acquisition, planning permission would have been granted for development of a specific kind. Some of these assumptions about planning permission depend directly upon the provisions of the development plan.

N. LEGAL CHALLENGE TO DEVELOPMENT PLANS

Under the provisions of s 287 of the 1990 Act, any person aggrieved by a unitary development plan or a local plan, or by any alteration or replacement of any such plan or structure plan, may question its validity by application to the High Court. The grounds of challenge under the section, however, are limited to two, namely, that the plan, alteration, repeal or replacement is not within the powers conferred by Part II of the 1990 Act, or that any requirement of Part II or of any regulations made thereunder has not been complied with. A further limitation on the use of this power is that the person aggrieved must make the application within six weeks from the date of publication of the first notices of the plan's approval or adoption or its alteration or replacement. The period of six weeks means precisely six weeks and not a day more. After the six-week period has elapsed, it is no longer possible to challenge the validity of the action taken. This is the result of s 284(1) of the 1990 Act which provides that, except as provided under s 287, the validity of a structure plan, local plan or unitary development plan or any alteration or replacement of any such plan, 'shall not be questioned in any legal proceedings whatsoever'. **4.185**

On an application under s 287, the High Court may, if satisfied that what has been done is outside the powers conferred by Part II of the 1990 Act, or that the interests of the applicant have been substantially prejudiced by the failure to comply with the requirements of Part II or the regulations thereunder, wholly or partly quash the plan, or as the case may be, the alteration or replacement either generally or in so far as it affects the property of the applicant. The Court also has the power, by interim order, wholly or partly to suspend the operation of the plan until the final determination of the proceedings. **4.186**

If part of a plan is quashed by the Court, the question arises as to whether the previous stages in the plan-making process which have not been challenged and quashed should remain valid. Is the local planning authority required to start the whole plan-making process again from the beginning in relation to that part, or can it proceed again to the adoption stage in order to comply with the court's order in the light of all the information then available? The Court has no power to amend the plan. In *Charles Church Developments Ltd v South Northamptonshire DC* [2000] PLCR 40, the High Court held that the term 'plan' in s 287 of the 1990 Act comprised the plan both in draft and adopted form, so that where part of a local plan is quashed, it has the effect of quashing that part of the plan both in draft and as adopted. **4.187**

Since 1984, there have been a growing number of challenges to the validity of new-style development plans. Apart from the cases referred to earlier, some other early cases include the following. **4.188**

4.189 In *Edwin H. Bradley & Sons Ltd v Secretary of State for the Environment* (1982) 47 P & CR 374, the main allegation made was that in approving a structure plan with modifications, the Secretary of State had failed to comply with his duty under what is now s 35(10) of the 1990 Act to give 'such statement as he considers appropriate of the reasons governing his decision'. Glidewell J held that the Secretary of State was entitled to give 'short reasons' for his decision, so long as he had complied with the tests laid down in *Re Poyser & Mills' Arbitration* [1964] 2 QB 467, and given reasons which were adequate and intelligible. His lordship found that the Secretary of State had done so.

4.190 In *Barnham v Secretary of State for the Environment* [1985] JPL 861, however, the Secretary of State had approved an alteration to a structure plan in a way that made it conflict with policy guidance contained in a government Circular. Farquharson J held that he should have referred to that guidance in the statement of reasons for his decision, and that the failure to do so was a breach of his duty under what is now s 35(10). Accordingly, his lordship quashed part of the alterations to the structure plan which the Secretary of State had approved.

4.191 In *Fourth Investments Ltd v Bury MBC* [1985] JPL 185, McCullough J held that the Inspector who had conducted the inquiry into a local plan had erred in failing to balance the local green-belt significance of the applicant's land against the possibility that further land than that already allocated in the plan for housing might be needed in the future, and that in that event the applicant's land might be required for that purpose. In quashing the policy in the local plan in so far as it related to the applicant's land, McCullough J held that on the Inspector's findings (or on his inability to make findings far enough into the future) about housing land requirements and upon his findings about the green-belt significance of the applicant's land, the chances that the land might be needed for future housing were sufficiently high for it to have been wrong to have given the land a green-belt notation in the plan.

4.192 A recent example of a policy in a development plan being quashed was in *Charles Church Developments plc v Hart DC* [1994] JPL B133 where the High Court held that the local planning authority had failed to give substantive reasons for including an area of land within their strategic gap policy, contrary to the clearly expressed view of the Inspector who had conducted the local plan inquiry. Another example is *Thames Water Utilities v East Hertfordshire DC* [1995] JPL 706, where the applicants had been substantially prejudiced because the local planning authority had changed their mind during the course of the local plan inquiry about the precise boundaries of a Green Belt.

4.193 Probably the most important legal challenge made to the provisions of a development plan occurred in *Westminster City Council v Great Portland Estates plc* [1985] AC 661. There the respondent company challenged both the industrial and the office policies contained in the Westminster City local plan. With regard to industrial development, the general policy was that applications for planning permission for new industrial floor space and the creation of new industrial employment were to be encouraged. That general policy was modified, however, in the case of applications for planning permission to rehabilitate or redevelop existing industrial premises. There, the authority's general policy was supplanted where it was considered necessary to maintain the continuation of industrial uses important to the diverse character, vitality and functioning of Westminster. The policy was intended to protect 'specific industrial activities' from redevelopment. The company challenged this latter aspect as being outside the purposes of planning law. The essence of its argument was that the protection of specified industrial activities was not a policy concerned with the development and use of land, but one concerned with the protection of particular users of land. It was irrelevant, it was claimed, to have regard in this way to the interests of individual occupiers.

Giving the only speech, but one concurred in by all the other Law Lords, Lord Scarman adopted the general principle enunciated by Lord Parker CJ in *East Barnet UDC v British Transport Commission* [1962] 2 QB 484 that, in considering whether there had been a change of use, 'what is really to be considered is the character of the use of the land, not the particular purposes of a particular occupier'. It was a logical process, Lord Scarman thought, to extend the ambit of that statement to the formulation of planning policies and proposals. However, like all generalisations, he said, the statement of Lord Parker had its own limitations. Personal circumstances of the occupier, personal hardship, the difficulties of business which are of value to the community were not to be ignored in the administration of planning control. **4.194**

Lord Scarman thought the human factor was always present, though indirectly as the background to the consideration of the character of land use. Yet in exceptional or special circumstances it would have a direct effect. But such circumstances, he said, fell to be considered not as a general rule but as exceptions to a general rule to be met in special cases. Such cases *may* be mentioned in a plan, he said, but it would only be necessary to do so where prudent to emphasise that, notwithstanding the general policy, exceptions could not be wholly excluded from consideration in the administration of planning control. He therefore disagreed with the view of the Court of Appeal that the council's real concern was the protection of existing occupiers. He thought the council had made a strong planning case for its proposal, and that the linkage (i.e., between the general policy and the exceptions) was 'a powerful piece of positive thinking within a planning context'. Accordingly the challenge to the industrial policy failed. **4.195**

As regards the challenge to the authority's office policy, the plan had divided the City of Westminster into two zones, a 'central activities' zone and elsewhere. The policy was expressed in the plan as being 'to guide office development to location within the central activities zone'. Elsewhere, in order to ensure that land use and development were compatible with residential use, the policy was to prescribe (almost) any office development, save in exceptional or special circumstances. The plan had stated that those exceptional circumstances were to be set out in non-statutory guidelines to be prepared after consultation following the adoption of the plan. **4.196**

In quashing the office policies in the plan, Lord Scarman held (after admitting that the point had caused him some difficulty) that the authority had failed to comply with the duty imposed on them to formulate in the plan its development and land use proposals. The authority had, he said, 'deliberately omitted some'. By so doing they had deprived persons such as the respondent company from raising objections and securing a public inquiry into such objections. **4.197**

A further argument raised by the respondent company in its challenge to the office policies in the plan, namely, that in commenting upon the Inspector's report the authority **4.198** had failed to give an adequate statement of their reasons for rejecting his views and recommendations, was rejected by their Lordships.

4.199 The decision of the House of Lords was important for a number of reasons. First, the recognition that the personal circumstances of an occupier or the character of an occupier can be taken into account, which until then had never been clear. It was no doubt partly legal uncertainty on this point that led the Secretary of State at one time to decline to approve policies in a number of structure plans which sought to restrict the occupation of new residential development to local persons. More importantly, however, the judgment strengthens the hand of local planning authorities wishing to protect from redevelopment the many and varied small businesses found in inner city areas, be it the bookshop, the violin maker or the local store.

4.200 Secondly, the judgment makes clear that the duty of a local planning authority to formulate in a plan 'their proposals for the development and other use of land' means *all* proposals, not merely some of them. Other proposals, it seems, ought not to be left to influence development control decisions from the sidelines if they are proposals capable of being included in the plan. As a result of the Great Portland Estates decision, policy on the use of supplementary planning guidance (SPG) is now contained in PPG12 Development Plans. The PPG deals with SPG in paras 3.14 onwards. It urges that local plan policies in development plans should avoid excessive detail, concentrating on the matters relevant to determining planning applications.

> Local authorities should therefore consider the use of supplementary planning guidance as a means of setting out more detailed guidance on the way in which the policies in the plan will be applied in particular circumstances or areas.

4.201 In paragraph 3.15, the role of SPG is discussed:

> Supplementary planning guidance (SPG) does not form part of the plan. It can take the form of design guides or area development briefs, or supplement other specific regional policies in a plan. SPG must itself be consistent with national and regional planning guidance, as well as the policies set out in the adopted development plan.

4.202 The procedures which should be followed are then set out:

> It should be issued separately from the plan and made publicly available; consultation should be undertaken and the status of the SPG should be made clear . . . SPG should be prepared in consultation with the general public, businesses, and other interested parties and their views should be taken into account before it is finalised. It should then be the subject of a Council resolution to adopt it as supplementary guidance. On adoption a statement of the consultation undertaken, the representations received and the local authorities response to those representations should be made available with each copy of the SPG.

4.203 The significance of SPG thus prepared is in the weight which the Secretary of State would then give it. Paragraph 3.16 states:

> While only the policies and the development plan can have the status that Section 54A of the 1990 Act provides in deciding planning application, SPG may be taken into account as a material consideration.The Secretary of State will give substantial weight in making decisions on matters that come before him to SPG which derives out of and is consistent with the development plan arlo has been prepared in the proper manner.

Paragraph 3.17 then sounds this note of caution: **4.204**

> SPG can play a valuable role in supplementing plan policy and proposals. However it is emphasised that SPG must not be used to avoid subjecting to public scrutiny in accordance with the statutory procedures, policies and proposals which should be included in the plan. Plan policies should not attempt to delegate the criteria for decisions on planning applications to SPG or to development briefs.

In one recent case, *R (on the application of JA Pye (Oxford) Ltd, Bellway Homes and the House-builders Federation) v Oxford City Council* [2003] JPL 4–5, the High Court held that a local planning authority was under a duty to include all policies in the local plan. It did not prevent, however, the production of policies in another document on an interim basis or in parallel with the local plan. **4.205**

O. THE PROPOSED NEW SYSTEM

In the consultation paper, 'Delivering a Fundamental Change', published in December 2001, the Government decides to make a far-reaching reform of the development plan system. The Govermnent's main criticism of the existing system centred on the role of local plans. According to the consultation paper, the system of local plans was over-complex; they were often inconsistent with policies set out at national or regional levels; they were too long; preparation was slow and expensive; and they contained too many policies. As a result they were failing their users. Furthermore, preparation of local plans was being overtaken by new local authority policies and programmes such as community strategies and regeneration and neighbourhood renewal initiatives. **4.206**

Accordingly, the Government decided to fundamental reform the development plan system. The proposal was to abolish all structure plans, local plans, and unitary development plans with a new single level of plan to be known as the Local Development Plan Framework. This Framework would consist of: **4.207**

— a statement of core policies setting out the local authority's vision and strategy in promoting and controlling development throughout its area;
— more detailed action plans for further smaller local areas of change such as urban extensions, town centres and neighbourhoods undergoing renewal; and
— a map showing the areas of change for which action plans are to be prepared and existing designations, such as conservation areas.

The consultation paper criticised the local development plan public local inquiry system at which objections to the plan can be heard, as often time-consuming and adversarial. So this too was to be reformed. **4.208**

On 18 July 2002, the Government reaffirmed the intention to proceed with the abolition of structure plans and the replacement of local and unitary development plans with a Local Development Framework. They also announced their intention to retain the right of objectors to be heard at plan inquiries. It was also announced that Regional Planning Guidance was to be replaced by a statutory Regional Spatial Strategy. These proposals were given effect to in the Planning and Compulsory Purchase Act 2004. **4.209**

5

DEVELOPMENT PLANS: AFTER THE PLANNING AND COMPULSORY PURCHASE ACT 2004

5.01 The Planning and Compulsory Purchase Act 2004 has introduced a sea-change to the development plan system of the past. It provides for the replacement of the non-statutory regional guidance, structure plans, local plans, waste plans, mineral plans and unitary development plans by regional spatial strategies and local development documents. Part I of the Act provides for the new regional spatial strategies; Part II for local development documents.

5.02 The provisions in the Act for the introduction of the new development plan system allow for structure plans to be 'saved' (i.e. continued in force) for a period of three years from the date of commencement of the Act, unless within that period revisions to the regional spatial strategy are expressed to replace structure plan policies in whole, or in part or the Secretary of State by direction extends the three-year period to such policies as are specified in the direction. With regard to local plans, the Secretary of State by regulations, may require that within a prescribed period, local planning authorities submit to him a timetable for the preparation of local development documents over the following three years. Local plans may also be 'saved' (continued in force) during the three-year period but subject to replacement of policies in the plans by approved development plan documents. In some cases after the three-year period has ended the Secretary of State may continue policies in the local plan which are compliant with an authority's local development framework (see para. 5.42).

A. REGIONAL SPATIAL STRATEGIES

5.03 A main principle of the new system for regional spatial strategies (RSSs), is to give more weight to regional policy previously contained in non-statutory regional planning guidance with a new statutory basis for that policy. Section I of the Act (which applies only to England) provides for there to be an RSS for every region. A region is designed as a region specified in Schedule I to the Regional Development Agencies Act 1998. The regions as so defined are East Midlands; Eastern; North East; North West; South East; South West; West Midlands and Yorkshire and Humber. A region may therefore, as now, cover the area or parts of the area of more than one authority. Furthermore, there is an exception in the case of National Parks, where a single RSS may cross regional boundaries. The provisions of Part I do not apply to London. This is because in London, the Mayor's Spatial Development Strategy when adopted, will become the strategic planning document for the capital.

By virtue of s.38 of the Act, the RSS is made part of the development plan and is thus a material consideration in the determination of planning applications. In addition, the integrity of a plan-led system of development control is secured by the requirement in Part II of the Act that local planning authorities in preparing a local development document must have regard to national policies and advice contained in guidance issued by the Secretary of State, and that the document must be in general conformity with the RSS. **5.04**

Section I of the Act provides that the RSS must set out the Secretary of State's policies (however expressed) in relation to the development and use of land within the region. These policies could include therefore, Answers to Questions in Parliament given by planning Ministers, Government responses to Reports of Select Committees of Parliament are Ministerial contributions to relevant Parliamentary debates. Section 1 also provides that from the date of the commencement of Part I of the Act (which occurred on 28 September 2004), existing regional planning guidance issued by the Secretary of State is to become the RSS for the region. One effect of this is that whereas regime planning policy contained in an RPG did not form part of the development plan, but fell merely to be considered as a material consideration in the determination of an application for planning permission, much greater weight is now given to the policy by its inclusion within the statutory framework of an RSS, which itself forms part of the development plan. **5.05**

However, only that part of the existing regional planning guidance prescribed by regulations is to become part of the RSS. This latter provision is intended to allow the Secretary of State to decide where there is a range of regional planning guidance within a region, which part of it is to become the RSS for the region. The section also contains a proviso that if a policy sets out in the RSS conflicts with any other statement or information in it, the conflict must be resolved in favour of the policy. This may become of greater significance following the revision of an RSS by the Regional Planning Body (RPB). **5.06**

The RSS is intended to provide a broad development strategy for the region for a period of at least fifteen years. Among other things, the RSS is to identify the scale and distribution of provision for new housing and priorities for the environment, transport, infrastructure, economic development, agriculture, minerals extraction and waste treatment and disposal. It will be confined to regional or sub-regional matters, leaving local issues to be addressed in a local development document. It should not deal with detailed development issues or be site specific. The RSS should also include policies which contribute to the achievement of sustainable development in line with the provision of section 39 of the 2004 Act (see 5.19). **5.07**

One advantage seen for the new RSS system is the provision of better integration between transport and spatial planning, in that transport planning will now take into account the spatial strategies in the RSS, and the RSS and local development documents will take into account plans for the development of the transport network. **5.08**

Even though the start to the new system will benefit from the translation of regional planning guidance into RSS, revisions to the RSS will be required periodically, particularly if **5.09** changes are made to 'national' policy. PPS 11 Regional Spatial Strategies advises that whilst a RSS should have regard to national policy, it should not simply repeat them nor resort to platitudes. It should provide spatial specific policies applying national policies to the circumstances of the region. The revision may be to parts of the RSS or may be a comprehensive revision of the entire RSS. Most of Part I of the Act therefore, deals with the revision of the RSS, as does the Town and Country Planning (Regional Planning) (England) Regulations 2004. In addition (PPS 11) gives details of the preparation, implementation, monitoring and review of the RSS, along with policy and guidance on the topics to be covered by it.

B. THE REGIONAL PLANNING BOARD

5.10 The RSS is to be revised by the Regional Planning Board (RPB). Section 2 of the Act enables the Secretary of State to make a direction recognising a body (which may be corporate or otherwise) as the RPB for a region. The RPB in all regions outside London will be the Regional Chamber (otherwise known as the Regional Assembly). These bodies are not to be confused with any proposed elected Regional Assemblies provided for in the Regional Assemblies (Preparation) Act 2003. The section authorises the Secretary of State to establish the criteria that a body must satisfy in order for it to be recognised as the RPB. The criteria that he is likely to require include a consideration of whether the body is sufficiently representative; whether the RPB will consult a sufficiently broad rage of regional stakeholders; whether the RPB will be able to work sufficiently closely with all groups to ensure delivery of the regional strategy; and whether the RPB will be able to take a sufficiently strategic regional view where it becomes necessary to distinguish between difficult regional choices. Section 2 also includes an overriding requirement that the Secretary of State cannot recognise a body as the RPB for a region unless not less than 60 per cent of the persons who are to be members of it are drawn from members of a district council, a county council, a metropolitan district council, a National Park authority or the Broads authority, whose areas fall within the region.

5.11 The Act also provides for regional planning bodies to be statutory consultees on certain planning applications.

The Regional planning body is required to be consulted on any development which would be of major importance for the implementation of the Regional Spatial Strategy or a relevant regional policy, because of its scale or nature or the location of the land. Furthermore, each regional planning body may notify local planning authorities in writing of other descriptions of development in relation to which it wishes to be consulted. It is expected that these descriptive criteria will be linked to development likely to impinge on the implementation of the regional spatial strategy or a relevant regional policy, but they may also cover other types of development.

5.12 Section 3 of the 2004 Act sets out the general function of an RPB. In particular, the section requires the Board to keep under review the RSS and those matters which may be expected to affect the development in its region or any part of it, and the planning of that development. The Board is also required to monitor the implementation of the RSS throughout the region, and to prepare and submit to the Secretary of State an annual report in its implementation.

It should be noted that under Section 4 the RPB is authorized to make arrangements with specified authorities within the region for the discharge by the authority of any of its functions (save for the draft revision of an RSS and its submission to the Secretary of State). The authorities specified as able to exercise functions on behalf of the RPB are a county council, a district council, a metropolitan district council and a National Park authority. The RPB is also required to seek the advice of those authorities in the monitoring of the RSS, in keeping the RSS under review, and in the preparation of a draft revision. The specified authorities also have the right to give the RPB advice relating to the inclusion within the RSS of specific policies relating to any part of the region. 5.13

C. THE REVISION OF THE RSS BY THE RPB

The main function of the RPB is to revise the RSS. The Town and Country Planning (Regional Planning) (England) Regulations 2004 prescribe in more detail the form and content of a draft revision of the RSS and the procedure to be followed. 5.14

Under section 5 the RPB must prepare a draft revision where it appears to the Board to be necessary or expedient to do so. Notice of the Board's intention to do so must be given to the Secretary of State. Revision may also take place where prescribed by regulation, or if the Board is directed to do so by the Secretary of State. 5.15

In preparing a draft revision, the RPB is required to have regard to: 5.16

(a) national policies and advice contained in guidance issued by the Secretary of State;
(b) the RSS for each adjoining region;
(c) the spatial development strategy if any part of its region adjoins Greater London;
(d) the Wales Spatial Plan if any part of its region adjoins Wales;
(e) the resources likely to be made available for implementation of the RSS.

Section 5 contains an important provision where the RPB decides to make different provision for different parts of the region. In such cases the detailed proposals for such different provision must first be made by an authority specified in section 4 (see 5.13).

Revision of the RSS must also take into account European Union legislation, policies, programmes and funding regimes to the extent that they impact on the region. In addition, an RSS requires Strategic Environmental Assessment in accordance with the EC Directive (see Chapter 14). 5.17

The regulations also require the RPB to have regard to the regional economic strategy proposed by the regional development agency. Additional matters to be taken into account in preparing the RSS are given below D–F: 5.18

D. SUSTAINABLE DEVELOPMENT

Section 39 of the Act requires persons or bodies responsible for exercising any function in relation to a regional spatial strategy, to exercise that function with the objective of contributing to the achievement of sustainable development. 5.19

5.20 For a number of years planning policy guidance has contained a number of specific references to this concept. It has now received express statutory recognition in section 39.

5.21 The idea behind the expression is the wish to ensure that everybody enjoys a better quality of life both now and in the future. A widely used definition of the term is that drawn up by the World Commission on Environment and Development in 1987, as being 'development that meets the needs of the present without compromising the ability of future generations to meet their own needs.'

5.22 A commitment to the concept of sustainable development was established in May 1999 with the publication by the Government of 'A Better Quality of Life – a Strategy for Sustainable Development for the UK' CM 4345. That strategy identified four broad objectives all of which have to be achieved at the same time. They are:

social progress which recognises the needs of everyone;
effective protection of the environment;
the prudent use of natural resources; and
maintenance of high and stable levels of economic growth and employment.

5.23 The Government consider that the planning system can make a major contribution to the achievement of these objectives. Practical guidance on how to achieve this was given in 'Good Practice Guide on Sustainability Appraisal of Regional Planning Guidance' which published by the Secretary of State in October 2000. The Government sees one of the objectives in using the term 'sustainable development' to be the provision for the first time of a statutory definition of the purposes of the planning system. It sees the preparation by the RPB of the RSS and the content of the RSS to contribute towards the achievement of sustainable development. PPS 11 contains further guidance (and explanation) as to how this is to be done.

E. RACE RELATIONS

5.24 In preparing a draft revision of the RSS, the RPB must comply with a general duty in the Race Relations (Amendment) Act 2000 to promote racial equality. In effect it requires compliance with the duty to have due regard to the need to eliminate unlawful racial discrimination and promote equal opportunities between persons of different racial groups.

F. COMMUNITY INVOLVEMENT

5.25 Section 6 of the 2004 Act requires the RPB in exercising its functions to prepare, publish and keep under review a statement of its policies as to the involvement of persons who appear to the RPB to have an interest in the exercise of those functions. The section requires the RPB to comply with the statement. The importance of the statement is emphasised in PPS 11 which states:

> It is essential that the public is able to be involved throughout the RSS revision process and this should include broad public consultation rather than relying on targeted consultation with

particular groups. The statement of public participation should set out how the RPB intends to achieve this, including the stages of public participation in the Sustainability Appraisal process.

The statement may be also relevant in the preparation of Local Development Documents and in consultation on planning applications.

PPS1 gave guidance on this aspect under the heading 'Principles of Community Involvement in Planning'. The guidance has been expanded in a document 'Community Involvement in Planning: The Government's Objectives' issued in February 2004. The guidance recognizes that the 'community' could be made up of many different interest groups, relating to a particular place, issues, values or religion. The statement says that 'An inclusive approach is needed to ensure that different groups have the opportunity to participate and are not disadvantaged in the process'. 5.26

The Government's key principles for community involvement outlined in PPS1 are: 5.27

— Community involvement that is appropriate to the level of planning. Arrangements need to be built on a clear understanding of the needs of the community and to be fit for purpose;
— Front loading so that there are opportunities for early community involvement in the revision process;
— Using methods which are relevant to the experience of communities;
— Clearly articulated opportunities for continuing involvement. Recognition that this is not a one-off event;
— Transparency and accessibility; and
— Planning for involvement so that it is planned into the process for revising the RSS from the start.

G. SUBMISSION OF DRAFT RSS TO SECRETARY OF STATE

Section 7 of the Act and the relevant regulations require the RPB to send the draft revision of the RSS to the Secretary of State. Detailed advice on the practice and procedure is obtained in Planning Policy Statement (PPS II) Regional Spatial Strategies. The draft revision must be accompanied by the sustainability appraisal report, the pre-submission consultation statement and any supporting technical documents which support the draft revision. An electronic copy of the draft must also be sent to the Secretary of State. In the regulations this material is called the 'draft revision documents'. 5.28

The regulations go on to require the draft revision documents should be made available for inspection at the RPB's principal office (and other offices within the region considered to be appropriate), during normal office hours. The draft revision documents must also be published on the RPB's website along with information on such matters as details of where hard copies of the draft may be inspected; the period within which representations on the draft must be made; the address for representations to be sent; and the likely place, start date and place for the examination-in-public, if the Secretary of State decides that this should be held. 5.29

The regulations also provide for local planning authorities to make the draft revision 5.30

documents available for inspection at their offices. To that end the RPB must send a copy to them. Section 7 provides that any person may make representations on the draft

5.31 Note that the Secretary of State can vary the period within which representations may be made. It seems that this will depend on whether the draft revision constitutes a minor amendment or not. For this reason, the RPB should send to the Secretary of State a 'near final' version of the draft revision before formal submission of the final draft. If then the Secretary of State considers an examination-in-public will be held, members of the Panel may be appointed on a 'shadow basis' prior to the Secretary of State's formal decision to do so.

5.32 Where an examination-in-public does take place, the Secretary of State, following receipt of recommendations from the Panel conducting the examination, will select the matters which the Panel will examine. PPS 11 outlined when this is likely to be done. It includes issues involving significant controversy and conflict between national policies and the draft revision. The panel will also draw up a list of those people invited to appear at the examination. Both the list of matters to be examined and the list of participants will be published, allowing for representations to be made on those matters. Then, after representations have been received, a final list will be drawn up and published.

5.33 The procedure to be followed to a great extent mirrors the procedure followed at an examination-in-public into structure plans. PPS 11 says that the 'examination-in-public will be conducted in an informal manner to create the right atmosphere for discussion . . . [S]ome participants may wish to present their views on the selected matters through an agent or adviser. However, it is essential that this does not undermine the informal nature of the examination-in-public. Formal legal advocacy, and cross-examination is inappropriate to a "round table" discussion.'

5.34 At the close of the examination-in-public the Panel will report to the Secretary of State. Normally, this will be done within two months of the end of the examination.

5.35 Section 9 of the Act provides that the Secretary of State must then consider the report of the Panel; and any representations which were not considered by the Panel. The latter of course would include representations made on matters not selected for examination-in-public and representations by persons not invited to participate in the examination.

5.36 If the Secretary of State then wishes to make changes to the draft, he must publish them, together with his reasons for the changes. Following consideration of any representations, the Secretary of State will them approve and issue the revised RSS.

H. INTRODUCTION TO THE LOCAL DEVELOPMENT FRAMEWORK

5.37 Part 2 of the 2004 Act contains the provisions relating to local development. In order to provide for the proper planning of an area by the local planning authority. The authority is required by 5.13 of the Act to keep under review the matters which may be expected to affect the development of their area or the planning of its development. Section 14 details the matters to be included in that review. They are:

(a) the principal physical, economic, social and environmental characteristics of the area of the authority;
(b) the principal purposes for which land is used in the area;
(c) the size, composition and distribution of the population of the area;
(d) the communications, transport system and traffic of the area;
(e) any other considerations which may be expected to affect those matters;
(f) such other matters as may be prescribed or as the Secretary of State (in a particular case) may direct.

The matters are also to include: **5.38**

(a) any changes which the authority think may occur in relation to any other matter; and
(b) the effect such changes are likely to have on the development of the authority's area or on the planning of such development.

Where in any area, planning functions are shared between a county council and a district council, the county council must similarly keep under review matters in so far as they relate to county matters (i.e. minerals and waste).

I. LOCAL DEVELOPMENT SCHEMES

Local planning authorities are required to submit to the Secretary of State a local development scheme within six months of the commencement of the date of Part 2 of the Act (namely by 28 March 2005) regardless of where they are in terms of their current development plan. In those areas where the county council is a local planning authority, a duty is placed on the county council to submit a minerals and waste development scheme. Once prepared, the schemes must be kept under review by the authority, and revised as appropriate. The Act is supplemented by the Town and Country Planning (Local Development) (England) Regulations 2004 (S.I. 2204). The Regulations prescribe the form and content of the local development scheme and the procedure to be followed to bring it into effect. **5.39**

A local development scheme must specify: **5.40**

(a) the documents which are to be local development documents;
(b) the subject matter and geographical area to which each document is to relate;
(c) which documents are to be development plan documents;
(d) which documents (if any) are to be prepared jointly with one or more other local planning authorities;
(e) any matter or area in respect of which the authority have agreed (or propose to agree) to the constitution of a joint committee under section 29;
(f) the timetable for the preparation and revision of the documents;
(g) such other matters as are prescribed.

Central government control over the extent of a local development scheme is ensured by requiring its submission to the Secretary of State. It has also be submitted to the Regional Planning Board. Under the regulations, this must be done by 28 March 2005. The Act and **5.41** the regulations give the Secretary of State wide powers. He may prescribe (and has done so) other matters to be included in a scheme (see reg. 6 and 8); publicity to be given to the same (reg. 12); and for bringing a scheme into effect (reg. 11). The Secretary of State is given wide powers in relation to local development schemes. Above all, he has the power to direct the local planning authority to make such amendments to the scheme as he thinks appropriate. These powers ensure that local development schemes are consistent with the policies of the regional spatial strategy.

J. LOCAL DEVELOPMENT DOCUMENTS (LDDs)

5.42 Detailed provisions relating to local development documents are also contained in the Town and Country Planning (Local Development) (England) Regulations 2004. In addition, Planning Policy Statement (PPS 12) Local Development Frameworks give advice on the nature of and preparation of local development frameworks.

5.43 Although the term local development framework is not referred to in the Act, elsewhere the term has been used to refer to the system by which local and unitary development plans are to be replaced by providing for the creation of LDDs. These are in effect a portfolio of documents which collectively set out the local planning authority's planning strategy for their area. PPS 12 Local Development Framework set out the policies to be taken into account in the preparation of the framework.

5.44 Section 17 of the 2004 Act makes provision for the making of LDDs. A local planning authority must include in the local development scheme as LDDs:

(a) documents of such description as are prescribed; and
(b) the local planning authority's statement of community involvement.

In addition, the authority may also specify in the scheme such other documents as it thinks are appropriate.

5.45 An important provision in the section requires the LDDs (taken as a whole) to set out the authority's policies (however expressed) relating to the use and development of land in their area.

5.46 Where the local development scheme is prepared by the county council in any area, the LDD must set out that authority's policies relating to minerals and waste development.

5.47 The section also provides that if to any extent a policy set out in a LDD conflicts with any other statement or information in the document, the conflict must be resolved in favour of the policy.

5.48 The Secretary of State has power to prescribe the form and content of LDDs. He may also prescribe which descriptions of documents are development plan documents. (See 5.51.)

5.49 Section 19 of the 2004 Act provides that local development documents must be prepared in accordance with the local development scheme. The section sets out matters which the local planning authority must have regard to. These include:

- national policies and advice contained in guidance issued by the Secretary of State;
- the RSS for the region in which the area of the authority is situated, if the area is outside Greater London;
- the spatial development strategy if the authority is a London borough or if any part of the authority's area adjoins Greater London;
- the community strategy prepared by the authority;
- any other local development document which has been adopted by the authority;
- the resources likely to be available for implementing the proposals in the document;
- such other matters as the Secretary of State prescribes.

In addition, the local development documents are required to comply with the statement of community involvement once that statement has been adopted (see 5.52). **5.50**

Development plan documents

Some local development documents will be 'development plan' documents. Development plan documents are those documents which are to form part of the authority's development plan once they have been subject to independent review (see 5.62). They are to be spatial planning documents. **5.51**

Statements of community involvement

In the same way as section 6 of the Act requires all RPB to prepare and publish a statement of community involvement in carrying out their functions, section 18 of the 2004 Act requires local planning authorities to do likewise. This statement of community involvement must set out the authority's policy for involving the community in the preparation and revision of local development documents and in the taking of development control decisions. It is not a development plan document, but the section provides that it should be subject to independent examination as if it were. The regulations set out the minimum requirements for public involvement which have to be complied with, although it is possible for authorities to exceed those requirements if they so wish. The regulations contain, *inter alia*, detailed provision for pre-submission consultation with specific named bodies and pre-submission participation by members of the public. **5.52**

Strategic Environmental Assessment

Mention should also be made of the need for local development documents to comply with Strategic Environmental Assessment now required under EC Directive No. 2001/42 (see Chapter 14). **5.53**

The procedure leading to the adoption of a local development plan document is contained in the Act and in the Regulations. Planning Policy Statement PPS 12 also contains advice on the practical implications of the procedures. **5.54**

The Regulations contain detailed provisions relating to the procedures for pre-submission consultation, pre-submission public participation, the making of representations, the submission of documents and information to the Secretary of State and the handling by the authority of any representations made. Given below are the main features of this process. **5.55**

5.56 Local planning authorities are advised that following the taking of key decisions on their spatial strategy, and on proposals and land allocations at an early stage in their preparation of development plan documents, they should publish their preferred options and proposals and invite comments over a specified period of six weeks. An authority must have regard to those comments at the preparation stage. Although comments made are not part of any representations to be considered at the independent examination, the authority should explain how the comments received have been dealt with and how they have affected the policies and proposals in the development plan document.

K. PREPARATION OF LOCAL DEVELOPMENT PLAN DOCUMENTS

5.57 As previously stated, development plan documents are documents which are to form part of the authority's development plan. These documents are spatial planning documents, so that in preparing them local authorities are not just to be concerned with physical aspects of location and land use, but also economic, social and environmental matters. Development plant documents will be required to contain the following.

(a) *A core strategy*

The core strategy sets out the key elements of the planning framework for the area. It must be kept up-to-date and once adopted, all other development plan documents must be in conformity with it. The core strategy will thus comprise a set of primary policies. Those policies may be set out in one document covering a range of policy areas, or a number of individual documents. Having a portfolio of policies in individual development plan documents should make it easier for a document to be reviewed independently of other documents, though it would still be possible to review independently the coherent parts of a single development plan document.

(b) *Action area plans* (where needed)

Action area plans should be used to provide a planning framework for areas of change and areas of conservation. They should be used for planned growth areas, to stimulate regeneration, to protect areas sensitive to change, to resolve conflicting objectives in areas subject to development pressures, or to indicate areas for regeneration.

(c) *Site specific allocation of land*

A development plan document may specifically allocate land for specific and/or mixed uses. Policies relating to critical access requirements, any broad design principles or any planning obligations which may be sought should be set out in the development plan document. The document may be a separate development plan document or form part of the core strategy document. To meet the case of 'windfall' site which may become available for development, the document should contain criteria-based policies by which they can be assessed.

(d) *Proposals map*

The proposals map should be on an Ordnance Survey base and illustrate all the policies and proposals contained in development plan documents and any 'saved' policies from the pre-2004 Act development plans. The proposals map should identify areas to which specific policies apply.

Being a separate development plan document, it must be revised as new development plan documents are prepared. The proposals map should identify areas of protection such as nationally protected landscape and local nature areas, Green Belt and Conservation Areas. It should also illustrate locations and define sites for particular land uses and development proposals included in any development plan document and identify the areas to which specific policies apply.

Separate inset maps may be used and the geographical area covered by them will be identified on the main proposals map. Inset maps may be used to show all the proposals for part of an authority's area, such as policies and proposals for action area plans.

Supplementary planning documents

Supplementary planning documents may be included in local development documents. These documents can provide further details of policies and proposals in a development plan document. They may take the form of design guides, area development briefs or other documents supplementing policies which are in a development plan document. What they cannot do is to avoid the need to include policies and proposals which should be included within a development plan document. They must also be consistent with national and regional planning policies. It should be emphasized that supplementary planning documents are not subject (as are development plan documents) to independent examination, and they do not form part of the statutory development plan for the area. Technically therefore they are not development plan documents. **5.58**

The process of preparing and adopting a supplementary planning document therefore differs somewhat from other local development documents. The local planning authority is required to publish the draft supplementary planning document which should be accompanied by an appraisal of sustainability and by a statement outlining how the authority has complied with the statement of community involvement. The authority must also ensure that the document is in general conformity with the regional spatial strategy. Once the local planning authority has made such representations in the draft supplementary planning document and made changes considered appropriate, the authority may proceed to adoption. The regulations (Part 5) contain detailed provisions with regard to public participation in the preparation of supplementary planning guidance before its adoption. **5.59**

L. THE EXAMINATION OF DEVELOPMENT PLAN DOCUMENTS

On completion of the pre-submission consultation process, s.20 of the 2004 Act requires that the development plan document should be submitted for independent examination. For that purpose two copies of the development plan document must be sent to the Planning Inspectorate, along with: **5.60**

(a) the report of the sustainability proposal;
(b) any supporting technical documents such as urban capacity studies and housing needs surveys; and
(c) a copy of the statement of community involvement and a statement of compliance.

5.61 The local planning authority should at that same time publish a notice that the development plan document has been submitted for independent examination and invite representations to be made within a specified period of six weeks. Where the representations include proposals for alternative site allocations, the authority should publish them and invite representations. All representation on a development plan document that seeks changes to it should specify precisely the changes being sought.

M. THE INDEPENDENT EXAMINATION

5.62 The purpose of the examination is to determine whether the development plan document satisfies the requirements of the Act with regard to its preparation; and 'whether it is sound'. According to PPS 12, the criteria for assessing soundness is whether the document:

(a) is a spatial plan, i.e. does it properly take into account the various strategies which relate to meeting the community's needs for its area in economic, environmental and social terms where those strategies have an impact on the development and use of land;

(b) conforms generally with national planning policy and the regional spatial strategy or spatial development strategy in London;

(c) contains a coherent statement of core strategy (if the development plan document includes the core strategy) or is consistent with the core strategy or saved policies (if it is a development plan document which deals with site specific allocations or areas of change or conservation);

(d) is founded on a robust and credible evidence base;

(e) has clear mechanisms for implementation;

(f) is realistic and able to be implemented without compromising its objectives;

(g) is robust and able to deal with changing circumstances;

(h) is consistent with other development plan documents within the authority's area and those elements of neighbouring authorities' development plan documents where cross boundary issues are relevant;

(i) has taken proper account of views of the community; and

(j) has been prepared following the proper procedures, including sustainability appraisal/strategic environment assessment.

5.63 The examination will be carried out by 'a person appointed by the Secretary of State'. This will normally be an inspector drawn from the Planning Inspectorate. Any person who made representations seeking to change the development plan document must be given the opportunity to appear before and be heard by that person.

5.64 At the conclusion of the examination, the person appointed must make recommendations; and give reasons for those recommendations.

N. THE BINDING NATURE OF INSPECTORS' REPORTS

Unlike the position under the pre-2004 Act system where a local planning authority was not obliged to accept an inspector's proposed modifications to a local plan, under the post-2004 Act system, the modifications proposed by the Inspector following examination of a development plan document are binding on the authority. This is probably the key feature of the development plan reforms. Section 23 of the 2004 Act provides that the authority has power to adopt a development plan document as originally prepared if the person carrying out the examination so recommends. Or the authority has power to adopt a development plan document with modifications if the person carrying out the examination has recommended the modifications. Subject only to intervention by the Secretary of State, the authority has no choice in the matter and should proceed to adopt the development plan as soon as practical. Once adopted, the local development plan document then becomes part of the local development framework. **5.65**

O. POWERS OF THE SECRETARY OF STATE WITH REGARD TO LOCAL DEVELOPMENT DOCUMENTS

Section 21 of the 2004 Act gives the Secretary of State wide powers of intervention in the preparation of local development documents. If he considers a document to be unsatisfactory, he may at any time before it is adopted, direct the local planning authority to modify it in accordance with the direction. With regards to any development plan document, he has the additional power to direct that it should be submitted to him for his approval. It would also be noted that under section 27 of the 2004 Act, the Secretary of State is given wide power to prepare or revise a development plan document if he considers those functions are not being properly carried out by the local planning authority themselves. **5.66**

P. MISCELLANEOUS PROVISIONS OF PART 2

5.67

(a) *Withdrawal*
A local planning authority may withdraw a local development document at any time before adoption. This power is not available however where a development plan document has been submitted for independent examination, unless the Inspector carrying out the examination so recommends or the Secretary of State directs that the document should be withdrawn (s.22).

(b) *Adoption*
A local planning authority may adopt a local development document that is not a local development plan document either as originally prepared or as modified to take into account representations made in relation to the document or any other relevant matter.

(c) *Revocation*
The Secretary of State may at any time revoke a local development plan at the request

of the local planning authority. He may also prescribe the descriptions of local development documents which may be revoked by the authority themselves (S.25).

(d) *Revision*

A local planning authority may at any time prepare a revision of a local development document, and indeed must do so if the Secretary of State directs it to do so and in accordance with any timetable as he directs. They must also revise a local development document if an enterprise zone scheme is created within the area of the authority, or an existing enterprise zone scheme is modified (s.26).

(e) *Joint committees*

Sections 28–31 of the Act deal with the setting up of arrangements for two or more local planning authorities to jointly prepare a local development document. It also provides for the establishment of joint committees of one or more local planning authorities and one or more county councils in relation to any area of the country council for which there is a district council.

(f) *Urban Development Corporations*

Section 33 allows the Secretary of State to direct that Part 2 of the Act shall not apply to the area of an Urban Development Corporation, in which case the local planning authority will not be required to prepare a local development scheme for that area.

(g) *Implementation*

Section 35 requires local planning authorities to report annually to the Secretary of State on the implementation of their local development scheme and whether the policies in the local development documents are being achieved. Finally, Section 36 enables the Secretary of State to make regulations in connection with the exercise by any person of functions under the Act.

Q. LEGAL CHALLENGE

5.68 Any person may challenge the validity of a development plan document on the ground that it is not within the powers conferred by Part 2 of the 2004 Act, or that the requirements of the Act or regulations made under it have not been complied with. The application must be made within six weeks of the date of the publication of the advertisement stating that the development plan document has been adopted. This is similar to the right given to persons to challenge development plans prepared under the pre-2004 Act system (see 4.184).

R. DEVELOPMENT PLANS

5.69 Section 38 of the Planning and Compulsory Purchase Act provides that the development plan for any area in England (other than Greater London) shall be the regional spatial strategy for the region in which the area is situated, and the development plan documents (taken as a whole) which have been adopted or approved in relation to that area. With regard to Greater London, the development plan is to be the spatial development strategy, and the development plan documents described above. The section applies this definition of the development plan to other relevant legislation.

The section provides that where regard has to be had to the development plan in any determination made under the Planning Acts, the determination must be made in accordance with the plan unless material considerations indicate otherwise. Additionally the section provides that where there is a conflict in a development plan between any one policy and another, the conflict should be resolved in favour of that in the last document to be adopted, approved or published (as the case may be). **5.70**

It should be noted that as the new development plan system envisaged by the 2004 Act begins to be introduced, special transitional provisions apply to the relevance of development plans effective under the 1990 Act. This is dealt with in schedule 8 of the 2004 Act, and referred to below. **5.71**

S. TRANSITIONAL PROVISIONS: TRANSFERRING TO THE NEW SYSTEM

The Government's main objectives underlying the arrangements made in the 2004 Act for transferring to the new system of development plans are to move as quickly as possible from the old system of regional planning guidance, structure plans, local plans, waste and minerals plans and unitary development plans to a system of regional spatial strategies and local development documents and in addition, to maintain continuity in the development plan system as a framework for the exercise of development control until the new system has been introduced. **5.72**

The Act received Royal Assent on 13 May 2004. Section 121 of the Act enables the Secretary of State to bring the provisions of the Act into force on such day as he appoints. The key date in these transitional arrangements therefore, was the date when Parts 1 and 2 of the Act and section 38 (definition of development plan) were brought into effect, name of 28 September 2004. **5.73**

The transitional arrangements are contained in Schedule 8 to the Act. The provisions are elaborate and complicated. The schedule provides that with one minor exception, whatever constitutes the development plan in an area at the date of commencement of section 38 of the Act retains that development plan status. This status, however, will survive for whatever is the earlier of: **5.74**

(a) the end of a period of three years from the commencement of the Act;
(b) the day when in relation to an old policy, a new policy which expressly replaces it is published, adopted or approved.

It should be noted here that an old policy referred to above is one which immediately before the commencement of section 38 formed part of the development plan for the area. A new policy is one that is contained in a revision of the regional spatial strategy or in an alteration or replacement of a spatial development strategy or in a development plan document. It should be noted here that local development documents cannot replace saved policies as they do not form part of a development plan. Development plans in place on the bringing into effect of section 38 therefore, will be 'saved' for a period of three years or later if the Secretary of State so directs. During that time, the policies in a saved structure plan will be progressively replaced by revisions to the regional spatial strategy with other plans. The appropriate authorities will begin to replace policies in other saved plans with the preparation of development plan documents based on the local development scheme. The following summarizes the position:

T. STRUCTURE PLANS

Existing plans

5.75 Structure plans which have been approved or adopted will be saved for three years. During this period they will continue to form a part of the development plan. Within that same period, regional planning boards will be considering whether any elements of the saved plan should be saved for a longer period. If they do so decide, they will request the Secretary of State to direct that those policies should be saved for a further period beyond the three years. In addition, county planning authorities may during the preparation of a development document, consider the document to be inconsistent with a saved structure plan. If this is the case they may make representations to the Secretary of State who will then consider whether the inconsistency would in fact bring the development plan document out of general conformity with the regional spatial strategy.

Plans in preparation

5.76 Where the alteration or replacement of a structure plan had not reached the deposit stage (under section 33(2) of the 1990 Act) before the commencement of Part I of the Act, all plan preparation must cease. If by that time the alteration or replacement of a structure plan has reached the deposit stage, it may continue to be prepared under the 1990 Act and, once adopted, the three-year 'saved' period for the plan will start from that date. Alternatively, the county planning authority may decide not to take the preparation beyond the deposit stage and withdraw the draft plan. Whether or not they do so is likely to depend upon how far the work they have undertaken so far contributes to a revision of the regional spatial strategy by the regional planning board.

U. LOCAL PLANS, UDPs, WASTE AND MINERAL PLANS

Existing plans

5.77 Regulations made by the Secretary of State will require that within a prescribed period from that date, local planning authorities must submit to him a local, waste or minerals development scheme strategy setting out their timetable for producing local development documents over the following three years. Local planning authorities will then in accordance with that programme, produce development plan documents complying with those schemes. The development plan documents will, after independent explanation, then be adopted incrementally, replacing any corresponding policies of their 'saved' plans.

At the end of the three-year period, all saved plans will cease to be part of the development plan. However, there may be cases where the local planning authority wish certain policies which are compliant with their local development framework to continue beyond the three-year saved period. If so, the Secretary of State may use his power to so direct. **5.78**

V. PLANS IN PREPARATION

As with structure plans, transitional arrangements will vary according to the stage the adoption process has reached before commencement of Part 2 of the Act. Where proposals for the alteration or replacement of a plan had not reached the first deposit stage, all preparatory work should cease. However, work done on these plans might well assist the local planning authority in the preparation of local development documents in accordance with the authority's local development scheme or their minerals and waste development scheme. **5.79**

If on the other hand the first deposit stage has been reached before the commencement of Part 2 of the Act the position will vary according to circumstances: **5.80**

(a) If the plan has reached the first deposit stage and a hearing or inquiry is not required, it will continue to progress under the old statutory procedures.
(b) If a hearing or inquiry is required and an inspector has already been appointed the statutory procedures will continue and the plan may proceed to adoption or approval.
(c) If the plan has reached the first deposit stage and a hearing or inquiry is required but no Inspector has been appointed before the commencement of Part 2, the plan will continue under the existing procedures, but subject to changes in these procedures. The most important change is that the Inspector's report will be binding upon the local planning authority and the modification stage will not apply. This is because one of the mainstays of the new system is the binding nature of Inspectors' reports.

In all the above cases, once plans in preparation have been adopted, the three-year 'saved' period will begin. **5.81**

W. REGIONAL FUNCTIONS AND LOCAL DEVELOPMENT: WALES

The National Assembly for Wales cannot pass primary legislation. Planning is, however, a function within the competence of the National Assembly and therefore, is a function for which it has the power to pass delegated legislation. Accordingly, Parts 1 and 2 do not apply to Wales. Instead the provisions of Part 6 apply only to Wales. The provisions of this Part thus reflect the differences which allow the National Assembly for Wales to exercise the powers given in England to the Secretary of State, as much as reflecting the different ways in which the development plan system operates from that in England. **5.82**

The provisions of Part 6 of the Act provide for the National Assembly for Wales to prepare a **5.83**

Wales Spatial Plan setting out such of the policies of the National Assembly as it thinks appropriate in relation to the use and development of land in Wales. The basic pattern of development plans (including the single tier of local government and the uniform pattern of unitary development plans introduced in 1994) is to be retained but reformed. Under the provisions of Part 6, every local planning authority is required to prepare a development plan to be known as a local development plan, and to review it and revise it as necessary. The local planning authority will be required to have regard to the Wales Spatial Plan in preparing their local development plan. Part 6 also provides for the independent examination of local development plans, and procedures for their preparation have been simplified.

6

DEFINITION OF DEVELOPMENT 1: OPERATIONAL DEVELOPMENT

A. NEED FOR PLANNING PERMISSION

Section 57(1) of the 1990 Act provides that, subject to the following provisions of that section, 'planning permission is required for the carrying out of any development of land'. This planning permission may be granted following the determination of an express application for permission made to the local planning authority for the area in which the land is situated. In other cases, however, it is not necessary for an express application to be made. This is because planning permission for the development in question may have been granted by a development order, which may be a special, local or general order, (such development is generally known as 'permitted' development), or by some other specific statutory provision (as in the case of enterprise zones or simplified planning zones), or be deemed to have been granted under other powers contained in the Act (as in the case of the display of certain advertisements), or authorised by some Private Act of Parliament. **6.01**

B. DEFINITION OF DEVELOPMENT

The term 'development' is central to the power of local planning authorities to control the use and development of land. It is defined in s 55 (see Appendix A) and in s 336(1) (the interpretation section) of the 1990 Act. Section 55(1) contains the central core of the definition and provides that development may take one of two forms, namely, 'the carrying out of building, engineering, mining or other operations in, on, over or under land' or 'the making of any material change in the use of any buildings or other land'. **6.02**

6.03 The scheme of the Act is to keep these two forms of development separate and distinct. So in order to prevent confusion which might otherwise arise between the two forms by way of overlap, s 336(1) of the 1990 Act provides that the expression 'use' in relation to land, 'does not include the use of land for the carrying out of any building or other operations thereon'. Hence, any planning permission granted solely for the making of a material change in the use of land or buildings will not authorise the carrying out of an operation on the land in order to secure the better enjoyment of that new use. On the other hand, the Act recognises that the enjoyment of a building erected under a grant of planning permission will almost inevitably involve a change in the use of the land on which the building has been erected. Accordingly, s 75(2) of the 1990 Act provides that:

> Where planning permission is granted for the erection of a building, the grant of permission may specify the purposes for which the building may be used.

6.04 Section 75(3) then goes on to say:

> If no purpose is so specified, the permission shall be construed as including permission to use the building for the purpose for which it is designed.

6.05 The two forms of development, namely, a building, engineering, mining or other operation or a material change of use, are often referred to as two limbs in order to emphasise their related but independent characteristics. The first limb is often referred to as 'operational development'.

6.06 The fact that the two forms of development are kept separate and distinct, however, does not exclude the possibility of a single process comprising both operational development and a material change of use. In *West Bowers Farm Products v Essex County Council* (1985) P & CR 368, Nourse LJ said:

> The planning legislation is not impressed by the indivisibility of single processes. It cares only for their effects. A single process might for planning purposes amount to two activities. Whether it did so or not was a question of fact and degree. If it involved two activities, each of substance, so that *one is not merely ancillary to the other*, then both required permission (author's emphasis).

6.07 The *West Bowers* case is, however, exceptional. There the owners were carrying out operations on farmland consisting of digging a reservoir to contain water for agricultural irrigation. This operation constituted an 'engineering operation requisite for the use of land for the purpose of agriculture'. In the course of digging the reservoir the owners were extracting and selling huge quantities of gravel which constituted 'the use of land for the winning and working of minerals', a different class of development. The owners needed planning permission and the issue was on what basis to make the application. If the application related 'solely' to engineering operations requisite to the use of the land for agricultural purposes, no fee had to be paid, nor did the application need to be advertised. The local planning authority, however, contended successfully that the owner was also using the land for the winning and working of minerals. Thus in the *West Bowers* case the one individual process had two physical aspects, each of which fell into a different specific category. As was subsequently explained in *R v Durham CC and Lafarge Redland Aggregates Ltd, ex p Lowther* [2002] JPL 197, it is correct to analyse the *West Bowers* case as involving two separate and sequential activities. In the *West Bowers* case there were two aspects of one activity, each of which had different consequences according to the express terms of the planning regulations, so that each had to be separately considered.

Although the core of the definition is contained in s 55(1) of the 1990 Act, it is qualified by important provisions contained in sub-sections (2) to (5) of that section. Sub-section (2) lists three operations (paras (a) to (c)), three uses (paras (d) to (f)), and then one further operation (para (g)) added to the sub-section by the Planning and Compensation Act 1991, which are not to be taken to involve the development of land. Sub-section (3) lists two uses which, for the avoidance of doubt, are declared to involve a material change of use. Sub-section (4) amplifies the meaning of the term mining operations; subsection (4A) brings certain fish-farming activities within the definition of development; and sub-section (5) provides that the display of certain advertisements shall constitute a material change of use. 6.08

C. OPERATIONAL DEVELOPMENT

As already stated, the first limb of the definition of development is the 'carrying out of building, engineering, mining or other operations in, on, over or under land'. 6.09

Building operations

Sub-section (1A) of s 55 of the Act provides that the term 'building operations' includes: 6.10

(a) demolition of buildings;
(b) rebuilding;
(c) structural alterations of or additions to buildings; and
(d) other operations normally undertaken by a person carrying on business as a builder.

Two points about this definition should be noted. First, the use of the word 'includes' shows that the words that follow it are not exhaustive of its meaning; secondly and somewhat surprisingly, the erection of an entirely new building is not specifically mentioned as being within the term. It seems fairly clear, however, that such activity must fall within the concluding clause of the definition as being work normally undertaken by a person carrying on business as a builder. 6.11

Buildings

As recognised in the definition given to the words 'building operations', the work done will normally involve work to a 'building'. The meaning of the word 'building', therefore, may also be relevant to the question of whether a particular activity constitutes development. 'Building' is defined in s 336(1) to include 'any structure or erection, and any part of a building, as so defined, but does not include plant or machinery comprised in a building'. The word 'building' therefore, has been given in this context a wider meaning than is normally given to it in everyday parlance. It will thus include 'erections' which may not normally be regarded as 'buildings'. 6.12

As might be expected, therefore, a number of significant judicial decisions have been made on its precise meaning and application. 6.13

6.14 In *Buckinghamshire County Council v Callingham* [1952] 2 QB 515 the Court of Appeal held that the model village and railway at Bekonscot near Beaconsfield was a structure or erection, and therefore a building within the meaning of that word. In *James v Brecon County Council* (1963) 15 P & CR 20, however, it was held that a battery of six swing-boats erected at a fairground was not a structure or erection. An important factor in that decision was that the entire battery could be dismantled by six men in no more than half an hour.

6.15 Thus in determining whether a structure or erection exists, factors likely to be considered dominant by the courts are size and permanence. That much seems clear from two of the most important judicial decisions made in this area.

6.16 In *Cheshire CC v Woodward* [1962] 2 QB 126, a coal merchant installed a coal hopper and conveyor equipment in his coal yard without first obtaining a grant of planning permission to do so. The hopper, which was some 16 to 20 feet in height and mounted on wheels, traversed and delivered coal to stationary lorries beneath. An enforcement notice was then served on behalf of the county council alleging a breach of planning control and requiring the removal of the hopper and conveyor. The coal merchant appealed to the Minister against the enforcement notice and the Minister, after holding an inquiry, accepted the recommendation of the Inspector and quashed the notice. The Council then appealed to the High Court on the point of law that the Minister had erred in holding that the installation was not development. In dismissing the appeal, Lord Parker CJ said:

> . . . the Act is referring to any structure or erection which can be said to form part of the realty, and to change the physical character of the land.

6.17 It seems, however, that an object may be affixed to land and not be a building, or not be affixed to land and be a building. According to Lord Parker CJ in *Cheshire CC v Woodward*:

> The mere fact that something is erected in the course of a building operation which is affixed to the land does not determine the matter. Equally, as it seems to me, the mere fact that it can be moved and is not affixed does not determine the matter . . . There is no one test; you look at the erection, equipment, plant, whatever it is, and ask: in all the circumstances is it to be treated as part of the realty? So here, . . . one must look at the whole circumstances, including what is undoubtedly extremely relevant, the degree of permanency with which it is affected.

6.18 The decision in *Cheshire CC v Woodward* was later considered by the courts in *Barvis Ltd v Secretary of State for the Environment* (1971) 22 P & CR 710. In that case the appellant company had erected at its depot a mobile crane normally used by it for erecting pre-cast concrete structures on contract sites. The crane was some 89 feet high and ran on a steel track permanently fixed in concrete. The crane could be dismantled in sections and re-erected, but took several days to do so. The local planning authority maintained that the erection constituted development and served an enforcement notice on the appellant requiring its removal. Following an appeal, the notice was upheld by the Secretary of State. The appellant company then challenged the decision of the Secretary of State in the High Court. It maintained that the crane was intended to be moved on and off land as requirements demanded; that it was not fixed to the land, nor did it form part of the realty. Furthermore, its degree of permanence was slight and had not altered the physical character of the land. Dismissing the appeal, Bridge J said he did not wish in the slightest degree to question the validity or usefulness of the tests propounded in *Cheshire CC v Woodward*, which he considered it might be necessary to apply in a borderline case. He felt, however, that here it was not necessary to apply the tests propounded in that case. One must ask, he said:

> . . . was the crane, when erected, a 'building' within the definition . . .? 'Building' includes any structure or erection. If, as a matter of impression, one looks objectively at this enormous crane, it seems to me impossible to say that it did not amount to a structure or erection.
>
> . . . in my judgment, this crane was not the less a structure or erection by reason of its limited degree of mobility on rails on the site, nor by reason of the circumstance that at some future date, uncertain when it was erected, the appellants contemplated that it would be dismantled . . .

The *Barvis* case is the strongest authority for the view that the key elements in deciding whether something is a building or not are size, permanence and physical attachment to the land. Indeed, this approach is at one with that taken by the court in a rating case, *Cardiff Rating Authority v Guest Keen Baldwin Iron and Steel Co. Ltd* [1949] 1 KB 385, where the three factors identified in deciding what consistututed a structure, were size, permanence and physical attachment. **6.19**

In *R v Swansea City Council, ex p Elitestone Ltd* (1993) 66 P & CR 422, the question arose whether chalets were buildings and therefore capable of being protected from demolition by conservation area status. The Court of Appeal considered the chalets were buildings and that the degree of permanence was a highly material factor in so deciding. Other significant facts may, however, be size and composition by component parts, as where a structure results from the assembly on site of the various parts which go to make it up. **6.20**

The relevance of permanence as a factor to be considered can be seen in *Skerritts of Nottingham Ltd v Secretary of State for the Environment, Transport and the Regions* [2000] JPL 1025. There a question arose as to whether the erection of a marquee every year to remain on site between February and October amounted to a building operation. An enforcement notice served by the local planning authority requiring its removal had been upheld on appeal by an Inspector acting on behalf of the Secretary of State. The marquee measured 40m by 17m with a ridge height of 5m. Its erection required several people to work for several days. The 16 feet of metal portal frames sat on square metal plates spiked into the soil beneath. This, together with internal bracing and its considerable weight held the marquee in place. Inside the marquee was a timber floor, supported by metal ground beams resting on the land. The Inspector had concluded, as a matter of fact and degree, that the marquee was a building due to its dimensions, its permanence (rather than its fleeting nature); and the secure nature of its anchorage. Accordingly, since the marquee was a building operation, Skerritts were carrying out building operations every year when it was erected. Skerritts then appealed successfully to the High Court on the question of the Inspector's approach to permanence. Reinstating the decision of the Inspector, however, the Court of Appeal rejected the argument by Skerritts that the annual removal of the marquee deprived it of the quality of permanence. That term, according to the Court, carried with it a degree of flexibility between temporary on the one hand and everlasting on the other, and it did not mean that an object had be on the land for 365 days in the year. To hold otherwise, would mean that any object, however large and well-constructed, which was built in a way that it could be dismantled and removed annually for a short time, would be outside planning control. **6.21**

6.22 Despite what was said in *Cheshire CC v Woodward* and *Barvis Ltd v Secretary of State for the Environment*, one can envisage many situations in which the question of whether or not an object is a structure or erection will be finely balanced and where it may be difficult to decide on which side the scales should be brought down.

6.23 More recently, the High Court held in *Tewkesbury Borough Council v Keeley* [2004] EWHC 2594 (QB), that a mobile shed was not a structure or erection falling within the definition of a building. The Court accepted that in none of the cases to which it had been referred had a structure been held to be a building which was mobile to the extent of having wheels so that it could be freely moved about on site. This accords with the view the courts have taken with regard to the position of caravans.

6.24 It should be remembered here that the decision-making processes in the planning law field allows the Secretary of State, in determining such matters as appeals against enforcement notices or the refusal of an authority to issue a certificate of lawfulness of a proposed use or development under s 192 of the 1990 Act, to make an initial determination on whether or not a particular activity constitutes development. Although this is a determination on a point of law, landowners and local planning authorities may be willing to accept his decision and be reluctant to pursue the matter further by challenging his decision in the courts. Hence, the Secretary of State's decision in a particular case is often final.

6.25 In that capacity, he has held that such things as a carport, a portakabin, a slide (erected on a pier at a seaside resort), a plastic tree (erected in the children's playing area in the grounds of a public house), a steel frame supporting a polythene cover over a swimming-pool, a model railway track, a radio mast and a large area of timber decking in the grounds of a hotel were structures or erections and thus within the definition of a building. More recently, an Inspector has held that tunnels assembled on agricultural land to protect growing stock from wind and rain was an operation within s.55(i) of the 1990 Act (Ref: APP/Y2620/4/04/1142007). In another case, an Inspector held that the erection in the garden of a public house of three large umbrellas, attached together with canvas side shades, each of which was in a concrete footing fell within the definition of a building in s.336 of the 1990 Act (Ref. APP/H5390/C/03/1128513). On the other hand, the Secretary of State has held that the erection of benders (a woven timber framework covered with tarpaulins and anchored down by posts driven into the ground and sealed with turf sods) used for the purpose of human habitation, constituted not operational development but a material change of use. This last decision was later upheld by the High Court in *Britton v Secretary of State for the Environment* [1997] JPL 617.

6.26 From a practical point of view, in considering operational development, it should be borne in mind that the General Permitted Development Order grants planning permission for such minor matters as the erection or construction of gates, fences, walls or other means of enclosure. However, this is not in itself conclusive proof that in law minor work of this kind necessarily constitutes a building operation: the content of an order made under the Act cannot be used to try to discover the meaning of the Act itself.

Building operations which are not development

6.27 Mention was made earlier that s 55(2) of the 1990 Act specified three operations (paras (a) to (c)) and three uses (paras (d) to (f)) and then a further operation (para (g)), which were not to be taken to involve the development of land. The operation mentioned in paragraph (a) of s. 55(2) is:

> the carrying out for the maintenance, improvement or other alteration of any building of works which—
>
> (i) affect only the interior of the building, or
> (ii) do not materially affect the external appearance of the building,
>
> and are not works for making good war damage or works begun after 5th December 1968 for the alteration of a building by providing additional space in it underground.

This provision makes it clear that it is not development to remove, say, an internal wall of a building. The provision however, is sometimes misunderstood. There are many activities which may affect only the interior of a building or do not materially affect its external appearance. These activities will not constitute development, not because of the provisions in s 55(2)(a) but because the work involved does not constitute a building operation. In other words, one must first consider whether the work involved falls within the meaning of development as defined in ss 55(1) and 336(1). If it does, one has then to consider whether it is excluded from that definition by being an activity which falls within s 55(2)(a). Thus it is not development to replace a broken pane of glass in the window of a dwellinghouse. The reason is that it is not an operation as defined in ss 55(1) and 336(1), and the fact that the replacement does not materially affect the external appearance of the building is not relevant. 6.28

The value of following this approach is best seen with regard to the concluding provision in s 55(2)(a), namely the words 'and are not . . . works begun after 5th December 1968 for the alteration of a building by providing additional space in it underground'. These words were introduced into the law by the Town and Country Planning Act 1968. The need to do so arose from the wishes of a provincial department store to extend its premises. Because policy or site limitations respectively prevented the store from extending upwards or outwards it decided to obtain the additional space it needed by excavating downwards. On the completion of the work and the opening of the store's household basement the additional custom generated by the extension caused considerable congestion in the surrounding streets. 6.29

The work done by the store was not development and the local planning authority were powerless to prevent it. Although it constituted a building (and possibly also an engineering) operation under s 55(1), it was excluded from the definition of development by virtue of being work for the alteration of a building which affected only its interior. During the passage of the 1968 Act through Parliament, the opportunity was taken to close this lacuna in the law by, as it were, excluding that exclusion for the future. Thus after 5 December 1968, the work carried out by the store would require planning permission. Such work would be a building operation, but one to which the provisions of para (a) of s 55(2) would not apply. 6.30

The limitations of this exclusion became to be realised when changes were made to Government policy with regard to retail development. It became clear that the creation in an existing retail store of additional internal floor space to be used for that purpose was not affected by the changes made in 1968. Since the additional space was not being created below ground. So that, for example, the erection of a mezzanine floor within retail buildings and its use for that purpose would not normally require planning permission. Where a local 6.31

planning authority wished to control such additions, only an appropriate condition which limited the amount of floor space to be used for retail purposes imposed in the original grant of permission could do so. Few permissions did that.

6.32 Amendments made by the Planning and Compulsory Purchase Act 2004 now enable the Secretary of State to remedy that mischief. Section 49 of the 2004 Act added new subsections 2A and 2B to section 55 of the 1990 Act by allowing the Secretary of State by a development order to specify 'any circumstances or description of circumstances in which s.55 subsection 2 is not to apply to operations mentioned in paragraph (a) of the subsection which would have the effect of increasing the gross floor space of the building by such amount or percentage amount as is so specified.' When a development order is made under this amendment, it may make different provision for different purposes.

6.33 The question of whether or not carrying out works for the maintenance, improvement or other alteration of a building materially affects the external appearance of the building is one which will normally be determined by the local planning authority or, on appeal, by the Secretary of State. In two rare cases, however, the question has come to be determined by the courts.

6.34 In *Kensington & Chelsea RLBC v C. G. Hotels* [1981] JPL 190 the owners of a West London hotel installed floodlights without planning permission. The local planning authority then served an enforcement notice requiring their removal. Some of the floodlights were attached to the basement area of the hotel; others simply stood under their own weight on first floor balconies but were not attached to the building other than by the electricity supply cable.

6.35 The owners of the hotel had appealed to the Secretary of State and an Inspector, acting on his behalf, had concluded that there was no breach of planning control and quashed the notice. In dismissing an appeal against the decision of the Secretary of State, the Divisional Court held that assuming, without actually deciding, that the installation of floodlights constituted development within s 55(1) of the 1990 Act, the placing of electric cables and floodlights in position and the fixing of some of them to the building, did not 'materially affect the external appearance of the building'. If the external appearance of the building had been materially affected, it was caused by the running of electricity through the cables, not by the positioning and fixing of the floodlights.

6.36 Further help as to the interpretation of this provision has now been given by the High Court in *Burroughs Day v Bristol City Council* [1996] 1 PLR 78, where the occupiers of a building proposed an alteration to the roof of the building and replacement of windows to the front elevation in order to accommodate the installation of a lift in the building. A question then arose as to whether the occupiers were entitled to compensation for the refusal of listed building consent to carry out those works under statutory provisions now repealed. That in turn required a consideration of whether the work was development under s 55(1) of the 1990 Act. The Court held that in interpreting the words of the provision and in applying them to particular facts, the following points should be taken into account, namely:

(a) what had to be affected was the 'external appearance of the building, not the "exterior" of the building'. The use of the word 'appearance' meant that it was not sufficient for the external surface of a building to be affected by the proposed alteration. The alteration had to be one which affected the way in which the exterior of the building could be seen by an observer outside the building;

(b) the external appearance of the building had to be 'materially' affected. That effect must be more than *de minimis*;

(c) whether the effect of the alteration was 'material' must depend in part on the degree of visibility; and

(d) the effect on the external appearance must be judged for its materiality in relation to the building as a whole and not by reference to a part of a building taken in isolation.

The old problem of demolition

The problem of whether or not the demolition of a building *simpliciter* constitutes development has for many years been uncertain yet important. 'Building operations', it may be recalled, is defined in s 55(1A) to include 'demolition of buildings; rebuilding; structural alterations of or additions to buildings; and other operations normally undertaken by a person carrying on business as a builder'. **6.37**

Prior to the 1991 Act, the definition of building operations (previously found in s 336(1) of the Act) did not include 'demolition of buildings' and this led to much uncertainty. **6.38**

The leading case in this area was without doubt that of *Coleshill & District Investment Co. Ltd v Minister of Housing and Local Government* [1969] 1 WLR 746. The facts are particularly crucial to the decision. A site had consisted of six separate buildings used during the last war as an ammunition depot. Four of the buildings had been used as magazines, the other two for the storage of explosives. Around each building was a blast wall nine feet in height. Against each wall and on its outside was a sloping embankment of rubble and soil extending out about eight feet from the base. The functional relationship between the wall with its embankment and the buildings which it surrounded is only too self-evident. **6.39**

There was no dispute between the parties that the original use having been discontinued, the six buildings had an existing use for storage purposes. The appellant company wished to remove the embankments and walls. As a first step it started to remove the embankments. Following complaints by residents, the local planning authority served an enforcement notice on the company requiring it to cease the removal. The company, having taken the view that this activity did not constitute development and that no planning permission was necessary, appealed against the enforcement notice to the Minister, who refused to grant planning permission for the development and upheld the notice. **6.40**

The company had also wished to demolish the walls. It therefore applied to the local planning authority, under what was then s 64 of the 1990 Act, for a determination whether that operation would constitute development. Having heard nothing from the authority within the period prescribed for doing so, the company appealed to the Minister against non-determination of their application. The Minister then determined that the removal of the walls would constitute development and that planning permission was required. Thus, by two separate procedural routes, the Minister had given a decision that the removal of the embankments and walls constituted development. In the High Court the company again contended that an act of demolition was not development. The case eventually reached the House of Lords. Their Lordships thought that the question of whether demolition was or was **6.41** not development was a neat and arresting question, but not one that needed to be answered on the facts of the case. According to their Lordships, the true path of inquiry was not to crystal-gaze or to ask hypothetical questions. One had to see exactly what had been done, and then see whether it came within the statutory definition of development. They pointed out that it was unnecessary (and possibly misleading) to give work a single label like demolition, and then try to apply the definition to that label. Their Lordships were clearly right. Nothing is to be gained by asking, for example, whether renovation, or repair, or rehabilitation constitutes development.

6.42 The House of Lords went on to find that the Minister had made no error of law in holding:

(a) that the blast walls and embankments were an integral part of the buildings and that the removal of the blast walls would constitute a building operation; and
(b) that the removal of the embankments was an engineering operation.

6.43 The decision proved difficult to interpret. There was no doubt that an important feature of the case was the upholding of the Minister's finding that the blast walls and embankments formed an integral part of the buildings. Hence it was inevitable that their removal would constitute development, since a building operation was then defined in s 336(1) to include 'structural alterations . . . to buildings'.

6.44 The decision thus raised the important question of whether or not it would be development to remove the whole of a building or a building complex. Leaving aside the possibility that its removal might constitute an engineering operation (see 6.56) it is difficult to see how, if the whole of a building were demolished, it could be said to be 'a rebuilding operation, a structural alteration or an addition to a building'. It could be, however, that the courts would regard that activity as an 'other operation normally undertaken by a person carrying on business as a builder'. No one, it seems, could be sure. There was an *obiter* statement which suggested that, unless the total removal of a building constituted an engineering operation, the work would not be regarded as development. In *Iddenden v Secretary of State for the Environment* [1972] 1 WLR 1433 the appellant had demolished a Nissen hut and workshop and erected in its place a new building. The local planning authority had served an enforcement notice upon him requiring him to demolish the new building which had been erected without planning permission. Iddenden claimed that the notice was invalid because it did not also require him to re-erect the buildings he had demolished. It was held that the local planning authority had a discretion to decide what steps were required to restore the land to its condition before the development took place. They could if they wished, decide that all that was necessary was the pulling down of the new building. That effectively disposed of the appellant's argument. For good measure, however, Lord Denning MR added that 'Whilst some demolition operations may be development . . . the demolition of buildings such as these was not'. In other words, it was not a breach of planning control to remove these old buildings.

6.45 The difficulty of knowing whether or not the law regarded the *total* demolition of a building as development had important consequences for development control. The demolition of buildings sometimes took place in order to remove an impediment to the grant of planning permission for the redevelopment of the land on which the building stands. Planning permission, for example, might be refused for the redevelopment of land with an existing community use such as shops and theatres, because of a desire to retain those uses; and this even though the redevelopment proposal was in accordance with the provisions of the development plan for the area. If the shops and theatres are first demolished, no valid reason would then exist for the refusal of the permission. Nowhere was this more of a problem than with regard to buildings having some architectural or historical interest, but which were not considered to possess such special qualities as to warrant their inclusion in the statutory list of buildings (called listed buildings) kept by the Secretary of State under the provisions of s 1 of the Planning (Listed Buildings and Conservation Areas) Act 1990. The significance of this was that if the buildings were within the list they could not be demolished without listed building consent to do so first being obtained. A somewhat similar rule applied to the demolition, without conservation area consent, of a non-listed building situated within a conservation area. It often happens that once an application for planning permission is made for redevelopment of land on which there stands a building which, although not listed, has some architectural or historical interest, the application will generate suggestions that the building has sufficient special qualities to warrant it being added to the list, and so subject to the special protection which is given to listed buildings. If it is added, the prospect of obtaining listed building consent for its demolition to enable the redevelopment to go ahead is not likely to be high. It follows, therefore, that in these situations there is pressure on landowners and developers to first demolish the building and then make an application for planning permission for the redevelopment of the land on which it stood. In this way no one is alerted to the possibility that an important building would be lost to the public heritage if planning permission was granted, and by the time the public are alerted, it has already been lost.

In past years, further concern was expressed over the wanton demolition of existing houses, **6.46** prior to the submission of applications for planning permission for residential development of the land on which the houses stood with much higher housing densities. In a consultation paper issued in 1989 by the Secretary of State, various ways to deal with this problem were then canvassed.

As it so happened, the Secretary of State's consideration of the views expressed by consultees **6.47** was quickly overtaken by events. In *Cambridge City Council* v *Secretary of State for the Environment* (1991) 89 LGR 1015, Mr David Widdicombe QC, sitting in the High Court as a deputy judge, described the question whether demolition was development within the Act as 'a question which like a ghost has haunted planning law for many years . . . The time has now come when the ghost must be laid to rest'. He then went on to hold that the demolition of houses was a 'building operation' being (as per the definition in s 336(1)) an 'other operation normally undertaken by a person carrying on business as a builder'. Although an appeal against that decision was subsequently allowed by the Court of Appeal (1992) 90 LGR 275, the Government decided after the High Court decision to include a provision in the Planning and Compensation Act 1991 amending the definition of building operations, then contained in s 336(1) of the 1990 Act, to include the 'demolition of buildings' and to include that definition in the body of s 55.

The new problem of demolition

It was not the intention of the Government that the demolition of every type of building **6.48** should be development and therefore require planning permission. Accordingly, the 1991

Act amendment gave the Secretary of State power to make directions enabling him to provide that the demolition of particular types of building was not to involve development. Thus the following new paragraph (g) was added to the three operations listed in s 55(2) (in paras (a) to (c)) which are *not* to be taken to involve development:

> . . . the demolition of any description of building specified in a direction given by the Secretary of State to local planning authorities generally or to a particular local authority.

6.49 The Secretary of State has now issued the Town and Country Planning (Demolition — Description of Buildings) Direction 1995, published in a circular letter to local planning authorities dated 6 March 1995. It has subsequently been published again as Appendix A to Circular No 10/95, 'Planning Controls over Demolition'. The effect of the Direction, is to provide that the demolition of the following types of building shall *not* be taken to involve development of land:

(a) Listed buildings, buildings in conservation areas and any building which is a scheduled monument as defined in the Ancient Monuments and Archaeological Areas Act 1979. The demolition of all such buildings is subject to control under other legislation.

(b) A building of less than 50 cubic metres (when measured externally). Clearly this is intended to be a *de minimis* provision.

(c) Any building other than a dwellinghouse or a building adjoining a dwellinghouse. Thus the demolition of buildings used as offices, factories, shops or warehouses are outside the definition of development. But a building is not to be regarded as a dwellinghouse if the use of that building or part of that building, as a dwellinghouse is ancillary to any non-residential use of that building or other buildings on the same site.

(d) The whole or any part of any gate, fence, wall or other means of enclosure.

6.50 It should be noted that for the purposes of the Direction, the term 'building' includes each house in a pair of semi-detached houses, and every house in a row of terrace houses (whether or not, in either case, the house is in residential use). Also, the term 'dwellinghouse' includes a residential home or hostel, and a building containing a flat.

6.51 The remaining control over demolition is intended in the main to apply to the demolition of dwellinghouses and of buildings adjoining dwellinghouses. However, because the demolition of most dwellinghouses does not justify the full application of these new controls, the Secretary of State has, with one important exception, exercised his power in relation to the General Permitted Development Order to include as permitted development the demolition of all buildings which are not already excluded from control by the Direction described above. With that one exception, namely, where a building has been made unsafe or uninhabitable, either through deliberate action or neglect by anyone having an interest in the land on which the building stands and the building can be made secure through temporary repairs or support, the demolition of a dwellinghouse or of a building adjoining a dwellinghouse is permitted without the need for express planning permission by virtue of Part 31 of Sch 2 to the Order. Before such permitted development rights may be used, however, the Order provides that the developer must first apply to the local planning authority for a determination of whether the prior approval of the authority is required as to the *method* of the proposed demolition and any proposed restoration of the site. The authority are then given 28 days to consider the matter. If the developer is not notified within the 28-day period that prior approval is required, he may proceed to demolish the building in accordance with the details submitted by him to the authority in his application for the determination. If, on the other hand, the authority require prior approval to be obtained before demolition, the only remedy available to the developer is to seek that prior approval and then, if approval should not be given, to appeal to the Secretary of State.

The purpose of this prior-approval requirement is to give local planning authorities the opportunity to regulate the details of demolition and restoration in order to minimise the impact of that activity on local amenity. It must be emphasised, however, that the need to seek prior approval does not in fact prevent demolition from taking place once the prior-approval process has been negotiated. In order to do that, there must be in place an Article 4 direction (see Chapter 7), withdrawing the permitted development right. **6.52**

Refusal of approval cannot be based on the absence of an approved scheme of redevelopment. At the application for approval stage demolition is not an issue. It is concerned solely with details of the method of demolition and the restoration of the site. Approval could be withheld for example, if the demolition proposals did not include measures to protect trees, the erection of fencing on the perimeter of the land to provide a safe and secure environment during demolition, an undertaking not to carry out site burning, a provision relating to hours of work, the removal of demolition rubble and an undertaking to level the site and to leave it clean and tidy and clear of all hazards on completion of the demolition. **6.53**

It should be noted too that the prior-approval procedure described above, does not apply where demolition is: **6.54**

(a) urgently necessary in the interests of health or safety, provided that the developer gives a written justification of the demolition to the local planning authority as soon as reasonably practicable after the demolition has taken place;
(b) on land which is the subject of planning permission, for the redevelopment of the land granted on an application or deemed to be granted under Part III of the Act;
(c) required or permitted to be carried out by or under any enactment (e.g., as the result of an enforcement notice); or
(d) required to be carried out by virtue of a relevant obligation (e.g., a s 106 agreement).

The above changes do not affect the need to obtain planning permission for the partial demolition of a building which is generally regarded as a 'structural alteration' to a building. Furthermore, demolition of a building may still constitute an engineering operation. However, the demolition of a building within the Town and Country Planning (Demolition — Description of Buildings) Direction 1995 will not involve development, whether or not the demolition is a building or an engineering operation. Subject to this proviso and to that extent, the decision of the House of Lords in the *Coleshill* case continues to have some legal relevance. **6.55**

Engineering operations

The 1990 Act gives little guidance on the meaning of the expression 'engineering operations' save that s 336(1) provides that it includes 'the formation or laying out of means of access to **6.56** highways'. It will be recalled that in *Coleshill & District Investment Co. Ltd v Minister of Housing and Local Government* [1969] 1 WLR 746, the House of Lords found that the Minister had not erred in law in holding the removal of an embankment to be an engineering operation. In this case it was shown that the removal of the embankment would require many lorries to be used over a prolonged period to transport the debris away from the site. On the other hand, the removal of a mere shovelful of earth from one spot to another is unlikely to be considered an engineering operation. Somewhere in between lies the demarcation line that separates an activity which is not an engineering operation from one which is. The meaning of the term has until recently received little judicial consideration. The absence of judicial guidance led at one time to much uncertainty and inconsistency in cases where the term had to be applied. In 1983, however, the meaning of the term was clarified by the decision in *Fayrewood Fish Farms Ltd v Secretary of State for the Environment* [1984] JPL 267, in which the High Court had to consider whether the excavation and removal of topsoil for the purpose of extracting underlying gravel constituted an 'engineering operation'. The Secretary of State had thought that it did. In remitting the matter back to the Secretary of State with the opinion of the court, Mr David Widdicombe QC, sitting as a Deputy High Court judge, accepted that the Secretary of State was basically right to hold that engineering operations called for engineering skills, but that he had gone too far in requiring that there had to be a 'specific project which is of sufficient predetermined size and shape that a conception of the finished project can be illustrated on a plan or drawing'. In his view, the term 'engineering operations' should be given its ordinary meaning in the English language. It must mean, he said, 'operations of the kind usually undertaken by engineers, i.e., operations calling for the skills of an engineer'. These would normally be civil engineers, but could be traffic engineers or other specialist engineers who applied their skills to land. It did not mean, he said, 'that an engineer must actually be engaged on the project, simply that it was the kind of operation on which an engineer could be employed, or which would be within his purview'.

6.57 In the exercise of his appellate functions, the Secretary of State has held that the removal of part of an embankment supporting a railway bridge and the deposit of subsoil and topsoil on land constituted an engineering operation [1983] JPL 616. In a recent decision (Ref. APP/Q3 115/X/04 /1149901), an Inspector held that the demolition of a bridge carrying a disused railway line over a road was not development, since the bridge was a building within the Demolition of Buildings Directive 1995. However, the alteration to the contours of the adjacent embankment abutting the bridge was an engineering operation requiring planning permission.

6.58 Although the deposit of refuse or waste materials on land is regarded by the 1990 Act as being, if anything, a material change of use, it was suggested by the High Court in *Ratcliffe* v *Secretary of State for the Environment* [1975] JPL 728 that the deposit of refuse could amount to an 'engineering operation'.

6.59 In *R. F. W. Copper (Trustees of the Thames Ditton Lawn Tennis Club) v K. J. Bruce-Smith* [1998] JPL 1077, the Court of Appeal held that contrary to the finding of the High Court, the proposed breaking up and digging out of tennis courts was more aptly considered to be an engineering or other operation than demolition and a building operation.

6.60 Whatever the meaning of the term 'engineering operation' its compass is limited by the provisions in paras (b) and (c) of s 55(2) of the 1990 Act, the two remaining operations specified in that sub-section as not to be taken to involve the development of land. The provisions are as follows:

(b) the carrying out on land within the boundaries of a road by a highway authority of any works required for the maintenance or improvement of the road, but in the case of any such works which are not exclusively for the maintenance of the road, not including any works which may have significant adverse effects on the environment;

(c) the carrying out by a local authority or statutory undertakers of any works for the purpose of inspecting, repairing or renewing any sewers, mains, pipes, cables or other apparatus, including the breaking open of any street or other land for that purpose.

As regards the activity mentioned in paragraph (b), it should be remembered that, particularly in country areas, the boundaries of a road may frequently be much wider than that part of the road which is actually 'made up'. This provision may enable the local highway authority, therefore, to make important alterations to the line of a road by such activities as ironing out a curve or removing old walls and hedges, without the need to apply for planning permission to do so. This freedom from planning control is compounded by a provision in the General Permitted Development Order. Part 13 of the Order grants planning permission for the carrying out by a local highway authority: **6.61**

(a) on land within the boundaries of a road, of any works required for the maintenance or improvement of the road, where such works involve development by virtue of s 55(2)(b) of the Act; or

(b) on land outside but adjoining the boundary of an existing highway, of works required for or incidental to the maintenance or improvement of the highway.

Although the local highway authority would, unless it already owned adjacent land, have to purchase it from the owner before being able to avail itself of the permission granted by the order, the two provisions taken together give a wide latitude to highway authorities to alter the lay-out of a road without the public being able to influence its proposals.

The problem has been ameliorated to some extent by the amendments made to s 55 and Part 13 of the Order (and incorporated in this text above) by the Environmental Impact Assessment Regulations 1999. The result is that such development may form part of or be Sch 1 or Sch 2 development and require environmental impact assessment, or otherwise have adverse environmental effects and therefore require an express grant of planning permission. **6.62**

It will be recalled that s 336(1) provides that engineering operations includes 'the formation or laying out of means of access to highways'. It would seem, therefore, that the simple driving of a vehicle on to the highway from adjoining land without more such as the laying of hardcore or the removal of a hedge is not in itself an engineering operation. However, under the Highways Act 1980 the highway authority has power to erect fences or posts to prevent access to the highway from adjacent land. **6.63**

Prior to the Planning and Compensation Act 1991, doubts also existed about the extent to which fish farming constituted development, and thus an activity subject to development control. **6.64**

6.65 Section 14 of the 1991 Act inserted into s 55 of the 1990 Act a new sub-section (4A) to bring fish tanks (cages) in inland waters within the definition of development. The new sub-section (4A) provides:

> Where the placing or assembly of any tank in any part of any inland waters for the purpose of fish farming there would not, apart from this sub-section, involve development of the land below, this Act shall have effect as if the tank resulted from carrying out engineering operations over that land; and in this sub-section—
>
> 'fish farming' means the breeding, rearing or keeping of fish or shellfish (which includes any kind of crustacean and mollusc);
>
> 'inland waters' means waters which do not form part of the sea or of any creek, bay or estuary or of any river as far as the tide flows; and
>
> 'tank' includes any cage and any other structure for use in fish farming.

6.66 Allied to the decision to make the placing or assembly of fish tanks development, Part 6 of Sch 2 to the General Permitted Development Order provides that such activity should be permitted development under the Order when carried out on land outside national parks. However, under the Order, a person wishing to exercise such permitted development 'rights' must give prior notice to the local planning authority. This prior-notification procedure allows the local planning authority to decide within a period of 28 days whether or not they wish to make the activity subject to their prior approval. If the authority do so decide, it allows them to exercise control over the siting and appearance of the development.

Mining operations

6.67 As originally enacted the definition of development contained no definition of the term 'mining operations'. In s 336(1) however, minerals are defined to include 'all minerals and substances in or under land of a kind ordinarily worked for removal by underground or surface working, except that it does not include peat cut for purposes other than sale'.

6.68 The Town and Country Planning (Minerals) Act 1981 amended the definition of development by adding a new provision. This is now contained in s 55(4) which states:

> For the purposes of this Act mining operations include—
>
> (a) the removal of material of any description—
>   (i) from a mineral-working deposit;
>   (ii) from a deposit of pulverised fuel ash or other furnace ash or clinker; or
>   (iii) from a deposit of iron, steel or other metallic slags; and
>
> (b) the extraction of minerals from a disused railway embankment.

6.69 The 1981 Act was passed after the Government had considered the report of the Stevens Committee on Planning Control over Mineral Workings. Concern was there expressed about whether the definition of development and particularly mining operations, was wide enough to include the recovery of material originally removed or extracted from the land and then deposited on it, such as a slagheap from a coal-mine or a coal deposit on a railway line. The amendment made to the definition of development by the 1981 Act makes clear that this and other like activities over which there was similar doubt now fall within that definition.

Other operations

It is clear that there must be some restriction on the words 'other operations'. As was pointed out by the House of Lords in *Coleshill & District Investment Co. Ltd v Minister of Housing and Local Government* [1969] 1 WLR 746, the use of the words 'building, engineering, mining or other operations', makes it clear that not every operation constitutes development since to hold otherwise would be to render the words 'building, engineering and mining' superfluous. Their Lordships also pointed out that since 'mining' operations differed substantially from 'building' operations, it was not possible for a single genus to fit all three words. Accordingly 'other operations' could not be construed *ejusdem generis*. Their Lordships all agreed, however, that there must be some restriction on the meaning of 'other operations'; that it must be construed by reference to building, engineering and mining, and that the maxim *noscitur a sociis* might apply even though it is not *ejusdem generis*. Lord Pearson also suggested that although no single genus would fit all three preceding words, it was possible that there were three separate genera, and that 'other operations' would connote an activity similar to 'building operations', or to 'engineering operations' or to 'mining operations'. 6.70

In *Cambridge City Council v Secretary of State for the Environment*, the Court of Appeal, having concluded that there had been no evidence before the Deputy Judge upon which he had been entitled to make a finding of fact that the demolition of houses constituted work normally undertaken by a person who carried on business as a builder, went on to consider whether the work constituted an 'other operation' on land. On the basis of authority (i.e., the *Coleshill* decision), the Court of Appeal concluded that it did not. The Court emphasised that 'other' operations in s 55 of the 1990 Act did not mean all other operations; and that other operations had to be '. . . at least of a constructive character, leading to an identifiable and positive result' or be '. . . similar to building operations or to engineering operations'. 6.71

Because of the wide definition given in the Act to the words building, engineering and mining, there is no recorded judicial decision of any particular activity being held to be an 'other operation'. In fact, there are few known examples of an activity found to be an 'other operation' and these are contained in Ministerial decisions given on appeal. 6.72

When making decisions on appeal in this area, it is not uncommon for the Secretary of State (or the Inspector) to confine himself to a statement that the activity which he is considering is or is not development; or, at best, to confine himself to a reference to one of the specific operations listed in s 55(1). In one Ministerial decision, however, the Inspector held that the deposit of waste materials on land for the purpose of raising the level of the land to make it suitable for agricultural use was not a building or engineering operation, but an 'other operation' for which planning permission was required [1982] JPL 741. That decision, however, was made before the Inspector had the benefit of the judgment in *Fayrewood Fish Farms Ltd v Secretary of State for the Environment* [1984] JPL 267. Had that been available, he might well have held that the deposit in question was an engineering operation. 6.73

In another Ministerial decision reported at [1985] JPL 129 it was held that the installation of a protective grille over a shop window and door was an 'other operation' within the meaning of s 55(1) of the 1990 Act. In a later decision in 1996 (unreported), a golf club had constructed a further tee to their golf course, which had an existing nine-hole capacity, in order to enable golfers more conveniently to use the course for a full 18 holes. The Inspector 6.74

rejected the local planning authority's contention that the construction works constituted an 'engineering operation', but held instead that the works amounted to an 'other operation' within the definition in s 55(1). More recently, an Inspector held that freestanding parasols (with heaters installed) in sunken bases, were works falling within the definition of 'other operations' (Ref: APP/R1038/C/03/1136482).

7

DEFINITION OF DEVELOPMENT 2: MATERIAL CHANGE OF USE

7.01 The term 'material change of use' is not defined in the Act. Its meaning has to be ascertained, therefore, by reference to the many cases in which the courts have had to consider its significance. In *Parkes v Secretary of State for the Environment* [1978] 1 WLR 1308, Lord Denning MR said that 'operations' comprised activities which resulted in some physical alteration to the land, which had some degree of permanence to the land itself; whereas 'use' comprised activities which are done in, alongside or on the land but which did not interfere with the actual physical characteristics of the land. Accordingly, he held that, for the purposes of serving a discontinuance order under what is now s 102 of the 1990 Act, the sorting, processing and disposal of scrap materials was a 'use' of land.

A. MATERIAL CHANGE OF USE

7.02 It must be emphasised that the activity which constitutes the second limb of the term 'development' is not merely a 'change of use' but a 'material change of use'. The attitude of the courts to the question of whether or not a change of use is material is that it is largely a matter of fact and degree for the local planning authority to decide, and they will only interfere if the decision is one to which the authority could not reasonably have come. In *Bendles Motors Ltd v Bristol Corporation* [1963] 1 WLR 247 an application for planning permission had been made to the local planning authority for permission to erect an egg-vending machine on the forecourt of garage premises. After permission had been refused, the owners of the garage proceeded nevertheless to erect the machine on the forecourt. The machine measured some six feet in height, two feet seven inches deep and two feet seven inches wide. Since it was both free-standing and gravity-fed, it could not be considered to be operational development. The local planning authority had served an enforcement notice requiring the removal of the machine and, on appeal, the Minister had upheld the notice. The owners then appealed to the High Court against the Minister's decision on a point of law.

7.03 The Minister had upheld the enforcement notice on the ground that the stationing of the egg-vending machine on the site involved a change of use of the land on which it stood and that its introduction on the site involved a material change of use of the land, since the use of the machine was in the nature of a 'shop use', in that it attracted customers not necessarily concerned with the motoring service provided by the garage. In dismissing the appeal Lord Parker CJ quoted his own words in *East Barnet UDC v British Transport Commission* [1962] 2 QB 484:

> 'It is a question of fact and degree in every case and . . . the court is unable to interfere with a finding . . . on such a matter unless it must be said that they could not properly have reached that conclusion.' That was dealing with a case stated from justices, but in my judgment the same is true of an appeal from the Minister himself. This court can only interfere if satisfied that it is a conclusion that he could not, properly directing himself as to the law, have reached.

Later, the Lord Chief Justice went on to say:

> I confess that at first sight, and indeed at last sight, I am somewhat surprised that it can be said that the placing of this small machine on this large forecourt can be said to change the use of these premises in a material sense from that of a garage and petrol filling station by the addition of a further use. It is surprising, and it may be, if it was a matter for my own personal judgment, that I should feel inclined to say that the egg-vending machine was *de minimis*; but it is not a question of what my opinion is on that matter, it is for the Minister to decide.

7.04 It is submitted that this was clearly a sensible decision. The court held that the Minister had not erred in law in holding that the change of use from a garage and petrol filling-station, to a garage, petrol filling-station and 'shop use' was material. Had the Lord Chief justice given precedence to his personal feelings, it would have been difficult for the local planning authority to control a later installation on the forecourt of other types of vending machines.

Furthermore, if the garage and petrol filling-station use were then to be abandoned, a change to an exclusively shop use would have been achieved.

The case demonstrates that whether or not a change of use is material is a question of fact and degree in every case for decision by the local planning authority, or on appeal by the Secretary of State. It also demonstrates that a material change of use may not only occur where a change is made from, say, use A to use B, but also where a change is made from use A to use A and B by the addition of a further use. **7.05**

The same approach was followed in *Hidderley v Warwickshire CC* (1963) 14 P & CR 134, where the installation of an egg-vending machine on farm land adjacent to a lay-by on a public road was held to constitute a material change of use. **7.06**

In this area it is important to bear in mind two cardinal principles. First, that the assessment of facts and matters of planning judgment have always been regarded as exclusively for the decision-maker. Secondly, the courts have a limited ability to intervene, as indicated by Nourse LJ in *Moore v Secretary of State for the Environment, Transport and the Regions* [1998] JPL 877, where he said at p. 70: **7.07**

> A question of fact and degree, although it is a question of fact, involves the application of a legal test. If the Secretary of State applies the correct test, the court, on an appeal under section 289, can only interfere with his decision if the facts found are incapable of supporting it. If, on the other hand, he applies an incorrect test, then the court can interfere and itself apply the correct test to the facts found.

A question that has recently arisen again is whether, when determining whether a change of use is material, it is proper to consider the effect of the change on adjacent land. Some early cases indicated that it was. However, it seemed sensible to consider the change merely in relation to the planning unit in question; and to consider the off-site effects that the change would bring as relevant to the question of whether planning permission should be granted. But it is otherwise. In *Devonshire CC v Allens Caravans (Estates) Ltd* (1962) 14 P & CR 440, Lord Parker said: **7.08**

> The materiality to be considered is a materiality from the planning point of view and, in particular, the question of amenities.

In the same case, Gorman J said:

> It seems to me that one of the criteria for determining what is a material change may well be in effect the planning of the neighbourhood.

A later case is *Blum v Secretary of State for the Environment* [1987] JPL 278 which has a more explicit passage on the relevance of off-site effects. Simon Brown J said:

> The Inspector here had plainly addressed himself, as he was in law obliged to do, to the character of the use. He did so in large part, but not in fact exclusively, by reference to the extent to which the additional use of the premises as a riding school intensified certain aspects of the activity both on and off site. He referred to the additional staff required, the additional facilities required, and he observed that there would be more horse activity, more horse traffic, more rides out, more car traffic, more car parking. Not exclusively, though, because he also referred to the introduction of a sanded paddock which had been provided on site for instructional purposes. True, that in itself had not been felt by the planning authority to amount to a material

> change of use; but that could not prevent their having regard to it in assessing the overall impact of the introduction of the new use on the overall character of the use of the land.

Both cases and the statements made in them were considered with approval by David Widdicombe QC sitting as a deputy High Court judge in *Forest of Dean DC v Secretary of State for the Environment* [1995] JPL B184. In that case the Secretary of State's decision in respect of an enforcement notice relating to a change of use of a caravan park from holiday use to permanent residential use was remitted to him because the Inspector had failed to take into account the relevance of off-site effects in determining whether a material change of use had occurred.

7.09 Quite apart from the approach taken by the courts to the meaning of the word 'material', a number of propositions may be advanced with regard to the expression 'change of use':

(a) A change of use will take place where the nature or the character of the use is changed. So that to move from a residential use to a commercial use or to an industrial use, or within any permutation of those uses, will, if the change is material, fall within the definition of development.

(b) In determining whether any activity constitutes a change of use, it is the character of the use which has to be considered, not the particular purpose of a particular occupier. In *East Barnet UDC v British Transport Commission* [1962] 2 QB 484 the Divisional Court refused to interfere with the decision of justices (who had quashed enforcement notices served on the company) that to use land as a transit depot for the handling and storage of crated motor vehicles, following upon the use of the land for the storage and distribution of coal, did not constitute development. In expressing the view that what really had to be considered was the character of the use of the land, not the particular purpose of a particular occupier, Lord Parker CJ quoted with approval a statement by Glyn-Jones J in *Marshall v Nottingham Corporation* [1960] 1WLR707 where he said:

> The mere fact that a dealer in the course of his business begins to deal in goods in which he had not dealt before does not necessarily involve a change, still less a material change, in his use of the land or premises where the business is carried on. A dealer in musical instruments might 50 years ago have begun to deal in gramophones or phonographs, as I suppose they would then have been called; and then in the course of time in radio sets and later in television sets. A dealer in electrical appliances, as demand changed and fresh appliances were invented, might have successively added vacuum cleaners, refrigerators, washing machines and the like to his stock-in-trade, and he too might have begun to deal in radio and television sets. Each of them may have ceased to sell goods formerly sold for which there is no longer an adequate demand. Yet neither, in my view, has thereby altered the use he is making of his premises.

The position may be far less clear, however, where a retail business is carried on but a change takes place in the type of business, as might occur, for example, where the business of a baker is substituted for that of a butcher. Fortunately for most practical purposes the problem is dissolved by the existence of the Use Classes Order (see 7.52).

B. USES EXCLUDED FROM DEVELOPMENT

Whatever may be the meaning of the term 'material change of use', its scope is restricted by paras (d) to (f) of s 55(2) of the 1990 Act, in which three uses are expressly stated *not* to involve the development of land. The three uses are: **7.10**

(d) A use incidental to the enjoyment of a dwellinghouse.
(e) A use for agriculture or forestry.
(f) A change of use within the same use class.

Use incidental to the enjoyment of a dwellinghouse

By s 55(2)(d) of the 1990 Act, 'the use of any buildings or other land within the curtilage of a dwellinghouse for any purpose incidental to the enjoyment of the dwellinghouse as such' is not to be taken to involve development of the land. **7.11**

Under this provision, it is not a material change of use to convert, say, a henhouse into a workshop or an outhouse to provide additional sleeping accommodation for one's family. The provision refers, however, to the *use of* buildings or other land, so that if the occupier finds it necessary to carry out operational development for the better enjoyment of that use, planning permission will be needed for that operation. The paragraph also refers to the use of any buildings or other land within the *'curtilage'* of a dwellinghouse. Precisely what constitutes the curtilage may not always be clear. The definition of the term most usually referred to is that given in a Scottish case of *Sinclair-Lockhart's Trustees v Central Land Board* (1950) 1 P & CR 195, as: **7.12**

> ground which is used for the comfortable enjoyment of a house . . . and thereby as an integral part of the same, although it has not been marked off or enclosed in any way. It is enough that it serves the purposes of the house . . . in some necessary or reasonably useful way.

It has also been held in *Dyer v Dorset County Council* [1989] QB 346 that the definition in the *Oxford English Dictionary* is adequate for most purposes. That definition is: **7.13**

> a small court, yard, garth or piece of ground attached to a dwellinghouse and forming one enclosure with it, or so regarded by the law; the area attached to and containing a dwellinghouse and its outbuildings.

It seems from *Stephens v Cuckfield RDC* [1959] 1QB 516, however, that land may be a garden but not be within a curtilage. In *James v Secretary of State for the Environment* (1990) 61 P & CR 234, it was held that there are three criteria for determining whether land is within the curtilage of a building, namely: **7.14**

(a) physical layout,
(b) ownership, past and present,
(c) use or function, past and present.

In an unpublished Ministerial decision in 1993, an Inspector took the view that the cases contain a certain amount of common ground which assists in forming a view on the question of whether land lies within the curtilage of a building. From *Dyer v Dorset CC* comes the notion of the curtilage of a building being essentially small in extent. From **7.15**

Sinclair-Lockhart's Trustees v Central Land Board comes the concept of land which serves the purpose of a house or building in some reasonably useful way being part of the building's curtilage, and from *James v Secretary of State for the Environment* there is the idea of the curtilage of a dwellinghouse being an area forming an enclosure with the building.

7.16 In the case of *McAlpine v Secretary of State for the Environment* [1995] 1 PLR 16 (concerning the interpretation of the word 'curtilage' in the GDO1988, Sch 2, Part 1, Class E) it was said that 'curtilage is constrained to a small area about a building, it is not necessary for there to be physical enclosure but the land needs to be regarded in law as part of one enclosure with the house, and overall the term has a restrictive meaning'.

7.17 The criteria for defining a curtilage has, however, been restated by the Court of Appeal in *Secretary of State for the Environment, Transport and the Regions v Skerritts of Nottingham* [2000] JPL 789, where it was held that although the decision in *Dyer* was plainly correct, the court in that case had gone further than was necessary in expressing the view that the curtilage of a building must always be small, or that the notion of smallness was inherent in the expression. No piece of land could ever be within the curtilage of more than one building, and if houses were built to a density of twenty or more to an acre, the curtilage of each house could be extremely restricted. But as was said in *Dyer*, the definition of a curtilage in relation to a building must remain a question of fact and degree in each case. In this case the Court of Appeal held that the curtilage of a large building was likely to extend to what were, or had in the past been, in the context of ownership and function, ancillary buildings.

7.18 Possibly the most important part of paragraph (d) of s 55(2), however, is the last two words. The requirement is that use must be incidental to the enjoyment of the dwellinghouse 'as such' i.e., as a dwellinghouse. Hence to use land within the curtilage of a dwellinghouse for the parking of a commercial vehicle used for business purposes is not within this provision, although as a matter of fact and degree it might not be considered to be material. This is an area of particular difficulty where a person uses outbuildings or a room in a dwellinghouse to carry on a hobby or an activity having a business or commercial element. Artists' studios and the giving of music lessons are classic examples of this problem. The use of outbuildings for mending cloth, carrying on a tailoring business or dog breeding, the use of a room for a nursing agency and the use of a kitchen to prepare sandwiches and salads for local firms, have all been held by the Secretary of State to constitute development.

7.19 In all these cases it is necessary for the authority to look at the nature and scale of the hobby or non-domestic use being carried on, and then to judge whether as a matter of fact and degree a further use has been added to the existing dwellinghouse use. It seems that an activity carried out by the occupier of a dwellinghouse is not automatically incidental to the enjoyment of the dwellinghouse as such merely because it is a hobby.

7.20 The application of the provision in s 55(2)(d) was considered by the Court of Appeal in *Wallington v Secretary of State for Wales* [1991] JPL 942, where a challenge was made to a decision by an Inspector appointed by the Secretary of State to uphold an enforcement notice which had alleged the making of a material change in the use of a dwellinghouse by the addition of a further, wholly non-commercial use, namely the keeping within the curtilage of the dwellinghouse of some 44 dogs. It was argued on behalf of the appellant that in applying s 55(2)(d), the Inspector had regarded the question as being whether as a matter of fact and degree it was *reasonable* to regard the relevant activity as the use of the premises for a purpose incidental to the enjoyment of the dwelling as such. It was claimed that to apply an objective test of reasonableness was erroneous, since it would place an unjustifiable restriction on an enthusiast who had an eccentric hobby of his own.

In rejecting the argument and dismissing the appeal, Slade LJ in the Court of Appeal, held that the Inspector had been entitled to have regard to what people *normally* do in dwellinghouses to decide whether, as a matter of fact and degree on the one hand, (a) the keeping of 40 or more dogs should be regarded as reasonably incidental to the enjoyment of the dwellinghouse, or on the other hand, (b) the number of dogs kept exceeded what could reasonably be so regarded. **7.21**

The court also made reference to a decision of Sir Graham Eyre QC, sitting as a Deputy High Court judge, in *Emin v Secretary of State for the Environment* [1989] JPL 909. That decision concerned the criteria set down in Class 1.3 of then General Development Order 1977, which dealt with development within the curtilage of a dwellinghouse 'required for a purpose incidental to the enjoyment of the dwellinghouse as such', although a distinction might be drawn between the wording of that order and of s 55(2)(d), which does not include the word 'required'. Nevertheless, according to Slade LJ, certain observations of Sir Graham Eyre were helpful and apposite in the present case, where he had said (at p. 913): **7.22**

> The fact that such a building had to be required for a purpose associated with the enjoyment of a dwellinghouse could not rest solely on the unrestrained whim of him who dwelt there but connoted some sense of reasonableness in all the circumstances of the particular case. That was not to say that the arbiter could impose some hard objective test so as to frustrate the reasonable aspirations of a particular owner or occupier so long as they were sensibly related to his enjoyment of the dwelling. The word 'incidental' connoted an element of subordination in land use terms in relation to the enjoyment of the dwellinghouse itself.

According to Farquharson LJ in the Court of Appeal in the *Wallington* case, in approaching the question of whether a use was for a purpose incidental to the enjoyment of a dwellinghouse, it was sensible to consider what would be the normal use of a dwellinghouse, although this was not determinative of the question. In his view, consideration of whether the use was subjective or objective merely complicated matters. In his judgment, the word 'incidental' meant subordinate in land use terms to the enjoyment of a dwellinghouse as a dwellinghouse. In considering whether a use came within s 55(2)(d), one had to have regard to such things as where the dwellinghouse was situated, its size and how much ground was included in its curtilage, the nature and scale of the activity said to be incidental to enjoyment of the dwellinghouse as such and the disposition and character of the occupier. He might also have added that in the case of dogs, their breed and prolixity to barking would also be relevant considerations. **7.23**

It will be seen that the judgments in the *Wallington* case do not make clear the precise criteria to be applied in determining whether a use falls within para (d) of s 55(2). Slade LJ appeared to favour taking an objective view of whether an activity was incidental, whereas Farquharson LJ clearly thought little help was to be gained by considering any subjective/objective dichotomy. **7.24**

Since the keeping of 44 dogs in the *Wallington* case was held to be outside the provisions of **7.25** s 55(2)(a), the question that arises is how many dogs may a person keep in order to come within the paragraph. In the *Wallington* case the Inspector had expressly accepted that to impose any specific limiting number would be 'arbitrary'; but had gone on, in order to be sure not to over-enforce, to agree with the planning authority that the requirement section of the enforcement notice should enable up to six dogs to be kept on the premises without the need for planning permission.

7.26 In a later Ministerial decision, an Inspector upheld an enforcement notice alleging a material change of use within the curtilage of a dwellinghouse by the keeping of dogs, and requiring that the number kept at the premises at any one time should be reduced to not more than three. The Inspector, who had the benefit of having seen the decision in the *Wallington* case, considered that the main issue was whether the continued keeping of the dogs (which over the years had varied between six and eight excluding puppies) would be likely to be harmful to the amenities which occupiers of neighbouring houses would reasonably be expected to enjoy. Although the Inspector considered that the figure of three dogs cited in the notice as the number which would be acceptable might be regarded as arbitrary, the number was not inappropriate to a normal domestic situation, even allowing for the fact that this figure might be exceptional when not every household had dogs.

7.27 In yet another Ministerial decision [1993] JPL 901, an Inspector again upheld an enforcement notice which had required that the number of dogs kept within the curtilage of a dwellinghouse be reduced to not more than three. The property in question was a two-bedroom mid-terrace property with a small front garden and a hard-surfaced yard area to the rear. In his decision letter, the Inspector considered it important to distinguish between the enjoyment of the dwellinghouse as such and the enjoyment of the occupier. Put another way, the occupier of a dwellinghouse might well be enjoying himself in some way which was not related to the dwellinghouse *as a dwelling*. In this particular case, for example, the evidence showed that the occupation of the dwellinghouse had been given over to a very large degree to the keeping of animals associated with an animal welfare charity.

7.28 Another recent (but unreported) Ministerial decision, involved the keeping of nine German shepherd dogs at a small semi-detached house with modest curtilage located in an urban estate of similar houses in Banbury. The Inspector's view was that the house appeared to have been given over to the dogs, to the point where the interior accommodation looked more suited to housing dogs than people; and he found that the garden was largely given over to dog runs and kennels. In his view, the scale of the dog keeping in relation to the modest size of this suburban property went well beyond that which may be considered incidental to the enjoyment of the dwelling.

7.29 Mention should also be made of *South Oxfordshire DC v Secretary of State for the Environment, Transport and the Regions* [2000] PLCR 315, where the Deputy Judge upheld a decision by an Inspector that the use of land around a dwellinghouse for the landing and taking off of helicopters was a use incidental to the enjoyment of the dwellinghouse taking into account the nature of the house and the purposes of the helicopter use, namely as a personal means of transport for the owner and members of his family. This case should be contrasted with *Harrods v Secretary of State* (see 7.120) where the Court of Appeal refused to interfere with a finding by the Secretary of State that the introduction of a helicopter use to the roof of a department store amounted to a material change in the use of the store. The Court considered that the correct approach was to consider on general principles whether there had been a material change of use. Here one had to concentrate not on what was incidental to a particular shop (Harrods) bearing in mind its particular mode of operation, but to see what activities were reasonably incidental to shops in general.

The principal was followed in *R (I'm Your Man Ltd.) v The International Helicopter Museum* [2004] EWHC 342 (Admin), where the High Court held that the local planning authority had been entitled to decide that the use of land at a helicopter museum for helicopter 'air experience' flights, with passengers who were visitors to the museum and helicopter flights to and from the museum with or without passengers who were visitors to the museum, were incidental to the primary use of land as a museum which did not constitute a material change of use. Whether this was a change of use was a question of fact and degree for the authority to decide. **7.30**

In another judicial decision, *Croydon LBC v Gladden* [1994] JPL 723, the Court of Appeal, upholding an enforcement notice served by the local planning authority, held that placing a replica Spitfire aeroplane in the garden of a dwellinghouse was not a use incidental to the enjoyment of the dwellinghouse as such. The Court held that the concept of what was incidental to such enjoyment included an element of reasonableness. It could not rest solely on the unrestrained whim of the occupier, and no one could regard it as reasonable to keep a replica Spitfire as incidental to the enjoyment of the dwellinghouse. The Court also considered that any pleasure, however exquisite, derived from defying the local authority was not enjoyment of the dwellinghouse as such. **7.31**

Another issue which is now topical is whether land within the curtilage of a dwellinghouse can be used by the owner as a private burial ground for himself and his family without the need to apply for planning permission. In a Ministerial decision [1994] JPL 305, a Scottish inquiry reporter held that it could be so used. The reporter made no mention of the Scottish provision equivalent to s 55(2)(d) of the 1990 Act, it being unlikely, following the decision in the *Wallington* case, to be a use incidental to the enjoyment of the dwellinghouse as such. The reporter held, however, that since the proposed project would involve the digging of only a very limited number of graves (by hand), it would not amount to an 'engineering or other operation'; and since there would be no change in the surface land use, nor any upstanding physical features resulting from the intending burials, it could not be said that the proposal amounted to a 'material change of use'. **7.32**

In a later Ministerial decision reported at [1996] JPL 1083, the Secretary of State held that a proposal to dig two trenches for the burial of two bodies within the curtilage of a dwellinghouse did not constitute development. In that case there was no intention to mark the site with a headstone or memorial and it was proposed to level the site after interment. The Secretary of State decided that the proposed activity could not be regarded as incidental to the enjoyment of the dwellinghouse as such on the basis that that use could not be regarded as a normal element of residential use. However, since the burial site would after interment be indistinguishable from its surroundings, the small area of land affected was within a general residential curtilage and the scale of the proposal was small, he had concluded as a matter of fact and degree that any change in the character of the planning unit was '*de minimis*' and that no change of use had occurred. **7.33**

7.34 In the past few years there has been a growing interest in the number of categories of lawful use issued by local planning authorities for non-commercial burials on private land where operational development is not considered significant. So whether planning permission is required in order to be buried in the garden of a dwellinghouse, is a question of fact and degree in every case, taking into consideration the nature of any memorial to be erected on the site. Quite apart from planning law considerations, however, any death must be registered with the Registrar of Births and Deaths and a certificate of disposal obtained, and objections may be raised to the burial by environmental health officers if there is a risk of danger to public health, having regard to such matters as having a sufficient depth of soil on top of the body, the height of the water table and the distance from watercourses.

Use for agriculture or forestry

7.35 The second of the three uses listed in paragraphs (d) to (f) of s 55(2) which are expressly stated *not* to involve the development of land is:

> (e) the use of any land for the purposes of agriculture or forestry (including afforestation) and the use for any of those purposes of any building occupied together with land so used.

7.36 Again the provision refers to the *use* of land for the purposes of agriculture or forestry, so operational development on land used for agriculture or forestry is not within the exclusion. Certain operational development on land used for those purposes is however, permitted development under the General Permitted Development Order.

7.37 Some disputes have arisen about whether particular activities fall within this exemption. Section 336(1) of the 1990 Act provides that 'agriculture' includes horticulture, fruit growing, seed growing, dairy farming, the breeding and keeping of livestock (including any creature kept for the production of food, wool skins or fur, or for the purpose of its use in the farming of land), the use of land as grazing land, meadow land, osier land, market gardens and nursery grounds, and the use of land for woodlands where that use is ancillary to the farming of land for other agricultural purposes.

7.38 There have been many cases where the courts have had to consider this agriculture or forestry exclusion: In *Williams v Minister of Housing and Local Government* (1967) 18 P & CR 514 the owner of a nursery garden used a timber building situated on the land as a retail shop selling produce grown on the land. When he started to sell produce grown elsewhere, the local planning authority issued an enforcement notice which the Minister subsequently upheld. The High Court there agreed with the Minister that the use of land for agricuture necessarily includes the selling of produce grown on the land, but that the selling of products grown elsewhere was not an agricultural use.

7.39 In *Allen v Secretary of State for the Environment and Reigate and Banstead Borough Council* [1990] JPL 340 the court declined to interfere with an Inspector's judgment that a material change of use had occurred where the revenue from the sale of imported plants reached about ten per cent of total turnover.

7.40 In *Wealdon District Council v Secretary of State for the Environment and Colin Day* [1988] JPL 268, the Court of Appeal upheld the decision of an Inspector to quash an enforcement notice requiring the removal of a caravan placed upon agricultural land for the purpose of providing a weatherproof place for the storage and mixing of cattle food and to provide shelter for Mr Day, on the ground that the caravan was used for animal feed preparation and shelter and as such was ancillary to the agricultural use of the land.

In *Gill v Secretary of State for the Environment* [1985] JPL 710 the High Court held that the occasional killing of animals which had been reared and bred on a farm might be within the normal use of land used for agricultural purposes, but that the wholesale slaughter of large numbers of foxes, kept on land for the purpose of producing skins or furs, was not within the definition of agriculture. **7.41**

In *Salvatore Cumbo v Secretary of State for the Environment* [1992] JPL 366, the High Court refused to interfere with the decision of an Inspector that the establishment on a farm of a cheese making business would be outside the realms of wholly agricultural use and be in the nature of a mixed farming and manufacturing use for which planning permission was necessary. **7.42**

In a more recent case, *Millington v Secretary of State for the Environment, Transport and the Regions* [2000] JPL 297 the Court of Appeal had to decide whether the Secretary of State was right in considering an enforcement notice appeal, to proceed on the basis that where land is used for the creation of a new product (wine), from produce grown on the land (grapes), the land was therefore no longer being used for the purposes of agriculture and as such not exempt from planning control. The Court considered the Secretary of State had not been right. According to the Court: **7.43**

> the proper approach to the root question in this case is . . . to consider whether what the Millingtons were doing can, having regard to ordinary and reasonable practice, be regarded as ordinarily incidental to the growing of grapes for wine included in the general term agriculture, ancillary to normal farming activities, reasonably necessary to make the product marketable or disposable to profit or whether it had come to the stage where the operations cannot reasonably be said to be consequential on the agricultural operations of producing crops.

Since the Secretary of State had not adopted that approach, the enforcement notice was remitted back to him to make a new decision in the light of the Court's judgment.

In *Crowborough Parish Council v Secretary of State for the Environment* [1981] JPL 281, it was held that the use of land for allotments was an agricultural use falling within the definition of agriculture and that in determining an appeal against what was then called a s 64 determination, the Secretary of State had erred in law in holding otherwise. **7.44**

In *Sykes v Secretary of State for the Environment* [1981] JPL 285, the Divisional Court had to consider whether the use of land for grazing horses was within the definition of agriculture. The Secretary of State had held that it was, and his view was supported by the Court. The case raises, however, important issues with regard to the use of land for what is sometimes referred to as 'horsiculture'. This usually refers to the practice of keeping horses on land for horse-riding purposes. If the land is used intensively for that purpose the horses may need to be supplied with extra food. In such cases the question to be asked is: What use is being made of the land? Is it for the purpose of grazing? If not, then the activity may amount to a material change of use. **7.45**

Donaldson LJ said: **7.46**

> If . . . horses are being kept on the land and are being fed wholly or primarily by other means so that such grazing as they do is completely incidental and perhaps achieved merely because there are no convenient ways of stopping them doing it, then plainly the land is not being used for grazing but merely being used for keeping the animals.

It follows, therefore, that land will not normally be treated as being used for the 'grazing' of horses and thus an agricultural use, if the horses are primarily kept on it for some other purpose such as recreation or exercise when the grazing is seen as completely incidental and inevitable. It would be otherwise, however, if little or no extra food was provided for horses kept on the land, but which were being used for riding or associated activities elsewhere, such as on adjacent bridleways.

7.47 Another significant case on the definition of agriculture was *North Warwickshire BC v Secretary of State for the Environment* [1984] JPL 435, where it was held that the use of a *building* for the purposes of agriculture also fell within the paragraph. The paragraph refers to the use of land for the purposes of agriculture 'and the use for any of those purposes of any building occupied together with land so used'. The Court considered that because the definition of land in s 336(1) of the 1990 Act meant 'any corporeal hereditament, including a building', the two phrases had to be construed disjunctively. If this decision is correct, it would be possible to convert a disused building in suburbia into a chicken farm without the change amounting to development.

7.48 It should be noted that the statutory definition of agriculture in s 336(1) of the 1990 Act does not include any requirement that the activity should be carried on in connection with a trade or business, or that it should be profitable, viable or sustainable. This is in marked contrast to the definition of agricultural land for the purposes of permitted development rights under parts 6 and 7 of Sch 2 to the GDPO.

Leisure plots

7.49 As the restrictive nature of planning control became clearer in the post-war period, a practice developed whereby owners of land in certain parts of the country sought to obtain a greater profit from their land than that obtained from its agricultural use, by selling small parcels to others, the sales often being accompanied by suggestions that the parcels could be used for a variety of leisure purposes. Areas particularly affected included the Thames Estuary and the New Forest. The purchasers of each parcel were likely to be town dwellers, who believed that they might in future be able to build on the land or use it for camping or for siting a caravan on it.

7.50 In the late 1970s and the early 1980s, the Minister responsible for Planning held on appeal from decisions of local planning authorities that a change from agricultural use to leisure use amounted to a material change of use. In *Pitman et al v the Secretary of State for the Environment* [1989] JPL 831, leisure plots were defined as pieces of land where leisure activities were carried on with some degree of frequency, and leisure activities were defined as activities which people carry on in their free time for the primary purpose of pleasure or amusement rather than the acquisition of money or money's worth; the Court gave the examples of enjoying the view and the sunshine. It upheld the decision that the change of use from agriculture to use as leisure plots was a material change.

There is now some evidence that a resumption of the practice of farmers and others subdividing land into small plots and then selling them (sometimes over the internet) to unsuspecting purchasers, is again beginning to take place. **7.51**

Extensions to gardens of dwellinghouses

Under the present law the extension of a domestic garden to include adjacent land may well constitute a material change of use requiring planning permission. This situation commonly arises where land being used for agricultural purposes is incorporated with land forming part of the curtilage of a dwellinghouse. The problem for planning control with this situation is that unless challenged the landowner would benefit from permitted development rights in Parts 1 and 2 of Sch 2 to the GDPO over a much larger curtilage, thus enabling him to erect porches, garden sheds, tennis courts, garages and oil tanks on the 'added' land, and to fence the boundary of the larger residential curtilage without the need for an express grant of planning permission. **7.52**

In November 1996, the Government expressed sympathy with the concern felt that the requirement to obtain planning permission for extensions to domestic gardens to be an unnecessary burden. In a consultation paper then issued, the Government invited views on a proposal to include the extension of a garden of a dwellinghouse onto adjoining land as permitted development under the GDPO. In June 1997, however, a new Government decided not to proceed with the implementation of this proposal. **7.53**

Change of use within the same use class

The third of the three uses listed in paragraphs (a) to (f) of s 55(2) which are expressly stated *not* to involve the development of land is: **7.54**

> (f) in the case of buildings or other land which are used for a purpose of any class specified in an order made by the Secretary of State under this section, the use of the buildings or other land or, subject to the provisions of the order, of any part of the buildings or the other land, for any other purpose of the same class.

The relevant order is now the Town and Country Planning (Use Classes) Order 1987, which came into force on 1 June 1987 (see Appendix B, to which reference should be constantly made). It replaced a previous order which had not been substantially changed since introduced in 1948. The 1987 Order now specifies 11 different classes of use for the purposes of paragraph (f), so that a change of use within the same use Class is not to be taken to involve the development of land. It should be noted that the effect of the Use Classes Order is to specify that a change of use which results in the old and the new uses falling within the same use Class is not development. It does not specify that a change of use involving a change from one use Class to some other use Class is necessarily development. Whether or not it is depends upon whether a material change of use has taken place. This was made clear in *Rann v Secretary of State for the Environment* [1980] JPL 109. The Use Classes Order is thus a liberalising measure freeing certain activities from planning control. It does not seek to restrict activities by making them subject to planning control when they would otherwise not be so. **7.55**

The order is divided into four parts, which correspond broadly with (a) shopping area uses; (b) other business and industrial uses; (c) residential uses; and (d) social and community uses **7.56** of a non-residential kind. This classification makes it more likely that a change of use from one part of the order to another will be regarded as a material change of use, particularly where the different uses have sharply contrasting environmental effects. This would accord with the approach in *Scrivener* v *Minister of Housing and Local Government* (1966) 18 P & CR 357 in which it was held that the division of the old Use Classes Order 1963 into 'light', 'general' and 'special' industrial uses classified such uses according to the extent to which they caused nuisance or inconvenience in the neighbourhood.

7.57 It should be noted that not all uses of buildings or other land are allocated to a particular Class in the order. Those uses not allocated to a particular Class are known as *sui generis*. Indeed, Art 3(6) of the order specifically identifies a number of uses not included in any class of the order. They are the use of buildings or other land:

(a) as a theatre,
(b) as an amusement arcade or centre, or a funfair,
(c) as a launderette,
(d) for the sale of fuel for motor vehicles,
(e) for the sale or display for sale of motor vehicles,
(f) for a taxi business or business for the hire of motor vehicles,
(g) as a scrapyard, or a yard for the storage or distribution of minerals or the breaking of motor vehicles,
(h) for any work registrable under the Alkali, etc., Works Regulation Act 1906,
(i) as a hostel,
(j) as a waste disposal installation for the incineration, chemical treatment (as defined in Annex IIA to Directive 75/442/EEC under heading D9), or landfill of waste to which Directive 91/689/EEC applies,
(k) as a retail warehouse club being a retail club where goods are sold, or displayed for sale, only to persons who are members of that club,
(l) as a night-club.

7.58 There are no doubt many other uses that can be regarded as *sui generis*. In *London Residuary Body v Secretary of State for the Environment* [1988] JPL 637 it was held that London's County Hall did not fall within the office use class of the order as its office use was incidental to the primary 'London governmental use' to which the building had been put. A significant feature of the County Hall case was that the building had a high public profile as the seat of a local government function with a considerable amount of public involvement and access. That decision was considered in a later Ministerial decision [2003] JPL 920, where the question arose as to whether a building occupied by the Public Trust Office could be used for general office work without the need for planning permission. The Inspector held that it could so be used, on the ground that the use by the Public Trust Office led to no involvement of, or access for, members of the general public.

Part A — Shopping area uses

Class A1. Shops

7.59 Under this heading, the order lists, in paragraphs (a) to (j), the following specified uses, where the sale, display or service is to visiting members of the public:

(a) for the retail sale of goods other than hot food,
(b) as a post office,
(c) for the sale of tickets or as a travel agency,
(d) for the sale of sandwiches or other cold food for consumption off the premises,
(e) for hairdressing,
(f) for the direction of funerals,
(g) for the display of goods for sale,
(h) for the hiring out of domestic or personal goods or articles,
(i) for the washing or cleaning of clothes or fabrics on the premises,
(j) for the reception of goods to be washed, cleaned or repaired,
(k) as an internet café; where the primary purpose of the premises is to provide facilities for enabling members of the public to access the internet.

where the sale, display or services is to visiting members of the public.

Hence, for example, a butcher's shop can become a travel agent or hair-dresser and remain within the same use class. **7.60**

Building societies are included in Class A2 (financial and professional services); and shops for the sale of hot food in Class A3 (food and drink) (see below). **7.61**

In *Cawley v Secretary of State for the Environment* [1990] JPL 742 it was held that the scope of Class A1 is restricted to retail uses which take place in a building and not on open land. This is because the heading of the class, 'Shops', necessarily refers to buildings. So the use of open land for retail sales is a *sui generis* use. **7.62**

In one high-profile case, *R v Thurrock BC, ex p Tesco Stores Ltd* [1994] JPL 328, it was necessary to consider the scope of the phrase 'visiting members of the public'. A retailer named Costco had been granted planning permission to operate a warehouse club selling a limited selection of products within a wide range of product categories only to members of the club who had paid a subscription and were within categories of person specified by Costco. Tesco argued that the development was essentially a retail use on an industrial and commercial site which would be contrary to the authority's development plan policy which sought to promote wholesale cash and carry warehousing on the site but to exclude retail uses within Class A1 which would affect the vitality and viability of existing shopping centres. As a *sui generis* use, it was neither a warehouse use nor a retail use. In dismissing Tesco's application for judicial review of the grant of planning permission, Schiemann J held that if there was a restriction on persons who were able to enter and buy then the premises were not prima facie properly described as being used for the sale of goods to visiting members of the public. Hence, the use did not fall within Class A1. **7.63**

Class A2. Financial and professional services

This Class is intended to provide flexibility in the use of buildings for a sector of the economy which is rapidly expanding, particularly that part which needs to be accommodated in shop-type premises in a shopping area. It embraces use for the provision of: **7.64**

(a) financial services, or
(b) professional services (other than health or medical services), or
(c) any other services (including use as a betting office) which it is appropriate to provide in a shopping area

where the services are provided principally to visiting members of the public.

7.65 This Class includes use by banks, building societies, betting shops, accountants, architects, surveyors, mortgage and insurance brokers and law centres. Since membership of this Class depends also upon services being provided primarily to visiting members of the public, barristers' chambers do not come within it.

7.66 In *Kalra v Secretary of State for the Environment* [1996] JPL 850, the Court of Appeal had to consider the question of whether use of land as a solicitors' office was an A2 use or a B1 (Business Use) or whether some were one and some were the other. Staughton LJ there addressed the difficulty for planning authorities in resolving the problem. He pointed out that Class A2 required the provision of services principally to visiting members of the public. It was, he said, like the difference between an 'on licence' and an 'off-licence' for the sale of wines and spirits. The practice of some solicitors would currently not be an 'on licence' practice, where services were provided by letter or telephone or fax or E-mail. But some solicitors did provide services principally to visiting members of the public, so it is a matter of fact whether a solicitor's office is covered by the definition and much will depend upon the level of pedestrian flow. Quite apart from considering the differences between an A2 use and a B1 use, the Court found that in upholding the refusal of a local planning authority to grant planning permission for a change of use of a retail shop to a solicitors' office (within Class A2), the Inspector had not applied the correct tests. In particular, he had erred in holding that to be within Class A2(b) the use had also to be a use which was appropriate to provide in a shopping area, a requirement which applied only to uses within Class A2(c). In a subsequent redetermination of the appeal, the Secretary of State granted the planning permission the applicant had sought.

7.67 The requirement that the services must be provided primarily to visiting members of the public is always likely to cause difficulty. Access by the public to financial institutions or professional offices may not be constant and the order does not lay down a prescribed level of access. A bank, for example, may be a building mainly for internal administration of trust accounts with little public access. It would appear not to be a use within Class A2 and any change by the bank to use for normal banking services used by the public may constitute a material change of use.

7.68 Class A3. Restaurants and cafes

Use for the sale of food and drink for consumption on the premises.

Class A4. Drinking establishments

Use as a public house, wine-bar or other drinking establishment.

Class A5. Hot food takeaways

Use for the sale of hot food for consumption off the premises.

Part B — Other business and industrial uses

Class B1. Business

7.69 This Class embraces use for any of the following purposes:

(a) as an office other than a use within Class A2 (financial and professional services),

(b) for research and development of products or processes, or
(c) for any industrial process,

being a use which can be carried out in any residential area without detriment to the amenity of that area by reason of noise, vibration, smell, fumes, smoke, soot, ash, dust or grit.

This Class brings together many of the uses which in the previous order were found in the office and light industry classes which now no longer exist. The Class also includes other uses broadly similar in their environmental impact, such as the use of buildings for the manufacture of computer hardware and software, computer research and development, consultancy and after-sales services, micro-engineering, biotechnology, and pharmaceutical research, development and manufacture. **7.70**

An important qualification, however, is that to come within the Class, the use has to be one which can be carried out in any residential area without detriment to the amenity of that area by reason of noise, vibration, smell, fumes, smoke, soot, ash, dust or grit. **7.71**

Class B2. General industrial

This Class includes any use for the carrying on of an industrial process, other than one which falls within Class B1 (the Business Class). **7.72**

Class B3 to B7. (Special industrial groups A to E)

When the order was made in 1987 it contained Classes B3 to B7 but they have since been repealed. The uses previously within those classes are now all contained within Class B2. **7.73**

Class B8. Storage and distribution

This Class comprises buildings and other land used for storage or as a distribution centre. Retail warehouses, where the main purpose is the sale of goods direct to members of the public visiting the premises fall within the Shops Use Class (A1), even though a limited part of the building may be used for storage. This would follow from the decision of the High Court in *Monomart (Warehouses) Ltd v Secretary of State for the Environment* [1977] JPL 524 in which it was held that a warehouse is not a building in which retail selling is the principal activity carried on, so that sales are acceptable only on a scale which is incidental to the main permitted use. **7.74**

Part C — Residential uses

Class C1. Hotels

This Class includes boarding-houses and guest-houses, but does not include the use of a building as a hotel, boarding-or guest-house where a significant element of care is provided. Article 2 of the order provides a definition of the word 'care'. Until April 1994, 'hostels' were included in this particular use Class. Because of the threat to the amenity of tourist areas from the use made of the freedom to change the use of premises from that of a hotel to a hostel without the need to obtain planning permission, it was decided to exclude hostels from the Class; and also to provide that a hostel was not included within *any* class of the Schedule to the Order. In short, use as a hostel became a *sui generis* use under Art 3(6) of the Order. **7.75**

Class C2. Residential institutions

7.76 The uses contained in this Class are the use for the provision of residential accommodation and care to people in need of care (other than a use within Class C3 (dwellinghouses)); the use as a hospital or nursing home; and use as a residential school, college or training centre.

Class C3. Dwellinghouses

7.77 This Class groups together use as a dwellinghouse by a single person or by people living together as a family, with use as a dwellinghouse by no more than six residents living together as a single household (including a house where care is provided for residents).

7.78 The grouping together of these uses in the same Class means that it is not development when a dwellinghouse occupied by a family or a single person is used as a small community care house providing support for disabled and mentally disabled people, provided that all the residents live together as a single household and that they number no more than six including resident staff. Similarly, other groups of people, up to a maximum of six, such as students, not necessarily related to each other, may live in a dwellinghouse on a communal basis, so long as they do so as a single household. Sharing a communal living-room, toilet facilities, kitchen etc., sharing the cost of electricity, gas and telephone by the occupiers, a common doorbell, the common purchase and consumption of food, may all be evidence indicating that persons are living together as a single household. Other forms of multiple occupation, however, will generally remain outside the scope of the order.

7.79 The interpretation of terms in Class C of the Order has given rise to a certain amount of litigation. In *R (Hossack) v Kettering Borough Council and English Churches Housing Group* [2002] JPL 1206, the Court of Appeal had to consider, with regard to Class C3 the nature of the relationship required between residents before they could be said to be 'living together as a single household'. The Court considered that the fact that the residents had been brought together because of a common need for 'accommodation, support and resettlement' was not necessarily determinative of their status. There was according to the Court, no certain indicia, the presence or absence of any of which, was by itself conclusive.

7.80 In *North Devon District Council v the First Secretary of State* [2003] JPL 1191, the High Court had to consider whether a dwelling used for providing care for two children fell within Class C2 or Class 3(b) of the Order. The evidence was that two non-resident staff were on duty at all times in the dwelling and that the children were under continuous supervision by a team of six or eight adult carers who operated in eight-hour shifts. The Court held that notwithstanding *R v Bromley London Borough Council ex p Sinclair* [1991] 3PCR60 which had held otherwise, Class C3 required at least one non-residential carer, together with of course those who were being cared for. The use here more properly fell within Class C2. It was said that the concept of living together as a household meant a proper functioning household had to exist, and in the context of this case, meant that the children and a carer had to reside in the premises.

7.81 The Housing and Planning Act 1986, amended the provisions of para (f) of what is now s 55(2) to make it clear that, subject to the provisions of the order, planning permission is not required where premises are subdivided; provided that both the existing and proposed use fall within the same use Class. Article 4 of the Order, however, provides that this general rule shall not apply in the case of a building used as a dwellinghouse (Class C3). The benefit of this exclusion, therefore, is not available wherever a dwellinghouse is subdivided. This accords with the special provision found in sub-section (3)(a) of s 55 of the 1990 Act.

Part D — Social and community uses of a non-residential kind

Class D1. Non-residential institutions

The common element in the uses included in this Class is that the buildings are visited by members of the public on a non-residential basis. It includes use as a crêche, museum and public reading room. **7.82**

Class D2. Assembly and leisure

Uses in this Class include places of mass assembly such as cinemas and concert halls (but not theatres which are *sui generis*) and all indoor and outdoor sports uses except motor sports and sports involving firearms. **7.83**

The Court of Appeal has held that the use of land as a concert hall (Class D2(b)) must necessarily be restricted to buildings with the degree of enclosure required to function as such; hence, the use of land at Twickenham rugby stadium could not be held to be within that use category (*Rugby Football Union v Secretary of State for the Environment, Transport, Local Government and the Regions* [2003] JPL 96). Furthermore, it was held that the holding of concerts did not fall within Class D2(e), use as an 'area for . . . outdoor sports or recreation'. The Class made a distinction between watching and playing. Concert performances were neither sport nor recreation; recreation required some physical effort from those involved. **7.84**

General considerations

In *City of London Corporation v Secretary of State for the Environment* (1971) 23 P & CR 169, it was accepted that a local planning authority and the Secretary of State could grant planning permission subject to a condition that restricted the rights which would otherwise be available under the Use Classes Order. The Court upheld as valid the grant of planning permission to use premises as an employment agency, but subject to a condition that the premises should be used 'as an employment agency and for no other purpose'. In Circular 11/95 the Secretary of State makes it clear, however, that there is a presumption against conditions designed to restrict future changes of use, which, by virtue of the order, would not otherwise constitute development. Unless there is clear evidence that the uses excluded would have serious adverse effects on the environment or on amenity which was not susceptible to other control, the Secretary of State says he will consider the imposition of such conditions to be unreasonable. **7.85**

It should also be noted that Part 3 of Sch 2 to the General Permitted Development Order provides that certain changes made between different Use Classes is permitted development. These changes are: **7.86**

From	*To*
Sale of motor vehicles *(sui generis)*	A1 (shops)
A2 (financial and professional services) so long as the premises have a display window at ground-floor level	A1 (shops)
A3 (restaurants and cafes)	A1 (shops)
A4 (drinking establishments)	A1 (shops)
A5 (hot food takeaways)	A1 (shops)
B1 (business) but limited to changes of use relating to not more than 235 square metres of floorspace in the building	B8 (storage and distribution)
B2 (general industrial)	B1 (business)
B2 (general industrial) but limited to changes of use relating to not more than 235 square metres of floorspace in the building	B8 (storage and distribution)
B8 (storage and distribution) but limited to changes of use relating to not more than 235 square metres of floorspace in the building	B1 (business)

Many of the above provisions are unilateral in form, in the sense that they mainly allow a change from one specified use Class to another, but not normally vice versa.

C. USES INCLUDED WITHIN DEVELOPMENT

7.87 Sub-section (3) of s 55 of the 1990 Act specifies two uses (in paragraphs (a) and (b)), which, for the avoidance of doubt, are declared to involve a material change of use: namely, use of a single dwellinghouse as two or more separate dwellinghouses and the deposit of refuse and waste material.

Use of a single dwellinghouse as two or more separate dwellinghouses

7.88 By s 55(3)(a) of the 1990 Act:

> . . . the use as two or more separate dwellinghouses of any building previously used as a single dwellinghouse involves a material change in the use of the building and of each part of it which is so used.

7.89 This provision is intended to bring under planning control the use of houses for multiple occupation. The utility of the provision, however, has been much restricted by the decision of the Divisional Court of the Queen's Bench Division in *Ealing LBCv Ryan* [1965] 2QB486. Multiple occupation, it seems, is in itself not enough to fall within this provision. Here, the Court had to consider the application of the provision to a dwellinghouse part of which had been let out to an old lady and to another family. An enforcement notice had been served sometime earlier requiring the respondent to discontinue the use of the house as two or more separate dwellings. On the failure to comply with the notice, the respondent had been prosecuted by the local planning authority for non-compliance with it, but acquitted by the justices. On an appeal by the authority by way of case stated, the Court, in upholding the decision of the justices that there had been no breach of planning control, considered that the important phrase in the provision was the term 'separate dwellinghouses'. According to Ashworth J:

> . . . a house may well be occupied by two or more persons, who are to all intents and purposes living separately, without that house being thereby used as separate dwellings.

In other words, people may live separately under one roof without occupying separate dwellings. His lordship then went on to say that in considering whether these were separate dwellings:

> The existence or absence of any form of physical reconstruction is a relevant factor; another is the extent to which the alleged separate dwellings can be regarded as separate in the sense of being self-contained and independent of other parts of the same property.

It should be remembered here that work for the maintenance, improvement or other alteration of a building which affects only the interior of the building, or which does not materially affect its external appearance, is itself not development by virtue of s 55(2) of the 1990 Act. **7.90**

As a result of this case, local planning authorities have sought to control multiple occupation through other means, and in particular by alleging that there has been material change of use under s 55(1) of the 1990 Act. **7.91**

Section 55(3)(a) of the 1990 Act deals with the use of a single dwellinghouse as two or more separate dwellinghouses. No similar provision applies to the use of two or more separate dwellinghouses as a single dwellinghouse. Whether or not this change of use is a material change of use has not been entirely free from doubt. In *Richmond LBC v Secretary of State for the Environment, Transport and the Regions and Richmond Churches Housing Trust* [2001] JPL 84, the High Court held that if a change of use gave rise to a planning consideration, for example the effects on the residential character of the area, a strain on the welfare services or a reduction in the stock of private accommodation available for renting, they were all relevant factors to be taken into account in considering whether or not the change amounted to a material change of use. The position is that whereas the conversion of a single dwellinghouse is by express statutory provision a material change of use, the reverse situation is a question of fact and degree for the decision-maker. And if a particular use fulfils a legitimate or recognised planning purpose, it is relevant to the decision to be made. **7.92**

Deposit of refuse and waste material

By s 55(3)(b) of the 1990 Act: **7.93**

> . . . the deposit of refuse or waste materials on land involves a material change in its use, notwithstanding that the land is comprised in a site already used for that purpose, if
>
> (i) the superficial area of the deposit is extended, or
> (ii) the height of the deposit is extended and exceeds the level of the land adjoining the site.

It seems reasonably clear that under the first part of this provision, the deposit of refuse or waste materials on land constitutes development. But the paragraph may also be important, **7.94** not for what it says, but for what it does not say. The implication of the second part of the provision is that if a hole in the ground is already being used for the deposit of refuse or waste, any further deposit of waste or refuse in that same hole does not involve development of the land unless the limitations mentioned above are exceeded.

D. ADVERTISING

7.95 Sub-section (5) of s 55 of the 1990 Act contains a special provision with regard to the display of certain advertisements:

> Without prejudice to any regulations made under the provisions of this Act relating to the control of advertisements, the use for the display of advertisements of any external part of a building which is not normally used for that purpose shall be treated for the purposes of this section as involving a material change in the use of that part of the building.

7.96 With reference to this provision, s 222 of the 1990 Act provides that where the display of advertisements in accordance with the regulations relating to the control of advertisements involves the development of land, planning permission for that development shall be deemed to be granted, so that no application for planning permission is necessary. If however, the erection of an advertisement affects the character of a listed building to which it is attached, listed building consent will be required.

7.97 Under the regulations for the display of advertisements, the person responsible can be prosecuted if he displays an advertisement without 'consent'. The purpose of s 55(5), therefore, seems to be to give a local planning authority alternative methods of proceeding in cases where an advertisement is displayed on an external part of a building not normally used for that purpose, without any 'consent' for its display having been granted. In such a case, the authority may proceed either by way of an enforcement notice for breach of planning control, or by prosecution for breach of the advertising regulations.

7.98 The use of an enforcement notice to control the unlawful display of advertisements as opposed to prosecution may have advantages. Enforcement action can be quick and inexpensive if there are multi-advertisements. In such a case prosecution of each separate advertiser may take much longer and be more costly. In addition, under the provisions relating to advertisements, there is no power whereby the local planning authority can physically remove them. It is of course, possible, though probably unnecessary, for the authority to pursue both proceedings.

E. INTENSIFICATION

7.99 The question whether the intensification of a use constitutes a material change of use has until quite recently given rise to much uncertainty, misunderstanding and ambivalence. In one of the early cases, *Guildford RDC* v *Penny* [1959] 2 QB 112, the Court of Appeal refused to interfere with the finding of justices that an increase in the number of caravans in a field from 8 to 27 was not development. In this case the Court was prepared to concede that intensification could be relevant to the question of whether there had been a material change of use, but thought that whether or not it was relevant depended upon the particular circumstances of the particular case. The Court gave as example the Oval cricket ground being used to provide a greater number of cricket pitches with contemporaneous playing on each pitch, or an increase of housing estate density. Later, in *Glamorgan CC v Carter* [1963] 1 WLR 1, the Court had to consider whether planning permission was needed for a caravan use commenced before 1 July 1948. The question of intensification was raised before the Court and in the course of his judgment Salmon J said:

> Although I do not express any concluded view on the point, I very much doubt whether intensification of use — . . . confining what I say to this caravan site — could be a material change of user. Once it is established that the whole site is used as a caravan site, it does not seem to me that the use is materially changed by bringing a larger number of caravans upon the site.

The early cases in this area continued to be dominated by caravans. In *James v Secretary of State for Wales* [1966] 1 WLR 135, the Court of Appeal recognised that an intensification of an existing use could be a material change of use. In referring to this aspect, Lord Denning MR said, 'I think that a considerable increase in the number of caravans would be a material change of use'. Russell LJ said 'I would agree that . . . it is possible in law for the Minister to consider that the use of land for stationing . . . three other caravans is a material change of use. One swallow does not make a summer.' The latter phrase was a colourful reference to the fact that a grant of planning permission to station one caravan on land did not entitle the owner to add any more. **7.100**

Yet another caravan case was *Esdell Caravan Parks Ltd v Hemel Hempstead RDC* [1966] 1 QB 895. In dealing with the question of intensification, Lord Denning MR said: **7.101**

> . . . I doubt very much whether the occupier could increase from 24 to 78 without permission. An increase in intensity of that order may well amount to a material change of use — see the recent case of *James v Secretary of State for Wales*.

He then went on to assume that a material change of use had not taken place.

Perhaps the first important non-caravan case was *Birmingham Corporation v Minister of Housing and Local Government* [1964] 1 QB 178. There the local planning authority had served enforcement notices alleging the making of a material change in the use of two houses, from use as single dwellinghouses to use as houses let in lodgings, and directing that the latter use should cease. At the inquiry into the appeal the Inspector had the assistance of a legal assessor, who advised him that, because of shared facilities in one of the houses, it could not be said that there was within it separate dwellinghouses; and that as regards the other house, while it was used intensively, in the matter of residential use, intensification of use did not amount *per se* to a material change of use. Acting on this legal advice the Inspector concluded that what was alleged in the enforcement notices did not constitute development. The Minister accepted the Inspector's recommendation and quashed the enforcement notices, whereupon the local planning authority appealed to the High Court against the decision of the Minister. Allowing the appeal, Lord Parker CJ said that in his judgment the Minister had erred in law in saying that because the houses remained residential, in the sense of a dwellinghouse in which people lived, there could not be a material change of use. In his opinion, the case should go back to the Minister with the opinion of the Court and it **7.102** would then be for him to find whether what had taken place in each of the houses amounted to a material change in their use, despite the fact that they both remained dwellinghouses. The Minister would take into consideration the use to which they were put; that private dwellinghouses were being used for multiple paying occupation, or that houses which had been used for private families were now being used for gain by the letting out of rooms.

7.103 It will be seen, therefore, that a house may have a residential use both before and after the making of a material change of use. In considering how this can be so, it may be possible to divide up a single genus of residential use into various species of residential use, so that even though a general residential user remains, the change from a private dwellinghouse to multiple paying occupation may nevertheless constitute development. One should note that although the Inspector in his recommendation, and the Minister in his decision, both used the phrase 'intensification', the term is not used in Lord Parker's judgment. The decision did not justify, therefore, the proposition that intensification may constitute development. What happened here was that there was a change (which could be considered to be material) in the *character* of the residential use. This approach was borne out in the later case of *Clarke v Minister of Housing and Local Government* (1966) 18 P & CR 82. On 1 July 1948, the lodge of a large private house had been occupied by a gardener employed in connection with the commercial exploitation of the garden attached to the house. In September 1948, the lodge was sold and used as a private residence. In 1953, the house was converted into a hotel, and in 1963 the lodge was bought and used for the purpose of accommodating waiters employed by the hotel. The district council, acting as agents for the local planning authority, thereupon served an enforcement notice on the occupier alleging that there had been a material change in the use of the lodge to a use for the purpose of providing living accommodation for the hotel staff. The occupier appealed to the Minister who, in dismissing the appeal, accepted the 'conclusion' of the Inspector that a material change in the use of the lodge had taken place in 1963, from that of a use by a single family into that of multiple occupation by staff of the hotel. In dismissing an appeal to the High Court from the decision of the Minister, Lord Parker CJ said:

> I see no reason to criticise the Minister's decision . . . It seems to me that he was perfectly entitled to say here that there was a single family unit occupation before; that that ceased and that the change to staff accommodation was a material change of use. It is a case, as it seems to me, that does not involve a change by intensification, but by reason of totally different character of the user. I cannot see anything in law which prevented the Minister from saying that there was a change, and that that was a material change from the planning point of view.

7.104 Perhaps the only case decided on the basis that an intensification of use *per se* involved a material change of use is *Peake v Secretary of State for Wales* (1971) 22 P & CR 889. The case involved the part-time use of a garage in a garden for the repair by the owner of his car and occasionally his friends' cars. When the owner became redundant from his employment, he started repairing cars on a full-time basis. It was held that a change in activity from part-time to full-time could not of itself amount to a material change of use, but that the Secretary of State was entitled to conclude on the facts that there had been a change in the use of the garage for repair work by reason of the intensification of use. Clearly, the court was right to hold that there had been development. But it was not the intensification of the use that amounted to development. What had taken place was a change in the character of the use, from that of premises used as a dwellinghouse with ancillary private garage, to that of premises used as a dwellinghouse and a commercial garage.

Perhaps the greatest contribution made to the understanding of this area of law was made by Donaldson LJ in *Kensington and Chelsea RBC v Secretary of State for the Environment* [1981] JPL 50. Here, the borough council had served an enforcement notice alleging a material change in the use of a garden adjacent to a restaurant for the purposes of a restaurant. On appeal, the Inspector had decided that the planning unit comprised the restaurant and the garden, so there was no breach of planning control in using the garden as ancillary to the restaurant. The borough council did not appeal from that part of the Inspector's decision, but they complained that the Inspector had erred by failing to consider the council's alternative argument that there had been a material change of use by intensification of the restaurant use. In dismissing the appeal, Donaldson LJ is reported to have said: **7.105**

> Similarly, in *Peake's* case, the original use of the planning unit had been as a private garage. What had been objected to in the enforcement notice had been the use of the premises as a commercial garage. In a sense the vice of changing a private garage into a commercial garage was that one had far more cars coming and going. In that sense it might be said to be intensification, but half the trouble in this case (and perhaps in other cases) was that the word 'intensification' had a perfectly clear meaning in ordinary language. It had a wholly different meaning in the mouths of planners. In ordinary language, intensification meant more of the same thing or possibly a denser composition of the same thing. In planning language, intensification meant a change to something different. It was much too late no doubt to suggest that the word 'intensification' should be deleted from the language of planners, but it had to be used with very considerable circumspection, and it had to be clearly understood by all concerned that intensification which did not amount to a material change of use was merely intensification and not a breach of planning control.
>
> He (Donaldson LJ) hoped that, where possible, those concerned with planning would get away from the term and try to define what was the material change of use by reference to the *terminus a quo* and *terminus ad quem*. Indeed, if the planners were incapable of formulating what was the use after 'intensification' and what was the use before 'intensification', then there had been no material change of use.

The intensification of a use, therefore, may act as a catalyst of a material change. But for that to take place, there must be a change in the character of the use. For that change to take place, one ought to be able to give a name to the use before the change, and a name to the use after the change, and they must be of an essentially different character. **7.106**

The settled nature of this principle in planning law was recognised by Simon Brown J in *Lilo Blum v Secretary of State for the Environment* [1987] JPL 278, where he said: **7.107**

> It is well recognised in law that the issue whether or not there had been a material change of use fell to be considered by reference to the character of the use of land. It is equally well recognised that intensification was capable of being of such a nature and degree as itself to affect the character of the land and its use and thus give rise to a material change of use. Mere intensification, if it fell short of changing the character of the use, would not constitute a material change.

F. THE PLANNING UNIT, AND PRIMARY OR DOMINANT AND ANCILLARY USES

7.108 Problems occasionally arise as to the precise geographical area to be considered in determining whether the carrying out of a new activity on land constitutes a material change of use. The smaller the area to be considered, the greater the justification for holding that, as a matter of fact and degree, the new activity involves the development of land. The problem was demonstrated in *Bendles Motors Ltd v Bristol Corporation* [1963] 1 WLR 247 (the case of the freestanding, gravity-fed, egg-vending machine, see 7.02). There, counsel for the garage owners had claimed that the Minister had made a fatal error in considering only the 9 square feet upon which the egg-vending machine stood, and that in considering whether the change was material, he should have considered the premises as a whole. The evidence showed, however, that though the Minister had looked at the 9 square feet in considering whether there had been a change of use, he had in fact looked at the total area of the garage forecourt in considering whether the change was material. Hence the Minister's approach had disclosed no error of law.

7.109 An early case on the planning unit was that of *East Barnet UDC v British Transport Commission* [1962] 2 QB 484. In that case the court had to consider whether there had been a material change of use when land previously used as a coal depot was used for the handling and storage of crated motor vehicles. The land in question had been divided into seven distinct parcels, of which only six had been used as a coal depot, whilst the seventh had remained unoccupied. It was argued on behalf of the local planning authority that because the vacant parcel had been unoccupied, it was impossible to say that no material change of use had taken place. Dismissing that argument, Lord Parker CJ said:

> Whatever unit one considers in these cases is always a matter of difficulty, but looked at as a matter of common sense in the present case it seems to me that this [i.e., the vacant parcel] was merely an unused part of the unit in question.

7.110 Almost side by side with the development of the law relating to the planning unit has been the development of the principle that land may have a dominant or primary use, to which other uses may be subservient or ancillary. Hence, in determining the use of buildings or land, it may be that regard should be had to a larger unit of which the building or land in question is merely a part. So that if land and buildings are together used for a single dominant or primary purpose, it is that purpose which determines the character of the use of the whole unit, without regard to any ancillary uses to which individual parts of the unit may be put.

7.111 One of the earliest cases to address this problem was *Vickers-Armstrong* v *Central Land Board* (1957) 9 P & CR 33, where the Court of Appeal had to consider whether a claim for loss of development value under the Town and Country Planning Act 1947 could be made in respect of a building which, although situated within the company's aviation works complex, had been used for administrative purposes. It was agreed by both parties that the highest value that could be placed on the administrative building was its value for use as a general industrial building, and that, if planning permission would have been required before it could have been used for that purpose, the loss of development value would have been £15,000. If, on the other hand, planning permission would not have been required, no loss of development value would have occurred. Crucial to the resolution of this dispute, therefore, was the nature of the use to which the administrative block had been put. If the use was that of a general industrial building, planning permission would not be required to change to that use. If, however, its use was that of general offices, planning permission would be required. The Court of Appeal, upholding the decision of the Lands Tribunal, held that the appellant's works 'as a whole' had been used for general industrial purposes and that the use of the administrative block was incidental to that main purpose. Hence, the owner had suffered no loss of development value.

It seems, from this decision, therefore, that once the planning unit has been established, the character of the primary use which is carried on in the unit colours the character of every part of that unit, notwithstanding that some parts of it may be devoted entirely to some incidental or ancillary use. An example may be taken of a factory complex, comprising a factory where the main manufacturing processes are carried on, a car park for employees' cars, a canteen or refectory and a sports ground for recreational use by employees. The unit has a primary (industrial) use, to which the other uses are all ancillary. It follows that the occupier of the unit may change the location of those ancillary uses without any material change of use being involved. Any operational development, of course, will need planning permission but, subject to that, planning permission will not be needed if the occupier of that unit decides that the location of the car park and sports ground should be exchanged: he might also decide that due to the additional demand for car parking spaces, the sports ground should also be used for that purpose. This too would not be development, so long as the ancillary car parking use remains a use ancillary to the dominant 'industrial' use. Should that ancillary use, however, itself become dominant (as would happen if the owner of the factory complex allowed members of the general public to use the car park), a change of use would have occurred from that of industrial use, to that of industrial use and car-parking. **7.112**

It has to be said that the implications of the *Vickers-Armstrong* case were not at first generally recognised. It was, after all, a case more concerned with compensation for the loss of development rights than with the application of general principles of planning law. It was not until 1966 in *G. Percy Trentham Ltd v Gloucestershire CC* [1966] 1 WLR 506 that the principle in the *Vickers-Armstrong* case was first considered to be of more general application. The facts involved a site which comprised a farmhouse, a farmyard and farm buildings. Prior to its purchase by building and civil engineering contractors, the farm buildings had been used to house tractors and livestock associated with the farm. After purchase, the farm buildings were used by the contractors for the storage of building materials. Since planning permission to use the land for that purpose had not been granted, the local planning authority sought its discontinuance by an enforcement notice served on the building contractors. The notice alleged that a material change of use had taken place from agricultural purposes (namely, the storage of farm machinery) to the storage of plant and machinery of building contractors. On appeal against the notice and in the courts, the contractors had argued that, by virtue of the then Use Classes Order, planning permission for the change was not required. They claimed that the use of the buildings and other land for the storage of tractors and for the storage of building materials, both fell within the then Class X of the Order, which spoke of 'use as a wholesale warehouse or repository for any purpose'. Accordingly, no development had taken place. Dismissing this argument, the Court of Appeal held that a repository is a **7.113** place where goods are stored as part of a storage business, so that the term did not cover the use of farm buildings to store tractors where the storage was ancillary to the use of the farm. But then, after having decided the issue in narrow terms in favour of the local planning authority, the Court of Appeal went further in holding that, looked at in isolation, even if the buildings did constitute a repository or warehouse, they could not be severed from the rest of the farmhouse buildings. The Court thought that, in considering the Use Classes Order, it was necessary to look at the whole of the unit being used, the whole area on which a particular activity was carried on, including uses incidental to, or included in the activity. The Court gave, as an example, a baker's shop with a flour store and a dwellinghouse above in one unit, which could be changed into a butcher's shop with a meat store and dwelling-house above without the need for planning permission. In this case, it was clear that the planning unit being considered comprised the farmhouse, farm buildings and yard, and in no sense could the unit be regarded as a warehouse or repository.

7.114 Buttressed by a further decision of the Court of Appeal in *Brazil (Concrete) Ltd v Amersham RDC* (1967) 18 P & CR 396, where the court followed the principles it had enunciated earlier in *G. Percy Trentham Ltd v Gloucestershire CC*, it became settled law that in order to see whether a change of use was permitted under the Use Classes Order, regard should be had to the whole area in which a particular activity is carried on and the primary purpose for which the whole area is used. The character of the user is then determined by that primary purpose and not by any ancillary uses.

7.115 The question that then remained to be answered was whether a similar principle applied in cases where the Use Class Order was not in issue. In *Williams v Minister of Housing and Local Government* (1967) 18 P & CR 514, the Queen's Bench Divisional Court decided that it did.

7.116 Williams owned a nursery garden and made his living by selling, from a timber building which was situated in one corner, fruit, vegetables and flowers grown in the garden. Then, in order to give his customers a wider choice of produce, he purchased from a market imported fruit such as bananas, oranges and lemons and placed them on sale alongside the home-grown produce. The local planning authority thereupon served an enforcement notice on Williams which, as subsequently upheld by the Minister, alleged the carrying out of development by the use of the timber building as a retail shop without planning permission and prohibiting the use of the building as a shop, except for the sale of indigenous agricultural produce grown on the land.

7.117 On appeal, the Minister took the view that the building should not be looked at in isolation and that the building and garden should be taken as a whole. He then proceeded to uphold the notice on the ground that the established use of the building was restricted to the sale of agricultural produce grown on the land and was a use incidental to the use of the premises as a nursery and market garden; and that the sale of imported fruit had effected a change in the character of the use to that of a greengrocer's shop, which constituted a material change of use.

7.118 The Divisional Court refused to interfere with the Minister's decision, taking the view that he had acted correctly in looking at the premises as a whole. The Court held that the primary use of the premises was agriculture, the use of the timber building for selling produce was ancillary to that use, and that the Minister was entitled to find that although the quantitive change was small, a change which involved selling fruit not grown on the premises constituted a material change of use. In the *Williams* case it was not entirely clear what percentage of total sales was accounted for by imported fruit. A figure of 10 per cent was mentioned, however; and it seems that anything less than that order of proportion will tend to be regarded as *de minimis* and insignificant from a planning point of view.

There is now a well-established principle that the right to use land for some dominant or primary purpose includes the right to use it for any purpose which is ancillary to that primary or dominant purpose. The addition of an ancillary use, therefore cannot be a material change of use. Neither can the substitution of one ancillary use for another. But if an ancillary use becomes a primary use, a material change of use may have taken place. This is seen not only in *Williams v Minister of Housing and Local Government* but also in *Jillings* v *Secretary of State for the Environment* [1984] JPL 32. There land and buildings in the Norfolk Broads had been used for boat-hire purposes, but included an ancillary use of boat manufacture. Later the manufacturing of boats increased to such an extent that it had become a primary purpose. Instead of the land being used for boat-hire purposes, it was being used for a dual purpose of boat hire and the manufacture of boats for sale. As one use had now given way to two, the Divisional Court had no qualms about upholding the validity of an enforcement notice alleging that a material change of use had taken place. **7.119**

If a use of land or buildings is not incidental or ancillary to the primary use, then if the use is material, planning permission will be required. In *Harrods v Secretary of State for the Environment, Transport and the Regions and the Royal Borough of Kensington and Chelsea,* [2002] JPL 1258, the Secretary of State had refused on appeal an application for a lawful development certificate for the proposed use of the existing roof of Harrods department store for helicopter landing, solely for the use of the owner of the store in connection with his position of Chairman and his work in directing the day to day operations of the store. The Secretary of State had regard in making his decision to the 'ordinary and reasonable practice' or to what was 'normally done' at inner city department stores. The Court of Appeal refused to interfere with the Secretary of State's decision. It held that the Secretary of State was entitled to come to the conclusion that introducing a helicopter pad on the roof of Harrods world constitution material change in the use of the store. **7.120**

In developing the above principles, the courts have often had to consider the precise boundaries of the planning unit. Take, for example, a block of flats; or that current shopping centre phenomenon, shops located within a shop. Is the planning unit the whole building or is each individual flat or shop a planning unit? In a recent case, *Church Commissioners v Secretary of State for the Environment* (1995) 71 P & CR 73, it was held that a shop in the Metro-Centre in Gateshead constituted an individual planning unit so that planning permission was required to change the use from Class A1 to A3. **7.121**

Similarly, where a motorway services area includes a variety of shops providing a range of facilities for travellers such as eating areas, general shops and an amusement arcade, each individual shop may constitute a separate planning unit, so that a change of use from any unit to a betting office would involve a change of use and, if material, require planning permission. **7.122**

In many cases the question may pose something of a conundrum.On the one hand, one is **7.123** looking at the planning unit in order to determine its use. On the other, one is looking at the use in order to determine the planning unit. Fortunately, some important guidelines in resolving this problem were given by Bridge J in *Burdle v Secretary of State for the Environment* [1972] 1 WLR 1207. His Lordship had been involved as counsel in many cases concerning disputes about the planning unit. As a judge, he used this opportunity to set out firm guidelines for its determination. According to his Lordship there were three criteria for determining the correct planning unit:

(a) Whenever it is possible to recognise a single main purpose of the occupier's use of his land to which secondary activities are incidental or ancillary, the whole unit of occupation should be considered.
(b) Even though the occupier carries on a variety of activities and it is not possible to say that one is incidental or ancillary to another, the entire unit of occupation should be considered.
(c) Where there are two or more physically separate and distinct uses, occupied as a single unit but for substantially different and unrelated purposes, each area used for a different main purpose (together with its incidental and ancillary activities) ought to be considered a separate planning unit.

7.124 Bridge J recognised that deciding which of the three categories applied to the circumstances of a particular case at any given time might be difficult. On this he said:

> Like the question of material change of use, it must be a question of fact and degree. There may indeed be an almost imperceptible change from one category to another. Thus, for example, activities initially incidental to the main use of an area of land may grow in scale to a point where they convert the single use to a composite use and produce a material change of use of the whole. Again, activities once properly regarded as incidental to another use or as part of a composite use may be so intensified in scale and physically concentrated in a recognisably separate area that they produce a new planning unit the use of which is materially changed. It may be a useful working rule to assume that the unit of occupation is the appropriate planning unit, unless and until some smaller unit can be recognised as the site of activities which amount in substance to a separate use both physically and functionally.

7.125 In propounding the first criterion, Bridge J had in mind the commonest situation of all, where an occupier carries on a single dominant use on the land he occupies. With regard to the second criterion, Bridge J had in mind the situation that existed in *Wipperman v Barking London Borough Council* (1965) 17 P & CR 225, where an occupier of land was using it for a number of unrelated and different purposes, none of which was ancillary to any other and which were not confined to any particular location on the land. Furthermore, it was not possible to identify any particular part of the land as the site of any particular primary use. In such cases, the planning unit is the entire area of occupation with the whole unit being used for a number of planning purposes.

7.126 With regard to the third criterion, Bridge J had in mind the situation where an occupier of land was using it for a number of unrelated and different purposes but it was possible to identify the particular part of the site where each purpose was carried on. In such cases it would be right to divide the unit of occupation into as many different planning units as there were different purposes carried on.

7.127 Despite the guidelines given in the *Burdle* case, problems continue to arise in particular cases.

In *Fuller v Secretary of State for the Environment* [1987] 2 EGLR 189, land was being farmed by the appellant as an agricultural unit. The holding, however, comprised a widely scattered number of farms, some as much as eight miles apart. A question arose as to whether the Secretary of State in upholding an enforcement notice, was correct in holding that the agricultural unit comprised a number of separate planning units. Dismissing an appeal against the Secretary of State's decision, Stuart-Smith J held that there was clearly material evidence upon which he could come, as a question of fact and degree, to the conclusion he did. According to his Lordship, the Secretary of State had been right to regard the physical separation of the farms as an important consideration, but not the only one. In so finding, he quoted with approval from the judgment of Glidewell J in *Duffy v Secretary of State* [1981] JPL 811 where he said:

> In my judgment when buildings lie on opposite sides of a road, at some distance from each other, separated by other properties, that geographical separation must be a major, and may be the main factor in deciding whether they form one planning unit.

An interesting issue may arise where an occupier uses his land for a variety of uses, none of which is incidental or ancillary to any other. If he then proceeds to add another use to those which are already carried on, is there a requirement that in determining whether there has been a material change in the use of the land, one has merely to consider the addition of that use without regard to its effect on existing uses; or must that effect be considered against the totality of the existing uses? In *Beach v Secretary of State for the Environment and the Regions and Runnymede Borough Council* [2002] JPL 185, Ouseley J. stated the correct approach: **7.128**

> In my judgment, the law is as follows: where in respect of one planning unit a use comprises A, B and C together is joined by use D, there is a change of use, which may or may not be a material change of use to uses A, B, C. But whether there is a material change of use or not involves a comparison of uses A, B and C with uses A, B, C and D. If the change does involve a material change of use, it is to a new use which comprises both the old and the new uses, whether they are separate uses within the one planning unit or mixed or composite uses within the one planning unit. If, as time goes on, another use is added so that the use being carried on is A, B, C, D, plus now E, the same issues arise. Whether a material change of use has occurred is to be judged by whether the uses A, B, C, D and E are materially different in planning terms from the use A, B, C and D. If it is, it is a new use again comprising old and new uses. Uses A, B and C are not treated as distinct uses unaffected by the additional uses unless they are carried out in a distinct planning use. That is not the issue that arises here.

A question may sometimes arise as to whether the Use Classes Order has any application to a mixed or composite use of land. In conceptual terms the Use Classes Order would appear to relate to single uses, which suggests that the Order has no application to a component part of a mixed use, unless of course the component part can be identified as being carried on within its own planning unit.

Another question that may arise is whether a single planning unit can cover an area of land in the separate occupation of two or more people. Within the context of an enforcement notice, it was held in *Rawlings v Secretary of State for the Environment and Tandridge District Council* (1990) 60 PCR 413, that the selection of the appropriate planning unit was essentially a matter of fact and degree, and that the Secretary of State had not erred in dismissing (through his Inspector) an appeal against an enforcement notice in respect of a piece of land which had been divided into small plots for occupation by caravan dwellers. **7.129**

7.130 More recently in a Ministerial decision reported at [1996] JPL 429, an enforcement notice had alleged:

> a change of use of part of a beach for the sale and display of sundry beach goods including surfboards and wetsuits, and for the sale of hot dogs and ice-creams, other than in accordance with permitted rights.

Whilst recognising that the identification of the correct planning unit was often assisted by the coincidence of ownership, occupation and user, the Inspector found that rather than determining the planning unit by reference to the area of land occupied by the recipient of the notice, it was as a matter of fact and degree proper to regard the unit as including, 'the entire beach, including the area devoted to car parking'.

7.131 In another recent case, *Ralls v Secretary of State for the Environment* [1998] JPL 444, the Court of Appeal upheld a decision of an Inspector to treat as one planning unit a total of five parcels of land, some of which were not contiguous and whose unity of ownership was not present. The Inspector had found that the co-ordinated pattern of land use for the holding of a market in excess of 14 days in any calendar year overcame the physical separation of the various land parcels and their separate occupancy. In this case, the appellant had owned all five parcels prior to his disposal of some of the parcels, including one to his mother. The Court emphasised that what was the proper planning unit was essentially a matter of fact and degree for the decision-maker, and that occupation and ownership were not conclusive.

7.132 With regard to the concept of dominant and ancillary uses, it should be noted that this can only apply to activities within the same planning unit. In *Westminster City Council v British-Waterways Board* [1985] AC 676, Lord Bridge of Harwich said:

> The concept of a single planning unit used for one main purpose to which other uses carried on within the unit are ancillary is a familiar one in planning law. But it is a misapplication of this concept to treat the use or uses of a single planning unit as ancillary to activities carried on outside the unit altogether.

Also, in *Essex Water Co. v Secretary of State for the Environment* [1989] JPL 914, Sir Graham Eyre QC said 'treating the use of a single planning unit as ancillary to activities carried on outside the unit altogether is a misapplication of the concept'.

G. INTERRUPTION AND ABANDONMENT OF A USE

7.133 If a use of land or buildings is temporarily discontinued, the resumption of that use is not development. If, however, a use is permanently discontinued, it would appear that the revival of that use is development.

7.134 One of the earliest cases to consider the interruption or temporary discontinuance of a use was *Fyson v Buckinghamshire CC* [1958] 1 WLR 634. The facts were that from 1943 to 1949, land within the county had been used for storage purposes. From 1949 to 1956, the land was not used at all, except for a brief period of four months from the end of 1953 to March 1954. In 1956, the land was once again used for storage purposes. Subsequently, an enforcement notice was served on behalf of the local planning authority requiring the use of the land for storage purposes to be discontinued, on the ground that in 1956 a material change had been made in the use of the land without planning permission. The authority claimed that the previous storage use was discontinued in 1949, and that when the land was once again used for storage in 1956 a new use had been instituted.

On appeal to the magistrates' court, the justices found as a question of fact that no material change in the use of the land had taken place since 1948, so that no planning permission was required to carry on the storage use in 1956. On an appeal from the decision of the justices, the Divisional Court held that they were fully entitled to come to that decision. The Court pointed out that since 1943 there had never been a use of the land by anyone except for a storage use; and that all that had happened was a rather long interruption of the storage use without any change having taken place. **7.135**

Although *Fyson v Buckinghamshire CC* shows that a use of land may survive a physical interruption of that use, the courts soon began to suggest that there might be situations where a use of land could be lost through the process of abandonment. In *Clarke v Minister of Housing and Local Government* (1966) 18 P & CR 82 a lodge in the garden of a large house was occupied successively by a gardener engaged in the commercial exploitation of the house, as a single family dwelling having no connection with the house, and lastly as residential accommodation for waiters employed at the house, which by then had been converted into a hotel. In upholding the validity of an enforcement notice in relation to the last of these three uses the Court held that a change of occupation from that of a single family unit to staff accommodation was a change to a different character of use, and that, accordingly, there had been a material change of use. The occupier, however, had also contended that one had the right in law to go back to the use of the lodge as it existed on 1 July 1948 (the appointed day under the Town and Country Planning Act 1947), namely its use by a servant engaged in the exploitation of the garden attached to the house; and he claimed that there was no difference in use between that activity and that of waiters employed in the exploitation, not of the garden, but of the hotel. The Court held that it was questionable whether there could be a right to revert back to the use of land as it existed on 1 July 1948, but that even assuming the user of the lodge on that date was that of user by a servant, that use had been wholly abandoned when it began to be used as a private residence. **7.136**

The notion of abandonment was again referred to in *Webber v Minister of Housing and Local Government* (1967) 19 P & CR 1. Here the appellant owned and occupied a four-acre field which since 1960 had been used for a variety of seasonal activities. Between Easter and the end of September the field was used for camping. Between September and Easter, it was used for grazing livestock, except on Saturdays when it was used as a football pitch. In addition, the field was used somewhat infrequently for local events such as flower shows. In September 1965, shortly before the campers were due to depart for the winter, the local planning authority served an enforcement notice on the appellant requiring him to remove all tents, caravans and Dormobiles from the land within 28 days. Now before 1968, if an authority had allowed four years to pass without serving an enforcement notice, it was then too late for the authority to put a stop to the contravening use. The appellant maintained that since he had been using the land in the same way since 1960, it was no longer open to the authority to take enforcement action. The local planning authority, however, maintained **7.137** that a change of use was being made twice a year, from grazing to camping and then from camping back to grazing, and that since planning permission had not been obtained for the latest change of use from grazing to camping (which had taken place only six months previously), the enforcement notice could not be challenged on the ground that it had not been served within four years. The Court of Appeal held that the purpose for which land is normally used had to be ascertained by looking at its use from year to year over a considerable period of time. Here the normal use of the field was for two purposes, namely, camping in summer and grazing in winter. So long as that continued, there could not be a material change of use. Hence the seasonal change of use from grazing to camping was not a change that required planning permission. But having thus disposed of the matters in contention, Lord Denning MR, went on to suggest that if the normal use of the land were to be abandoned for a time, the resumption of it afterwards would require planning permission.

7.138 The concept of abandonment was finally recognised by the Court of Appeal in the celebrated case of *Hartley v Minister of Housing and Local Government* [1970] 1 QB 413. The facts were that prior to 1961, land had been used for the dual purpose of a petrol filling-station and for the display and sale of cars. In March of that year a Mr Fisher purchased the property and until his death a few months later continued to use the land for both purposes. After his death, his widow, Mrs Fisher, ran the business with the help of her 19-year-old son. Because he lacked experience in the business, however, Mrs Fisher did not allow her son to sell cars. Together, they continued to use the land for the business of a petrol filling-station only, until finally disposing of the land to Hartley in 1965. Immediately the new purchaser, in addition to continuing the petrol filling-station business, resumed the business of the display and sale of cars. Thereupon the local planning authority served an enforcement notice on Hartley, alleging a material change of use of the land without planning permission and requiring him to cease that use. On appeal to the Minister against the notice, the Minister found that by 1965 the use of the land for the purpose of car sales had been abandoned and that the present use of the site was that of a petrol filling-station only. On that ground the Minister held the enforcement notice to be valid.

7.139 Hartley then appealed to the High Court, and from there to the Court of Appeal, which held that the Minister was entitled to find that the use for car selling had been abandoned and that once a use has been abandoned, it cannot be resurrected without planning permission. Lord Denning MR said:

> . . . when a man ceases to use a site for a particular purpose and lets it remain unused for a considerable time, then the proper inference may be that he has abandoned the former use. Once abandoned, he cannot start to use the site again, unless he gets planning permission: and this is so, even though the new use is the same as the previous one.

7.140 According to Lord Denning, whether the cessation of a use amounted to abandonment depended on the circumstances. If land remained unused for a considerable time, in such circumstances that a reasonable man might conclude that the previous use had been abandoned, it was open to the local planning authority or the Minister to do so as well. As regards the date for determining whether or not a use had been abandoned, Lord Denning thought that the material time for doing so was when the new use was started.

7.141 A number of points can be made with regard to this decision. First, although it was concerned with the abandonment of one of two dual uses and its subsequent resumption, the same reasoning would clearly apply to the abandonment and subsequent resumption of a single use of land. Secondly, the recognition that it is possible to abandon a use means that, where it does occur, the land could be left with no planning use at all, other than its use for some purpose such as agriculture or forestry, which does not involve its development. Thirdly, although planning permission is required to resume an abandoned use, it is not required for the abandonment of the use. In *Hartley's* case it was unsuccessfully argued that there could be no material change of use between a 'nil' use of land (i.e., after abandonment) and the resumption of the previous use for car sales, unless there was a similar but opposite material change of use when the use of the land for car sales ceased. That point was dealt with forcibly by Widgery LJ who said:

> No one can make a man continue with a branch of his business if he does not wish and no one is going to interpret this legislation as though it gave a local authority that power.

That statement echoed what his Lordship (then Widgery J) had said in the Divisional Court in *Wipperman v Barking LBC* (1965) 17 P & CR 225. In that case the planning history of the land involved the following three stages:

Stage 1	1958 to 1961	Land used for: (a) Storage of farming materials. (b) Storage of building materials. (c) Residential caravan by person engaged in building and fencing work
Stage 2	1961 to 1962	Land used for: (a) Storage of farming material. (b) Storage of building materials. (c) Car breaking and the storage of car parts.
Stage 3	1962 to date of enforcement notice	Wipperman and Buckingham, trading as Five Star Conservatories go into occupation, give up the car-breaking use, and use the whole of the land for storage of materials used in the manufacture of conservatories and house extensions.

It will be seen that the caravan use in stage 1 had given way to a car-breaking use in stage 2; and that the car-breaking use in stage 2 had given way to a storage use in stage 3.

The Court had to consider the validity of an enforcement notice which had alleged that a material change of use had taken place between stages 2 and 3. The Court said that if it had merely been a case of suspension of the car-breaking use with the storage use being maintained at its former intensity, no material change of use would have occurred. The reason for this is that merely to cease one of a number of component activities in a composite use of land did not in itself amount to a material change of use. This was the very same principle which was accepted again by the Court of Appeal in *Hartley v Minister of Housing and Local Government* when it expressed the view that the abandonment of a use would not amount to a material change of use. **7.142**

With regard to the actual validity of the enforcement notice in *Wipperman v Barking LBC*, the Court held that although the car-breaking use had been suspended, the storage use had not been maintained at its former intensity. Instead, it had taken over the whole of the unit **7.143** including that part previously used for car breaking. So, as a matter of law, it seems that where there is a site with a number of component uses, there can be a material change of use if one component is allowed to absorb the entire site to the exclusion of the other use or uses. It should, of course, be pointed out that in such cases the material change of use would result not from the intensification of that one component use but from the fact that the absorption of the entire site by that component use to the exclusion of the others has resulted in a change in the character of the use.

7.144 One further matter to be considered in relation to abandonment is the circumstances when abandonment will be held to have taken place. According to Lord Denning MR in the *Hartley* case, it is open to the local planning authority or the Minister to conclude that a use has been abandoned if land has remained unused for a considerable time in such circumstances that a reasonable man might conclude that it had been abandoned. It is submitted that in considering whether a use has been abandoned one has also to consider the intention of the party concerned, and in subsequent decisions in this area this is a factor to which much weight has been given.

7.145 In *Hall v Lichfield DC*, noted at [1979] JPL 426, a woman had lived in a cottage since at least 1935. In 1961 she had entered hospital as a voluntary patient, where she remained until her death in 1974, apart from occasional visits to the cottage, the last of them in 1968. The deceased's sister and niece had been correctly advised by the council that if they removed the furniture from the cottage it would not attract rates. This they had duly done, but without informing the deceased for fear of upsetting her. Their intention at all times had been to return the furniture to the cottage if the deceased were ever to recover sufficiently to be able to live there again on her own, which had been her hope. Shortly after the deceased's death, the property was put on the market (though not sold) as a result of which doubts had been raised by the council about the lawful use of the property.

7.146 As might be envisaged, the cottage was in a dilapidated condition. It was also situated in a green belt. The view of the authority was that planning permission was necessary before residential use of the property could be resumed, and it appeared that this was not likely to be granted. The authority also took the view that because of the state of the cottage, even if residential use had not been abandoned, any works of renovation would constitute a rebuilding operation and require planning permission.

7.147 Counsel advising the personal representatives took the view that in order to prevent any confusion arising between questions relating to residential use of the property and those relating to structural alterations, it was appropriate to seek a declaration that the residential use of the cottage had not been abandoned and that there was an existing right to occupy it for that purpose. That declaration was duly granted.

7.148 That approach has also been followed in decisions made by the Secretary of State on appeal. In one such case the local planning authority had made a determination that the resumption of residential use would constitute a material change of use [1980] JPL 759. The owner of the property in question had vacated the property and, whilst empty, the property had been vandalised. The owner, however, had taken the trouble to board up the premises and had reported the vandalism to the police. Allowing the appeal against the authority's determination, the Minister held that the owner had not disclosed a firm intention to abandon the residential use of the property and he in turn granted a declaration that the resumption of residential use would not constitute development.

It seems, however, that the intention of the party concerned is just one of the factors, albeit a very important factor, which has to be taken into account. In *Trustees of the Castell-y-Mynach Estate v Secretary of State for Wales* [1985] JPL 40, the Queen's Bench Divisional Court, in considering the validity of a determination that the resumption for residential use of a disused derelict house required planning permission, gave judicial acknowledgement to the submission of counsel that, in deciding whether a use had been abandoned, it was necessary to take into account: (a) the physical condition of the building; (b) the period of non-use; (c) whether there had been any other intervening use; and (d) evidence regarding the owner's intention. **7.149**

In *Hughes v Secretary of State for the Environment, Transport and the Regions* [1999] JPL 83, the Court of Appeal emphasised that in considering the issue of abandonment, it was necessary to have regard to all the relevant circumstances and that it would be wrong to elevate the intentions of an owner to a paramount status, or conversely to subordinate other relevant considerations to that of intention. Although intention was relevant, the Court said that it could not be decisive, because at the end of the day the test must be the view to be taken by a reasonable man with knowledge of all the relevant circumstances. **7.150**

The doctrine of abandonment continues to be affirmed by the courts. Other past examples include *White v Secretary of State for the Environment* (1989) 58 P & CR 281 and *Northavon DC v Secretary of State for the Environment* [1990] JPL 579. **7.151**

H. SUB-DIVISION OF A PLANNING UNIT

Except in those rare cases where a personal planning permission has been granted, planning law is concerned with the use of land, not with the identity of the person who occupies or owns it. It follows that if a large parcel of land used for a particular purpose is divided into smaller parcels, and each parcel is conveyed to a number of different purchasers, those purchasers should be able to continue to use the land for that same purpose without the need for planning permission. **7.152**

This principle, however, may not apply where land which is used for both a dominant and ancillary purpose is divided into two and each part sold, so that one purchaser acquires that part of the land used for the primary purpose and the other purchaser acquires that part used for the ancillary purpose. **7.153**

In principle, it would seem that the purchaser of the part of the land previously used for the ancillary purpose cannot continue to use it for that purpose without first obtaining planning permission since he has converted what was previously an ancillary use into a dominant use. The position may be less clear, however, as regards the position of the purchaser of the part of the land previously used for the dominant purpose. What was previously a dominant purpose continues to be a dominant purpose despite the change of ownership, which should suggest that no development has occurred. **7.154**

7.155 It is, of course, a problem not confined to the subdivision of a planning unit consequent upon the sale of part of the unit. The problem can also arise (though less commonly so) where the owner divides up a unit without selling any part. Unfortunately the law on this issue is even less clear.

7.156 These issues have been considered by the courts on two known occasions. In *Wakelin v Secretary of State for the Environment* [1978] JPL 769, a large house set in its own grounds had been used as a single family unit. Planning permission was then granted for the erection in the grounds of garages and additional residential accommodation subject to a condition that it should only be occupied by a close relative or member of the household staff of the main house. The additional buildings were later converted into self-contained flats, and the question then arose whether the change to separate occupancy amounted to a material change of use. The Court of Appeal thought it did. According to Lord Denning MR, the division of a large planning unit into two separate units was beyond question a material change of use. Browne LJ also considered that on the facts there had been a material change of use, but he did not think it necessary to decide whether the creation of a new planning unit out of an existing unit would *always* amount to a material change of use.

7.157 In *Winton v Secretary of State for the Environment* [1984] JPL 188, a building formerly used to make breeze-blocks had been divided into two. One part was then used for metal working; the other part for car conversions. The local planning authority then served separate enforcement notices in relation to each part alleging a material change of use without permission. The appellants appealed to the Secretary of State against the notices and he, after an inquiry, concluded that when the new uses were instituted, there was, as a matter of fact and degree, in each case a material change of use from the permitted use. Nevertheless, he quashed the notices on the ground that planning permission should be granted for a limited period. The appellants then appealed to the High Court to quash the Secretary of State's decision. Rejecting the appeal, the High Court held that although the mere subdivision of a single planning unit into two separate planning units did not of itself amount to development, whether the subdivision amounted to a material change of use was a matter of fact and degree, which in the normal circumstances of an appeal to him was a matter exclusively for the Secretary of State to decide.

7.158 It should be noted that the appellants also argued that since the uses both before and after the subdivision fell within the same Use Class, by virtue of the then s 22(2)(f) of the 1971 Act and Art 3(1) of the Order, no development had taken place. This argument the High Court rejected on the grounds that to hold otherwise could mean that a large factory complex with a multiplicity of separate uses but within the same Class could be subdivided into smaller units without development being involved, and that this would be inconsistent with the approach to development control indicated in the *Wakelin* case. It should be noted, however, that Parliament has now intervened in relation to uses falling within the same Use Class of the Use Classes Order. Except in the case of dwellinghouses, planning permission is not required where premises are subdivided, so long as both the old and the new use fall within the same Use Class. The provision does not, of course, affect the law as it relates to the subdivision of a planning unit outside the Use Classes Order.

8

THE NEED FOR PLANNING PERMISSION 1: GENERAL PERMITTED DEVELOPMENT ORDERS; LOCAL DEVELOPMENT ORDERS

Section 57(1) of the 1990 Act provides that, subject to the provisions of the section, planning permission is required for the carrying out of any development of land. Planning permission may be granted in three main ways, namely by development order without the need for any application to be made, by a deemed grant of planning permission, or as the result of an express application for planning permission made to the local planning authority. **8.01**

A development order is made by the Secretary of State. It may be a special development order or a general development order. Section 59(3) provides that a development order may be either: **8.02**

(a) as a general order applicable, except so far as the order otherwise provides, to all land, or
(b) as a special order applicable only to such land or descriptions of land as may be specified in the order.

Section 60(1) of the 1990 Act provides that planning permission granted by a development order may be granted either unconditionally or subject to such conditions or limitations as may be specified in the order.

8.03 Examples of the use made by the Secretary of State to grant planning permission by special development order have been given in Chapter 2.

A. TOWN AND COUNTRY PLANNING GENERAL PERMITTED DEVELOPMENT ORDER

8.04 The current Order (SI 1995/418) came into effect on 3 June 1995. It replaced and re-enacted with amendments part of the General Development Order 1988 which was repealed. This new Order specifies in Sch 2, in 33 separate Parts, various classes of development which may be undertaken upon land without the permission of the local planning authority or the Secretary of State. Each Part may itself include a number of Classes of development. Development falling within the Classes is known as 'permitted development'. The whole of the General Permitted Development Order is set out in Appendix C. In considering the application of development control procedures it may be necessary to refer to the Order. The Parts are as follows:

Part
1 Development within the curtilage of a dwellinghouse
2 Minor operations
3 Changes of use
4 Temporary buildings and uses
5 Caravan sites
6 Agricultural buildings and operations
7 Forestry buildings and operations
8 Industrial and warehouse development
9 Repairs to unadopted streets and private ways
10 Repairs to services
11 Development under local or private Acts or orders
12 Development by local authorities
13 Development by local highway authorities
14 Development by drainage bodies
15 Development by National Rivers Authority
16 Development by or on behalf of sewerage undertakers
17 Development by statutory undertakers
18 Aviation development
19 Development ancillary to mining operations
20 Coal mining development by the Coal Authority and licensed operators

21 Waste tipping at a mine
22 Mineral exploration
23 Removal of material from mineral-working deposits
24 Development by telecommunications code system operators
25 Other telecommunications development
26 Development of the Historic Buildings and Monuments Commission for England
27 Use by members of certain recreational organisations
28 Development at amusement parks
29 Driver information systems
30 Toll road facilities
31 Demolition of buildings
32 Schools, colleges, universities and hospitals
33 Closed-circuit television cameras

B. GENERAL CONSIDERATIONS

Before considering in more detail the application of the General Permitted Development Order, a number of important general points should be borne in mind, all of which may have the effect of rendering the Order inapplicable in particular circumstances. 8.05

(a) Under Art 4 of the Order, if either the Secretary of State or the local planning authority is satisfied that it is expedient that development described in any Part, Class or paragraph in Sch 2, other than Class B of Part 22 or Class C of Part 23 should not be carried out unless permission is granted for it on an application, he or they may give a direction that the planning permission granted by the Order shall not apply. A direction so made is referred to as an 'article 4 direction'. Where such a direction has been made, its effect is to require an application for planning permission to be made for the development specified in the direction, which, if the development were to take place elsewhere, would not be required. Article 4 directions are commonly found in conservation areas, nearly half of the total number of directions currently in force covering residential properties in such areas. In such areas, if no directions existed, the extension of a dwellinghouse (within the prescribed limits) would be permitted development under Part 1 of Sch 2. The owner could, therefore, build an extension which was out of character with the dwellinghouse and any surrounding buildings. If an Art 4 direction has been made in relation to that development, the owner must apply for express planning permission to build the extension and the local planning authority will be able to refuse permission or otherwise secure (e.g., through conditions) that the proposed extension is in harmony with the surrounding buildings.

Article 4 directions are also commonly used in rural areas to prevent damage to vulnerable areas from the indiscriminate siting of buildings; from the sub-division of agricultural land; or from temporary uses such as car boot sales and motor sports. 8.06

Where an Art 4 direction is made by a local planning authority, the Secretary of State's approval is normally required (Art 5). It is not required, however, where the direction relates to a listed building or to development within the curtilage of a listed building. The Secretary 8.07

of State's approval is also not required for development within Parts 1 to 4 or Part 31 of Sch 2 if, in the opinion of the local planning authority, the development would be prejudicial to the proper planning of their area or constitute a threat to the amenities of their area. In this latter case, however, the direction remains in force for only six months, unless before the end of that period it has been approved by the Secretary of State.

8.08 In addition Art 4(2) now gives local planning authorities a discretionary power to restrict certain specific permitted development rights in relation to dwellinghouses in conservation areas where the permitted development would front a highway, waterway or open space. The approval of the Secretary of State is not required, but the authority must first notify residents and consider their views before confirming any such direction.

8.09 One of the problems with the making of an Art 4 direction is that if an application for planning permission is made for development covered by the direction, the refusal of permission or a grant subject to conditions other than those previously imposed by the Order, may allow the landowner affected to claim compensation under ss 107 and 108 of the 1990 Act for abortive expenditure, or other loss or damage directly attributable to the withdrawal of the 'permitted development rights'. Although claims are fairly rare, where they are made substantial sums may be involved.

(b) Article 3(4) of the Order provides that nothing in the Order shall operate to permit any development which is contrary to any condition imposed by any planning permission granted or deemed to be granted under Part III of the Act.

8.10 Local planning authorities and the Secretary of State not infrequently impose conditions on the grant of planning permission to restrict the scope of development which would otherwise be permitted under the Order. For example, a grant of planning permission for residential development may contain the following condition:

> Pursuant to Art 3(4) of the Town and Country Planning General Permitted Development Order 1995, the provisions of Art 3(1) and Part 1 of Schedule 2 to the said Order (relating to development within the curtilage of a dwellinghouse) shall not apply to any dwellinghouse to which this permission relates and no such development within the curtilage of any such dwellinghouse shall be carried out without the permission of the local planning authority being first obtained.

8.11 The reason for these conditions is often that the local planning authority in granting permission for the development may feel that they have allowed the maximum possible development of the site and have no wish to see the landowner, having implemented the planning permission, now use his permitted development 'rights' to enlarge the size of the building. The condition is thus often imposed to restrict the amount of site coverage by buildings in relation to the size of the plot.

8.12 It should be noted, however, that for permitted development rights to be withdrawn on a grant of planning permission, the condition must expressly exclude those rights (*Dunoon Developments v Secretary of State for the Environment* [1992] NPC 22).

(c) Under Art 3(5) of the Order permitted development rights may only be exercised in relation to an existing use or building if the use or the construction of the building is lawful (Art 3(5)).

(d) Development is not permitted under the Order if an application for planning permission for that development would be for a project listed in Sch. 1 or Sch 2 to the Town and Country Planning (Environmental Impact Assessment) (England and Wales) Regulations 1999 and thus be subject to environmental assessment.

(e) In a number of cases before permitted development rights can be exercised, the developer must first apply to the local planning authority for a determination of whether the authority's 'prior approval' is required (see, for example, Part 6: Agricultural Buildings; Part 7: Forestry Buildings; Part 11: Development under local or private Acts or Orders; and Part 24: Telecommunications Code System Operators). Where the authority determines that prior approval is not required, or no determination is made by the authority within the time specified for doing so in the relevant Part of the Order, the developer may then proceed to exercise those permitted development rights. A failure to seek prior approval from the local planning authority will mean that the development will be in breach of planning control and permitted development rights will not apply (*Cowan v Secretary of State for the Environment and Peak District National Park* (QBD 12 February 1998)). In cases where the authority refuses approval for the proposed development there is a right of appeal to the Secretary of State.

(f) Some of the development which is permitted under the Order (e.g., Part 1, Class A — the enlargement, improvement or other alteration of a dwellinghouse) has a size restriction or a tolerance related to the size of the original building. 'Original' is defined in the order as meaning, in relation to a building existing on 1 July 1948, as existing on that date; and in relation to a building built on or after 1 July 1948, as so built. The effect of this is that if, say, a dwellinghouse has been erected under a grant of planning permission in 1970, the size of the permitted development is calculated in relation to the size of the dwellinghouse as then built. An owner cannot, therefore, claim the benefit of 'permitted development rights' to extend the dwellinghouse, and then once extended claim further permitted development rights calculated on the basis of the dwellinghouse as extended. He may, however, extend a dwellinghouse on more than one occasion, so long as in total the size of all the extensions taken together, does not exceed the tolerances permitted by the order.

(g) The extent of the permitted development which is allowed by the Order has been modified in a number of special cases. This is particularly so in relation to what is called article 1(5) land. This is defined in the Order as land within a National Park, an area of outstanding natural beauty, a conservation area, an area specified by the Secretary of State for the purposes of s 41(3) of the Wildlife and Countryside Act 1981, and the Broads. In Parts 1, 8, 17, 24 and 25 of Sch 2 to the Order, the development permitted where the land is article 1(5) land is more restricted than in other cases. This is because of the need to exercise greater control over minor development in highly sensitive areas.

It should be remembered that where the development carried out exceeds that permitted by **8.13**
the Order, the breach of planning control is not just the excess beyond what is permitted by the Order, but the whole of the development carried out. Unless the excess is considered by the local planning authority to be '*de minimis*', the whole of the development may become subject to enforcement action. In *Garland v Ministry of Housing and Local Government* [1968] 20 P&CR 93, the Court of Appeal held that once the cubic capacity permitted under the Order had been exceeded, demolition of the entire structure could be required and not

simply that part of the extension which fell outside the permitted capacity. The Court considered that specified limits to the size of development permitted formed part of the definition of permitted development.

C. FURTHER CONSIDERATION OF SOME OF THE PARTS

8.14 Only the heading of each Class of permitted development is given here. Most Classes are subject to detailed limits on such matters as size, height, proximity to curtilage boundaries and in some cases external appearance. If those limits are not met the development will not be permitted by the Order. Reference to Appendix C is therefore essential when reading the text.

8.15 No attempt has been made in the sections that follow to deal with every aspect of Sch 2 to the Order, but the following are particular points to note.

Part 1 — Development within the curtilage of a dwellinghouse

8.16 Many of the Classes of permitted development set out in Part 1 of Sch 2 (particularly Classes A and B) are so detailed that there are many problems of interpretation and application. It is not always a simple matter to decide whether or not a building is actually a dwellinghouse. In *Gravesham BC v Secretary of State for the Environment* (1982) 47 P&CR 142 it was said, 'whether a building was or was not a "dwelling-house" . . . was a question of fact; that a distinctive characteristic of a dwellinghouse was its ability to afford to those who used it the facilities required for day-to-day private domestic existence . . .'. It should be noted too that the definition of a dwellinghouse in the Order does not include a building containing one or more flats, or a flat contained within such a building.

8.17 Part 1 is the Part most frequently used in day-to-day development control. It contains eight classes of permitted development from Class A to Class H as set out below:

Class A The enlargement, improvement or other alteration of a dwellinghouse.

Class B The enlargement of a dwellinghouse consisting of an addition or alteration to its roof.

Class C Any other alteration to the roof of a dwellinghouse.

Class D The erection or construction of a porch outside any external door of a dwellinghouse.

Class E The provision within the curtilage of a dwellinghouse of any building or enclosure, swimming or other pool required for a purpose incidental to the enjoyment of the dwellinghouse as such, or the maintenance, improvement or other alteration of such a building or enclosure.

Class F The provision within the curtilage of a dwellinghouse of a hard surface for any purpose incidental to the enjoyment of the dwellinghouse as such.

Class G The erection of provision within the curtilage of a dwellinghouse of a container for the storage of oil for domestic heating.

Class H The installation, alteration or replacement of a satellite antenna on a dwellinghouse or within the curtilage of a dwellinghouse.

It will be seen that Class A permits the enlargement, improvement or other alteration of a dwellinghouse, as long as the work does not infringe the limitations set out in Al (paras (a) to (h)), or A2.

8.18 A particular problem which sometimes arises with the application of Class A, is where an owner begins to repair or renovate a disused or dilapidated dwellinghouse in a piecemeal fashion over a prolonged period of time. The question then is whether the owner is 'improving' the dwelling and is thus within the Class, or whether he is re-erecting the dwellinghouse by stages so as to embrace its entirety and thus be outside the Class. In *Larkin v Basildon DC* [1980] JPL 407, the appellant rebuilt all the four external walls of a dwellinghouse in two distinct stages. This involved first pulling down and rebuilding two walls of the dwellinghouse and then subsequently rebuilding another two walls. The appellant contended that the works were permitted development under Class I (1) of what was then Sch 1 to the General Development Order as the 'enlargement, improvement or other alteration' of a dwellinghouse. The Divisional Court considered that whether the activities with which they were concerned amounted to improvement or rebuilding depended almost entirely on matters of fact and degree. It concluded that the Secretary of State's decision that the original building had virtually ceased to exist and the operations amounted to the construction of a new dwelling and did not therefore come within the class was valid.

8.19 In *Hewlett v Secretary of State for the Environment* [1985] JPL 404 an enforcement notice was served by the local planning authority in respect of the works carried out to a very small building which had only three walls. This work apparently involved jacking up the roof, then undertaking certain operations to the walls in turn, and then at a later stage probably working on the roof itself. The appeal was based on the Town and Country Planning Act 1971 s 22(2)(a) which was the forerunner to s 55(2)(a) of the 1990 Act and it was submitted that the operations amounted to the 'maintenance, improvement or other alteration' of the building not materially affecting the external appearance. The Court of Appeal held, *inter alia*, that improvement works of rebuilding done to a building, albeit in stages, amounted to the erection of a new building and not the original building in an improved form and that this was a matter of fact and degree for the Secretary of State to decide.

8.20 Another point to note concerns the effect of the clause headed 'Interpretation of Part I' at the conclusion of that Part. For the purposes of Class A house extensions, the definition of the 'resulting building' includes all enlargements of the 'original dwellinghouse', whether or not they had received express planning consent, so its effect is to secure that in calculating the tolerance allowed, any development carried out under an express planning permission is to be taken into account. In other words if a dwellinghouse is extended by virtue of an express planning permission, the size of the extension will eat into the tolerance allowed by the Part and may exhaust it altogether. It seems, however, that if the planning permission has not been implemented then an owner can take advantage of the full tolerance allowed by the Part and then proceed to implement the permission. This could be avoided, of course, if the local planning authority, by condition in the planning permission, excluded the operation of that part of the Order. The wisdom of using permitted development rights prior to the implementation of a planning permission can be seen in the case of *R (Watts) v the Secretary of State for the Environment, Transport and the Regions* [2002] JPL 1473. There it was recognised that there was inherent in the Order a degree of artificiality in the way in which it might or might not be available depending upon which works were carried out first, be it the works authorised by the express planning permission or the works comprising permitted development under the Order. The legislative framework however, made the sequence and timing of these events of crucial significance. In the *Watts* case, the owner of a dwelling constructed simultaneously a roof extension (which was permitted under the Order) and a side and rear extension for which express planning permission had been granted. The local planning authority claimed that the roof extension was outside the scope of the Order and served an enforcement notice on the ground that the two extensions together constituted a single operation which had not been authorised. On appeal an Inspector took the same view as the authority. The High Court, however, thought that he had been wrong and so remitted the matter back to the Secretary of State. So that if an extension or an enlargement for which express planning permission has been given is to be included in the calculation of the cubic content of the building, the extension or enlargement must have existed or have been substantially completed before any permitted development rights can be claimed. In other words, the extent of any permitted development rights will be reduced or excluded once the express planning permission has been implemented.

8.21 Problems have also occurred in relation to Class E. This Class typically includes garages, garden sheds, domestic stores or games rooms to be used by residents. In *Pêche d'Or Investments v Secretary of State for the Environment* [1996] JPL 311, it was held that whether a building fell within Class E was a matter of fact and degree in every case. In this case the provision of a study room was not excluded from the Class. In *Rambridge v Secretary of State for the Environment* [1997] 74 P & CR 126, however, it was held that the Class did not include buildings designed for primary residential accommodation or additions to basic living accommodation, such as bedrooms or kitchens. In other words, the building is only permitted if it is required for a purpose incidental to the enjoyment of the dwellinghouse.

8.22 There have been frequent changes to Class H of Part I. The present position is that the Class permits the installation, alteration or replacement of a satellite antenna on a dwellinghouse, or within the curtilage of a dwellinghouse, subject to certain limits and conditions. The main conditions are:

(a) the size of the antenna (excluding any projecting feed element, reinforcing rim, mountings and brackets) when measured in any dimension must not exceed:
   - 45cm if it is installed on a chimney;
   - 90cm if it is installed on land other than on a chimney;

(b) the highest part of the antenna, if installed on the roof, must not exceed the highest part of the roof (or the highest part of the chimney, if installed on the chimney);

(c) there is no more than one antenna on the dwellinghouse or within its curtilage;

(d) on article 1(5) land, an antenna must not be installed:
   (i) on a chimney;
   (ii) on a building which exceeds 15m in height;
   (iii) on a wall or roofslope facing a highway;
   (iv) on a wall or roofslope facing a waterway in the Broads; or

(e) an antenna installed on a building shall, so far as is practicable, be sited so as to minimise its effect on the external appearance of the building, and shall be removed as soon as reasonably practicable when no longer needed.

Part 2 — Minor operations

Part 2 contains three classes of permitted development as set out below. **8.23**

Class A The erection, construction, maintenance, improvement or alteration of a gate, fence, wall or other means of enclosure.

Class B The formation, laying out and construction of a means of access to a highway which is not a trunk road or a classified road, where that access is required in connection with development permitted by any class in this Schedule (other than by Class A of this Part).

Class C The painting of the exterior of any building or work.

In *Shepherd v Secretary of State for the Environment and Three Rivers DC* [1997] JPL 764, the High Court held that Class B was not confined to the formation of a means of access to a highway which was adjacent to the land on which the permitted development was to take place. The right was available under the Class even where there was intervening land between the highway and the land on which the permitted development was to take place.

Part 3 — Changes of use

Under the Town and Country Planning (Use Classes) Order 1987, a change of use within the same use class does not involve the development of land. A change of use between two use classes, however, will only constitute development if it involves a material change of use. Under Classes A to D in Part 3 of the General Permitted Development Order, the following unilateral changes between different use classes are permitted development. This aspect has been mentioned earlier. **8.24**

Class A Development consisting of a change of use of a building to a use falling within Class A1 (shops) of the Schedule to the Use Classes Order from a use falling within Class A3 (restaurants and cafes), A4 (drinking establishments) or A5 (hot food takeaways) of the Schedule.

Class AA Development consisting of a change of use of a building to a use falling within Class A3 (restaurants and cafes) of the Schedule to the Use Classes Order from a use falling within Class A4 (drinking establishments) or Class A5 (hot food takeaways) of that Schedule.

Class B Development consisting of a change of the use of a building—

(a) to a use for any purpose falling within Class B1 (business) of the Schedule to the Use Classes Order from any use falling within Class B2 (general industrial) or B8 (storage and distribution) of that Schedule;

(b) to a use for any purpose falling within Class B8 (storage and distribution) of that Schedule from any use falling within Class B1 (business) or B2 (general industrial).

Class C Development consisting of a change of use to a use falling within Class A2 (financial and professional services) of the Schedule to the Use Classes Order from a use falling within Class A3 (restaurants and cafes), Class A4 (drinking establishments) or Class A5 (hot food takeaways) of that Schedule.

Class D Development consisting of a change of use of any premises with a display window at ground floor level to use falling within Class A1 (shops) of the Schedule to the Use Classes Order from a use falling within Class A2 (financial and professional services) of that Schedule.

Class E Development consisting of change in the use of any building or other land from a use permitted by a planning permission granted on an application, to another use which that permission would have specifically authorised when it was granted.

8.25 Class E of Part 3 should be noted even though it is little used. Its purpose is to encourage the use of planning permission granted in the alternative. It has always been possible for a local planning authority to grant more than one planning permission for the same parcel of land, e.g., for a change of use from use A to use B; also for a change of use from use A to use C. If the owner implements the first change by moving from use A to use B, he cannot subsequently move to use C without first obtaining planning permission to do so. To overcome this difficulty, Class E envisages that a local planning authority may grant planning permission for say, a change of use from use A to use B *or* C. If then, the owner implements the change to use B, he may subsequently change from use B to use C as permitted development. Two limitations on the right, however, require that the second change (to use C) must be carried out within 10 years of the grant of planning permission, and that the second change must not be in breach of any condition, limitation or specification imposed in the permission.

Part 4 — Temporary buildings and uses

8.26 This Part of Sch 2 to the Order contains the following two Classes:

Class A The provision on land of buildings, moveable structures, works, plant or machinery required temporarily in connection with and for the duration of operations being or to be carried out on, in, under or over that land or on land adjoining that land.

Class B The use of any land for any purpose for not more than 28 days in total in any calendar year, of which not more than 14 days in total may be for the purposes referred to in paragraph B.2, and the provision on the land of any moveable structure for the purposes of the permitted use.

8.27 Under Class A of this Part, a builder's hut, used for administrative purposes on a construction site during the course of building operations, would be permitted development during the period of construction.

8.28 Class B of Part 4 permits the use of land for certain temporary purposes. The permission does not apply, however, where the land in question is a building or is within the curtilage of a building, or to the use of land as a caravan site. There is no doubt that the 28 days' grace allowed for the temporary use (or 14 in some cases) does not allow land to be used for that period on a permanent basis. In *Tidswell v Secretary of State for the Environment* [1977] JPL 104 an enforcement notice had been served requiring the discontinuance of land for use as a market. At the time of service of the notice, the contravening development had operated for a total of nine Sundays, but the use of the land for that purpose on Sundays had continued after service of the notice for at least another nine months. By the date of the appeal, the use had continued far beyond the Order limits (every Sunday from 23 June 1974 until 15 April 1975, i.e., 37 Sundays in 1974 and 15 in 1975). The Queen's Bench Divisional Court upheld the Secretary of State's view that the benefit of the Order was not available to the appellant.

In this case all the evidence suggested that the use was not a temporary use but a permanent one. The decision upheld the validity of the enforcement notice served after use of the land as a market for the first nine Sundays. In upholding the enforcement notice, Forbes J quoted Upjohn LJ in *Miller-Mead v Minister of Housing and Local Government* [1963] 2 QB 196, 231 where he said, '. . . a permanent user for a purpose not permitted and a temporary casual user up to 28 days in any one year are quite different things'. He went on to hold that, from the evidence available, it must have been apparent that what was there was a permanent use for a purpose not permitted and not a temporary casual user.

In deciding whether or not a change of use is temporary or permanent, it may be relevant to consider the use in the light of the way in which the land is likely to be used in practice. In *Ramsay v Secretary of State for the Environment and Suffolk DC* [1998] JPL 60 it was held in a challenge to the refusal by the Secretary of State on appeal to grant a lawful development certificate for 'the use of land for vehicular sports and leisure activities on not more than 28 days in any calendar year' that he was entitled to conclude that the use was a permanent, intermittent use which was not permitted by the General Permitted Development Order. The site had retained throughout the year the physical features of the use on a permanent basis, e.g., rope around the track enclosures, moveable huts used for the collection of entry fees and the sale of refreshments to spectators, vehicle track, and tyres. It had all the hallmarks of a permanent, if intermittent, change of use. **8.29**

Subsequently, however, the appellants applied for and were granted a lawful development certificate in respect of the earlier operational development of the land, namely, 'the creation of a circuit or track by mechanical excavation and raising the banks and jumps on formerly level or graded field or meadow'. The certificate thus established the lawful existence of the physical changes that had been made. **8.30**

Thereafter, the appellants sought a lawful development certificate in identical terms to that which they had applied for earlier and which had been refused. The evidence again was that between each use of the land for vehicle sports and leisure activities, the land continued to be used for the grazing of sheep. The application for that certificate was again refused by the Secretary of State on the ground that the proposed use was a permanent use falling outside Part 4 of Class B of the schedule. **8.31**

In *Ramsay v Secretary of State for the Environment, Transport and the Regions and Suffolk Coastal District Council* [2000] JPL 1123, the Court of Appeal quashed the Secretary of State's decision, holding that if the physical changes were allowed to take place and they did not prevent the normal permanent use from continuing for most of the year (in this case agricultural) there was no reason in principle why rights under Part 4 should not be available for another use which did not take place for more than 28 days of the year. The Court emphasised that the critical factors were the duration of the proposed use of the land and the reversion in between times to its normal use. **8.32**

In *South Bucks DC v Secretary of State for the Environment* [1989] JPL 351, the Court of Appeal held that the effect of Part 4 was to grant as many planning permissions as there were changes of use, so that where land was used at intervals of one week for a Sunday market, a change of use occurred every time the market was held. The significance of this decision is that it enables the local planning authority to issue an article 4 direction withdrawing the **8.33** permitted development rights, even where the landowner has begun to use the 'temporary permission' but not exhausted it completely. In effect, therefore, the provision does not grant a single permission for temporary use of land for each calendar year. It allows the landowner to make up to 28 changes of use for the same activity, on each of the days permitted in any year.

8.34 In a consultation paper issued in August 1992, the Government invited views on whether further control should be introduced over the temporary use of land for clay pigeon shooting, markets and car boot sales, war games and the use of land by helicopters landing and taking-off. When being carried out, these activities can generate excessive traffic and noise, causing concern to local residents in the area. It will be seen that Part 4 permits these activities to occur on land with the following specified frequencies in any one calendar year:

	On Sites of Special Scientific Interest	Elsewhere
Markets	14 days	14 days
Motor sports	nil	14 days
Clay pigeon shooting	nil	28 days
War games	nil	28 days
All others (including helicopters)	28 days	28 days

After considering responses received to that consultation paper, the Government decided not to introduce any change.

8.35 In January 2002 the Government issued a consultation paper seeking views on whether any changes were desirable to this Part of the Order. In August 2000 however, the Government announced that there would be no changes made to any of the existing provisions in Part 4.

Part 6 — Agricultural buildings and operations

8.36 This Part of Sch 2, extracts from which are set out below, gives permitted development rights (where the development is, or the winning and working of minerals are, as the case may be, reasonably necessary for the purposes of agriculture) in relation to

— certain building works and excavation or engineering operations on agricultural units of 5 hectares or more in area (Class A);

— the extension or alteration of agrictultural buildings, the installation of certain plant and machinery, the provision of sewers etc, and certain other works, on agricultural units of not less than 0.4 but less than 5 hectares in area (Class B); and

— the winning and working of minerals on certain land (Class C).

8.37 Class A The carrying out on agricultural land comprised in agricultural unit of 5 hectares or more in area of—

(a) works for the erection, extension or alteration of a building; or

(b) any excavation or engineering operations, which are reasonably necessary for the purposes of agriculture within that unit.

8.38 Class B The carrying out on agricultural land comprised in an agricultural unit of not less than 0.4 but less than 5 hectares in area of development consisting of—

(a) the extension or alteration of an agricultural building;
(b) the installation of additional or replacement plant or machinery;
(c) the provision, rearrangement or replacement of sewer, main, pipe, cable or other apparatus;
(d) the provision, rearrangement or replacement of a private way;
(e) the creation of a hard surface;
(f) the deposit of waste; or
(g) the carrying out of any of the following operations in connection with fish farming, namely, repairing ponds and raceways; the installation of grading machinery, aeration equipment or flow meters and any associated channel; the dredging of ponds; and the replacement of tanks and nets,

where the development is reasonably necessary for the purposes of agriculture within the unit.

Class C The winning and working on land held or occupied with land used for the purposes of agriculture of any minerals reasonably necessary for agricultural purposes within the agricultural unit of which it forms part. **8.39**

At one time Part 6 of Sch 2 to the Order granted a single permission allowing certain buildings or engineering operations to be carried out on agricultural land comprised in an agricultural unit having an area of 0.4 of a hectare or more, where reasonably necessary for the purposes of agriculture within the unit. The present Part 6 was substituted for the old as from 2 January 1992. It will be seen that under the new provisions, the development allowed is divided. In particular, in Class A the permitted development is restricted to agricultural units of 5 hectares or more, subject to a minimum size of 1 hectare where the development would be carried out on a separate parcel of land within and forming part of that larger unit. Class B permitted development is restricted to agricultural land comprised in an agricultural unit with an area of 0.4 hectares or more, but less than 5 hectares in area. It should be noted that under both Class A and B it may be necessary, before exercising permitted development rights, to first apply to the local planning authority for a determination as to whether the authority's prior approval is required for certain details of the development proposed. In particular, the provisions for prior notification apply where it is proposed to erect, extend or alter an agricultural building. If the authority gives notice that prior approval is needed for such development, the applicant is required by the Schedule to display a site notice on or near the land on which the proposed development is to be carried out, leaving the notice in position for not less than 21 days in the 28 days from the date on which the local planning authority gave notice to the applicant. **8.40**

The development rights permitted by Class A of Part 6 of Sch 2 apply only to building operations 'reasonably necessary for the purposes of agriculture within that unit'. In *Clarke v Secretary of State for the Environment* (1992) 65 P & CR 85 it was held that to qualify as permitted development, the buildings did not have to be reasonably necessary for the particular agricultural enterprise being undertaken on the unit at the time the buildings were erected; they simply have to be reasonably necessary for, and designed for, the purposes of agriculture within that unit. It is essentially a question of fact and degree, to be decided with regard to the circumstances prevailing at the date when the building was erected, and relating to the particular building on the particular unit. It seems that this assessment can refer to the future intended agricultural use of the land since there is no requirement that the **8.41** building should be intended to accommodate only an existing use (*Jones v Stockport MBC* [1984] JPL 274).

8.42 For a building to be permitted development, it has to be designed for the purposes of agriculture. According to *Belmont Farms Ltd* (1962) 13 P & CR 417, this relates to its physical appearance and layout. In *Harding v Secretary of State for the Environment* [1984] JPL 503, it was said that design related to appearance rather than function 'to ensure that buildings in the countryside should look like farm buildings and not dwelling houses'.

8.43 One other provision should be particulary noted. Development under Class A and B is not permitted by the Order if it involves the provision of accommodation for livestock or the storage of slurry and sewerage sludge within 400 metres of the curtilage of a 'protected building'. The purpose of the provision is to maintain a 'cordon sanitaire' between livestock and livestock slurry and nearby residential accommodation.

Part 7 — Forestry buildings and operations

8.44 This Part of Sch 2 gives permitted development rights to certain operational development carried out on land used for forestry, as follows:

Class A The carrying out on land used for the purposes of forestry, including afforestation, of development reasonably necessary for those purposes consisting of—
(a) works for the erection, extension or alteration of a building;
(b) the formation, alteration or maintenance of private ways;
(c) operations on that land, or on land held or occupied with that land, to obtain the materials required for the formation, alteration or maintenance of such ways;
(d) other operations (not including engineering or mining operations).

Part 24 — Development by telecommunications code system operators

8.45 Part 24 of Sch 2 provides for the installation of apparatus by licensed telecommunications code system operators. Development will only be permitted under this Part of the Order if it is undertaken either on the operator's own land or in accordance with conditions subject to which Sch 2 to the Telecommunications Act 1984 ('the Telecommunications Code') has been applied by the operator's licence. Failure by an operator to comply with the code-related conditions in his licence when carrying out development would mean that the development was unauthorised and would be open to the normal planning enforcement procedures.

8.46 Part 24 covers mainly the installation, alteration and replacement of 'telecommunications apparatus' as defined in Sch 2 to the Telecommunications Act 1984 which are 15 metres or lower in height. All types of apparatus required for the code system operator's telecommunications system may be installed in, on, over or under land (including on buildings and on other structures, such as radio masts, electricity pylons or water towers), or altered or replaced, subject to a number of limits and conditions.

8.47 A number of important changes have been made to Part 24 of Sch 2 to the Order since 1995, in particular in 1999 and 2001. The most important of many important changes include the introduction of a 56-day prior-approval procedure in respect of ground-based masts which it is proposed to erect under the permitted development rights granted in Part 24, including a requirement for the operator to erect a site notice to publicise the development proposed. If, however, the authority fails to notify a decision within 56 days, approval will be deemed to have been granted for the installation.

In understanding permitted development rights in this area reference should be made to Planning Policy Guidance Note 8: 'Telecommunications' (PPG8) issued in August 2001. **8.48**

Part 25 — Other telecommunications development

Part 25 of Sch 2, which does not apply if Part 24 applies, permits the installation, alteration or replacement of an antenna on any building (or structure) other than a dwellinghouse or within the curtilage of a dwellinghouse, subject to certain limits and conditions, the main limits and conditions being as follows: **8.49**

(a) in the case of buildings over 15m in height:
- — there would be no more than 2 antennas on the building;
- — in the case of a satellite antenna, the size of the antenna must not exceed 1.3 metres;
- — in the case of a terrestrial microwave antenna, the size of the antenna should not exceed 1.3m, and the highest part of the antenna should not be more than 3m higher than the highest part of the building on which it is installed;
- — the antenna is not installed on article 1(5) land;

(b) in the case of buildings less than 15 metres in height:
- — the size of the antenna must not exceed 90cm;
- — the highest part of the antenna should not exceed the highest part of the roof;
- — there is no more than one antenna on the building;
- — the antenna is not installed on a chimney;
- — the antenna should not be installed on a wall or roofslope facing a highway;
- — the antenna should not be installed on a wall or roofslope facing a waterway in the Broads;

(c) in all cases, an antenna must, so far as practicable, be sited so as to minimise its effect on the external appearance of the building, and should be removed as soon as reasonably practicable when no longer needed.

D. PROPOSALS FOR CHANGE

In July 2002, the Government announced that the General Permitted Development Order was to be updated. This has not yet been done. **8.50**

E. LOCAL DEVELOPMENT ORDERS

Introduction

8.51 Section 40 of the Planning and Compensation Act 2004 will introduce a new procedure to allow for the making of local development orders. It has inserted into the 1990 Act three new Sections 61A, 61B and 61C, the purpose of which is to give local planning authorities power to expand on the permitted development rights given in the General Permitted Development Order. A local development order may only be made to implement the policies in one or more development plan documents or in a local development plan. An order may grant planning permission for development specified in the order or for development of any class so specified. The order may relate to all land within the area of the authority, or to any part of it, or to a site specified in the order. The permission granted by the order may be granted either unconditionally, or subject to such conditions or limitations as are specified in the order. The new Section 61A however, provides that an order may specify any area or class of development for which an order must not be made. That power is intended to prescribe that a local development order may not be made in respect of development related to listed buildings and in conservation areas, and to Environmental Impact Assessment development for which an environmental statement is required.

8.52 The new provisions provide that at any time before a local development order is adopted by a local planning authority, the Secretary of State may direct that the order be submitted to him for its approval. He also has the power to revoke a local development order if he thinks it expedient to do so.

Procedure

8.53 The new Section 61A also introduces into the 1990 Act a new schedule 4A, which allows the Secretary of State to make regulations as to the procedures to be followed in preparing and in submitting the order to the Secretary of State where he so directs. Regulations may also be made relating to the approval or adoption of an order or the revision or withdrawal of an order. It also allows regulations to be made in respect of such matters as notice requirements, publicity, inspection and consultation. It is expected that the procedures in respect of the preparation of an order will generally mirror those in respect of the local plan document to which it relates, save that an independent examination will not be required.

8.54 The regulations are likely to provide:

(a) that the local planning authority should inform any person required to be consulted in respect of a development plan document to which the local development order relates: and any person who would be a statutory consultee for any application for planning permission which would no longer be required if the order is adopted, by sending them a copy of the draft order and the justification for it. The local planning authority would be required to take into account any representations received.

(b) the draft order must be sent to the Secretary of State who may direct that the order be sent to him if appropriate.

(c) the draft and the order when adopted and the related justification for it will be required to be placed on the planning register by the local planning authority.
(d) the local planning authority will be required to report on the extent to which the order is achieving its purpose as set out in the justification note.

Completion of development after revision of revocation of order

With regard to all development orders, whether local, general or specific, the new section 61C of the 2004 Act provides that a development order or a local development order may include provisions which permit the completion of development if the planning permission is withdrawn after the development is started but before it is completed. This provision will therefore apply where planning permission granted by the order is withdrawn or if the order is amended so that it ceases to grant planning permission for the development or materially changes any condition or limitation to which the permission was subject. **8.55**

Sections 44 to 46 of the 2004 Act providing for the making of local development orders have not yet been fully brought into effect. This is expected to follow the carrying out of a consultation exercise during 2005. **8.56**

9

THE NEED FOR PLANNING PERMISSION 2: CASES OF DOUBT

Given the complexities of the definition of development and the difficulties which may arise in deciding whether in any particular case proposed development is permitted development, landowners may be in doubt about whether they need to make an express application for planning permission to the local planning authority before carrying out some activity. In most circumstances there is an opportunity to put the matter beyond doubt. **9.01**

A. CERTIFICATE OF LAWFULNESS OF PROPOSED USE OR DEVELOPMENT (CLOPUD)

Under s 192 of the 1990 Act, if any person wishes to ascertain whether: **9.02**

(a) any proposed use of buildings or other land; or
(b) any operations proposed to be carried out in, on, over or under land,

would be lawful, he may make an application for the purpose to the local planning authority specifying the land and describing the use or operations in question. Then, if the local planning authority are satisfied on the information provided that the use or operations described in the application would be lawful if instituted or begun at the time of the application, they must issue a certificate to that effect; and in any other case they must refuse the application. A certificate may be issued therefore if the proposed use or operation does not constitute development or if it does but the development is 'permitted development' under the GDPO, or the carrying out of it would be in accordance with an existing planning permission. The certificate procedure enables people to ascertain whether specified operations or activities stated in the application would be lawful under planning law. The certificate procedure cannot be used to ask the question 'what is or what would be' lawful on the land.

9.03 As with the certificate of lawfulness of *existing use or development* available under s 191 of the Act (see Chapter 18), the onus of proof will be on the applicant, who will need to describe his proposal in sufficient detail and with sufficient precision to enable the authority to make its decision. It was held by the Court of Appeal in *R v Thanet DC and Kent International Airport plc, ex p Tapp and Britton* [2002] PLCR 88 that it was not open to a local planning authority to require an application for a s 192 certificate to be modified. (This is in contrast to the position under s 191 where that power exists.) The local planning authority may instead refuse the application and suggest the applicant amend the description of the proposed development in a fresh application. In another case, *Broads Authority v Secretary of State for the Environment, Transport and the Regions and David Phillips Investments Ltd* [2001] PLCR 66, it was held that an application under s 192 could be granted even if it related to a grant of planning permission requiring the submission of further details such as with an outline planning permission.

9.04 Section 193 of the 1990 Act contains various provisions to enable the form of application and the procedure for dealing with applications for both ss 191 and 192 certificates to be prescribed by development order, for a certificate to be issued in respect of whole or part of the land specified in any application, for applications to be entered in the planning register, for certificates to be revoked if based on an application containing a falsehood in some material particular and for offences to be created where a person gives false information in order to obtain a certificate. A certificate issued under the section must specify the land to which it relates; describe the use or operations in question (by specific use class if appropriate); give reasons for determining the use or operation to be lawful, and specify the date of the application for the certificate.

9.05 The section also provides that the lawfulness of any use or operations for which a certificate is in force shall be conclusively presumed unless there is a material change, before the use is instituted or the operations begun, in any of the matters relevant to determining such lawfulness.

9.06 In dealing with an application the local planning authority has no discretion, since it is making a determination of law based on established fact. If the applicant is aggrieved by the determination of the local planning authority, he may appeal to the Secretary of State under s 78 of the 1990 Act, and from his determination to the High Court under s 288.

9.07 An important limitation to the scope of a s 192 certificate procedure is that it is not available where the proposed activity has already been carried out. In such a case the owner may either do nothing, and then if an enforcement notice is served appeal against it to the Secretary of State on the ground that the matters alleged in the notice do not constitute a breach of planning control.

9.08 The provision in s 192 allowing 'any person' to apply for a certificate is intended to allow the procedure to be used by prospective purchasers of land in addition to owners. It does, however, also allow interested third parties to do so, as happened a few years ago in a somewhat unique case involving Railtrack plc (ref. APP/X/98/X/5210/3059). The company wished to remodel the existing main railway lines between Euston station and Primrose Hill tunnels,

Camden. They considered that an application for planning permission to carry out the work was unnecessary, since the proposed works constituted permitted development by virtue of Class A of Part 11 and Class A of Part 17 of Schedule 2 to the Town and Country Planning (General Permitted Development) Order 1995. Local residents thought otherwise, on the ground that permitted development rights had no application where the development was such as to require environmental assessment by virtue of the Town and Country Planning (Assessment of Environmental Effects) Regulations 1998, SI 1998/1199. They maintained that the works proposed by Railtrack required such an assessment, so that the development could only be lawful if express planning permission was granted. To help resolve the issue, the residents applied for a certificate under s 192. The local planning authority, however, failed to determine the application within the required eight-week period, resulting in the residents appealing to the Secretary of State against non-determination. At the subsequent public inquiry, Railtrack adopted the role of appellants, with the residents acting as a major interested party and being in the position of asking the Secretary of State to dismiss their own appeal. In the event the Secretary of State determined that the proposed work did not require environmental assessment, whereupon he issued a certificate that the proposed works were lawful as being permitted under the General Permitted Development Order.

The s 192 certificate procedure replaced the previous procedure (known as a s 64 determination) as a result of charges made by the Planning and Compensation Act 1991. The s 192 procedure is considered further in Chapter 18. **9.09**

B. ACTION FOR A DECLARATION

In *Pyx Granite Co Ltd v Ministry of Housing and Local Government* [1960] AC 260, the House of Lords decided that as an alternative to seeking a determination under planning legislation that no planning permission was required for a particular activity on land, a landowner could by way of an originating summons apply to the courts for a declaration to the same effect. The right to use this alternative has now long since been removed and any advantage it may have had is now provided for by the landowner's right to apply for a certificate under s 192. An action for a declaration, however, may be used in order to determine the scope of a planning permission. **9.10**

In one case, *Thames Heliport v Tower Hamlets LBC* [1997] JPL 448, an application for a number of declarations was sought by way of originating summons to determine whether planning permission was needed for a vessel floating but not moored in the tidal River Thames for helicopters to take off from and land on. Declarations were also sought on whether, if planning permission was required for that activity, the 28 days' use permitted under the then General Development Order 1988, Art 3(1) and Sch 2, Part IV, Class B, applied to each of the 20 different sites on the river where the helicopters might take off and land, or was restricted to the whole length of the tidal River Thames on which that activity might take place. The decision of the High Court was that planning permission was required and that the 28 days' permitted use would cover the whole of the tidal river. On appeal, however, the Court of Appeal was only prepared to grant a declaration (and duly did so) that the use of the vessel for the purposes stated *could* constitute a material change of use of the River Thames for the **9.11** purposes of s 55 of the 1990 Act. Mindful that the question of whether a change of use is material or not was one of fact and degree which Parliament had entrusted to the local planning authorities, the Court declined to grant a declaration that the use of the River Thames for the purposes stated *would* constitute a material change of use.

9.12 The Court of Appeal also refused to make a declaration with regard to the question of whether the 28 days' permitted use covered the whole of the tidal River Thames or a lesser stretch of it. In the Court's view the extent of permitted development rights depended upon the determination of the appropriate planning unit. This again was a question of fact and degree to be determined by the local planning authority. The Court felt that it would be inappropriate to attempt to use the mechanism of securing a declaration from the court, so as to inhibit the decision-takers primarily entrusted with the task of deciding those matters from forming their own view.

9.13 Following that decision, it is clear that an application for planning permission does not include either expressly or by implication, a request that the authority should determine whether or not planning permission is required for what has been applied for.

9.14 There is now no doubt that although the courts will decline to answer the question, 'Is the activity proposed development?' (since the s 192 procedure should be available to answer that question), they will consider whether or not planning permission has been granted for particular development or what is actually authorised by the permission.

9.15 In *Burhill Estates Ltd v Woking BC* [1995] JPL 147, the Court of Appeal granted a declaration that an outline permission for development, which involved work on a listed barn, was a valid permission capable of being implemented notwithstanding the destruction of the barn in a severe gale.

9.16 In *R (Gregan and others) v Hartlepool Borough Council and Able UK Ltd.* [2003] EWHC 3278/(Admin), an application was made to quash a decision by the Council that planning permission granted in 2002 to Able UK Ltd., provided permission for a site on the north bank of Seaton Channel (which runs into the River Tees at Teesmouth) to be used for 'dismantling and refurbishment of ships'. The action had been brought to halt the dismantling and recycling of a number of ships at the site which had formed part of the U.S. National Defence Reserve Fleet. The first of these ships had in fact already set off from the United States under tow to cross the Atlantic.

9.17 The High Court heard that the words 'marine structure' used in the earlier grant of planning permission to describe the activity which would be carried on at the site was not wide enough to include the term 'ships'. However, because the Council's decision was not a grant of planning permission but merely an informal expression of the view of an officer of the Council, the Court could not make an order quashing the 'decision'. Instead, it granted a declaration that the earlier permission did not allow the dismantling and refurbishment of ships.

C. APPLICATION FOR PLANNING PERMISSION

This procedure, of course, does not resolve the question of whether an application was necessary in the first place. So if planning permission were refused, any concern that it was needed at all would still have to be resolved by some formal action. In *Wells v Minister of Housing and Local Government* [1967] 1 WLR 1000, it was held that an application for planning permission could be treated by the local planning authority as an application for a (s 64) determination. In *David Saxby v Secretary of State for the Environment and Westminster City Council* [1998] JPL 1132, however, it was held that it would no longer be consistent with the scheme under the 1990 Act for an applicant to be able to require the local planning authority to determine whether planning permission was required as part of a planning application. Should the applicant require a binding determination of the issue he should apply for a certificate of lawful use under s 192 of the 1990 Act. **9.18**

D. CARRYING OUT AN ACTIVITY WITHOUT ASCERTAINING WHETHER IT NEEDS PERMISSION

There may be advantages but also considerable disadvantages in going ahead with an activity without ascertaining whether it requires planning permission, bearing in mind the power of the local planning authority to take enforcement action in respect of any breach of planning control. From a cost point of view it should be recognised that operational development is expensive to carry out and, in the event of an enforcement action being taken, it is expensive to have to reinstate the land to its former condition. A change of use, on the other hand, can often be carried out, and if necessary the earlier use reinstated, at much less cost. **9.19**

Another difference however, is with regard to the application of the four-year rule. Enforcement action cannot be taken in respect of operational development unless served within four years of it being carried out. As regards the making of a material change of use, however, enforcement action against the contravening development may not be taken more than ten years after it has been carried out. **9.20**

Lastly, however, the unknown factor in this area is not only whether the local planning authority would take enforcement action in respect of the contravening development, but whether if an enforcement notice were served, the notice would be upheld by the Secretary of State on appeal. There is no doubt that where there is evidence of a breach of planning control, a local planning authority is duty bound to consider taking enforcement action. It does not have to do so. The 1990 Act provides that an authority 'may' issue an enforcement notice where it 'appears to them that there has been a breach of planning control' and 'it is expedient to do so', having regard to the development plan and other material considerations. **9.21**

This is an aspect of planning law which affects not only those in doubt about whether they must make an express application for planning permission, but also those who are in no doubt that their activity requires any planning permission but who nevertheless develop **9.22** without it. The position is that before serving an enforcement notice, a local planning authority will often ask the owner to submit an application for planning permission under s 73A of the 1990 Act in respect of development carried out before the date of the application. This procedure enables the local planning authority to publicise the application and listen to the views of third parties on the development which has already taken place, and then to weigh up the strength of opposition to that development before deciding whether to grant or refuse permission. Where the decision taken is to refuse permission, the authority will normally also take a decision to issue an enforcement notice in respect of the development. When this procedure under s 73A is followed, however, the owner may be able to show that the environmental effects of the development are not as bad as might have been anticipated, or the authority may consider that the development already carried out can be made more acceptable by the imposition of conditions and accordingly grant retrospective planning permission subject to those conditions.

9.23 The local planning authority's position has been admirably explained by Schiemann LJ in *R v Leominster District Council, exp Pothecary* [1998] JPL 335 at p. 345 where he said:

> It is not rare that buildings are put up without the appropriate planning permission. Sometimes there is no planning objection at all. Sometimes there is an insuperable objection. There are many situations between the two ends of what is a continuum. There are situations where the authority would not have given permission for the development if asked for permission for precisely that which has been built, but the development is not so objectionable that it is reasonable to require it to be pulled down. To require this would be a disproportionate sanction for the breach of the law concerned. That is why Parliament has imposed the requirement of expediency. What weight the authority gives to the existence of the building is a matter for the authority. There are policy reasons . . . for not giving much weight to the existence of a building put up without the necessary planning permission, but these will not prevail in every case. . . . [T]here can . . . be cases where the authority can say that, while it would not have granted the permission for that precise building there, it is not expedient to require it to be pulled down. Circumstances vary infinitely.

10

APPLICATIONS FOR PLANNING PERMISSION 1: PRE-SUBMISSION REQUIREMENTS

In the year ending 31 March 2004, local planning authorities in England received some 675,000 applications for planning permission and related consents. Eighty-four per cent were granted, the vast majority subject to conditions. **10.01**

The content and form of applications for planning permission are governed by s.62 of the 1990 Act and regulations made thereunder. The current regulations are the Town and Country Planning (Applications) Regulations 1988, SI 1988/1812 which provide that an application for planning permission shall: **10.02**

(a) be made on a form provided by the local planning authority;
(b) include the particulars specified in the form and be accompanied by a plan which identifies the land to which it relates and any other plans and drawings and information necessary to describe the development which is the subject of the application; and
(c) except where the authority indicate that a lesser number is required, be accompanied by three copies of the form and the plans and drawings submitted with it.

Under the above regulations, the local planning authority may direct an applicant to supply further information or require him to verify particulars of information given before determining an application. **10.03**

In accordance with the Town and Country Planning (Electronic Communications) (England) Order (SI 2003/956), applications for planning permission may now be made by e-mail. **10.04**

10.05 Section 42 of the Planning and Compulsory Purchase Act 2004 when fully implemented will substitute a new section 62 to replace the old section 62 in the 1990 Act. Under the new section, instead of the form used to apply for planning permission being left to the discretion of the authority, the Secretary of State is given the power to prescribe by development order alone the content and form of applications, and the manner in which they are handled. This allows details of the application procedure to be dealt with in the same statutory instrument.

10.06 Other changes to be made by the 2004 Act include an amendment to section 63, to provide that a development order may require applications for planning permission for such development as is specified in the order to be accompanied by such of the following as specified below—

(a) a statement about the design principles and concepts that have been applied to the development;

(b) a statement about how issues relating to access to the development have been dealt with.

Furthermore, section 42 of the 2004 Act is to repeal s 73(4) of the 1990 Act which allowed special provision to be made in relation to applications for planning permission provision to develop land without complying with conditions previously attached.

10.07 Lastly, section 42 of the 2004 Act introduces a new section 327A into the 1990 Act. The new section provides that the local planning authority must not entertain an application if it fails to comply with any provision in the law which implies a requirement as to the form or manner in which an application is needed; or the form or content of any development or other matter which accompanies the application.

10.08 The new sections 62 and 327A also provide like powers to prescribe the form of applications for consent under tree preservation orders, for the display of advertisements and for listed buildings and conservation area consents.

A. OUTLINE PLANNING PERMISSION

10.09 Where the permission sought is for the erection of a building, and the applicant so desires, an application may be made for 'outline planning permission'. An application for outline planning permission can only be made where the permission sought is for the erection of a building. It is not available for other forms of development. However, it seems that the outline procedure may properly be used to cover operational development carried out on what might be called an ancillary basis along with the construction of a building. For example, an application for outline planning permission for a supermarket might include development of a car park to serve the development. The purpose in allowing an application for outline planning permission to be made is that it gives a prospective developer the opportunity to find out at an early stage, and before he has incurred substantial cost, whether or not a proposal is likely to be approved by the local planning authority. When such an application is made the applicant need not submit details of any proposed 'reserved matters'.

An *application* for outline planning permission may result in the *grant* of outline planning permission (as opposed to what is often referred to as 'full' planning permission). An outline planning permission is defined in Art 2 of the Town and Country Planning (Applications) Regulations to mean: 10.10

> . . . planning permission for the erection of a building, subject to a condition requiring the subsequent approval of the local planning authority with respect to one or more reserved matters . . .

'Reserved matters' are then defined to mean:

> (a) siting, (b) design, (c) external appearance, (d) means of access, (e) the landscaping of the site.

No development may commence until all reserved matters have been approved. It is well-settled case law that the grant of outline permission constitutes a commitment by the local planning authority to the principle of the development, thus preventing the authority from refusing to approve any reserved matter on grounds which go to the principle of the development (*Lewis Thirkwell v Secretary of State for the Environment* [1978] JPL 844). In granting outline planning permission, therefore, the local planning authority have committed themselves to the form of development which is comprised in the permission subject only to the subsequent approval of those specified reserved matters. A local planning authority, however, may consider that they are unable to determine an application for outline planning permission independently of any reserved matters. This view is frequently taken with regard to applications for the erection of buildings in conservation areas. In such cases, the local planning authority can require the applicant to submit further details with regard to all the reserved matters or any of them before proceeding to consider the development proposal. 10.11

It is not uncommon for appellants to submit with an application for outline planning permission details of the proposed development 'for illustrative purposes only'. The purpose is to illustrate the likely form of the development or to show that the proposed development can be carried out in a manner likely to comply with acceptable planning standards. As such, illustrative plans or other details can be a material consideration in determining whether or not to grant the outline permission being sought. If, however, the applicant has not indicated that details are submitted for illustrative purposes only or has not otherwise indicated that they are not formally part of the application, the local planning authority should treat the detail as part of the proposed development; and cannot reserve the matter by condition for subsequent approval unless the application is amended by the withdrawal of the details. 10.12

Although outline planning permission is a permission granted subject to a condition requiring approval of reserved matters, it was held in *R v Newbury DC, ex p Stevens* (1992) 65 P & CR 438 that, contrary to previous doubts, the authority had the power under s 78 of the 1990 Act to impose a condition on the grant of approval of a reserved matter, even though that aspect had not been mentioned in the outline permission, so long as the condition did not derogate from the outline permission already granted. Accordingly, it would be within the powers of a local planning authority, for example, to remove permitted development rights at the reserved matters stage. 10.13

Within the last two years, the courts have had to consider several matters relating to the scope and effect of outline planning permissions. In *R v Newbury DC and Newbury and District Agricultural Society, ex p Chievely Parish Council* [1999] PLCR 51, the Court of Appeal held it to 10.14

be unlawful for a local planning authority to grant an outline planning permission with a reserved matters condition when details of the reserved matters had already been given in the outline application. Furthermore, the Court went on to consider whether (as had been suggested in the High Court) the scale or quantum of development, in that case the gross floor space, was a reserved matter. According to the Court of Appeal, gross floor space could not be brought within the words 'siting' or 'design', especially when those words were read with the words 'external appearance', 'means of access' and 'landscaping of the site'. None of these words was appropriate to govern the scale of the development in a statutory context. Accordingly, if a local planning authority wished to limit, at the outline stage, the scale of the development, it must do so by an appropriate condition. So too, an outline application which specifies the floor area commits the applicant to development on that scale, subject to minimal changes and to such adjustments as can reasonably be attributed to siting, design and external appearance. If, on the other hand, the outline permission does not incorporate any floor space figures, that matter is open for determination at the reserved matters stage. In a later case, *Christchurch BC v Secretary of State for the Environment, Transport and the Regions and Morris* [2001] JPL 606, the High Court considered the meaning of the term 'design' and held that there was no reason for excluding from that term the length, width or height of a building.

10.15 Yet another question the courts have had to consider is what considerations are relevant in determining an application for approval of reserved matters. In *McClean Homes (East Anglia) Ltd v Secretary of State for the Environment, Transport and the Regions and Chelmsford BC* [1999] PLCR 372, the Deputy Judge, Mr George Bartlett QC, put it this way:

> In such cases the principle of the development is established by the grant of outline planning permission, so that the parties, applicant and planning authority, have moved from the question of whether any development of the type proposed may be acceptable to the question of the form that the development should take. That there is at least one such form that is acceptable is implicit in the grant of planning permission.

It is also implicit, therefore, that some forms of development will not be acceptable. Whether any precise form of development is acceptable or non-acceptable at the reserved matters stage must, of course, depend upon the provisions of the current development plan and any other material considerations. Although the courts do not appear so far to have expressly considered the question, material considerations would include the provisions of any development plan which has been amended since the outline planning permission was granted, together with those other material considerations existing at the time the application for approval of reserved matters is determined. This is subject, however, to the overriding requirement that the consideration of any new policies at the detailed application stage does not enable the local planning authority to derogate from the principle of the development already established by the grant of outline permission.

10.16 In *R (Redrow Homes Ltd) v First Secretary of State and South Gloucestershire Council* [2003] EWHC 30/4(Admin) the Secretary of State in determining an appeal on an application for approval of reserved matters, had sought to impose a condition that the site 'shall be used by public service vehicles only'. The High Court quashed the determination because the condition would have the effect of modifying the grant of outline planning permission which had imposed no restriction as to the particular types of traffic able to use the access.

It should also be borne in mind that the definition of the words 'reserved matters' is exclusive and does not include any other matters. Thus a condition in an outline planning permission which provides for subsequent approval by the local planning authority of mitigation measures or the substitution of other land, is not a reserved matter. 10.17

The Government has long accepted that the use of outline planning permission had significant faults. In particular it allows the 'redlining' on a map of an area or development site for a particular use or uses with few details of the development being shown. In such circumstances local communities are given little opportunity to influence the details of the proposed development. For developers too there is the problem that if an environmental impact assessment is required for the development, an outline planning permission may not provide sufficient detail to comply with the relevant regulations (see Chapter 13). 10.18

In the consultation paper, 'Delivering a Fundamental Change', published in December 2001, the Government floated the idea of replacing outline planning permissions with a system whereby a developer might obtain a certificate or a statement of development principles from the local planning authority that it has the authority's agreement to work up a detailed scheme against parameters determined by the agreement. Any formal application would subsequently be submitted in detail and the existence of the certificate would weigh heavily in the determination of planning permission. 10.19

The Government carried the proposal forward when it introduced the 2004 Act into Parliament. The Bill contained a clause to remove outline planning permissions from planning law. During the passage of the Bill through Parliament the clause was withdrawn from the Bill. The Government is now expected to require developers to provide more detail at the application for outline planning permission stage. The new section 62 is likely to provide that at the application for outline planning permission stage, the applicant must submit details of the proposed development which cover the key design principles, such as massing, layout, relationship to public space, density, building heights, access and movements, landscape strategy and the mix and distribution of uses. 10.20

Apart from completing the appropriate application form, the following further requirements are imposed on the applicant. 10.21

B. NOTIFICATION OF OWNERS

It is sometimes said that anyone can make an application for planning permission. If this be so, the prospect that a beggar might apply for planning permission for the redevelopment of land be it in Bermondsey or Belgravia (if he can afford the fee to do so) is unlikely to raise much enthusiasm with the local planning authority for the area. The consideration of applications for planning permission is a time consuming business for local planning authorities. Nevertheless, applications for planning permission have been made by persons with little capacity to implement the permission should it be granted. In 1980, the British Airports Authority, which is responsible for airport development in the country, made an application for outline planning permission to extend the airport capacity of Stansted Airport. The Town and Country Planning Association's view was that the expansion of airport capacity in the 10.22

South-east would be better accommodated by building a new airport at Maplin Sands in Essex. In order that consideration should be given to this at the same time as the proposed development at Stansted, the Association applied for planning permission (which was subsequently withdrawn) for that development. Furthermore, the local authority within whose area Stansted was located, the Uttlesford District Council, thought that a better solution to the expansion of Stansted was an expansion of the terminal facilities at London Heathrow Airport. Accordingly, the district council submitted an application to the local planning authority for the Heathrow area for the building of a fifth passenger terminal complex at the airport. Both that application and the application submitted by the British Airports Authority were then called in by the Secretary of State for his own decision and treated for all practical purposes as one.

10.23 Although it is probably incorrect to say that anyone can apply for planning permission, it is not necessary that the applicant should have any present interest in the land that is the subject of the application. In *Hanily v Minister of Local Government and Planning* [1952] 2 QB 444, where a third party had applied for and been granted planning permission to develop land without the knowledge of the owner of the land, the High Court thought that anybody who genuinely hoped to acquire an interest in the land could properly apply for planning permission.

10.24 Whatever the applicant's position, however, if he is not the owner of an interest in every part of the land to which the application relates, he has been required since 1962 to give notice of the application to the holders of certain interests in the land.

10.25 Under s 65 of the 1990 Act and Art 6 of the General Development Procedure Order it is provided that:

> (1). . . an applicant for planning permission shall give requisite notice of the application to any person (other than the applicant) who on the prescribed date is an owner of the land to which the application relates, or a tenant,—
>
> (a) by serving the notice on every such person whose name and address is known to him; and
>
> (b) where he has taken reasonable steps to ascertain the names and addresses of every such person, but has been unable to do so, by local advertisement after the prescribed date.

10.26 The 'prescribed date' under the article is defined as being 'the day 21 days before the date of the application', and the 'requisite notice' means 'notice in the appropriate form which is set out in Part 1 of Sch 2 to the Order.

10.27 Under the Order, the applicant or the person applying on his behalf is required to serve on an owner or tenant of any land to which the application relates, notice that he is applying to the local planning authority for planning permission for development, details of which must be specified. The notice must also inform the owner of the land or tenant, that if he wishes to do so he may make representations about the application to the local planning authority within 21 days of service of the notice.

10.28 For the purpose of these provisions the term 'owner' means the estate owner in respect of the fee simple or a leasehold interest the unexpired term of which is not less than seven years. Where a leasehold interest exists in land, therefore, an applicant who owns the freehold interest in the land to which the application relates will not be required to give specific notice to the owner of any leasehold interests with less than seven years to run. If, on the other hand, the applicant is himself the owner of a leasehold interest then, irrespective of the length of his term he must give specific notice of his application to the freeholder.

In addition, if any of the land to which the application relates is or forms part of an agricultural holding, specific notice must be given to the tenant thereof, irrespective of the length of his interest. The purpose in giving notice of an application to the tenant of an agricultural holding, whatever his interest, is that the tenant may lose his security of tenure if the landlord can show that he wishes to put the land to some non-agricultural use. **10.29**

The effect of the Order is to require applicants not only to notify owners and agricultural tenants of a planning application they intend to submit in relation to the owner's or tenant's land, but also requires the applicant to certify (see Art 7), in the appropriate form prescribed in Sch 2 to the Order, that the notification requirements have been satisfied. The Schedule also lists the certificates which must be completed in order to inform the local planning authority, and on appeal the Secretary of State, that the notification requirements have been fulfilled. The four certificates, only one of which is required to be submitted with the application for planning permission are as follows: **10.30**

Certificate A This certificate states that on the day 21 days before the date of the accompanying application nobody, except the applicant, was the owner (as earlier defined) of any part of the land to which the application relates. **10.31**

Certificate B This certificate states that the applicant has given the requisite notice to everyone else who, on the day 21 days before the date of the accompanying application, was the owner (as earlier defined) of any part of the land to which the application relates. The certificate further requires the applicant to list the owners to whom notice has been given, the address at which notice was served and the date of service.

Certificate C This certificate applies where the applicant is able to discover and give notice to some but not *all* persons owning an interest in the land. It states that the applicant is unable to issue certificate A or B; also that the applicant has given the requisite notice to persons (who must be specified) who on the day 21 days before the date of the application were owners (as earlier defined) to which the application relates.

As well as listing the names of owners notified, along with their addresses at which they were served and the date notice was served, the certificate must also state that the applicant has taken all reasonable steps open to him (which must be specified) to find out the names and addresses of the *other* owners of the land or of a part of it, but that he has been unable to do so. The steps taken must include publication in a newspaper circulating in the locality in which the land is situated.

Certificate D This certificate applies where the applicant is unable to discover the names of *any* of the persons owning an interest in the land. It states that the owner is unable to give certificate A; also that he has taken the reasonable steps open to him (which must be specified and include publication of notice of the application in a newspaper circulating in the locality), to find out the names and addresses of everyone else who on the day 21 days before the date of the application was the owner (as earlier defined) of any part of the land to which the application relates, but that he has been unable to do so.

It should be noted that, under Art 7 of the Order, a further certificate must be given (in addition to certificates A to D) stating either that none of the land to which the application **10.32** relates is, or is part of an agricultural holding or that the applicant has given the requisite notice to every person who on the day 21 days before the date of the application was a tenant of an agricultural holding on all or part of the land to which the application relates.

10.33 The above procedures also apply to any appeal made to the Secretary of State under s 78 of the 1990 Act. Furthermore, under the Order, the above procedures apply to applications for planning permission for development consisting of the winning and working of minerals, but with some variations.

10.34 There is no point in giving an owner notice of an application to develop land in which he has an interest, unless he is also given the opportunity to make representations with regard to the development proposed. Hence, Art 19 of the Order provides that where a certificate contains a statement that notice of the application has been given to another, the local planning authority shall not determine the application before the end of a period of 21 days beginning with the date when the notice was served on that person. In addition, the Order provides that, in determining the application, the local planning authority must take into account any representations made to them during that period by such persons.

10.35 It should be noted that, other than for certificate A, the procedure merely requires the applicant to state in a certificate that notice of the application has been given to the appropriate persons. Under the Order, authorities are required to notify their decisions to the applicants, but apart from notifying owners and agricultural tenants who have made representations on any application for planning permission affecting their land, there is no statutory requirement for authorities to notify their decision to other parties. The system does not guarantee that the applicant has actually given notice and, because acknowledgement of the authority's decision is restricted, the owner of an interest in the land may remain unaware that an application has been made. In practice it is known that the certificate procedure does not work particularly well, particularly where applications are submitted by an agent on behalf of the applicant.

10.36 It seems that non-compliance with these provisions may have a variable effect. Section 65(6) provides that if a person issues a certificate which purports to comply with any requirements imposed by virtue of the section and contains a statement which he knows to be false or misleading in a material particular; or recklessly issues a certificate which purports to comply with any such requirement and contains a statement which is false or misleading in a material particular, he shall have committed an offence and be liable on summary conviction to a fine not exceeding level 5 on the standard scale. Of more importance than any criminal sanction, however, is the effect of a certificate containing a false, misleading or inaccurate statement on any planning permission which has been granted. In *R v Bradford-on-Avon UDC, ex p Boulton* [1964] 1 WLR 1136, an application was made for an order of certiorari to quash a grant of planning permission for residential development. A certificate which had been signed on behalf of the applicant, stated that he was the owner of the fee simple in the land. In fact the applicant was not the owner of the fee simple. He had been negotiating for the purchase of the land from the owner, who was in fact privy to the application. Refusing to grant the order sought, the Divisional Court held that, on the true construction of the statutory provisions, a planning authority had jurisdiction to entertain an application for planning permission if it was accompanied by a genuine certificate in the approved terms signed by the applicant, and that a factual error in the certificates did not deprive the authority of that jurisdiction.

One factor which seemed to influence the decision was that a grant of planning permission runs with the land and is relied on by subsequent purchasers. If a purchaser was to be required to investigate whether the certificate submitted with the application was correct in its factual averments before being able to rely on the grant, the conveyancing difficulties would be formidable. 10.37

Following the *Bradford-on-Avon* case it was generally recognised, though with some reluctance, that the grant of planning permission would survive any factual error in the content of a certificate, at least as long as there was no actual dishonesty. The later case of *Main v Swansea City Council* [1985] JPL 558, however, has done much to clarify the position. In this case outline planning permission had been granted for residential development. The certificate which had accompanied the application stated that notice of the application had been given to all other owners of land, namely, the city council. It transpired that the land the subject of the application also included land owned by a person whose identity was unknown, and that the certificate did not specify that notice of the development had been published in a local newspaper circulating in the locality as was required. The appropriate certificate was thus certificate C, not B which had been submitted. The applicant had applied for judicial review to quash the grant of planning permission. The Court of Appeal held that in considering the failure of the applicant to comply with the statutory requirements, one had to look not only at the nature of the failure, but also at such matters as the identity of the applicant for relief, the lapse of time before proceedings were taken and the effect on other parties and on the public. In this case the Court had no doubt that the defect in the certificates was sufficient to enable it to strike down the subsequent grant of planning permission in certain circumstances, as where, for example, a prompt application had been made by the owner of the non-council owned land. Although the defects were not such as to render the grant a nullity, the Court held that it had discretion whether to grant the relief sought. In refusing to exercise that discretion in favour of the applicant, the Court took into account the fact that, throughout the period between the grant of the outline permission and the approval of reserved matters (over three years), the applicant had not objected; that the scheme which had been approved did not involve the development of the land not owned by the city council; and that the Secretary of State in full knowledge of the position had not sought relief. It was too late, therefore, for the applicant to obtain the necessary relief to quash the permission and with it the subsequent approval of reserved matters. 10.38

Although the courts are now able, in the exercise of their discretion, to give relief to a petitioner where there is an error in the certificate submitted, in an appropriate case a remedy in private law may be available. 10.39

In *English v Dedham Vale Properties Ltd* [1978] 1 WLR 93, the prospective purchaser of a parcel of land submitted an application for planning permission to develop the land in the vendors' names and without their authority. The application, which was subsequently granted, was signed by an employee of the prospective purchaser stating himself to be the vendors' agent. The accompanying certificate described the applicants (i.e., the vendors) as the estate owners in fee simple of the land to which the application related. The certificate would in fact have been accurate had it been made with the vendors' authority. Without 10.40

that authority, however, the application should have been accompanied by a certificate stating that the vendors had been given notice of the making of the application.

10.41 In making the application, the purchaser's employee had asked that the decision notice be sent to him at the purchaser's address. Hence the vendors remained ignorant of the application for planning permission and of its subsequent grant and, whilst still unaware, conveyed the land in question to the purchaser for a price lower than they would have done had they known the true position. As a result, the surviving vendor (one having died) brought an action against the purchaser claiming, *inter alia*, damages for fraudulent misrepresentation in regard to the prospects of obtaining planning permission, and an account of the profits which had accrued to the purchasers as a result of the grant. In the Chancery Division it was held by Slade J that whilst there had not been any misrepresentation by the purchaser as to the prospect of obtaining planning permission and he was therefore absolved from any charge of fraud, he was accountable to the vendors for the profit he had received as a result of making the planning application. This was because, in relation to the application, he had assumed the character of self-appointed agent of the vendors, thereby placing himself in a fiduciary relationship with them; and he had failed to disclose to them the fact that the application had been made. Slade J also held that where, during the course of negotiations for a contract for the sale and purchase of a property, the proposed purchaser, in the name of and purportedly as agent for the vendor but without the vendor's consent or authority, took some action in regard to the property such as making a planning application, which, if it had been disclosed to the vendor might reasonably have been likely to influence him in deciding whether or not to conclude a contract, a fiduciary relationship arose between the two parties which gave rise to a duty on the purchaser to disclose to the vendor before the conclusion of the contract what he had done as the vendor's purported agent; and, in the event of non-disclosure, the purchaser was liable to account to the vendor for any profit he made in the course of the purported agency, unless the vendor had consented to his retaining the profit.

C. FEES FOR PLANNING APPLICATIONS

10.42 Under s 303 of the 1990 Act, the Secretary of State may make regulations for the payment of a fee to local planning authorities in respect of applications made to them for any permission, consent, approval, determination or certificate.

10.43 The Town and Country Planning (Fees for Applications and Deemed Applications) Regulations 1989, SI 1989/193, as amended, now provide for fees to be payable where an application is made for planning permission, for a certificate of lawful use or development, for the approval of reserved matters, for consent to the display of advertisements and on a deemed application for planning permission which arises when an appeal is made against an enforcement notice.

10.44 The fees charged are based on broad categories of development and are designed to relate the fee to the approximate cost of dealing with applications. These costs cover the whole development control process from the validation of the application and its registration, through to the issue of the decision letter.

Before the 2004 Act the power of the Secretary of State under section 303 to prescribe a fee payable to a local planning authority related only to an authority's handling of planning applications. The Planning and Compulsory Purchase Act 2004 will, when fully implemented, amend section 303 to widen the scope of the Secretary of State's power to enable him to provide for the payment of charges and fees relating to any other function of local planning authorities under the 1990 Act, the Planning (Listed Building and Conservation Areas) Act 1990 and the Planning (Hazardous Substances) Act 1990. **10.45**

In September 2004, the Government published a consultation paper setting out proposals to improve the resourcing of planning work in local planning authorities. The proposals include the raising of planning fees by an average of 17 per cent. The size is intended to help recover the cost of planning applications, particularly with regard to larger developments. Another proposal is to allow authorities that meet Government targets for handling major applications to be allowed to increase the application fee they charge by up to 10 per cent. to help them meet more of the costs of handling large and often complex applications. In addition, authorities willing to offer the facility for applications to be made online will also be able to offer a reduction in fees to encourage this. **10.46**

D. TWIN-TRACKING

With some of the more important development proposals, it was not uncommon for a developer to submit two identical or near identical applications for planning permission for the same development. The purpose of this was that if the local planning authority has not determined either application for planning permission within the prescribed period of eight weeks for doing so, the developer could exercise his right to appeal to the Secretary of State against non-determination of one of the applications. The authority could then determine that application and the developer knew that he had a place in the appeal queue. It allowed the authority and developer to continue to negotiate over the second application. If the authority subsequently granted planning permission for the development on the second application, the developer could then withdraw his appeal against non-determination of the other. **10.47**

The use of twin tracking by developers has effectively ended by giving local planning authorities additional powers in handling planning applications. This is dealt with in Chapter 11. **10.48**

E. CONSULTATIONS WITH THE LOCAL PLANNING AUTHORITY

It is common practice to hold discussions with the local planning authority before formally submitting an application for planning permission. Circular 28/83 advises applicants to do this so that guidance can be given on how the authority's planning policies should influence the applicant's proposals before a formal application is made; that information required by the authority for proper consideration of the application can be agreed and provided with **10.49** the formal application; and that applications are submitted in the correct form and accompanied by the correct fee. It may also be that, after informed discussions with the local planning authority, applicants may decide to adjust their proposals in order to meet the authority's objections to their original scheme.

10.50 The House of Lords has held that where pre-planning application discussions are held with the local planning authority, the authority had no power to make a charge for so doing (*R v Richmond upon Thames LBC, ex p McCarthy & Stone (Developments) Ltd* [1992] 2 AC 48).

10.51 The effect of this decision has now been reversed. Section 98 of the Local Government Act 2003 gives local authorities the power to charge for pre-planning application consultations.

10.52 If informal planning advice is given to a member of the public by officers of a local planning authority, no general duty of care exists to make the authority liable to the person advised if the advice is negligent. In *Tidman v Reading BC* [1994] 3 PLR 72, the High Court dismissed an action brought by a member of the public who claimed he had been given negligent advice as to the need for planning permission for land he was trying to sell and had not been advised on the steps he could take to clarify the position. Negligent advice by a local planning authority may, however, be the subject of a complaint to the Local Government Ombudsman alleging maladministration. Many such complaints have succeeded and have resulted in authorities making *ex gratia* payments to those affected.

F. THE PLANNING REGISTER

10.53 Under s 69 of the 1990 Act, every local planning authority must keep in such manner as may be prescribed by development order, a register containing such information as may be prescribed with respect to applications for planning permission made to the authority. The register must be kept available for inspection by members of the public at all reasonable hours.

10.54 Under the General Development Procedure Order, the register of applications for planning permission is to be kept in two parts. Part I must contain a copy of every application for planning permission and of any application for approval of reserved matters submitted to the authority and not finally disposed of, together with copies of plans and drawings submitted with them. Part II must contain in respect of every application for planning permission,

(a) a copy (which may be photographic) of the application and of plans and drawings submitted in relation thereto;
(b) particulars of any direction given under the Act or the Order in respect of the application;
(c) the decision (if any) of the local planning authority in respect of the application, including details of any conditions subject to which permission was granted, the date of such decision and the name of the local planning authority;
(d) the reference number, the date and effect of any decision of the Secretary of State in respect of the application, whether on appeal or on a reference under s 77 of the 1990 Act;

(e) the date of any subsequent approval (whether approval of reserved matters or any other approval required) given in relation to the application.

Registers also keep details of such matters as environmental impact assessment statements, simplified planning zone schemes, enforcement notices and stop notices. Under the 1990 Act, the registers must be kept open for public inspection at all reasonable times. **10.55**

11

APPLICATIONS FOR PLANNING PERMISSION 2: PROCEDURE ON RECEIPT OF APPLICATIONS BY THE LOCAL PLANNING AUTHORITY

A. ACKNOWLEDGEMENT OF RECEIPT OF APPLICATION

An application for planning permission is made to the authority with responsibility for determining the application. In the case of a nonmetropolitan area with a two-tier division of planning responsiblity, most applications fall to be determined by the district planning authority for the area in which the land is situated. If the application relates **11.01** to a county matter, application must be made to the county planning authority for the area.

11.02 On receipt of the application, the local planning authority is required to send an acknowledgement to the applicant in the terms (or substantially in the terms) set out in Part 1 of Sch 1 to the General Development Procedure Order. A requirement of Art 20 of the Order is that the authority shall notify the applicant of their decision on the application within eight weeks from the date on which the application was received, or such extended period as may be agreed upon in writing between the applicant and the local planning authority. Accordingly, the acknowledgement states that if notice of the decision has not been given by the appropriate date, the applicant may appeal to the Secretary of State in accordance with s 78 of the 1990 Act within a further period of three months.

11.03 The precise effect of the provision that the authority shall give notice of their decision within the prescribed period was considered by the Court of Appeal in *James v Secretary of State for Wales* [1966] 1 WLR 135. Under the special provisions of the Caravan Sites and Control of Development Act 1960, where express planning permission for the use of land as a caravan site had not previously been given, an application for a site licence under the Act also operated as an application for planning permission. Then if, within six months of the application having been made, express planning permission had not been given, permission for the use of the land as a caravan site was deemed to have been given.

11.04 James claimed that by virtue of these provisions he had deemed permission for the use of his land as a caravan site without restriction. The authority maintained, however, than an express planning permission for a restricted number of caravans had previously been granted, so that James could not claim the benefit for any larger number. James thereupon contended, but unsuccessfully, that since the express planning permission had not been given within two months of the application, the permission was, therefore, null and void. In his judgment, which examined the effect of the requirement to give notice of the decision within the prescribed period, Lord Denning MR said:

> The grant or refusal of permission after two months is not void, but at most voidable. If a planning authority allow more than two months to go by, and then *give* permission, with or without conditions, the permission is good. At any rate it is good, if it is accepted and acted upon. Or if an appeal is made against it, for it is then too late to avoid it. If a planning authority allow more than two months to go by, and then *refuse* permission, the party aggrieved can appeal against the refusal. Alternatively he can treat the failure to determine within two months as a refusal and appeal on that ground. If he does not appeal, he cannot afterwards say that the grant or refusal was bad because it was made after the two months.

11.05 The two-month period mentioned by Lord Denning in the *James* case has now been reduced to the eight weeks mentioned earlier. It is a decision of some importance. Unless the applicant has appealed against non-determination of the planning application, it enables the local planning authority to grant a valid planning permission after the eight-week period has expired; but it also gave the applicant the option of either implementing the permission or appealing against any conditions which it might contain. If planning permission is refused after the eight-week period, the applicant may appeal against the refusal. If no decision has been given by the end of the period of eight weeks, the applicant can appeal against non-determination of his application under s 78 of the 1990 Act. If he does so, this deprives the authority of the power to take a decision upon it.

Local planning authorities are determining about 65 per cent of applications for planning permission within the statutory eight-week period. One of many reasons why they fail to determine more within that period is the obligation placed upon them to consult with or notify others with regard to different kinds of application. **11.06**

When a local planning authority fails to determine an application for planning permission within the prescribed period of eight weeks, the applicant may appeal to the Secretary of State against non-determination. The general position is that once the appeal has been made, the local planning authority loses jurisdiction to determine the application, despite the fact that the authority might subsequently be in a position to do so itself. **11.07**

Section 50 of the Planning and Compulsory Purchase Act 2004 will, when implemented, make a limited amendment to this position by inserting a new section 78A in the 1990 Act. The purpose of this new section is to allow a short additional period of time (which is to be prescribed by development order) in which the local planning authority can still issue a decision even though an appeal against non-determination has been made. During that short period following the lodging of the appeal, a local planning authority and the Secretary of State both have jurisdiction to determine the application. If the local planning authority refuses planning permission, the appeal against non-determination becomes an appeal against refusal. In such a case the Secretary of State must give the appellant the opportunity to raise the grounds of appeal and to change any option he has chosen relating to the procedure on appeal. If the authority grants permission subject to conditions, the applicant may proceed with the appeal against the grant of planning permission subject to conditions, revise the grounds of appeal and change his options as to the appeal procedure. **11.08**

Section 50 also provides for a similar provision to be inserted as section 20A in the LBCA Act 1990. **11.09**

B. POWER TO DECLINE TO DETERMINE APPLICATIONS

Before the Planning and Compensation Act 1991, a local planning authority could not refuse to determine an application for planning permission. Every application had to be considered on its merits, despite the fact that the merits may have already been considered and rejected on a previous application made for the same or similar development. It was thought that by making repeat applications for the same development, developers were sometimes able to wear down the resistance of local planning authorities and neighbours to the development, so that planning permission for it would eventually be granted. **11.10**

Under a change made by the 1991 Act, a new s 70A was inserted into the 1990 Act to provide that a local planning authority may decline to determine an application for planning permission for the development of any land if: **11.11**

(a) within a period of two years ending with the date on which the application is received by the authority, the Secretary of State had refused a similar application referred to him under s 77; or had dismissed an appeal against the refusal of a similar application; and

(b) in the opinion of the authority there has been no significant change since the refusal or, as the case may be, dismissal mentioned in paragraph (a) in the development plan, so far as material to the application, or in any other material considerations.

11.12 For the purposes of this provision, an application for planning permission for the development of land was only to be taken to be similar to a later application if the development and the land to which the application relates are, in the opinion of the local planning authority, the same or substantially the same.

11.13 Under s 70A no appeal could be made to the Secretary of State if the local planning authority had given notice to the applicant that it has declined to determine an application under the provisions of this section. Judicial review would appear to be the only method of challenge.

11.14 The power of a local planning authority under the 1990 Act to decline to determine an application for planning permission will be greatly extended by section 43 of the Planning and Compulsory Purchase Act 2004.

11.15 When fully implemented, that section will substitute in the 1990 Act a new section 70A for the old. It retains the powers given to local planning authorities by the old section, but in addition it extends the power of authorities to decline to determine an application for planning permission in those cases where in the past two years the authority have refused more than one similar application and there has been no appeal to the Secretary of State against any refusal. The provisions will allow an authority to decline to determine an application if they think that it is similar to another application which has not been finally determined either by the authority or by the Secretary of State on appeal, and the time within which an appeal could be made to the Secretary of State (six months) has not expired. Similar provisions to those of this new section are made applicable to applications for listed building consent and conservation area consent (by a new section 81A inserted in the LBCA Act 1990); the provisions apply also to applications for the prior approval of the local planning authority for development which is permitted by the General Permitted Development Order.

11.16 A decision of the Scottish Court of Session in *Noble Organisation Ltd v Falkirk District Council* 1994 SLT 100 was the first to consider the power given to local planning authorities to decline to determine an application for planning permission. Although the case was concerned with the Town and Country Planning (Scotland) Act 1992, s 26A, the provisions of s 70A of the 1990 Act are identical.

11.17 In the Scottish case an application had been made to change the use of vacant shop premises to an amusement centre with ancillary retail sales. Following the refusal of permission by the local planning authority and on appeal by the Secretary of State, the petitioners submitted a second application for change of use to an amusement centre/snack bar with exclusive retail sales area, claiming that it went a substantial way to meet some of the objections made to the first application. In judicial review proceedings the petitioners sought to have the decision by the authority to decline to determine the second application quashed on the ground that the authority had acted unreasonably, or *ultra vires*. Rejecting the petition, the Court of Session held that on the facts and having regard to all relevant considerations, including a ministerial circular on the operation of the new provision, the second application was similar to the first and that the amendments made to the second were merely cosmetic.

The Court emphasised that the application of the section might involve a two-stage process. First, the local planning authority had to make a judgment on a matter of fact as to whether or not the second application was the same or substantially the same as the first application. Then, if the answer to that was that the second application was the same or substantially the same, the authority had a discretion to decide whether they should decline to determine the application at all, or alternatively, deal with it on its merits as an application for planning permission. **11.18**

C. PUBLICITY FOR PLANNING APPLICATIONS

Prior to the Planning and Compensation Act 1991, publicity for planning applications was limited to a number of special situations, such as applications described as 'bad neighbour' development. There was no general duty placed on local planning authorities to give publicity to an application for planning permission, the matter being regarded as being purely a matter between the applicant and the local planning authority as guardian of the public interest. Some local planning authorities, however, adopted a policy of consulting with third parties such as neighbours where, in the opinion of the authority, the proposed development would be likely to affect them adversely. There was no statutory requirement that this should be done, but was regarded by many a local planning authority as a feature of good administration. **11.19**

If a local planning authority had a policy of notifying third parties of an application, the failure to do so did not give rise to any legal consequence. A complaint might be made, however, to a Local Commissioner (the Local Government Ombudsman), who has held that an authority's failure to comply with their own policy in this regard amounted to maladministration. If it could be shown that the complainant had suffered injustice as a result of that maladministration, the report of the Local Government Ombudsman could result in a remedy being provided by the local planning authority. Sometimes this leads to an authority making a payment to the complainant which reflected the depreciation in the value of his property caused by the development carried out. **11.20**

In Scotland there had been for many years a formal system of neighbour notification of all planning applications. The responsibility for notification was on the applicant, who had to serve, on any party holding a notifiable interest in neighbouring land, a copy of the application, together with a notice stating that the plans or drawings relating thereto may be inspected in the planning register or other specified place. **11.21**

The position in England and Wales was radically altered as a result of the Planning and Compensation Act 1991. By the 1991 Act, the Secretary of State was given power in a new s 65 of the 1990 Act to make provision by development order requiring notice to be given of any application for planning permission. At the same time, the Government expressed a wish to extend publicity requirements to cover all types of application. This is now achieved in the General Development Procedure Order, under which responsibility for publicising **11.22** planning applications is imposed on the local planning authority. The relevant provisions are to be found in Art 8 of the Order, which provides:

> An application for planning permission shall be publicised by the local planning authority to which the application is made in the manner prescribed by this article.

11.23 The article requires three different levels of publicity according to the nature of the development applied for, namely, development of a kind specified in Art 8 (called para 2 applications), major development, and other development not falling under either of these two heads.

Development specified in article 8 (paragraph 2 applications)

11.24 Article 8(2) of the Order provides that in the case of an application for planning permission for development which:

(a) is the subject of an application falling within Sch 1 or 2 to the Town and Country Planning (Environmental Impact Assessment) (England and Wales) Regulations 1999,
(b) does not accord with the provisions of the development plan in force in the area in which the land to which the application relates is situated, or
(c) would affect a right of way to which Part III of the Wildlife and Countryside Act 1981 applies,

the publicity given to the application shall be by giving notice (in the form set out in Sch 3 to the Order) by posting a site notice in at least one place on or near the land to which the application relates for not less than 21 days, *and* by publishing the notice in a newspaper circulating in the locality in which the land to which the application relates is situated.

Major development

11.25 Under Art 8(4) of the Order, in the case of an application for planning permission other than a para 2 application (see 10.3.1), if the development proposed is major development the application shall be publicised by giving notice (in the form set out in Sch 3 to the Order) by posting a site notice in at least one place on or near the land to which the application relates for not less than 21 days, *or* by serving the notice on any owner or occupier of any land adjoining the land to which the application relates. In addition to the above alternatives, a notice must also be published in a newspaper circulating in the locality in which the land to which the application relates is situated.

11.26 Article 8 defines 'major' development as development involving any one or more of the following:

(a) the winning and working of minerals or the use of land for mineral working deposits;
(b) waste development;
(c) the provision of dwellinghouses where—
  (i) the number of dwellinghouses to be provided is ten or more; or
  (ii) the development is to be carried out on site having an area of 0.5 hectare or more and it is not known whether the development falls within paragraph (c)(i);
(d) the provision of a building or buildings where the floor space to be created by the development is 1,000 square metres or more; or
(e) development carried out on a site having an area of 1 hectare or more.

As indicated earlier, the General Development Procedure Order no longer contains a list of 11.27 developments classified as 'bad neighbour'. It is considered, however, that applications for certain types of development may warrant the wider publicity now accorded to 'major development' as described above.

In Circular 15/92, 'Publicity for Planning Applications', the Secretary of State expressed the 11.28 view that it is the responsibility of local planning authorities to decide, on a case-by-case basis, whether developments falling outside the categories of major development listed above, were likely to create wider concern and require publicity beyond the minima set out in the Order (see 11.29). The Circular then lists types of development where a newspaper advertisement may be required in addition to either a site notice or neighbour notification namely development:

(a) affecting nearby property by causing noise, smell, vibration, dust or other nuisance;
(b) attracting crowds, traffic and noise into a generally quiet area;
(c) causing activity and noise during unsocial hours;
(d) introducing significant change, for example, particularly tall buildings;
(e) resulting in serious reduction or loss of light or privacy beyond adjacent properties;
(f) affecting the setting of an ancient monument or archaeological site;
(g) affecting trees subject to tree preservation orders.

Other development

In the case of development not falling within 11.24 or 11.25 above, Art 8(5) of the Order 11.29 provides that the application for planning permission shall be published by giving notice (in the form set out in Sch 3 to the Order) by posting a site notice in at least one place on or near the land to which the application relates for not less than 21 days, *or* serving the notice on any owner or occupier of any land adjoining the land to which the application relates.

Summary

The following is a summary of the above publicity requirements for planning applications 11.30 under the provisions of Art 8.

Nature of development	*Publicity required*
Development where application accompanied by an environmental statement Development involving a departure from the development plan Development affecting a public right of way	Advertisement in a local newspaper *and* site notice
Major development	Advertisement in local newspaper *and* either site notice *or* neighbour notification
Minor development	Site notice or neighbour notification

It should be noted that in all cases where a site notice is required or given, Art 8 provides that 11.31

the local planning authority are not to be treated as having failed to comply with that requirement if the notice is, without fault or intention of the authority, removed, obscured or defaced before the period of 21 days has elapsed, if the authority have taken reasonable steps for its protection and, if need be, replacement.

11.32 Furthermore, Art 8 is applied by the Order to any appeal made to the Secretary of State under s 78 of the 1990 Act as it applies to any application for planning permission. Article 19 of the Order also provides that the local planning authority should take into account any representations made within 21 days from the date notice of the application is given or 14 days from the date any advertisement appeared in a local newspaper, and that the local planning authority shall not determine an application for planning permission until the expiration of those periods.

11.33 One criticism of the provisions relating to publicity for applications for planning permission is that no obligation is placed on a local planning authority to publicise:

(a) changes to applications made after they have been submitted and accepted by the authority;
(b) applications to discharge or amend a condition imposed in a permission previously granted; or
(c) applications made for the approval of reserved matters following the grant of outline planning permission.

11.34 Circular 15/92 recognises that in such cases the local planning authority has discretion to decide whether further publicity is desirable, and they should take into account the following considerations:

(a) Were objections or reservations raised at an earlier stage substantial and, in the view of the local authority enough to justify further publicity?
(b) Are the proposed changes significant?
(c) Did earlier views cover the matters now under consideration?
(d) Are the matters now under consideration likely to be of concern to parties not previously notified?

In addition, it should be noted that the publicity requirements do not apply where a local planning authority decides to issue an enforcement notice on an owner or occupier of land, despite the fact that if the person appeals against the notice and pays the appropriate fee, he is deemed to have made an application for planning permission for the development being enforced against.

11.35 It seems that the failure to comply with art. 8 could be a sufficient reason for the courts to quash a grant of planning permission, so long as the claimant for relief could show that he had been substantially prejudiced by the failure, and his application was made timely (see *R (Seamus Gavin) v London Borough of Haringey and Wolseley Centres Ltd* [2003] EWHC 2591 (Admin).

D. NOTIFICATION REQUIREMENTS

Development affecting highways

Under Article 15 of the General Development Procedure Order, the local planning authority is required to notify the Secretary of State of applications for planning permission for development which consists of or includes the formation, laying out or alteration or a means of access to certain trunk roads or special roads or the development of land within 67 metres of certain roads. The procedure enables the Secretary of State to consider whether to give a direction under the Order restricting the power of the local planning authority to grant planning permission for the development. **11.36**

Parish and community councils

Under para 8 of Sch 1 to the 1990 Act, a local planning authority must, if requested to do so by the council of any parish or community situated in their area, notify the council of any relevant planning application and any alteration to that application which has been accepted by the authority. For this purpose a relevant planning application includes not only an application for planning permission, but an application for approval of any reserved matter under an outline planning permission. **11.37**

Under these provisions a parish or community council may ask the local planning authority to notify it of all applications for planning permission or for a particular category, such as applications for industrial development. In practice, however, it is not uncommon for local planning authorities to whom a request has been made to be notified of a particular category of application, to notify the parish or community council without restriction to any particular category of development. This is no doubt done to avoid the possibility that a mistake might otherwise be made. Further provisions on this matter are made in Art 13 of the General Development Procedure Order. **11.38**

Development affecting the character or appearance of a conservation area

Under s 73(1) of the Planning (Listed Buildings and Conservation Areas) Act 1990, where an application for planning permission is made to a local planning authority and the development would, in the opinion of the authority, affect the character or appearance of a conservation area, the authority must publish in a local newspaper circulating in the locality in which the land is situated, and display on or near the land for not less than seven days, a notice indicating the nature of the development in question and naming a place where a copy of the application can be seen. **11.39**

Here, the local planning authority may have to take two independent decisions. First, to decide if the proposed development would, if granted, affect the character or appearance of a conservation area. If so, the application must be given publicity. Secondly, and after publicity has been given to the application and any representations received taken into account, to decide whether planning permission should be granted. **11.40**

Development affecting the setting of a listed building

11.41 Under s 66(1) of the Planning (Listed Buildings and Conservation Areas) Act 1990, the local planning authority, in considering whether to grant planning permission for development which affects a listed building or its setting, are required to have regard to the desirability of preserving the building or its setting or any features of special architectural or historic interest which it possesses.

11.42 Under s 67 of that Act, if the local planning authority are of the opinion that the development would affect the setting of a listed building, they must publish in a local newspaper circulating in the locality in which the land is situated and for not less than seven days display on or near the land, a notice indicating the nature of the development in question and naming a place where a copy of the application can be seen.

Applications relating to county matters

11.43 Under the General Development Procedure Order, a county planning authority must, in relation to a county matter, give the district planning authority an opportunity to make recommendations as to how the county should determine applications for planning permission, applications for certificates of lawfulness of existing use or development, certificates of lawfulness of proposed use or development and the approval of reserved matters.

Duplication of publicity and notice requirements

11.44 The provisions of Art 8 of the General Development Procedure Order, referred to earlier, may result in a degree of overlapping or duplication with other statutory requirements, or indeed within the article itself. For example, 'major' development may also require an environmental assessment, and the article applies different publicity requirements to each. Again, the publicity for development which is not specified within Art 8(2) (para 2 applications) and is not major development may be different from the publicity required under the Planning (Listed Buildings and Conservation Areas) Act 1990 in respect of applications for development affecting the character or appearance of a conservation area or the setting of a listed building. Clearly, in order to be within the law, the more demanding of the publicity requirements should be followed. Conversely, in the case of 'twin-tracking', it is not necessary to advertise the two applications separately, so long as they are made simultaneously, and the publicity should make it clear that there are two applications. If not made simultaneously, both applications will need to be separately published.

E. CONSULTATION

11.45 The provisions of Art 10 of the General Development Procedure Order allow for the views of various specialist bodies to be obtained on particular types of development. It is an important provision which provides that, before granting planning permission for certain specified types of development, a local planning authority should consult with named authorities or persons. For example, where the development would involve the manufacture, processing, keeping or use of a hazardous substance likely to lead to a notifiable quantity of such substance, the authority are required to consult with the Health and Safety Executive. So, for example, in a case involving a proposal to develop the site of the former Staveley Central Station for residential purposes, the Secretary of State, in dismissing an appeal against the refusal of the local planning authority to grant planning permission, had regard to the view of the Health and Safety Executive that the potential hazards arising from the proximity of the site to land presently being used for the manufacture and storage of highly flammable liquids precluded the use of the site for housing.

Of more general application is the requirement to consult with the local highway authority where the development involves the formation, laying out or alteration of any means of access to a highway; with the Coal Authority where the development consists of a building or pipeline in an area of coal working notified by the authority to the local planning authority; and with the Minister of Agriculture, Fisheries and Food where the development is not development for agricultural purposes and is not in accordance with the provisions of the development plan and would involve the loss of not less than 20 hectares of grades 1, 2 or 3a agricultural land. According to a written answer to a Parliamentary question in the House of Commons in January 1992, the Ministry of Agriculture, Fisheries and Food objected to only 26 planning applications in 1990, as opposed to 489 in 1981. More recently, a study carried out by the Council for the Preservation of Rural England has shown that between 1985 and 1995 the Ministry was consulted on development proposals involving a total area of 150,730 hectares. The Ministry objected to proposals covering 13,795 hectares. **11.46**

It should also be noted that under this article the Secretary of State may give a direction to a local planning authority requiring them to consult with any person or body named in the direction. Where consultation is required, the consultee must be given at least 14 days' notice to make representations, which must be taken into account by the local planning authority before they determine the application. **11.47**

Although the provisions of Art 10 are statutory requirements, local planning authorities are advised in Appendix B of Circular 9/95 to consider nonstatutory consultation in certain other cases. The Circular also advises statutory undertakers proposing to exercise permitted development rights, to inform the local planning authority of their intention to do so and for the authority to consider advertising the proposal. **11.48**

Consultation responses

Because no statutory time scale is imposed on bodies required to be consulted within which responses are to be made, much of the delay in determining planning applications has been laid at the door of statutory consultees, some of whom are statutory bodies, others nonstatutory. This is now to be changed. **11.49**

Section 54 of the Planning and Compulsory Purchase Act 2004, when fully implemented, will introduce a new requirement that those persons or bodies which are required to be consulted by the Secretary of State or local planning authority (as the case may be) before the grant of any planning permission, approval or consent required under the Planning Acts, must respond to consultation request within a prescribed period. The new provision will apply also to consultation by any person prior to an application for permission approval or **11.50** consent. The provision will enable the Secretary of State to prescribe, by development order, the consultation requirements which will trigger the duty to respond, and the period within which each statutory consultee must reply. It allows the Secretary of State to prescribe: the procedures to be followed; the information to be provided by the consultee; and the requirements of the substantive response which the provisions require the consultee to provide. It is expected that the provisions will be made to apply to anyone who is at present a statutory consultee by virtue of arts. 10 and 12 (including directions under artical 10(3) of the Town and Country Planning (General Development Procedure) Order 1995; and Part 24 of the Town and Country Planning (General Permitted Development Order) 1995 (consultation in respect of prior approval applications for planning permission).

11.51 Based on the existing statutory provisions, it may be expected to apply to the following statutory consultees.

British Waterways
Coal Authority
County Planning Authorities
DCMS
District Planning Authorities
English Heritage
English Nature
Environmental Agency
Garden History Society
Health and Safety Executive
Highways Agency
Local Highway Authorities
Local Planning Authorities
Rail Network Operators
Regional Development Agencies
Sport England
Theatres Trust
Toll Road Concessionaries

These provisions will not change the right of bodies like parish councils and the national amenity societies to be notified of planning applications.

11.52 The Government are proposing that the deadline for response be 21 days after the date on which the statutory consultee receives the consultation. This period can be extended by agreement between both parties.

11.53 The new provision will allow the Secretary of State, by development order to require statutory consultees to report to him on their compliance with the duty to respond within the prescribed period and to prescribe the form and content of the report and the times when the report must be made.

11.54 Consultees will also be required to provide an annual report to the Secretary of State. They will be required to provide the number of consultation requests received, the number which were responded to with the prescribed period, and (if appropriate) a summary of reasons why the statutory deadline has not been met in all cases.

F. DEVELOPMENT NOT IN ACCORDANCE WITH THE PROVISIONS OF THE DEVELOPMENT PLAN

Section 74(1)(b) of the 1990 Act authorises the local planning authority, in such cases and subject to such conditions as may be prescribed by a development order, or by directions given by the Secretary of State thereunder, to grant planning permission which does not accord with the provisions of the development plan. In addition Art 17 of the General Development Procedure Order authorises local planning authorities to grant permission for development not in accordance with the development plan in such cases and subject to such conditions as may be prescribed by directions given by the Secretary of State. The relevant directions for England are the Town and Country Planning (Development Plans and Consultation) (Departures) Directions 1999, which were issued as Annex 1 to Circular 07/99. **11.55**

The new Directions apply to 'departure applications', that is an application for planning permission for development which does not accord with one or more provisions of the development plan in force in the area in which the application site is situated. **11.56**

Where a departure application which a local planning authority do not propose to refuse is for— **11.57**

(a) development which consists of or includes the provision of—
  (i) more than 150 houses or flats; or
  (ii) more than 5,000 square metres of gross retail, leisure, office or mixed commercial floor space;
(b) development of land belonging to a planning authority by that authority or any other party, or for the development of any land by such an authority, whether alone or jointly with any other person; or
(c) any other development which, by reason of its scale or nature or the location of the land, would significantly prejudice the implementation of the development plan's policies and proposals,

the authority shall send to the Secretary of State—

(i) a copy of the application (including copies of any accompanying plans and drawings);
(ii) a copy of the requisite notice;
(iii) a copy of any representations made to the authority in respect of the application;
(iv) a copy of any report on the application prepared by an officer of the authority;
(v) unless contained in a report supplied pursuant to sub-paragraph (iv), a statement of the material considerations which the authority consider indicate otherwise for the purposes of s 38(6) of the Town and Country Planning Act 1990;
(vi) copies of any statement of any views expressed on the application by a government department, another local planning authority or a parish council.

Annex 2 of the Circular provides policy guidance on the Directions. In particular, it advises that where applications are referred under para (c) above, only significant departures should be notified. The Circular then gives examples of the types of development proposed which might have the effect described in para (c). **11.58**

11.59 After following the above procedure, and subject only to the Secretary of State's call-in power, the local planning authority are free to grant planning permission after the expiration of a period of 21 days, beginning with the date notified to the local planning authority by the Secretary of State as the date of receipt of the documents which are required to be sent to him by the authority ((i)–(vi) above) and after considering any objections received.

11.60 It should, of course, be noted that departure applications are subject (like all applications) to the statutory publicity required under Art 8 of the General Development Procedure Order (see 10.3).

11.61 An important question raised in the past is the precise consequences that flow from a failure to comply with the Directions. Does a failure to do so render the subsequent grant of planning permission void? In an old case, *Gregory v Camden LBC* [1966] 1 WLR 899, it was held that a neighbour did not possess the necessary standing to challenge a grant of planning permission for development which involved a departure from the development plan, but had been granted without compliance with the procedure required by the Direction. In a more recent case, *R v St Edmundsbury BC, ex p Investors in Industry Commercial Properties Ltd* [1985] 1 WLR 1168, an application was made to the High Court for judicial review to quash outline planning permission granted to J. Sainsbury plc for the erection of a supermarket on land in Bury St Edmunds town centre. One of the many grounds for challenge alleged that there had been a defect in the statutory advertisement required by the then Town and Country Planning (Development Plans) (England) Direction 1981, in that it had not included any reference to the fact that the application conflicted with the development plan. It was contended by the applicants for judicial review that the requirements of the Direction were mandatory and a condition precedent to the grant of a valid planning permission. Rejecting that contention, Stocker J thought that to construe the Direction as mandatory would involve difficulties likely to lead to practical and commercial problems. He had no doubt that the words 'in the opinion of the local planning authority' did require that proper consideration be given to the problem, but it seemed to him inappropriate for a Direction, the breach of which involved the proposition that planning permission granted was void, should be regarded as mandatory since this might involve investigating the committee's opinion and whether such opinion was based upon full and proper consideration. The words themselves suggest that a directive and procedural order, rather than a mandatory one, arose.

11.62 After expressing the view that the absence of information in the statutory advertisement had had no effect because a wide section of the public were aware that the development would involve a departure from the town map, Stocker J went on to say that if he was wrong in his conclusion that the direction was a procedural one, and not mandatory involving a condition precedent, he would, in the exercise of discretion, not have made an order for judicial review on this ground.

11.63 The approach of Stocker J in *R v St Edmundsbury BC* was followed later by Macpherson J in *R v Carlisle City Council, ex p Cumbrian Co-operative Society Ltd* [1986] JPL 206, where it was held that a failure to comply with the Direction did not invalidate the grant of a deemed planning permission by the local planning authority for development of a superstore on a site owned by the authority.

G. AMENDMENT OF APPLICATIONS

It is common practice for an application for planning permission to be amended by agreement following negotiations between the applicant and the authority's planning officer. In *Britannia (Cheltenham) Ltd v Secretary of State for the Environment and Tewkesbury* [1979] JPL 534 it was recognised that it was competent for the applicants and planning authority to agree a variation of an application at any time up to the determination of the application. 'To take any other view', it was said, 'would fly in the face of everyday practice and make the planning machine even more complicated than it was.' In *British Telecommunications plc v Gloucester CC* [2001] EWHC Admin 1001, the limitations on this practice were considered. In the view of the High Court, where the change is substantial the procedure cannot be used to sidestep the rights of third parties, or in circumstances where the statutory requirements (eg, for consultation) have not been complied with. **11.64**

12

DETERMINATIONS OF APPLICATIONS FOR PLANNING PERMISSION

A. DELEGATION

Under s 101 of the Local Government Act 1972, a local authority may arrange for the discharge of any of its functions by a committee, a subcommittee, an officer of the authority, or by any other local authority. **12.01**

In *R v Secretary of State for the Environment, ex p Hillingdon LBC* [1986] 1 WLR 807, it was held that a committee meant more than one person, so that a local authority has no power to delegate any of their functions to any individual member of the authority. To overcome this difficulty, however, many local planning authorities have now made delegation arrangements authorising an officer of the Council (such as the chief planning officer) to exercise functions on the Council's behalf but only after consultation with a particular member of **12.02** the Council (such as the Chairman of the Planning Committee). The inability of a Chairman of a Council to act under delegated power had an unusual impact ten years later in the case of *R v Hillingdon LBC, ex p Denham* (CO/1557/96) where, on it being shown that two enforcement notices had been issued on the instructions of the Chairman of the appropriate Committee, the High Court granted leave some 23 years after the date they had been issued to move for judicial revision of the two notices. The case, however, never went to trial, the applicant and the Council arriving at a compromise solution which disposed of the planning issues.

12.03 Every local planning authority has made arrangements for their planning functions to be delegated to a committee. Many local planning authorities have also made arrangements for the delegation of functions to subcommittees. Delegation to subcommittees may be a useful exercise where it is desired to divide the geographical area of an authority into sub-areas, with planning functions in respect of each sub-area being exercised by a separate subcommittee.

12.04 Most local planning authorities have also made arrangements for the discharge of many of their functions by an officer of the authority. Current statistics show that 87 per cent of all planning decisions are determined by officers under schemes of delegation, without reference to a committee. The actual scope of an officer's delegated powers will, like all delegated arrangements, depend upon the terms of the particular scheme of delegation. Frequently those arrangements give an officer power to decide applications for planning permission which do not conflict with the development plan or other planning policies of the authority. In many cases the scale or size of the development proposed may also be relevant to whether the delegation of authority is available.

12.05 In *R (Carlton Conway) v London Borough of Harrow* ([2002] JPL 1216) the Court of Appeal quashed the decision of the authority's Chief Planning Officer to use his delegated power to grant planning permission for a residential extension. The terms of delegation provided that the officer could determine all applications other than those where approval of the development is recommended and written objections have been received, except where the proposals do not conflict with agreed policies, standards and guidelines. It was claimed that the development proposed did conflict with the authority's agreed policies and should therefore have been decided by the appropriate committee of the authority. The Court of Appeal agreed, Dill LJ stating 'When [as here] there are real issues as to the meaning of planning policies and as to their application to the facts of the case, reference to the appropriate committee was required.'

12.06 In cases where planning functions are not delegated to an officer but are exercised by a committee or a subcommittee of the authority, the role of officers will be to ensure that all considerations material to the decision to be made are brought to the attention of the committee or subcommittee together with (in most cases) a recommendation as to how the application should be dealt with. The Local Government Ombudsman has rightly advised local authorities that any report to a committee should provide all the material that members need to make an informed decision. The report should be in clear terms and should cover as necessary the relevant law and policy; sufficient and accurate information to enable members to understand the issues to be considered or determined; a summary of the outcome of any consultation or seeking of advice; a reference to all the considerations which have to be taken into account; the identification of possible approaches which could be adopted; the reasons for any recommendations; and an analysis of any financial or other significant implications which are relevant. The question of the material the Committee should have available to it before reaching its decision has been subject to a number of judicial decisions. In *Oxton Farms v Selby District Council* (18 April 1997) Pill LJ said:

> It is important that those who make determinations under the planning acts are familiar with sections 70(2) and 54A of the 1990 Act and apply the test imposed by Parliament. It follows that a planning officer reporting to and advising council members who are to make a relevant decision must keep the test in mind in the information and advice he provides and in the manner in which he provides it.
>
> Clear mindedness and clarity of expression are obviously important. However that is not to say that a report is to be construed as if it were a statute or that defects of presentation can often render a decision made following its submission to the council liable to be quashed. The overall fairness of the report, in the context of the statutory test, must be considered.
>
> It has also to be borne in mind that there is usually further opportunity for advice and debate at the relevant council meeting and that the members themselves can be expected to acquire a working knowledge of the statutory test.

Judge LJ agreed, and he added these observations: **12.07**

> The report by a planning officer to his committee is not and is not intended to provide a learned disquisition of relevant legal principles or to repeat each and every detail of the relevant facts to members of the committee who are responsible for the decision and who are entitled to use their local knowledge to reach it. The report is therefore not susceptible to textual analysis appropriate to the construction of a statute or the directions provided by a judge when summing a case up to the jury.

The content of an officer's report was again considered in *R v Mendip DC* [2000] JPL 810, **12.08**
where Sullivan J said:

> Whilst planning officers' reports should not be equated with inspectors' decision letters, it is well established that, in construing the latter, it has to be remembered that they are addressed to the parties who will be well aware of the issues that have been raised in the appeal. They are thus addressed to a knowledgeable readership and the adequacy of their reasoning must be considered against that background. That approach applies with particular force to a planning officer's report to a committee. Its purpose is not to decide the issue, but to inform the members of the relevant considerations relating to the application. It is not addressed to the world at large but to council members who, by virtue of that membership, may be expected to have substantial local and background knowledge. There would be no point in a planning officer's report setting out in great detail background material, for example, in respect of local topography, development planning policies or matters of planning history if the members were only too familiar with that material. Part of a planning officer's expert function in reporting to the committee must be to make an assessment of how much information needs to be included in his or her report in order to avoid burdening a busy committee with excessive and unnecssary detail.

The need for officers' reports to include all information on relevant considerations relating **12.09**
to the application is the General Development Procedure Order. Article 22 of the Order requires that where a local planning authority gives notice of a decision or determination of an application for planning permission (or approval of reserved matters) and the application

is refused or granted, the authority must specify, in addition to stating its full reasons, 'all policies and proposals in the development plan which are relevant to the decision'. In addition, if planning permission is granted subject to conditions, the authority must state clearly and precisely their full reasons for each condition imposed.

12.10 As with the exercise of all delegated power, the actions of the delegatee, acting within the four corners of his power, will bind the delegator. Furthermore, where power to discharge functions has been delegated to another, the donor of the power is usually free to withdraw that power before it has been exercised. Under s 101(4), where a power to discharge a function has been delegated to a committee, a subcommittee or an officer, this does not prevent the authority or the committee (as the case may be) discharging the function themselves. In *R v Yeovil BC, ex p Trustees of Elim Pentecostal Church, Yeovil* (1971) 23 P & CR 39 the Church had made two applications for planning permission. The minutes of the planning committee of the council recorded its decision that 'the town clerk be authorised to approve the application subject to [certain] conditions when evidence of an agreement about the car-parking facilities has been received'. At a subsequent meeting the planning committee, after having heard evidence that the development would be detrimental to the amenities of the area, changed its mind and decided to refuse the application. The applicants thereupon applied for an order of mandamus requiring the authority to issue conditional planning consent for the development, contending that the committee had already committed themselves, and that as all that remained was for the town clerk to issue notices of approval, the council were in no position to change their mind.

12.11 The Queen's Bench Divisional Court held that, on the facts, there was no question of planning permission having been granted at any time before the town clerk had expressed a view with regard to the adequacy of any evidence presented to him. Moreover, the council had delegated the final determination of the application to the town clerk, and unless and until he had made such determination within the authority granted to him, no question of planning permission having been granted arose; and the clerk not having finally determined the matter before the later committee meeting, it was open to the council to change their mind and to withdraw their provisional approval and refuse the application.

12.12 Officers of the local planning authorities also exercise many functions of a magisterial nature, as where they transmit to the applicant the decision made by the local planning authority. In *Norfolk CC v Secretary of State for the Environment* [1973] 1WLR1400, a company made an application for planning permission to build an extension to a factory. The planning committee refused the application. Then, by mistake, the planning officer sent a notice to the applicant saying planning permission had been granted. As soon as the mistake was discovered the council sent a letter to the applicant apologising, together with a proper notice of refusal. The company immediately cancelled, without penalty, an order for new machinery. But it continued to maintain that it had the benefit of a valid planning permission. In order to bring matters to a head, the company commenced development. This enabled the council to serve an enforcement notice against which the company appealed to the Secretary of State. He duly proceeded to quash the notice, so the council appealed to the High Court against that decision. Allowing the appeal, the Court held that the council were entitled to serve the enforcement notice because the officer concerned only had authority to transmit to the applicant the decision of the planning committee. He had no authority himself to make a decision on the planning application so that the notice given by him could not be regarded as a grant of planning permission.

A similar approach was taken in *Attorney-General v Taff-Ely BC* (1981) 42 P & CR 1. The facts were that in 1975, Co-operative Retail Services Ltd (CRS) applied for planning permission to develop land as a superstore. A few months later, Sir Robert McAlpine Ltd (with Tesco stores in mind) applied for planning permission to develop other land for the same purpose just half a mile away from the CRS site. It was clear that only one of the two applications could be granted and that it was the Tesco site that was favoured by the local planning authority. Accordingly they refused planning permission for the CRS site. On the very same day, the authority considered and adopted a recommendation of a subcommittee of their planning committee that planning permission be granted for the development of the Tesco site. A dispute then arose as to the exact status of the subcommittee's decision. CRS took the view that it had merely expressed the authority's preliminary views on the application, prior to discussions taking place between the authority and the Mid-Glamorgan County Council who were the county planning authority for the area. Tesco's agents, however, took the view that the action of the subcommittee constituted a grant of planning permission for the development, and threatened the authority that if they did not issue the grant they would bring an action for mandamus to compel them to do so and for damages for the loss they had suffered. The town clerk then duly issued the grant of planning permission that Tesco had sought. Once this had been done, Tesco proceeded to buy the land for which the permission had been granted. CRS now threatened the authority that it would sue for a declaration that Tesco had not been granted a valid planning permission; whereupon the authority resolved to ratify the earlier action of the town clerk. CRS then did what it had threatened and brought an action for a declaration. The Court of Appeal (1979) 39 P & CR 223 held that on the true construction of the relevant minutes of the planning subcommittee the local planning authority had not resolved to grant planning permission for the development of the Tesco site. Furthermore, since the town clerk could only transmit to the applicant the decision of the local planning authority, the authority could not ratify what was in fact a nullity. On appeal to the House of Lords, the decision of the Court of Appeal was upheld. **12.13**

There was then a rather surprising aftermath. The decision of the House of Lords had left the application for the Tesco site still to be determined. At that stage, the Secretary of State intervened and called in the application for his own decision. Also outstanding was an appeal to the Secretary of State by CRS against the decision of the authority to refuse planning permission for its site. In October 1982, following a local inquiry into both applications, the Secretary of State granted planning permission for the Tesco site, but refused to grant it for the CRS site. **12.14**

That, however, was not the end of the matter. Even before the decision of the Secretary of State was known, Tesco maintained it had suffered loss through the negligence of the clerk in purporting to issue notice of a grant of planning permission when no grant had in fact been made. Tesco maintained that it had bought the land on the strength of what it thought to be a grant of planning permission. If the company were eventually to lose on the planning merits, its loss of development value would be considerable. If it were eventually to win (as it **12.15** did) it would still suffer loss as land purchased with planning permission is plainly more valuable than land with only the chance of permission at some later date. In the ensuing action for damages in the Queen's Bench Division, Beldam J in an unreported decision, held that the clerk had been negligent in issuing the notice, despite the fact that he had been stampeded into doing so by threats that if he did not his ratepayers would be faced with a very large claim for damages.

12.16 The Court went on to hold, however, that the plaintiff could not recover damages for the clerk's negligence, because it had, by its agents, been aware of the circumstances in which the notice had been issued and could not, therefore, be said to be bona fide purchasers of the land for value without notice of the particular circumstances in which the notice to grant planning permission had been issued.

B. ESTOPPEL BY REPRESENTATION

12.17 An issue which bedevilled planning law for many years was the extent to which a representation made by an officer of a local planning authority could bind the authority. The long-established principle was that a public authority could not be stopped from exercising statutory powers by the representations of an officer. From 1967 however, a number of exceptions began to be made to that principle. In *Lever Finance Ltd v Westminster (City) London Borough Council* [1971] IQB 222 Lord Denning MR said:

> I know that there are authorities which say a public authority cannot be estopped . . . from doing its public duty. . . . But those statements must now be taken with considerable reserve. There are many matters which public authorities can now delegate to their officers. If an officer, acting within the scope of his ostensible authority, makes a representation on which another acts, then a public authority may be bound by it, just as much as a private concern would be.

12.18 The judgment of Lord Denning was thereafter taken at its face value, particularly by the Secretary of State in dealing with appeals against enforcement notices. *Any* representation made by an officer within the scope of his ostensible authority was regarded as capable of binding the authority. The doctrine of estoppel was poised to run wild and duly did so. That in turn led to extreme caution by the officers of local planning authorities in giving advice and guidance to prospective applicants for planning permission. Eventually, the judgment of a strong Court of Appeal in *Western Fish Products Ltd v Penwith DC* [1978] JPL 623 was able to limit the situations where representations by officers of an authority might bind the authority.

12.19 The whole basis of estoppel in public law, however, and indeed the extent to which there are exceptions to the general principle that public authorities cannot be estopped from performing their statutory duties was raised again by judgement of the House of Lords in *R v East Sussex CC, ex p Reprotech (Pebsham) Ltd* [2002] JPL 821. The case was concerned, inter alia, with the question of whether a resolution of a committee of the local planning authority to agree to amend a condition subject to which an earlier planning permission had been granted, could be inferred as a determination under s 64 of the Town and Country Planning Act 1990 (a section now replaced by s 192). The Court of Appeal considered it could be. The

House of Lords thought otherwise, holding that it was impossible to say that a conditional resolution to grant planning permission (under s 73 of the Act) which itself did not bind the authority, could by implication constitute a binding determination under s 64.

On the general question of estoppel in public law, Lord Hoffmann said: **12.20**

> I think that it is unhelpful to introduce private law concepts of estoppel into planning law. As Lord Scarman pointed out in *Newbury DC v Secretary of State for the Environment* [1981] 578, 616, estoppels bind individuals on the ground that it would be unconscionable for them to deny what they have represented or agreed. But these concepts of private law should not be extended into 'the public law of planning control, which binds everyone'.

Later, he said:

> It is true that in early cases . . . Lord Denning MR used the language of estoppel in relation to planning law. At that time the public law concepts of abuse of power and legitimate expectation were very undeveloped and no doubt the analogy of estoppel seemed useful. In the *Western Fish* the Court of Appeal tried its best to reconcile these invocations of estoppel with the general principle that a public authority cannot be estopped from exercising a statutory discretion or performing a public duty. But the results did not give universal satisfaction . . . *It seems to me that in this area, public law has already absorbed whatever is useful from the moral values which underlie the private law concept of estoppel and the time has come for it to stand upon its own two feet.* (author's emphasis)

Commenting upon the judgment of the House of Lords in the *Reprotech* case, Richards J in **12.21**
Coghurst Wood Leisure Park Limited v Secretary of State for Transport, Local Government and the Regions [2002] EWHC 1091 (Admin) said:

> It is obvious that the judgments in Powergen and Reprotech mark an important change in direction in this area of planning law. Looked at together, they emphasise not just the need to apply public law *concepts* rather than private law *concepts* but also the importance attached in public law to a statutory body's powers and duties and to the wider public interest. It cannot be assumed that exceptions previously found to exist will still apply. Substantial reappraisal is required.

Again, in Wandsworth London Borough Council & Secretary of State for Transport Local Government and the Regions and BT Cellnet, the High Court held that following the approach of the House of Lords in Reprotech there would now be no statutory jurisdiction to allow a planning appeal simply on the grounds of estoppel. [*NB*] Case ref is [2003] EWHC 622

Whatever the ramifications may be of the House of Lords decision in *Reprotech*, the giving of **12.22**
misleading advice may nevertheless be a ground for making a complaint to the Local Government Ombudsman. In one report (No 627/H/80) the planning officer of a local planning authority had told a prospective purchaser of land during discussions that he could see no objection to the erection of a two-storey building on the land. The prospective purchaser acted on that advice and completed the purchase. Then, the planning officer, contrary to his earlier advice, recommended to the authority that planning permission be granted only for a bungalow. After a finding by the Local Government Ombudsman of injustice suffered as a result of maladministration, the local planning authority made an *ex gratia* payment of £2,000 to the complainant to compensate him for his loss.

12.23 Concurrently with the demise of estoppel as a principle to be applied in planning law by the judgement of the House of Lords in the *Reprotech* case, attention has turned to the question of whether another principle of public law, namely that of legitimate expectation can be used to achieve the same result. A legitimate expectation may be said to occur where a public body leads someone to believe that a certain practice or a particular situation exists or may come about. As was said in the public law case of *CSSU v Minister for the Civil Service* [1985] Ac 374, a legitimate expectation may arise 'either from an express premise given on behalf of a public authority or from the existence of a regular practice which the claimant can reasonably expect to continue'.

12.24 The approach taken by the courts as expressed in *Coghurst Wood Leisure v Secretary of State* [2003] JPL 206 is to accept that whilst situations may occur in planning law where the principle of legitimate expectation might apply it is likely to be very rare. In *Henry Boot Homes Ltd v Bassetlaw District Council* [2003] JPL 1030, it was unsuccessfully claimed that the local planning authority, in approving an application for the approval of reserved matters and subsequently, had conducted itself in such as way as to give rise to a legitimate expectation on the part of the developers that it would not be prevented from developing the site pursuant to the outline planning permission, despite the fact that it had not complied with the relevant conditions in the outline permission prior to the commencement of operations. In effect, what the claimants were seeking was a non-statutory variation of a condition. Giving judgement against them, Keane L J said:

> The interests of third parties and the public in such matters also greatly reduce the potential for a legitimate expectation, such as is contended for in the present appeal, to arise. One of the reasons is that it is difficult to see how a legitimate expectation, said to derive from the conduct of the local authority, could operate so as to prevent an interested third party from questioning whether development has validly begun and whether the planning permission is still extant. . . .
>
> Mr Lowe invited us to say that legitimate expectation could never operate so as to enable the developer to begin development validly and effectively in breach of condition. I am not prepared to adopt so absolute a proposition. It is possible that circumstances might arise where it was clear that there was no third party or public interest in the matter and a court might take the view that a legitimate expectation could then arise from the local planning authority's conduct or representations. But, as was said in the *Coghurst Wood* case, one suspects that such cases will be very rare.

12.25 In another recent case, *R (Kabbell Developments Ltd) v Secretary of State* (2004 unreported) the Court of Appeal accepted that once a s 106 obligation had been entered into, the landowners who had entered into it (and their successors) had a legitimate expectation that an application for outline planning permission for residential development (which the s. 106 objection was intended to facilitate) would be granted. The court however, held that in this case if the time for submission of an application for approval of reserved matters had expired, in considering an application under s.73 of the Act for some later date for submission, there was no legitimate expectation that it would be granted. The only legitimate expectation the landowners would have was that the application would be dealt with in accordance with legal principles and the provisions of the Act. In other words, in determining the application for approval of reserved matters, an authority would take into account all material considerations, including any changes in planning policy since that grant of the outline planning permission and the fact that since the grant the developer may have already fulfilled his duty under the s 106 obligation.

In *Cox v First Secretary of State* [2003] EWHC 1290 Admin, the High Court accepted that a greivance as a result of misleading advice given unintentionally could not properly amount to a legitimate expectation such as to warrant a grant of planning permission, though it might well found a justified complaint to the Local Government Ombudsman. **12.26**

Perhaps, however, the courts may be less likely to take such a robust view of the application of legitimate expectations in planning law in requiring persons to be consulted, where there has been a promise to do that, or where it derives from an established practice to do so. **12.27**

C. DETERMINATION OF A PLANNING APPLICATION

Section 70(1) of the 1990 Act provides that where an application is made to a local planning authority for planning permission: **12.28**

(a) . . . they may grant planning permission, either conditionally or subject to such conditions as they think fit; or
(b) they may refuse planning permission.

As alreadt stated by virtue of amendments made in 2003 to the General Development Procedure Order, there is now a general obligation on local planning authorities to give along with the notice of a grant of planning permission, a summary of their reasons for so doing, together with a summary of the policies and proposals in the development plan. **12.29**

Where planning permission is granted subject to conditions, the notice must state full reasons for each condition imposed and specify all policies and proposals in the development plan which are relevant to that decision. Where planning permission is refused the local planning authority is required in the notice of refusal to state clearly and precisely their full reasons for refusal, specifying any policies and proposals in the development plan which are relevant to the decision. **12.30**

Section 70(2) of the 1990 Act provides that the local planning authority, in dealing with an application for planning permission, 'shall have regard to the provisions of the development plan, so far as material to the application, and to any other material considerations'. For the meaning of the term 'development plan', see Chapters 4 and 5. **12.31**

As stated earlier, the courts have held that the expression 'shall have regard to the provisions of the development plan', does not require that the plan should be slavishly adhered to. As long as the development plan was considered, an authority have been able to base their decision on 'other material considerations'. It also enabled local planning authorities and the Secretary of State, as a matter of policy during the 1980s when development plans were beginning to get out of date, to give rather less weight to the provisions of the development plan than had formerly been the case. Indeed, this is recognised in s 74(1) of the 1990 Act, which gives the Secretary of State power to regulate the manner in which applications for planning permission are dealt with by local planning authorities, and in particular **12.32** applications for planning permission for developments which do not accord with the provisions of the plan.

12.33 When the term 'material considerations' was first introduced into the law by the Town and Country Planning Act 1947, the intention may have been to allow local planning authorities, when determining applications for planning permission, to have regard to any amendments the authority were proposing to make to the approved development plan. In other words, the term was seen mainly as an adjunct to the preceding phrase, 'the provisions of the development plan'. The position was altered as a result of a provision inserted into the 1990 Act by the Planning and Compensation Act 1991, which gave the development plan a place of primacy over other material considerations in the exercise by local planning authorities of their development control functions.

12.34 Section 26 of the 1991 Act provided that the following provision should be added at the end of Part II of the 1990 Act:

> **54A.** Where, in making any determination under the planning Acts, regard is to be had to the development plan, the determination shall be made in accordance with the plan unless material considerations indicate otherwise.

The effect of s. 54A was clear. It plainly increased the emphasis to be given to the provisions of the development plan in the exercise of development control functions, and emphasises that decisions should be 'plan-led', rather than, as in the past, regarding the development plan as just another material consideration carrying no special weight. This interpretation would accord with the obligation now placed on all local planning authorities to prepare development plans for the whole of their area. The effect of the provision was to raise a presumption that if proposed development accords with the provisions of the current development plan, planning permission should be granted; unless, that is, material considerations indicate otherwise. Contrariwise, it would seem that if the development proposal does not accord with the development plan planning permission should be refused, unless material considerations indicate otherwise.

12.35 Section 54A, however, has now itself been repealed by the Planning and Compulsory Purchase Act 2004. Section 37(6) of that Act now provides as follows:

> If regard is to be had to the development plan for the purpose of any determination to be made under the planning Acts the determination must be made in accordance with the plan unless material considerations indicate otherwise.

Compared with the provision found in s. 54(A), the significant change made by s. 37(6) is the substitution of the word *shall* and its replacement with the word *must*. Neither the purpose nor the significance of this change is clear, which must now await further for a judicial comment.

12.36 The s. 54 provision has been considered by the courts on a number of occasions. In *St Albans DC v Secretary of State for the Environment* [1993] JPL 374, considering the effect of s 54A, the Deputy Judge, Mr David Widdicombe QC, after accepting as common ground that the section had no relevance to applications for consent to the demolition of a listed building under the Planning (Listed Buildings and Conservation Areas) Act 1990, felt it was clear that s 54A did set up a presumption in favour of the development plan, but for its rebuttal it was sufficient if there were 'material considerations which indicate otherwise'.

The effect of the Scottish equivalent of England's s 54A was considered by the House of Lords in *City of Edinburgh v Secretary of State for Scotland* (1997) 3 PLR 71. In that case their Lordships made it quite clear that the provision gave rise to a presumption in favour of the plan. They went on, however, to say that the presumption was in essence one of fact; it still left the assessment of the facts and the weighing of the considerations in the hands of the decision-maker. As Lord Hope said: **12.37**

> The only questions for the court are whether the decision taker had regard to the presumption, whether the other considerations which he regarded as material were relevant considerations to which he was entitled to have regard and whether, looked at as a whole, his decision was irrational. It would be a mistake to think that the effect of [section 18A] was to increase the power of the court to intervene in decisions about planning control.

The function of the court, therefore, was to see whether the decision taker had regard to the presumption, not to assess whether the decision maker gave enough weight to it where there were other material considerations indicating that the determination should not be made in accordance with the development plan. **12.38**

The decision of the House of Lords was considered by the Court of Appeal in *R v Leominster DC, ex p Pothecary* [1998] JPL 335 to also represent English law. The position, therefore, is that the development plan carries greater weight than it would otherwise do if there were no s 54A, but that the weight to be given to it is a matter for the decision-maker. **12.39**

It seems clear from *R v Canterbury City Council, ex p Springimage Ltd* [1994] JPL 427 that to disregard the presumption by merely considering the requirement to be, 'to have regard to the provisions of the development plan . . . unless material considerations indicate otherwise,' in considering an application for planning permission, would be an incorrect application of the law. It seems, too, that the decision-maker does not have to state expressly that he has had regard to the presumption by indicating whether or not a proposal is in accordance with the development plan (see *Spelthorne BC v Secretary of State for the Environment* (1994) 68 P & CR 211). He must, however, indicate in some way that he has considered s 54A and reached a clear finding on its application. *James v Secretary of State for the Environment and Saunders* (1998) 1 PLR 33, makes it clear, too, that although the decision-maker is not required specifically to state that he has considered s 54A, he must at least make clear the outcome of applying the presumption by indicating whether the proposed development is, or is not, in accordance with the relevant development plan. As was said in *Jones*: **12.40**

> . . . if an Inspector makes no conclusion as to whether or not a proposal is in accordance with the development plan, it may depending upon a full reading of the decision letter, be difficult to infer that he has determined the case properly upon the basis of section 54A. In order to be helpful, I would urge that it is safer in those cases where regard is to be had to the development plan, which in practice is a majority of cases, that a conclusion should be reached in the decision letter as to whether or not the proposal is in accordance with it.

Since s 54A was couched in mandatory terms, there could be no question of it being applied or disapplied as a matter of discretion. There was probably only one situation where the section could be properly disregarded, namely if the development plan should contain no policies relevant to the application in question. More problematical, is where policies in the development plan pull in different directions, so that conflicting guidance is given on the question of whether or not planning permission should be granted. **12.41**

12.42 Development plans often contain exceptions, qualifications, overlapping or even contradictory policies and issues on which value judgments have to be made. In *R v Rochdale MBC ex p Milne* (2001) 81 P & CR 27, Sullivan J said:

> It is not at all that unusual for development plan policies to pull in different directions. A proposed development may be in accord with development plan policies which, for example, encourage development for employment purposes, and yet be contrary to policies which seek to protect open countryside. In such cases there may be no clear cut answer to the question: is this proposal in accordance with the plan?. The local planning authority has to make ajudgment bearing in mind such factors as the importance of the policies which are complied with or infringed, and the extent of compliance or breach.

12.43 The same approach was taken in *City of Edinburgh Council v Secretary of State for Scotland* [1997] 1 WLR 1447. Lord Clyde (with whom the remainder of their Lordships agreed) said this as to the approach to be adopted under s 18A of the Town and Country Planning (Scotland) Act 1972 (to which s 54A is the English equivalent):

> In the practical application of section 18A, it will obviously be necessary for the decision-maker to consider the development plan, identify any provisions in it which are relevant to the question before him and make a proper interpretation of them. His decision will be open to challenge if he fails to have regard to a policy in the development plan which is relevant to the application or fails properly to interpret it. He will also have to consider whether the development proposed in the application before him does or does not accord with the development plan. There may be some points in the plan which support the proposal but there may be some considerations pointing in the opposite direction. He will require to assess all of these and then decide whether in the light of the whole plan the proposal does or does not accord with it.

12.44 It should also be emphasised that a development plan in course of preparation is only a material consideration, and did not become part of the development plan for the purpose of s 54A until it was adopted. The point was recognised in *Nottingham CC and Brostowe BC v Secretary of State for the Environment, Transport and the Regions* [1999] EGCS 35 by Sullivan J when he said:

> But there is a clear difference, in my judgment, between a statutory obligation to determine an appeal in accordance with Development Plan policies unless material considerations indicate otherwise, and an obligation to have regard to emerging policies as material considerations, even if the emerging policies are accorded considerable weight.

Other material considerations

12.45 In determining applications for planning permission, it is also necessary to consider the term 'other material considerations'. Whatever the genesis of the term may have been, it is now recognised to have a much wider connotation.

12.46 In *Stringer v Minister of Housing and Local Government* [1970] 1 WLR 1281, Cooke J, in upholding a decision to refuse planning permission for development which would have interfered with the working of the Jodrell Bank telescope said,

> It may be conceded at once that the material considerations to which the Minister is entitled and bound to have regard in deciding the appeal must be considerations of a planning nature. I find it impossible, however, to accept the view that such considerations are limited to matters

> relating to amenity . . . it seems to me that any consideration which relates to the use and development of land is capable of being a planning consideration.

Among the matters commonly regarded as relating to the use and development of land are the siting of buildings, their number, area, height, mass, design and external appearance; means of access; landscaping; impact on neighbouring land; availability of infrastructure; traffic considerations and communications. **12.47**

The following are other examples of considerations held by the courts to be material: **12.48**

(a) The safeguarding of land required for a road-widening scheme (*Westminster Bank Ltd v Minister of Housing and Local Government* [1971] AC 508).
(b) The protection of an ancient monument (*Hoveringham Gravels Ltd* v *Secretary of State for the Environment* [1975] QB 754).
(c) The likelihood of the proposed development being carried out (*Sovmots Investments Ltd v Secretary of State for the Environment* [1979] AC 144).
(d) The risk of flooding to neighbouring landowners (*George Wimpey & Co. Ltd v Secretary of State for the Environment* [1978] JPL 776).
(e) Disturbance or annoyance to neighbouring occupiers from a casino (*Ladbroke (Rentals) Ltd v Secretary of State for the Environment* [1981] JPL 427).

The following are some examples of considerations held by the courts not to be material: **12.49**

(a) The question of whether development was economically worthwhile (*Walters v Secretary of State for Wales* [1979] JPL 171). However, although the financial viability of development may not be a material consideration, in *Sosmo Trust v Secretary of State for the Environment* [1983] JPL 806, it was held that the lack of financial viability could be material where a failure to grant planning permission for development would result in a building being left unoccupied and derelict. Finance is also material where funds are being provided by development being allowed contrary to the development plan, in order to enable development which is not contrary to the plan to proceed (enabling development).
(b) In *R v Essex CC, ex p Tarmac Roadstone Holdings Ltd* [1998] JPL B23, the High Court held that a planning permission the sole or primary purpose of which was to legitimise a previous breach, to make lawful that which was not lawful, did not relate to the development's planning merits. If something were brought to the attention of an authority as being in breach of planning laws, the authority's duty was to consider in the circumstances of the case whether any form of enforcement is appropriate. It was not lawful for the authority, instead of doing that, to decide to confer a mantle of legality upon what has been done by a further grant of planning permission, and for no perceptible reason other than to confer such a mantle.
(c) The cost to a local planning authority of modifying or revoking a planning permission as in *Alnwick DC v Secretary of State for the Environment, Transport and the Regions* [1999] JPL B190.

Note too that the Race Relations Act 1976, s 19A, makes it unlawful for a planning authority to discriminate against a person in carrying out their planning functions. This provision was inserted into the 1976 Act by the Housing and Planning Act 1986 following concern that the 1976 Act might permit such discrimination. **12.50**

12.51 Circulars too are very much a material consideration in the taking of planning decisions. However, as Schiemann J indicated in *R v Poole Borough Council, ex p Beebee* [1991] JPL 643, planning Circulars are full of broad statements with many presumptions, many of which are mutually irreconcilable, so that in a particular case one may have to give way to another. That statement is also apposite to apply to Planning Policy Guidance Notes and Planning Policy Statements. Given the language used in s 70(2) of the 1990 Act and the original intent behind the use of the words 'other material considerations' it is not surprising that government policy should lie fairly and squarely within that term. The main vehicle for the articulation of government policy is Planning Policy Guidance Notes and Planning Policy Statements, and these will always be a material consideration in making development control decisions. But, as Jowett J indicated in *R v Wakefield MDC, ex p Pearl Assurance plc* [1997] JPL B131, PPGs are not delegating legislation and do not have the force of statutes. They are 'guidelines not tramways. They do not purport to deal definitively with every situation which may arise.' He went on to say that whether a piece of guidance amounts as a matter of law to a material consideration has to be judged by reference to the content of the particular case. It followed, therefore, that part of a PPG which amounts to a material consideration in one case, may not necessarily be a material consideration in every case, though certain elements of the guidance may be of universal application.

12.52 It must be borne in mind too, that a Guidance Note or statement can in no way remove from the local planning authority or Secretary of State the obligation to consider the development plan for the area, which must always be pre-eminent. Furthermore, in *E.C. Gransden & Co. Ltd v Secretary of State for the Environment* (1987) 54 P & CR 86, Woolf J (as he then was) made it clear that a policy statement in a Guidance Note or Circular cannot turn what would otherwise be a material planning consideration into an irrelevant consideration. But it seems from that case that a Guidance Note or Circular can decide that more weight should be given to one or to some material considerations than to others, though the authority would not act *ultra vires* if it preferred some other weighting.

12.53 In *E.C. Gransden & Co. Ltd v Secretary of State for the Environment*, Woolf J set out *in extenso* the proper approach to policy considerations at that time embodied in Circulars. He said (at pp. 93–4):

> . . . it seems to me, first of all, that any policy, if it is to be a policy which is a proper policy for planning purposes, must envisage that in exceptional circumstances the Minister has the right to depart from that policy. If the situation was otherwise . . . it would be an improper attempt to curtail the discretion which is provided by the Act, which indicates that in determining planning applications regard is not only to be had to the provisions of the development plan so far as material, but also to any other material considerations.
>
> What then is the significance of the inspector having failed to follow the policy? Does that mean that this court has to quash his decision? The situation, as I see it, is as follows: first, section 29 [now s 70] lays down what matters are to be regarded as material, and the policy cannot make a matter which is otherwise a material consideration an irrelevant consideration. Secondly, if the policy is a lawful policy, that is to say if it is not a policy which is defective because it goes beyond the proper role of a policy by seeking to do more than indicate the weight which should be given to relevant considerations, then the body determining an application must have regard to the policy. Thirdly, the fact that a body has to have regard to the policy does not mean that it needs necessarily to follow the policy. However, if it is going to

depart from the policy, it must give clear reasons for . . . not doing so in order that the recipient of its decision will know why the decision is being made as an exception to the policy and the grounds upon which the decision is taken.

Fourthly, in order to give effect to the approach which I have just indicated it is essential that the policy is properly understood by the determining body. If the body making the decision fails to properly understand the policy, then the decision will be as defective as it would be if no regard had been paid to the policy.

Fifthly, if proper regard, in the manner in which I have indicated, is not given to the policy, then this court will quash its decision unless the situation is one of those exceptional cases where the court can be quite satisfied that the failure to have proper regard to the policy has not affected the outcome in that the decision would in any event have been the same.

The materiality of Circulars and Planning Policy Guidance Notes was also considered in **12.54**
Carpets of Worth Ltd v Wyre Forest DC (1991) 62 P & CR 334, where Purchas LJ said:

> I must consider the status of these documents. They are not issued under statutory authority. 'Prescribed' considerations involve regulations made by the Secretary of State under section 287 of the 1971 Act and are therefore subject to resolution of each House of Parliament. Ministerial circulars as published or as summarised in PPGs have therefore no formal statutory force and should therefore not be treated as such for any purpose. This includes in my judgment the manner in which they should be construed and/or applied. They constitute announcements of the current ministerial planning policy. The only statutory obligation upon the local planning authority is 'to have regard to them'. They are in no way bound by them.

Then later he said:

> Although the local authority is not bound by the policy circulars, it should observe them and depart from them only if there are clear reasons, which should be stated, for so doing.

Although it is a requirement of the law that in order for a decision-maker to have regard to a **12.55**
policy or to determine an application in accordance with it the policy must be properly understood, the court's role is limited to construing the policy in question, leaving the decision-maker to apply the policy to the planning issues as a matter of fact.

It is important also to emphasise that the law makes a clear distinction between the question **12.56**
of whether something is or is not a material consideration, and the weight which should be given to it. As Lord Hoffman said in *Tesco Stores Ltd v Secretary of State of the Environment* [1995] 1 WLR 759:

> The former is a question of law and the latter is a question of planning judgment, which is entirely a matter for the planning authority. Provided that the planning authority has regard to all material considerations, it is at liberty (provided that it does not lapse into Wednesbury irrationality) to give them whatever weight the planning authority thinks fit or no weight at all. The fact that the law regards something as a material consideration therefore involves no view about the part, if any, which it should play in the decision-making process.

A case in practice where a problem commonly occurs as to the weight to be given to a **12.57**
material consideration, is when a development plan is being prepared but has not yet been formally adopted (or approved). The precise weight to be given to the emerging development plan is, of course, a matter for the decision-maker.

Paragraph 48 of PPG1 gives guidance on the Secretary of State's view as to the weight to be **12.58** given, by making the somewhat obvious point that this will depend upon the stage in the preparation and adoption process that the plan has reached, and the more weight should be given to the plan as each successive stage is reached. If an application for planning permission would, if granted, prejudice the outcome of the development plan process, that would represent a case for refusing the application on the grounds of prematurity.

Previous appeal decisions

12.59 In *North Wiltshire DC v Secretary of State for the Environment* (1992) 65 P & CR 137, the Court of Appeal held that it was indisputable that a previous appeal decision concerning the same application site was a material consideration in determining a subsequent application for the development of the same site. The reason is the need for like cases to be decided in a like manner so that there is consistency in the appellate process. In his judgment Mann LJ said:

> Consistency is self-evidently important to both developers and development control authorities. But it is also important for the purpose of securing public confidence in the operation of the development control system. I do not suggest and it would be wrong to do so, that like cases *must* be decided alike. An Inspector must always exercise his own judgment. He is therefore free upon consideration to disagree with the judgment of another but before doing so he ought to have regard to the importance of consistency and to give his reasons for departure from the previous decision.
>
> To state that like cases should be decided alike presupposes that the earlier case is alike and is not distinguishable in some relevant respect. If it is distinguishable then it usually will lack materiality by reference to consistency, although it may be material in some other way. Where it is indistinguishable then ordinarily it must be a material consideration. A practical test for the inspector is to ask himself whether, if I decide this case in a particular way, am I necessarily agreeing or disagreeing with some critical aspect of the decision in the previous case?

12.60 The *North Wiltshire* case concerned an earlier decision on the same site. In *R v Secretary of State for the Environment, ex p David Baber* [1996] JPL 1032, the Court of Appeal had to consider an earlier appeal decision on a site that was different from but close to the second appeal site. There, Glidewell LJ referred to the test proposed by Mann LJ in *North Wiltshire* and continued:

> He [Glidewell LJ] suggested that the test which the inspector ought to have posed to himself was slightly different. It was: a previous decision having been drawn to my attention, do I take the view that it may well be sufficiently closely related to the matters in issue in my appeal that I ought to have regard to it and either follow it or distinguish it?

12.61 In *Beaulieu Property Management v Secretary of State for the Environment* (1997) EGCS 129 it was accepted that the decision-maker, and ultimately the Court, must first determine that the first appeal decision is 'alike and not distinguishable in some relevant respect' (*North Wiltshire*) or 'sufficiently closely related to the matters in issue' (*Baber*) such that it was a material consideration. If it was material, then the decision-maker is under a duty to give reasons if his decision departs from the previous decision. A failure to give reasons could lead to the Court quashing a decision if there was substantial prejudice to the applicant.

12.62 The principle is based on the need for consistency in the appellate process. It was only a question of time before the principle was extended to the decision-making power of local planning authorities. In *R (Edward Rank) v East Cambridgeshire District Council* [2003] JPL 454 the High Court held that a local planning authority must take into account a previous decision of the authority where it was refused. Quite apart from the need for consistency, the need to have regard to previous decisions can be important elsewhere particularly where land has the benefit of a previous planning permission which has not been implemented and a new development proposal has to be considered, the argument being that implementation of a new planning permission would be better than the implementation of an old permission. This gives rise to what has been called the fall-back principle, and it requires the decision-maker in determining the second application for planning permission to have regard to the merits of the previous decision and the reasons for it. Recent examples of the operation of this rule occurred in *Postwood Developments Ltd v Secretary of State for the Environment* [1992] JPL 823, and *Haven Leisure Ltd v Secretary of State for the Environment and North Cornwall DC* [1994] JPL 148. This latter case is one authority for the proposition that not only has the existence of the 'previous' planning permission to be shown, but also that the permission is likely to be implemented if permission for the later development is refused.

In *P. F. Ahern (London) Ltd v Secretary of State for the Environment and Havering BC* [1998] JPL 351, it was said that in the context of fallback cases, the question to be answered was: 'is the proposed development in its implications for impact on the environment, or other relevant planning factors, likely to have implications worse than or broadly similar to any use to which the site would or might be put if the proposed development was refused?' In considering this question, the word 'might' did not mean a mere possibility; there had to be a finding of an actually intended use as opposed to a mere legal or theoretical entitlement. **12.63**

Then again in *South Buckinghamshire DC v Secretary of State for the Environment and Berkeley Homes Ltd* [1999] JPL 1340, it was said that it was not sufficient for the decision-maker to rely on the theoretical possibility that an authorised use may be resumed. He had to assess the probability that it would, and give it appropriate weight. In *Windsor and Maidenhead RBC v Secretary of State for the Environment, Transport and the Regions and Amalgamated Holdings Ltd* [2001] PLCR 497, it was said that the mere existence of a planning permission was not, of itself, conclusive. **12.64**

Protection of private interests

It is constantly said that the object of planning control is to restrict private development in the public interest and not in the private interest. Examples of public-interest matters include acceptable standards of privacy, adequate daylight or sunlight and freedom from excessive noise. The preservation of open views, however, is a private interest which the law is not intended to protect. Occasionally, of course, public and private interests overlap. **12.65**

Although it is not the proper function of planning law to protect private interests, in the course of protecting the public interest a landowner may obtain a benefit which he would not otherwise enjoy. In *Stringer v Minister of Housing and Local Government* [1970] 1 WLR 1281, the director of the Nuffield Radio Astronomy Laboratories, which operated the Jodrell Bank radio telescope, sought to persuade the local planning authority that in considering applications for planning permission in the surrounding area, they should have regard to the efficient operation of the telescope. It appeared that the efficiency of the telescope was **12.66** affected by electrical sparks and other forms of disturbance which emanated from terrestrial sources in the neighbourhood, since those sources produced signals similar to the signals the telescope received from outer space. The danger of interference from such things as radios, televisions and motor vehicles, however, diminished the more distant they were from the telescope. So the local planning authority, the rural district council and the University of Manchester (which owned the telescope) entered into an agreement whereby the local planning authority undertook to discourage development within a certain radius of the station. Stringer became a victim of this agreement. His application for planning permission was refused on the ground that, if granted, the development would interfere with the efficient running of the telescope. His appeal against the refusal to the Minister was dismissed. Stringer then appealed to the High Court under what is now s 288 of the 1990 Act for an order quashing the Minister's decision.

12.67 The Court held that the agreement between the local planning authority and the University was null and void because its intention was to bind the local planning authority to disregard considerations which it was required to have regard to under what is now s 70(2) of the 1990 Act. The agreement breached the basic principle that a public authority cannot by contract bind itself to disregard its statutory duties. The Court went on, however, to consider that the Minister's decision was valid. The Minister had not been party to the improper agreement and had not bound himself to follow any particular course of action. In determining the appeal, which included the determination of the planning application as if it were made to him *de novo*, the Minister was entitled to have a policy with regard to the proposed development and here that policy was to discourage development in the vicinity of the telescope. As long as that policy was not followed blindly so as to exclude the consideration by him of all material considerations, his decision could not be faulted.

12.68 Faced with the likely success of that argument, however, Stringer also argued that the Minister had taken into account a consideration which was not material, namely the private interests of Jodrell Bank radio telescope. Dismissing that argument, Cooke J held that the term 'material considerations' was not limited to considerations of amenity and that in a proper case might take into account private interests as well as public interests. The fact that the proposed development would interfere with the operation of the telescope was a material consideration in determining the application.

12.69 The decision was followed shortly after in *RMC Management Services Ltd v Secretary of State for the Environment* (1972) 222 EG 1593. The company had applied to the High Court to quash a decision of the Secretary of State dismissing an appeal from a refusal by the local planning authority to grant planning permission for the erection of a ready-mixed concrete batching plant. The reason given for the dismissal of the appeal was that the development would generate an abnormal level of airborne abrasive dust which would affect the operations of four neighbouring establishments. The four establishments had been attracted to that area by the relatively clean air needed to carry on their high-precision engineering work. The company alleged that in so deciding the Secretary of State was seeking to protect the extraordinary requirements of adjacent occupiers in the use and enjoyment of their land at the expense of and to the detriment of the company in the use and enjoyment of its land. It was not disputed that the proposed use would have been normal for an industrial estate and that it would not have given rise to an actionable nuisance by escape of dust, even if carried out in a residential area. In dismissing the application Bristow J adopted the language of Cooke J in *Stringer v Minister of Housing and Local Government* where he said:

> In principle, it seems to me that any consideration which relates to the use and development of land is capable of being a planning consideration. Whether a particular consideration falling within that broad class is material in any given case will depend upon the circumstances.

In dealing with the application before him, Bristow J thought that the Secretary of State was entitled to ask himself whether the proposed development was compatible with the proper and desirable use of other land in the area. In his view the risks to the four special clean-air neighbours was a planning consideration which the Secretary of State was entitled to consider and right to consider material. **12.70**

So the fact that the special interests of adjoining occupiers of land in clean air was protected, gave them (as a side-effect) a benefit under planning law they would not have enjoyed at common law. **12.71**

Although it is clear law that planning control is concerned only with the public interest, where private rights are being interfered with the proper question to ask is whether the public interest requires that the interests of that party should be considered. In *Wood-Robinson v Secretary of State for the Environment and Wandsworth LBC* [1998] JPL 976, the applicant had been refused planning permission for the construction of a dwellinghouse within the curtilage of a block of flats. On appeal the Inspector had upheld the refusal, holding that although the proposed development would not have an adverse effect on the surrounding locality, it would have an adverse effect on the amenity of local residents. Refusing to quash the decision of the Secretary of State, the High Court held that it was legitimate for the Secretary of State to take into account the effects on local residential amenity. **12.72**

Creation of a precedent

The courts have accepted the principle that although land may be suitable for the development proposed, the local planning authority may refuse planning permission for that development if to grant it would be likely to lead to a proliferation of applications for similar development, which the authority would then find it difficult to refuse. **12.73**

In *Collis Radio Ltd v Secretary of State for the Environment* [1975] JPL 221, the owners of a warehouse, who had used it for storing electrical goods, began to use it to carry on a cash and carry business. The local planning authority had served an enforcement notice on the owners requiring them to cease and to restore the land to its former user. The Secretary of State dismissed the owners' appeal against the notice on the ground, *inter alia*, that while the development on the appeal site was unlikely to have a particularly harmful effect on the existing shopping centres, a proliferation of such developments might well do. The owners appealed to the Secretary of State against the notice solely on the ground that 'planning permission ought to be granted' for the development. Their appeal to the court against the Secretary of State's decision to uphold the enforcement notice was based on the ground that, if planning permission were to be granted, the effect of possible future developments of the type enforced against, was not a material consideration. In dismissing the appeal, Lord **12.74**

Widgery CJ said that it was of great importance when considering a single planning application to ask what the consequences in the locality would be and what side-effects would flow if permission were granted. In so far as planning permission for the one site was judged by the Secretary of State in the light of the consequences for other sites, no error of law had been disclosed. It seems, however, that something more than a mere assertion or generalised concern is needed.There must be evidence to indicate that if planning permission were granted, it would make it more difficult to refuse other planning applications for similar development which may have damaging effects.

12.75 The decision of the Divisional Court in *Collis Radio Ltd v Secretary of State for the Environment* was followed by Woolf J in *Anglia Building Society v Secretary of State for the Environment* [1984] JPL 175, where planning permission for a change of use from retailing to that of a building society branch office was refused on the ground that to grant the permission would create a precedent that might adversely affect the authority's planning policy for the area, which was to preserve primary shopping areas and to resist non-retail uses except in exceptional cases. Here, although the presence of building society offices in the area was not in itself objectionable, other building societies might use the grant of permission as a lever to establish offices in the area, and this would have led to a dilution of the predominantly retailing character of the area.

12.76 In *Poundstretcher v Secretary of State for the Environment* [1988] 3 PLR 69, Deputy Judge David Widdicombe QC, in a well-known statement, said:

> Be that as it may, in the present case the inspector clearly did rely on precedent. I accept Mr Hobson's proposition that where precedent is relied on, mere fear or generalised concern is not enough. There must be evidence in one form or another for the reliance on precedent. In some cases the facts may speak for themselves. For instance, in the common case of the rear extension of one of a row or terrace of dwellings, it may be obvious that other owners in the row are likely to want extensions if one is permitted. Another clear example is sporadic development in the countryside.

Existence of alternative sites

12.77 The operation of the planning control system relies heavily on the local planning authority responding to development proposals made by individual landowners or developers for individual sites. Hence, as a matter of principle, it would seem that the question of alternative sites ought not to be a material consideration in determining whether planning permission should be given for the development of the land the subject of the application. The courts, however, have not followed that approach. In *R v Royal County of Berkshire, ex p Mangnall* [1985] JPL 258, the applicant sought judicial review to quash a grant of planning permission for the extraction of sand given in favour of a neighbouring landowner on the ground that the authority had failed to have proper regard to the existence of an alternative site. It was alleged that before granting planning permission, the authority should have made a comparative evaluation of both sites. According to Nolan J, there was no hard-and-fast rule governing the evaluation of alternative sites, but the statutory duty to have regard to material considerations would, in certain cases, more easily recognised than defined, require the consideration of another possible site than that for which permission was sought. In his judgment, there were serious environmental disadvantages in allowing the development of the neighbouring land. He thought that here the requirement to 'have regard to the provisions of the development plan . . . and to any other material considerations', could not be complied with unless the authority had regard to the merits or demerits of the other site, but that it was reading too much into the section to say that an equal evaluation of that site was required. Since it was shown that the authority had in fact considered the merits of the alternative site, the application for judicial review failed.

It seems, therefore, that the merits or demerits of an alternative site *can* be a material consideration, but that the authority is under no duty to evaluate the alternative site in the same way as it must do with the application site. This seems reasonable, since there would be no practical way of securing that without the submission of a planning application for the development of the alternative site. An early case, *Rhodes v Minister of Housing and Local Government* [1963] 1 WLR 208, established that there is no duty on the local planning authority to 'rout around' to see whether there may be an alternative site. On the other hand, it was said in *Trusthouse Forte Hotels Ltd v Secretary of State for the Environment* (1986) 53 P & CR 293 that it 'may be possible for the authority to decide in certain cases that a particular need can be satisfied elsewhere than on the appeal site even though no other specific sites are identified and established as preferable alternatives'. **12.78**

The law was summarised by Simon Brown LJ in that case (and was quoted with approval by Laws LJ in the Court of Appeal in *R (Scott Jones) v North Warwickshire BC* [2001] PLCR 509) and by Richards J in *Laing Homes Ltd v Secretary of State for Transport, Local Government and the Regions* [2003] JPL 559 in the following terms: **12.79**

> (1) Land (irrespective of whether it is owned by the applicant for planning permission) may be developed in any way which is acceptable for planning purposes. The fact that other land exists (whether or not in the applicant's ownership) upon which the development would be yet more acceptable for planning purposes would not justify the refusal of planning permission upon the application site.
>
> (2) Where, however, there are clear planning objections to development upon a particular site then it may well be relevant and indeed necessary to consider whether there is a more appropriate alternative site elsewhere. This is particularly so when the development is bound to have significant adverse effects and where the major argument advanced in support of the application is that the need for the development outweighs the planning disadvantages inherent in it.
>
> (3) Instances of this type of case are developments, whether of national or regional importance, such as airports . . . coalmining, petro-chemical plants, nuclear power stations and gypsy encampments . . .
>
> (4) In contrast to the situations envisaged above are cases where development permission is being sought for dwelling houses, offices (see the *GLC* case itself) and superstores (at least in the circumstances of and *R v Carlisle City Council and the Secretary of State for the Environment, ex p Cumbrian Co-operative Society Ltd*).
>
> (5) There may be cases where, even although they contain the characteristics referred to above, nevertheless it could properly be regarded as unnecessary to go into questions of comparability. This would be so particularly if the environmental impact was relatively slight and the planning objections were not especially strong . . .

Later, Pill LJ in the Court of Appeal in *Kyte v Secretary of State for the Environment* (14 March 1997, ref QB COF 96/1633/D) opined: **12.80**

> When considering possible alternative sites, there can be no universally applicable rule as to the area to be considered or the range of detail of inquiry required . . . Potentially the exercise upon alternative sites is an exercise without limits.

An early example of the difficulties in this area was seen in *R v Carlisle City Council, ex p Cumbrian Co-operative Society Ltd)* [1986] JPL 206 where Macpherson J held that on an application to consider the use of land as a superstore there was no need for the authority to consider *in detail* the merits of alternative sites. Precisely when the merits or demerits of an alternative site can be material was not exhaustively spelt out in the *Mangnall* case. Some help in this area, however, has been given in *Greater London Council v Secretary of State for the Environment* [1986] JPL 193. Here, Cable Cross Projects Ltd had applied to the London Docklands Development Corporation for planning permission for office development. The Secretary of State had called in the application and an Inspector, after holding an inquiry, had recommended that permission be refused. The Secretary of State, however, after considering the Inspector's report, had decided to grant permission. The local council then appealed unsuccessfully to the High Court under what is now s 288 of the 1990 Act for an order to quash the Secretary of State's decision. One of the grounds of challenge was that the Secretary of State had failed to have regard to a material consideration by not examining other comparable sites. In the Court of Appeal, Oliver LJ thought that there were cases where a comparable site had to be a material consideration; an obvious example was an airport. Without seeking to lay down a test for every case, because definition was always dangerous in these circumstances, he thought it might be that comparability was appropriate generally to cases having the following characteristics: first of all, the presence of a clear public convenience, or advantage, in the proposal under consideration; secondly, the existence of inevitable adverse effects or disadvantages to the public or to some section of the public in the proposal; thirdly, the existence of an alternative site for the same project which would not have those effects, or would not have them to the same extent; and fourthly, a situation in which there could only be one permission granted for such development, or at least only a very limited number of permissions.

12.81 The question of alternative sites was considered by the High Court in *Edwards v Secretary of State for the Environment* (1993) 66 P & CR 393. A number of applications had been made for planning permission for the construction of roadside service areas on different sites along an improved trunk road. All had been refused by the local planning authority and appeals were pending. In one case the appeal was by the written representation procedure but another applicant had elected for a planning inquiry and requested that all the appeals be considered at the same inquiry. The Secretary of State had refused this request and the appeal by written representation went ahead before an Inspector and succeeded. However, the High Court quashed the Inspector's decision because he should have taken account of the alternative proposals: the case had the four characteristics set out in *Greater London Council v Secretary of State for the Environment*. An appeal by the Secretary of State from the decision of the High Court was subsequently dismissed by the Court of Appeal. That decision has been reported at [1994] 1 PLR 62.

12.82 All the cases suggest that as a general proposition, consideration of alternative sites will only be relevant to exceptional circumstances. Nevertheless, the problem of alternative sites has become more topical with the Government's decision to allow private-sector operators to develop as well as operate motorway service areas. In one case, six different applications were made for the development of one service facility between junctions 4 and 8 on the M40. In order to meet the difficulty of having to consider with regard to each application all the alternative sites, the Secretary of State decided to hold a joint multiple public inquiry into five of the six applications. The sixth application was dealt with at a later separate inquiry, at which much of the evidence given at the multiple inquiry was again covered. The problem of alternative sites could also arise in relation to competing applications for superstore development where the applicants and authority are all agreed that no more than one should be permitted.

Risk of piecemeal development

It seems that if a landowner makes an application for planning permission to develop only part of his land, there may be circumstances where the authority would be justified in refusing permission until such time as the landowner has indicated to the authority his proposals for the remainder of his land. **12.83**

In *Rugby School Governors v Secretary of State for the Environment* [1975] JPL 97, the school had applied for planning permission to develop part of the school estate. The local planning authority had decided to deal with it on the ground that piecemeal development of the estate was bad planning practice and that individual applications should await a master plan, the preparation of which had been agreed earlier with the applicants. The school then appealed to the Secretary of State against with — determination of the application by the authority, who directed that it be determined by an Inspector. He dismissed the appeal. The school then applied to quash his decision on the ground that the Inspector had, while purporting to give a considered refusal, failed to determine the appeal or that he had taken into account irrelevant considerations. Refusing the application, Willis J held that by his endorsement of the authority's policy, the Secretary of State could not be said to have failed to comply with his statutory obligation to determine the appeal. He also held that given the background, it would require special circumstances to justify permitting an individual application to proceed in advance of agreement on a master plan. It should be noted that here the authority should have decided, like the Inspector on behalf of the Secretary of State, to refuse the application instead of deciding not to determine it. **12.84**

Preservation of existing uses

One of the first cases to consider the relevance of the existing use of land as a material consideration in determining an application for planning permission for the development of the land was *Granada Theatres Ltd v Secretary of State for the Environment* [1976] JPL 96. There, the owners of a cinema applied for planning permission to change its use to that of a bingo and social club. Following the refusal of the application, the owners appealed to the Secretary of State who, mainly as a result of a petition by children for the retention of the cinema, dismissed the appeal. The application to quash that decision was based on the grounds that the Secretary of State had taken a mistaken view that the refusal of the permission would ensure the continued use of the building as a cinema and that he had acted contrary to the rules of natural justice in that he had taken into account the petition without **12.85** giving the applicants an opportunity to comment on it. On both those grounds the Secretary of State consented to the decision being quashed by the court.

12.86 In *Clyde & Co. v Secretary of State for the Environment* [1977] JPL 521 planning permission had been granted to erect a building, the western half of which was to be used for offices, the eastern half to be used as dwellings. The applicants proceeded to build and occupy the western half, but the eastern half was not completed. The applicants then made a further application to change the permitted use of the eastern half from residential to office use. The application was refused, and an appeal to the Secretary of State against the refusal was not upheld. The applicants then applied to the High Court for the decision to be quashed on the ground that the Secretary of State had erred in law in basing his decision on the ground that the loss of residential accommodation ought to be resisted. The Divisional Court granted the application, but this was reversed by the Court of Appeal which restored the Secretary of State's decision. The Court of Appeal held that the Secretary of State's ground for refusal was not wrong in law. Housing need was a material consideration, and if permission for office use was refused, there was at least a fair chance that the building would be used for housing rather than be allowed to stand empty.

12.87 The next important case to be considered by the courts was *Granada Theatres Ltd v Secretary of State for the Environment* [1981] JPL 278. Here the applicants owned a cinema in Chichester where trade had declined to such an extent that it had become the second most unprofitable cinema in the Granada group. The company had applied for planning permission to change the use of the cinema to another bingo and social club. On refusal of the application, the applicants had appealed to the Secretary of State, but without any success. In his decision letter the Secretary of State had said that he did not regard as material the alleged demerits such as they might be of bingo as an activity, and he had not been influenced by unfavourable comments made about it in connection with the appeal. He did, however, consider public demand for the retention of a cinema facility in Chichester on the one hand and for the introduction of commercial bingo on the other as well as the availability of alternative suitable premises and ways and means of providing these facilities. He accepted that, notwithstanding the expression of public opinion in favour of retaining the cinema, the appellant company faced difficulties in running the cinema as it stood, but the company had already given some thought to the possibility of finding an alternative use which would still incorporate a cinema element. He also accepted that the proposed change of use to bingo was likely to be much more profitable than the present use. However, he concluded that it might well be that a cinema and bingo operation or a multiunit cinema were not the only possibilities, and despite the appellant's declared intention of closing the present cinema soon, the Secretary of State could not rule out the hope that, as the Inspector had suggested, an increased interest in the cinema or further examination of alternative ways of using the building could yet result in the retention of a viable cinema facility. He therefore rejected the appeal.

12.88 In an action to quash the Secretary of State's decision, Forbes J, referring to the decision in *Clyde & Co. v Secretary of State for the Environment*, confessed to be surprised that it should have been necessary for there to be an authority for the proposition that in a change of use case the desirability of preserving the existing use was a material consideration, because it seemed to him so self-evident a proposition. According to Forbes J, however, there could be situations where the question of desirability of retaining the existing use was not material. If all the parties agreed that the continuation of an existing use was undesirable, one need not consider the question of desirability further. It was a concluded question. But where there was a dispute between the parties about whether an existing use should be retained or not, it seemed to him inevitable that the desirability of retaining it was a material question. Here, the sole issue for the Secretary of State to decide was whether there was a possibility, a reasonable possibility perhaps, that the existing use would be preserved if planning permission was refused. Forbes J decided that it was reasonable for the Secretary of State to come to that conclusion and so refused to interfere with his decision.

The tests so far applied by the courts in considering the relevance of an existing use in determining planning applications has been whether, if permission were refused, there would be a 'fair chance' or 'a possibility' or 'a reasonable possibility' that the existing use would continue. **12.89**

In *Westminster City Council v British Waterways Board* [1985] AC 676 however, the House of Lords held that the preservation of an existing use which had been temporarily suspended could not afford a ground of refusal of planning permission for an otherwise acceptable change of use, unless it could be shown that the refusal might lead to a resumption of the suspended use. In dealing with the question of resumption, Lord Bridge of Harwich thought that the 'fair chance' test was, on the facts, an unnecessarily lax criterion. In his view, in a contest between the planning merits of two competing uses, to justify the refusal of permission for use B on the sole ground that use A ought to be preserved, it must be necessary at least to show 'a balance of probabilities' that if permission is refused for use B, the land in dispute will be effectively put to use A. **12.90**

In another case, *London Residuary Body v Lambeth LBC* [1990] 1 WLR 744, the House of Lords in allowing an appeal from a decision of the Court of Appeal, held that in exercising powers under s 29 of the 1971 Act (s 70 of the 1990 Act), a local planning authority was not bound to apply between two uses a competing needs test of whether in planning terms the desirability of preserving the existing use outweighs the merits of the proposed new use. After considering the cases of *Clyde & Co. v Secretary of State* [1977] JPL 521 and *Westminster City Council v British Waterways Board* [1985] AC 676, Lord Keith of Kinkel said: **12.91**

> In my opinion nothing in either the *Clyde* case or in the *Westminster Council* case is properly to be interpreted as laying down that the competing needs test exists as a matter of law. Such a proposition would involve putting an unwarranted gloss on the language of s 29(1) of the 1971 Act. The most that can be extracted from the two cases is that the desirability of preserving an existing use of land is a material consideration to be taken into account under that sub-section, provided there is a reasonable probability that such use will be preserved if permission for the new use is refused. If the Court of Appeal is right, it must follow that the presumption in favour of development can in law only receive effect where other planning considerations for or against a proposed use are evenly balanced. Such a straitjacket cannot properly be imposed on the Secretary of State. It must be left to him, in the exercise of a reasonable discretion, to form his own judgment whether any planning objections are of sufficient importance to overcome the presumption. This was the view taken, in my opinion correctly, by Simon Brown J. It should be kept in mind that in the case of many individual planning applications, for example to build a single house somewhere in the country, there is no question of it being possible to prove a need for the development. There may, however, be some planning objection to it which is not

of very great weight. In such a situation it must surely be open to the determining authority to decide that the presumption may properly receive effect and to grant planning permission.

12.92 Whether or not there is a 'reasonable probability' or 'perhaps a realistic prospect' that an existing use will be preserved will depend on the individual facts of each case. Factors like the institution of a new use in breach of planning control, the demolition of a building in which an old use took place, a sustained period of disuse and evidence that the old use ceased because it was not economically viable to carry it on and is unlikely to be resurrected, remain of great evidential value in determining the future use of a parcel of land.

12.93 In *South Buckinghamshire DC v Secretary of State for the Environment and Berkeley Homes Ltd* [1999] JPL B40, it was said that it was not sufficient for the decision-maker to rely on a theoretical possibility that an authorised use may be resumed. He had to assess the possibility that it would and give it appropriate weight.

12.94 The test laid down in the *British Waterways Board* case has in the past been exclusively related to the existing use of land, and the principle has been enunciated in that specific context. The question may also be posed, however, as to whether or not the same or a similar test was to be applied to competing future uses. That question could have important consequences for development control generally. Land may be considered by a local planning authority to be suitable for, say, future educational needs, yet it has to consider an application for planning permission to develop the land for housing. Attempts are often made to safeguard land for particular purposes, and faced with an application for a competing use for that land, the 'balance of probabilities' test would, as far as the future use of the land is concerned, be likely to require more speculation than if the test was applied to the preservation of an existing use.

12.95 One case which has considered this issue is *Nottinghamshire County Council v Secretary of State for the Environment, Transport and the Regions* [2002] JPL 161. There the High Court held that if a judgment was made, whether through the development plan process or outside it, that it appeared desirable to preserve the option of using a piece of land for a purpose seen to be of benefit to the public interest for the country or the local community, this was, in principle, a material planning consideration for the purposes of ss 70(2) and 54A of the Act. The weight given to that consideration would vary hugely from case to case. Each case would turn on its own merits. Therefore in considering whether to grant planning permission for a proposal which would pre-empt the possibility of the desirable future use, the relative desirability of the two uses would have to be weighed. In striking the balance, the likelihood of the desirable use actually coming about was doubtless a highly material consideration. However, there was no warrant to put a gloss on the wide statutory discretion by imposing the prohibition that the desirability of the future use could only be a material consideration if it had a 51 per cent probability of coming about.

12.96 The issue was again considered in *R (Mountcook Land Ltd) v Westminster City Council* [2003] [2004] JPL 470. There the Court of Appeal accepted that it would be irrational to have regard to an alternative proposal, and appeared to suggest that for some other use to be a material consideration, there had to be a likelihood or real possibility of that other use being achieved. In the words of Auld LJ:

If it were merely a matter of a bare possibility, planning authorities and decision-makers would constantly have to look over their shoulders before granting any planning application against the possibility of some alternative planning outcome, however ill-defined and however unlikely of achievement. Otherwise they would be open to challenge by way of judicial review for failing to have regard to a material consideration or of not giving it sufficient weight, however remote.

The fears of residents

In *West Midlands Probation Committee v Secretary of State for the Environment* [1998] JPL 388, the Court of Appeal held that the commission of criminal offences and anti-social behaviour by occupiers of proposed development may be a material consideration in the determination of applications for planning permission if it was intimately connected with the development. In that case planning permission which had been sought for a bail and probation hostel, had been refused on appeal because of the crime and disorder committed by the hostel's residents. The evidence had been that this was connected with the use of the land and did not arise out of the isolated and idiosyncratic behaviour of particular residents. **12.97**

Another case which considered how far residents' fears are a material consideration in determining applications for planning permission is *R v Broadlands DC, St Matthew Society Ltd and Peddars Way Housing Association, ex p Dove, Harpley and Wright* [1998] JPL B84. There, planning permission had been granted for a change of use from a hotel to a hostel, a bed group home with staff flats and a number of one-bedroom flats. An officer had reported to the relevant sub-committee that determined the application, that a common thread running through letters of objection to the proposed development suggested '. . . that the occupants of the development will be unemployed, unemployable, anti-social and morally unstable, thereby posing a security risk to persons in the locality'. The officer went on to say that concern over the nature and character of the potential residents of the proposed development was not a land and planning issue. In refusing an application for judicial review of the Council's decision, the High Court held that the officer's advice had been erroneous, and that the anti-social behaviour of the residents of the proposed hostel was a land use consideration and material to planning. However, the applicants had been unable to show that the sub-committee had not taken the residents' fears into account in arriving at their decision. **12.98**

What is not clear from the case law in this area is the extent to which it must be shown that residents' fears are justified. Even if their fears were unjustified, the case of *Newport Borough Council v Secretary of State for Wales* [1998] JPL 377 has established that they might still be a material consideration, though in that situation the decision-maker is likely to accord those fears much less weight. It has also been recognized that the planning system does not operate on the basis that development can proceed only if harm can be guaranteed never to occur. Furthermore, the system requires the decision-maker to have regard to other systems of statutory control that exist to deal with situations likely to generate residents' fear. **12.99**

Lastly, it seems that local planning authorities should not make moral judgments on the way in which property may be used if planning permission is to be granted. In *Finlay v Secretary of State for the Environment* [1983] JPL 802, the Secretary of State had dismissed an appeal against an enforcement notice which had alleged an unauthorised use of a house as a private members club. The club was known for showing sexually explicit films to members. **12.100**

In his decision letter the Secretary of State had referred to the fact that this could alter the environmental character of the area by introducing a use detrimental to residential amenities. In dismissing a challenge to the Secretary of State's decision, the High Court held that far from making any moral judgment on the type of films shown, he was making a planning judgment on whether the showing of such films adversly affected the local environment.

12.101 In *R v Tandridge DC, ex p Mohamed Al Fayed* [1999] JPL 825, objections had been made by the appellant to a grant of planning permission for the erection of a radio telephone base station tower on nearby land. The High Court whilst accepting that there had been a flaw in the Council's decision-making process in not consulting the Health and Safety Executive before granting permission, refused to exercise its discretion to quash the grant. In the Court of Appeal, [2000] JPL 604, Schiemann LJ recognised as common ground '. . . that the existence of objectively unjustified fears in the locality can, in some circumstances, be a legitimate factor for a local planning authority to take into account when deciding a planning application'. He then went on to dismiss the appeal from the decision of the High Court.

Personal circumstances of the applicant

12.102 Although in practice the personal circumstances of an applicant do occasionally result in his obtaining a favourable decision from the local planning authority, the legal authority for this practice is not of long standing.

12.103 In *New Forest DC v Secretary of State for the Environment* [1984] JPL 178, a Mr Clarke was the owner of a bungalow built with an occupancy condition restricting its use to past or present employees of an adjacent hotel, or to agricultural or forestry workers. He had made a number of applications for planning permission to use the bungalow without the occupancy condition and, save for the last, all had been refused. Finally, the Secretary of State had granted planning permission on appeal. The local planning authority claimed in the Queen's Bench Division that the Secretary of State had wrongly taken into account Mr Clarke's financial circumstances and that this was not a material consideration. Rejecting that argument, Taylor J held that it was proper to take into account personal circumstances and personal hardship where matters might be very evenly balanced, and to consider the effect the decision might have on the individual applicant. Obviously such a consideration could only be peripheral to the main planning issues which had to be taken into account.

12.104 In *Tameside MBC v Secretary of State for the Environment* [1984] JPL 180 it again was held that the Secretary of State was entitled to take personal hardship into account.

12.105 The consideration of personal circumstances, but only on a marginal basis, was given the seal of the highest judicial authority in *Westminster City Council v Great Portland Estates plc* [1985] AC 661. In that case the respondent company had challenged both the industrial and the office policies contained in the Westminster City local plan. With regard to industrial development, the general policy was that applications for planning permission for new industrial floor space and the creation of new industrial employment were to be encouraged. That general policy was modified in the case of applications for planning permission to rehabilitate or redevelop existing industrial premises. In these cases the authority's general policy was supplanted where considered necessary to maintain the continuation of industrial uses important to the diverse character, vitality and functioning of Westminster. There the policy was to be to protect 'specific industrial activities' from redevelopment. The respondent company challenged this latter aspect as being outside the purposes of planning law. The essence of the company's argument was that the protection of specified industrial activities was not a policy concerned with the development and use of land, but one concerned with the protection of particular users of land. It was irrelevant, it was claimed, to have regard in this way to the interests of individual occupiers.

In rejecting the challenge to the authority's industrial policy, Lord Scarman, giving the only speech, but one concurred in by all the other Law Lords, adopted the general principle enunciated by Lord Parker CJ in *East Barnet UDC v British Transport Commission* [1962] 2 QB 484 that in considering whether there had been a change of use, 'what is really to be considered is the character of the use of the land, not the particular purposes of a particular occupier'. It was a logical process, Lord Scarman thought, to extend the ambit of that statement to the formulation of planning policies and proposals. However, like all generalisations, he said, the statement of Lord Parker had its own limitations. Personal circumstances of the occupier, personal hardship, and the difficulties of business which are of value to the community were not to be ignored in the administration of planning control. **12.106**

A good example of the application of *Westminster City Council v Great Portland Estates plc* with somewhat unusual consequences is seen in decisions involving listed buildings in the Lake District. In December 1987, the South Lakeland District Council became aware that original windows in a row of listed terrace houses at Nos 1, 3 and 4 Eastside, The Square, Burton-in-Kendal, had been replaced by modern casement windows without listed building consent. Following a decision by the authority to take enforcment action to remedy the breaches of control, the owner of No 3 submitted an application for listed building consent to retain the new windows. On appeal to the Secretary of State, an Inspector allowed the appeal and granted the retrospective listed building consent applied for. **12.107**

In *South Lakeland DC v Secretary of State for the Environment and Rowbotham* [1991] JPL 440, the local planning authority then sought unsuccessfully to challenge that decision in the High Court, which held, *inter alia*, that the Inspector had not erred in regarding the personal circumstances of the elderly applicant, namely the costs and disruption which would be caused by having to put back the original windows and the loss of the comfort an aged resident would derive from double glazing, as material factors to be taken into account in applying planning legislation. The High Court also made it clear (as had the Inspector in his decision letter) that the granting of the consent afforded no precedent in relation to other pending cases. **12.108**

Accordingly, the local planning authority then proceeded to take listed building enforcement action against the owners of Nos 1 and 4 Eastside. Both owners appealed against the notice to the Secretary of State. The same Inspector in both cases concluded that the replacement windows were inappropriate and upheld the notices. In one of them, personal circumstances were advanced by the appellant but discounted by the Inspector. In both cases reference was made to replacement windows installed at No 3 Eastside with now listed building consent. On this aspect the Inspector said: **12.109**

> . . . the fact that inappropriate windows have been granted consent at No 3 makes it more, and

> not less, important to ensure that appropriate windows are installed elsewhere in the front façade. Consequently, I find no merit in the suggestion that, for uniformity, inappropriate windows should be installed in all the windows of the front elevation of Nos 1–4.

Following the decision the elderly occupant of No 3, whose personal circumstances were crucial to the decision to grant listed building consent vacated the premises, which were then put up for sale.

12.110 A more recent case on personal circumstances was *R v Vale of Glamorgan DC, ex p Adams* [2001] JPL 93, where a grant of planning permission to convert and change the use of three barns to residential use was quashed because members of the local planning committee had not been advised that 'personal circumstances of an occupier, personal hardship and the difficulties of business which are of value to the community' were capable of being material considerations even if to give effect to them would involve an exception from general policy. The application to quash had been made by a tenant farmer of the land who risked losing his security of tenure if planning permission were to be granted.

12.111 It should also be noted that although the variety of circumstances that might be described as 'personal' is probably extremely wide, there is as was recognised by the House of Lords in South Bucks District Council v Porter [2003] JPL 1412 now an overlap between the requirements of the Human Rights Act 1998 and decisions made previously by domestic courts in this area.

Affordable housing

12.112 One issue on which there could be a clearer and more authoritative statement of the law is the basis on which a local planning authority can use its powers to promote the provision of 'affordable housing'. Affordable housing is a term used to describe both low-cost market and subsidised housing (irrespective of tenure, ownership — whether it be exclusive or shared — or financial arrangements) that is made available to people who cannot afford to rent or buy houses available on the open market. This latter class is usually referred to in this context as 'general market housing'. In the beginning Government policy was that if a demonstrable need could be shown, then planning permission might be granted exceptionally for affordable housing on sites which would not normally receive permission and which would be additional to those provided for in development plans. It was recognised that where this took place secure arrangements would have to be made to ensure that subsequent occupants complied with the objectives of the policy.

12.113 The jurisprodential difficulty is that the policy may conflict with the principle that planning seeks to control the character of the use of land not the particular purpose of a particular occupier, though personal circumstances may also be a material consideration.

12.114 Some light was shone on this conflict by *Mitchell v Secretary of State for the Environment* [1994] EGCS 111. The local planning authority had a policy 'to resist proposals for the conversion into self-contained accommodation of houses in multiple occupation meeting a known and established need'. The authority had failed to determine an application for permission to change the use of a house in multiple occupation into self-contained flats and there was an appeal to the Secretary of State, who applied the authority's policy and dismissed the appeal. The High Court had then quashed the Secretary of State's decision on the ground that the authority's policy was not a material consideration which could be taken into account. An appeal by the Secretary of State against that decision, however, was upheld by the Court of Appeal. The Court held that 'material considerations' were not confined to questions of amenity and environmental impact. The need for housing in a particular area could be a material consideration. No sensible distinction could be drawn between a need for housing generally and a need for a particular type of housing, whether defined in terms of cost, tenure or otherwise. The fact that the need might be dictated by considerations of cost or type was irrelevant.

In the *Mitchell* case the local planning authority's policy had been contained in its draft Unitary Development Plan. In *ECC Construction Ltd v Secretary of State for the Environment* [1995] JPL 322, the High Court followed that decision, but went further in holding that although it was not necessary for the need for affordable housing to be included in formulated policies, it could arise by implication. The decision is thus authority for the proposition that the absence of affordable housing in a development proposal could render the development unacceptable. **12.115**

Again, in *R v London Borough of Tower Hamlets exp Barrett Homes Ltd* [2000] JPL 1050 the High Court refused to grant an application for a declaration that supplementary planning guidance which required the provision of affordable housing was unlawful and must not be taken into account as a material consideration in determining a planning permission application. **12.116**

It must now firmly be accepted, therefore, that the need for affordable housing can be a material consideration to be taken into account in determining applications for planning permission. PPG3, Housing, published in March 2000, contains advice to local planning authorities on the general approach to be taken in achieving affordable housing through the planning system. In addition, Circular 6/98 gives practical advice to local planning authorities on how to increase the supply of affordable housing through negotiation with developers and others. Now, local development plans contain policies relating to the provision of affordable housing. Circular 6/98 advises on the criteria which should be taken into account in assessing the suitability of housing development sites for an appropriate mix of affordable housing and general market housing. **12.117**

The procedure for providing affordable housing usually takes the form of the developer entering into a s 106 agreement, whereby either the land is transferred to a housing association, charitable organisation or similar body; or by the developers themselves undertaking the role of registered social landlords and managing the units as affordable housing then and in the future, or through an agent such as a housing association. The obligation is also likely to deal with the mix of the low cost housing and social rented housing, nomination rights, occupancy criteria, location and provision to ensure that the affordable housing remains affordable. **12.118**

Enabling development

In *R v Westminster City Council, ex p Monahan* [1988] JPL 107, the Court of Appeal made clear that 'any other material considerations' could properly include 'financial considerations'. In this case an application had been made to the High Court for judicial review to quash a grant **12.119** of planning permission and various consents for the demolition of a number of listed and unlisted buildings as part of a development scheme to improve the facilities at the Royal Opera House, Covent Garden. The main purpose of the scheme had been the redevelopment of the Opera House, but this could only proceed if permission were also granted for adjacent commercial development which would provide the funds needed to improve the Opera House. But for this essential link, planning policy would have dictated that planning permission would not have been granted for the commercial development alone. In the courts the appellants claimed unsuccessfully that the local planning authority had taken into account a consideration that was not material, namely the generation of finance from part of the proposed development to be used for the benefit of the Opera House; and had failed to consider a material consideration, namely that if finance was a material consideration, they had not considered other sources of finance available to the Opera House not involving the commercial development.

12.120 Upholding the decision of the High Court, the Court of Appeal held that financial constraints on the economic viability of a desirable planning development are unavoidable facts of life in an imperfect world and virtually all planning decisions involve some kind of balancing exercise. Provided that the ultimate determination of a planning decision is based on planning grounds and not on some ulterior motive, and that it is not irrational, there is no basis for holding it invalid in law solely on the ground that it has taken account of, and adjusted itself to, the financial realities of the overall situation. The meaning of 'material consideration' in the Town and Country Planning Act has been circumscribed in wide terms and these do not exclude financial considerations from being treated as material in appropriate cases. Hence, the financing of the development scheme was capable of being a material consideration, as it related to the use and development of land.

12.121 It is probable that the *Covent Garden* case has led to an increase in the number of cases where it is claimed that any detriment suffered by a grant of permission for part of a development scheme contrary to established policy, would be more than offset by the benefit to be gained from other aspects of the scheme if the whole were to be allowed to proceed.

12.122 In a number of later Ministerial decisions the '*Covent Garden* influence' can be seen. The first decision granted planning permission for the erection of eight houses in the walled kitchen garden of Croome Court, Worcester, a Grade 1 listed building, the construction of which was begun in 1751 by 'Capability' Brown, and was now unoccupied and in need of restoration. The Inspector found that the proposed development would be contrary to the policies of the approved structure plan for the area so that the proposal should normally fail. However, he accepted the applicant's contention that if the development were permitted the profit realised from the sale of eight building plots would generate enough cash to enable restoration of the house to proceed. At the inquiry, the parties had favoured a planning agreement to achieve this. In the event, this did not prove possible, so the Inspector dealt with it by conditions.

12.123 In another decision, the Secretary of State had to consider whether to grant planning permission to Wates Homes Ltd for the erection, *inter alia*, of a superstore at Broadlands, Hampshire. The applicants argued that by permitting the development, sufficient funds would be generated to secure the restoration and future maintenance of Broadlands House and surrounding estate, which included no less than 50 listed buildings.

In dismissing the appeal, the Secretary of State considered that whilst it was reasonable to take that into account, he could not agree with the Inspector's judgment that the needs of this historic house could justify the introduction of an inappropriate and intensive form of development, with all its attendant disturbance into a countryside area contrary to structure plan policies. 12.124

This decision raises the question of whether, if one is to take advantage of the *Covent Garden* approach, there has to be a functional link between the proposed development and the land to be benefited by it, or for both to be on the same site. In this instance, the site of the proposed development was approximately two miles from Broadlands House itself. 12.125

Another example of enabling development is a 1994 ministerial decision, where planning permission was given for a 36-hole golf-course with clubhouse and car parking on land at Mapledurham Estate, Mapledurham, near Reading, in an Area of Outstanding Natural Beauty. A significant reason for so doing was that some of the listed buildings in the estate's ownerhsip were in need of urgent repair, and the income from the proposed golf-course would enable a 20-year programme of repairs to be undertaken. The decision was later challenged unsuccessfully in the High Court in *South Oxfordshire DC v Secretary of State for the Environment* [1995] JPL 213 on grounds which included an allegation that the method chosen for securing that the programme of repairs would be undertaken (a s 106 agreement) was a nullity. 12.126

Again, in a Ministerial decision reported at [1996] JPL 158, the Secretary of State granted planning permission for residential development close to Henbury House, Sturminster Marshall, Dorset, a Grade II* listed building, contrary to planning policy governing development in the green belt, because the development would generate funds to enable repairs to be carried out. 12.127

In yet another Ministerial decision [1995] JPL 654, planning permission was granted for the construction of an education centre and car-parking spaces at Paignton Zoo, and for the construction of a 65,000 square foot food retail store on adjoining land. Although the Secretary of State accepted that the proposals involved a degree of conflict with certain development plan policies, he considered the benefits from the new development carried greater weight. Those benefits were that the future viability of the zoo would be ensured by allowing it to upgrade facilities which would be to the advantage of tourism and would avoid the job losses which would result from closing the zoo. 12.128

So far the use of the concept of enabling development appears to have been mainly restricted to the field of listed buildings. This may change, however, particularly in relation to the development of contaminated land. Government policy, set out in PPS23, Planning and Pollution Control, for dealing with contaminated land encompasses a 'suitable for use' approach, which requires remedial action to be taken only where the contamination poses unacceptable actual or perceived risks to health and to the environment, and where there are appropriate and cost-effective means available, taking into account the actual or intended use of the site. This may mean that planning permission could be given for development not otherwise acceptable, in order to ensure the 'clean-up' of land previously contaminated. 12.129

Apart from *R v Westminister City Council, ex p Monahan*, other cases where the courts have recognised the principle of enabling development as a material consideration include 12.130

Northumberland CC v Secretary of State for the Environment [1989] JPL 700 and *Wansdyke DC v Secretary of State for the Environment* [1992] JPL 1168.

12.131 Before granting planning permission a local planning authority must ensure that all material considerations are taken into account. Within the context of enabling development it was suggested by the High Court in *R v West Dorset DC, ex p Searle*, that although an authority may consider that before granting planning permission an independent evaluation or assessment of the financial appraisal submitted by the developer was a necessary tool by which to judge the appropriateness of the proposed development, there was no necessity for the authority to go that far. Latham J concluded that on the evidence before him, the authority was within its rights to conclude that the benefits of proceeding with the applicant's proposals as they stood outweighed the planning detriments: in this case the restoration of a Grade II* listed building. On appeal, the Court of Appeal [1999] JPL 331 upheld the decision of Latham J by a majority.

Planning and pollution control

12.132 Pollution controls in the United Kingdom are exercised through a range of organisations and a variety of mechanisms, including licensing and authorisation procedures which are applied to processes and substances which can have potentially harmful effects on the environment. In the past few years, a sustantial body of new legislation such as the Control of Pollution Act 1974, the Environmental Protection Act 1990 and the Water Resources Act 1991 have considerably extended the scope and effectiveness of pollution controls. The relation between planning and pollution control, however, is not particularly clear. An early case, *Ladbroke (Rentals) Ltd v Secretary of State for the Environment* [1981] JPL 427, established that disturbance or annoyances caused to other occupiers of land is a relevant planning consideration regardless of powers to control the source under other legislation. It should also be noted that under the Town and Country Planning (Assessment of Environmental Effects) Regulations 1999, a local planning authority must not grant planning permission for any development of land to which the regulations apply, unless they first take into account environmental information.

12.133 The problem was discussed in the case of *Gateshead MBC v Secretary of State for the Environment* (1993) 67 P & CR 179. The Northern Regional Hospital Authority had applied to the local planning authority for outline planning permission for a clinical waste incinerator which had been refused. On appeal to the Secretary of State by the Health Authority, an Inspector had concluded that whilst an appropriate plant could be built to meet the various standards relating to emission limits laid down by HM Inspectorate of Pollution under the Environmental Protection Act 1990, the effect on air quality and agriculture in the locality was insufficiently defined, and that public disquite about environmental pollution could not be sufficiently allayed to make the proposed development acceptable. Accordingly, he recommended to the Secretary of State that planning permission for the incinerator should be refused. The Secretary of State, however, declined to accept the recommendation and granted permission for the development on the grounds first, that the Secretary of State could not lawfully abdicate his planning responsibilities to the Environmental Protection Act 1990 regime; secondly, that there was no evidence on which he could be satisfied that controls under that regime would be adequate and thirdly, that if he could not properly be satisfied that these concerns could be dealt with under that regime, it followed that the proposal would not comply with structure plan requirements for the consequences in terms of environmental impact to be acceptable.

In an unsuccessful application to the High Court to quash the Secretary of State's decision, it was held that the environmental impact of emissions into the atmosphere was a material consideration in determining planning applications, but so too was the existence of pollution controls. After remarking that any attempt to draw a demarcation line between the two forms of control was not helpful, the learned deputy judge went on to say: **12.134**

> At one extreme there will be cases where the evidence at the planning stage demonstrates that potential pollution problems have been substantially overcome, so that any reasonable person will accept that the remaining details can sensibly be left to the EPA authorisation process.
>
> At the other extreme, there may be cases where the evidence of environmental problems is so damning at the planning stage that any reasonable person would refuse planning permission, saying, in effect, there is no point in trying to resolve these very grave problems through the EPA process. Between these two extremes there will be a whole spectrum of cases disclosing pollution problems of different types and differing degree of complexity and gravity.

This judgment was subsequently upheld by the Court of Appeal [1994] 1 PLR 85.

It seems, therefore, that the weight to be given to environmental issues and the power to control them under pollution legislation in determining applications for planning permission is a matter for the particular decision maker, be it local planning authority or Secretary of State. **12.135**

PPS23, Planning and Pollution Control, makes it clear that planning control and pollution control are separate but complementary procedures, with both being designed to protect the environment from the potential harm caused by development and other operations, but with different objectives. Although PPS accepts that the planning system should not be operated so as to duplicate environmental control, it acknowledges that the dividing line between the two systems is not always clear-cut. **12.136**

The PPS makes the point that the scope of the planning regime for protecting the environment is wider than that of the pollution control regime. For example, Her Majesty's Inspectors of Pollution are not likely to pay regard to the effect of noxious emissions on the development potential of an area, or to consider whether in any particular case the location of a particular process would make the area less attractive for securing its regeneration. **12.137**

It should also be remembered that the controls exercised under the regulatory pollution regime exist to prevent or mitigate harm from what are called 'prescribed processes'. Any grant of planning permission for development involving such processes in no way inhibits Inspectors of Pollution from refusing to authorise that process where they consider it would cause demonstrable harm. **12.138**

Where the development would not involve an authorisation requirement under pollution control, it would seem that local planning authorities still have some latitude to invoke the planning regime for amenity reasons. For example, it would seem acceptable for a local planning authority to seek to control through the planning system a shop for the sale of hot food to be located in a residential area, irrespective of whether the effects of that **12.139** development on the living conditions of neighbours would be susceptible to control as being a statutory nuisance.

12.140 With regard to pollution control, it should be noted that her Majesty's Inspectorate of Pollution, the National Rivers Authority and Waste Regulation Authorities are now part of the Environment Agency set up by the Environment Act 1995. The Agency has indicated that it will become involved with land use planning in the following ways:

(i) responding to a consultations by local planning authorities under the Town and Country Planning (Assessment of Environmental Effects) Regulations 1999;
(ii) responding to requests from developers for information relating to their applications under the regulations at (i) above;
(iii) responding to consultation on planning applications;
(iv) responding and providing input to the preparation of development plans;
(v) responding to general enquiries about proposed developments; and
(vi) provided technical advice to the Government at regional or national level in response to requests for information about the significance of any likely pollution from a proposed development.

Planning and licensing control

12.141 The decision in the Gateshead case (see above) suggests that the notion that the operation of planning law ought not to attempt to replicate the law on pollution and other environmental controls is essentially one of planning policy and practice than of law. The existence of alternative statutory means of controlling pollution continues to be therefore in law, a material consideration for authorities to take into account in dealing with applications for development which would also be subject to those other forms of statutory control.

12.142 In *Roger Lethem v Secretary of State and Worcester City Council* [2003] JPL 332, the High Court dismissed an application to quash a decision by an Inspector to dismiss an appeal against a refusal by the local planning authority to grant planning permission for a change of use of premises from a use within Class A1 of the Use Classes Order to a café/bar within use Class A3. The applicants unsuccessfully contended that the Inspector erred in failing to recognise that the objections he found to aspects of the proposed café/bar, were matters that fell to be dealt with under the Licensing Act 1964, and would not therefore, justify a refusal of planning permission.

Consolidation of undesirable uses

12.143 Uses which are undesirable in a particular area can only be required to cease if the local planning authority is prepared to serve a discontinuance order in respect of the use and to pay compensation for loss suffered as a result. Where, however, undesirable uses exist it has been held that a local planning authority can refuse planning permission for development of the site if to grant permission would perpetuate and consolidate the use being carried on on the land. For example, where a person carries on as an established use the business of storage and haulage of plant hire on open land, he might apply for planning permission to construct a building in which to carry out that activity. The authority may then refuse planning permission in the hope that the use will diminish or cease altogether. The principle was recognised in *W. H. Tolley & Son Ltd v Secretary of State for the Environment* (1998) 75 P & CR 533, where it was stated:

> The concept of consolidation of an undesirable use is familiar in planning. As I understand it, it implies not . . . an increase or an intensification in the current use, but a strengthening of the features that support it, thus making it less likely that the use will diminish in intensity or be replaced by a less undesirable use. By refusing planning permission for a development which it considers would consolidate the existing undesirable use, the planning authority seek to preserve the prospect of its diminution or replacement.

Environmental information

Under the Town and Country Planning (Environmental Impact Assessment) (England and Wales) Regulations 1999, a local planning authority or the Secretary of State must not grant planning permission for any development to which the regulations apply, unless they have first taken into consideration any environmental information. This area of law is dealt with in the next chapter. **12.144**

13

ENVIRONMENTAL IMPACT ASSESSMENT

A. INTRODUCTION

A requirement for the environmental impact assessment of certain major development projects, was a result of the first direct impact of European Community law on domestic town and country planning law. The terms of EC Directive No 85/337, *The Assessment of the Effect of Certain Public and Private Projects on the Environment,* have been implemented in the UK as far as possible within normal town and country planning procedures. Now there are in fact many sets of statutory provisions which implement the Directive, dealing with such matters as afforestation projects, highways, harbour works, land drainage, fish farming and electricity and pipeline works. The EC Directive came into force in 1988. The Directive was subsequently amended by EC Directive 97/11/EC, which came into force on 14 March 1999. The amendment extended the range of development to which EC Directive 85/337/EEC was to apply and made a number of small but important changes to EIA procedures. The main vehicle for the implementation of the Directive is now the Town and Country Planning **13.01**

(Environmental Impact Assessment) (England and Wales) Regulations 1999, SI 1999/293 (the Regulations). The Regulations came into force on 14 March 1999. At the same time the Secretary of State issued Circular 02/99 giving guidance on the procedures. Where the procedure for the approval of projects requiring environmental impact assessment under the Directive is dealt with under other legislation (e.g. highways under the Highways Acts), separate subordinate legislation has been introduced. These, however, fall outside the scope of this chapter.

13.02 The regulations apply to applications for development that require planning permission under the 1990 Act. They do not apply to decisions of local planning authorities not to take enforcement proceedings against contravening development, since such proceedings are not regarded as development consent for the purposes of the Directive.

13.03 Most of the regulations governing environmental impact assessment were introduced under powers given to Ministers by the European Communities Act 1972. During the passage of the Planning and Compensation Act 1991 through Parliament, however, the Government accepted the view that as regards planning legislation there should be some direct statutory authority for the implementation of the European Community Directive. In addition, it considered that there was an argument for extending environmental impact assessment to types of project beyond those specifically required by the Directive. Accordingly, s 15 of the 1991 Act inserted a new s 71A into the 1990 Act to give the Secretary of State power to make regulations about the consideration to be given, before planning permission for development is granted, of the likely environmental effects of the proposed development. He can thus at any time enlarge the classes of development for which environmental impact assessment may be required. He did in fact do so in 1994, when he amended the Regulations to add privately financed toll roads to Sch 1 and wind generators, motorway service areas and coast protection works to Sch 2. Following the amendment of the Directive in 1997 that amendment has now been repealed, the development mentioned having been subsumed within the latest Environmental Impact Assessment Regulations.

13.04 'Environmental Impact Assessment' can be seen as 'a technique for the systematic compilation of expert quantitative analysis and qualitative assessment of a project's environmental effects, and the presentation of results in a way which enables the importance of the predicted results, and the scope for modifying or mitigating them, to be properly evaluated by the relevant decision-making body before a planning application decision is taken'.

13.05 In order to understand the procedures that have to be followed, it is important to understand the following terminology expressed in legal terms in Regulation 2(1):

(a) *Environmental impact assessment* is essentially a process. It is the whole process required to reach a decision on whether or not to allow the project to proceed. Environmental assessment involves the presentation, collection, publication and assessment of information on the environmental effects of a project, and also the final judgment upon it. An important part of that process is the submission of an environmental statement.

(b) *Environmental statement* is the information which must be provided by the developer in conjunction with his application for planning permission for the project.

According to Regulation 2(1) an environmental statement is a statement:

(a) that includes such of the information referred to in Part I of Sch 4 as is reasonably required to assess the environmental effects of the development and which the applicant can, having regard in particular to current knowledge and methods of assessment, reasonably be required to compile, but
(b) that includes at least the information referred to in Part II of Sch 4.

Parts I and II of Sch 4 are as follows:

PART I

1. Description of the development, including in particular—
   (a) a description of the physical characteristics of the whole development and the land-use requirements during the construction and operational phases;
   (b) a description of the main characteristics of the production processes, for instance, nature and quantity of the materials used;
   (c) an estimate, by type and quantity, of expected residues and emissions (water, air and soil pollution, noise, vibration, light, heat, radiation, etc.) resulting from the operation of the proposed development.
2. An outline of the main alternatives studied by the applicant or appellant and an indication of the main reasons for his choice, taking into account the environmental effects.
3. A description of the aspects of the environment likely to be significantly affected by the development, including, in particular, population, fauna, flora, soil, water, air, climatic factors, material assets, including the architectural and archaeological heritage, landscape and the inter-relationship between the above factors.
4. A description of the likely significant effects of the development on the environment, which should cover the direct effects and any indirect, secondary, cumulative, short, medium and long-term, permanent and temporary, positive and negative effects of the development, resulting from:
   (a) the existence of the development;
   (b) the use of natural resources;
   (c) the emission of pollutants, the creation of nuisances and the elimination of waste, and the description by the applicant of the forecasting methods used to assess the effects on the environment.
5. A description of the measures envisaged to prevent, reduce and where possible offset any significant adverse effects on the environment.
6. A non-technical summary of the information provided under paragraphs 1 to 5 of this Part.
7. An indication of any difficulties (technical deficiencies or lack of know-how) encountered by the applicant in compiling the required information.

PART II

1. A description of the development comprising information on the site, design and size of the development.
2. A description of the measures envisaged in order to avoid, reduce and, if possible, remedy significant adverse effects.
3. The data required to identify and assess the main effects which the development is likely to have on the environment.
4. An outline of the main alternatives studied by the applicant or appellant and an indication of the main reasons for his choice, taking into account the environmental effects.
5. A non-technical summary of the information provided under paragraphs 1 to 4 of this Part.

(c) *Environmental information* is a term used to include the information provided by the developer in his environmental statement; any further information; any representations made by anybody who by the Regulations must be invited to make them; and any representations made by any other person about the environmental effects of the development. As such it is a material consideration in determining the application for planning permission.

13.06 It is thought that about 300 applications for planning permission for development requiring environmental impact assessment are now made each year; a number likely to increase following the extensive amendments to the Regulations in 1999.

B. PROJECTS REQUIRING ENVIRONMENTAL IMPACT ASSESSMENT

13.07 The Regulations apply to two separate lists of development projects:

(a) 'Schedule 1 development', for which environmental impact assessment is mandatory;
(b) 'Schedule 2 development', for which environmental impact assessment is required if the particular project is considered likely to give rise to significant effects on the environment by virtue of factors such as its nature, size or location or to development located wholly or partly in a 'sensitive area'.

Schedule 1 development

13.08 The following types of development require environmental impact assessment in every case:

The carrying out of development to provide any of the following—

1. Crude-oil refineries (excluding undertakings manufacturing only lubricants from crude oil) and installations for the gasification and liquefaction of 500 tonnes or more of coal or bituminous shale per day.
2. (a) Thermal power stations and other combustion installations with a heat output of 300 megawatts or more; and
   (b) Nuclear power stations and other nuclear reactors (except research installations for the production and conversion of fissionable and fertile materials, whose maximum power does not exceed 1 kilowatt continuous thermal load).
3. (a) Installations for the reprocessing of irradiated nuclear fuel.
   (b) Installations designed—
   (i) for the production or enrichment of nuclear fuel,
   (ii) for the processing of irradiated nuclear fuel or high-level radioactive waste,
   (iii) for the final disposal of irradiated nuclear fuel,
   (iv) solely for the final disposal of radioactive waste,
   (v) solely for the storage(planned for more than 10 years) of irradiated nuclear fuels or radioactive waste in a different site than the production site.
4. (a) Integrated works for the initial smelting of cast-iron and steel;
   (b) Installations for the production of non-ferrous crude metals from ore, concentrates or secondary raw materials by metallurgical, chemical or electrolytic processes.
5. Installations for the extraction of asbestos and for the processing and transformation of asbestos and products containing asbestos—

(a) for asbestos-cement products, with an annual production of more than 20,000 tonnes of finished products;

(b) for friction material, with an annual production of more than 50 tonnes of finished products; and

(c) for other uses of asbestos, utilisation of more than 200 tonnes per year.

6. Integrated chemical installations, that is to say, installations for the manufacture on an industrial scale of substances using chemical conversion processes, in which several units are juxtaposed and are functionally linked to one another and which are—

(a) for the production of basic organic chemicals;

(b) for the production of basic inorganic chemicals;

(c) for the production of phosphorous-, nitrogen- or potassium-based fertilisers (simple or compound fertilisers);

(d) for the production of basic plant health products and of biocides;

(e) for the production of basic pharmaceutical products using a chemical or biological process;

(f) for the production of explosives.

7. (a) Construction of lines for long-distance railway traffic and of airports with a basic runway length of 2,100 metres of more;

(b) Construction of motorways and express roads;

(c) Construction of a new road of four or more lanes, or realignment and/or widening of an existing road of two lanes or less so as to provide four or more lanes, where such new road, or realigned and/or widened section of road would be 10 kilometres or more in a continuous length.

8. (a) Inland waterways and ports for inland-waterway traffic which permit the passage of vessels of over 1,350 tonnes;

(b) Trading ports, piers for loading and unloading connected to land and outside ports (excluding ferry piers) which can take vessels of over 1,350 tonnes.

9. Waste disposal installations for the incineration, chemical treatment (as defined in Annex IIA to Council Directive 75/442/EEC under heading D9), or landfill of hazardous waste (that is to say, waste to which Council Directive 91/689/EEC applies).

10. Waste disposal installations for the incineration or chemical treatment (as defined in Annex IIA to Council Directive 75/442/EEC under heading20D9) of non-hazardous waste with a capacity exceeding 100 tonnes per day.

11. Groundwater abstraction or artificial groundwater recharge schemes where the annual volume of water abstracted or recharged is equivalent to or exceeds 10 million cubic metres.

12. (a) Works for the transfer of water resources, other than piped drinking water, between river basins where the transfer aims at preventing possible shortages of water and where the amount of water transferred exceeds 100 million cubic metres per year;

(b) In all other cases, works for the transfer of water resources, other than piped drinking water, between river basins where the multi-annual average flow of the basin of abstraction exceeds 2,000 million cubic metres per year and where the amount of water transferred exceeds 5% of this flow.

13. Waste water treatment plants with a capacity exceeding 150,000 population equivalent as defined in Article 2 point (6) of Council Directive 91/271/EEC.

14. Extraction of petroleum and natural gas for commercial purposes where the amount extracted exceeds 500 tonnes per day in the case of petroleum and 500,000 cubic metres per day in the case of gas.

15. Dams and other installations designed for the holding back or permanent storage of water, where a new or additional amount of water held back or stored exceeds 10 million cubic metres.

16. Pipelines for the transport of gas, oil or chemicals with a diameter of more than 800 millimetres and a length of more than 40 kilometres.
17. Installations for the intensive rearing of poultry or pigs with more than—
    (a) 85,000 places for broilers or 60,000 places for hens;
    (b) 3,000 places for production pigs (over 30 kg); or
    (c) 900 places for sows.
18. Industrial plants for—
    (a) the production of pulp from timber or similar fibrous materials;
    (b) the production of paper and board with a production capacity exceeding 200 tonnes per day.
19. Quarries and open-cast mining where the surface of the site exceeds 25 hectares, or peat extraction where the surface of the site exceeds 150 hectares.
20. Installations for storage of petroleum, petrochemical or chemical products with a capacity of 200,000 tonnes or more.

Schedule 2 development

13.09 The following types of development ('Schedule 2 development') require environmental impact assessment if likely to have significant effects on the environment by virtue of nature, size or location. The schedule sets out against each description of development the threshold or criteria for the purpose of classifying whether such development is within the schedule. Schedule 2 development may also include development which is listed in column 1 below, but is located wholly or in part in a 'sensitive area'. In such cases, the threshold and criteria mentioned in column 2 do not apply to the development.

Description of development and applicable thresholds and criteria for the purposes of the definition of 'Schedule 2 Development'

1. In the table below—

   'area of the works' includes any area occupied by apparatus, equipment, machinery, materials, plant, spoil heaps or other facilities or stores required for construction or installation;

   'controlled waters' has the same meaning as in the Water Resources Act 1991;

   'floorspace' means the floorspace in a building or buildings.
2. The table below sets out the descriptions of development and applicable thresholds and criteria for the purpose of classifying development as Schedule 2 development.

Column 1 *Description of development*	*Column 2* *Applicable thresholds and criteria*

The carrying out of development to provide any of the following—

1. *Agriculture and aquaculture*	
(a) Projects for the use of uncultivated land or semi-natural areas for intensive agricultural purposes;	The area of the development exceeds 0.5 hectare.
(b) Water management projects for agriculture, including irrigation and land drainage projects;	The area of the works exceeds 1 hectare.
(c) Intensive livestock installations (unless included in Schedule 1);	The area of new floorspace exceeds 500 square metres.
(d) Intensive fish farming;	The installation resulting from the development is designed to produce more than 10 tonnes of dead weight fish per year.
(e) Reclamation of land from the sea.	All development.

2. *Extractive industry*	
(a) Quarries, open-cast mining and peat extraction (unless included in Schedule 1); (b) Underground mining;	All development except the construction of buildings or other ancillary structures where the new floorspace does not exceed 1,000 square metres.
(c) Extraction of minerals by fluvial dredging;	All development.
(d) Deep drillings, in particular— (i) geothermal drilling; (ii) drilling for the storage of nuclear waste material; (iii) drilling for water supplies; with the exception of drillings for investigating the stability of the soil.	(i) In relation to any type of drilling, the area of the works exceeds 1 hectare; or (ii) in relation to geothermal drilling and drilling for the storage of nuclear waste material, the drilling is within 100 metres of any controlled waters.
(e) Surface industrial installations for the extraction of coal, petroleum, natural gas and ores, as well as bituminous shale.	The area of the development exceeds 0.5 hectare.

3. *Energy industry*	
(a) Industrial installations for the production of electricity, steam and hot water (unless included in Schedule 1);	The area of the development exceeds 0.5 hectare.
(b) Industrial installations for carrying gas, steam and hot water;	The area of the works exceeds 1 hectare.
(c) Surface storage of natural gas; (d) Underground storage of combustible gases; (e) Surface storage of fossil fuels;	(i) The area of any new building, deposit or structure exceeds 500 square metres; or (ii) a new building, deposit or structure is to be sited within 100 metres of any controlled waters.
(f) Industrial briquetting of coal and lignite;	The area of new floorspace exceeds 1,000 square metres.
(g) Installations for the processing and storage of radioactive waste (unless included in Schedule 1);	(i) The area of new floorspace exceeds 1,000 square metres; or (ii) the installation resulting from the development will require an authorisation or the variation of an authorisation under the Radioactive Substances Act 1993.
(h) Installations for hydroelectric energy production;	The installation is designed to produce more than 0.5 megawatts.
(i) Installations for the harnessing of wind power for energy production (wind farms).	(i) The development involves the installation of more than 2 turbines; or (ii) the hub height of any turbine or height of any other structure exceeds 15 metres.

4. *Production and processing of metals*	
(a) Installations for the production of pig iron or steel (primary or secondary fusion) including continuous casting; (b) Installations for the processing of ferrous metals— (i) hot-rolling mills; (ii) smitheries with hammers; (iii) application of protective fused metal coats. (c) Ferrous metal foundaries; (d) Installations for the smelting, including the alloyage, of non-ferrous metals, excluding precious metals, including recovered products (refining, foundary casting, etc.); (e) Installations for surface treatment of metals and plastic materials using an electrolytic or chemical process; (f) Manufacture and assembly of motor vehicles and manufacture of motor-vehicle engines; (g) Shipyards; (h) Installations for the construction and repair of aircraft; (i) Manufacture of railway equipment; (j) Swaging by explosives; (k) Installations for the roasting and sintering of metallic ores.	The area of new floorspace exceeds 1,000 square metres.

5. *Mineral industry*	
(a) Coke ovens (dry coal distillation); (b) Installations for the manufacture of cement; (c) Installations for the production of asbestos and the manufacture of asbestos-based products (unless included in Schedule 1); (d) Installations for the manufacture of glass including glass fibre; (e) Installations for smelting mineral substances including the production of mineral fibres; (f) Manufacture of ceramic products by burning, in particular roofing tiles, bricks, refractory bricks, tiles, stonewear or porcelain.	The area of new floorspace exceeds 1,000 square metres.

6. *Chemical industry (unless included in Schedule 1)*	
(a) Treatment of intermediate products and production of chemicals; (b) Production of pesticides and pharmaceutical products, paint and varnishes, elastomers and peroxides;	The area of new floorspace exceeds 1,000 square metres.
(c) Storage facilities for petroleum, petrochemical and chemical products.	(i) The area of any new building or structure exceeds 0.05 hectare; or (ii) more than 200 tonnes of petroleum, petrochemical or chemical products is to be stored at any one time.

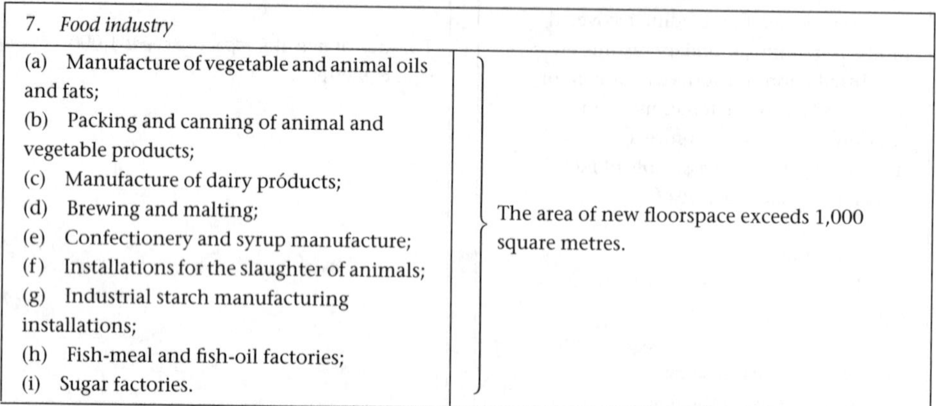

7. *Food industry*	
(a) Manufacture of vegetable and animal oils and fats; (b) Packing and canning of animal and vegetable products; (c) Manufacture of dairy próducts; (d) Brewing and malting; (e) Confectionery and syrup manufacture; (f) Installations for the slaughter of animals; (g) Industrial starch manufacturing installations; (h) Fish-meal and fish-oil factories; (i) Sugar factories.	The area of new floorspace exceeds 1,000 square metres.

8. *Textile, leather, wood and paper industries*	
(a) Industrial plants for the production of paper and board (unless included in Schedule 1); (b) Plants for the pre-treatment (operations such as washing, bleaching, mercerisation) or dyeing of fibres or textiles (c) Plants for the tanning of hides and skins; (d) Cellulose-processing and production installations.	The area of new floorspace exceeds 1,000 square metres.

9. *Rubber industry*	
Manufacture and treatment of elastomer-based products.	The area of new floorspace exceeds 1,000 square metres.

10. *Infrastructure projects*	
(a) Industrial estate development projects; (b) Urban development projects, including the construction of shopping centres and car parks, sport stadiums, leisure centres and multiplex cinemas; (c) Construction of intermodal transshipment facilities and of intermodal terminals (unless included in Schedule 1);	The area of the development exceeds 0.5 hectare.
(d) Construction of railways (unless included in Schedule 1);	The area of the works exceeds 1 hectare.
(e) Construction of airfields (unless included in Schedule 1);	(i) the development involves an extension to a runway; or (ii) the area of the works exceeds 1 hectare.
(f) Construction of roads (unless included in Schedule 1);	The area of the works exceeds 1 hectare.
(g) Construction of harbours and port installations including fishing harbours (unless included in Schedule 1);	The area of the works exceeds 1 hectare.
(h) Inland-waterway construction not included in Schedule 1, canalisation and flood-relief works; (i) Dams and other installations designed to hold water or store it on a long-term basis (unless included in Schedule 1); (j) Tramways, elevated and underground railways, suspended lines or similar lines of a particular type, used exclusively or mainly for passenger transport;	The area of the works exceeds 1 hectare.
(k) Oil and gas pipeline installations (unless included in Schedule 1); (l) Installations of long-distance aquaducts;	(i) The area of the works exceeds 1 hectare; or, (ii) in the case of a gas pipeline, the installation has a design operating pressure exceeding 7 bar guage.
(m) Coastal work to combat erosion and maritime works capable of altering the coast through the construction, for example, of dykes, moles, jetties and other sea defence works, excluding the maintenance and reconstruction of such works;	All development.
(n) Groundwater abstraction and artificial groundwater recharge schemes not included in Schedule 1; (o) Works for the transfer of water resources between river basins not included in Schedule 1;	The area of the works exceeds 1 hectare.
(p) Motorway service areas.	The area of the development exceeds 0.5 hectare.

11. *Other projects*	
(a) Permanent racing and test tracks for motorised vehicles;	The area of the development exceeds 1 hectare.
(b) Installations for the disposal of waste (unless included in Schedule 1);	(i) The disposal is by incineration; or (ii) the area of the development exceeds 0.5 hectare; or (iii) the installation is to be sited within 100 metres of any controlled waters.
(c) Waste-water treatment plants (unless included in Schedule 1);	The area of the development exceeds 1,000 square metres.
(d) Sludge-deposition sites; (e) Storage of scrap iron, including scrap vehicles;	(i) The area of deposit or storage exceeds 0.5 hectare; or (ii) a deposit is to be made or scrap stored within 100 metres of any controlled waters.
(f) Test benches for engines, turbines or reactors; (g) Installations for the manufacture of artificial mineral fibres; (h) Installations for the recovery or destruction of explosive substances; (i) Knackers' yards.	The area of new floorspace exceeds 1,000 square metres.

12. *Tourism and leisure*	
(a) Ski-runs, ski-lifts and cable-cars and associated developments;	(i) The area of the works exceeds 1 hectare; or (ii) the height of any building or other structure exceeds 15 metres.
(b) Marinas;	The area of the enclosed water surface exceeds 1,000 square metres.
(c) Holiday villages and hotel complexes outside urban areas and associated developments; (d) Theme parks;	The area of the development exceeds 0.5 hectare.
(e) Permanent camp sites and caravan sites;	The area of the development exceeds 1 hectare.
(f) Golf courses and associated developments.	The area of the development exceeds 1 hectare.

13.	
(a) Any change to or extension of development of a description listed in Schedule 1 or in paragraphs 1 to 12 of Column 1 of this table, where that development is already authorised, executed or in the process of being executed, and the change or extension may have significant adverse effects on the environment;	(i) In relation to development of a description mentioned in Column 1 of this table, the thresholds and criteria in the corresponding part of Column 2 of this table applied to the change or extension (and not to the development as changed or extended). (ii) In relation to development of a description mentioned in a paragraph in Schedule 1 indicated below, the thresholds and criteria in Column 2 of the paragraph of this table indicated below applied to the change or extension (and not to the development as changed or extended): *Paragraph in Schedule 1* — *Paragraph of this table* 1 — 6(a) 2(a) — 3(a) 2(b) — 3(g) 3 — 3(g) 4 — 4 5 — 5 6 — 6(a) 7(a) — 10(d) (in relation to railways) or 10(e) (in relation to airports) 7(b) and (c) — 10(f) 8(a) — 10(h) 8(b) — 10(g) 9 — 11(b) 10 — 11(b) 11 — 10(n) 12 — 10(o) 13 — 11(c) 14 — 2(e) 15 — 10(i) 16 — 10(k) 17 — 1(c) 18 — 8(a) 19 — 2(a) 20 — 6(c).
(b) Development of a description mentioned in Schedule 1 undertaken exclusively or mainly for the development and testing of new methods or products and not used for more than two years.	All development.

13.10 The Schedules (particularly sch.2) are very wide, and to some extent certain obscure expressions, so that a good deal of legitimate disagreement may be involved in applying them to the facts of any particular case. In *R (Anne-Marie Goodman) v London Borough of Lewisham and Big Yellow Property C. Ltd* [2003] JPL, the Court of Appeal had to consider whether the authority correctly interpreted the expression 'urban development projects' in deciding that the development of a storage and distribution centre fell within the ambit of para. 10(2) of Sch.2. In quashing a grant of planning permission for that development the Court of Appeal held that if an authority makes an understanding of expressions used in the regulations which is wrong in law, the court may correct it. However, if the meaning in law is imprecise (as opposed to determining what the meaning was in the first place) a range of different meanings may be legitimately available. In such a case the court will only interfere if the planning authority goes outside the range of legitimate meanings.

Identifying relevant Sch 2 projects

13.11 As already indicated the criteria for determiningwhether a Sch 2 project requires environmental impact assessment is whether or not it is likely to give rise to significant effects on the environment by virtue of its nature, size or location. With the exception of development which is located wholly or partly within a 'sensitive area', the test of whether development is likely to have significant effects on the environment depends upon whether it meets or exceeds the threshold or criteria listed in column 2 of Sch 2. No such test, however, is provided for the development of land for any of the activities set out in column 1 of Sch 2, where the land is located mostly or partly within a 'sensitive area'. A 'sensitive area' includes land within an area of Special Scientific Interest, a National Park, the Broads, an Area of Outstanding Natural Beauty, World Heritage sites, scheduled monuments and land to which Nature Conservation Orders apply.

13.12 Most helpfully, Sch 3 of the Regulations set out selection criteria which must also be taken into account in determining whether development is likely to have significant effects on the environment. Such criteria apply to all development within column 1 of Sch 2, and irrespective of whether the development takes place on land in a sensitive area.

13.13 The selection criteria set out in Sch 3 are as follows:

1. Characteristics of development

The characteristics of development must be considered having regard, in particular, to—

(a) the size of the development;
(b) the cumulation with other development;
(c) the use of natural resources;
(d) the production of waste;
(e) pollution and nuisance;
(f) the risk of accidents, having regard in particular to substances or technologies used.

2. Location of development

The environmental sensitivity of geographical areas likely to be affected by development must be considered, having regard, in particular, to—

(a) the existing land use;
(b) the relative abundance, quality and regenerative capacity of natural resources in the area;

(c) the absorption capacity of the natural environment, paying particular attention to the following areas—
   (i) wetlands;
   (ii) coastal zones;
   (iii) mountain and forest areas;
   (iv) nature reserves and parks;
   (v) areas classified or protected under Member States' legislation; areas designated by Member States pursuant to Council Directive 79/409/ EEC on the conservation of wild birds and Council Directive 92/43/EEC on the conservation of natural habitats and of wild fauna and flora;
   (vi) areas in which the environmental quality standards laid down in Community legislation have already been exceeded;
   (vii) densely populated areas;
   (viii) landscapes of historical, cultural or archaeological significance.

3. **Characteristics of the potential impact**

The potential significant effects of development must be considered in relation to criteria set out under paragraphs 1 and 2 above, and having regard in particular to—

(a) the extent of the impact (geographical area and size of the affected population);
(b) the transfrontier nature of the impact;
(c) the magnitude and complexity of the impact;
(d) the probability of the impact;
(e) the duration, frequency and reversibility of the impact.

The schedule identifies three broad criteria to be taken into account, namely: the characteristics of the development; the environmental sensitivity of the location; and the characteristics of the potential impact. The Secretary of State's view, expressed in Circular 02/99, is that in general, environmental impact assessment will be needed for Sch 2 developments in the following three main types of case: **13.14**

(a) for major developments which are of more than local importance;
(b) for developments which are proposed for particularly environmentally sensitive or vulnerable locations; and
(c) for developments with unusually complex and potentially hazardous environmental effects.

Given the range of Sch 2 projects and the importance of locational factors, it is (as Circular 02/99 emphasises) not possible to formulate criteria or thresholds which will provide a universal test of whether or not environmental impact assessment is required. The most that the Circular says can be offered is a broad indication of the type or scale of development which is likely to be a candidate for assessment and, conversely, an indication of the sort of development for which environmental impact assessment is unlikely to be necessary. The Circular does this by containing, in Annex A, 39 examples of when and when not environmental impact assessments are likely to be required, but it contains a warning that these thresholds should only be used in conjunction with the general guidance, and particularly that relating to 'environmentally sensitive locations'.

A diagram (reproduced from Circular 02/99) may be helpful in establishing whether development requires environmental impact assessment. **13.15**

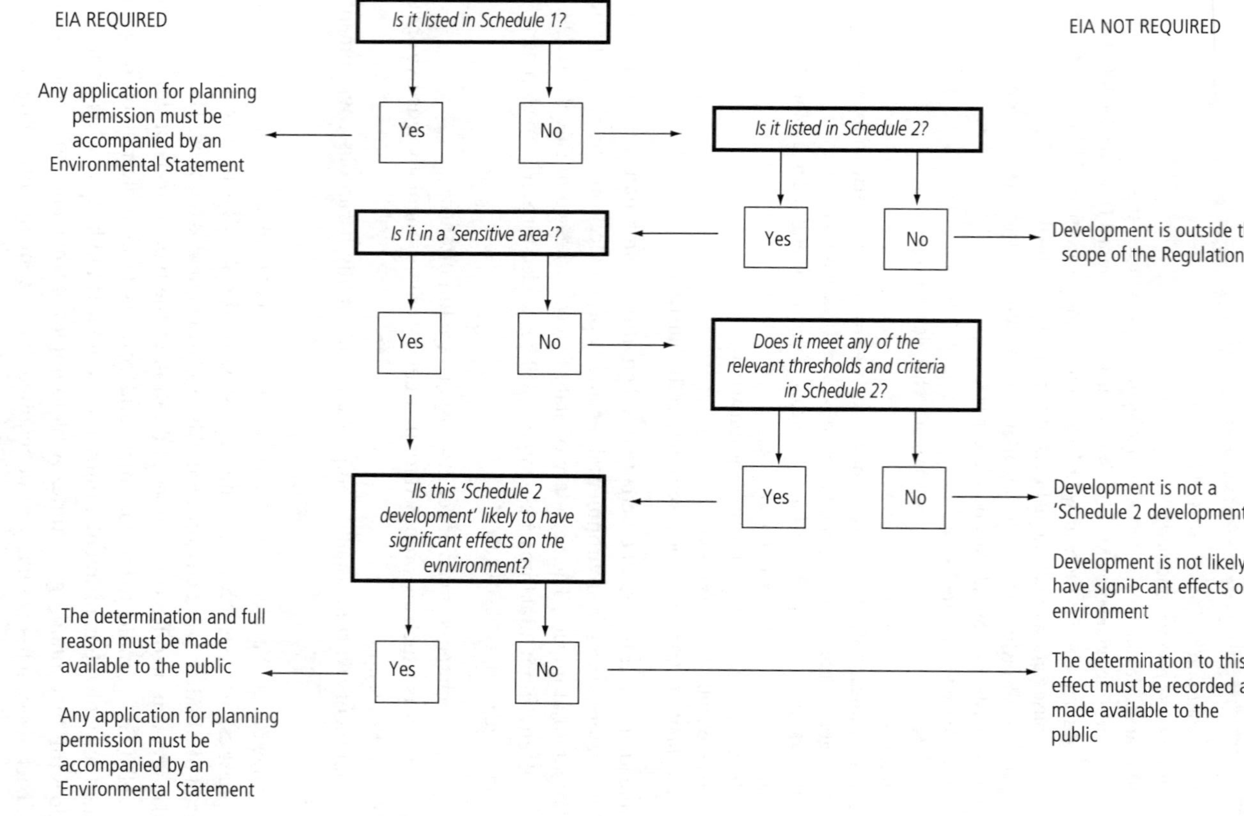
EIA REQUIRED
EIA NOT REQUIRED
Is it listed in Schedule 1?
Yes
No
Any application for planning permission must be accompanied by an Environmental Statement
Is it listed in Schedule 2?
Yes
No
Development is outside the scope of the Regulations
Is it in a 'sensitive area'?
Yes
No
Does it meet any of the relevant thresholds and criteria in Schedule 2?
Yes
No
Development is not a 'Schedule 2 development'
Development is not likely to have signiÞcant effects on the environment
IIs this 'Schedule 2 development' likely to have significant effects on the evnvironment?
Yes
No
The determination and full reason must be made available to the public
Any application for planning permission must be accompanied by an Environmental Statement
The determination to this effect must be recorded and made available to the public

Who decides whether environmental impact assessment is required?

Given the lack of a simple test for deciding whether or not environmental impact assessment is required, particularly for Sch 2 development, on whom does the decision depend? In the first instance and in the majority of cases, the local planning authority must 'screen' every application for Sch 2 development to determine whether environmental impact assessment is required. The determination is referred to as a 'screening opinion'. If an authority fails to screen a Schedule 2 application, with the consequence that no consideration is given to whether the development is likely to have a significant effect on the environment by virtue of factors such as its nature, size and location, the courts will quash a subsequent grant of planning permission if the grant is challenged timely. **13.16**

It is the responsibility of the local planning authority to ensure that planning applications are screened to establish whether environmental impact assessment is required. The central issue in many cases will be whether the proposed development is likely to have significant effects on the environment etc. To do this, an authority must be sure that it has sufficient information to enable it to form a sensible judgement as to the liklihood of the proposed development having a significant effect on the environment. Full knowledge of the project's likely significant effect on the environment is not however required at this stage. Thus the degree of information required at this stage will be less than that required at the later second stage once it has been decided that environmental impact assessment is required (*see R (Jones) v Mansfield District Council* [2003] EWHC Admin.) **13.17**

Again, in *British Telecommunications plc and Bloomsbury Land Investments v Gloucester City Council* [2002] JPL 993, it was pointed out that the regulations required that screening was necessary when the proposed development was likely to have significant effect on the environment, not whether the development was likely to have significant adverse effects. There was no justification it was held for treating the phrase 'significant effects' as though it was qualified by the word 'adverse'. For that reason the High Court quashed a grant of planning permission for the redevelopment of Blackfriars area of the City. The Court thought that the wording used in the regulations was essential as it gave the public an opportunity to form their own view as to whether the effects were adverse or beneficial. Furthermore, it was not for the authority at this stage to conclude that the liklihood of significant adverse effects could be mitigated or removed by mitigating methods. The purpose of environmental assessment was to consider the mitigating measures and to enable public discussion of their effectiveness. **13.18**

The matter was again considered by the Court of Appeal in *Gillespie v First Secretary of State* [2003] EWCA Civ. 400. There the Secretary of State had considered that the proposed development relating to an area of contaminated land in a densely populated urban area was unlikely to cause significant effects on the environment and that therefore no environmental impact assessment was necessary. He expressed himself satisfied that remediation of the land could be cured by a condition. The Court held that in deciding whether environmental impact assessment was necessary, the Secretary of State was not obliged to 'shut his eyes' to the remedial measures, or 'put into separate compartments' the development proposed and the proposed remedial measures and to consider only the first when making his screening decision. The extent to which remedial measures can be taken into account when making a screening decision will therefore depend upon their nature. If they are 'modest in **13.19** scope or . . . plainly and easily achievable' or 'plainly established and plainly uncontroversial' or 'of limited impact or well established to be easily achievable with . . . the development, then the decision maker can properly take them into account in forming the decision that the project would not be likely to have significant adverse effect on the environment'.

13.20 A developer may well decide that environmental impact assessment will be required for his proposed development and submit an environmental statement with his application for planning permission. If the applicant states that the information he has submitted is intended to constitute an environmental statement for the purposes of the Regulations, then, unless the Secretary of State otherwise directs, the local planning authority is required to treat it as such and the statement is an essential part of the environmental impact assessment of the development. If on the other hand, the applicant has not made it clear that the information submitted is an environmental statement for the purposes of the Regulations, and the local planning authority considers the development does not require environmental impact assessment, none will be necessary, although the information given by the applicant may still be taken into account by the local planning authority in determining the application for planning permission.

13.21 Often, however, a developer may, before submitting a planning application, be in doubt as to whether his proposed development requires environmental impact assessment. In such cases, Regulation 5 provides that he may request a 'screening opinion' from the local planning authority. The request must be accompanied by a plan sufficient to identify the location of the land and a brief description of the nature and purpose of the development and its possible environmental effects. The authority may ask the developer for further information in order to formulate an opinion. Then, unless the authority and developer so agree to extend, the authority must give its opinion within three weeks of the request, and give clearly and precisely the full reasons for adopting that opinion. Should the local planning authority decide that environmental impact assessment is required and the developer disagrees or the authority fails to give a screening opinion within the three-week period, the developer may request the Secretary of State to make a 'screening direction'. Should he then direct that environmental impact assessment is required (but not otherwise) the Secretary of State must give a clear and precise statement of his full reasons for doing so.

13.22 A third possibility is that a developer may submit an application for planning permission for development which could be a Sch 1 or 2 development without submitting an environmental statement. Where the local planning authority considers the application to be within Sch 1 or 2 of the Regulations it is required to proceed as if an application had been made to it under Regulation 5 requesting the authority to give a 'screening opinion' as to whether an environmental impact assessment is required for the development. If the authority considers that it is so required, the applicant must within three weeks either provide an environmental statement or ask the Secretary of State for a screening direction.

13.23 In two situations the Secretary of State may have to deal with a development proposal which is not accompanied by an environmental statement. First, if an application for planning permission is called in for determination by the Secretary of State under s 77 of the 1990 Act and secondly, where an appeal is made to the Secretary of State under s 78 of the 1990 Act and in either case is not accompanied by an environmental statement and the development is considered by the Secretary of State to be a Sch 1 or 2 development. In both cases the

Secretary of State will notify the applicant accordingly, who will then have three weeks to provide an environmental statement which, if not complied with, will result in the Secretary of State losing jurisdiction to deal with the application or appeal, save to refuse it.

Essentially, therefore, it is for the local planning authority to decide whether a proposed development falls within the descriptions of development set out in Schs 1 and 2 to the Regulations and, in the latter case, whether or not the development would be likely to have significant effects on the environment. It was held in *Berkeley v Secretary of State for the Environment* [2001] JPL 58 that the decision is only reviewable by the courts on *Wednesbury* grounds. **13.24**

In the *Berkeley* case no environmental statement had been submitted when it should have been. In the House of Lords. Lord Hoffmann was prepared to accept that 'an EIA by any other name will do as well'. But he added '. . . it must in substance be an EIA'. In *R (Blewett) v Derbyshire District Council* [2004] JPL 751, Sullivan J opined that 'it was important that decisions on EIA applications are made on the basis of 'full information' but the Regulations are not based on the premise that the environmental statement will necessarily contain the full information. The process is designed to identify any deficiencies in the environmental statement so that the local planning authority has the full picture . . . when it comes to consider the 'environmental information of which the environmental statement will be but a part'. **13.25**

Environmental impact assessment and permitted development rights

Because the majority of permitted development rights largely concern development of a minor nature, such development is unlikely to fall within Sch 1 or 2 of the Regulations. However, the GDPO provisions in so far as they relate to Sch 1 or 2 development, provide that Sch 1 development is not permitted development. The GDPO also provides that Sch 2 development is not permitted development under the Order unless the local planning authority has adopted a screening opinion to the effect that environmental impact assessment is not required. **13.26**

If the authority's opinion is that environmental impact assessment is required, permitted development rights are withdrawn and a planning application accompanied by an environmental statement must be made. There are, however, a number of types of permitted development in the GDPO which are not subject to these restrictive provisions relating to Sch 2 development. **13.27**

'Scoping opinions' and preparing an environmental statement

Before making a planning application, a developer may ask the local planning authority to state in writing their opinion as to the information to be provided in the environmental statement. The opinion so given is called a 'scoping opinion' (Regulation 10). The request for this opinion must include the same information as would be required to accompany a request to the local planning authority for a 'screening opinion'. Indeed, both requests may be made at the same time. This will include a plan indicating the proposed location of the development, a brief description of the nature and purpose of the proposal and its possible **13.28** environmental effects, giving a broad indication of their likely scale. The local planning authority may seek further information from the developer.

13.29 Where a scoping opinion is sought from a local planning authority, the authority must respond within five weeks of the request, failing which the developer may apply for one to the Secretary of State. There is, however, no provision for the Secretary of State to intervene if the developer and local planning authority disagree as to the content of a scoping opinion provided by the authority, though if the application for development is called in or goes to the Secretary of State by way of appeal, the Secretary of State will be in a position to form his own opinion on the matter at that stage.

13.30 Lastly, it should be noted that under the Environmental Information Regulations 1992, a number of public bodies must make environmental information already in their possession available to any person who requests it. This obligation is supplemented by Regulation 12, under which the local planning authority is required to give those bodies notice where a developer intends to submit an environmental statement and that they should if requested make that information available to him. The bodies under this obligation are statutory consultees under Art 10 of the GDPO; any principal council for the area in which the land is situated; English Nature; the Countryside Commission; and the Environment Agency.

Publicity requirements

13.31 When an environmental statement accompanies a planning application, the applicant must submit in addition to the statement three copies of it to the local planning authority, together with the names of every body to whom the applicant has already sent or intends to send a copy of the statement. In addition he must send such further copies to the authority as are necessary to allow the authority to send one to other consultation bodies. Applicants must also make a reasonable number of copies of the environmental statement available to the public at a reasonable cost (Regulations 17 and 18).

13.32 On receipt of the application, the local planning authority must take a number of steps additional to those it is already required to take with any planning application, namely: publish the application and statement in accordance with the provisions set out in Art 8 of the GDPO; send copies of the statement and application to those consultation bodies who have not already received them from the applicant; send three copies of the statement and application to the Secretary of State; and place the statement and any related screening or scoping opinions or directions in Part I of the planning register. Similar publicity requirements are required for environmental statements which are submitted after a planning application.

Consideration of environmental impact assessment applications

13.33 The local planning authority should determine such applications within 16 weeks from the date of the receipt of the statement instead of the normal eight weeks prescribed for determining all other applications. If the local planning authority fails, to make a determination after 16 weeks (or such further period as agreed with the applicant), the applicant may appeal to the Secretary of State against non-determination. Under Regulation 3(2), planning permission cannot be granted unless the local planning authority (or the Secretary of State, as the case may be) has taken environmental information into consideration. Furthermore, the fact that they have done so is required to be stated in their decision. Environmental information, it will be recalled, means the environmental statement, including any further information, any representations made by any body required by the Regulations to be invited to make representations (the consultation bodies) and any representations made by any other person about the environmental effects of the development.

Publicising determinations of environmental impact assessment applications

Once the application has been determined, the local planning authority must in addition to notifying the applicant, notify the Secretary of State. The authority must also publish a notice in the local press giving the content of the determination and saying where the documents relating to the determination may be inspected. Under Regulation 21(1) these documents shall include a statement containing the content of the decision and any conditions attached thereto; the main reasons and considerations upon which the decision was based; and a description, where necessary, of the main measures to avoid, reduce and, if possible, offset the major adverse effects of the development. In cases where the Secretary of State makes the determination a copy is sent to the authority who then has responsibility for its publication. **13.34**

Special cases

A number of modifications to the environmental impact assessment regime described above apply in some special cases. These include local authorities' own development, development likely to have significant environmental effects in other Member States of the Community and development which is the subject of an enforcement notice. In the last of these cases, the Secretary of State, in dealing with an appeal against an enforcement notice, may not grant planning permission for the development enforced against, without first taking into account environmental information where the development is an EIA development. **13.35**

C. JUDICIAL CHALLENGE

The question of whether there has been compliance with the Environmental Impact Assessment Regulations has been considered by the courts on a number of occasions. Early cases mostly related to the question of whether proposals 'in the pipeline' (that is, development proposals made before 15 July 1988 but approved thereafter) were subject to the Environmental Assessment Regulations. One decision on the main stream application of the Regulations is *R v Swale BC, ex p the Royal Society for the Protection of Birds* [1991] JPL 39. The Royal Society had applied for judicial review of a grant of planning permission which had been issued by the Borough Council without any environmental assessment having been carried out. In rejecting the Royal Society's argument that the Town and Country Planning (Assessment of Environmental Effects) Regulations 1988 applied, Simon Brown J held that the decision whether any particular development was or was not within the **13.36** scheduled descriptions was a matter exclusively for the planning authority, subject only to *Wednesbury* challenge. He considered that questions of classification were essentially questions of fact and degree, not of law; and that the court was not entitled upon judicial review to act effectively as an appeal court and to reach its own decision so as to ensure that EEC obligations were properly discharged. This subjective approach to the implementation of the regulations in the United Kingdom could well mean the European Community Directive being interpreted differently in different member States of the European Community.

13.37 Simon Brown J also concluded that the question of whether or not development was of a category described in either schedule had to be answered strictly in relation to the development applied for, not for any development beyond that. But the further question arising in respect of Sch 2 development, namely the question whether it 'would be likely to have significant effects on the environment by virtue of factors such as its nature, size or location', should be answered differently. He thought the proposed development should not then be considered in isolation if in reality it was properly to be regarded as an integral part of an inevitably substantial development. If this were otherwise, developers would be able to defeat the object of the regulations by piecemeal development proposals.

13.38 The principle was considered again in *British Airports Authority plc v Secretary of State for Transport, Local Government and the Regions* [2003] JPL 610. There the Secretary of State had failed to consider whether the totality of two schemes of development were in fact capable of constituting one integral site and part of a single development. Had he done so, and then reached the conclusion that they were not a single development, the decision would have been vulnerable to legal challenge on the basis of irrationality. As a consequence of the Secretary of State's omission, the need for environmental impact assessment had been effectively side-stepped.

D. RECENT DEVELOPMENTS

13.39 More recently the courts appear to be adopting a more robust approach to the obligations imposed by the Environmental Impact Assessment regime which has resulted in a steady stream of litigation. In *Dido Berkeley v Secretary of State for the Environment* [2001] JPL 59, the Secretary of State had granted planning permission for residential development on part of Craven Cottage, the home of Fulham Football Club. Lady Berkeley (a third party) moved under s 288 of the 1990 Act to quash the decision, one of the grounds being that no environmental statement had been required of the applicant and that the proposed development was or could have been an 'urban development project' requiring submission of an environmental statement pursuant to EC Directive 85/337 because it was likely to have significant effects on the environment. The Secretary of State conceded that there had been a failure, which was not deliberate, to consider whether an environmental statement was required before the application for planning permission was considered. However, despite holding that there had been a breach of the regulations which had implemented the EC Directive into domestic law, the Court of Appeal refused to exercise the discretion to quash the grant of planning permission, holding that the objectives of the Directive had in substance been achieved by the procedure which had been followed. So although the procedures adopted had been flawed, they were nevertheless sufficiently thorough and effective to enable the Inspector (following a public local inquiry) to make a comprehensive judgment on all environmental issues. Hence the absence of an environmental statement in the circumstances of the case was of no significant practical importance. The House of Lords, however, found otherwise. In quashing the grant of planning permission, their Lordships held that the court was not entitled retrospectively to dispense with the requirements of an environmental impact assessment on the ground that the outcome would have been the same, or that the decision-maker had all the information necessary to enable him to reach a proper decision on the environmental issues.

A similar robust view was taken in *R v St Edmondsbury BC, ex p Walton* [1999] JPL 805, where it was held that it was not within the power of an officer of the Council to decide whether a Sch 2 application required environmental impact assessment. If an officer is to have the power to so decide, the authority must be formally delegated to the officer by the Council. In quashing the grant of planning permission which had followed the officer's decision, the High Court held that if an environmental impact assessment had been carried out it did not follow that the result of the planning application would have been the same. **13.40**

In *R v North Yorkshire CC, ex p Brown* [1999] JPL 616, the House of Lords seemed prepared to look more closely at the EC Directive itself, rather than the regulations implementing the Directive into domestic law. The case concerned an 'old mining permission'. Under s 22 of and Sch 2 to the Planning and Compensation Act 1991, owners of these permissions had to apply to the local planning authority for them to be registered. Once registered, the permission could then be made subject to conditions. A question arose as to whether the determination of the conditions by the local planning authority required an environmental impact assessment to be made in accordance with 85/337 EEC Directive. The House of Lords held that it did; that the determination of the conditions was a 'development consent' under the Directive, and that it was a 'decision of the competent authority or authorities which entitles the developer to proceed with the project'. Hence their Lordships upheld the decision of the Court of Appeal to quash the authority's determination. Following the House of Lords decision, changes to the Environmental Impact Regulations were subsequently made to bring applications to determine such conditions within domestic law (see Chapter 24: Minerals). **13.41**

Two further cases need to be mentioned. In *R v Hammersmith and Fulham LBC, ex p CPRE* ([2000] Env. LR 549), the Borough Council had granted outline planning permission for development of the White City area in London, which included a shopping centre of up to 600,000 square feet. The applicants claimed that permission had been granted without environmental assessment, contrary to the Environmental Assessment Directive 85/337/EEC. The applicants then asked the Council to consider exercising its powers to revoke the permission under s 97 of the 1990 Act. Upon its refusal to do so, the applicants sought judicial review of that decision. **13.42**

The High Court refused their request. It referred to the case of *Becker v Finanzamt Münster-Innerstadt* (Case 8/81 [1982] ECR I–53), when it had been held that an individual could rely on a directive as giving him an enforceable Community law right, only where the Member State had failed to transpose, or had failed to transpose properly, a directive into domestic legislation and where the provision of the directive upon which reliance was placed was **13.43** unconditional and sufficiently precise. Accordingly, since these preconditions were not justified, the applicant had no enforceable Community law right.

13.44 In *R v Durham CC and Sherburn Stone Company Limited, ex p Huddleston* [2000] JPL 1125, the question again for decision was whether the courts could intervene where the statutory regime for implementing the EC Directive on Environmental Impact Assessment in the United Kingdom enables a company to revive a mining permission by registering it with the mineral planning authority without providing an environmental impact assessment.

13.45 In this case the Sherburn Stone Company Ltd was the holder of a dormant planning permission to extract minerals on a large site in the County of Durham. The applicant lived close by. Under s 22, Planning and Compensation Act 1991 because no quarrying had taken place in the two years prior to 1 May 1991, that permission, known as an old mining permission, was suspended pending registration of the permission with the mineral planning authority and the setting of conditions to which the permission was to be subject.

13.46 On 15 February 1999 Sherburn made an application for registration and submitted with it a scheme of conditions. The County Council thereupon informed Sherburn that an environmental statement was required, Sherburn took the view however, that no environmental statement was required and on 24 May 1999, wrote to the County Council stating that because the three months period allowed by the 1991 Act had expired without them having determined the conditions to which the permission was to be subject, there was a deemed determination of those conditions as set out in the Sherburn application.

13.47 It will be recalled that in the North Yorkshire County Council case, the House of Lords decided that a mineral planning authority's determination under s 22 of the 1991 Act was a development consent falling within Directive 85/337/EEC and therefore required an environmental impact assessment as part of the registration process. Their Lordships, however, felt it unnecssary to decide the validity of the deeming provisions relating to the conditions to be imposed in a permission in the event of the minerals planning authority failing to determine them within the three month time limit for doing so. As a result of that decision, the County Council (acting on counsel's advice) moderated its stance and accepted that it could not of its own motion treat the Directive as effective or, therefore, the deeming provision as ineffective.

13.48 At an expedited hearing, however, the Court of Appeal reversed the decision of the High Court and gave direct effect to the Directive, so as to require an environmental assessment before the deeming provisions could apply. In the Court's view, the applicant was entitled to complain that the state had not set up the requisite machinery to give him the opportunity which should have been afforded to him (namely his right to be consulted) if the Directive had been properly implemented.

13.49 Environmental impact assessment was also the key issue in the recent decision of the High Court in *R v Rochdale MBC, ex p Tew* [2000] JPL 54. The case arose following the grant of outline planning permission by Rochdale MBC for a 'business park . . . with associated and complementary retail, leisure, hotel and housing . . .', with siting, design, means of access and external matters to be treated as reserved matters. An illustrative master plan accompanied the site plan, with an indicative schedule of floor space being provided later. The outline application, in a form which is sometimes described as a 'bare' application, reserved all detailed matters for subsequent approval, was accompanied by an environmental statement and was subsequently supplemented by an ecological survey. Local residents applied for judicial review to quash the grant of permission, the main ground of challenge being that the developers had failed to provide the information required by the Assessment of Environmental Effects Regulations 1988 (now superseded by the 1999 Regulations) and that accordingly, the Council was not entitled to grant planning permission for the development.

There was no dispute that the development was Sch 2 development likely to have significant effects on the environment by virtue of factors such as its nature, size or location. The objectors successfully contended that no application for planning permission to which Regulation 4 applied can be granted unless the applicant includes a description of the developments proposed, which must comprise, at a minimum, information as to the 'design and size or scale of the project' as well as data necessary to identify the main effects which the development was likely to have on the environment. Hence the environmental assessment had been based on an Illustrative Masterplan and Indicative Schedule of Uses, which was inadequate for the purposes of Sch 3. Although Sullivan J held that such a generalised description of the development was insufficient to comply with the regulations, he refused to go so far as to hold that it was not possible to make any application for outline planning permission for a development which fell within Sch 1 or Sch 2. The description of the proposed development must, however, be sufficient to enable the main environmental effects which the development is likely to have to be stressed and identified so as to enable mitigation measures to be taken to ameliorate any adverse effects. **13.50**

The decision raises questions of how far it is possible to seek outline planning permission for development projects falling within Schedules 1 or 2. Round 2 of this particular saga was to follow shortly. Instead of pursuing their right of appeal to the Court of Appeal (leave for which had been granted), the developers submitted an amended application for outline planning permission. Unlike the earlier 'bare' application, only details of landscaping, design and external appearance of the buildings were to be reserved. In addition, a new environmental statement accompanied the application. It contained much more detail. In particular, it contained a Schedule of Developments which set out the details of the buildings and their likely environmental effects; and the master plan was no longer merely illustrative. The local planning authority had also imposed conditions which was to tie the outline permission for the business park to the documents which comprised the application. The outline permission was further restricted so that the development that could take place would have to be within the parameters of the matters assessed in the environmental statement. Reserved matters would also be restricted to matters that had previously been assessed in the Environmental Statement. In a challenge to the decision of the local planning authority to grant planning permission, the High Court held in *R v Rochdale MBC, ex p Milne* [2000] 81 P & CR 365 that the application satisfied the requirements of the Environmental Assessment Regulations. **13.51**

In *R (Barker) v Bromley LBC* [2002] Env. LR 25, it was said that where an application was made for outline planning permission, the Regulations required the local planning authority to consider the full environmental effects of a proposed development at that stage. There was no scope therefore for a claim that the environmental impact of a development be **13.52** considered at the later stage of an application for approval of reserved matters. This accords with the rule that the principle of the development cannot be reopened at the reserved matters stage.

13.53 The problem of outline applications and environmental assessment was again emphasised in *R v Waveney DC, ex p Bell* [2001] PLCR 292, where the High Court quashed a grant of outline planning permission for new printing works because the document which had accompanied the application and which purported to be an environmental statement, contained no information about the design of the development.

13.54 In an attempt to deal with the problem of the extent to which an outline planning permission can comply with the Directive and the Regulations, the Government in 2002 issued an aide-memoir to local planning authorities giving advice as to the approach authorities should take in considering applications for outline planning permission. That advice was as follows:

i) An application for a 'bare' outline permission with all matters reserved for later approval is extremely unlikely to comply with the requirement of the EIA Regulations;
ii) When granting outline consent, the permission must be 'tied' to the environmental information provided in the ES, and considered and assessed by the authority prior to approval. This can be usually done by conditions although it would also be possible to achieve this by a section 106 agreement. An example of a condition was referred to in ex parte Milne (2000). 'The development on this site shall be carried out in substantial accordance with the layout included within the Development Framework document submitted as part of the application and shown on (a) drawing entitled "Master Plan with Building Layouts".' The reason for this condition was given as 'The layout of the proposed Business Park is the subject of an Environmental Impact Assessment and any material alteration to the layout may have an impact which has not been assessed by that process.' (see paras 28 and 131 of the judgment);
iii) Developers are not precluded from having a degree of flexibility in how a scheme may be developed. But each option will need to have been properly assessed and be within the remit of the outline permission
iv) Development carried out pursuant to a reserved matters consent granted for a matter that does not fall within the remit of the outline consent will be unlawful.

It should also be noted that the Planning and Compulsory Purchase Act 2004 now provides that a development order may make provision as to applications for planning permission made to a local planning authority. When made, the order is likely to require that more information be supplied at the outline application stage, including a statement about design principles and access issues relevant to the proposed development.

14

STRATEGIC ENVIRONMENTAL ASSESSMENT

A. INTRODUCTION

In addition to EC Directive No. 85/337/EEC The Assessment of the Effect of Certain Public and Private Projects on the Environment, now implemented in the United Kingdom as far as possible within normal town and country planning procedures (see Chapter 13), a later EC Directive No. 2001/42, The Assessment of the Effects of Certain Plans and Programmes on the Environment, has now been similarly implemented through normal town and country planning procedures. **14.01**

Whereas Directive No. 85/337 dealt with the environmental assessment of projects, Directive No. 2001/42 deals with the environmental impact of plans and programmes. Although the latest Directive does not use the term 'strategic environmental assessment', this is the term likely to be used to describe the environmental assessment which complies with it. **14.02**

The Directive was brought into effect on 20 July 2004 by the Environmental Assessment of Plans and Programmes Regulations 2004 (S1 No 1633). **14.03**

The requirement for environmental assessment applies, in particular, to any plan or programme prepared for agriculture, forestry, fisheries, energy, industry, transport, waste management, water management, telecommunications, tourism, town and country planning or land use, which sets the framework for future development consent of projects listed in Annex I or II to Council Directive 85/337/EEC on the assessment of the effects of certain public and private projects on the environment, as amended by Council Directive 97/11/EC; and to any plan or programme which, in view of the likely effect on sites, has been determined to require an assessment pursuant to Article 6 or 7 of Council Directive 92/43/EEC on the conservation of natural habitats and of wild flora and fauna, as last amended by Council Directive 97/62/EC (regulation 5(1) to (3); Article 3.2 of the Directive). **14.04**

14.05 The Directive therefore impacts in particular on local plans, unitary development plans, regional planning guidance, the spatial development strategy for London, local development documents and regional planning strategies. Although the provision of the Directive are required to be applied to plans and programmes and to any modifications to them where formal preparation began after 21 July 2004, they will also normally apply to plans and programmes whose formal preparation began before that date, if they have not been adopted (or submitted to a legitimate procedure leading to adoption) by 21 July 2006.

14.06 Because the retroactive provision of the Directive is likely to affect many plans now in the course of preparation, the Government published in advance of the bringing into force of the Directive 'The Strategic Environmental Assessment Directive: Guidance for Planning Authorities'. This was done in order to help authorities become familiar with its requirements and to prepare for them.

14.07 The Directive, and accordingly the Regulations, does not apply to plans and programmes whose sole purpose is to serve national defence or civil emergency, or to financial or budget plans and programmes. An exception is also made for plans and programmes that determine the use of a small area at local level and for minor modifications, if the authority responsible for preparing the plan or programme has determined that the plan or programme is unlikely to have significant environmental effects.

B. SCHEDULE I

14.08 In this connection Regulation 9 requires the responsible authority to determine whether or not a plan, programme or modification is likely to have significant environmental effects. In making this determination the authority is required to take into account the criteria specified in schedule I to the Regulations, and the views of the 'consultation bodies'. Schedule I is as follows:

Criteria for determining the likely significance of effects on the environment

14.09 1. The characteristics of plans and programmes, having regard, in particular, to:
   (a) the degree to which the plan or programme sets a framework for projects and other activities, either with regard to the location, nature, size and operating conditions or by allocating resources;
   (b) the degree to which the plan or programme influences other plans and programmes including those in a hierarchy;
   (c) the relevance of the plan or programme for the integration of environmental considerations in particular with a view to promoting sustainable development;
   (d) environmental problems relevant to the plan or programme; and
   (e) the relevance of the plan or programme for the implementation of Community legislation on the environment (for example, plans and programmes linked to waste management or water protection).

2. Characteristics of the effects and of the area likely to be affected, having regard, in particular, to:

(a) the probability, duration, frequency and reversibility of the effects;
(b) the cumulative nature of the effects;
(c) the transboundary nature of the effects;
(d) the risks to human health or the environment (for example, due to accidents);
(e) the magnitude and spatial extent of the effects (geographical area and size of the population likely to be affected);
(f) the value and vulnerability of the area likely to be affected due to:
  (i) special natural characteristics or cultural heritage;
  (ii) exceeded environmental quality standards or limit values; or
  (iii) intensive land-use; and
(g) the effects on areas or landscapes which have a recognised national, Community or international protection status.

Regulation 10 enables the Secretary of State to require a responsible authority to provide him with relevant documents. It also enables him to direct that a particular plan or programme is likely to have significant environmental effects. In the latter case, any determination to the contrary made under regulation 9(1) by a responsible authority ceases to have effect. If a responsible authority has not made any determination under that provision, the Secretary of State's direction relieves it of the duty to do so. **14.10**

Regulation 5 provides that where the first formal preparatory act of a plan or programme is after 21 July 2004, the responsible authority shall carry out, or secure the carrying out of, an environmental assessment, in accordance with Part 3 of the Regulations during the preparation of the plan or programme and before its adoption. The plans or programmes to which this provision is made to apply include those prepared for town and country planning or land use which set the framework for future development projects listed in Annex I or II to Council Directive 85/337/EEC (see chapter 14, p.000). The regulation is also made to apply to plans or programmes which, in view of the likely effect on sites, have been determined to require an assessment pursuant to Articles 6 or 7 of the EC Habitats Directive. **14.11**

Under Part 3 of the Regulations, an environmental assessment requires the responsible authority to prepare an environmental report. Regulation 12 (2) and (3) provides as follows: **14.12**

(2) The report shall identify, describe and evaluate the likely significant effects on the environment of:
  (a) implementing the plan or programme; and
  (b) reasonable alternatives taking into account the objectives and the geographical scope of the plan or programme.
(3) The report shall include such of the information referred to in Schedule II to these Regulations as may reasonably be required, taking account of:
  (a) current knowledge and methods of assessment;
  (b) the contents and level of detail in the plan or programme;
  (c) the stage of the plan or programme in the decision-making process; and
  (d) the extent to which certain matters are more appropriately assessed at different levels in that process in order to avoid duplication of the assessment.

C. SCHEDULE II

14.13 Schedule II to the Regulation contains the information required to be included in the Report.

Schedule II
Information for environmental reports

14.14 1. An outline of the contents and main objectives of the plan or programme, and of its relationship with other relevant plans and programmes.
2. The relevant aspects of the current state of the environment and the likely evolution thereof without implementation of the plan or programme.
3. The environmental characteristics of areas likely to be significantly affected.
4. Any existing environmental problems which are relevant to the plan or programme including, in particular, those relating to any areas of a particular environmental importance, such as areas designated pursuant to Council Directive 79/409/EEC on the conservation of wild birds (a) and the Habitats Directive.
5. The environmental protection objectives, established at international, community or Member State level, which are relevant to the plan or programme and the way those objectives and any environmental considerations have been taken into account during its preparation.
6. The likely significant effects on the environment, including short-, medium- and long-term effects, permanent and temporary effects, positive and negative effects, and second, cumulative and synergistic effects, on issues such as:
   (a) biodiversity;
   (b) population;
   (c) human health;
   (d) fauna;
   (e) flora;
   (f) soil;
   (g) water;
   (h) air;
   (i) climatic factors;
   (j) material assets;
   (k) cultural heritage, including architectural and archaeological heritage;
   (l) landscape; and
   (m) the inter-relationship between the issues referred to in sub-paragraphs (a) to (l).
7. The measures envisaged to prevent, reduce and as fully as possible offset any significant adverse effects on the environment of implementing the plan or programme.
8. An outline of the reasons for selecting the alternatives dealt with, and a description of how the assessment was undertaken including any difficulties (such as technical deficiencies or lack of know-how) encountered in compiling the required information.
9. A description of the measures envisaged concerning monitoring in accordance with regulation 17.
10. A non-technical summary of the information provided under paragraphs 1 to 9.

Part 3 also provides that every draft plan or programme for which an environmental report has been prepared and its accompanying environmental report shall be made available for consultation. As soon as is reasonably practicable after the preparation of the relevant documents, the responsible authority is required to: **14.15**

(a) send a copy of those documents to each consultation body;
(b) take such steps as it considers appropriate to bring the preparation of the relevant documents to the attention of the persons who, in the authority's opinion, are affected or likely to be affected by, or have an interest in the decisions involved in the assessment and adoption of the plan or programme concerned, required under the Environmental Assessment of Plans and Programmes Directive ('the public consultees');
(c) inform the public consultees of the address (which may include a website) at which a copy of the relevant documents can be viewed, or from which a copy may be obtained; and
(d) invite the consultation bodies and the public consultees to express their opinion on the relevant documents, specifying the address to which, and the period within which, opinions must be sent.

The period referred to in paragraph (2)(d) above must be of such length as will ensure that the consultation bodies and the public consultees are given an effective opportunity to express their opinion on the relevant documents. **14.16**

The consultation bodies referred to in (a) above, are defined in Regulation 34 as being the Countryside Agency; the Historic Buildings and Monuments Commission (English Heritage) English Nature; and the Environmental Agency. **14.17**

Regulation 8 prevents the adoption or submission for adoption of a plan or programme for which environmental assessment is required before the completion of that assessment. **14.18**

Part 4 of the Regulations deals with the procedures to be followed after the adoption of a plan or programme which has been subject to environmental assessment. In particular, it requires the person by whom the plan or programme has been prepared to give notice of its adoption and to make it and other specified information available for inspection. In addition the Regulations requires the person who prepared the plan or programme to monitor the significant environmental effects of the implementation of the plan or programme with a view to identifying, at an early stage, unforeseen adverse effects and being able to undertake appropriate remedial action. **14.19**

Special provision is made in the Regulations for dealing with cases where draft plans and programmes prepared in the United Kingdom are likely to have significant effects on the environment in other Member States; and where draft plans and programmes prepared in another Member State are likely to have significant effects on the environment in any part of the United Kingdom. **14.20**

15

CONDITIONS

Almost all planning permissions that are granted are granted subject to conditions. It often happens that the problem with decisions relating to land use is not over the question of whether the development should be permitted at all, but on what terms it should be permitted. Conditions may be imposed, therefore, not only to enhance the quality of the development but to ameliorate any adverse effects that might otherwise flow from the development. It is not uncommon, for example, for the grant of planning permission for mineral working to contain as many as 100 conditions in order to achieve that purpose. Local planning authorities are often criticised for imposing unnecessary conditions, and it may be that a reported grant of a permission subject to a condition that 'before any of the dwellings are **15.01** occupied a rear wheelbarrow access shall be provided for each dwelling without going through the dwelling', lends some credibility to that view. But this is a matter of administrative discretion, not of law. In order to assist local planning authorities in the exercise of their power, extensive advice has been given to them by the Secretary of State. The latest advice is contained in Circular 11/95 dated 20 July 1995. The Circular takes account of the most important judicial decisions and includes an appendix containing model conditions for local planning authority use.

15.02 Section 70(1) of the 1990 Act provides that in dealing with an application for planning permission, a local planning authority:

(a) . . . may grant planning permission, either unconditionally or subject to such conditions as they think fit; or
(b) . . . may refuse planning permission.

15.03 In addition to the power to impose such conditions as the authority think fit and without prejudice to the generality of that power, the Act gives the authority power to impose a number of specific conditions on the grant of planning permission.

15.04 An analysis of the definition of development contained in s 55 of the 1990 Act, whether it be operational development or a material change of use, will show that development is essentially a process; and a process which is begun and completed, so that with the full implementation of that process the planning permission authorising it is spent. The fact that development is a process allows a local planning authority to impose, by way of conditions, restrictions which not only define the limits of what is authorised on the completion of the process, but also to control the way in which the process itself is carried out. Examples of the latter include conditions relating to hours of work, noise levels and access to the site during the construction process, the erection of protective fencing around trees and the provision of adequate space on site for the parking of vehicles, equipment and materials of the contractors.

A. THE GENERAL POWER

15.05 Although couched in the widest of all possible terms, the power to impose conditions is not unlimited.

15.06 In *Pyx Granite Co. Ltd v Ministry of Housing and Local Government* [1958] 1 QB 554 Lord Denning said at p. 572:

> Although the planning authorities are given very wide powers to impose 'such conditions as they think fit', nevertheless the law says that those conditions, to be valid, must fairly and reasonably relate to the permitted development. The planning authority are not at liberty to use their powers for an ulterior object, however desirable that object may seem to them to be in the public interest.

The law was later restated in this form by the House of Lords in *Fawcett Properties Ltd v Buckingham CC* [1961] AC 636.

15.07 In *Newbury DC v Secretary of State for the Environment* [1981] AC 578, the House of Lords were required to consider again the validity of a condition imposed under the general power now given by s 70(1) of the 1990 Act. According to their Lordships, conditions must comply with the following tests:

(a) They must be imposed for a planning purpose and not for an ulterior one.
(b) They must fairly and reasonably relate to the development permitted.
(c) They must not be so unreasonable that no reasonable authority could have imposed them.

Although the legal tests for the validity of a condition have been laid down in the *Newbury* case, Circular 11/95 sets out a six-fold test the conditions should meet. They are that conditions should be necessary, relevant to planning, relevant to the development to be permitted, enforceable, precise and reasonable in all other respects. In effect the Circular attempts to amplify and slightly reclassify the legal tests set down in *Newbury*, although the tests of enforceability and precision are not in themselves free-standing grounds of legal validity. The Circular, however, also contains policy guidance on when conditions should or should not be used. As such, this guidance is a material consideration in determining planning applications. **15.08**

Imposed for a planning purpose

Like all statutory powers, a power can only be exercised for the purpose for which it is given. Conditions which are imposed for some ulterior purpose, therefore, are not exercised within that power. One of the leading cases in this area is *R v Hillingdon LBC, ex p Royco Homes Ltd* [1974] QB 720. Here, the applicant was able to obtain an order of certiorari to quash a grant of planning permission which had been made subject to *ultra vires* conditions. **15.09**

The planning permission in question had permitted the development of land for residential purposes. It had been granted subject to two conditions which had required that the dwellings approved by the permission be designed to conform to space and heating standards laid down by the Department of the Environment for local authority housing, and that they be constructed at a cost which did not exceed the relevant cost yardstick for such housing. A further two conditions required the dwellings be first occupied by persons on the housing waiting list of the authority, and that for a period of ten years from the date of first occupation they be occupied as the residence of a person who occupied by virtue of a tenure which would not be excluded from the protection of the Rent Act 1968 by any provision of s 2 of the Act. In the Queen's Bench Divisional Court, Lord Widgery CJ was in no doubt that the latter two conditions were *ultra vires* the authority and, although he considered that the first two conditions did not have a clear badge of *ultra vires* upon them, was unable to sever one set of conditions from the other because they had all been designed for a single purpose. Furthermore, he held that since the conditions were fundamental to the planning permission, the planning permission fell with the invalid conditions. Although the Lord Chief Justice considered the conditions to be *ultra vires* because they were unreasonable, Bridge J based his finding of *ultra vires* upon improper motive, namely, the attempt by the authority to transfer on to the shoulders of the applicant a duty (of housing people in need) which Parliament had placed upon the authority as a housing authority. **15.10**

In 1987, Brent London Borough Council sought to impose a condition in a planning **15.11** permission for residential development which provided that '25 per cent of the units the construction of which is hereby permitted shall not, without the written consent of the council, be occupied for a period of 10 years from the date that they were first occupied, otherwise than by a tenant or tenants on a periodic tenancy'. The reason for the condition was expressed to be 'To ensure that new residential developments contribute to meeting the needs of the borough's residents for low-cost housing and to offset the decline in the level of rental housing in the borough'. In discharging the condition the Secretary of State considered that it did not serve a planning purpose, did not fairly relate to the permitted development and was an unreasonable inter-ference with a landowner's normal rights. He also had serious doubts about its legality ([1988] JPL 222).

15.12 The application of the first of the three *Newbury* tests was considered in *R v Bristol CC, ex p Anderson* [2000] PLCR 104. There, the Court of Appeal held that a condition in the grant of planning permission for the erection of flats to be occupied by students, which required the prior approval of the Council of a management agreement which included a prohibition on students residing on the site from keeping motor vehicles, did fulfil a planning purpose. Allowing an appeal from a decision of the High Court quashing the grant of planning permission given by the Council, the Court held that the management agreement was necessary to enable the student development to operate effectively and consonantly with the interests of nearby residents and others.

Fairly and reasonably relate to the permitted development

15.13 This test was first approved in *Pyx Granite Co. Ltd v Ministry of Housing and Local Government* [1958] 1 QB 554, where the courts had to consider the validity of conditions attached to a grant of planning permission for quarrying for a limited period. The conditions in question limited the hours each day between which quarrying should be carried on, and required that all plant and machinery be removed from the site when no longer required and that the site be left in a tidy condition. The Court of Appeal, upholding the legality of the conditions, made it clear that they would have been quashed if they had not fairly and reasonably related to the development permitted. Although the case eventually reached the House of Lords, their Lordships held for the company on another ground, which relieved them of having to express an opinion on the validity of the conditions.

15.14 The principle was accepted by the House of Lords, however, in *Fawcett Properties Ltd v Buckingham CC* [1961] AC 636. There, the local planning authority had granted planning permission for the erection of cottages in the green belt subject to a condition that 'the occupation of the houses shall be limited to persons whose employment or latest employment is or was employment in agriculture . . . or in forestry, or in an industry mainly dependent upon agriculture and including also the dependants of such persons'. Fawcett Properties Ltd then purchased the properties and asked for a declaration that the condition was *ultra vires*. The House of Lords refused to grant the declaration, holding that the condition fairly and reasonably related to the permitted development.

15.15 In granting permission, the authority had recognised that agricultural workers need to live close to their place of work. The purpose of the authority in imposing the condition (now known as an agricultural occupancy condition) was to prevent the cottages being occupied by commuters, which would have infringed their policy of preserving green-belt land from development.

In *British Airports Authority v Secretary of State for Scotland* [1980] JPL 260, the Scottish Court of Session took the view that a condition attached to a grant of planning permission for development at Aberdeen Airport which restricted the hours between which aircraft might take off or land, fairly and reasonably related to the development permitted. A clear case where there was no connection between the condition and the development permitted was seen in *Newbury DC v Secretary of State for the Environment* [1981] AC 578. There, planning permission had been granted for a period of 10 years for a change in the use of hangars previously used for the storage of civil defence vehicles, to use for the storage of synthetic rubber. The permission was subject to a condition that at the end of the 10-year period the hangars should be demolished. The House of Lords held that the Secretary of State had been right to quash an enforcement notice requiring the removal of the hangars after the expiry of the permission on the ground that the occupiers were entitled to use the hangars for storage during their occupancy without relying upon the grant of planning permission. Their Lordships, however, went on to express (as *obiter*) their further view that had the planning permission been in operation, the condition would have been *ultra vires* as it did not fairly and reasonably relate to the development permitted. It is difficult to see how on the facts their Lordships could have arrived at any other conclusion. The planning permission which was given related to the use of the property for a 10-year period. The requirement to demolish the hangars at the end of the period in no way restricted the quality or the nature of that use. The essential nexus between the permission without the condition and the condition was not just tenuous but non-existent. A condition will not be relevant to the permitted development if it seeks to control something not created by the proposed development. **15.16**

In the *Newbury* case the House of Lords, whilst recognising that it would be unusual for a condition requiring the demolition of a building to fairly and reasonably relate to a permission granted for a change of use, considered that, exceptionally, a condition might do so. The question of whether a particular condition could be described as exceptional was considered in *Delta and Design and Engineering Ltd v Secretary of State for the Environment and South Cambridgeshire DC* [2000] JPL 726. **15.17**

In that case planning permission had been granted for a change of use of a listed building, Newton Hall. A condition attached to the permission required the demolition of an adjacent barn. The local planning authority considered the change of use would have an adverse effect on the character of the Hall and its setting, but that effect could be offset in part, by an improvement to the setting of the building by the demolition of the barn. The company had sought the removal of the condition. Following the refusal of the local planning authority to do so, the company appealed unsuccessfully to the Secretary of State. They then appealed to the High Court to quash the decision of the Inspector, but again unsuccessfully. One of the grounds of appeal to both the Secretary of State and the High Court was that the condition did not reasonably relate to the permitted development and was therefore ultra vires. In overturning the decision of the High Court and quashing the Inspector's decision, the Court of Appeal held that the Inspector determining the appeal had failed adequately to address the question of whether the desirable action of enhancing the setting of Newton Hall had **15.18** fairly and reasonably related to the change of use which the permission had granted. In addition, the trial judge at first instance had been wrong to decide that issue himself, which was a duty imposed on the Inspector as decision-maker, subject only to interference by the court on the well established grounds identified in the *Newbury* case. Furthermore, in deciding the issue of lawfulness of the condition, his reasoning was contrary to the *Newbury* case. On the facts the court found great difficulty in seeing how the condition which the Council sought to impose could be said to relate fairly and reaonably to the permitted development.

15.19 However, this case does not rule out the possibility that occasion may arise where planning permission for a change of use of land or buildings could lawfully include a condition requiring the demolition of ancillary buildings, but it would require a much clearer and closer relationship between the change of use and the demolition of the building than that which occurred in the *Delta* case in order to be justified.

15.20 In a more recent case, *Tarmac Heavy Building Materials Ltd UK v Secretary of State for the Environment, Transport & the Regions* [2000] PLCR 157, land had been used prior to 1 July 1948 and subsequently, for the manufacture of ready mixed concrete for which purpose a concrete batching plant had been erected. In 1952 planning permission had been granted for sand and gravel extraction on the land subject to a condition that at the completion of working, 'all building, huts or other structures on the site . . . should be removed from the site'. The local planning authority considered that the implementation of that condition required that on the cessation of working, the concrete batching plant should also be removed. Following the service of an enforcement notice which required removal of the concrete batching plant, the Secretary of State rejected an appeal by Tarmac and upheld the notice. In subsequent proceedings, however, the High Court held that the condition could not possibly be said to fairly and reasonably relate to the permission granted in 1952 and quashed the decision of the Secretary of State.

Not be unreasonable

15.21 It will be recalled that in *R v Hillingdon LBC, ex p Royco Homes Ltd* [1974] QB 720, the Lord Chief Justice considered that the imposition of conditions which gave to the occupiers of houses erected under a planning permission rights to security of tenure were *ultra vires* because they were unreasonable. A further example of a condition held to be void because it was unreasonable occurred in *Hall & Co. Ltd v Shoreham-by-Sea UDC* [1964] 1 WLR 240. There, the company had been granted planning permission for industrial development subject to a condition requiring it to construct an ancillary road over the entire frontage of the site at its own expense and to give a right of passage over it to persons proceeding to and from adjoining properties. The Court of Appeal held the condition to be unreasonable because its effect was to require the company to construct and dedicate a public road at its own expense. A similar view was taken in *City of Bradford Metropolitan Council v Secretary of State for the Environment* [1986] JPL 598 where it was held that a condition which required a highway maintainable at public expense to be widened by the applicant was manifestly unreasonable and *ultra vires*.

15.22 It is now quite clear that a condition in a planning permission which requires the developer to carry out or fund a public function of a local planning authority as a price for getting that permission is unlawful. This is so, irrespective of whether the initiative for the imposition of the condition comes from the local planning authority or, as it did in *City of Bradford Metropolitan Council* v *Secretary of State for the Environment* from the applicant himself. In such circumstances, however, it may be possible for the applicant to fund that function by the parties entering into what has for long been known as a s 106 obligation.

Another case which fell four-square within the situation considered in *Hall & Co. Ltd v Shoreham-by-Sea UDC* was *M.J. Shanley Ltd v Secretary of State for the Environment* [1982] JPL 380. Here, the company had proposed to the local planning authority that if it was granted planning permission for residential development for 10 acres of land in the green belt, it would lay out a further 40 acres of land for recreational purposes and then, having done so, would donate the 40 acres to the public as public open space. The proposal having met with a favourable response from the authority, the company proceeded to buy additional land, but was then surprised when the authority refused to grant the planning permission. The company appealed to the Secretary of State who, in upholding the authority's refusal, held that a condition requiring the provision of 40 acres of open space would be invalid and unenforceable. On a subsequent application by the company to quash the decision of the Secretary of State, Woolf J supported the view taken by the Secretary of State of the invalidity of the condition. **15.23**

Other tests of the validity of conditions

Apart from the three tests laid down in *Newbury DC v Secretary of State for the Environment* [1981] AC 578 for the validity of a condition, it seems that a condition may also be void because it is either uncertain or unenforceable. In addition, it was thought at one time that a condition could not take away existing use rights. **15.24**

Uncertain conditions

A condition may be void for uncertainty if it can be given no meaning at all, or no sensible or ascertainable meaning. A condition which is merely ambiguous will not fail for uncertainty, though the courts may be required to resolve the ambiguity. In *Fawcett Properties Ltd v Buckingham CC* [1961] AC 636, it was agreed that the condition limiting occupation of houses to workers (or the dependants of workers) in agriculture or forestry, or industries mainly dependant upon agriculture or forestry, could mean that a retired sheep farmer from New Zealand or a retired furrier from London would qualify, but not a telephone operator from Chalfont St Giles. The House of Lords held that in the context agriculture meant agriculture in the locality and so on, so that the condition was not void for uncertainty. **15.25**

In *Alderson v Secretary of State for the Environment* [1984] JPL 429 the Court of Appeal applied *Fawcett Properties Ltd v Buckingham CC* in reversing a decision of the High Court that a condition attached to a planning permission which limited the occupation of premises to persons employed locally in agriculture was void, because the word 'locally' had no ascertainable meaning. Although it was said on behalf of the respondents that some authorities preferred to spell out a precise boundary to the area in which the agriculture was being carried on, the court held that the word locally had a perfectly intelligible meaning even though some doubtful cases might arise. **15.26**

15.27 In *David Lowe & Sons Ltd v Musselburgh Corporation* 1974 SLT 5, the Scottish Court of Session was required to construe a grant of planning permission for residential development of three agricultural sites subject to a condition that:

> The sites are approved for the burgh's estimated future local authority and private housing needs over the next 20 years which cannot be accommodated within the existing burgh boundaries, in the proportion of one private house to four local authority houses.

Although one judge thought that it was a statement of the reason why planning permission was granted rather than a condition, the condition was held to be void on the ground that it was not capable of any certain or intelligible interpretation.

Unenforceable conditions

15.28 There are a number of instances where the Secretary of State has discharged a condition in a planning permission on the ground that it is unenforceable. It seems that in law such a condition may also be invalid. It is likely that in most cases a legal challenge to a condition alleging uncertainty would need to be based on the grounds of *Wednesbury* 'unreasonableness' (i.e., perversity).

15.29 A condition may be unenforceable on the ground that the local planning authority has no power to secure compliance with the condition. In *British Airports Authority v Secretary of State for Scotland* [1980] JPL 260, a condition was imposed in the grant of permission for development at Aberdeen Airport concerning the flight path of aircraft taking off and landing at the airport. The condition was concerned with matters over which the applicants had no control, since statutory authority to prescribe the direction of flight or aircraft lies with the Civil Aviation Authority. Since there were no steps the applicants could take to secure the result required by the condition for that additional reason, the authority was held to have no power to impose it under the relevant statutory provisions.

15.30 A condition would only be unenforceable if, for example, it required 'a landscape scheme to be submitted for the approval of the local planning authority', since it does not require a scheme to be actually approved by the authority. So too, is it difficult to see how a condition that the development should be completed by a given date can be enforced since, once the time limit has expired, it is to late to require compliance with the condition.

Existing use rights

15.31 At one time it was thought that a condition in a planning permission could not take away existing use rights. In *Allnatt London Properties Ltd v Middlesex CC* (1964) 15 P & CR 288, planning permission had been granted for the demolition and replacement of industrial buildings forming part of a factory complex. The permission was granted subject to a condition that the replacement buildings were to be used only in conjunction with the main factory and, for the first 10 years, only by persons or firms who at the date of the permission occupied industrial premises in Middlesex. The purpose of the condition was to restrain any further influx of industrial development into the county without inhibiting the rebuilding of existing industrial premises. The effect of the condition, however, was to restrict for 10 years the number of potential purchasers of the company's property. Glyn-Jones J held that the condition was void. The company had a right to continue with the existing use of the factory complex and that right could not be taken away without compensation.

15.32 It was perhaps unfortunate that no appeal was made from this decision. A planning permission granted without conditions would also, if implemented, take away existing use rights without compensation. The owner would have the option not to implement the permission and to retain existing use rights, or to do so and lose them. Logically, it should make no difference where the planning permission has a condition attached to it.

15.33 The authority of *Allnatt London Properties Ltd v Middlesex CC* was not to last too long. In *Kingston-upon-Thames RLBC v Secretary of State for the Environment* [1973] 1WLR1549, planning permission had been granted to rebuild a station subject to a condition that land to the south of the station should be used for car-parking. When the condition was not complied with the authority served an enforcement notice. On appeal, the Secretary of State discharged the condition, because the land was being used to carry the electric traction cable and, on the authority of *Allnatt London Properties Ltd v Middlesex CC*, that right could not be taken away without compensation. The local planning authority then sought to challenge the Secretary of State's decision. The Divisional Court allowed the appeal and returned the case to the Secretary of State for reconsideration. In considering *Allnatt London Properties Ltd v Middlesex CC*, Lord Widgery CJ considered it correctly decided but for the wrong reason. The defect in the condition was that it did not reasonably relate to the development permitted. Bridge J, on the other hand, considered the decision to be wrong. He referred to the power of the local planning authority to regulate the use of land other than land in respect of that for which planning permission is granted, the exercise of which must encroach on the existing use rights of that other land. So long as a condition in a planning permission fairly and reasonably relates to the development permitted, the effect on existing use rights in no way affects its validity.

15.34 Reaffirmation of the principle was given in *Peak Park Joint Planning Board v Secretary of State for the Environment* [1980] JPL 114 where, after calling in an application for development for his own decision, the Secretary of State granted planning permission for the development but refused to impose certain conditions (as sought by the authority) on the ground that they would have affected existing use rights and were *ultra vires*. On a challenge to that decision, Sir Douglas Frank QC, sitting as a Deputy High Court judge, held that the Secretary of State was wrong to hold that the conditions would be *ultra vires* because they derogated from existing use rights and remitted the matter back to him for further consideration.

The need for precision

15.35 As stated earlier, Circular 11/95 contains a number of suggested models of acceptable conditions for use by local planning authorities in appropriate circumstances. The list is not exhaustive and authorities need to show care in the wording of other conditions if they are to be effective for the purposes intended. This can be difficult. In *R v Ealing LBC, ex p Zainuddin* [1995] JPL 925, the local planning authority had granted planning permission for a mosque, subject to a condition that no ceremonial gatherings or acts of worship should take place except within the buildings. The owners erected merely the frame of the building, with no roof and no sides, and then proceeded to hold a gathering of 1,500 devotees. The High Court held that the owners had not been in breach of the condition and granted judicial review of the authority's decision to serve a breach of condition notice.

B. SPECIFIC POWERS TO IMPOSE CONDITIONS

15.36 Although specific powers to impose conditions are also given to local planning authorities, it seems that their use should be subject to the same limitations as is the use of the general power, namely, that they must be imposed for a planning purpose, be fairly and reasonably related to the permitted development and not be manifestly unreasonable. The following specific powers are given to authorities.

Regulating other land

15.37 Section 72(1)(a) of the 1990 Act provides that a condition may be imposed on the grant of planning permission:

> for regulating the development or use of any land under the control of the applicant (whether or not it is land in respect of which the application was made) or requiring the carrying out of works on any such land, so far as appears to the local planning authority to be expedient for the purposes of or in connection with the development authorised by the permission.

An example of its use would be where an owner of land applies for planning permission to erect a dwelling house with cesspit arrangements for the disposal of sewage. The authority may grant permission subject to a condition that the owner lays a sewer under adjoining land in his control to connect the dwellinghouse to the public sewer system. For the condition to be imposed, the land must be under the 'control' of the applicant. This requirement does not necessarily require the applicant to own an estate or interest in the land. In *George Wimpey & Co. Ltd v New Forest DC* [1979] JPL 313, Sir Douglas Frank QC held that the question of whether land was in the applicant's control became a question of fact and degree for the Secretary of State and depended upon whether the control was of a degree and kind sufficient to satisfy him that the condition could be complied with.

15.38 In a Ministerial decision in 1988, the Secretary of State in an appeal against an enforcement notice, considered *ultra vires* on the grounds of unreasonableness a condition in a grant of planning permission for a change of use of three floors of the old Derry and Toms building in Kensington High Street, London, from 'retail use' to 'use for exhibition purposes and ancillary restaurant'. The condition required that 'The loading or unloading of vehicles visiting the premises, including those delivering fuel, shall not be carried out otherwise than from within the curtilage of the building'. The Secretary of State considered that the condition was dependent upon the action of others, such as the police or the highways authority, and since it purported to regulate use of the public highway, was unreasonable.

15.39 Similarly, in a Ministerial decision [2001] JPL 241, the Secretary of State discharged a condition in a grant of planning permission for a change of use from a petrol filling station to a car sales showroom that 'there shall be no deliveries or collections of vehicles to and from the application site by car transporters', because deliveries to and from the site might well take place by persons who were not necessarily the occupiers of the appeal site.

15.40 It would be otherwise, however, if it were within the power of the beneficiary of the permission to comply with the condition. In *John & Joseph Davenport v Hammersmith & Fulham LBC* [1999] JPL 1112, planning permission had been granted to Joseph Davenport for the retention of a building in connection with the use of land for motor vehicle repairs. A condition in the planning permission prohibited vehicles which had been left with or in the control of the applicant being parked in the access road to the premises. The access road, which was a cul-de-sac, was a vehicular highway owned by the Borough Council. Following non-compliance with the condition, the Council served a breach of condition notice and then, subsequently, prosecuted the Davenports for non-compliance with that notice. Following their conviction, the Davenports appealed by way of use stated to the Queen's Bench Divisional Court. Central to the appeal was whether the condition prohibiting the parking and storage of vehicles could lawfully be imposed under s 70(1). The Divisional Court held that it could, since although the condition did not require that the Davenports should have control of the land in question, the condition was one that they were able to comply with, namely to ensure that they did not use the access road for the parking of vehicles left with them or which were within their control. So, too, would a condition in a planning permission for a change of use to a 'taxi information and booking office' which sought to prevent the collection of passengers from the taxi office.

A not uncommon condition imposed in planning permissions for new uses sited in busy town centre locations which meets the test of validity would be 'no vehicles which are in the control of XYZ at [address of XYZ], shall be left or parked in the following "named" streets'. **15.41**

Grampian-type conditions

The ability of a local planning authority to impose conditions under the general power to do so, over land not under the control of the applicant was again raised in *Grampian Regional Council v City of Aberdeen District Council* (1984) 47 P & CR 633. In this case planning permission had been made for a change of use of land from agricultural use to industrial use. The applicants had appealed to the Secretary of State for Scotland against non-determination of the application within the statutory time-limit, and he had delegated the determination of the appeals to a reporter (Inspector) who took the view that traffic to and from the site would constitute such a hazard as to justify the refusal of planning permission. He considered that the hazard would be removed if an existing road could be closed, but concluded that it would not be competent to grant planning permission subject to a condition requiring the closure of the road since it did not lie wholly within the power of the first respondents to secure the closure, any closure order that they might make requiring confirmation by the Secretary of State under s 198(1) of the Town and Country Planning (Scotland) Act 1972, which would not necessarily be granted. He accordingly dismissed the appeals. The First Division of the Inner House of the Court of Session allowed an appeal by the first respondents, holding that, while a condition requiring something to be done that was not within the control of the first respondents would be incompetent, a condition requiring that no development be commenced until the road had been closed would be competent. The appellants appealed, contending that the imposition on the grant of planning permission of any negative condition related to the occurrence of an uncertain event was unreasonable and, therefore, invalid and that in any event it was undesirable that there should be prolonged uncertainty as to whether the development would be able to go forward or not. **15.42**

In dismissing the appeal the House of Lords held that there was a crucial difference between a positive and a negative type of condition in that the latter was enforceable while the **15.43** former was not; that the reasonableness of any condition had to be considered in the light of the circumstances of the case and that in the present case, where the proposals for development had been found by the reporter to be generally desirable in the public interest, it would have been not only not unreasonable but highly appropriate to grant planning permission subject to the condition in question; that, moreover, it was impossible to view such a condition as unreasonable and not within the scope of s 26(1) of the Town and Country Planning (Scotland) Act 1972 if regard was had to s 198(1), from which it was reasonable to infer that it was precisely that type of condition that had been envisaged by the legislature when enacting s 26(1). (Note that ss 26(1) and 198(1) of the Scottish Act were identical to ss 29(1) and 209(1) of the Town and Country Planning Act 1971, now ss 70(1) and 247(1) of the 1990 Act.)

15.44 Since the *Grampian* case, the imposition of negative conditions (known colloquially as *Grampian*-type conditions) has risen in popularity, particularly with regard to highway works necessary on other land before any development on the application land can begin. Their utility, however, was restricted by the advice contained in Appendix A to PPG 13: *Highways Considerations in Development Control* that such conditions should not be imposed where such works are unlikely to be done within a reasonable period, usually five years — the normal lifetime of a planning permission.

15.45 In *Jones v Secretary of State for Wales* (1990) 88 LGR 942, the Court of Appeal upheld the advice in PPG 13, holding that it was unlawful for a local planning authority to grant planning permission subject to a condition which prevented development until some obstacle had been removed, unless there was a reasonable prospect of that obstacle being removed within the time limit imposed by the permission. The decision was purportedly based on the *Grampian* case, where it was said that the question whether a condition was unreasonable depended upon the circumstances of the case.

15.46 This approach was taken by the Secretary of State in *British Railways Board v Secretary of State for the Environment* [1994] JPL 32, where he took the view that, as a matter of law, a *Grampian* condition could not be validly attached to a permission unless there was a reasonable prospect of it being fulfilled. The House of Lords, however, held that the mere fact that a desirable condition appeared to have no reasonable prospects of fulfilment did not mean that planning permission must necessarily be refused. Their Lordships went on to hold that *Jones v Secretary of State for Wales* was wrongly decided.

15.47 Lord Keith, after referring to the earlier decision in *Grampian* and the Court of Appeal decision in *Jones*, said:

> The owner of the land to which the application related might object to the grant of planning permission for reasons which might or not be sound on planning grounds. If his reasons were sound on planning grounds no doubt the application would be refused. But if they were unsound, the mere fact that the owner objected and was unwilling that the development should go ahead could not in itself necessarily lead to a refusal. The function of the planning authority was to decide whether or not the proposed development was desirable in the public interest. The answer to that question was not to be affected by the consideration that the owner of the land was determined not to allow the development so that permission for it, if granted, would not have reasonable prospects of being implemented. That did not mean that the planning authority, if it decided that the proposed development was in the public interest, was

> absolutely disentitled from taking into account the improbability of permission for it, if granted, being implemented. For example, if there were a competition between two alternative sites for a desirable development, difficulties of bringing about implementation on one site which were not present in relation to the other might very properly lead to the refusal of planning permission for the site affected by the difficulties and the grant of it for the other. But there was no absolute rule that the existence of difficulties, even if apparently insuperable, had to necessarily lead to refusal of planning permission for a desirable development. A would-be developer might be faced with difficulties of many different kinds, in the way of site assembly or securing the discharge of restricted covenants. If he considered that it was in his interests to secure planning permission notwithstanding the existence of such difficulties, it was not for the planning authority to refuse it simply on their view of how serious the difficulties were.

This statement was subsequently translated into Circular 11/95 (at para 40 of the Annex) in the following form and following a reference in the Circular to the possibility of imposing negative conditions: **15.48**

> It is the policy of the Secretaries of State that such a condition should only be imposed on a planning permission if there are at least reasonable prospects of the action in question being performed within the time-limit imposed by the permission.

To that paragraph there is appended a foot-note referring to the *British Railways* case and observing that: **15.49**

> The House of Lords established that the mere fact that a desirable condition, worded in a negative form, appears to have no reasonable prospects of fulfilment does not mean that planning permission must necessarily be refused as a matter of law. However, the judgment leaves open the possibility for the Secretary of State, to maintain as a matter of policy that there should be at least reasonable prospects of the action in question being performed within the time-limit imposed by the permission.

However, the issue was again raised in *Merritt v Secretary of State for the Environment, Transport and the Regions* [2000] JPL 371 where Robin Purchase QC, sitting as a Deputy Judge, quashed the decision of an Inspector to dismiss an appeal against non-determination of a planning application made by the applicants, on the ground that the Inspector had erred in law in rejecting a *Grampian* condition relating to the provision of access to the site because he was not convinced that there was a reasonable prospect that the condition would be fulfilled within the time limit imposed on any permission. The Deputy Judge pointed to the danger that in promulgating a policy in an absolute form, such as in para 40 of the Annex to Circular 11/95, a decision-maker may regard himself as bound to follow that policy. The Deputy Judge had no doubt that on the face of the decision letter, the Inspector had simply applied the policy as a mandatory requirement, without considering whether there was scope for the exercise of discretion. In applying policy, the Inspector should have considered the actual implications of imposing a *Grampian* condition and whether it would, in fact, cause demonstrable harm. **15.50**

A similar view of para. 40 of circular 11/95 was expressed by Sullivan J. in the case of *R (Shina) v Secretary of State for the Environment, Transport and the Regions and the Royal Borough of Kensington and Chelsea* [2002] JPL 1132. There the court quashed a decision of the Inspector to dismiss an appeal against a refusal to grant planning permission for the development of a site, because of the need for access to the site to be provided over adjoining land not in the applicant's control. As in the *Merritt* case, the Inspector had regarded himself bound by the **15.51** mandatory terms of para. 40 and in doing so, had failed to have regard to the applicant's argument that the grant of planning permission subject to a *Grampian* condition would actually facilitate the problem of land assembly which needed to be resolved before the development could be carried out.

15.52 The law relating to the imposition of a *Grampian* condition seems from the cases to be that it is not ultra vires to impose a negative condition even though there is no reasonable prospect of it being fulfilled within the time limit of the permission; but that the fact that it is unlikely to be fulfilled within that period is material to whether or not one should be imposed. Put another way, in deciding whether or not to impose a negative style condition, the policy statement in para 40 of the Annex to Circular 11/95 should be taken into account, but the decision-maker should not consider himself bound by it in mandatory terms. He must consider all relevant circumstances and the likelihood of the condition being fulfilled within the time limit of the permission is only one of the factors to be taken into account.

Permission granted for a limited period

15.53 Section 72(1)(b) of the 1990 Act provides that a condition may be imposed on the grant of planning permission:

> for requiring the removal of any buildings or works authorised by the permission, or the discontinuance of any use of land so authorised, at the end of a specified period, and the carrying out of any works required for the reinstatement of land at the end of that period.

In order for the life of a planning permission to be limited to a term of years, it is necessary to impose an express condition in the permission requiring the authorised use of the land to be discontinued or the removal of any authorised building or works, etc., at the end of some stated period. The dangers of not doing so are seen in *I'm Your Man Ltd v Secretary of State for the Environment* [1999] PLCR 109, where the local planning authority had granted planning permission in 1995 for the use of buildings for sales, exhibitions and leisure activities for a temporary period of seven years. No express condition was imposed which required that use to cease at the expiration of that period. Before the expiration of the seven years, however, the owners applied for planning permission for the permanent use of the premises for those purposes. On appeal against the refusal of the local planning authority to grant planning permission for permanent use, it was argued that despite the fact that the 1995 permission was expressed to be for a temporary period, the permission was in effect a permanent permission. On dismissal of the applicants' appeal to the Secretary of State, the applicants successfully applied to the High Court for the decision to be quashed. It was held that the temporary period identified in the 1995 permission was a 'limitation' rather than a condition, and that local planning authorities had no power to impose a limitation on a grant of planning permission. This could only be done by way of a development order. Accordingly, the permission granted in 1995 was effectively a permanent permission.

15.54 The decision by the Courts that a limitation in the description of the development does not operate as a condition of the planning permission could have a significant impact in other cases. A planning permission granted for the use of a holiday cottage between April and September each year for example, would not prevent its unrestricted residential use throughout the year, unless an appropriate condition was imposed on the permission limiting the occupancy to its use during that period as a holiday cottage.

In a recent Ministerial decision in April 2004 (Ref. APP/J 2210/X/03/1134471) an Inspector held that a grant of planning permission for the 'continued use as an occasional caravan camp in accordance with the application for planning permission, would not prevent the use of the land as a caravan site throughout the year, since the wish to restrict occupancy in this way had not been expressed as a condition of the permission. **15.55**

In another Ministerial decision (Ref. APP/D0515/X/1124089), planning permission had been granted for the use of a site as an airport and parachute drop zone using one light aircraft. An Inspector allowed an appeal against the refusal of a lawful development certificate for the use of a second light aircraft. The planning permission had contained a limitation to one aircraft, but this would only be enforced by way of a condition. Furthermore, an increase in the number of aircraft from one to two, could not be described as development. **15.56**

The kind of planning permission authorised by s 72(1)(b) is called a 'term consent' or 'a permission granted for a limited period'. It was this kind of condition that was successfully challenged in *Newbury DC v Secretary of State for the Environment* [1981] AC 578. It has several advantages in practice. First, where land is awaiting redevelopment, planning permission can be granted for a limited period for development which would not otherwise be allowed, such as for a charity shop in an area zoned for residential development. In such cases, the temporary permission is normally sought by the applicant himself. Secondly, where there have been strong objections to proposed development, the term consent enables the parties to 'have a trial run', so that it becomes clear during the currency of the term whether or not the objections made were well founded. If not, at the end of the term, another planning permission without a similar condition can be granted. **15.57**

A somewhat unusual example of such a condition being imposed occurred in 1994, when consent (for three years) was granted for the retention of a fibreglass fish attached to the side extension of a dwellinghouse on land in Norbury, London SW16. The local planning authority had served an enforcement notice requiring its removal on the ground that its presence was detrimental to the amenities of nearby residents. It appeared that the fibreglass fish was a reproduction of a marlin caught by the appellant in the Pacific Ocean, and he wished to retain it as a work of art commemorating this achievement. The appellant had earlier attracted some notoriety by placing at various times on or near the appeal site, a military tank, a self-propelled gun, a large replica Spitfire and an assortment of smaller items, some lit up at night. All had attracted traffic and activity and media attention to the site. **15.58**

In dealing with the planning merits of the case, the Inspector concluded that the presence of unauthorised developments at the appeal site, including the fish, had caused demonstrable harm to residential amenity and traffic safety in the area. He felt, however, that there was insufficient evidence available for him to come to a proper view of the extent to which that harm was attributable to the presence of the fish and to assess the future impact of the fish alone. In the circumstances, he decided to grant planning permission for the fish on a temporary basis, thus giving a proper opportunity for the impact of the fish alone to be tested. **15.59**

Subsequently the local planning authority were to seek a 'planning injunction' against the **15.60** occupier requiring him, *inter alia,* to remove the replica Spitfire. This was the subject of further proceedings in *Croydon LBC v Gladden* [1994] JPL 723 (see Chapter 21).

15.61 Where a term consent has been granted, planning permission is not normally required to revert to the previous use. Section 57(2) of the 1990 Act deals with the right to revert in these terms.

> Where planning permission to develop land has been granted for a limited period, planning permission is not required for the resumption, at the end of that period, of its use for the purpose for which it was normally used before the permission was granted.

The effect of these provisions was considered in *Smith v Secretary of State for the Environment* [1983] JPL 462. It is clear that if a landowner has been granted a term consent no planning permission is required to return to the last normal use of the land. But the provision requires no account to be taken of any use of land begun in contravention of planning control. So if a term consent has been granted to change from a use of land which has been begun in contravention of planning control, the owner cannot under the section revert to that use at the end of the term without a grant of planning permission. It would be otherwise, of course, if the previous contravening use had become immune from enforcement action by virtue of the time limits now laid down in the Act for the taking of enforcement action.

Requiring the development to be commenced

15.62 Section 72(3) of the 1990 Act provides that where:

> (a) planning permission is granted for development consisting of or including the carrying out of building or other operations subject to a condition that the operations shall be commenced not later than a time specified in the condition; and
> (b) any building or other operations are commenced after the time so specified,
>
> the commencement and carrying out of those operations do not constitute development for which that permission was granted.

15.63 It should be noted that the provision only applies to building or other operations. Furthermore, the provision is concerned with the commencement of such development, not its completion.

15.64 In practice little use has ever been made of this statutory power. Since 1968 its purpose has been met by new mandatory conditions relating to the commencement of development which have been imposed in most planning permissions granted since April 1969. These provisions are now to be found in ss 91 to 95 of the 1990 Act, to which reference is made later.

Limiting the benefit to a particular person

15.65 It may sometimes be appropriate to confine the benefit of a planning permission to a particular person. The power to do so derives from the wording of s 75(1) of the 1990 Act which provides:

> Without prejudice to the provisions of this Part [of the 1990 Act] as to the duration, revocation or modification of planning permission, any grant of planning permission to develop land shall

(except in so far as the permission otherwise provides) enure for the benefit of the land and of all persons for the time being interested in it.

In *Knott v Secretary of State for the Environment and Caradon DC* [1997] JPL 713, the District Council had granted planning permission for the erection of a dwelling subject to a condition that the 'permission should enure solely for the benefit of Mr & Mrs Knott'. The assumption had been that the condition controlled both the initial construction of the dwelling and its subsequent occupation for the benefit of the Knotts and they alone. The High Court thought otherwise, however, holding that once the permission had been implemented by the construction of the house and its occupation by the Knotts, the condition did not prevent persons other than the Knotts from occupying the dwelling. What the Council should have done was to impose a condition limiting the occupation of the dwelling when completed solely to the Knotts.

Let no one say that planning law is dull. In the aftermath of the decision of the High Court, the District Council, after taking into account the views of the Secretary of State that the grant of planning permission could be said to have been grossly wrong, decided to make a revocation order to annul the permission and a discontinuance order requiring removal of the uncompleted dwelling. Both orders were then confirmed by the Secretary of State. **15.66**

However, the Council then became aware that the dwelling was being constructed outside the boundaries of the application site and, mindful of the obligation to pay compensation for loss caused by the revocation and discontinuance orders, decided to issue an enforcement notice under s 174(2) of the 1990 Act on the ground that there had been a breach of planning control. If effective, this could, of course, have relieved the District Council of any compensation liability. **15.67**

The applicants then applied to the High Court for relief by seeking a declaration that the Council's resolution to take enforcement action was contrary to law and certiorari to quash the enforcement notice. In *R v Caradon DC, ex p Knott* (2000) 80 P & CR 154, Sullivan J granted the relief that had been sought. **15.68**

The High Court held that the Council had not taken the decision to issue the enforcement notice in order to secure any planning objective, that having been achieved by the revocation and discontinuance orders. Furthermore, Sullivan J held that under the doctrine of estoppel, the Council was barred from taking enforcement action. Compensation for the revocation and discontinuance orders has now been settled, although the Council itself undertook the remedial works. **15.69**

Personal planning permissions are comparatively rare, because if it is thought desirable to avoid a perpetuation of a use of land, a term consent can best achieve that purpose. The power is a statutory recognition, however, that planning permission may be granted in circumstances where permission would otherwise be refused. A personal planning permission may sometimes be granted on hardship grounds, and may sometimes be linked to a term consent. **15.70**

Sometimes a personal planning permission may result from service of an enforcement notice issued by the local planning authority. One such case concerned contravening development of an industrial nature located in a rural area. In quashing the enforcement notice the **15.71**

Secretary of State granted a temporary and personal planning permission for a period of two years for the contravening development in order to allow the owner to search for an alternative location for his business during that period.

Specifying the use to which a building may be put

15.72 Mention has previously been made of s 75(2) and (3) of the 1990 Act which provides that:

(2) Where planning permission is granted for the erection of a building, the grant of permission may specify the purposes for which the building may be used.

(3) If no purpose is so specified, the permission shall be construed as including permission to use the building for the purpose for which it is designed.

The question is sometimes asked whether, if a building is demolished, the existing use rights associated with the building's previous lawful occupation survive to benefit the land itself or the use is extinguished with the building's demolition. The matter is not entirely free from doubt, but it is considered that the demolition ends a chapter in the land's planning history and that a new chapter is then commenced. The result, of course, is that as with the abandonment of a use, the land cannot be used for any purpose without planning permission, save for those activities and uses that are not development.

C. CHALLENGING AN INVALID CONDITION

15.73 The validity of a condition may be challenged following an appeal from a decision of the Secretary against an adverse decision of a local planning authority on a planning application. It may also follow an appeal to the Secretary of State against an enforcement notice alleging a breach of condition. It may also be challenged as a defence to a prosecution for failure to comply with a breach of condition notice, by an application for a certificate as to the lawfulness of proposed operations or uses; and of course, by an application for a declaration in the High Court.

D. EFFECT OF AN INVALID CONDITION

15.74 Where a condition is held to be invalid, the question arises whether the condition can be severed from the planning permission so that the permission survives shorn of its invalidity, or whether the condition cannot be severed so that the whole planning permission is void *ab initio*.

15.75 In *Hall & Co. Ltd v Shoreham-by-Sea UDC* [1964] 1 WLR 240, a condition which required the company effectively to dedicate a road to the public at the company's expense was held to be invalid. The local planning authority had argued that if the condition was void, then the whole planning permission was a nullity. The Court of Appeal was persuaded by that argument because the invalid condition was fundamental to the whole of the planning permission. The suggestion in this and later cases was that if the invalid condition was incidental or trivial then it could be severed from the permission; if it were fundamental then the whole permission fell.

In *Allnatt London Properties Ltd v Middlesex CC* (1964) 15 P & CR 288, a condition was held to be void because it took away existing use rights. In argument, the local planning authority were unable to give any grounds on which a reasonable planning authority could have refused planning permission assuming the condition to be void. Not surprisingly, therefore, the court held that the permission could stand free of the condition. Since the authority would have been prepared to grant the permission in the absence of the condition, the impugned condition was clearly not one which was fundamental to the permission, so that the test to be applied may well be whether the local planning authority would have been prepared to grant planning permission in the absence of the condition. **15.76**

The trivial/fundamental dichotomy was eventually supported by the House of Lords in *Kent CC v Kingsway Investments (Kent) Ltd* [1971] AC 72. Here the House of Lords held that conditions in an outline planning permission requiring details of proposals to be submitted to and approved by the authority before any work began and that the permission should cease to have effect after the expiration of three years unless within that time notice of approval of the detailed proposals had been given, were valid. Their Lordships went on, however, to consider the position if they had found otherwise. According to their Lordships, if the invalid conditions are unimportant, incidental or merely superimposed on the permission, then the permission might endure. If the conditions are part of the structure of the permission, then the permission falls with it. **15.77**

In *R v St Edmundsbury BC, ex p Investors in Industry Commercial Properties Ltd* [1985] 1 WLR 1168 it was said (*obiter*) that if a condition requiring the developer of a superstore to provide three independent retail units was invalid, it could be severed from the permission. **15.78**

A more recent example of non-severability occurred in *Fisher v Wychavon District Council* [2001] JPL 694, where planning permission had been granted for a residential caravan, subject to a condition that that use be discontinued not later than 'F' years from the date of the permission. The permission had been issued some 13 years earlier and it was unclear as to what was intended by the 'F' in the condition. The Court of Appeal refused to apply a blue line to strike out all reference to what was a temporary consent so as to leave a consent which was permanent, and so upheld a decision of the High Court that the planning permission was of no effect. **15.79**

E. REMOVING CONDITIONS PREVIOUSLY ATTACHED

Under s 73 of the 1990 Act an application may be made to the local planning authority for the development of land without complying with conditions subject to which a planning permission was granted. On an application the authority must only consider the question of the conditions, and they may decide that the permission shall be subject to the same conditions as were previously imposed, that the permission should be granted subject to different conditions, or that permission should be granted unconditionally. There is a right of appeal to the Secretary of State and a right of challenge in the normal way to the courts on a point of **15.80** law. Jurisdiction in all cases is limited to the conditions and decisions relating to those conditions.

15.81 A successful application under s 73 results in a fresh grant of planning permission. However, in considering whether to grant a fresh planning permission, the local planning authority can only consider the question of conditions subject to which the earlier planning permission was granted. An authority can, if it so wishes, impose new conditions in the fresh planning permission, subject to the conditions being those which it could have lawfully imposed upon the earlier permission and which do not amount to a fundamental alteration to the proposal put forward in the original application (*R v Coventry City Council, ex p Arrowcroft Group plc* [2001] PLCR 113). It is also clear that an application under s 73 cannot be used by a local planning authority to have a 'second bite of the cherry', nor to plug any perceived holes in the earlier permission.

F. RETROSPECTIVE PLANNING APPLICATIONS

15.82 S. 73A of the 1990 Act provides for an application to be made to a local planning authority for planning permission for development which has already been carried out. This procedure applies not only to development carried out without planning permission, but to development carried out without complying with some condition subject to which planning permission was granted. It would seem that a developer must implement the permission and breach the condition before making an application under the section.

15.83 An application for planning permission under s. 73A is in all respects, apart from the fact that development will have commenced, a conventional planning application. In dealing with it the local planning authority must have regard to the provisions of the development plan, so far as material, and to any other material considerations. Hence if the trigger for a s.73A application arises not from the fact that development has been undertaken without planning permission, but that there has been a breach of a condition subject to which an earlier planning permission was granted, the local planning authority in considering the merits of the application, is not required to confine its attention to the appropriateness of the conditions (see *Brenda Wilkinson v Rossendale Borough Council* [2003] JPL 82. The authority's role is to consider the planning merits of permitting the development to continue, and under what conditions, if any.

G. DURATION OF PLANNING PERMISSIONS

15.84 Prior to 1969, one of the risks a local planning authority faced in granting planning permission was that the permission might never be implemented. This could be important in practice where development had to be restricted because of inadequate infrastructure. For example, a planning permission given to A (but not implemented) might prevent planning permission being given later to B because the existing infrastructure might not support both developments. In 1968, power was given to local planning authorities to impose conditions which it was thought would alleviate that problem. The statutory provisions are now to be found in the 1990 Act as amended by the Planning and Compulsory Purchase Act 2004.

Full planning permissions

Section 91 of the 1990 Act as originally enacted provided that every planning permission granted, or deemed to be granted, shall be subject to the condition that the development to which it relates must be begun not later than the expiration of: **15.85**

(a) five years beginning with the date on which the permission is granted or . . . deemed to be granted; or
(b) such other period (whether longer or shorter) beginning with that date as the authority concerned with the terms of planning permission may direct.

The period of five years mentioned in (a) above is to be reduced to three years once s. 51 of the Planning and Compulsory Purchase Act 2004 is fully implemented. **15.86**

The period mentioned in (b) above is to be the period which the authority consider appropriate having regard to the provisions of the development plan and to any other material considerations. **15.87**

The section further provides that if planning permission is granted without such a condition, it shall be deemed to have been granted subject to the condition in paragraph (a) above. Exceptionally, if legal proceedings are brought to challenge the validity of a grant of planning permission (or a deemed grant of permission) the time limit for beginning the development is to be taken to be extended by one year. **15.88**

The above provisions do not, for reasons which are in most cases self-evident, apply to: **15.89**

(a) any planning permission granted by a development order;
(b) any planning permission granted under s 73A for development carried out before the making of an application;
(c) any planning permission granted for a limited period;
(d) any planning permission granted for the winning and working of minerals (which is subject to special provisions relating to the commencement of the development);
(e) any planning permission granted by an enterprise zone scheme;
(f) any planning permission granted by a simplified planning zone scheme;
(g) any outline planning permission (which is subject to special rules).

It should be noted that the standard three-year period may be varied at the discretion of the local planning authority or on appeal by the Secretary of State. This power to vary may be useful where it is desired to phase the commencement of large-scale development over a prolonged period of time. **15.90**

The existence of time-limits with which development must be begun imposes pressure on the developer to do so, since s 93(4) provides that development carried out after the date by which the condition requires it to be carried out shall be treated as not authorised by the permission. In other words, if the condition is not complied with, the benefit of the permission will be lost. This may be of little consequence to the landowner, who may reapply for planning permission which, if granted, will contain a like condition. The problem arises, **15.91** however, where there has been a change in planning policy by the local planning authority since the first grant of permission, which results in the renewal application being refused. In such a case land which had a value which reflected the right to develop will no longer have that value. It will often be important, therefore, to ensure that development is begun by the date specified in the condition. If it is, then the planning permission will be kept alive. If not, then the permission will be lost.

15.92 This is of particular importance in view of s 54A of the 1990 Act (now to be repealed and substituted by s. 38(6) of the Planning and Compulsory Purchase Act 2004). In *Kirkman v Secretary of State for Wales* [1995] EGCS 127, developers found to their cost that although in 1988 the local planning authority were prepared to grant planning permission for residential development, in 1992, as a result of s 54A, the dominance of the provisions of the development plan as a material consideration was sufficient to justify a later refusal.

15.93 Section 56 of the 1990 Act prescribes the activities that constitute compliance with the requirement that the development should be begun. It provides that development shall be taken to be begun on the earliest date on which any 'material operation' (previously called a 'specified operation') comprised in the development begins to be carried out. 'Material operation' is defined in s 56(4) to mean:

(a) any work of construction in the course of the erection of a building;
(aa) any work of demolition of a building;
(b) the digging of a trench which is to contain the foundations, or part of the foundations, of a building;
(c) the laying of any underground main or pipe to the foundations, or part of the foundations, of a building or to any such trench as is mentioned in paragraph (b);
(d) any operation in the course of laying out or constructing a road or part of a road;
(e) any change in the use of any land which constitutes material development.

15.94 In the context of paragraph (e), material development means any development other than:

(a) development for which planning permission is granted by a general development order for the time being in force and which is carried out so as to comply with any condition or limitation subject to which planning permission is so granted;
(b) development of a class specified in paragraph 1 or 2 of Schedule 3;
(c) development of any class prescribed for the purposes of this sub-section.

15.95 It is also provided that if the development consists both of the carrying out of operations and a change of use, the development of land shall be taken to be initiated by the commencement of the operations or the carrying out of the change of use, whichever is the earlier. It is clear that great care must be taken to ensure compliance with the section.

15.96 In *High Peak BC v Secretary of State for the Environment* [1981] JPL 366, Courtdale Developments Ltd wished to exploit a planning permission with a time-limit for commencement of development within five years, and so, within that time, the company arranged for a mechanical digger to dig a trench of the requisite width and depth to contain foundations. It had then proceeded to fill in the trench with the earth which had been excavated. The trench had been dug in order to keep the planning permission alive but back-filled to prevent animals and children falling into it. The Queen's Bench Divisional Court held that the company's action in digging the trench was an operation under what is now s 56(4) of the 1990 Act so that the permission had not expired.

In *South Oxfordshire DC v Secretary of State for the Environment* [1981] JPL 359 trenches had been dug which appeared to fulfill the requirements of what is now s 56(4), but they had not been dug for the development to which the planning permission related. Accordingly, the Secretary of State did not consider that that was sufficient to comply with the provisions, a conclusion which Woolf J was prepared to accept. **15.97**

In *Malvern Hills DC v Secretary of State for the Environment* [1982] JPL 439, an enforcement notice had been served by the local planning authority on a company alleging a breach of planning control. The Court of Appeal was required to decide whether or not marking out with pegs the line of part of a proposed road constituted a 'specified operation'. The pegs had been placed in position so that a road could be constructed with machines which would be guided by the pegs. This was part of an overall operation, namely the laying out of a road. If it did do so, the planning permission was still alive and there would be no breach. A divided court held that the work was a specified operation and found that, contrary to the view of the authority, the Secretary of State had not erred in law in so finding. **15.98**

In this case the company had always believed that the condition which required the development to be begun by a set date had been complied with and so proposed to continue with the development despite its dispute with the authority. The local planning authority, who thought otherwise, had not only served an enforcement notice on the company requiring the cessation of all construction work on the site, but also a related stop notice. Now, under s 186 of the 1990 Act, compensation is payable for loss suffered due to the service of a stop notice if it is quashed on the ground that the matters alleged in the enforcement notice do not constitute a breach of planning control. Following a dispute over the amount of the company's loss, compensation was eventually determined by the Lands Tribunal, which awarded the company £42,562. **15.99**

In a more recent case (*Commercial Land Ltd v Secretary of State for Transport, Local Government and the Regions and Royal Borough of Kensington and Chelsea* [2002] EWHC 1264 (Admin)), the Court allowed for a relevant start to be made when the work was not in accordance with the plans, though it seems that the work bore some relationship to the development proposed. **15.100**

In the early 1990s the Courts began to require that in addition to the need for a start to be made to the development in question, there had to be a continuing intention at that time to carry out the development for which the planning permission had been granted. As expressed in a number of cases, there had to be an 'earnest of intention to develop', failing which the act of starting the development would be 'colourable'. **15.101**

The application of a colourability test is one which would always be extremely difficult to apply. Could, for example, the intention with regard to the carrying out of the development be passed on from the developer who obtained planning permission to another? Many developers of course undertake a specified operation prior to the likely expiry of a planning permission in the expectation of completing the development at a later date. On the other hand, a developer without the necessary finance to complete the development may carry out a specified operation in the hope of being able to raise the finance subsequently, or to dispose of the land to somebody who can. Intention is unlikely to be limited in application **15.102** to the recipient of a planning permission, in the same way that a personal planning permission is limited to the recipient.

15.103 Issues of colourability now, however, no longer need to be considered in England following the lead given in a Scottish case. In *East Dunbartonshire Council v Secretary of State for Scotland and MacTaggart & Mickel Ltd* [1999] 1 PLR 53, the Inner House of the Court of Session (the equivalent of the English Court of Appeal) held, interpreting equivalent statutory provisions in Scottish legislation to those in England, that planning legislation does not impart into the relevant provisions of the Planning Acts any test of intention. The Court held that Parliament had laid down precisely what was required to be done on the site to keep the planning permission alive, and that was all that was required, no more and no less. In the *East Dunbartonshire* case the court rejected the need for a subjective intention test and ruled that the test was an objective one. The objective test was satisfied by first considering whether the work done was done in accordance with the planning permission and secondly whether it was material in the sense of not being de minimis.

15.104 One did not have to wait long to see whether English courts would follow the Scottish decision. In *Riodan Communications Ltd v South Bucks & District Council* [2000] JPL 594 Mr David Vaughan QC, sitting in the High Court as a Deputy Judge considered that the unanimous decision of the Inner House in the *East Dunbartonshire* case was, if not actually binding upon him, a decision which should be treated with such a high degree of respect as to make little difference to a judge of first instance in England. There is the Deputy Judge considered, 'no justification in the terms or the structure of the legislation for the ill-defined requirement that some operation should be carried out with some particular intention'. The approach taken in the *East Dunbartonshire* case that the question must be approached objectively and not subjectively has now been followed by the Court of Appeal in *Staffordshire CC v Riley* [2002] PLCR 75.

15.105 But indeed one that has far wider implications than the requirements imposed by s 56 is what is called the *Whitley* principle, namely that the operations to which the planning permission relates are the operations which it authorises, not those which contravene the conditions of the permission. In *F. G. Whitley & Sons Co. Ltd v Secretary of State for Wales* [1990] JPL 678, planning permission had been granted for mineral extraction, subject to a number of conditions, including one which provided that no working should take place except in accordance with a scheme to be agreed with the local planning authority or, in the absence of agreement, by the Secretary of State. The developers were unable to reach agreement with the local authority. In an attempt to prevent the permission expiring, the developers carried out work on the site. An enforcement notice was served in relation to those works and was upheld by the Secretary of State. In a subsequent judicial challenge to the notice,Woolf LJ said:

> As I understand the effect of the authorities to which I am about to refer, it is only necessary to ask a single question: are the operations (in other situations the question would refer to development) permitted by the planning permission read together with its conditions? The permission is controlled by and subject to the conditions. If the operations contravene the conditions they cannot properly be described as commencing the development authorised by the permission. If they do not comply with the permission they constitute a breach of planning control and for planning purposes will be unauthorised and thus unlawful.

His Lordship went on to say that works carried out under a planning permission could never qualify as 'development to which it relates' unless the works were also carried out in compliance with the conditions subject to which the permission was granted. Hence works carried out before the condition precedent had been satisfied do not save a permission which would otherwise be time-expired.

A similar view of the law was taken in *Handoll and Suddick v Warner, Goodman & Streat, Cook and East Lindsey DC* [1995] JPL 930, where the High Court took the view that 'works which do not comply with the permission and any conditions to which it is subject do not constitute the implementation or commencement of a planning permission'. This is of course a principle of general application. It applies to a condition precedent, a commencement condition or a limitation. The principle was applied in somewhat different circumstances in *Handoll*, where planning permission had been granted for a bungalow subject to an agricultural occupancy condition. In the event the bungalow was built 90 feet away from where it should have been built. When the new owners decided they wanted to use the land for dog kennels they were told by the authority of the condition. Since this was the first they knew of the condition they decided to sue the solicitors who had acted for them for negligence. The defendants raised a preliminary point as to whether any loss had been suffered by the plaintiffs, it being contended that as the bungalow had not been built in accordance with the planning permission, namely on the land for which planning permission had been granted, it was not subject to the agricultural condition imposed by the authority. The Court of Appeal accepted that contention. So because the particular planning permission had not been implemented, the conditions imposed on that planning permission were unenforceable. **15.106**

In a later case of *Wycombe District Council v Williams* [1995] 3 PLR 19, however, the High Court held that where a development does not comply to a material extent with a planning permission, a condition which was attached to development the subject of that planning permission cannot be applied to the unauthorised development that was carried out. It appears, however, that the decision in *Handoll* would have no application where the difference between the approved development and the development which was carried out falls within the normal tolerances or minor variations inherent in the laying-out and construction process. **15.107**

It is however with regard to commencement conditions that the principle has had its greatest impact. In this connection the *Whitley* principle was applied in *Oldham MBC v Roland Bardsley (Builders) Ltd* [1996] JPL B119, where planning permission had been granted subject to conditions relating to the fencing of trees and the provision of a drainage scheme and emergency access, all of which were to be in accordance with a scheme approved by the authority. None of the conditions had been met, but development had been begun within the period specified in the planning permission for doing so. In granting an application for judicial review of a decision of the authority, the High Court held that the authority had been given wrong advice by their Director of Environmental Services to the effect that the permission had not expired when in fact, under the law, the site operations undertaken within the period for so doing were unauthorised and unlawful. Within a few days of that decision the Court of Appeal in *Daniel Platt Ltd v Secretary of State for the Environment and Staffordshire CC* [1996] JPL 349 showed no inclination to depart from the *Whitley* principle. **15.108**

15.109 The courts have, however, recognised limited exceptions to this general principle. In *Agecrest Ltd v Gwynedd CC* [1998] JPL 325 conditions of a planning permission required a number of schemes to be submitted and approved before development could commence. Subsequently however, the local planning authority agreed that the development could commence without full compliance with those conditions. The High Court held that the authority had a discretion in the way in which it dealt with such conditions and that the work did amount to a start of the development. Further in *R v Flintshire CC, ex p Somerfield Stores Ltd* [1998] EGCS 53, a condition in a planning permission required a study to be made and approved by the Council of projected traffic generation and highway effects and of the implications of the development before the development commenced. The study had been carried out with the full knowledge and co-operation of the Council and the highway authority. However, the developers had made no actual application to the Council for approval of the study, nor was there a record of the Council communicating approval to the developer. Nevertheless, the High Court refused an application for judicial review to quash the Council's decision not to consider taking enforcement action against the development, holding that the general principle had to be applied with common sense and with regard to the facts of the particular case. In the instant case it would have been unreasonable for the Council to have decided that the planning permission had not been implemented.

15.110 In *Leisure Great Britain plc v Isle of Wight CC* [2000] PLCR 88 the Court considered that any exception to the general *Whitley* principle should be on a clearly identifiable basis and not simply because the Court considered it unfair on the merits to apply the general principle. The exceptions are therefore, essentially limited to circumstances where the local planning authority has subsequently approved unlawful work, or agreed in advance of the works to waive the requirements in question or where the conditions have been complied with in substance albeit without observing the usual formalities.

Outline planning permissions

15.111 The provisions relating to the duration of planning permission are slightly modified with regard to outline planning permission. Section 92(2) of the 1990 Act originally provided that where outline planning permission is granted for development consisting in or including the carrying out of building, or other operations, it shall be granted subject to conditions:

(a) that, in the case of any reserved matter, application for approval must be made not later than the expiration of three years beginning with the date of the grant of outline planning permission; and
(b) that the development to which the permission relates must be begun not later than—
   (i) the expiration of five years from the date of grant of outline planning permission;
   (ii) if later, the expiration of two years from the final approval of the reserved matters or, in the case of approval on different dates, the final approval of the last such matter to be approved.

Once s. 51 of the Planning and Compulsory Purchase Act 2004 has been fully implemented, subsection 2(b), sub-paragraph (i) is to be repealed, along with the words 'if later' in subsection 2(b), sub-paragraph (ii).

15.112 Again, it is provided that the standard period of three years mentioned in the section may be varied at the discretion of the local planning authority or, on appeal, by the Secretary of State.

In addition, in the condition which requires applications for approval of reserved matters to be made within three years (para (a) above), the local planning authority may specify separate periods in relation to separate parts of the development. This flexibility can be particularly useful where the proposed development is on a large scale and is of a mixed nature. **15.113**

It is important to remember that in order to keep the planning permission alive, the final approval of all reserved matters, whether given by the local planning authority or by the Secretary of State on appeal, must result from an application or applications for approval made to the authority within three years from the date of the grant of outline planning permission. If a landowner applies within the three year period for approval of reserved matters and approval is not given, he cannot submit further applications for approval of matters reserved by that permission, unless they are also submitted within three years of the date of the grant of the outline permission. A landowner may submit any number of applications for approval of reserved matters within the three-year period. One application, however, need not cover every reserved matter requiring approval. A landowner may wish to submit a series of applications, each for the approval of specific reserved matters. For example, he may wish to obtain approval of matters relating to layout, siting, design and external appearance before applying for the approval of matters relating to landscaping. All such applications, however, must be submitted within the specified three-year period if the permission is to be kept alive. **15.114**

It is clear in the light of the judgment in *Heron Corporation Ltd v Manchester City Council* [1978] 1 WLR 937, that an application for approval of reserved matters need only cover a part of a site for which outline planning permission has been given. This indeed is recognised in the statutory provision (see above) which enables different time periods to be specified in relation to different parts of the development site. Where this power has not been exercised, however, the question arises as to whether once all reserved matters have been approved in relation to part of a site within the specified time period, further application for approval of reserved matters can be made for the remaining part or parts of the development site. It would seem not. A question also arises as to whether once all reserved matters have been approved in relation to a specific part of the site, development of that part can be commenced. Section 92 contains no prohibition against doing so. However, the ability to do so may be constrained if a local planning authority as well as imposing the statutory condition requiring submission of applications for approval of reserved matters within a specified period (and without using its powers to set different time periods for different parts of the development), requires that all reserved matters should be submitted to and approved by the authority before the development is begun (see *Powergen United Kingdom plc v Leicester City Council and Safeway Stores* [2000] JPL 1037). **15.115**

It seems from the case of *Etheridge v Secretary of State for the Environment and Torbay BC* [1984] JPL 340, that a later grant of full planning permission (i.e., where all details have been approved) may act as an approval of details of developmentwhich had been reserved in an **15.116** earlier outline permission. For this to happen, it appears that the full planning permission must approve exactly those matters (but not necessarily all of them) which, in respect of the landto which they related, would have had to have been approved on an application for approval of reserved matters. Furthermore, the fact that full planning permissionmay relate to only part of the landcovered by the earlier outline permission, does not affect its validity in relation to the whole of the site, as was made clear in *R v Secretary of State for the Environment, ex p Bilton* (1975) 31 P & CR 154.

15.117 It should be noted that local planning authorities sometimes grant planning permission subject to conditions on matters that require the prior approval of the authority before development can be commenced. If those matters are not matters that come within the definition of 'reserved matters', s.92 has no application to that matter. Hence the condition would be subject to s.91.

Extending time conditions

15.118 It was held by the High Court in *R v Secretary of State for the Environment, ex p Corby BC* [1995] JPL 115, that the power available to a developer under s 73 of the 1990 Act to apply to the local planning authority for planning permission for the development of land without complying with a condition imposed on the grant of a previous planning permission could, subject to sub-section (4) of that section, be used with regard to conditions imposed requiring the submission of applications for approval of reserved matters to be made within a specified period, in addition to a condition requiring commencement of the development within a specified period.

15.119 Sub-section (4) of s 73 then provided:

> This sub-section does not apply if the previous planning permission was granted subject to a condition as to the time within which the development to which it related was begun *and that time has expired without the development having been begun* (author's emphasis).

15.120 Section 51 Planning and Compulsory Purchase Act 2004 when fully implemented will add to s.73 the following subjection:

> (5) Planning permission must not be granted under this section to the extent that it has effect to change a condition subject to which a previous planning permission was granted by extending the time limit in which:
> (a) a development must be started;
> (b) an application for approval of reserved matters (within the meaning of section 92) must be made.

The effect of the changes made by the 2004 Act cannot be underestimated. In particular (subject to s. 92), it reduces the life of a planning permission to three years. Furthermore, the effect of adding subsection (5) to s.73, means that once planning permission has been granted for development, no conditions as to time is capable of being altered. If a developer finds that existing time conditions in a planning permission cannot be met, he must submit another application for planning permission for that development, which he may do at any time, even where the time limits for commencement imposed in the earlier planning permission have not expired. Any subsequent application will of course be dealt with by the authority in the same way as any other application, namely by having regard to the development plan so far as material and to any other material considerations.

The impact of this new provision means that henceforth the previous litigation which had been brought to clarify the effect of ss.(4) when a planning permission was sought to be renewed, in particular *Pye v Secretary of State for the Environment and North Cornwall District Council* [1999] PLCR 28, will in future be consigned to history.

Completion notices

The provisions considered so far operate to secure that, as far as possible, development is begun within the period stipulated in the permission. The provisions do not secure that the development once begun will actually be completed. Accordingly, s 94 of the 1990 Act provides that if the local planning authority are of opinion that the development will not be completed within a reasonable period, they may serve a completion notice on the owner and occupier of the land and any other person who in the opinion of the local planning authority will be affected by the notice, stating that the planning permission will cease to have effect at the expiration of a further period (being not less than 12 months) after the notice takes effect. A completion notice will only take effect after confirmation by the Secretary of State who, before confirming the notice, must give a person on whom the completion notice was served and the authority, an opportunity of appearing before, and being heard by, an Inspector appointed for that purpose. A completion notice cannot be served until the period allowed for the commencement of the development has passed. So that in the case of a full planning permission, this will normally be after five years, a period to be reduced to three years under the 2004 Act. **15.121**

Section 94(4) provides that if a completion notice takes effect, the planning permission referred to in it shall become invalid at the expiration of the period specified in the notice. Section 95(5) then goes on to provide that the previous sub-section shall not affect any permission so far as development carried out under it before the end of the period mentioned in that sub-section is concerned. Now, since planning permission is granted for development and not for a series of stages in the development process, that provision appears to mean that once a completion notice has taken effect, any act of development which has taken place in the process of partially implementing the permission will be development undertaken without planning permission, and thus be liable to enforcement notice procedure. So if, for example, planning permission has been granted for the erection of a two-storey building and only the ground floor has been built by the time a completion notice takes effect, no planning permission would exist for the single-storey building. It would be otherwise, however, if, as happened in another context in the case of *F. Lucas & Sons Ltd v Dorking & Horley RDC* (1964) 62 LGR 491, a grant of planning permission for the erection of a number of houses could be constructed as a grant of a number of mini-planning permissions, each of which authorised the construction of an individual house. **15.122**

This view of the law appears to be supported by the Ministerial Decision reported at [1985] JPL 496, where the Secretary of State upheld an enforcement notice requiring the removal of an uncompleted building erected pursuant to a planning permission for the building which had ceased to have effect as a result of the coming into effect of a completion notice. **15.123**

15.124 The alternative view is that a completion notice has no effect on that part of the development completed, but renders nugatory that part of the development which is uncompleted. Whichever is the better view, it is clear that the completion notice does not guarantee completion of a part-finished development. It is for that reason that completion notices are so rarely used.

15.125 Evidence given by the Department of the Environment to the Environment Committee of the House of Commons in June 1997, disclosed that there had only been 21 cases in the five years from 1992/97 where the confirmation of completion notices had been sought from the Secretary of State. Most of the cases involved housing development. In one case however, a completion notice had been confirmed where planning permission had been granted for shopping development in 1988, but by 1994 only the car park had been constructed. The Department's evidence gave no details for that period of non-contested cases, that is cases where there had been compliance with the completion notice without the need for the Secretary of State's confirmation of it.

16

THE CONSTRUCTION, SCOPE, EFFECT AND LIFE OF A PLANNING PERMISSION

A. CONSTRUCTION OF A PLANNING PERMISSION

Doubts may arise about the precise construction of a grant of planning permission. The construction will occasionally involve looking not only at the notification of the decision but also behind the notification at the application for planning permission. **16.01**

The rule established by the courts is that if the planning permission is on the face of it a complete and self-contained document, not incorporating by reference any other document, the planning permission will stand on its own. If, on the other hand, the planning permission incorporates other documents such as the application for planning permission, then those documents must be taken into account in construing the permission. **16.02**

In *Miller-Mead v Minister of Housing & Local Government* [1963] 2 QB 196, the Court of Appeal held that a planning permission runs with the land and cannot be cut down by reference to **16.03** the application pursuant to which it was granted. The reason for the Court taking that view was that the permission may come into the hands of people who have never seen the application and who must, therefore, rely on the actual words used in the grant. The decision ignored the fact that applications for planning permission (and also the grant) must be entered by the local planning authority in a planning register which is available for public inspection at all reasonable times.

16.04 Although ideally an applicant for planning permission should be able to see the precise terms of the permission from the permission itself (i.e. the notification of the decision to grant), the decision in *Miller-Mead v Minister of Housing and Local Government* could have created difficulties for the many local planning authorities who expressly link the grant of permission to the application to which it relates. Indeed, six weeks later, in *Wilson v West Sussex County Council* [1963] 2 QB 764, the Court of Appeal had to consider a grant of planning permission which said: 'The council hereby permit the following development, that is to say . . . in accordance with the plan and application No. . . . submitted to the council on . . .'.

16.05 Although the Court thought that the incorporation of the 'relevant correspondence' into the permission was a very unfortunate practice, it held that where the permission specifically incorporates the terms of the application for planning permission, it was proper, and indeed necessary, to refer to the terms of the application in construing the permission.

16.06 A few years later, in *Slough Estates Ltd v Slough BC (No 2)* [1971] AC 958, the House of Lords confirmed the later view of the Court of Appeal that it was proper to look at the application if it were incorporated in the permission itself.

16.07 In *Manning v Secretary of State for the Environment* [1976] JPL 634, planning permission had been granted for a limited period for the erection of a riding school, to be used by a private riding school together with disabled riders. The reason for the grant of the permission was that it would enable facilities for disabled riders to be provided. Later, towards the end of that period, an application was made for the renewal of the permission. The permission, when granted, referred to 'continued use of indoor riding school'. A dispute then arose over whether the later permission was to be construed as widely as the first and include the use, not only for the disabled but for the general riding school as well, or whether (as the local planning authority had maintained) the use was limited to disabled persons only. The plaintiff, contending that it was not so limited, obtained a declaration to that effect in the High Court. The Court of Appeal, upholding the decision of the High Court, held that in this case it was relevant not only to look at the planning permission, but also at the previous history, the previous application and the previous permission.

16.08 Although it is better to restrict the scope of this decision to the interpretation of 'renewal applications', it is significant that Stephenson LJ thought that because documents such as applications for and grants of permission were rarely drafted by lawyers, they should in his view 'be given a tolerant view'.

16.09 It also seems that, unless incorporated in the permission, it is not permissible to look at the resolution of the authority, or of the appropriate committee of the authority, in order to construe the permission. In *R v West Oxfordshire DC, ex p Pearce Homes Ltd* [1986] JPL 523 the planning committee of the authority adopted a resolution that planning permission be granted subject to the execution of an agreement under the then s 106 of the 1990 Act. Details of the resolution were then notified to the applicants by letter. Subsequently, the applicants were refused permission for the development on the ground that the site had now been scheduled by the Secretary of State under the Ancient Monuments and Archaeological Areas Act 1979. In an application for judicial review of the authority's decision to refuse planning permission, the company alleged that the resolution had the effect of granting the planning permission it was seeking, or alternatively that if it did not then permission had been granted by the subsequent letter.

Refusing the application, Woolf J held that, ordinarily, to decide what planning permission had been granted, all it was necessary to do was to look at the actual notification of the decision. Normally one could not look at the resolution except to determine other issues, such as whether or not an officer had authority to notify the grant of planning permission. Hewenton to hold that the letter subsequent to the resolution did not amount to a grant of planning permission. It had simply anticipated that a grant would be made once an agreement had been completed. **16.10**

In *Wivenhoe Port Ltd v Colchester BC* [1985] JPL 396, the Court of Appeal favoured the view that, if it were necessary to do so, it was appropriate to look at the application *as an aid* to the construction of a planning permission. The reason for this approach was the recognition that a grant of planning permission is made in response to an application, and that the permission granted cannot purport to grant something outside the terms of the application. **16.11**

In later cases, *Oakimber Ltd v Elmbridge BC* (1991) 62 P & CR 594 and *Staffordshire Moorlands DC v Cartwright* (1991) 63 P & CR 285, the Court of Appeal held that the terms of a planning permission had to be construed in the factual context of the application on which it was based. More recently, in *R v Secretary of State for the Environment, ex p Slough BC* [1995] JPL 135, Schiemann J considered that there was a strong public interest in the Court taking a grant of planning permission as granting what it purported to grant, though where the permission was not prima facie clear, or where an application was expressly incorporated in the permission, different considerations arose. The mere recital of the application number at the top of the permission did not incorporate the application into the planning permission. In order to do that, words such as 'in accordance with the plans and application' would be necessary. The decision of the High Court was subsequently upheld by the Court of Appeal [1995] EGCS 95. According to the Court the general rule was that, in construing a planning permission, regard might be had only to the permission itself, including the reasons stated for it. Since the breach of planning control might lead to criminal sanctions, the Court felt that the public should be able to rely on a document that was plain on its face without having to consider whether there was any discrepancy between the permission and the application. **16.12**

The law in this field has now been helpfully summarised by Keene J in *R v Ashford BC, ex p Shepway District Council* [1999] PLCR 12. According to Keene J, the legal principles applicable to the use of other documents to construe a planning permission were not really in dispute in the proceedings. It was nonetheless necessary to summarise them: **16.13**

1. The general rule is that in construing a planning permission which is clear, unambiguous

and valid on its face, regard may only be had to the planning permission itself, including the conditions (if any) on it and the express reasons for those conditions: See *Slough BC v Secretary of State for the Environment* [1995] JPL 1128, and *Miller-Mead v Minister of Housing and Local Government* [1963] 2 QB 196.

2. This rule excludes reference to the planning application as well as to other extrinsic evidence, unless the planning permission incorporates the application by reference. In that situation the application is treated as having become part of the permission. The reason for normally not having regard to the application is that the public should be able to rely on a document which is plain on its face without having to consider whether there is any discrepancy between the permission and the application: see *Slough BC v Secretary of State* (ante); *Wilson v West Sussex CC* [1963] 2 QB 764; and *Slough Estates Limited v Slough BC* [1971] AC 958.
3. For incorporation of the application in the permission to be achieved, more is required than a mere reference to the application on the face of the permission. While there is no magic formula, some words sufficient to inform a reasonable reader that the application forms part of the permission are needed, such as '. . . in accordance with the plans and application . . .' or '. . . on the terms of the application . . .', and in either case those words appearing in the operative part of the permission dealing with the development and the terms in which permission is granted. These words need to govern the description of the development permitted: see *Wilson* (ante); *Slough BC v Secretary of State for the Environment* (ante).
4. If there is an ambiguity in the wording of the permission, it is permissible to look at extrinsic material, including the application, to resolve that ambiguity: see *Staffordshire Moorlands DC v Cartwight* [1991] 63 P-CR 285; *Slough Estates Limited v Slough BC* (ante); *Creighton Estates Limited v London CC* (1958), *The Times*, 20 March 1958.
5. If a planning permission is challenged on the ground of absence of authority or mistake, it is permissible to look at extrinsic evidence to resolve that issue: see *Slough BC v Secretary of State* (ante); *Co-operative Retail Services v Taff-Ely BC* (1979) 39 P & CR 223 affirmed (1981) 42 P & CR 1.

16.14 Later he said:

The issue, however, is whether such recourse to resolve a particular ambiguity or inconsistency brings the application into play, so as to operate as a means of interpreting and, if appropriate, restricting the permission as a whole. There is no clear authority on this point, though such as there is suggests that that is not the consequence. In the *Staffordshire Moorlands DC* case (ante), Purchas LJ referred to the permission being construed 'where ambiguous' in the context of other material: see page 139. In *Creighton Estates* (ante) Danckwerts J (as he then was) referred to extrinsic material in order to resolve a specific ambiguity and no more.

I propose to deal with this as a matter of principle. It is important to recognise that when an application is being used for such a purpose, it is not being incorporated into the permission. This is a wholly different exercise from that involved in incorporation. The justification for such resort to extraneous material is to resolve a particular inconsistency or ambiguity. That being so, it would not be proper to regard other parts of the permission free from ambiguity as open to re-interpretation in the light of the application or, indeed, other extrinsic material. Such material is only being brought into play for a specific purpose. Such recourse does not make the application or other extrinsic material part of the permission generally. Otherwise the existence of an ambiguity on a single point or word in an otherwise complete and clear permission would mean that the extent of the development as a whole thereby permitted could be cut down by the application. That would be contrary to the general rule spelt out many years ago in *Miller-Mead* and endorsed by the Court of Appeal recently in *Slough Borough Council v Secretary of State for the Environment*. Moreover, any such exception to a general rule ought to be narrowly construed.

B. SCOPE OF A PLANNING PERMISSION

Although, as stated, the grant of planning permission cannot purport to grant something outside the terms of the application, this does not mean that the grant must replicate precisely what has been applied for. 16.15

In *Bernard Wheatcroft Ltd v Secretary of State for the Environment* [1982] JPL 37 an application for planning permission had been made for 'approximately 420 dwellings on 35 acres of land'. Permission was refused. On appeal the Inspector recommended the appeal be refused, but indicated that if it were possible to restrict the area to 25 acres and for the number of dwellings to be reduced to 250, then such development would not be objectionable. In accepting his Inspector's recommendation that the appeal be dismissed, the Secretary of State considered he had no power to grant planning permission for development on a smaller site and with houses at a lower density than that which was indicated on the original application form. In granting an application made to the High Court to quash the Secretary of State's decision, Forbes J held that it was permissible to grant planning permission subject to a condition that only a reduced development was to be carried out, provided that the result did not differ substantially from the development proposed in the original application. This was an aspect to which the Secretary of State had failed to have regard. What clearly cannot be done is to consider an amendment to an application which would have the effect of altering its whole character. 16.16

The main criterion the Secretary of State (or indeed a local planning authority) must have regard to is whether the development would be so changed that it would in substance be no longer what was applied for and that to grant planning permission would be to deprive those who should have been consulted on the changed development of the opportunity of such consultation. In a later case, *Wessex Regional Health Authority v Salisbury DC* [1984] JPL 344, Glidewell J upheld the decision of an Inspector to refuse planning permission for residential development. The appellants had invited the Inspector, during an appeal against a refusal of planning permission by the local planning authority, to consider the argument that if 48 houses were too many, but 37 were acceptable, he could grant planning permission subject to a condition limiting the number to 37. The Inspector decided that 48 houses were too many and dismissed the appeal. He also took the view that in the circumstances a reduction in number from 48 to 37 differed substantially from the development proposal and should rightly form the basis of a fresh application. 16.17

The principle has had ramifications in other situations which have not led to litigation. In the aftermath of the decision in *Bernard Wheatcroft Ltd v Secretary of State for the Environment*, the Secretary of State had to consider an application by the National Coal Board to exploit what became known as the Vale of Belvoir coalfield. 16.18

The National Coal Board had applied for planning permission to construct and work three mines at Hose, Saltby and Asfordby, and to tip spoil adjacent to those three sites. The Inspector had recommended the grant of permission for all three mines, but that permission be refused for the proposed spoil tips at Hose and Saltby. 16.19

After considering the report the Secretary of State concluded that the development of the 16.20

mine at Hose was environmentally unacceptable. In addition, before tipping at any of the sites could be contemplated, the possibility of other methods of spoil disposal should be further examined. So had there been acceptable proposals for the disposal of spoil, the Secretary of State would have been prepared to grant planning permission for the development of the mines at Asfordby and Saltby.

16.21 The National Coal Board had submitted, however, one application for planning permission covering all the underground coal extraction in Leicestershire, together with the three mine complexes and three spoil tips, thus opting to stand or fall by a strategy of developing the whole coalfield as one project. In his decision letter the Secretary of State said:

> in those circumstances the granting of planning permission for only part of the development would be in effect granting a permission for development which is significantly different in kind from the proposal which was the subject of the application. This may be a point which the Board would wish to bear in mind in future.

16.22 In a later case, *Breckland DC* v *Secretary of State for the Environment* (1992) 65 P & CR 34, the local planning authority sought to quash the decision of an Inspector whereby he had allowed an appeal for a 16-pitch gypsy caravan site in Norfolk. The case is believed to be the first to come before the courts where an amendment of a planning application by an Inspector involved the enlargement of the application site. The effect of the amendment was to increase the application site by 50 per cent, bringing it nearer to three nearby residences and increasing the number of pitches. In quashing the Inspector's decision Mr David Widdicombe QC, sitting as a Deputy Judge, considered that the legal validity of an enlargement might be harder to justify than a reduction. He thought the test of validity of the action was derived from *Bernard Wheatcroft Ltd v Secretary of State for the Environment* but it was an exercise of discretion which could only be challenged within the *Wednesbury* rules. He held that the parish council and local residents were deprived of the opportunity to be consulted on the proposed amendment, and it was *Wednesbury* unreasonable of the Inspector to hold that the amendment did not substantially alter the proposal. The decision to allow the amendment was unreasonable and therefore invalid.

Split decisions

16.23 A variant of the principle in *Bernard Wheatcroft Ltd v Secretary of State for the Environment* [1982] JPL 37 is the development of what may be called the 'split decision', whereby planning permission is granted not for reduced development as in *Wheatcroft*, but for only part of the land the subject of the application, whilst being refused for the remaining part.

16.24 An example is a Ministerial decision involving the North Wiltshire District Council, where an application had been made for the erection of 11 detached houses on land at Tetbury Hill, Malmesbury. In default of the decision within the prescribed period, the applicants had appealed to the Secretary of State. About half of the site was included within the 'limits of development' for the town of Malmesbury as identified on the proposals map in the Malmesbury local plan. The remainder of the site lay outside the limits. The Inspector took the view that that part of the development which lay within the limits-of development boundary would be acceptable, but not that which lay outside. Although the applicants had objected at the inquiry to the making of a split decision, the Inspector dismissed the appeal and refused planning permission for development of that part of the site which lay outside the limit-of development boundary, but at the same time allowed the appeal and granted planning permission for the erection of dwellinghouses in respect of that part of the application site which lay inside the boundary. For obvious reasons, the grant of planning permission was a grant of outline planning permission, with approval of details relating to siting, design, external appearance, means of access and landscaping being reserved for the approval of the local planning authority.

The legality of the practice of giving a split decision on an application for planning permission has not yet been tested in the courts, but it is thought that the principle to be applied would be the same as that in the *Wheatcroft* case, namely, whether it would be unreasonable to grant permission which would be substantially different from the development applied for. **16.25**

C. EFFECT OF A PLANNING PERMISSION

Until the decision of the Divisional Court in *Petticoat Lane Rentals Ltd v Secretary of State for the Environment* [1971] 1 WLR 1112, it had always been assumed, but with only slender authority for so doing, that the implementation of a planning permission destroyed the old use to which the land had previously been put. The case concerned a site which had been cleared after having been bombed during the Second World War. It had been leased to a company, which used it to let out stalls to street traders every day of the week. In 1963, planning permission had been granted for a new commercial building on the site supported on pillars. The open ground floor was to be used as a car parking and loading area ancillary to the commercial use of the building. Under the terms of the permission that area could continue to be used for market trading on Sundays, when the ground floor would not be needed for that ancillary purpose. Almost immediately after the building had been constructed,market traders began to use the ground floor not only on Sundays but also on every other day of the week. **16.26**

Almost inevitably the local planning authority served an enforcement notice on the company alleging the making of a material change of use without permission and requiring the discontinuance of weekday trading. The company appealed. After a public inquiry, the Secretary of State upheld the notice on the grounds that any existing use rights had been extinguished with the implementation of the permission. The Divisional Court held, dismissing an appeal by the company, that, where an area of open land was developed by the erection of a new building over the whole site, the land as such was merged into the new building and a new planning unit was created with a new use; and that any use to which the new building was put thereafter was a change of use which, if not authorised by the planning permission, could be restrained by planning control. **16.27**

In so holding, the Court relied heavily on one of its earlier decisions, namely *Prossor v Minister of Housing and Local Government* (1968) 67 LGR 109. This was a case of a petrol service station on a main road where the occupier sought and obtained planning permission to rebuild the petrol station. He was given such permission and an express condition was attached to the permission to the effect that no retail sales other than the sale of motor **16.28** accessories should be carried on on the site. In fact, having let the establishment, the occupier began to exhibit second-hand cars for sale on the site, which was clearly a breach of the condition if the condition was effective. It was argued in favour of the occupier that he was enabled to do that because there was a continuing and unbroken use of the land for the sale of second-hand cars, and in his contention the fact that he had had a new and inconsistent planning permission and had implemented it did not destroy that right. Lord Parker CJ, having dealt with a number of arguments not relevant to the present appeal, put the matter thus:

> Assuming . . . that there was at all material times prior to April 1964 [the date of the rebuilding] an existing use right running on this land for the display and sale of motor cars, yet by adopting the permission granted in April 1964, the appellant's predecessor, as it seems to me, gave up any possible existing use rights in that regard which he may have had. The planning history of this site, as it were, seems to me to begin afresh on 4 April 1964, with the grant of this permission, a permission which was taken up and used, and the sole question here is: has there been a breach of that condition?

16.29 Although in the *Prossor* case the use of the land for the display of second-hand cars had been expressly prohibited by a condition of the planning permission, the Court in *Petticoat Lane Rentals Ltd v Secretary of State for the Environment* thought that to be irrelevant. According to Widgery LJ, the fact that there was an express prohibition was no more than an indication of the fact that the draftsman of the permission had found it easier to express his wishes in that way.

16.30 Although the Court in the *Petticoat Lane Rentals Ltd* case was unanimous in holding that the existing use of the land had been extinguished by the erection upon it of a new building, both Bridge J and Lord Parker CJ drew a distinction between, on the one hand, a case where land formerly open and not built upon had been used for a certain purpose and subsequently the land itself had been built upon; and on the other hand, a case where open land had been used, that land had subsequently been embodied in the curtilage of a site developed by building for other purposes but the building had not extended over all the land used for the former purpose. It is quite clear that in the latter situation, the local planning authority can, by express condition, exclude the right to continue the former use of the land not built upon. Without such a condition being imposed, however, the position is far from clear.

16.31 The decision in *Prossor v Minister of Housing and Local Government* was considered by the House of Lords in *Newbury DC v Secretary of State for the Environment* [1981] AC 578. One of the three main issues to be determined in that case was whether the company concerned, having been granted planning permission to change the use of hangars from the storage of civil defence vehicles to use for the storage of synthetic rubber, could subsequently contend that no permission was necessary on account of existing use rights. In deciding that there was no bar to the right of the company to do so, their Lordships referred to the *Prossor* case. Relating that case to the facts before him, Viscount Dilhorne felt that *Prossor's* case was not sustainable on the basis that obtaining and taking up planning permission in itself prevents reliance on existing use rights. He went on:

> If, however, the grant of planning permission, whether it be permission to build or for a change of use, is of such a character that the implementation of the permission leads to the creation of a

> new planning unit, then I think that it is right to say that existing use rights attaching to the former planning unit are extinguished. It may be that in the *Prossor* case the erection of the new building created a new planning unit. If it did, and it is not very clear from the report, then in my view that case was rightly decided.
>
> It is clear that in this case the grant of the planning permission in May 1962 did not create a new planning unit and so, in my opinion, [the company] were not precluded from relying on the existing use rights attaching to the site.

The idea that the implementation of a planning permission may lead to the creation of a new planning unit was echoed by Lord Fraser of Tullybelton in the *Newbury* case when he said: 16.32

> The only circumstances in which existing use rights are lost by accepting and implementing a later planning permission are, in my opinion, when a new planning unit comes into existence.

The relevance of a new planning unit was again considered, this time by the Court of Appeal, in *Jennings Motors Ltd v Secretary of State for the Environment* [1980] JPL 521. There, land had been used for many years for the repair and maintenance of vehicles and the sale and hire of cars. In 1975, a new single-storey building was erected without planning permission on a small part of the site to replace an existing building. The new building was used for vehicle repair and servicing. Eventually the local planning authority served an enforcement notice which required not the demolition of the building, but the discontinuance of the use to which the building had been put. The occupiers appealed against the notice and, after an inquiry, the Inspector concluded that the planning unit was the site as a whole, and that the use could be carried on anywhere within the site, thus the appeal should be allowed. The Secretary of State, however, upheld the enforcement notice on the ground that when the new building was erected a new planning history was commenced in respect of it for which there had been a material change of use from 'no use'. The Divisional Court upheld the Secretary of State's decision, but on appeal by the occupiers the Court of Appeal allowed the appeal, holding that the erection of a new building on part of a whole site does not in itself constitute a new planning unit or a new chapter in the planning history and, accordingly, the Secretary of State had erred in law in holding that development had taken place. 16.33

The decision in the *Jennings* case was concerned with the question of whether an established use survived within the new building. It did not determine the question of whether the implementation of a planning permission on part of a site created a new planning unit or introduced a new chapter in planning history as regards the rest of the site. 16.34

This latter aspect was considered subsequently by the Divisional Court of the Queen's Bench Division in *South Staffordshire DC v Secretary of State for the Environment* [1987] JPL 635. Apart from preferring the term 'new chapter in planning history' to that of 'new planning unit', the Court considered that established use rights on the rest of a site would survive implementation of planning permission to erect a building on another part of the site, unless the development which took place was inconsistent with the established use. 16.35

Unfortunately, the cases subsequent to the *Petticoat Lane Rentals Ltd* case have not succeeded in resolving the problem there identified of the effect of implementing a planning permission which affects only part of the original planning unit, on the existing use rights of the part of the unit not affected by the development. Certainly *Pioneer Aggregates* (UK) Ltd v Secretary of State for the Environment [1985] AC 132, suggests that existing use rights on an 16.36

undeveloped portion of a site may remain extant when development of only a part of it is carried out. Until this problem is resolved, a person applying for planning permission to develop part of his land should consider restricting his application to that part only, leaving the authority to restrict the existing use rights of the other part by condition, if they should consider this to be necessary. Otherwise, it might be harder to maintain that the grant of permission and its implementation for the part has led to the creation of a smaller planning unit carved out of the old so that the existing use rights in what is left of the old still remain.

16.37 The risks that can be run by applying for planning permission to develop the whole of a parcel of land when the application could be limited to only part is seen in *Wiggins v Secretary of State for the Environment Transport and the Regions and Slough BC* [2001] PLCR 365. There, part of a parcel of land was being lawfully used for the crushing of concrete. In 1995 the claimant had sought planning permission for that activity to be carried out on the whole of the site. Permission was granted but made subject to a condition requiring the use of the land to be discontinued by 1998. When this did not occur the authority took enforcement action in respect of the whole site. An Inspector's refusal to allow an appeal against the enforcement notice was subsequently upheld in the High Court. In what may be seen as a somewhat unconvincing decision, the Court held that if the planning permission was strictly unnecessary because it covered the same site and gave permission only for the activities which could in any event be continued, the existing use rights cannot be extinguished. But if planning permission is required, different considerations apply. It was not possible to split the decision and say, because it was not needed for one part, the use of that part can continue. The reality in this case was that permission was required to continue the use of the two parts and that was a different site from one part of the parcel on its own.

D. PUBLIC RIGHTS OF WAY AND DEVELOPMENT

16.38 Under s 247 of the 1990 Act the Secretary of State may, by order, authorise the stopping up or diversion of any *highway*, if satisfied that it is necessary to do so in order to enable development for which planning permission has been granted to be carried out. A more limited power is given to local planning authorities by section 257 to make orders authorising the stopping up or diversion of any *footpath or bridleway* in order to enable development for which planning permission has been granted to be carried out. The grant of planning permission does not in itself authorise the stopping up or diversion of rights of way and if those rights are obstructed before any order has been made, the development cannot proceed until the obstruction has been removed. It should be emphasised that the grant of planning permission does not guarantee that any order will be made under these provisions. No assumption should be made that merely because planning permission has been granted, an order will invariably be made or confirmed under these provisions.

E. INTERFERENCE WITH EASEMENTS AND OTHER INTERESTS OR RIGHTS

Under s 237(1) of the 1990 Act, where land has been acquired or appropriated by a local authority for planning purposes, the erection, construction or carrying out or maintenance of any building or work on that land whether done by the local authority or by a person deriving title under them is authorised by virtue of the section if it is done in accordance with planning permission, notwithstanding that it involves an interference with the interest or right annexed to the land or a breach of the restrictions on the user of land arising by virtue of a contract. **16.39**

Under this section it is recognised that subject to the payment of compensation for any loss suffered by a third party, that party's rights can be interfered with by a local authority acting in the public interest. It seems that a neighbouring landowner may have to accept, therefore, the loss of his right to light where the local authority develops land for which planning permission has been granted. The provision is extensive and without time limits. In *R v Mayor and Commonality and the Citizens of London v Royal London Mutual Insurance Society, ex p The Master Governors and Commonality of the Mystery of the Barbers of London* [1996] 2 EGLR 128, the High Court, held that the application of s 237(1) was not restricted to the implementation of the planning permission which underlaid the original acquisition of the land by the authority, but that it was available to authorise further works for which planning permission is duly granted. Furthermore, s 227(1) was also available to persons deriving title from the local authority, subject only to the authority paying compensation for any loss suffered. **16.40**

In that case Dyson J referred as follows to s 237: **16.41**

> The statutory objective which underlies section 237 of the 1990 Act is that, provided that work is done in accordance with planning permission, and subject to payment of compensation, a local authority should be permitted to develop their land in the manner in which they, acting bona fide, consider will best serve the public interest. To that end, it is recognised that a local authority should be permitted to interfere with third party rights. A balance has to be struck between giving local authorities freedom to develop land held for planning purposes, and the need to protect the interests of third parties whose rights are interfered with by local authority development. Section 237(1) is the result of that balancing exercise. Parliament has decided to give local authorities the right to develop their land and to interfere with third party rights, but on the basis that work is done in accordance with planning permission (with the protection inherent in the planning process), but third parties affected are entitled to compensation under section 237(4).

It should be noted, however, that in *Thames Water Utilities Ltd v Oxford City Council and Oxford United Football Club Ltd* (1998) EGCS 133, the High Court expressed doubt as to the extent to which s 237 can be used to authorise a use in contravention of a restrictive covenant which would involve interference with third party rights. **16.42**

F. PLANNING AND HIGHWAYS

16.43 The development of land frequently requires the development site to be linked to an adjoining highway, or improvements to be made to the surrounding highway network. Not surprisingly, it is felt that the cost of such work should fall not on the highway authority but upon the developer. Section 278 of the Highways Act 1980, therefore, provides that if a highway authority are satisfied that it would be of benefit to the public for the authority to enter into an agreement with any person (who will normally be the developer) for the carrying out of highway works, the authority may do so on terms that that person pay the whole or part of the cost. Such agreements are independent of the system of planning obligations created under s 106 of the 1990 Act. Normally, agreements under s 278 are entered into by the Highways Agency on behalf of central government.

16.44 The discretion given to a highway authority to enter into a s 278 agreement is not unlimited. In *R v Warwickshire CC, ex p Powergen plc* [1998] JPL 131 the local planning authority for the area had refused to grant planning permission to Powergen for a supermarket on the site of a former power station. Satisfactory development would have required the widening of an existing highway and bridge over a canal, together with other minor highway works. Powergen appealed against the refusal of planning permission to the Secretary of State who, after the holding of a public local inquiry at which evidence on highway aspects had been submitted by the county council as highway authority, decided to allow the appeal and grant outline planning permission for the development. The permission was subject, however, to a condition requiring the carrying out of prescribed highway works, including the widening of the bridge over the canal.

16.45 In order for the condition to be satisfied, Powergen then sought from the county council as highway authority an agreement under s 278 of the Highways Act 1980, which the council then refused to enter into on the ground that the works would not satisfactorily minimise the risk of accidents.

16.46 On an application for judicial review the High Court quashed the decision of the county council not to enter into a s 278 agreement. Forbes J held that where the benefit to the public of the proposed highway works in respect of which a s 278 agreement had been sought, had been fully considered and determined during the planning process because the works had formed a detailed and related aspect of the application for which planning permission had been properly obtained, the highway authority's discretion to enter into the agreement was necessarily limited to matters likely to be of a relatively minor nature. Accordingly he held that the county council's refusal to enter into a s 278 agreement was *Wednesbury* unreasonable. That decision was then upheld by the Court of Appeal ([1998] JPL 131). According to the Court of Appeal, the county council as highways authority had no option but to co-operate in implementing the planning permission by entering into a s 278 agreement. Accordingly, although the highways authority's 'approval or consent' was still required before the condition could be satisfied, such approval or consent could not be unreasonably withheld.

16.47 Whether approval or consent is unreasonably withheld will, of course, depend upon the particular circumstances of each case. In *R v Cardiff CC, ex p Sears Group Properties Ltd* [1998]

PLSCS 92, the highway authority had not objected to development proposed subject to the developer entering into a s 278 agreement. Accordingly, the planning permission had been granted. Then, due to local government reorganisation, both the local planning authority and the highway authority had changed. The new highway authority then decided to review the traffic implications of the proposed development and decided that before completion of the s 278 agreement, the developer should submit for consideration an updated traffic impact analysis. In an unsuccessful challenge to that decision, the High Court considered that the wish of the highway authority to see whether there had been a change in circumstances since the planning permission was granted which would justify them not entering into s 278 agreement, was not unreasonable in the *Wednesbury* sense.

G. PLANNING PERMISSION AND ACTIONS IN NUISANCE

Where planning permission is given for the development of land and subsequently implemented, the question whether the use of the land amounted to an actionable nuisance is decided by reference to the neighbourhood following implementation of the permission and not as it was before implementation of the permission. In *Gillingham BC v Medway (Chatham) Dock Co. Ltd* [1993] QB 343, a local authority unsuccessfully brought proceedings for a declaration and injunction that the defendants' operation of their premises around the clock as a commercial port amounted to a public nuisance because of noise and vibration from heavy vehicular traffic using residential roads leading to the port.The Court held that the grant of planning permission for the use of the premises as a commercial port operating 24 hours a day changed the character of the residential area, and that the question of nuisance fell thereafter to be decided by reference to a neighbourhood with that development or use and not as it was previously. **16.48**

Prior to the *Gillingham* case, it had been generally assumed that the grant of planning permission, if implemented, did not take away the rights of owners affected by the development to sue in the tort of nuisance for any loss suffered. The effect of the *Gillingham* case, however, was to call that assumption into question, particularly where the planning permission granted was for major development which had the effect of altering the character of the immediate neighbourhood. Did the decision mean that thereafter, where planning permission for development has been implemented, the question of whether it amounted to a nuisance was to be considered by reference to the character of the neighbourhood with the development; or was the decision to be interpreted to mean that no action in nuisance could be brought following the implementation of any planning permission? In *Wheeler v J. J. Saunders Ltd* [1995] JPL 619, the Court of Appeal confined the implications of the *Gillingham* case to the former interpretation, in holding that where planning permission had been granted and implemented for building a row of 20 pens each of which was capable of containing 20 pigs close to a row of holiday cottages, the owner of the cottages could sue for actionable nuisance caused by smell. **16.49**

In an even more recent case, *Hunter v Canary Wharf Ltd* [1996] 1 All ER 482, the Court of Appeal shed further light on the extent to which a grant of planning permission for development gives immunity from an action based on nuisance resulting from that development. **16.50**

16.51 The plaintiffs had claimed from Canary Wharf damages in nuisance for television interference caused to their homes by the presence of the Canary Wharf tower, and from the London Docklands Development Corporation, damages in nuisance resulting from dust created by the construction of link roads in the area. One of the defences raised, which was tried as a preliminary issue, was whether, once a local planning authority had balanced the interests of the community against those of individuals and granted planning permission for development, members of the community had a claim in nuisance with respect to structures build in accordance with that permission.

16.52 Even though the views expressed by the Court of Appeal were *per curiam*, the Court came firmly down in favour of the view that whilst the question of whether a nuisance exists falls to be decided by reference to the character of the neighbourhood after the development has been implemented, implementation of the permission does not in itself grant an immunity from nuisance actions. Although the case finally went to the House of Lords on appeal, the argument that a grant of planning permission should be a defence to proceedings in nuisance under existing law was not pursued.

H. PLANNING PERMISSION AND ACTIONS FOR NEGLIGENCE

16.53 It would seem that no action for negligence will lie against a local planning authority as a result of a grant of planning permission to another. In *Ryeford Homes Ltd v Sevenoaks DC* [1990] JPL 36, the High Court held that in exercising their regulatory planning functions the local planning authority did not have that sufficiently special relationship or a sufficient 'proximity' to owe an individual landowner any duty of care.

16.54 There have been a number of more recent cases, in some of which the courts have held local authorities liable for loss caused to others by the conduct of their officers, under the doctrine of *Hedley Byrne & Co. v Heller & Partners Ltd* [1964] AC 465. In *Welton v North Cornwall DC* (CA, 17 July 1996) the Court upheld an award against the council of £34,000 damages, where the council's environmental health officer had in the purported exercise of his powers under public health legislation, negligently and unreasonably required the owner of the restaurant to carry out substantial alterations and modifications to his kitchen. Again, in *Lambert v West Devon BC* [1997] JPL 735, the Borough Council were held liable for negligent advice given by a building control officer to the owner of a building and then acted upon, that he could proceed to carry out work to a building, even though the owner's application to amend an existing grant of planning permission for work to the building had not yet been determined by the Borough Council. In both these two cases the officers responsible for the negligent misstatements had stepped well outside the boundaries of their duties.

16.55 The difficulty in holding planning authorities liable for the negligence of their officers and servants has been underlined, however, in other recent cases. In *R v Chung Tak Lam v Borough of Torbay* [1998] PLCR 30 the Court of Appeal upheld a decision of the High Court dismissing a claim against the Borough alleging negligence, nuisance and breach of duty in granting planning permission to a neighbour which had caused the claimants damage when the permission was implemented. It was held that no private law right of action for breach of statutory duty existed in respect of any statutory duties imposed on the Borough by the relevant statutory regimes under which their officers had acted, and that no additional claim for breach of the common law duty of care lay in the circumstances of the case.

In *Haddow v Secretary of State for the Environment* (1998) 95(7) LSG 33 the High Court dismissed a claim against the Secretary of State (and at the same time a related action against Tendring District Council), seeking damages in respect of alleged misstatements by an officer from the Department of the Environment and by an officer of the Council respectively. The claimant contended that she had received misleading advice that she should amend a planning application so that a direction made by the Secretary of State that the proposed development required environmental impact assessment could be withdrawn. In his judgment, Peter Lever QC, sitting as a Deputy Judge, quoted with approval part of the judgment of Collins J in the High Court in *Chung Tak Lam*, where he said: **16.56**

> It seems to me that it would be wholly detrimental to the proper process of considering planning applications if the local authority, in addition had to have regard to the private law interests of any persons who might be affected by the grant of permission, and to ask itself in each case whether it had properly had regard to the individual rights of those concerned. If it were potentially liable to actions in negligence in those circumstances, it seems to me that the carrying out of its important functions in the public interest would be likely to be adversely affected.

In dismissing the claim, the Deputy Judge held, *inter alia*, that the claimant had not shown a relationship with the Secretary of State which gave rise to a duty of care, or that the Secretary of State had assumed responsibility to her in the giving of advice, or that what his officer had said had been wrong. Likewise, he found that the officer of the Council had not assumed any responsibility to the claimant and that there had been no duty of care and so no breach of duty on his part.

The courts have not gone so far as to allow local planning authorities to shelter behind a general blanket of immunity in respect of anything done in the exercise of their planning functions. In *Kane v New Forest District Council* [2002] JPL 409, the Court of Appeal held that the authority owed a duty of care to a pedestrian injured following the negligent construction of a footpath which emerged on to the highway at a dangerous place. In subsequent proceedings, the authority was held to be in breach of that duty. **16.57**

I. PLANNING PERMISSION AND ACTIONS IN DECEIT

In dealing with all matters, a local planning authority should act with integrity and evenhandedness. Any failure to do this may make the authority liable in damages in an action based on the tort of deceit, as indeed happened in *Slough Estates plc v Welwyn Hatfield DC* [1996] EGCS 132. **16.58**

The case concerned two major shopping centres. One was called the Howard Centre and was built by the plaintiffs, Slough Estates, in Welwyn Garden City. The other, called A1 Gallerias, was located only a mile away from the Howard Centre and was built on land in respect of which the defendant council were head-leaseholders. **16.59**

In response to concern expressed by Slough Estates that the area did not have the capacity to support two retail developments, the council agreed that in order to reduce competition **16.60** which would affect the Howard Centre, they would enforce a 'tenant mix agreement' made with the developers of A1 Gallerias whereby the occupants of that centre would be restricted to 'leisure' retailing.

16.61 Subsequently, however, the council resolved not to enforce the terms of the tenant mix agreement; but they failed to inform Slough Estates that they had done so, with the result that Slough Estates continued with their construction of the Howard Centre.Worse still, the council decided to keep the decision to relax enforcement of the terms of the tenant mix agreement to themselves and to pretend to other parties, including particularly Slough Estates, that the agreement was still in force and that it was their intention to enforce it.

In the words of May J:

> From July 1987 [the council] were nursing a lie and had set themselves a time bomb. . . . Thereafter there was a policy to tell lies about the tenant mix agreement if it was necessary to do so. The lies were watered down wherever possible, but they were conscious lies.

16.62 May J proceeded to find for the plaintiffs and to award them agreed damages believed to be £29.75m against the council in respect of the loss the company had suffered as a result of the council's deceit.

J. LIFE OF A PLANNING PERMISSION

16.63 Once granted, planning permission will continue in force until one of the following events deprive it of its effectiveness:

(a) Where the development authorised by the permission has been carried out and completed. Here the permission is spent. The benefit of the permission has been accepted and the development which has been carried out in accordance with the terms of the permission becomes part of the existing use rights in the land. Where a personal planning permission has been granted, the benefit of the permission will cease on the death of the person concerned.

(b) Where planning permission has been granted subject to a condition imposed under ss 91 and 92 of the 1990 Act requiring development to be begun within a specified period, and the development has not been begun within that period, development carried out after the end of that period is to be treated as not authorised by the permission.

(c) Where planning permission is revoked under s 97 of the 1990 Act. This provision empowers a local planning authority to revoke or modify any planning permission to develop land granted on an application under Part III of the Act at any time in the case of permission for the carrying out of building or other operations, before the operations are completed and, in the case of permission for a change of use, before the change of use has taken place. The revocation or modification, however, will not affect any building or other operations carried out before the coming into force of the revocation or modification order. Unless an order is unopposed it will not come into effect until confirmed by the Secretary of State. The revocation or modification of a planning permission entitles any person interested in the land to claim compensation from the local planning authority under s 107 of the 1990 Act for any expenditure, loss or damage incurred in carrying out work rendered abortive by the revocation or modification, and any other loss or damage sustained which is directly attributable to the revocation or modification. In calculating the latter head of claim, the value of any other planning permission granted or likely to be granted for the development of the land must be taken into account. The willingness of the local planning authority, therefore, to grant an alternative permission to the one to be revoked or modified will reduce the compensation payable and may, at the same time, lead to the order being unopposed.

Where the development permitted by a planning permission has been carried out and completed, the local planning authority cannot serve a revocation or modification order. Under s 100 of the 1990 Act, however, the authority can require that any use of land should be discontinued, or that conditions should be imposed on the continuance of a use of land or that any buildings or works should be altered or removed. Any such discontinuance order is required to be confirmed by the Secretary of State. As with revocation or modification orders, compensation must be paid to any person who has suffered damage in consequence of the order under s 115 of the 1990 Act.

(d) Every planning permission for the winning and working of minerals or the deposit of mineral waste is made subject to a condition limiting the duration of the permission to 60 years (Schedule 5(1) to the 1990 Act).

(e) Where more than one planning permission has been granted in respect of land, and the carrying out the development authorised by one permission makes it impossible to carry out the development authorised by another. This may extend beyond cases where the implementation of the planning permission makes it physically impossible to implement another. In *Pilkington v Secretary of State for the Environment* [1973] 1 WLR 1527 the owner of land was granted planning permission to build a bungalow on part of the land, site B. It was a condition of the permission that the bungalow should be the only house to be built on the land. He built the bungalow. Later the owner discovered the existence of an earlier permission to build a bungalow and garage on another part of the same land, site A. That permission contemplated the use of the rest of the land as a smallholding. He began to build the second bungalow and was then served with an enforcement notice alleging a breach of planning control. The Divisional Court held that the two permissions could not stand in respect of the same land, once the development sanctioned by the second permission had been carried out. The effect of building on site B was to make the development authorised in the earlier permission incapable of implementation. The bungalow built on site B had destroyed the small holding: and the erection of two bungalows on the site had never been sanctioned.

In *Pioneer Aggregates (UK) Ltd v Secretary of State for the Environment* [1985] AC 132, Lord Scarman thought the *Pilkington* decision was a common-sense decision and correct in law. **16.64**

Mere incompatibility of the planning permission with another planning permission already implemented may thus invalidate it. It may of course also arise where, because one planning permission has been implemented, it is physically impossible to implement the other. **16.65**

The decision in the *Pilkington* case was also considered and followed by the Court of Appeal in *Staffordshire CC v NGR Land Developments Limited and Roberts* [2003] JPL 56. **16.66**

It should be noted that although existing use rights may be abandoned, it is not possible to abandon a planning permission. In *Pioneer Aggregates (UK) Ltd v Secretary of State for the* **16.67**

Environment [1985] AC 132, the respondent company, after a long period of non-user, had resumed the use of land for mining operations. The local planning authority alleged that the resumption constituted development and served an enforcement notice on the company requiring the use to be discontinued. The issue reached the House of Lords which held that there was no general rule of law that a planning permission which is capable of being implemented according to its terms can be abandoned. Their Lordships thought that the clear implication of what is now s 75(1) of the 1990 Act was that only the statute or the terms of the permission itself could stop the permission enduring for the benefit of the land and for all persons for the time being interested therein.

16.68 The principle that a valid permission capable of implementation could not be abandoned by the conduct of the owner or occupier was followed in *Camden LBC v McDonald's Restaurants Ltd* (1992) 65 P & CR 423. The case concerned property used as a restaurant between 1972 and 1987. In December 1987 the Secretary of State had granted planning permission for a single storey rear extension which had never been implemented. Between 1987 and 1991 when McDonald's had taken a lease of the premises, the property had either remained vacant or been used as a bookshop. When McDonald's sought to implement the permission to build the extension, the local planning authority maintained that the permission had lapsed. In granting declarations that the planning permission for the extension was valid and subsisting and that the ground floor of the premises could lawfully be used for restaurant purposes, the Court of Appeal held that one had to 'look back at the permission . . . and see whether in fact the development there contemplated can now be carried out'. Here the premises were still in existence and it remained physically possible to build the extension.

16.69 The authority had also claimed that the use of the premises as a bookshop fell within Class A1 of the Use Classes Order and that it would not be lawful to change the use of the premises back from A1 to A3 without planning permission. The Court held, however, that the permission for the extension was for operational development, not a grant of permission for a material change of use.

17

DEVELOPMENT BY THE CROWN, STATUTORY UNDERTAKERS AND LOCAL AUTHORITIES; PUBLIC WORKS ORDERS; MAJOR INFRASTRUCTURE PROJECTS

A. THE CROWN

The 1990 Act does not bind the Crown. This is an application of a fundamental principle of the constitution that the Crown is not bound by statute unless expressly named or bound by necessary implication. Government departments however, that proposed to carry out development (of a kind other than that permitted by the General Development Order) were required (as a matter of good administration) to consult the local planning authority in accordance with the arrangements set out in Circular 18/84. **17.01**

The procedure ensured that as far as possible proposals are dealt with within the spirit of town and country planning law and in accordance with the policies contained in the development plan and to any other material considerations. **17.02**

The procedure followed also sought to ensure that development proposals by Government departments receive the same publicity as development proposals made by private individuals. Although it is true that the local planning authority have no power to prevent the development taking place, the power of the Secretary of State to determine the matter if the authority should object to the proposed development accords with his power to grant **17.03** planning permission to a private person on appeal, where the local planning authority have decided to refuse it.

17.04 In June 1992 the Government decided, as part of a policy outlined in the Citizen's Charter to progressively remove any immunities which sheltered departments and Crown bodies from regulations, inspection and enforcement requirements placed on others and to bring to an end the exemptions now granted to the Crown under planning legislation. This will now been done by the provisions of Part 7 of the Planning and Compulsory Purchase Act 2004, so that subject to a number of important modifications, the planning Acts will, when the provisions of Part 7 are brought into force, bind the Crown. This is not expected to be before the end of 2005. The planning Acts are the Town and Country Planning Act 1990, the Planning (Listed Building and Conservation Areas) Act 1990 and the Planning (Hazardous Substances) Act 1990. In addition, Schedule 3 to the Act amends a number of provisions in the planning Acts to take account of the unique character of the Crown.

17.05 The main modifications relate to the following aspects:

(a) *National security*
The planning Acts provide that planning inquiries should normally be held in public. In this way oral and documentary evidence can be heard or seen by those attending the inquiry. These provisions however, are now to be modified in cases where the public disclosure of information would relate to national security or to the security of any premises or property, and the disclosure of this information would be contrary to the national interest. In such cases it is provided that the Attorney General may appoint a person to represent the interests of those who would be prevented from being able to hear or inspect such material. Where that is done, the Secretary of State may require the person or persons prevented from seeing the sensitive material to pay the fees and expenses of the person appointed by the Secretary of State.

(b) *Urgent Crown development*
Where the appropriate authority certifies that the development is of national importance, and that it is necessary that the development is carried out as a matter of urgency, the appropriate authority may, instead of making an application for planning permission to the local planning authority, make it instead to the Secretary of State. Where the appropriate authority proposes to take this course, it must publish in one or more newspapers circulating in the locality of the proposed development a notice describing the proposed development and stating their intention to make an application to the Secretary of State. The appropriate authority must also provide the Secretary of State with all necessary documentation, including if required, an environmental statement.

The Secretary of State may then require the authority to provide further information; make documents or other material available for inspection by the public and publish a notice to that effect; and consult the local planning authority and such other persons as are specified in a development order. Thereafter, the application is in effect treated as if it were a called-in application, though it may be expected that the Inquiry Procedure Rules may be amended to shorten the period for the holding of the public inquiry.

(c) *Enforcement*
Although the Crown may be subject to enforcement action, the Act provides that it should remain immune from prosecution for any offence under the planning Acts. However, a local planning authority, before taking any step for the purposes of enforcement in relation to Crown land must first obtain the consent of the appropriate authority for the purpose of enforcement. These steps include entering land; bringing proceedings; and the making of an application, but not the service of a notice or the making of an order (other than a court order).

(d) *Trees: enforcement*
Parallel to the other provisions of the Planning and Compulsory Purchase Act 2004 which will make the Crown subject to the planning Acts, the Act will amend the 1990 Act to prohibit the Crown from doing any act to a tree in a conservation area which might be prohibited by a tree preservation order, unless it serves notice of its intention to do so on the local planning authority and carries out the act either with the consent of the authority, or between six weeks and two years after the date of the notice.

(e) *Old mining permissions*
The Planning and Compulsory Purchase Act 2004 will modify Section 22 and Schedule 2 to the Planning and Compensation Act 1991 to allow Crown bodies holding old mining permissions (i.e. those granted between 1943–1948) the opportunity to register such permissions and apply for the determination of new conditions on the same terms as applied to other old mining permissions.

B. STATUTORY UNDERTAKERS

The expression 'statutory undertakers' is defined in s 262(1) of the 1990 Act to mean: **17.06**

> persons authorised by any enactment to carry on any railway, light railway, tramway, road transport, water transport, canal, inland navigation, dock, harbour, pier or lighthouse undertaking or any undertaking for the supply of hydraulic power and a relevant airport operator. . . .

In addition, for the purposes of many of the Act's provisions, any gas supplier, water or sewerage undertaking, the National Rivers Authority, the Post Office and the Civil Aviation Authority are deemed to be statutory undertakers. **17.07**

Statutory undertakers wishing to develop land must normally apply for planning permission to do so to the local planning authority. Modifications to the normal procedures are made in relation to applications for the development of 'operational land' of such bodies. **17.08**

Where an application for planning permission for the development of operational land comes before the Secretary of State, as with an appeal against an adverse decision by the local planning authority or because the application has been called in under s 77 of the 1990 Act, the Secretary of State is required to act in relation to the appeal or called-in decision jointly with the appropriate Minister; that is, the Minister responsible for the operations of the particular statutory undertaker. **17.09**

Apart from the above modification, planning permission for certain development of statutory undertakers is granted under various classes of the General Permitted Development **17.10**

Order. Much of that permitted development is extensive in character. In addition, other legislation may require development by statutory undertakers to be authorised by a government department. In such cases, s 90(1) of the 1990 Act provides that the department concerned may, in granting that authorisation, direct that planning permission for the development shall be deemed to be granted, subject to such conditions as may be specified. The value of this procedure is that it enables the authorising department to consider all matters relating to the proposed development at the same time, many of which may not be related to the land use matters, such as the significance of the proposed development to the strategic functions and responsibilities of the industry concerned.

C. LOCAL AUTHORITIES

17.11 Local authorities, like statutory undertakers, must obtain planning permission for any development they propose to carry out. As with statutory undertakers, certain development by local authorities is permitted development under the various classes of the General Permitted Development Order. Furthermore, where other legislation requires development by a local authority to be authorised by a government department, s 90(1) of the 1990 Act provides that the department concerned may, in granting the authorisation, direct that planning permission for the development be deemed to be granted.

17.12 There are other special provisions, however, which apply to other development. Section 316 of the 1990 Act empowers the Secretary of State to make regulations governing development of local planning authorities' land and development of any land by local planning authorities jointly with another person. The current regulations are the Town and Country Planning General Regulations 1992, SI 1992/1492. The regulations revoke and replace regulations made in 1976 which had been subject to much criticism.

17.13 In essence the old regulations gave a local planning authority the power, by passing two resolutions, to grant themselves planning permission for development carried out by them or by others on their land. It was alleged that local planning authorities were not able to act impartially in such matters when they were plaintiff and jury in their own cause. Moreover, because a local planning authority might gain financially when disposing of land with the benefit of planning permission, it was claimed that planning permission might be granted which would be refused if the 'applicant' were not the authority.

17.14 The requirements of the Town and Country Planning General Regulations have always been regarded as fundamental and strict, and a failure to comply with them has been regarded by the courts as fatal. Many of the cases, whilst still relevant to the new statutory provisions, turn on the interpretation of the old 1976 Regulations and the provisions of the 1990 Act, before amendments were made to that Act by the Planning and Compensation Act 1991. In *Steeples v Derbyshire County Council* [1985] 1 WLR 256, Webster J held that the failure to place notices in the planning register as required by the regulations rendered the deemed grant of planning permission *ultra vires* and void.

17.15 In *R v Lambeth LBC, ex p Sharp* [1987] JPL 440, the authority proposed to construct a floodlit synthetic athletics track with seats for 1,100 spectators in some 6 acres of parkland. Among a number of irregularities committed by the authority in the process of obtaining deemed planning permission for the development was a failure in a newspaper advertisement required by the regulations to specify the period within which objections to the proposed development should be made to the authority. Croom-Johnson LJ granted *certiorari* to quash the deemed grant of permission. Unanimously upholding that decision, the Court of Appeal held that the breach of the regulations had been fundamental.

A few months later in the High Court in *R v Doncaster MDC, ex p British Railways Board* [1987] JPL 444, Schiemann J followed the approach of the Court of Appeal in the *Lambeth* case and quashed a resolution of the authority to carry out development involving the building of a superstore in the town centre, in the light of a host of irregularities in the procedures followed by the authority. **17.16**

The process by which authorities were able in effect to grant planning permission to themselves was subject to much criticism. In this area local planning authorities were seen by many to be partial to their own development proposals. The stakes were high, since the value of a grant of planning permission can be considerable. This is particularly so where development proposals were made for under-used, county-council owned playing fields. Until the law was changed by the Planning and Compensation Act 1991, such development proposals were determined not by the district council as local planning authority for their area but by the county council. **17.17**

The problem however was best seen with regard to the growth in the desire for superstores and hypermarkets. Although it is no part of the planning system to protect commercial interests from competition, the effect of such development on shopping outlets in existing town centres is something which must be taken into account in deciding whether they should be allowed. The problem becomes acute in cases where there are a number of proposals for superstore development in the same area, since the greater the number, the greater the impact on the existing centre. **17.18**

Frequently because of this impact, there is general agreement between authorities and developers that the number of superstores in any area should be limited. When this is followed by a number of applications for such development by different developers, the question of which one is to be preferred can often pose a difficult decision for the authority.To meet this difficulty, a local planning authority may fail to issue a decision within the prescribed period for doing so, in the hope that at least one of the applicants will appeal to the Secretary of State against the non-determination of the application, and that other applications not determined will be called in by the Secretary of State. It is he who will then make the decision, after holding a composite local inquiry into all the applications. **17.19**

A further difficulty arises, however, when one of the proposed sites for such development is on land in which the local planning authority has an interest. Inevitably if an authority deals with an application in which it has an interest and grants planning permission, it is difficult for the authority to avoid suggestions of bias. **17.20**

The test originally applied by the courts was whether a reasonable man would consider that there was a real likelihood of bias. However the correct test to be applied in judging an authority's actions was outlined in *R v Sevenoaks DC, ex p Terry* [1985] 3 All ER 226. In that case, the council as local planning authority had granted planning permission to a company **17.21** called Fraser Wood Properties in respect of a site known as the Old Post Office Yard for the purpose, *inter alia*, of erecting a supermarket. The council had, on an earlier date, approved a recommendation that an offer by Fraser Wood to purchase a lease of the site should be accepted and the officers were authorised to take all necessary action. The formal agreement between the council and Fraser Wood was not entered into until after the date on which planning permission was granted. In an application for judicial review of the council's decision, the applicant contended that the planning permission was void on the grounds that the council had fettered the discretion of the planning committee and further, or alternatively, that the council gave to reasonable people the appearance that they regarded themselves as committed.

17.22 Dismissing the application, Glidewell J said in relation to these situations:

> . . . but it is not uncommon for a local authority to be obliged to make a decision relating to land or other property in which it had an interest. In such a situation, the application of the rule designed to ensure that a judicial officer does not appear to be biased would, in my view, often produce an administrative impasse. In my judgment, the correct test to be applied in the present case is for the court to pose to itself the question: had the district council before 5 January 1982 acted in such a way that it is clear that, when the committee came to consider Fraser Wood's application for planning permission, it could not exercise proper discretion? . . . if the answer to the question is No, it is in my judgment neither necessary nor desirable for the court to go further and consider what the opinion of a reasonable man would be.

17.23 The issue again arose for determination in the Queen's Bench Division in *R v St Edmundsbury BC, ex p Investors in Industry Commercial Properties Ltd* [1985] 1 WLR 1168. There the council's planning committee had granted outline planning permission to J. Sainsbury plc for the erection of a supermarket on land owned by the council. The applicants for relief had applied for judicial review to quash the council's decision. The circumstances which gave rise to their application were that at the meeting at which the committee had considered the matter, the committee had before it seven applications for supermarkets in respect of six sites, one of which was made on the applicants' behalf. Each of the applications was refused, save for that made by Sainsbury's for a supermarket on land owned by the council, who had entered into a contract to sell a 125-year lease of the site to Sainsbury's in the event of planning permission being obtained. The applicants contended that the council had thereby fettered themselves from proper exercise of their discretion and that the decision in favour of Sainsbury's had given rise to the inference of bias.

17.24 Dismissing the application and applying the dictum of Glidewell J in *R v Sevenoaks DC, ex p Terry*, Stocker J held that the test of what a hypothetical reasonable man would apprehend had no application in determining the validity of an administrative decision such as the grant of planning permission. The sole test was whether, despite its interests or its previous actions, the planning authority genuinely and impartially exercised its discretion, since there were many cases in which a local authority's own interests and land were likely to be affected by a favourable planning decision made by it. Accordingly, once a planning authority's decision was found or conceded to be fair there was no requirement to pose some further test by which the decision might be impugned as unlawful or void, either by reference to what the reasonable man would suspect or by reference to whether viewed through some other eyes, such as those of the judge, there was a real likelihood of bias.

The present procedures whereby local planning authorities obtain planning permission for development on their own land are now contained in the Town and Country Planning General Regulations 1992. The amendments made by the new regulations were intended to allay the disquiet caused by the operation of the old. The main features of the regulations are: 17.25

(a) a local planning authority must make an application to itself for planning permission to develop land within its area. Local planning authorities therefore, can continue to grant themselves planning permission for development carried out by them, such as schools or local authority housing, and will also be able to grant themselves permission for development undertaken jointly with another person, such as a joint venture with a housing association where the authority's interest is significant. Circular 19/92 suggests that the authority's level of financial commitment could be a useful test of whether the interest is significant or not;
(b) for all other development proposed to be carried out on local-authority-owned land by other parties, planning permission now has to be sought from the responsible development control authority (thus a county council which is, for example, seeking to dispose of land with planning permission has to apply to the district council, unless the development is a 'county matter'; and the district council has to apply to the county council for development which is a 'county matter');
(c) local planning authorities which now have to make a planning application to themselves or to another local planning authority will be subject to broadly the same statutory procedures as other applicants;
(d) applications are required to be publicised as prescribed by a development order in the same way as applications from the public;
(e) to avoid a conflict of interest, Regulation 10 provides that:

> Notwithstanding anything in s 101 of the Local Government Act 1972 (arrangements for the discharge of functions by local authorities), no application for planning permission for development may be determined by a committee or sub-committee of the interested planning authority concerned if that committee or sub-committee is responsible (wholly or partly) for the management of any land or buildings to which the application relates; or by an officer of the interested planning authority concerned if his responsibilities include any aspect of the management of any land or buildings to which the application relates.

The effect of this regulation is that where there is a conflict, the decision may only be made by the full Council;

(f) planning permission granted to local planning authorities for development by them or jointly may not pass to subsequent owners of the land; for example, an authority will not be able to grant itself planning permission for council housing then change its mind and sell the land with planning permission to a developer. The purpose of this provision is probably to prevent unimplemented planning permissions passing with the land to third parties. Once the permission has been implemented by the authority, however, the authority may sell the land on with the benefit of the completed development. It seems also that if a third party wishes to buy land from an authority with an unimplemented permission which they propose to 'implement' themselves, they must apply to the local planning authority for a similar permission which they then implement. It is likely that in such a case, the local planning authority would find the grant of the permission difficult to refuse. An important amendment to the general rule, however, was made in the Town and Country Planning General (Amendment) Regulations 1998. The effect of the amendment is that unitary authorities are no longer subject to the rule that a grant of planning permission to themselves for development by them is personal to the authority concerned. So that where an authority is the sole local authority for their area, they may grant themselves planning permission which runs with the land and enures for its benefit.

17.26 Despite these new provisions, allegations of bias continue to be made. A recent example, but one in which the allegations were not established, is to be found in *R v Canterbury CC, ex p Springimage Ltd* [1995] JPL 20, where the court applied the test set out in *R v Sevenoaks DC, ex p Terry*.

17.27 Allegations of bias may arise also not from the authority's ownership of land proposed to be developed, but from the position of members of the authority responsible for making decisions. In *R v Secretary of State for the Environment, ex p Kirkstall Valley Campaign* [1996] 3 All ER 304, an Urban Development Corporation had granted planning permission for retail development of land belonging to a rugby club. It was claimed that because of the private interests of three members of the council and an officer of the council in the decision taken, it was tainted by bias. In an application for judicial review to quash the decision to grant planning permission, the High Court held that the principle that a person was disqualified from participating in a decision if there was a real danger that he would be influenced by a pecuniary or personal interest in the outcome was of general application and not limited to judicial or quasi-judicial bodies or proceedings. Where members had an interest, it had to be declared and the member concerned could not participate in the decision unless it was remote or insignificant. In this case, the Court refused to grant judicial review of the decision on the ground that the personal interest of members had either disappeared by the time the decision was made, or that it was too remote.

17.28 Despite the changes brought about by the new regulations local authority development continues to give cause for concern. In view of this, the Nolan Report on Standards of Conduct in Local Government recommended that the Government should require authorities to notify the appropriate Secretary of State of all planning aplications in which they had an interest, either in the development or in the land, where the proposed development is contrary to the local plan, or has given rise to a level of objections regarded by the Secretary of State as substantial.

D. PUBLIC WORKS ORDERS

17.29 Until 1992, a private Act of Parliament was the normal method used to obtain powers to construct public works such as the provision of railways, tramways, inland waterways, ports and harbours. Such Acts would often be required because of the need for the promoters of the development to obtain powers to compulsorily acquire the land on which the development was to take place; to obtain immunity from actions in nuisance or other torts which would otherwise be available to those affected by the development; and to extinguish public or private rights of way likely to be interfered with by the development.

As far as development control was concerned, the General Development Procedure Order (as it is now called) provided that where the Act specifically designated the nature of the development and the land upon which it was to be carried out, the development was 'permitted' under the Order. Hence the private Act procedure was in effect determining questions of development control, without the promoters of that development being required to obtain express planning permission from the local planning authority or Secretary of State. 17.30

During the 1980s, the procedures for obtaining these powers came to be increasingly criticised. An increase in the number of schemes being proposed led to considerable pressure on Parliamentary time. In addition, it was felt that the procedures themselves were archaic and not the most suitable way of examining effectively this kind of proposal. In particular, the process ignored the development of the planning inquiry system and the role it played in assessing the impact of major proposals which involved the development of land. 17.31

In 1992, following a report of the Joint Committee on Private Bill Procedure, the Government introduced in Part I of the Transport and Works Act 1992 (the 1992 Act), an entirely new procedure allowing the Secretary of State to make orders for the authorisation of transport and other works and the making of related provisions. 17.32

Under s 1 of the 1992 Act the Secretary of State was given power to make orders relating to the construction or operation of railways; tramways; trolley vehicle systems; or systems using a mode of guided transport prescribed by order made by the Secretary of State under s 2 of the Act. Guided transport systems currently prescribed under s 2 include aerial cableway; lift; monorail; magnetic levitation; road based with cable or rail guidance; road based with side guidance and track based with side guidance. 17.33

In addition, under s 3 of the 1992 Act the Secretary of State is given power to make orders relating to the construction or operation of inland waterways and the carrying out of certain prescribed works which interfere with rights of navigation in inland and territorial waters. 17.34

The content of Works Orders

Works Orders contain provisions very similar to those previously found in private Acts of Parliament. Section 5 of the 1992 Act provides that they may include such provisions as the application, modification or exclusion of other statutory provisions; the acquisition of land, whether compulsorily or by agreement; the creation or extinguishment of rights over land; the abrogation and modification of agreements relating to land; the payment of compensation; the charging of tolls, fares and other charges; and the making of byelaws and their enforcement. 17.35

Although a Works Order will not in itself grant planning permission for any development involved in implementing the proposals, planning permission may be deemed to be granted by the Secretary of State at the time of making the order (see 17.45). 17.36

The procedure for applying for a Works Order

Any body with power to promote or oppose Bills in Parliament has the power to apply for a Works Order. This includes private individuals as well as corporations. Under s 7 of the 1992 Act, applications must be made in accordance with rules made by the Secretary of State. The 17.37

present rules are the Transport and Works (Applications and Objections Procedure) Rules 2000, SI 2000/2190 and provide for the submission of a draft order with the application, a memorandum explaining the powers sought, a statement as to the status of the applicant, an affidavit stating that the prior consultation and notification procedure required by rules have been followed, a list of consents, permission or licences which have been sought, the appropriate fee, an environmental statement similar to that required by the Town and Country Planning (Environmental Impact Assessment) (England and Wales) Regulations 1999, plans etc., of the proposed works, particulars of how the works are to be funded and an estimate of the length of time the works are expected to take. The applicant must also state whether he seeks a decision from the Secretary of State that planning permission should be deemed to be granted for any development proposed.

17.38 Provision is also made under s. 10 for allowing anybody to object to a draft order. Under s. 11, the Secretary of State may hold a public inquiry for the purposes of an application for a Works Order. The Transport and Works (Inquiry Procedure) Rules 2004 (SI 2078) prescribe the procedure to be followed in connection with public local inquiries held under s. 11 of the Act. The Secretary of State is indeed obliged to hold such an inquiry if objections to the order are received from statutory objectors such as local authorities, or landowners whose land is proposed to be acquired. Otherwise, objectors may have to be content with the opportunity to appear before and be heard by a person appointed by the Secretary of State by way of a hearing.

Schemes of national significance

17.39 Although for most Works Orders, Parliamentary approval will not be required for the proposals contained in them, it is otherwise where, in the opinion of the Secretary of State, the application relates to proposals which are of national significance. Under s 9 of the 1992 Act, such proposals must be approved by both Houses of Parliament.

17.40 Where the Secretary of State takes the view that aproposal in an application for a Works Order is of national significance, he would normally place a motion before Parliament asking for approval of the proposal before any public local inquiry is held into objections. The purpose of this process is that it enables Parliament to decide at an early stage whether it wishes to endorse the need for the project, leaving questions of detail to be dealt with at the inquiry. The Secretary of State has a residual power, however, to refer aproposal in a Works Order back to Parliament for further consideration after the holding of a public local inquiry so that any earlier resolution by Parliament may be modified before the Order is made by him.

17.41 So far few proposals in applications for a Works Order have been subject to the s 9 process. In July 1996 it was used in connection with the Central Railway Works Order. That order contained proposals for the construction of a railway between Leicester and the Channel Tunnel via Rugby on a dismantled railway alignment to link with the existing Chiltern line, and then on to Olympia in London and Ashford and Folkestone.

17.42 The 'draft' Order contained powers for Central Railway to build and operate the railway and terminals, to acquire land compulsorily, to create new accesses to motorways and other roads, and temporarily or permanently to stop up or divert streets and footpaths. The draft

Order also sought to disapply parts of public general legislation, including the regulating regime for licensing and track access in the Railways Act 1993.

The motion to approve, brought first in the House of Commons, was rejected by 172 votes to seven. If the draft Order had been approved by both Houses, the proposals would then have been considered at a public inquiry, with the final decision on whether to approve the Order then being made by the Secretary of State. **17.43**

Throughout the proceedings the Government maintained a neutral stance, unwilling to either support or damn the proposals. According to the Minister for Railways and Roads, for the Government to support such a scheme, 'they would need to be persuaded that the merits of the proposal were so overwhelming as to justify unequivocal support'. Without Government support, therefore, any scheme of national significance is unlikely to receive Parliamentary approval and thus proceed further. **17.44**

Planning permission

Quite apart from the s 9 process, where any proposals in a Works Order involve the development of land, planning permission must of course be obtained before these proposals can be implemented. Applicants for a Works Order may decide to seek express planning permission from the local planning authority. Given the scale and nature of proposals contained in a Works Order, however, it is much more likely that applicants for an Order will seek the involvement of the Secretary of State. **17.45**

In any event, under the rules for the submission of applications for the making of a Works Order, an applicant is required to consult the local planning authority before applying for the Order; to obtain from them a statement of their views as to whether the proposal in the Order would be consistent with the policies in the development plan; and to provide details of any planning permissions already obtained. **17.46**

The power of the Secretary of State to grant planning permission for any development involved in the implementation of proposals in an Order is contained in sub-section (2A) of s 90 of the 1990 Act which provides: **17.47**

> On making an order under sections 1 or 3 of the Transport and Works Act [1992] the Secretary of State may direct that planning permission for the development shall be deemed to be granted, subject to such conditions (if any) as may be specified in the direction.

This power of the Secretary of State to grant 'deemed' planning permission when making a Works Order is facilitated by a provision in the regulation for the making of an application for a Works Order requiring the applicant to state specifically whether he wishes the Secretary of State to grant deemed planning permission for development proposed in the Order. He must also identify in the application any matters which he is content should be reserved for subsequent approval by the local planning authority. **17.48**

Although the power contained in sub-section (2A) above is expressed in permissive terms and the Secretary of State may in theory withhold deemed planning permission when making an Order, it is inconceivable that he would do so given the importance of the planning issues to most applications for a Works Order. Indeed during the debate on the 1992 Act in the House of Commons, an unqualified assurance was given on behalf of the Secretary of **17.49**

State that where an application for planning permission was sought as part of the Order, the Secretary of State would determine the Works Order and the deemed planning permission at the same time.

17.50 It should be noted however, that the Secretary of State's power to grant planning permission under s.90 (2A) of the 1992 Act, does not circumvent the need to obtain listed building consent where the development proposed will affect a listed building.

18

PLANNING AGREEMENTS; PLANNING OBLIGATIONS; PLANNING CONTRIBUTIONS

A. INTRODUCTION AND ENABLING POWERS

Planning obligations are a development from the power first given to local planning authorities by s 34 of the Town and Country Planning Act 1932 to enter into planning agreements with landowners for regulating the development or use of their land. From that Act, the power found its way into the Town and Country Planning Act 1947; and thence into the Town and Country Planning Act 1971 as s 52. On the consolidation of planning legislation in 1990, s 52 of the 1971 Act was replaced by s 106 of the Town and Country Planning Act 1990 as the new statutory authority for the power to enter into planning agreements. Now, following the passing of the Planning and Compensation Act 1991, the original s 106 of the 1990 Act has been replaced in its entirety by new ss 106, 106A and 106B which have been inserted into the 1990 Act in its place. The replacement sections also introduced new arrangements and new terminology. From 25 October 1991, the power to enter into a 18.01

'planning agreement' under the 1990 Act has been repealed and replaced by the power to enter into a 'planning obligation'.

18.02 It should be emphasised that the current statutory provisions relating to planning obligations do not affect planning agreements entered into under either s 52 of the Town and Country Planning Act 1971, or the original s 106 of the 1990 Act (now repealed). These agreements may continue to play a part in regulating the use and development of land.

18.03 Section 52 of the 1971 Act and the original s 106 of the 1990 Act provided that a local planning authority could enter into an agreement with any person interested in land in their area for the purpose of restricting or regulating the development or use of the land, either permanently or during such period as may be prescribed by the agreement. It further provided that an agreement made under this section with any person interested in land could be enforced by the local planning authority against persons deriving title under that person in respect of that land as if the local planning authority were possessed of adjacent land and as if the agreement had been expressed to be made for the benefit of such land.

18.04 As subsequently amended by later legislation, a local planning authority's power under s.52 to enter into a planning agreement was extended to enable it to require a landowner not only to refrain from carrying out works on the affected land, but also to require him to do so.

18.05 As regards the exercise of these powers following their initial introduction in 1932, there is evidence that they provided a useful mechanism for controlling development in advance of the preparation by a local planning authority of a development plan for its area. Once that point had passed, however, the need for such agreements largely disappeared. Indeed, it has been estimated that in the 25 years up until 1968, no more than 500 agreements were made. In the 1970s, however, the position began to change dramatically, and there was evidence that the statutory provision was being used in a way quite unconnected with its original purpose. Local planning authorities saw the statutory provision as an opportunity for obtaining a 'planning gain' for their community. In some cases, the grant of planning permission was made conditional upon the applicant entering into a planning agreement. So no agreement, no planning permission. In return for the grant of planning permission, the developer would be expected to enter into an agreement to provide some public benefit, which might or might not be related to the development for which planning permission was to be granted. He might, for example, be required to contribute towards the provision of infrastructure or the restoration of a listed building or a church, or to provide public amenities such as open spaces or community centres. For the most part planning agreements were sought and obtained for a proper and legitimate planning purpose. For example, it might take the form of a requirement that the applicant should pay for improvements to a nearby (off-site) road junction to accommodate traffic to be generated by the development; or that he should pay for a new sewer which would be needed if the development was to take place; or that after the building authorised by the planning permission has been erected, existing buildings on the site should be demolished; all constitute examples of planning agreements entered into for a legitimate planning purpose.

18.06 Occasionally, however, planning agreements were sought for purposes which could be considered of doubtful legality. Examples might include a requirement that the applicant provide new roads or sewers in excess of that required to serve the additional demand generated by the particular development in question; or that he be allowed an increase in the density or plot ratio normally permitted in return for the dedication of land as open space or as a footpath.

It will be seen that the use of planning agreements linked to the grant of planning permission raised both moral and legal issues. It raised a moral issue where used by a local planning authority to circumvent the general principle that landowners are entitled to planning permission for the development of their land unless there is a substantial planning objection to the development, by the addition of a requirement that they should contribute something in return for that entitlement. It raised a legal issue in the sense that there is vagueness and uncertainty over the extent of authorities' power to require a planning agreement to be entered into as part of a 'planning permission package'. It is not surprising, therefore, that from the beginning of the 1970s, commentaries on the use of s 52 agreements were sometimes characterised by such terms as 'the sale of planning permissions' or 'cheque-book planning'; and in severe cases, their use was regarded by developers as little short of blackmail. **18.07**

On the other hand the system was not universally disliked by developers. The giving of a public benefit was often seen as a small price to pay in return for a grant of planning permission, and often enabled development which would otherwise have been controversial to be more readily accepted by the community. This may explain why so few attempts were made to challenge such agreements in the courts. The question of planning gain was raised in *Westminster Renslade Ltd v Secretary of State for the Environment* [1983] JPL 454. The appellant developer had sought planning permission for comprehensive development involving offices, car-parks, a bridge, a new station and a transport interchange at Feltham railway station in Hounslow. On appeal, the Inspector upheld the decision of the local authority to refuse permission, on the ground, *inter alia*, that the plans did not show sufficient provision for car-parking that would be under public control. In the High Court, Forbes J, quashing the decision, held that the Inspector was not entitled to treat the provision of publicly controlled car-parks as a valid material consideration in determining the appeal. According to Forbes J, if a developer freely chose to give away his rights because he considered it more likely he would be granted planning permission if he did so, it might be legitimate to take into account what the developer was providing as planning gain. But it was not right to say that planning permission could be refused unless a landowner took on a burden which should more properly be shouldered by the local planning authority. The decision suggested that if there is a genuine planning objection to proposed development, but that objection could be overcome by some action taken by the developer, then that was a legitimate consideration to be taken into account by the authority. For example, if lack of infrastructure is the sole reason for refusing planning permission for development, but the developer agrees to provide it himself or to meet the cost of providing it, that is a proper consideration to be taken into account. If, on the other hand, the authority is seeking a contribution from the developer towards the provision of public facilities (as by requiring the dedication of open space) which the authority is required to provide, that is not a proper consideration to be taken into account. **18.08**

So prolific became the use made of planning agreements to obtain planning gain from a developer, that provisions covering the matter were often contained in development plans. **18.09**

18.10 In *Richmond upon Thames LBC v Secretary of State for the Environment* [1984] JPL 24, an application was made for planning permission for the addition of an entrance hall and offices to an existing building in Richmond. The local planning authority had refused planning permission, because, *inter alia*, the development proposed did not provide adequate planning advantages as required by the development plan for the area. The relevant policy in the plan stated that 'all office developments will normally be required to provide planning advantage which is considered most appropriate to the site'.

18.11 On appeal, the Inspector felt unable to regard the development-plan policy requirement of planning gain as a prerequisite for the grant of planning permission as being a valid reason for its refusal. It seems that the Inspector took the view that in the light of a then recently published report by the Property Advisory Group on the subject of planning gain, the development plan policy might not be a valid policy. In the High Court, Glidewell J held that if that were the case it was a view the Inspector was not entitled to take. In the exercise of the Court's discretion, however, he decided not to quash the decision.

18.12 Whatever the limits of the power to enter into a planning agreement, they could not be used to fetter the exercise by a local planning authority of their statutory powers.

18.13 In *Windsor & Maidenhead RBC v Brandrose Investments Ltd* [1983] 1 WLR 509, a developer and the local planning authority entered into a s 52 agreement under the Town and Country Planning Act 1971, whereby the developer undertook to demolish existing buildings and redevelop the site on which the buildings stood. The authority then granted the developer outline planning permission to develop its property along the lines contemplated in the agreement. But then later, the authority designated land as a conservation area pursuant to what is now s 69 of the Planning (Listed Buildings and Conservation Areas) Act 1990, which included the developer's land. This meant that buildings in the conservation area could not be demolished without the authority's consent. When the developer started to demolish in accordance with the permission and the agreement, the authority sought an injunction restraining it from proceeding with the demolition. The Court of Appeal held that a s 52 agreement could not fetter an authority's discretion in the exercise of their statutory powers and the agreement could not bind the authority not to exercise their powers to designate a conservation area, even though the effect of so doing might be to frustrate the purposes of the agreement.

18.14 Nevertheless, the legal contours within which planning agreements operate remained far from certain. In *R v Gillingham BC, ex p Parham Ltd* [1988] JPL 336, a comparison was made between the powers of a local planning authority to impose conditions in a grant of planning permission, and the power of an authority to enter into statutory planning agreements. In the view of the court, an agreement had to satisfy two of the three requirements for the imposition of a valid condition as set out in the decision of the House of Lords in *Newbury DC v Secretary of State for the Environment* [1981] AC 578. First, since the power to enter into a statutory agreement was given by planning legislation, an agreement can only be entered into for a planning purpose, not an extraneous one. Secondly, as with the exercise of all public law powers, the power has to be exercised reasonably in accordance with *Wednesbury* principles (*Associated Provincial Picture Houses Ltd v Wednesbury Corporation* [1948] 1 KB 223). In the view of the court, however, it was not necessary that the purposes of a statutory planning agreement should 'fairly and reasonably be related to the permitted development'.

In *R v Wealden DC, ex p Charles Church (South East) Ltd* [1989] JPL 837, it was again held that the test of a fair and reasonable relationship to the development proposed did not apply to the making of statutory planning agreements. If that was correct, then no legal fetter existed on the power of the local planning authority to seek planning gain, other than the test of reasonableness and the knowledge that if the authority attempts to extract too much in the way of gain, the Secretary of State on appeal may grant planning permission without any planning agreement at all. If, on the other hand, the courts were to decide that a planning agreement must fairly and reasonably relate to the permitted development, the advantages of a planning agreement as opposed to the imposition of conditions in the planning permission becomes otiose, apart from the fact that a condition cannot require monetary payments to be made by a developer whereas a developer, may agree to do so via a planning agreement; and the fact that it was easier for an authority to enforce the terms of a planning agreement (by an injunction) than it is to enforce compliance with a condition (by an enforcement notice or breach of condition notice). **18.15**

Later, in *Safeway Properties Ltd v Secretary of State for the Environment* [1991] JPL 966, the Court of Appeal allowed an appeal from the refusal of the High Court to quash a decision by the Secretary of State to refuse outline planning permission for a superstore, petrol filling station and ancillary development, on the ground that the Inspector who had conducted the inquiry into the appeal had wrongly excluded from consideration an offer by the developers to provide financial assistance for the implementation of traffic management measures which, it was claimed, would go some way to alleviate the effects of increased traffic in the vicinity of the site and would benefit the already overcrowded traffic system in the locality generally. The Court of Appeal held that there were insufficient reasons for the Inspector to conclude that the measures to be financed by Safeways were not so directly related to the proposed development of the site that the superstore ought not to be permitted without them. Unfortunately, because the Court was concerned merely with the correctness of the interpretation given by an Inspector to the then current Ministerial Circular on Planning Agreements (22/83), it did not have an opportunity to clarify the legal uncertainty over the precise relationships between the determination of applications for planning permission and planning gain. **18.16**

The precise legal contours within which planning applicants operated continued to be in doubt. In *R v Plymouth City Council, ex p Plymouth and South Devon Co-operative Society* [1993] JPL 1099 (a case concerned with planning obligations and referred to later), the Court of Appeal held that the test of materiality for the purpose of s 70(2) of the 1990 Act was, as with a condition imposed in a grant of planning permission, that (a) it had to serve a planning purpose, (b) it had to relate fairly and reasonably to the development permitted, and (c) it had to be not *Wednesbury* unreasonable. Yet in *Good v Epping Forest DC* [1994] JPL 372 (a case concerned with planning agreements) the Court of Appeal accepted that planning agreements could be valid even though they went beyond what could be required by condition. Indeed Ralph Gibson LJ, who gave the leading judgment, said: **18.17**

> . . . it is not surprising that section 52 agreements might go to matters beyond those that fairly and reasonably relate to the development . . . because there would be little point in enacting section 52 . . . if section 52 agreements were confined to those matters which could be dealt with by way of conditions.

B. PLANNING OBLIGATIONS

18.18 One of the many problems associated with planning agreements was that only the developer and local planning authorities could be parties to it. A developer was not obliged to enter into an agreement when applying for planning permission and if a local planning authority decided to hold out for one, he could only appeal against non-determination of the application or its refusal, whichever was the case. The Inspector or the Secretary of State could then conclude, however, that permission could only be given if there was an agreement to meet some requirement that could not be met by the imposition of a condition. In such cases, the only action the Inspector could take, was to grant permission without any agreement or to refuse permission altogether.

18.19 Accordingly, the Government decided that there should be statutory provision to enable a developer to give a unilateral undertaking (which would be binding on him and on successors in title) to carry out certain works or to do whatever the undertaking may specify. The advantage of such an undertaking, which would be enforceable by the local authority, was that it would not be necessary for the local planning authority to agree its terms. In considering the related planning application or appeal, the authority or the Secretary of State respectively would be required to have regard to the terms of any unilateral undertaking offered by the developer before or during the course of appeal proceedings.

18.20 Another difficulty with s 52 planning agreements related to the power given by s 299 of the 1990 Act for an application for planning permission to be made for the development of Crown land prior to its disposal. The provision did not, however, enable a Government department to enter into a planning agreement with the local planning authority. Difficulties had arisen in cases where the local planning authority considered that such an agreement was needed before planning permission could be granted. The Government decided, therefore that s 299 should be amended to enable Government departments to enter into agreements in appropriate circumstances and to give unilateral undertakings as proposed above.

18.21 The Government's other proposal was to amend the law concerning the extent to which s 52 agreements could be discharged or modified. A party to such an agreement could apply to the Lands Tribunal for the agreement (or part of it) to be discharged if it was obsolete, but there was no provision for appeal against an agreement which, while not obsolete in legal terms, no longer had utility or validity for planning purposes. For example, an individual might have bought land which enjoyed planning permission for residential development but was subject to a s 52 agreement to maintain access to a community building beyond the site. If in the time elapsed since the permission was granted and the agreement was made, a different access to the community building had been provided across other land, the need for the planning agreement in connection with the residential permission will have disappeared. Furthermore, the Lands Tribunal had no jurisdiction either to modify or discharge a *positive* covenant contained in a planning agreement.

18.22 Accordingly, the Government legislated to enable a party entering into or giving the new planning obligation to apply to the local planning authority for the obligation (or part of it) to be discharged on the ground that its planning purpose has ended or was no longer relevant, so that the permission would become (to that extent) unencumbered.

C. PLANNING OBLIGATIONS (THE DETAILED REGIME)

Section 106 of the Town and Country Planning Act 1990 did no more than replace s 52 of the Town and Country Planning Act 1971 in the consolidating legislation. **18.23**

Section 12 of the 1991 Act however, replaced s 106 of the 1990 Act with new ss 106, 106A and 106B. The new s 106 amended the law relating to 'planning agreements' by enabling a developer to enter into a 'planning obligation', which could be *either* agreed with the authority, or by the developer giving a unilateral undertaking. The section also provided for planning obligations to include positive obligations. The new provisions, however, did not affect planning agreements entered into on or before 25 October 1991. These agreements continue to be governed by the old law. **18.24**

The new s 106A of the 1990 Act enabled a person bound by a planning obligation to apply to the local planning authority for its modification or discharge, and the new s 106B enabled a person bound by an obligation to appeal to the Secretary of State where the local planning authority refuse or fail to determine an application for its modification or discharge. **18.25**

Sections 106, 106A and 106B introduced into the 1990 Act by the Planning and Compensation Act 1991 are themselves now to be replaced by the Planning and Compulsory Purchase Act 2004. That Act is to replace them with new sections 106, 106A and 106B containing the permissions relating to 'planning contributions' (see 18.54). **18.26**

D. CREATION OF PLANNING OBLIGATIONS

Section 106 of the 1990 Act provided that any person interested in land in the area of a local planning authority could, by agreement or otherwise, enter into an obligation (defined as 'a planning obligation'). The section provided that such obligation could restrict the development or use of land in some specified way; require specified operations or activities to be carried out in, on, under or over land; require the land to be used in some specified way; or require a sum or sums to be paid to the authority on a specified date or dates or periodically. It is interesting to note that the section set out in rather more detail than did the old provisions the purpose of a planning obligation. The obligation could provide for money payments to be made, either of a specific amount or by reference to a formula, and require periodical payments to be paid indefinitely or for a specific period. There is no specific requirement, however, that the payments relate to the land itself or to the development which is to be carried out. **18.27**

It will be apparent that it was open to a developer to agree with a local planning authority to enter into a planning obligation. Such agreement, however, was no longer essential. It could be, therefore, that after negotiation with a developer the local planning authority **18.28** declined to accept a planning obligation offered by the developer. Under these provisions however, on an appeal to the Secretary of State against the refusal of planning permission (or perhaps an appeal against non-determination of an application), the Secretary of State was able, at the same time as granting planning permission, to accept under s 106 an undertaking by the developer to which the local planning authority was not a party but which, when accepted by the Secretary of State, was enforceable by the authority against the party giving it and any of their successors in title. It should be noted that there was no power for the Secretary of State, or any other person, to enforce the obligation.

18.29 The section provided also that in the event of a breach of any requirement in a planning obligation to carry out any operations, the local planning authority could enter the land and carry out the operations and recover the cost of doing so from the person against whom the obligation was enforceable. The authority was also given the power to enforce the obligation by injunction. The section further provided that a planning obligation could not be entered into except by way of a deed (presumably to ensure enforceability should there be an absence of consideration from the authority); that the deed should state that the obligation is a planning obligation for the purposes of the section; that it identified the land concerned; that it identified the person entering into the obligation and stated his interest; and that it identified the authority by whom the obligation was enforceable. Under the section a planning obligation could be unconditional or subject to conditions. It could also impose restrictions or requirements for an indefinite or specified period, thus enabling, for example, an obligation to end when a planning permission expired.

18.30 Following the cases of *R v South Northamptonshire DC, ex p Crest Homes plc* [1995] JPL 200, and *Wimpey Homes Holdings Ltd v Secretary of State* [1993] JPL 919, it seems that a planning obligation expressed in positive terms to transfer land was within s 106, as it would not directly impose any restriction on the development or use of land. A requirement to transfer land could, it seemed, be imposed indirectly under s 106, by means of an obligation restricting the use or development of land until such a transfer occurs.

18.31 A problem arose, however, if a s 106 obligation or agreement sought to transfer land to a person who is not a party to it. In *Jelson Ltd v Derby City Council* [2000] JPL 203, it was considered that whilst the provisions of s 106 were based in public law, it took effect subject to the ordinary rules of contract. One of the key contractual rules arises from s 2 of the Law of Property (Miscellaneous Provisions) Act 1989. The section requires, *inter alia*, a contract for the sale of land to be in writing and to be signed by or on behalf of each party to the contract. In the *Jelson* case, the company had agreed to transfer land to the Council's then undisclosed nominee housing association. Because the s 106 agreement lacked the signature of the intending 'purchaser' it was held to have fallen foul of s 2 of the 1989 Act. The Court held, however, that apart from the agreement to transfer the land, the agreement remained in effect between the parties.

18.32 Section 106 also provided that a planning obligation shall be a local land charge for the purposes of the Local Land Charges Act 1975. If, therefore, it is not registered as a local land charge, it remains binding upon a bona fide purchaser of the land for value, but such purchaser will be entitled under the Act to compensation for non-registration.

E. MODIFICATION AND DISCHARGE OF PLANNING OBLIGATIONS

Under the pre-1991 law, any person wishing to secure the modification or discharge of a restrictive covenant entered into as part of a s 52 agreement, could apply to the Lands Tribunal under s 84 of the Law of Property Act 1925. This procedure was considered to be unsatisfactory, since, as previously stated, the discharge or modification of positive covenants in an agreement was outwith the jurisdiction of the Lands Tribunal; and in determining whether or not to allow discharge or modification of restrictive covenants, the courts have taken the view that a restrictive covenant such as one not to build on land is not necessarily obsolete because planning permission has since been granted for the development of that land. **18.33**

Accordingly, it was decided that, since covenants are entered into exclusively for a planning purpose, the jurisdiction of the Lands Tribunal should not apply to planning obligations. Section 106A of the 1990 Act, therefore, provided that any person against whom a planning obligation was enforceable at any time after the 'relevant period', could apply to the local planning authority by whom the obligation was enforceable for the obligation to be modified in some specified way or to be discharged. The 'relevant period' was such period as may be prescribed by the Secretary of State, or a period of five years from the date the obligation was entered into. No 'relevant period' has even been prescribed. **18.34**

Where an application was made to a local planning authority to modify or discharge a planning obligation, the authority could determine that the obligation should continue to have effect without modification; or if the obligation no longer serves a useful purpose, that it should be discharged; or if the obligation continued to serve a useful purpose but would serve that purpose equally well if it had effect subject to the modifications specified in the application, that it should have effect subject to those modifications. **18.35**

In Circular 1/97 however, it was considered that the term 'useful purpose' should be understood in land-use planning terms. It seems therefore, that if the sole remaining purpose of a planning obligation was to meet a non-planning objective, it should be discharged. Finally, an application to modify had to be considered in its entirety. It was not possible for an authority to approve an application on the basis of accepting some of the proposed new definitions, but rejecting others. **18.36**

F. APPEALS

Section 106B of the 1990 Act provided for a right of appeal to the Secretary of State when a local planning authority failed to determine an application for the discharge or modification of a planning obligation within the prescribed period for so doing, or determined that a planning obligation should continue to have effect without modification. On an appeal, the Secretary of State had the same powers in relation to the application as had the local planning authority. Where an appeal was made under these provisions, the applicant or the authority had to be given an opportunity of appearing before and being heard by a person appointed by the Secretary of State for that purpose. **18.37**

18.38 The statutory provisions enabled the Secretary of State to make regulations governing applications to a local planning authority to modify or discharge a planning obligation and appeals to the Secretary of State when such applications are refused or not determined. The regulations made provision with regard to the form and content of applications and appeals, notification of and publicity for applications, determination of applications and determination of appeals by persons appointed by the Secretary of State.

18.39 It should be noted that the 1991 Act also altered the position with regard to Crown land. Once an obligation was entered into, the obligation could be enforced against any person with a private interest in the land. In any other case, however, enforcement of the obligation, whether by injunction or by entering land, requires the consent of the appropriate authority.

G. AMENDMENT OF PLANNING OBLIGATIONS

18.40 It seems clear that the parties to a s 106 obligation may by agreement amend the original agreement entered into. What is not clear is whether a s 106 agreement can be used to amend an existing s 52 agreement. In *R v Merton LBC, ex p Barker* [1998] JPL 440, Latham J held, without deciding the issue, that the question seemed to him to be 'at the very least arguable'.

H. THE SECRETARY OF STATE'S POLICY

18.41 In order to seek to prevent the kind of abuse with planning obligations as had occurred in the case of planning agreements, namely that planning permissions might be bought and sold, the policy of the Government contained in Circular 1/97 was to require a fair, open and reasonable negotiation of planning obligations, so that the obligations enhanced the quality of the development and enabled proposals to go ahead which might otherwise be refused. In particular, the circular advised that local planning authorities should not seek a contribution through a planning obligation unless it was:

- relevant to planning;
- directly related to the proposed development;
- fairly and reasonably related in scale and kind to the proposed development; and
- reasonable in all other respects.

A recent example of the application of the Secretary of State's policy, occurred in considering whether a developer contribution towards the provision of primary health care to serve the needs of new residents in the proposed development could be justified. The Secretary of State took the view that the decision test in that matter was whether the development would give rise to the need for additional investment in primary health care services which would not have been needed had the development not gone ahead.

18.42 That policy has become known as the 'necessity test'. Decisions of the courts in two landmark cases however, have established that the failure to comply with the requirements by an earlier Circular 16/91 which had set out the same test, would not invalidate a planning permission as a matter of law. The two cases were:

(a) *R v Plymouth City Council, ex p Plymouth and South Devon Co-operative Society* [1993] JPL 1099

In 1992, the market leaders in the food retailing business J. Sainsbury plc and Tesco Stores Ltd were each granted planning permission by Plymouth City Council, the local planning authority for the city, for the erection of a superstore on the city's outskirts. Both permissions were dependent upon the companies entering into an agreement under s 106 of the 1990 Act as amended whereby each company covenanted to provide, or provide funding for, various projects which formed no part of the development itself. In particular, J. Sainsbury plc agreed to provide the city with a tourist information centre, an Art gallery display and a bird-watching hide. The company also agreed to make contributions towards the development of the city's park-and-ride facilities and a much-needed increase in the city's crèche provision for working mothers. The total cost to the company of meeting these and other covenants was to be in excess of £3.6 million. Tesco Stores Ltd too agreed to provide, following the grant of planning permission, a variety of benefits not directly related to the development for which the company had applied.

Not surprisingly, the third major food retailer present in the area, the Plymouth and South Devon Co-operative Society, sought (albeit unsuccessfully) both in the High Court and the Court of Appeal to challenge the Council's decision. The society had found itself faced with two competitors, whereas previously it had expected that there would, at most, be only one. **18.43**

It will be recalled that s 70(2) of the 1990 Act provides that in determining an application for planning permission, the local planning authority 'shall have regard to the provision of the development plan, so far as material to the application, and to any other material consideration'. The Society's case was that the City Council had acted unlawfully by taking into account immaterial considerations, namely, the offers by the other two food retailers to provide some or all of the community benefits. The Society argued that in order for a benefit to be taken into account it had to be 'necessary', that is, needed in order to overcome what would otherwise be a planning objection to the development or some harm which would flow from it. Both the High Court and the Court of Appeal rejected the Society's argument. A unanimous Court of Appeal [1993] JPL 1099 held that the test of materiality was (as with a condition imposed in a grant of planning permission by the *Newbury* case) threefold, namely, it had to serve a planning purpose; it had to fairly and reasonably relate to the development permitted; and it had to be not *Wednesbury* unreasonable. The Court of Appeal held that all the benefits offered by Sainsbury's and Tesco met that threefold test. **18.44**

The decision of the Court of Appeal was thought by many as likely to have far-reaching consequences. It would seem that in determining applications for planning permission, a local planning authority could take into account any benefit (including those not necessary for the development to proceed) provided that it fairly and reasonably relates to the permitted development. The benefit no longer had to be one whose absence would justify the refusal of planning permission. The decision suggested that the advice contained in the then Circular 16/91 was, at best, inaccurate. At worst, it indicated an avenue whereby the test laid down in the Circular could be circumvented by a developer anxious to secure planning **18.45** permission from a local planning authority who are themselves anxious to obtain a contribution from developers to meet the cost of other socially desirable benefits. Above all, despite judicial statement in the case that planning permission cannot be bought or sold, it raised the spectre that this indeed could happen, particularly in those cases where the scales between a grant or refusal of planning permission were evenly balanced.

(b) *Tesco Stores Ltd v Secretary of State for the Environment* [1995] 1 WLR 759

Here both Tesco Stores Ltd and Tarmac Properties Ltd sought planning permission to build a retail store on the outskirts of Witney in Oxfordshire. Following a public inquiry into both proposals, the Inspector recommended permission for Tesco but not for Tarmac. Contrary to those recommendations the Secretary of State refused Tesco's application but granted Tarmac permission.

18.46 At the public inquiry, the county council had argued that full private funding for a new road to the west of the town (the West End Link Road) had to be provided if a superstore was to be built on either of the proposed sites. Tesco was willing to provide such funding if it was permitted to develop its site.

18.47 The Secretary of State considered that, given the distance between the link road and the proposed store, the relationship between them was tenuous. Using the tests of reasonableness set out in Circular 16/91, the Secretary of State did not consider that the link road was necessary to enable any of the superstore proposals to go ahead, or was otherwise so directly related in scale to any of the proposed developments that they might not be permitted without it. Full funding of the link road was not, according to the Secretary of State, fairly and reasonably related in scale to any of the proposed developments. Furthermore, given that the increase in traffic using the link road as a result of building the superstore might be less than 10 per cent, it would be unreasonable to seek even a partial contribution from developers towards the cost.

18.48 Tesco applied under s 228 of the 1990 Act for the Secretary of State's decisions to be quashed. It argued that its offer to fund the link road was a material consideration which the Secretary of State should have taken into account and that he had erred in applying the tests Circular 16/91, in particular, that he had applied an inappropriate test of necessity. This challenge was upheld in the High Court but rejected by the Court of Appeal.

18.49 In the High Court the learned deputy judge, following the *Plymouth* case, held that although the offer of full funding went beyond what was 'necessary', it was a material consideration because it was fairly and reasonably related to the proposed development. Although the tests in *Newbury District Council v Secretary of State for the Environment* [1981] AC 578 (which had been applied to planning obligations in the *Plymouth* case) were silent on the question of scale, the Secretary of State should have had regard to the Tesco offer. The Court of Appeal, however, held that he had indeed done so, but because the Secretary of State had found that there was only a tenuous connection between the link road and the proposed development, he must have concluded that the offer of full funding was material but had given it no weight, which he was entitled to do. Steyn LJ said that it was not open to the Secretary of State to dilute the *Newbury* requirements but, in the exercise of his wide statutory discretion, he could adopt a more stringent policy. However, Steyn LJ, considered that the Secretary of State had done this, but that his reasoning could not easily be reconciled with the decision in the *Plymouth* case, which he considered 'obliquely destroyed the core of the Circular' and 'became perilously close to emasculating the principle that planning permission may not be sold and bought'.

In the House of Lords, their Lordships upheld the decision of the Court of Appeal that the Secretary of State had not erred in law in dismissing Tesco's application for a retail store and in granting permission to Tarmac for similar development. According to their Lordships, the test to be applied in determining whether a planning obligation was a material consideration was whether it had some connection with the proposed development which was not *de minimis*. If that connection was established, the planning obligation had to be taken into account by the local planning authority. Their Lordships went on to say that once the link was established, the weight to be given to the planning obligation was a matter for the decision-maker, subject only to the obligation not to act unreasonably in the *Wednesbury* sense and to have regard to established planning policies. In the *Tesco* case their Lordships agreed that the Secretary of State had taken into account Tesco's offer to fund the link road but had given the offer little weight, as he was entitled to do. **18.50**

One effect of the House of Lord's judgment was that there was now no requirement that in order for a planning obligation to be within 'the law', it had to be necessary in order to enable the development proposed to proceed. In practice, the decision meant that local planning authorities had the same freedom to consider, but then still decline to follow, any government policy statements on planning obligations as they are on any other matter. **18.51**

Although it was recognised in the *Tesco* case that the Secretary of State's policy was a lawful policy, it was nevertheless more restrictive than the law. Ministerial policy is of course a material consideration to be taken into account in the determination of planning permissions. If local planning authorities decide to give that policy little weight, however, and to seek additional benefits outside the scope of that policy, they had no need to fear that courts would interfere simply because they did not follow that advice. No policy could control the scope of an obligation a developer is prepared to offer in an attempt to seek planning permission, other than the public law tests of relevance to the development proposed and *Wednesbury* unreasonableness. **18.52**

The onus of showing that in accepting a s 106 obligation a local planning authority has acted unlawfully, whilst extremely difficult to meet, was not entirely impossible. In *R v South Holland DC, ex p Lincoln Co-operative Society Ltd* [2001] JPL675, a developer had offered the local planning authority £100,000 to redress the harmful effect of granting planning permission for a supermarket. The development was contrary to the development plan and a previous application for permission for the same development without any s 106 offer accompanying it had been earlier refused. Quashing the grant of planning permission, the High Court held that although the planning obligation was one which the authority was entitled to take into account, it was at the very lower limit of materiality; but that the weight to be to given to it was entirely a matter for the decision-maker. However, there had been no evaluation of what could be achieved with that sum; and the decision was so much against the weight of the material before the authority that the only conclusion to be drawn was that the decision was obviously wrong. There were also no rational grounds for believing that the sum of £100,000 could significantly redress the harm envisaged by the development let alone outweigh it. The decision was such that no reasonable authority could have taken it. **18.53**

18.54 However, given the great difficulty there normally is in successfully challenging decisions of local authorities on grounds of *Wednesbury* unreasonableness (or perhaps perversity) the prospect of the purchase of planning permissions by developers was not discouraged by the decision.

18.55 There were a number of other problems associated with the system of planning obligations. One problem arose from the fact that development within the area of one local planning authority may also have consequences for adjacent land which is in the area of another local planning authority. The harmful effects can be diluted, removed or compensated for by the use of a s 106 obligation as regards land within the area of the local planning authority in which the development is to take place. It is more difficult, however, to provide like benefits by a s 106 obligation for land in the area of another local planning authority when that authority is not the body granting the permission.

18.56 A second problem could occur when a developer had entered into a s 106 obligation, whereby the developer has agreed to contribute to the road infrastructure costs associated with development for which planning permission was being granted. Subsequently, another developer applied for planning permission for nearby land, and benefits from the road infrastructure provided previously by the first developer. The result is that the road infrastructure costs which should be shared equitably between both developers, are in fact borne by the developer who applied for planning permission first. How this problem could arise can be seen by the facts of *R (on the application of Lichfield Securities Ltd) v Lichfield DC and Christopher JN Williams* [2001] PLCR 519. The issue in that case flowed from an agreement made under s 106, whereby a developer agreed to pay to the local planning authority a contribution towards the cost of improvements to the local highway network. A second developer wishing to develop adjacent land then sought details from the local planning authority as to the methodology of calculation and as to the amount of contribution which the first developer was being required to pay under the s 106 agreement, on the ground that this would affect the amount of their own contribution. Being dissatisfied with the local planning authority's response the second developer successfully obtained from the Court of Appeal judicial review of the authority's decision as being procedurally unfair. Although the case was not directly on the point, the system did not allow a local planning authority to require a developer to make a contribution to the case of a benefit that has already been provided by another developer's planning obligation.

I. EXAMPLES OF PLANNING OBLIGATIONS

18.57 Circular 1/97 contained examples of planning obligations that an authority may be able to seek in relation to particular kinds of development. They may include the provision or a contribution towards the cost of new access roads, bus shelters, open spaces, improving junction lay-outs, new or improved rail/bus stations or facilities, park and ride schemes, measures for cyclists/pedestrians of library facilities and the provision of social, educational, recreational, or sporting facilities. They may also be used to secure the inclusion of an element of affordable housing in large residential development. In addition, the Government had indicated that planning obligations could cover the provision of new shop fronts, payment for repairs to pavements and contributions towards local educational provision.

Examples of the use to which planning obligations have been put in recent Ministerial decisions include: **18.58**

- a contribution of £5m to public transport, mostly in respect of a station on a Metro to be built close to the development site;
- the provision of public conveniences;
- the inclusion of public Art works to a minimum of £100,000 in value;
- the provision of CCTV security to be connected to the central 'Citywatch' system;
- the payment of £265,000 per annum for three years towards a subsidy of bus services;
- the payment of £55,000 for traffic calming measures;
- the laying out and maintenance of public open space, amenity land and provision of a children's play area;
- the regulation of aircraft noise arising from an extension to buildings at an existing airport;
- the provision of cycleways and dedicated bus-lanes to ease congestion caused by the development proposed;
- a contribution towards the provision of additional educational facilities resulting from residential development;
- the restriction on flat occupancy to persons over the age of 60;
- the giving of instructions to drivers of heavy goods vehicles under the landowner's control, not to use specific roads and to make appropriate arrangements to ensure that they do not do so.
- Improving inadequate flood defenses to benefit both the development site and adjacent land.

Sometimes s.106 obligations have been used in an unusual way. In one recent case an Inspector held that an obligation which prohibited the occupants of a block of twelve flats from keeping cats and dogs or owning predatory animals was acceptable, because it would overcome the adverse impact of the development in a special area of conservation established under the European Habitat Directive (Ref. APP/U1240/A/03/1108797). In another case, planning permission had been sought for the replacement of a dwelling close to the cliff edge which was in danger of collapse within a few years. The new dwelling was to be situated further back from the cliff face where it would have an 'extended life'. The obligation would have sought to exonerate the local planning authority from any liability should the replacement dwelling subsequently collapse. The Inspector held that in the circumstances a s.106 obligation was justified, but since none had been provided, this counted against the grant of planning permission (Ref. APP/Q6810/A/03/1132068). **18.59**

In addition, it should be mentioned that, quite independent of s 106, where off-site highway works are required in order to enable development to proceed, s 278 of the Highways Act 1980 requires the developer to enter into an agreement with the highways authority that it will either carry out the highways work itself, or pay the cost of doing so to the highways authority. **18.60**

J. PLANNING CONTRIBUTIONS

18.61 The operation of the system of planning obligations showed not only a distinction between case law and Ministerial policy, but a lack of clarity about the sort of contributions that could be sought or offered. In addition, it was found that some agreements took an unacceptably long time to negotiate and could involve high legal costs. The Government decided therefore, that the old system should be overhauled and a new system called 'planning contributions' introduced which would retain some elements of the old but provide greater transparency, predictability and accountability.

18.62 Accordingly, the 1990 Act is to be amended by section 46 to 48 of the Planning and Compulsory Purchase Act 2004. When these provisions are fully implemented, they will allow for the introduction of an alternative to planning obligations whereby developers make contributions towards services and facilities relating to their proposed development. This will be done by repealing ss 106, 106A, and 106B and their replacement by new provisions. In particular the new s. 106 provides for two different forms or methods for developers' contributions in place of one, and both of these will be known as planning contributions.

18.63 The first form or method is defined as 'the prescribed means'. The prescribed means will involve either

> *the payment of a sum* calculated in accordance with the criteria set by the local planning authority in a development plan document or some other prescribed document; or
> *the provision of a benefit in kind*, the value of which is to be calculated in accordance with the criteria set out in a development plan document or some other prescribed document; or
> a combination of both the above.

18.64 In preliminary consultations during the passage of the legislation through Parliament, the term 'prescribed means' were there described as an optional (planning) charge. Although it may be misleading to use the term 'optional', it is certainly a planning charge and is likely to become known by that term henceforth.

18.65 The planning charge method of providing a planning contribution clearly requires that the local planning authority should have a contributions policy. This is achieved by a provision which enables the Secretary of State to require local planning authorities to include in a development plan document:

- the types of development for which it is likely to seek a contribution;
- development where a contribution via a charge will be sought;
- how funds obtained through planning contributions will be used by the local planning authority; and
- how any contribution will be calculated.

18.66 The second such form or method of planning contribution provides for a negotiated planning contribution, equivalent to the system of planning obligation. Because of that, it is likely to continue to be known as a planning obligation.

18.67 As with the planning charge the Secretary of State is given power to make regulations requiring a local planning authority to include in a development plan document, or other prescribed document, the types of development for which it is likely to seek a contribution, how funds obtained through the planning obligation form of planning contribution will be used by the local planning authority, and how the contribution will be calculated.

The new provisions provide for the possibility of a developer offering both a planning contribution by means of a planning charge, and also by way of a contribution via the new form of planning obligation. **18.68**

The provisions to be introduced by the Planning and Compulsory Purchase Act 2004 provide merely the outline of the new system of planning contributions. The detailed operation of the system will depend upon regulations to be made by the Secretary of State. The Government has indicated that the following regulations (all of which will be subject to the affirmative resolution procedure) are to be made: **18.69**

(a) to allow the Secretary of State to specify maximum and minimum amounts that may be prescribed by an LPA, where a planning contribution is offered by the prescribed means.

(b) to provide that the Secretary of State may make regulations allowing periodic adjustment of the criteria by which the LPA will determine the value of a contribution by the prescribed means. This is intended to allow amounts set by the prescribed means to be automatically uprated according to an index such as the RPI or a construction prices index without having to review the document in which the planning contributions policy (and therefore the amounts prescribed) are published.

(c) to provide that the Secretary of State may require LPAs to publish an annual report on planning contributions. Regulations would set out the matters on which local planning authorities should report — these might include the matters in relation to which a planning contribution has been sought, and how receipts from the prescribed means have been spent.

(d) to provide for the Secretary of State to make regulations relating to the means by which a planning contribution may be made. The regulations will provide that the person making the planning contribution must indicate that he wishes to make the contribution by paying the optional planning charge (the prescribed means) set by the LPA, rather than negotiate the terms of his contribution; regulations to provide that where a contributor makes a contribution through the charge (prescribed means), he is not also required to make the same contribution through a negotiated agreement (the relevant requirements), and vice versa. (This provision is designed to ensure that developers are not asked to contribute twice in relation to the same matters); regulations to provide that where a contribution has been made by compliance with the relevant requirements it may not be made by the prescribed means. (Again, this provision is designed to ensure that developers are not asked to contribute twice in relation to the same matters); regulations to provide for circumstances when no contribution must be required by the LPA.

(e) to enable the Secretary of State, where a document other than a development plan document will contain the matters where a planning contribution will be sought, to set out the procedure for the preparation and publication of the LPA's policy on planning contributions. It also provides, that the Secretary of State may himself take steps in relation to the preparation of such a document — for example, where the local planning authority fails to prepare one.

(f) to empower the Secretary of State to make regulations concerning the enforcement of planning contributions. These may include binding persons deriving title in the land, to which the planning contribution applies, to the terms of the planning contribution; enabling the Secretary of State to attach a condition to a planning permission requiring the payment of the planning contribution prior to the commencement of development; and to include the enforcement of planning contributions made in relation to Crown Land.

(g) to enable regulation to provide that the LPA may only apply receipts of contributions obtained by prescribed means to the matters described by the local planning authority in its planning contributions policy set out in a development plan document or such other document prescribed.

(h) to enable the Secretary of State to make provisions as to how the terms of the planning contribution will be set out. In the case of a negotiated agreement as to relevant requirements, it is envisaged that the terms of the contribution will be through a legal document similar to the system contemplated by the now repealed section 106 of the Town and Country Planning Act 1990. In the case of contributions made by the prescribed means, it is envisaged that regulations will set out a standard form of agreement.

(i) to enable the Secretary of State to make provisions in relation to the modification and discharge of a planning contribution. These matters are currently covered by section 106A and 106B in the Town and Country Planning Act 1990, but will be replaced with similar provisions in Regulations.

(j) to enable the Secretary of State to provide different provisions for different areas or descriptions of local authorities and exclude the application of the regulations to particular areas or descriptions of local authorities.

18.70 The Government has indicated that it does not intend to use the powers contained in ss. 46 and 47 Planning and Compulsory Purchase Act 2004 and proceed with the making of regulations necessary to introduce planning obligations on the new statutory basis until some time in 2005. It is, however, proceeding with consultation on a draft Circular to replace Circular 1/97. The main changes proposed in the draft are as follows:

— Retention/simplification of policy tests
— New typology for the use of planning obligations
— Clarification of policy on contributions for affordable housing
— Clarification of guidance on use of maintenance payments
— Clarification of guidance on pooled contributions
— Stronger emphasis on national, regional and local plan policies
— Encouragement of joining up across all public sector infrastructure providers
— Encouragement of use of formulae and standard charges
— New guidance on use of standard agreements/undertakings
— New guidance on use of independent third parties
— New guidance on cost recovery
— Encouragement of the use of unilateral undertakings
— New guidance on monitoring of implementation of planning obligations

19

APPEALS; STATUTORY REVIEW; JUDICIAL REVIEW; THE OMBUDSMAN

A. APPEALS

19.01 From most decisions of local planning authorities there is an appeal to the Secretary of State and from him to the courts on a point of law. In determining an appeal, the Secretary of State may allow the appeal, dismiss it, reverse or vary any part of the decision of the local planning authority and generally deal with the appeal as if it were before him in the first instance.

19.02 The main right of appeal is that given by s 78 of the 1990 Act, which provides for an appeal against the refusal of planning permission or a conditional grant of planning permission. Circular 05/2000 gives advice on the procedures for handling appeals under s 78. Annexes to the Circular deal with each of the various forms of appeal; a Code of Practice on Preparing for Major Planning Inquiries; and a statement of Government policy on called-in planning applications.

19.03 The s 78 machinery is also available where the local planning authority have failed to give a decision on an application for planning permission within the period prescribed for so doing, and appeals against the refusal of any approval required under the General Development Procedure Order or an outline planning permission.

19.04 Other appeal machinery exists in relation to enforcement notices, listed buildings and conservation area consents, listed building enforcement notices, certificates of lawfulness of existing or proposed use or development, tree preservation orders and advertising consent.

19.05 It sometimes happens that a local planning authority may consider that for one reason or another an application for planning permission is invalid. This may occur, for example, if an authority considers insufficient detail has been submitted by the applicant for the authority to determine the application. The question then arises as to whether the Secretary of State has jurisdiction to entertain an appeal by the applicant as a result of the authority's non-determination. In two recent decisions, the Court of Appeal decided that he had. In *Geall v Secretary of State for the Environment* [1999] JPL 909 the Court held that an Inspector can decide whether an application is or is not valid. Thus, if he decides the application is invalid, he must (on behalf of the Secretary of State) refuse to entertain the appeal. In *R v Secretary of State for the Environment, ex p Bath and North Somerset DC* [1999] 1 WLR 1759, the Court of Appeal applied the principle to listed building applications and held that a local planning authority was required by statute to determine an application. The right of appeal to the Secretary of State was available even when the authority had formed the opinion that the application was invalid, and the applicant was entitled to have the opinion of the Secretary of State on the question of its validity.

19.06 Unless an application for planning permission is granted unconditionally, the applicant is told in addition to the decision a summary of policies and proposals in the development plan relevant to the discussion. This duty was emphasised by the High Court in *R (Wall) v Brighton and Hove District Council (Co)* 2924/2004. He is also told that he must give notice of appeal to the Secretary of State within a period of six months or, where there are extraordinary circumstances, such longer period as the Secretary of State may allow.

19.07 A notice of appeal, made by completing a form obtainable from the Secretary of State, should be accompanied by a copy of such of the following documents as are relevant to the appeal:

(a) the application made to the local planning authority which has occasioned the appeal;
(b) all plans, drawings and documents sent to the authority in connection with the application;
(c) all correspondence with the authority relating to the application;
(d) any notices or any certificates provided to the authority in accordance with the provisions of a development order made under s 65 of the Act;
(e) any other plans or drawings relating to the application which were not sent to the authority;
(f) the notice of the decision if any;
(g) if the appeal relates to an application for approval of reserved matters, the application for outline planning permission, the plans submitted with that application and the outline planning permission granted.

An applicant must also send a copy of the notice of appeal, and of any such plans or drawings mentioned in para (e) as accompany it, to the local planning authority on the same date as he gives notice to the Secretary of State.

The Secretary of State is not bound to entertain the appeal, though the occasions on which he has not done so are thought to be rare. Under s 79(6) of the 1990 Act, if the Secretary of State is of the opinion that, having regard to the provisions of ss 70 and 72(1) of the Act and the development order, planning permission could not have been granted by the local planning authority or could not have been granted by the authority otherwise than subject to the conditions imposed, he may decline to determine the appeal. This might occur, for example, where the local planning authority has been directed by the Secretary of State to refuse planning permission or to impose conditions on any permission granted. **19.08**

Furthermore, if an applicant fails to serve any of the documents (see (a) to (g) above) on the Secretary of State within the time limit of six months provided, the Secretary of State may refuse to accept the notice of appeal. **19.09**

Before determining an appeal under s 78, the Secretary of State is required by s 79(2), if either the applicant or the local planning authority so desire, to afford to each of them an opportunity of appearing before and being heard by, a person appointed by the Secretary of State for that purpose. In the more important cases where use is made of this facility, a public local inquiry takes place before a person appointed for that purpose, known as an 'Inspector'. **19.10**

Although in law the decision made on appeal is that of the Secretary of State, the majority of appeal decisions are made by Inspectors, that is, by members of the Department's Planning Inspectorate, standing in the shoes of the Secretary of State. In 1968 it was established that more than 90 per cent of the recommendations made by Inspectors to the Minister were accepted by him. It was decided, therefore, to give Inspectors the power to make decisions on behalf of the Minister. These cases are sometimes referred to as 'transferred cases'. Given originally for a limited class of development and a limited range of appeals, the power has been gradually extended and now by the Town and Country Planning (Determination of Appeals by Appointed Persons) (Prescribed Classes) Regulations 1997 (SI 1997/420), applies to all planning appeals (with the exception of appeals by statutory undertakers relating to the development of operational land), to all enforcement notice appeals made under s 78 of **19.11**

the 1990 Act (except those relating to development for which an environmental statement is required and to some appeals made against the refusal of listed building consent and listed building enforcement notices relating to Grade II (non-starred) listed buildings. Under the 1990 Act, however, the Secretary of State has the power to recover the jurisdiction to decide an appeal from an Inspector in any other particular case. These cases are known as 'recovered' cases.

19.12 Among the criteria for recovering jurisdiction are the following:

(a) Residential development of five or more hectares or of 150 or more dwellings regardless of size of site.
(b) Proposals for development of major importance having more than local significance.
(c) Proposals giving rise to significant public controversy.
(d) Proposals which raise important or novel issues of development control.
(e) Retail or leisure development over 9,000 sq m.
(f) Proposals for significant development in the Green Belt.
(g) Major proposals involving the winning and working of minerals.
(h) Proposals which raise legal difficulties.
(i) Proposals against which another Government Department has raised major objections.
(j) Cases which can only be decided in conjunction with a case over which Inspectors have no jurisdiction (so-called 'linked' cases). The most common example of this is where a s 78 appeal is being processed concurrently with consideration of a draft public path diversion order under ss 247 and 253 of the 1990 Act, where Inspectors have no jurisdiction to decide.
(k) Other cases which merit recovery because of the particular circumstances.

19.13 In the year 2003/04, of 18,200 appeals decided in England, 97.8 per cent were decided by Inspectors on behalf of the Secretary of State. Only 264 appeals were recovered and decided by the Secretary of State.

19.14 Not every case recovered by the Secretary of State for his own decision necessarily involves the Secretary of State personally making the decision. It will often be made by a senior official in the decision branch of the Department, acting for the Secretary of State. Recovered cases which are likely to be referred personally to the Secretary of State include:

(a) Cases in which the decision branch propose to go against the Inspector's recommendation on the planning merits.
(b) Cases involving significant development in the green belt.
(c) Where the proposed decision is to refuse permission for a development involving more than 150 dwellings, or covering more than 6 hectares.
(d) Where it appears that there is considerable political interest because of representations received from a Member of Parliament.
(e) Sensitive or major appeals.

B. DISMISSAL OF APPEALS IN CASES OF UNDUE DELAY

19.15 The 1991 Act introduced a provision in the 1990 Act to deal with delay by developers in the determination of appeals. In the past this occurred with twin-tracking, the tactical device whereby developers submit two identical applications for planning permission to the local planning authority. The intention of doing so was to allow negotiations with the authority to continue on one application after the expiry of the eight-week period for the authority to determine the application, whilst at the same time lodging an appeal to the Secretary of State against non-determination of the other application. Once an appeal was lodged, the developer would do no more than the minimum necessary to pursue the appeal until the authority have either granted planning permission, in which case the appeal was withdrawn; or refuse planning permission, in which case the preparation for the appeal was reactivated. Such action may impose considerable additional costs on both the authority and the Planning Inspectorate. In order to deal with this problem, s 79 of the 1990 Act provides that if at any time before or during the determination of an appeal it appears to the Secretary of State that the appellant is responsible for undue delay in the progress of the appeal, he may give the appellant notice that the appeal will be dismissed unless the appellant takes within the period specified in the notice such steps as are specified in the notice for the expedition of the appeal. Then, if the appellant failed to take those steps within that period, the Secretary of State could dismiss the appeal without any consideration of its merits. The Planning and Compulsory Purchase Act 2004 makes further provision which, when fully implemented, will effectively end the practice of twin tracking.

C. NATURAL JUSTICE

It is a long-established principle that in the interval between the decision of the local planning authority and the decision of the Secretary of State (or Inspector), the Secretary of State should not 'listen to one party behind the back of the other'. In short, the decision-maker is required by the rules of natural justice 'to hear both sides'. **19.16**

One of the earliest cases to establish this was *Errington v Minister of Health* [1935] 1 KB 249, where the local authority had made a draft clearance order under housing legislation. Objections had been made to the order and a local inquiry held. After receiving the Inspector's report, the Minister had entered into correspondence with the authority and the Inspector, and an official of the Ministry and officers of the local authority had visited and conferred on the site. Subsequently, the Minister had confirmed the order. The objectors then successfully claimed that in hearing further evidence of one party (the local authority) behind the backs of the others (the objectors) the Minister had been guilty of a breach of natural justice and that his decision should not be allowed to stand. **19.17**

A landmark example is *Fairmount Investments Ltd v Secretary of State for the Environment* [1976] 1 WLR 1255. In this case the applicants owned a number of houses within an area declared to be a clearance area under the Housing Act 1957. The local planning authority had subsequently made a compulsory purchase order for the purpose of demolishing the houses which it considered to be unfit for human habitation. The applicants, who contended that the houses could be rehabilitated without demolition, objected to the order and an inquiry was duly held. At the inquiry the authority published documents showing the reasons for the order and a summary of the principal grounds of unfitness. This emphasised settlement **19.18** but did not suggest that it was a continuing problem. The summary did not refer to the foundations of the applicants' property nor did it suggest that they were defective and at the inquiry no reference was made to the foundations. Following the inquiry, the Inspector had visited the houses in question. In his report he had stated that the settlement in all the houses appeared to be due to the foundations 'not having been taken deeply enough into the clay'. He concluded that because of that it was his opinion that 'satisfactory rehabilitation would not be financially viable'. Following his report, the Secretary of State had confirmed the order.

19.19 In quashing the Secretary of State's decision, the House of Lords held that the decision had been made in breach of the rules of natural justice. It had been based on an opinion formed by the Inspector about the adequacy of the foundations which had not formed part of the authority's case and which the applicants had not been given an opportunity to refute. In the words of Lord Russell of Killowen, the applicants had not had 'a fair crack of the whip'.

19.20 Unfortunately, the application of the rules of natural justice to administrative decisions must remain uncertain both as regards their extent and scope. With thousands of appeal decisions to be made each year, administrators require something more concrete on which to base the conduct of the inquiry process than sporadic judicial decisions. Accordingly, the Lord Chancellor, after consultation with the Secretary of State, has exercised a power under s 9 of the Tribunals and Inquiries Act 1992 and other legislation to make rules for the conduct of appeals. In the field of s 78 appeals, the existence of statutory rules now means that appeals have to be conducted within the discipline of both the common law rules of natural justice and the statutory rules. Administrators know that if they comply with the statutory rules, they are not likely to infringe the rules of natural justice. But unfortunately, it does occasionally happen. The following cases are examples.

19.21 In *Hambledon & Chiddingfold Parish Councils v Secretary of State for the Environment* [1976] JPL 502, it was said that although compliance with the Inquiry Procedure Rules did not mean *ipso facto* that there must have been compliance with the rules of natural justice, a complainant attempting to show otherwise faced a heavy burden of proof.

19.22 In *Granada Theatres Ltd v Secretary of State for the Environment* [1976] JPL 96, it was held that taking into account petitions and letters not disclosed to the applicants was a breach of the rules of natural justice.

19.23 In *Hudson v Secretary of State for the Environment* [1984] JPL 258, it was held that the Inspector had erred in not giving the parties an opportunity to deal with a matter of substance which had influenced his decision.

19.24 In *Simmons v Secretary of State for the Environment* [1985] JPL 253, the Inspector was seen by the appellant in discussion with the chairman of the planning committee of the local planning authority after the close of the inquiry. Although the Inspector was totally absolved from any bias, the decision was quashed as being contrary to natural justice.

19.25 In *Furmston v Secretary of State for the Environment* [1983] JPL 49, the Secretary of State submitted to judgment and paid the applicant's costs where it was alleged the Inspector had discussed the applicant's development proposal with a representative of the district council before the site meeting and with a representative of the county council after the site meeting, without any representative of the applicant being present. Although in later correspondence with the applicant the Secretary of State had said that the discussion with the county council representative had been about the district council's lack of co-operation in forwarding documentation to them, the applicant pursued his challenge because he considered that justice must not only be done but seen to be done. In fact, the Secretary of State had nothing to lose by submitting to judgment; an identical planning application to the district planning authority having by then been granted.

In *Second City (South West) Ltd v Secretary of State for the Environment* (1990) 61 P & CR 498, the **19.26**
Secretary of State had dismissed an appeal against a refusal of planning permission for residential development. In his decision letter, the Secretary of State had referred to the site as being 'outside the village fence of Backwell as identified on the Woodspring Rural Areas Local Plan' which was on deposit, and where development would not be allowed. Because the applicants had not been given an opportunity to deal with this aspect, the High Court quashed the Secretary of State's decision.

In *Cadbury Schweppes Pension Trust Ltd v Secretary of State for the Environment* [1990] EGCS 86, **19.27**
an Inspector refused to relax a condition in a planning permission granted for mixed industrial and office use in adherence to a local policy statement for the provision of on-site car-parking. Because the applicant had not been given an opportunity to comment on the point or to show that it was fallacious the High Court quashed the decision.

In *Chartwell Land Development Ltd v Secretary of State for the Environment, Transport and the* **19.28**
Regions and Hillingdon LBC (16 April 1999), the High Court quashed a grant of planning permission on grounds that the decision was made contrary to natural justice, where an Inspector had failed to hear evidence from the applicants that a different road layout which they wished to propose would avoid disturbance to the living conditions of nearby residents.

A somewhat unusual case is *Rockhold Ltd v Secretary of State for the Environment* [1986] JPL 130, **19.29**
where three applications for planning permission had been made for the same site. Each had gone to appeal and different Inspectors had rejected the appeals for different reasons. The applicants had challenged the decision made by the last Inspector on a number of grounds, but in particular that the decision of an Inspector ought to be consistent with earlier decisions. Forbes J held that although Inspectors ought generally to be consistent in their decisions, each Inspector was free to exercise his own judgment on matters of planning merit. After the decision had been given, however, the appellants learnt that the Inspector who had determined the appeal had also acted as a field officer (planning) for a local amenity group, the Chiltern Society. His responsibilities there included the vetting of planning applications within the area covered by the Society. Although an appeal to the Court of Appeal from the decision of Forbes J was pending, the appellants sought and obtained leave to apply for judicial review of the Inspector's decision. One reason for so doing was that if an appeal under what is now s 288 of the 1990 Act were to succeed, it would not automatically follow that a fresh inquiry would be held. Another reason was that the additional ground of attack on the decision (namely the *appointment* of the Inspector) might not fall within the ambit of that section. The judicial review proceedings were subsequently abandoned, but only after the Court of Appeal had agreed (contrary to its normal practice) to quash the Inspector's decision by a consent order.

19.30 In another case, resolved without resort to the courts, the Inspector, accompanied by his architectural assessor, had, prior to the opening of a local inquiry into the applications for planning permission for the redevelopment of Limehouse Basin in London's East End, visited the site both on foot and by helicopter. The helicopter was, however, provided by the local planning authority and a representative of the authority had been present on the visit.

19.31 At the opening of the inquiry objectors to the application asked the Inspector to withdraw on the ground that there had been a breach of natural justice. The Inspector refused their request, but in turn offered them an opportunity to accompany him on a site visit by helicopter. This offer was accepted by some objectors but without prejudice to their rights, which they then pursued by asking the Secretary of State to intervene and remove the Inspector. This the Secretary of State duly did.

19.32 In a letter to the parties, the Secretary of State said he was satisfied that the Inspector did not in fact do anything on his original site visits which could in any way have resulted in unfairness to any of the parties at the inquiry; but he concluded that, in all the circumstances, the best course would be for him to close the inquiry and begin proceedings afresh, with a new Inspector and assessor.

19.33 The law does not require that Inspectors should deny themselves all social intercourse with the parties involved. In *Cotterell v Secretary of State for the Environment* [1991] JPL 1155, after a site visit, the Inspector had gone to a public house in the company of representatives of both sides. Before leaving the assembled company, the appellants' representative had offered to buy another round of drinks but this had been refused. In the event the Inspector remained in the pub with the other side for a further 20 minutes whilst they consumed another round of drinks bought by the Inspector. Dismissing an application to quash the Secretary of State's decision to uphold the local planning authority's refusal to grant planning permission for development, the learned deputy judge held that, bearing in mind the occasion started with everyone together and that the appellants' representative left the others alone, it fell on 'the right side of the line'.

19.34 In *Fox v Secretary of State* [1993] JPL 448, the High Court refused to quash a decision of the Secretary of State upholding the local planning authority's decision to refuse the appellant planning permission for residential development. The Inspector who conducted the inquiry had travelled to the appeal site in the company of the authority's planning officer and another witness. It appears that before doing so the Inspector had given the appellant assurances that he would not discuss the case during the journey; assurances which had been accepted by the appellant, who had travelled to the site on his own.

19.35 The Court took the view that in all the circumstances, a reasonable man would not have thought that anything might have taken place during the car journey which might have affected the Inspector's impartiality. Hence, there had been no breach of natural justice. The judge added, however, that he doubted the wisdom of the Inspector asking an unrepresented appellant whether he objected to him travelling without the appellant in a car with the council's witnesses.

D. WRITTEN REPRESENTATION PROCEDURE

Appeals may be dealt with by written representations, hearings or local inquiries. In most cases, the Secretary of State invites the appellant and the local planning authority to dispense with a local inquiry if he considers that he can obtain the information he needs to determine the appeal from written statements submitted by the parties. The advantage of this procedure is that it is often quicker, simpler and cheaper than proceeding by way of local inquiry. On average, inquiry appeals take twice as long to decide as written representation appeals. It is also advantageous if the matter in dispute is one of law rather than policy, since legal argument can be presented in written form at the outset, rather than presented orally before the Inspector. The disadvantage is that publicity and openness associated with the local inquiry are absent. So too, is the opportunity given to the parties to test the veracity of another party's evidence by way of cross-examination. Nevertheless, written representation procedure (as it is called) is extremely popular. Although either the appellant or the local planning authority can ask to be heard by an Inspector, in the year 2003/4 of 18,200 appeals decided under these provisions, 79 per cent were decided by way of written representation procedure, as against 5 per cent decided following a local inquiry and 16 per cent following a hearing. **19.36**

At one time the procedure depended upon informal agreement, subject only to compliance with the rules of natural justice. There were no procedural rules applicable as with local inquiries. Now s 323 of the 1990 Act provides that the Secretary of State may make regulations prescribing the procedure to be followed where an appeal is dealt with by this method. Under this power, the Secretary of State has made the Town and Country Planning (Appeals) (Written Representations Procedure) (England) Regulations 2000, SI 2000/1628. Circular 05/2000 (Annex 1) gives guidance on the operation of the regulations. **19.37**

One of the most recent examples of a breach of the rules of natural justice is *Jovy v Secretary of State for Transport, Local Government and the Regions and Asia House and Westminster City Council* [2003] JPL 549. There the High Court quashed the decision of an Inspector to grant planning permission for residential development after he had considered with the developer and the City Council the conditions subject to which the planning permission had been granted; but had not considered local residents who had appeared at the Inquiry and who had objected to the development. **19.38**

The procedure is best understood by refering to the following table which is reproduced from Annex 1 of Circular 05/2000. **19.39**

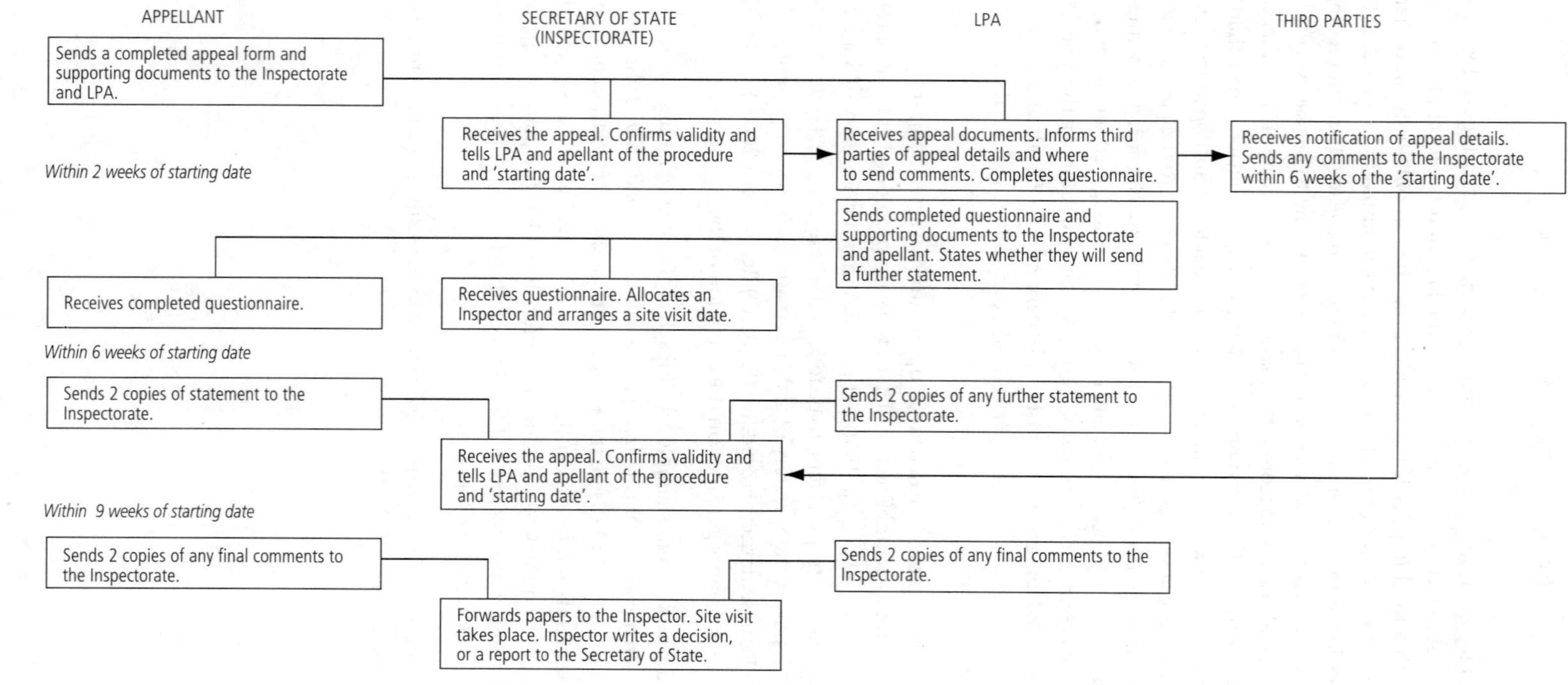
WRITTEN REPRESENTATIONS
APPELLANT
SECRETARY OF STATE (INSPECTORATE)
LPA
THIRD PARTIES
Sends a completed appeal form and supporting documents to the Inspectorate and LPA.
Receives the appeal. Confirms validity and tells LPA and apellant of the procedure and 'starting date'.
Receives appeal documents. Informs third parties of appeal details and where to send comments. Completes questionnaire.
Receives notification of appeal details. Sends any comments to the Inspectorate within 6 weeks of the 'starting date'.
Within 2 weeks of starting date
Sends completed questionnaire and supporting documents to the Inspectorate and apellant. States whether they will send a further statement.
Receives completed questionnaire.
Receives questionnaire. Allocates an Inspector and arranges a site visit date.
Within 6 weeks of starting date
Sends 2 copies of statement to the Inspectorate.
Sends 2 copies of any further statement to the Inspectorate.
Receives the appeal. Confirms validity and tells LPA and apellant of the procedure and 'starting date'.
Within 9 weeks of starting date
Sends 2 copies of any final comments to the Inspectorate.
Sends 2 copies of any final comments to the Inspectorate.
Forwards papers to the Inspector. Site visit takes place. Inspector writes a decision, or a report to the Secretary of State.

E. HEARINGS

19.40 As an alternative to written representation procedure or the formal local inquiry, the parties have in the past been invited by the Secretary of State to agree to the appeal being dealt with by a more informal procedure, namely a hearing. The procedure is now however, governed by formal rules, the Town and Country Planning (Hearings Procedure) (England) Rules 2000, SI 2000/ 1626. A hearing is likely to be suitable where the development is small-scale; there is little or no third party interest; complex legal, technical or policy issues are unlikely to arise; and there is no likelihood that formal cross-examination will be needed to test the opposing cases. Where a hearing takes place the Inspector takes a more active role in the proceedings by leading a discussion rather than by following the more formal procedures of the local inquiry. The proceedings are intended to be more relaxed than those of a local inquiry. These informal proceedings do not, however, absolve an Inspector from the duty to act fairly and to ensure that he takes into account all the information available to him before making his decision.

19.41 A reminder of the danger that the more relaxed atmosphere of non-inquiry procedures could lead not to a 'full and fair' hearing but to a less than thorough examination of the issues, so that the vigorous examination essential to the determination of difficult questions would be diluted, was given in *Dyason v Secretary of State for the Environment and Chiltern District Council* [1998] JPL 778. There, the Council had refused the applicant planning permission to carry out alterations to existing buildings to provide a single-storey building for ostrich breeding. Dyason appealed to the Secretary of State who held a hearing as opposed to a public inquiry. In advance of the hearing, Dyason submitted a business plan to the Inspector. During the hearing he called an expert to give his opinion on the business plan. The expert had not seen the business plan in advance and he explained to the Inspector that he could offer no assistance as he had not seen it. No opportunity was given for a short adjournment to enable the expert witness to consider it. Evidence was given by an expert witness on behalf of the Council, however, about similar development elsewhere. Refusing planning permission, the Inspector said in his decision letter that the evidence of the Council's witness that the proposed floor space would be approximately double that which was reasonably necessary 'had not been disputed'.

19.42 Allowing the appeal and quashing the Inspector's decision, the Court of Appeal considered the Inspector had not given the applicant's business plan the consideration it deserved and that the Inspector should have adjourned the hearing to allow the applicant's expert witness to see the plan so that he could comment upon it.

19.43 In coming to the conclusion that a fair hearing did not occur and that the decision must be quashed, Pill LJ said:

> Planning permission having been refused, conflicting propositions and evidence will often be placed before an Inspector on appeal. Whatever procedure is followed, the strength of a case can be determined only upon an understanding of that case and by testing it with reference to propositions in the opposing case. At a public local inquiry the Inspector, in performing that task, usually has the benefit of cross-examination on behalf of the other party. If cross-examination disappears, the need to examine propositions in that way does not disappear with it. Further, the statutory right to be heard is nullified unless, in some way, the strength of what

HEARING PROCEDURE

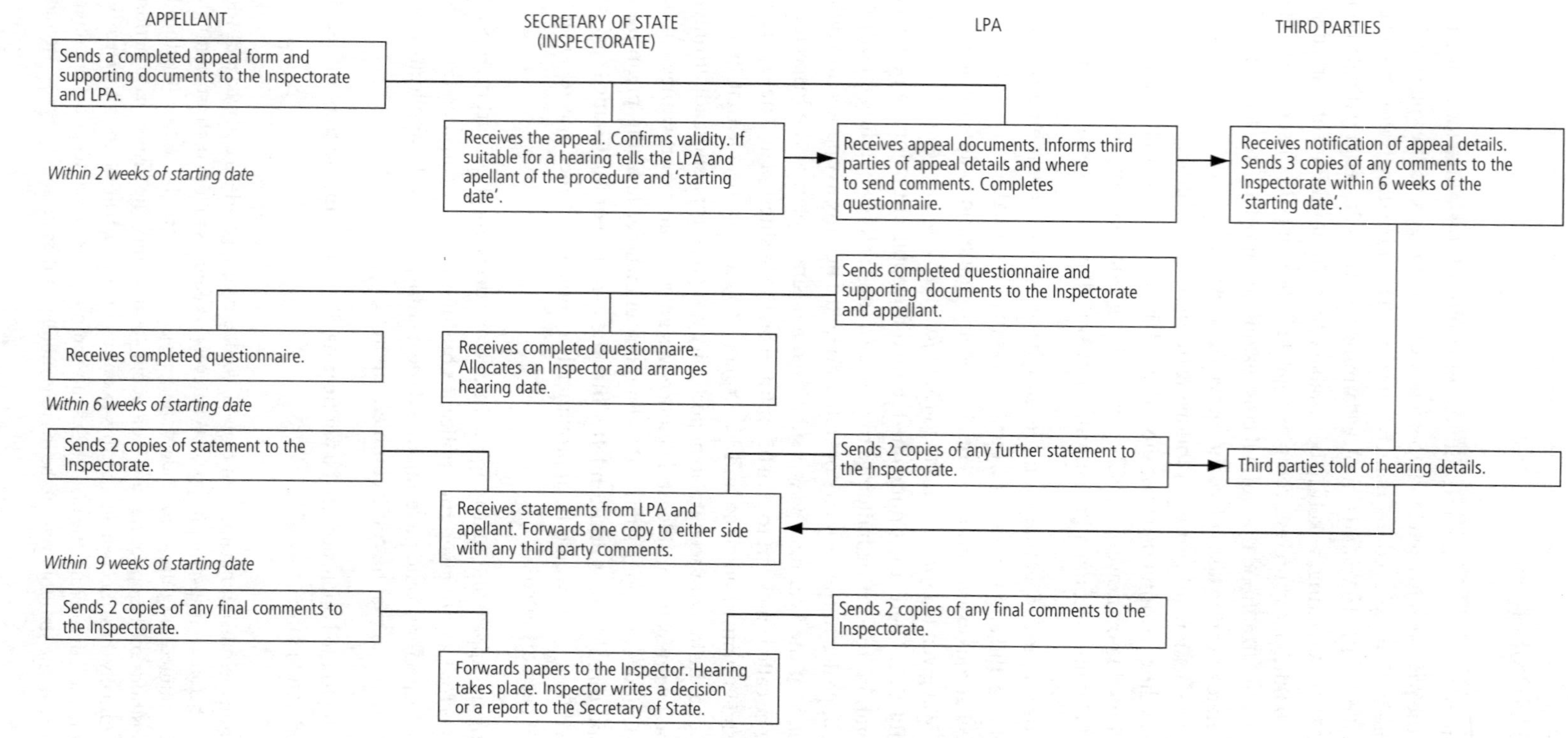

APPELLANT
SECRETARY OF STATE (INSPECTORATE)
LPA
THIRD PARTIES
Sends a completed appeal form and supporting documents to the Inspectorate and LPA.
Receives the appeal. Confirms validity. If suitable for a hearing tells the LPA and apellant of the procedure and 'starting date'.
Receives appeal documents. Informs third parties of appeal details and where to send comments. Completes questionnaire.
Receives notification of appeal details. Sends 3 copies of any comments to the Inspectorate within 6 weeks of the 'starting date'.
Within 2 weeks of starting date
Sends completed questionnaire and supporting documents to the Inspectorate and appellant.
Receives completed questionnaire.
Receives completed questionnaire. Allocates an Inspector and arranges hearing date.
Within 6 weeks of starting date
Sends 2 copies of statement to the Inspectorate.
Sends 2 copies of any further statement to the Inspectorate.
Third parties told of hearing details.
Receives statements from LPA and apellant. Forwards one copy to either side with any third party comments.
Within 9 weeks of starting date
Sends 2 copies of any final comments to the Inspectorate.
Sends 2 copies of any final comments to the Inspectorate.
Forwards papers to the Inspector. Hearing takes place. Inspector writes a decision or a report to the Secretary of State.

> one party says is not only listened to by the tribunal but is assessed for its own worth and in relation to opposing contentions.
>
> There is a danger, upon the procedure now followed by the Secretary of State of observing the right to be heard by holding a 'hearing', that the need for such consideration is forgotten. The danger is that the 'more relaxed' atmosphere could lead not to a 'full and fair' hearing but to a less than thorough examination of the issues. A relaxed hearing is not necessarily a fair hearing. The hearing must not become so relaxed that the rigorous examination essential to the determination of difficult questions may be diluted. The absence of an accusatorial procedure places an inquisitorial burden upon an Inspector.

The *Dyason* case was considered by Keene J (as he then was) in *Croydon LBC v Secretary of State for the Environment* [2000] PLCR 171. What that case established he said, '. . . is that, when there is an informal hearing which, as a matter of procedure, normally excludes cross-examination, the Inspector has to play an enhanced role in order to resolve conflicts of evidence. In addition, such an Inspector must not arrive at a finding adverse to a party without having put the point to the party in question or his witness . . .' **19.44**

The procedure at hearings is best understood by referring to the following table which is reproduced from Annex 2 of Circular 05/2000. **19.45**

F. LOCAL INQUIRIES

Local inquiries, it is said, are most suited to complex development proposals and to cases which generate substantial third-party representation, or where it is desirable to cross-examine those giving evidence. **19.46**

The procedure followed at a local inquiry held under s 78 is regulated substantially by the common law rules of natural justice and by the Town and Country Planning (Inquiries Procedure) (England) Rules 2000, SI 2000/1624 or the Town and Country Planning (Determination by Inspectors) (Inquiries Procedure) (England) Rules 2000, SI 2000/1625. Both sets of Inquiry Procedure Rules deal with the procedure to be followed before, during and after an inquiry. Both sets also deal with the procedure where an inquiry is held by the Secretary of State in connection with listed buildings appeals, and conservation area consent appeals. The former set of rules apply when the Secretary of State is to make the decision after considering a recommendation of the Inspector (recovered cases), the latter set when the Inspector is making the decision on behalf of the Secretary of State (transferred cases). **19.47**

Because most appeals where a local inquiry is held are determined by Inspectors, the latter set of rules (SI 2000/1625) are dealt with below in some detail. **19.48**

It should be noted that all rules of procedure governing appeals have a dual purpose. As mentioned earlier, the parties involved know that by following the rules they are not likely to infringe the rules of natural justice. The second purpose of the rules, however, is to impose a discipline on the parties so that the inquiry process is conducted as efficiently and effectively as possible, which in turn should lead to speedier decisions. To help this process the Government announced on 18 July 2002, that they intended to give the Secretary of State a power to prescribe a time table for 'called in' and 'recovered' appeal decisions. The statutory **19.49** rules, which came into effect on 1 August 2000, were accompanied by an explanatory Circular 05/0002. The rules made in 2000 replaced rules made in 1992. Under the pre–1988 rules, once an appeal had been accepted by the Secretary of State, the parties needed to take little formal action until 42 days before the opening of the inquiry, when the local planning authority's statement of case became due. Under the rules made in 1988 and 1992 this became no longer possible, since all the major stages in the appeal process were programmed to take place from what was then called the 'relevant date'. This was the date of the Secretary of State's written notice to the applicant and the local planning authority that it is his intention to cause a local inquiry to be held. In short, the relevant date was the trigger for all subsequent stages of the inquiry process, so that the period between acceptance of the appeal and the inquiry itself is used to greater advantage. Under the 2000 Rules this date is now called the 'starting date'.

19.50 In order to best understand both sets of Inquiry Procedure Rules, reference should be made to the table below which is reproduced from Annex 3 of Circular 05/2000:

19.51 Because of the importance and use made of Inquiries where the Inspector makes the decision a more detailed commentary on the rules is required.

Transferred cases (SI 2000/1625)

Procedure before the inquiry

19.52 (a) On receiving the relevant notice from the Secretary of State that an inquiry is to be held, the local planning authority must inform the Secretary of State and the appellant in writing of the name and address of any statutory party who made representations to them. Statutory parties are the owners of the land or a tenant of an agricultural holding to which the application relates, who made representations to the local planning authority within 21 days of being served with a notice of the application as required by the General Development Procedure Order or, in a case to which the Environment Impact Assessment Regulations apply, adjoining owners or occupiers (see Rule 4(1)).

(b) The Secretary of State must notify the name of the Inspector to every person entitled to appear at the inquiry (Rule 5(1)).

(c) No later than six weeks after the starting date, the local planning authority must serve a statement of case on the Secretary of State, the appellant and any statutory party (Rule 6(1)). Under the rules a statement of case means a 'written statement which contains full particulars of the case which a person proposes to put forward at an inquiry and a list of any documents which that person intends to refer to or put in evidence'. According to the Ministerial guidance it is helpful if the parties provided with their statement, the data, methodology and assumptions used to support their submission. In addition, the rules provide that if the Secretary of State or any local authority has previously given to the local planning authority a direction restricting the grant of planning permission for which application was made, or the Secretary of State or any other Minister of the Crown or government department or local authority has expressed, in writing, to the local planning authority, the view that the application should not be granted either wholly or in part, or should be granted only subject to conditions, the local planning authority must include the terms of any direction; and any views expressed or

INQUIRIES PROCEDURE

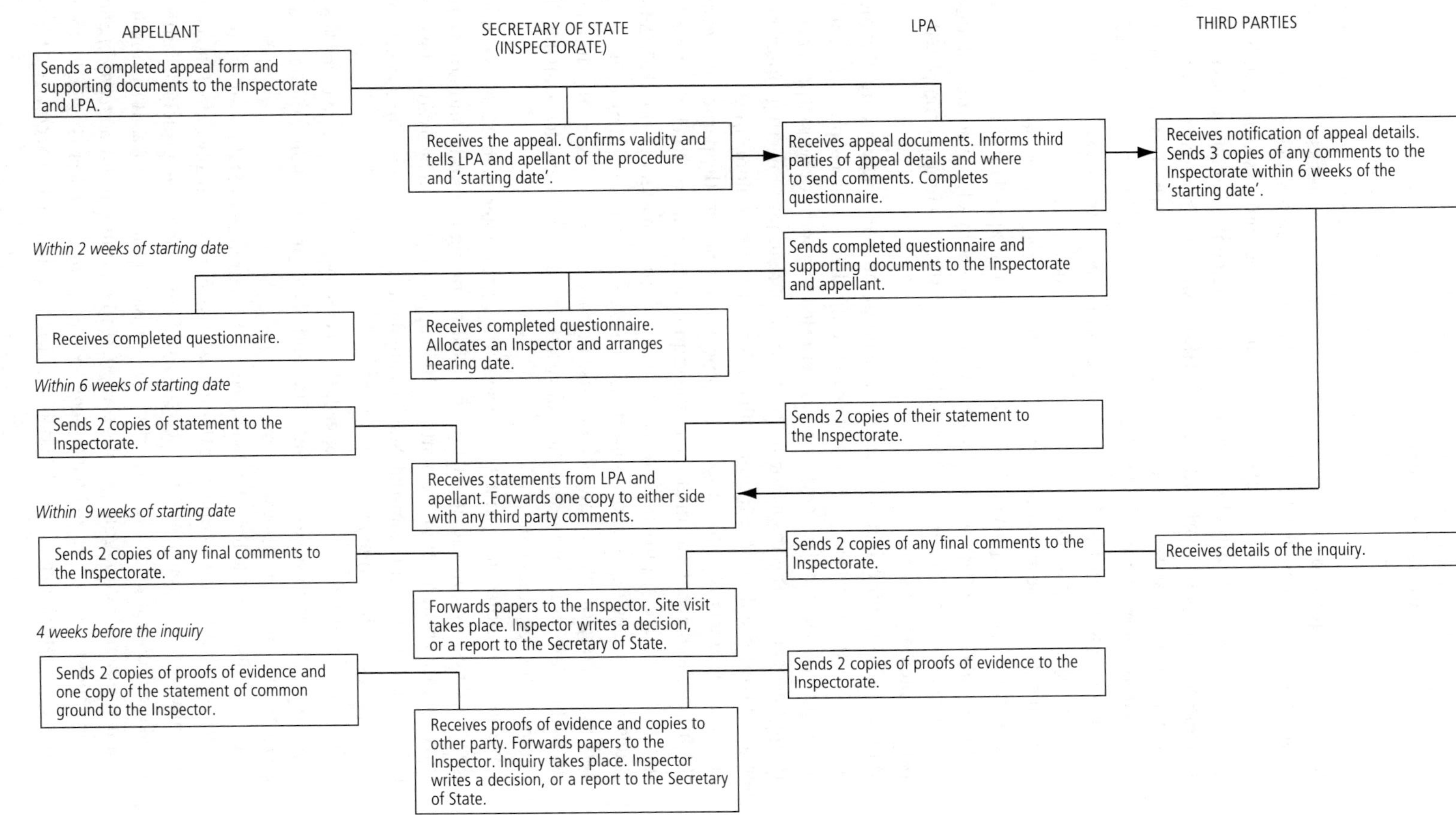

APPELLANT
SECRETARY OF STATE (INSPECTORATE)
LPA
THIRD PARTIES
Sends a completed appeal form and supporting documents to the Inspectorate and LPA.
Receives the appeal. Confirms validity and tells LPA and apellant of the procedure and 'starting date'.
Receives appeal documents. Informs third parties of appeal details and where to send comments. Completes questionnaire.
Receives notification of appeal details. Sends 3 copies of any comments to the Inspectorate within 6 weeks of the 'starting date'.
Within 2 weeks of starting date
Sends completed questionnaire and supporting documents to the Inspectorate and appellant.
Receives completed questionnaire.
Receives completed questionnaire. Allocates an Inspector and arranges hearing date.
Within 6 weeks of starting date
Sends 2 copies of statement to the Inspectorate.
Sends 2 copies of their statement to the Inspectorate.
Receives statements from LPA and apellant. Forwards one copy to either side with any third party comments.
Within 9 weeks of starting date
Sends 2 copies of any final comments to the Inspectorate.
Sends 2 copies of any final comments to the Inspectorate.
Receives details of the inquiry.
Forwards papers to the Inspector. Site visit takes place. Inspector writes a decision, or a report to the Secretary of State.
4 weeks before the inquiry
Sends 2 copies of proofs of evidence and one copy of the statement of common ground to the Inspector.
Sends 2 copies of proofs of evidence to the Inspectorate.
Receives proofs of evidence and copies to other party. Forwards papers to the Inspector. Inquiry takes place. Inspector writes a decision, or a report to the Secretary of State.

representations made on which they intend to rely in their submission at the inquiry, in their statement of case (Rule 4(1)).

(d) No later than six weeks after the starting date, the appellant must serve a statement of case on the Secretary of State, the local planning authority and any statutory party (Rule 6(3)). In addition, the Secretary of State may require *any other person* who wishes to appear at an inquiry to serve a statement of case within four weeks of being required to do so (Rule 6(6)). Previous rules allowed appellants and third parties nine weeks in order to serve a statement of case. This was to enable such persons to see more fully the local planning authority's case before preparing their statement. The change has been subject to some criticism particularly with regard to the position of third parties who could wish to comment upon statements made by the main parties. The Government has now accepted that third parties are disadvantaged by the change and have promised to alter the rules to allow third parties who have commented at the six-week stage a further opportunity to comment at the nine-week stage of the appeal.

Statements of case prepared under this rule are referred to colloquially as 'rule 6 statements'. It is also provided in Rule 6(5) that the appellant and local planning authority may each require the other to send them a copy of any document, or of the relevant part of any document referred to in the list of documents comprised in that party's statement of case.

(e) Where the Inspector considers it desirable to do so, he may hold a pre-inquiry meeting at not less than two weeks' written notice to the appellant, the local planning authority, any statutory party and any other person entitled to appear or whose presence at the inquiry appears to the Inspector to be desirable. Pre-inquiry meetings must be held where it is expected that the inquiry will last for eight days or more, unless the Inspector considers it unnecessary to do so. Its purpose is to encourage the parties to prepare for the inquiry and avoid wasting time at the inquiry with matters which are not relevant nor in dispute. Pre-inquiry meetings may deal with such matters as: the clarification of issues, nature of evidence to be submitted, exchange of proofs of evidence, presentation and numbering of plans and documents, normal sitting hours of the inquiry, its likely duration, order of presentation of cases or issues and facilities available (telex, photography, secretariat, etc.).

It should be noted too, that the Inspector may not later than 12 weeks after the relevant date serve on the appellant, the local planning authority and any statutory party a written statement of the matters which appear to him to be likely to be relevant to his consideration of the appeal. Such a statement is usually served in advance of any pre-inquiry meeting (Rule 7).

(f) Unless a lesser period of notice is agreed, the Secretary of State must give not less than four weeks' written notice of the date, time and place for the holding of the inquiry to every person entitled to appear.

The rules also provide that the date fixed by the Secretary of State shall be, unless he considers it impractical — not later than 20 weeks after the starting date. In exercise of that duty, it is the practice of the Secretary of State to give the principal parties (the appellant and local planning authority) one refusal to the date offered by him for the commencement and on-going consideration of the Inquiry. In *R v Secretary of State for the Environment, Transport and the Regions, ex p Borough of Kirklees* [1999] JPL 882, the Council sought unsuccessfully to challenge the decision of the Secretary of State to impose a second date for the Inquiry, after the Council had refused the first date offered. The Council's main ground for challenging the Secretary of State's decision had been the difficulty they faced in obtaining locally based counsel (there were others available in Birmingham and London) and the lack of availability of expert witnesses over that time. The Court held that judicial review, a remedy of last resort, should rarely be permitted to progress the sort of application made by the Council, where there was recourse to the Inspector, who had the power to arrange matters at the Inquiry in order to accommodate the unavailability of expert witnesses.

It should also be noted that the Secretary of State may require the local planning authority to serve notice of the inquiry on specified persons or classes of persons; publish notice of the inquiry in one or more newspapers circulating in the locality; and post a notice in a conspicuous place or places near to the land (Rule 10).

Procedure during the inquiry

(g) The appellant, the local planning authority, and if not the local planning authority the county or district council in whose area the land is situated, statutory parties and any other person who has served a statement of case, are among those entitled to appear at the inquiry (Rule 11(1)). In addition the rule also provides that nothing in Rule 11(1) 'shall prevent the Inspector from permitting any other person to appear at an inquiry, and such permission shall not be unreasonably withheld' (Rule 11(2)). The latter part of this rule allows the Inspector to permit any person who can make a contribution to the determination of the appeal to appear at the inquiry. **19.53**

(h) Where the Secretary of State or other body has given the local planning authority a direction restricting the grant of planning permission or the Secretary of State or any other Minister or any government department or local authority has expressed in writing to the local planning authority the view that the application should not be granted, the appellant may, not later than four weeks before the date of the inquiry, apply to the Secretary of State for a representative of the Secretary of State, Minister, department or other body concerned to be made available at the inquiry. The rule provides that the representative shall give evidence and be subject to cross-examination to the same extent as any other witness, but that the representative of a Minister or government department shall not be required to answer any question which in the opinion of the Inspector is directed to the merits of government policy (Rule 12).

(i) A person entitled to appear at an inquiry who proposes to give, or to call another person to give, evidence at the inquiry by reading a proof of evidence must send a copy of the proof to the Inspector together with a written summary. No written summary, however, is required where the proof of evidence proposed to be read contains no more than 1,500 words. Where a copy of a proof of evidence is sent to the Inspector in accordance with the rule (with or without a summary) this must normally be done no later than four weeks before the date fixed for the holding of an inquiry; and copies of that proof and any summary must be sent at the same time to the other party and to any statutory party. Where a written summary is so provided, only the summary is to be read at the inquiry, unless the Inspector permits or requires otherwise (Rule 14).

(j) The rules also provide that the local planning authority and the appellant shall jointly prepare an agreed statement of common ground which should be sent to the Secretary of State and any statutory party not less than four weeks before the date of the inquiry

(Rule 15). The statement is to contain agreed factual information about the subject of the appeal. The purpose of this is to save inquiry time on matters which are not in dispute.

(k) Except as is otherwise provided in the rules, the procedure at an inquiry is determined by the Inspector.

The rules provide that, unless the Inspector determines otherwise, the local planning authority shall begin and the appellant shall have the right of final reply; and that other persons entitled or permitted to appear shall be heard in such order as the Inspector may determine. The appellant, the local planning authority and statutory parties are entitled to call evidence and to cross examine persons giving evidence, but any other person appearing may do so only to the extent permitted by the Inspector. Where a person gives evidence at an inquiry by reading a summary of his evidence (which is the norm), his statement of evidence may be tendered in evidence and the person crossed-examined on it as if the statement were given orally. The Inspector may allow the local planning authority (or the appellant or both of them) to alter or add to any submissions made in their Rule 6 statement, but must give (if necessary by adjourning the inquiry) the other party and any statutory parties, an adequate opportunity of considering the fresh submission. If any person appearing or present at an inquiry, behaves in the opinion of the Inspector in a disruptive manner, he may be required by the Inspector to leave (Rule 16).

(l) The Inspector may make an unaccompanied site visit before or during the inquiry without giving notice of his intention to do so. Inspectors often visit the site on their own before the commencement of the inquiry. In addition, the rules provide that the Inspector may during an inquiry or after its close inspect the land in the company of the appellant, the local planning authority and any statutory parties (Rule 17).

The reason for site visits is to enable the Inspector to visually assess the impact of the proposed development on the immediate surroundings. No discussion of the merits of an appeal is allowed during a site inspection.

Procedure after the inquiry

19.54 (m) The rules provide that if, after the close of the inquiry, the Inspector proposes to take into consideration any new evidence or any new matter of fact (not being a matter of government policy) which was not raised at the inquiry and which he considers to be material to his decision, he shall not come to a decision without first notifying the persons entitled to appear at the inquiry who appeared at it of the matter in question; and affording them an opportunity within three weeks of the date of notification of making representations to him in respect of it or of asking for the reopening of the inquiry (Rule 18).

The genesis of this provision is to be found in the notorious *Chalk Pit* case in 1961. There, the owners of land in Essex applied for planning permission to develop land by quarrying chalk. The local planning authority refused the application on the ground that it would affect crops and livestock on neighbouring land. The owners appealed against the refusal to the Minister of Housing and Local Government, who appointed an Inspector to hold a local inquiry. Although the Inspector recommended that the appeal be rejected, the Minister allowed it and granted planning permission. It then became known that after the Inspector had made his recommendations, the Minister had had discussions with the Ministry of Agriculture, Fisheries and Food, who had convinced him that with proper safeguards the quarrying could be carried out without adversely affecting the neighbouring land. Adjacent landowners then applied to the High Court to set aside the Minister's decision. In *Buxton v Minister of Housing and Local Government* [1961] 1 QB 278, the court held that the statutory review procedure available under the Act to challenge the decision of the Minister was only available to a person aggrieved by that decision, and that Buxton (one of the neighbours affected) did not have the necessary standing to challenge the Minister's decision because he had not been aggrieved in the legal sense. Although the authority of that decision has since been progressively weakened, the landowners, having been defeated on a preliminary issue, secured detailed consideration of the problem by the Council on Tribunals, which led to a subsequent special report by the Council and the adoption of their proposals to amend the Inquiry Procedure Rules in the manner indicated above. This particular provision, however, has not been a fertile field of litigation. This is because Inspectors (and also the Secretary of State in recovered cases) are meticulously careful to ensure that they do not take into account new evidence or new issues of fact in breach of the rules. The distinction between 'fact' to which the rule applies, and 'opinion' to which it does not, is discussed in 19.58 below.

(n) The Inspector is required to notify his decision and his reasons for it, in writing, to all persons entitled to appear at the inquiry who did appear, and to any other person who, having appeared at the inquiry, had asked to be notified of the decision (Rule 19).

The obligation to state reasons for the decision has given rise to a considerable volume of litigation. In the much cited case of *Re Poyser and Mills' Arbitration* [1964] 2 QB 467, it was held that reasons must be adequate and intelligible and deal with the substantial points that have been raised. The obligation to give reasons was not met where they were scanty, uninformative and unintelligible.

The obligation to state the reasons for a decision has given rise to voluminous litigation. **19.55**
Fortunately, the most important of the subsequent cases on this aspect have been considered by the House of Lords in *South Bucks District Council and anon. v Porter* (FC) [2004] UKHL 33. There, Lord Brown summarized the judicial authorities governing the proper approach to a reasons challenge in the planning context as follows:

> The reasons for a decision must be intelligible and they must be adequate. They must enable the reader to understand why the matter was decided as it was and what conclusions were reached on the 'principal important controversial issues', disclosing how any issue of law or law or fact was resolved. Reasons can be briefly stated, the degree of particularity required depending entirely on the nature of the issues falling for decision. The reasoning must not give rise to a substantial doubt as to whether the decision-maker erred in law, for example by misunderstanding some relevant policy or some other important matter or by failing to reach a rational decision on relevant grounds. But such adverse inference will not readily be drawn. The reasons need refer only to the main issues in the dispute, not to every material consideration. They should enable disappointed developers to assess their prospects of obtaining some alternative development permission, or, as the case may be, their unsuccessful opponents to understand how the policy or approach underlying the grant of permission may impact upon future such applications. Decision letters must be read in a straightforward manner, recognising that they are addressed to parties well aware of the issues involved and the arguments advanced. A reasons challenge will only succeed if the party aggrieved can satisfy the court that he has genuinely been substantially prejudiced by the failure to provide an adequately reasoned decision.

It is of course, also necessary to show in a successful challenge for a failure to state reasons that the appellants' interests have been substantially prejudiced by that failure. In the House of Lords in *Save Britain's Heritage v Number 1 Poultry Ltd* [1991] IWLR 153, Lord Bridge said:

> Whatever may be the position in any other legislative context, under the planning legislation, when it comes to deciding in any particular case whether the reasons given are deficient, the question is not to be answered *in vacuo*. The alleged deficiency will only afford a ground for quashing the decision if the court is satisfied that the interests of the applicant have been substantially prejudiced by it. This reinforces the view I have already expressed that the adequacy of reasons is not to be judged by reference to some abstract standard. There are in truth not two separate questions: (1) were the reasons adequate? (2) if not, were the interests of the applicant substantially prejudiced thereby? The single indivisible question, in my opinion, which the court must ask itself whenever a planning decision is challenged on the ground of a failure to give reasons is whether the interests of the applicant have been substantially prejudiced by the deficiency of the reasons given. Here again, I disclaim any intention to put a gloss on the statutory provisions by attempting to define or delimit the circumstances in which deficiency of reasons will be capable of causing substantial prejudice, but I should expect that normally such prejudice will arise from one of three causes. First, there will be substantial prejudice to a developer whose application for permission has been refused or to an opponent of development when permission has been granted where the reasons for the decision are so inadequately or obscurely expressed as to raise a substantial doubt whether the decision was taken within the powers of the Act. Secondly, a developer whose application for permission is refused may be substantially prejudiced where the planning considerations on which the decision is based are not explained sufficiently clearly to enable him reasonably to assess the prospects of succeeding in an application for some alternative form of development. Thirdly, an opponent of development, whether the local planning authority or some unofficial body like *Save*, may be substantially prejudiced by a decision to grant permission in which the planning considerations on which the decision is based, particularly if they relate to planning policy, are not explained sufficiently clearly to indicate what, if any, impact they may have in relation to the decision of future applications.

Recovered cases (SI 2000/1624)

19.56 Where the Secretary of State has used his power to recover jurisdiction over the determination of the appeal, the Inspector, instead of determining the appeal himself, makes recommendations to the Secretary of State as to how the appeal should be determined. The procedure is regulated by the Town and Country Planning (Inquiries Procedure) Rules 2000, SI 2000/1624 and, of course, by the rules of natural justice. The Inquiries Procedure Rules relating to recovered cases differ from transferred cases in a number of ways.

19.57 Apart from the necessary differences (particularly in terminology) resulting from the position of the Secretary of State and the complex nature of the planning issues involved, the most significant change in these rules from the rules relating to transferred cases is that relating to the close of the inquiry. Rule 17 provides that after the close of the inquiry, the Inspector must make a report in writing to the Secretary of State which must include his conclusions and his recommendations or, if he makes no recommendations, his reasons for not doing so (Rule 16). Before he determines the appeal, the Secretary of State may take into account new evidence or new matters of fact. He may also, however, decide to differ from the Inspector on a matter of fact. The latter situation can only occur, of course, in recovered cases where the Secretary of State is considering the Inspector's report prior to making his decision. Accordingly if the Secretary of State does decide to:

(i) differ from the Inspector on any matter of fact mentioned in or appearing to him to be material to a conclusion reached by the Inspector, or
(ii) takes into consideration any new evidence or new matter of fact (not being a matter of government policy),

and is for that reason disposed to disagree with a recommendation made by the Inspector, he shall not come to a decision at variance with that recommendation without first notifying the persons entitled to appear at the inquiry and who appeared at it of his disagreement and reasons for it; and affording them an opportunity of making written representations to him (if the Secretary of State has taken into consideration any new evidence or new matters of fact, not being a matter of government policy) or of asking for the reopening of the inquiry. This must be done within three weeks of the Secretary of State's notification (Rule 17(5)).

The rules which impose obligations on the Secretary of State to give the parties an opportunity to make further representations, are concerned with matters of fact or new evidence or new matters of fact, not statements of opinion or the planning merits. The distinction has caused difficulty in the past, particularly in recovered cases. **19.58**

In *Lord Luke v Minister of Housing and Local Government* [1968] 1 QB 172 the Inspector in his report to the Minister had made two statements. The first was that the site of the proposed development was clearly defined behind walls. The second was that a well-designed house would add to the charm of the setting. He accordingly recommended that the appeal be allowed. In his decision letter, however, the Minister said he accepted the Inspector's findings of fact, but could not accept the Inspector's conclusions or recommendation. He considered the proposed development would lead to sporadic development in open countryside. He then dismissed the appeal, without giving the appellant the opportunity to make further representations. The appellant argued that in disagreeing with the second statement of the Inspector, the Minister had differed from him on a finding of fact. Although the High Court upheld the appellant's contention, the Court of Appeal held that the Minister's difference of opinion with the Inspector was not on a finding of fact, but on a question of opinion on the planning merits of the proposed development, and that he was not obliged to give the appellant a further opportunity to make representations. **19.59**

In *Pyrford Properties Ltd v Secretary of State for the Environment* (1977) 36 P & CR 28, the policy of the local planning authority was to restrict office development in its area, though exceptions were to be made for 'local firms'. The appellants were a firm with international ramifications, but the business had started in the locality. On an appeal against the refusal of planning permission, the Inspector had found that the appellants were and remained a local firm and recommended that the appeal be allowed. In his decision letter upholding the authority's refusal to grant planning permission, however, the Secretary of State said that he agreed with the Inspector's findings of fact but not his conclusions that the firm remained a local firm. Quashing the Secretary of State's decision for failing to comply with the relevant procedural rule, by providing the appellants with an opportunity to make further representations, Sir Douglas Frank QC, sitting as a deputy judge of the High Court, recognised that it **19.60** was not easy to draw from the *Lord Luke* decision any firm rules for distinguishing findings of fact from expressions of opinion on the planning merits, unless it were that the former depended on evidence of an existing state of affairs and the latter upon a subjective opinion of what would result from the proposed development.

G. MAJOR INFRASTRUCTURE PROJECTS

19.61 For many years concern has been expressed at the time taken to determine appeals into major development projects.

19.62 Apart from development which may be authorised by Parliamentary Bills or by Public Works Orders, most proposals for major infrastructure projects have been dealt with through the normal planning processes. Usually the application is called in for decision by the Secretary of State who then holds a public local inquiry into the proposal.

19.63 Although relatively infrequent, public inquiries at which such projects are considered are long, protracted and expensive. Inquiries into projects which have lasted more than 180 sitting-days, in addition to the inquiry into the Heathrow Airport Terminal 5 project which itself lasted 524 sitting-days, include Stansted, Sizewell B Nuclear Power Station and Hinkley Point Nuclear Power Station.

19.64 In addition to the main purpose of the inquiry, other related proposals linked to the project may also have to be considered. For example, the Terminal 5 inquiry involved the consideration of 21 planning applications, six highway orders, two transport and works applications, five Acquisition of Land Act 1981 orders, three applications under the Civil Aviation Act 1982 and Airports Act 1986, one scheduled monument order and three unopposed stopping up/diversion orders.

19.65 There is also the further difficulty that such developments are rarely the consequence of specific proposals in a development plan, and are usually in areas where there is an absence of specific national policy guidance.

19.66 Accordingly in July 2001, the Government announced a package of measures to improve the planning process for the determination of applications for planning permission for such projects.

19.67 In advance of more fundamental changes that may be made to the procedure for approving such projects, the Government introduced a new set of statutory rules governing major infrastructure projects. These rules are the Town and Country Planning (Major Infrastructure Project Inquiries Procedure) (England) Rules 2002. The Rules came into force on 7 June 2002. Major infrastructure projects are defined in the rules by using the Town and Country Planning (Environmental Impact Assessment) (England and Wales) Regulations 1999, which lists in Sch 1 to the Regulations those development projects for which environment impact assessment is mandatory. The new rules introduce a number of changes to the inquiry procedures that formerly applied to these projects and which were governed by the Town and Country Planning (Inquiry Procedure) Rules and the Code of Practice 'Preparing for Major Public Inquiries in England' contained in Annex 4 to Circular 05/02. Among the changes made is that people wishing to participate in the inquiry are required to register their interest and the part they wish to play; there is now a power to appoint a mediator to assist parties to reach agreement on matters relevant to the inquiry, or to define and narrow areas of disagreement; the timetable prepared by the Inspector (and any variation of it) is required to be approved by the Secretary of State and the Inspector is given the power to curtail cross-examination if he considers that permitting it (or allowing it) to continue, would have the effect that the timetable could not be adhered to.

The legislative provisions relating to major infrastructure projects will now be strengthened by the Planning and Compulsory Purchase Act 2004. When fully implemented, these provisions will insert into the 1990 Act new sections 76A and 76B. Neither section applies to Wales. The new provisions allow the Secretary of State to call in for his own determination, any application for planning permission or any application for the approval of a local planning authority required under a development order, if he thinks the development to which the application relates is of national or regional importance. It may also direct that any other application related to such development be referred to him instead of being dealt with by the local planning authority. Where the Secretary of State exercises his power under this section he must then appoint an Inspector to consider the application. Where the Secretary of State makes a direction requiring that an application for planning permission be referred to him, the applicant must prepare and send to him an 'economic impact report' in the form and contain such matter as is prescribed by the Secretary of State in a development order. **19.68**

Section 76B allows the Secretary of State to appoint more than one Inspector — a lead Inspector and such number of additional Inspectors as he thinks appropriate. Under the section, the lead Inspector's role is likely to largely consist of obtaining and considering outline evidence to be submitted to the Inquiry, holding a meeting to consider that evidence and considering the form the Inquiry should take. The lead Inspector will then make his recommendation to the Secretary of State, after which the additional Inspectors will be appointed. In this way the additional Inspectors may be asked to consider specific aspects of the proposed project and then to report to the lead Inspector on that matter. The details of such arrangements are to be set out in Regulations or by Rules made under the Tribunal and Inquiries Act 1992. **19.69**

The new provisions will not come into force until the Secretary of State has made the necessary regulations. The important changes made by the new ss. 76A and 76B include the possibility that concurrent inquiry sessions can be held dealing with different topics, and a requirement that economic impact reports be prepared and made available at the first pre-inquiry meeting. When implemented, the new procedures could apply to new airports and runways, trunk roads, rail schemes, power stations, radioactive waste disposal sites and reservoirs. **19.70**

H. TIME WITHIN WHICH THE SECRETARY OF STATE IS REQUIRED TO TAKE DECISIONS

19.71 The Secretary of State has never previously been subject to a time limit for the making of a decision on a planning issue which has come to him by way of appeal. Now, Section 55 and Schedule 2 of the Planning and Compulsory Purchase Act 2004, when fully implemented, will require him to prepare a timetable within which he should come to a decision in dealing with called in applications and appeals for which he has recovered jurisdiction. Under these provisions the Secretary of State must inform the parties of the timetable to be applied to the decision in question.

19.72 At this stage he may vary the standard timetable. He may also later revise the timetable if events occur that prevent the set timetable from being met. If the Secretary of State fails to meet the timetable, he must give reasons for that failure.

19.73 The provisions require the Secretary of State to prepare an annual report to Parliament on his performance under these provisions.

I. POWER TO CORRECT DECISION LETTERS

19.74 Sections 56 to 59 of the Planning and Compulsory Purchase Act 2004 introduce new provisions in planning law which allow an Inspector or the Secretary of State to correct an error in decision letters.

19.75 The rule is to apply to errors contained in decision letters issued by them, where the error is a 'correctable error'. The provisions define a correctable error as one which is contained in any part of the decision letter, but which is not part of any reasons for the decision. It has been suggested that this power is in the nature of a 'slip rule'.

19.76 The correction power may be exercised either where the Inspector or Secretary of State has written to the applicant to explain the error and to say he is considering making the correction, or he has been requested to do so by any person. In the former case, the applicant must agree to the correction.

19.77 A formal correction notice specifying the error to be corrected or the notice of a decision not to correct an error in the decision letter (as the case may be) must then be sent by the Inspector or Secretary of State to the applicant, the owner of the land in respect of which the decision was made, the local planning authority and, if the correction was sought by any other person, to that person.

19.78 The effect of issuing a notice correcting an error is that the original decision is taken not to have been made, but is replaced for all purposes by the correct decision and one which becomes effective on the date that the correction notice was issued. The statutory period for challenging the decision, therefore, operates from that date. Where a decision has been made not to correct an error, the statutory period is not affected.

J. AWARD OF COSTS

Very often, particularly following an inquiry, one or even both of the major parties involved will seek to recover from the other side their costs incurred in pursuing the appeal. In England and Wales the award of costs is governed by s 250(5) of the Local Government Act 1972, and is applied to planning appeals and other proceedings under the 1990 Act by s 320(2) and Sch 6 to the 1990 Act. Section 250(5) empowers the Secretary of State to 'make orders as to the costs of the parties at the inquiry and as to the parties by whom the costs are to be paid, and every such order may be made a rule of the High Court on the application of any party named in the order'. The purpose in making an order as to costs a rule of the High Court is to enable a party to sue and be sued on an award. Similar provisions are to be found in s 89 of the Planning (Listed Buildings and Conservation Areas) Act 1990. **19.79**

Prior to 1986, the Secretary of State's powers to make an award of costs were limited to local inquiries. The power has since been extended and under s 322 of the 1990 Act the Secretary of State has the same powers to make orders as to costs with regard to hearings and written representations as apply to local inquiries. An order has been made applying this power to hearings. It is the Government's intention to make awards of costs available in all written representation appeals also, as soon as resources allow. In addition, Inspectors have now been given the right to exercise the Secretary of State's power to award costs. **19.80**

The principles on which the power to award costs are exercised are based substantially on the general principles set out by the Council on Tribunals in 1964 in their *Report on the Award of Costs at Statutory Inquiries* (Cmnd 2471). **19.81**

The award of costs in planning appeals is becoming more common. The view is taken that the award of costs should not necessarily follow the decision on the planning merits of the appeal, so that the appellant would be awarded costs if his appeal was successful and would have costs awarded against him if he was unsuccessful. Costs of a planning appeal will normally be borne, therefore, by the party that incurs them. **19.82**

Before the Planning and Compensation Act 1991, the Secretary of State was able to make an award of costs against a party, requiring that party to pay the costs of another party, only where an inquiry or hearing had taken place. He had no power to do so where an inquiry or hearing had been cancelled as a result of the appellant abandoning the appeal or the local planning authority abandoning their case. The abandonment of an appeal by the appellant, or an objection to the development by the authority, could lead to the party not at fault incurring considerable costs preparing for the appeal which had now been aborted. Accordingly, the Planning and Compensation Act 1991, introduced a new s. 322A into the 1990 Act giving the Secretary of State power to make an award of costs where an inquiry or hearing has been arranged, but is then cancelled and does not take place. **19.83**

The criteria the Secretary of State uses in exercising his power to award costs, both in relation to cases where an appeal or hearing has taken place and where it has not, are now set out in **19.84**

Circular 8/93. The Circular contains seven annexes each dealing with specific circumstances. The annexes are:

Annex 1: general principles for awards of costs for unreasonable behaviour.
Annex 2: general procedural requirements of appeals: unreasonable behaviour.
Annex 3: unreasonable behaviour relating to the substance of the case, including action prior to submission of appeal.
Annex 4: application of costs policy to third parties in proceedings.
Annex 5: the costs application.
Annex 6: costs in respect of compulsory purchase and analogous orders (including a list of examples of analogous orders).
Annex 7: list of proceedings in which costs may be awarded where an inquiry or hearing is held.

19.85 The test of reasonableness for an Inspector in dealing with an application for costs is different from that where the courts examine the reasonableness of the decision. For an Inspector, unreasonable means what it means in the ordinary sense of the word. For the courts, unreasonableness means unreasonableness in the *Wednesbury* sense.

19.86 The following is a brief summary of the criteria for awards of costs on grounds of unreasonable behaviour contained in the Circular.

19.87 Appellants are at risk of an award of costs against them if, for example, they:

(a) fail to comply with normal procedural requirements for inquiries or hearings; do not provide a pre-inquiry statement when asked to do so, if the proceedings have to be adjourned or are unnecessarily prolonged; or are deliberately or wilfully uncooperative, such as refusing to discuss the appeal or provide requested, necessary information;
(b) fail to pursue an appeal or attend an inquiry or hearing;
(c) introduce new grounds of appeal, or new issues, late in the proceedings;
(d) withdraw the appeal, or legal grounds in an enforcement appeal, after being notified of inquiry or hearing arrangements, without any material change in circumstances;
(e) pursue an appeal which obviously had no reasonable prospect of success, including one which clearly 'flies in the face' of national planning policies.

19.88 Planning authorities are at risk of an award of costs against them, on appeal, if, for example, they:

(a) fail to comply with normal procedural requirements for inquiries or hearings, including compliance with relevant regulations;
(b) fail to provide evidence, on planning grounds, to substantiate each of their reasons for refusing planning permission, including reasons relying on advice of statutory consultees; or to demonstrate that they had reasonable grounds for considering it expedient to issue an enforcement notice;
(c) fail to take into account relevant policy statements in Departmental guidance or relevant judicial authority;
(d) refuse to discuss a planning application or provide requested information, or seek additional information, as appropriate;

(e) refuse permission for a modified scheme when an earlier appeal decision indicated this would be acceptable, and circumstances have not materially changed;
(f) fail to carry out reasonable investigations of fact, or to exercise sufficient care, before issuing an enforcement notice;
(g) at a late stage, introduce an additional reason for refusal, or abandon a reason for refusal, or withdraw an enforcement notice unjustifiably;
(h) impose conditions which are unnecessary, unreasonable, unenforceable, imprecise or irrelevant;
(i) pursue unreasonable demands or obligations in connection with a grant of permission;
(j) fail to renew an extant or recently expired planning permission, without good reason;
(k) unreasonably refuse to grant permission for reserved matters or pursue issues settled at outline stage.

Applications for award of costs should normally be made to the Inspector at the inquiry. **19.89** Later claims will be entertained only if the party claiming costs can show good reason for not having made the claim earlier. If an award of costs is made, the parties endeavour to agree on the amount to be recovered. If agreement is not possible, either party can refer the matter for determination to the Supreme Court Taxing Office. An application is a two stage process. The first stage requires an application to have the costs award made an order of the High Court. This act will enable the party in whose favour the award has been made to sue upon it if necessary. It also enables the party to claim interest on the amount of the award from that date. The second stage involves applying to the Taxing Office to commence assessment proceedings. Under the Civil Procedure Rules, an award of costs under s 250(5) of the Local Government Act 1972 is assessed on what is known as the 'standard basis'.

It was held in *R v Secretary of State for the Enviroment, ex p North Norfolk DC* [1994] EGCS 131, **19.90** that the Inspector must give clear and intelligible reasons for a decision on costs, just as he must do on the issues in the appeal.

Most awards of costs are made against local planning authorities. In *R v Secretary of State for* **19.91** *the Environment, ex p Wakefield MBC* (1998) 75 P & CR 78, the High Court held that there was an evidential threshold which, if reached, was likely to put a planning authority beyond the risk of finding that it had been guilty of unreasonable conduct. What was required of the authority, it was said, was a 'sufficient evidential basis', that is, evidence not lacking in substance, which is capable of belief and which, if accepted, would be capable of making good the planning authority's objection.

K. STATUTORY REVIEW

The 1990 Act contains a number of provisions under which the decision of the Secretary of **19.92** State may be challenged in the courts. The procedures are often referred as proceedings for statutory review, in order to distinguish them from judicial review proceedings which are normally available to a person wishing to question the validity of a public authority's actions.

Section 288 of the 1990 Act provides the only means whereby a person may question the **19.93** validity of a decision made by the Secretary of State on an appeal under s 78. This is because s 284(1) prescribes that, except in so far as may be provided by this part of the Act, the validity of any decision on an appeal under s 78 'shall not be questioned in any legal proceedings whatsoever'. Once a decision has been made on a s 78 appeal, therefore, whether it be a transferred or recovered case, the decision can only be questioned by using the machinery available under s 288.

19.94 Section 288 (1) provides:

> If any person—
>
> (a) is aggrieved by any order to which this section applies and wishes to question the validity of that order on the grounds—
> (i) that the order is not within the powers of this Act, or
> (ii) that any of the relevant requirements have not been complied with in relation to that order; or
>
> (b) is aggrieved by any action on the part of the Secretary of State to which this section applies and wishes to question the validity of that action on the grounds—
> (i) that the action is not within the powers of this Act, or
> (ii) that any of the relevant requirements have not been complied with in relation to that action,
>
> he may make an application to the High Court under this section.

19.95 In the context of appeals relating to decisions under the 1990 Act, it should be noted that in addition to appeals under s 78 of the 1990 Act, s 288 covers:

(a) revocation and modification orders (s 97);
(b) discontinuance orders (s 102);
(c) tree preservation orders (s 198);
(d) orders defining Areas of Special Advertisement Control (s 221(5));
(e) discontinuance, prohibition and suspension orders in respect of mineral workings (paras 1, 3, 4 and 6 of Sch 9);
(f) decision on planning merits of called-in applications (s 77);
(g) decision of Secretary of State to confirm completion notice (s 95);
(h) decision on appeal ground (a) on enforcement appeals (s 177);
(i) any decision of Secretary of State on a purchase notice (s 141);
(j) any decision on appeal in respect of certificate of lawfulness of existing use or development or certificate of lawfulness of proposed use or development (s 195);
(k) any decision made by Secretary of State in respect of tree preservation orders; and
(l) appeals against refusal of express consent or the issue of a discontinuance notice (Regulation 15 of 1992 Advertisement Regulations).

Section 288(3) also provides that an application under the section must be made within six weeks from the date on which the action is taken.

19.96 It will be seen that action must be commenced within six weeks of the decision. In *Griffiths v Secretary of State for the Environment* [1983] 2 AC 51, it was held that time begins to run from the date the Secretary of State takes an irreversible step in relation to the decision, as by typing, signing and dating the decision letter, and not when it is received by the appellant.

19.97 The period of six weeks means precisely six weeks, and there would appear to be no discretion available to the court to extend the period. It cannot in any circumstances be extended. Thereafter, for reasons of public policy, the decision becomes unimpeachable, as it is then immune from judicial attack even if the appellant alleges fraud (see *Smith v East Elloe RDC* [1956] AC 736 and *R v Secretary of State for the Environment, ex p Ostler* [1977] QB 122, both of which were cases of compulsory purchase with an identical time bar). More recently, the finality of the six-week time bar has been approved by the Court of Appeal in *R v Secretary of State for the Environment, ex p Kent* [1990] JPL 124 and applied by the High Court in *R v Cornwall CC ex p Huntington* [1992] 3 All ER 566.

Not everyone may use s 288 to challenge the Secretary of State's decision. The section gives **19.98** the right to 'any person aggrieved'. That clearly includes the appellant and the local planning authority. The position of others, particularly third parties, is not clear. In *Buxton v Minister of Housing and Local Government* [1961] 1 QB 278 it was held that an aggrieved person is not one dissatisfied with an act or decision, but one wrongfully deprived of something to which he is legally entitled. The appellant, a neighbour, was therefore denied review. A somewhat different view was taken by Ackner J in *Turner v Secretary of State for the Environment* (1973) 28 P & CR 123, where the chairman of a local amenity society was held to be an aggrieved person and able to apply for the review of the Secretary of State's decision. In *Bizony v Secretary of State for the Environment* [1976] JPL 306 the court were prepared to regard a neighbour (Bizony) as a person aggrieved, but held, before dismissing a weak case, that if it had been necessary to do so they would have required further argument on the question of whether or not he had the necessary standing.

Since the *Bizony* case there has been little further judicial discussion of the scope of the term **19.99** and whether or not people such as neighbours fall within it. In the light of the relaxation of the rules relating to *standing* in judicial review proceedings, however, it is thought the courts now take a more expansive view of the term than previously. Note, however, that in *Greater London Council v Secretary of State for the Environment* [1985] JPL 868, the council had applied under the earlier provision equivalent to s 288 to quash a decision made by an Inspector to dismiss an appeal by the developers against the failure of the Harrow London Borough Council to determine an application for planning permission. Although the Greater London Council had supported the dismissal of the appeal, it had sought review because it feared adverse consequences would flow from the reasoning of the Inspector. Granting leave to strike out the action, the Court held that the council was not a person aggrieved in relation to the Inspector's decision, but that it might challenge the decision by judicial review proceedings.

The decision of the Secretary of State under s 288 may be challenged either on the ground **19.100** that 'the action is not within the powers of this Act' or, that 'any of the relevant requirements have not been complied with.' Relevant requirements means any requirements of the Act or of the Tribunals and Inquiries Act 1992, or of any order, regulations or rules made under either Act (s 288(9)). It includes, therefore, not only a failure to comply with the main Town and Country Planning Inquiry Procedure Rules but also the Town and Country Planning (Enforcement) (Inquiry Procedure) Rules; the Town and Country Planning (Enforcement) (Notices and Appeals) Regulations; the Town and Country Planning (Control of Advertisements) Regulations; and Town and Country Planning (Appeals) (Written Representations Procedure) Regulations where these are relevant. Where a challenge is made on the grounds that the relevant requirements have not been complied with, the person aggrieved must, if he is asking for the order to be quashed, also show that he has been substantially prejudiced by the failure to comply with those requirements.

19.101 Traditionally, the two grounds of challenge available are referred to as substantive *ultra vires* and procedural *ultra vires*. In practice, however, there is some overlap, since allegations that there has been a breach of natural justice (as opposed to a breach of the Inquiry Procedure Rules) may properly be regarded as being outside the powers of the Act rather than a failure to comply with any relevant requirements.

19.102 The principles on which the court will act in deciding whether or not to quash a planning decision under s 288 is contained in the judgment of the Forbes J in *Seddon Properties Ltd v Secretary of State for the Environment* (1978) 42 P & CR 26 approved by the Court of Appeal in *Centre 21 v Secretary of State for the Environment* [1986] JPL 915. Although the application made in *Seddon* was a challenge of a Secretary of State's decision, the principles laid down in the case apply equally to decisions of Inspectors. The principles stated by Forbes J were:

> (1) The Secretary of State must not act perversely. That is, if the court considers that no reasonable person in the position of the Secretary of State, properly directing himself on the relevant material, could have reached the conclusion that he did reach, the decision may be overturned, see, for example, *Ashbridge Investments Ltd v Minister of Housing and Local Government* [1965] 1 WLR 1320, *per* Lord Denning MR and Harman LJ at pp. 1326 and 1328. This is really no more than another example of the principle enshrined in a sentence from the judgment of Lord Greene MR in *Associated Provincial Picture Houses Ltd v Wednesbury Corporation* [1948] 1 KB 223 at p. 230: 'It is true to say that, if a decision on a competent matter is so unreasonable that no reasonable authority could ever have come to it, then the courts can interfere.'
>
> (2) In reaching his conclusion the Secretary of State must not take into account irrelevant material or fail to take into account that which is relevant, see, for example, again the *Ashbridge Investments* case *per* Lord Denning MR at p. 1326.
>
> (3) The Secretary of State must abide by the statutory procedures, in particular by the Town and Country Planning (Inquiries Procedure) Rules 1974 [now the Inquiries Procedure Rules 2000]. These rules require him to give reasons for his decision after a planning inquiry, and those reasons must be proper and adequate reasons that are clear and intelligible and deal with the substantial points that have been raised, *Re Poyser and Mills' Arbitration, Re* [1964] 2 QB 467.
>
> (4) The Secretary of State in exercising his powers which include reaching a decision such as that in this case must not depart from the principles of natural justice: *per* Lord Russell of Killowen in the *Fairmount Investment* case.

19.103 Many applicants for statutory review (and judicial review) mistakenly assume that the courts are entitled to substitute their own judgment on the planning merits for that of the decision-maker; or they assume that a court is entitled to interfere with the decision of an Inspector or local planning authority on the basis that the decision-maker has given insufficient weight, or too much weight, to a particular material consideration or to a part or parts of the evidence. As was said in *Tesco Stores v Secretary of State for the Environment* [1995] IWLR 759 at 780, 'if there is one principle of planning law more firmly settled than any other, it is that matters of planning judgment are within the exclusive province of the local planning authority or the Secretary of State'.

The courts will only intervene to quash a decision on recognised legal principles (see *City of Edinburgh v Secretary of State for Scotland* [1997] 1 WLR 1447). One of the recognised grounds on which the courts may quash a decision is on grounds of *Wednesbury* unreasonableness. The *Wednesbury* principle, as it is known, is founded on the decision of the Court of Appeal in *Associated Provincial Picture Houses Ltd v Wednesbury Corporation* [1948] 1 KB 223. **19.104**

The case was not about town and country planning, but its importance lies in the control of administrative discretion generally. Although text books have been written on the meaning and application of the principle, the essence of it is that administrators should not make discretionary decisions which are so unreasonable that no reasonable person, properly understanding the law, would make them. For a decision to be quashed on *Wednesbury* grounds, therefore, it is necessary to show that the decision made was perverse. It has been said that the threshold to be overcome by a person alleging unreasonableness, is to show that the decision 'defies comprehension' or 'borders on absurdity'. Many attempts to quash decisions on this ground have failed because the decision-maker was able to show that the decision under challenge was within the scope of reasonable responses available to any reasonable decision-maker. **19.105**

Another ground on which the courts may quash a decision is where an Inspector misconstrues or misapplies a planning policy in reaching a decision as happened in *South Somerset DC v Secretary of State for the Environment* [1993] 1 PLR 80, and more recently in *Lancashire Alderney Estates Ltd v Secretary of State for Transport, Local Government and the Regions* [2002] EWHC 2104. It sometimes happens that the wording of a relevant policy is capable of having more than one meaning. If so, and the meaning adopted by the decision-maker is capable as a matter of law of having that meaning, the courts will not intervene. In *R v Derbyshire CC, ex p Woods* [1997] JPL 958, Brooke LJ said, at p. 967: **19.106**

> If there is a dispute about the meaning of the words included in a policy document which a planning authority is bound to take into account, it is of course for the court to determine as a matter of law what the words are capable of meaning. If the decision maker attaches a meaning to the words they are not properly capable of bearing, then it will have made an error of law, and it will have failed properly to understand the policy (see *Horsham DC v Secretary of State for the Environment* [1992] 1 PLR 80 *per* Nolan LJ at 88). If there is room for dispute about the breadth of the meaning the words may properly bear, then there may in particular cases be material considerations of law which will deprive a word of one of its possible shades of meaning in that case as a matter of law.

Then later, his Lordship said:

> If in all the circumstances the wording of the relevant policy document is properly capable of more than one meaning, and the planning authority adopts and applies a meaning which it is capable as a matter of law of bearing, then it will not have gone wrong in law.

The law concerning the approach to policy has also been set out by Mr George Bartlett QC, sitting as a deputy judge of the High Court, in *Virgin Cinema Properties Ltd v Secretary of State for the Environment* [1998] 2 PLR 24, especially at pages 28H–29E, where he said this: **19.107**

> I readily adopt the approach set out by Auld J, and I would add this. Since a planning policy does

> not confer rights or impose duties that are legally enforceable, I cannot see that it could ever be a matter for the court to determine its meaning as a matter of law for the purposes of deciding an issue arising from the making of a planning application. The decision whether to grant or refuse planning permission is an administrative decision which is only susceptible of review on the well-established principles of administrative law. Any conclusion that is formed by the decision maker as part of that decision can, in my judgment, be challenged only on *Wednesbury* grounds unless it is a conclusion of law. A conclusion on the meaning to be attached to a statute or a statutory instrument or a planning permission (which confers a legal privilege) is a conclusion of law, and a court can, accordingly, determine whether the conclusion is correct. A conclusion on the meaning of a planning policy on the other hand, is a matter for the decision maker in the case. On review, the role of the court, in my judgment, is to say whether the decision maker has attributed to the policy a meaning which he could not reasonably have attributed to it or, in forming his conclusion, has taken into account irrelevant matters or disregarded matters that were relevant. The court thus determines the ambit of reasonableness, which is a matter of law.
>
> If the point of interpretation that is at issue is simply the meaning of ordinary words, it may be the ambit of reasonableness is narrow or nil — that there is only one reasonable meaning. Such, I think, was the 'matter of pure construction' to which Mr Read QC was referring in *HJM Caterers* and the reference by Auld J in *Northavon* to 'the ordinary and natural meaning of words'. Formally, it seems to me, in such a case the court is not determining the meaning of the words in the policy, as suggested in *HJM Caterers*, but is saying that they cannot reasonably be construed in some other way — although, of course, in practice the result does not depend upon this formal distinction. On the other hand are policies which may require for their interpretation an understanding of the thinking and purposes that underlie them. In such cases the expertise of the decision maker will play an important part, and the ambit of reasonableness will be determined taking this into account. The court will also be concerned to see that the decision maker, in interpreting the policy, has taken relevant matters into account and has disregarded irrelevant matters.

19.108 It should also be noted that just as questions of weight are exclusively for the decision-maker, so too are findings of fact. The courts will not intervene unless there is simply no evidence at all to support the findings, or the findings are irrational or perverse in the narrow (*Wednesbury*) sense.

19.109 A question is sometimes asked as to whether there is a duty on the decision-maker to consider whether, and to what extent, any detriment or objection he may find as likely to arise from proposed development, could be dealt with by the use of appropriate conditions. The question has been considered by the courts on a number of occasions, particularly in *M. J. Shaney v Secretary of State for the Environment* [1982] JPL 380 and *Marie Finlay v Secretary of State* [1983] JPL 802. The latter decision was confirmed by the Court of Appeal in *Topdeck Holdings Ltd v Secretary of State* [1991] JPL 961 where, having referred to the judgment of Forbes J in the *Marie Finlay* case, Mann LJ said:

> He [Mann LJ] respectfully agreed with the view expressed by Forbes J. Such an approach had to work sensibly in practice. An Inspector should not have imposed upon him an obligation to cast about for conditions not suggested before him. He emphasised 'obligation'. If, of his own motion, he wished to impose a condition, then, as Forbes J suggested, different considerations would arise, including perhaps the reopening of the appeal.

It is now usual in the case of public inquiries for the Inspector to ask the parties if they wish to suggest conditions to be imposed in any grant of permission, if that should be his decision. This will generally result in the local planning authority suggesting appropriate conditions to which the applicant may or may not agree.

A similar approach is applied where an Inspector may not have before him all the information he considers necessary to arrive at a proper decision. Although it is not possible to lay down general rules in such circumstances, it was said in *John Taylor v Secretary of State for Wales* [1985] JPL 792 that 'an Inspector has no duty to seek to put the parties' own representations in order to give them assistance. However, if an Inspector came to a conclusion that he was unable to come to a fair decision on the issue on the basis of the material before him . . . [he was not] . . . necessarily entitled to sit back and hold that because of a lacuna which could easily be filled, the party had failed to fulfil a burden placed upon him.' **19.110**

Section 288(5) of the Act provides that: **19.111**

> On any application under this section the High Court—
>
> (a) may . . . by interim order suspend the operation of the order or action, the validity of which is questioned by the application, until the final determination of the proceedings;
> (b) if satisfied that the order or action in question is not within the powers of this Act, or that the interests of the applicant have been substantially prejudiced by a failure to comply with any of the relevant requirements in relation to it, may quash that order or action.

Despite the wording of the sub-section, the courts have held that they have a residual discretion not to quash a decision where an application is made under the section. The general rule, however, is that unless the grounds of challenge are purely technical, or the applicant has suffered no real harm, the decision of the Secretary of State should be quashed. Where a decision of the Secretary of State is quashed under these provisions, its effect is to leave the appeal outstanding, so that a further lawful decision has then to be made. Where a decision is quashed by the courts, both sets of Inquiry Procedure Rules require the Secretary of State to give those who were entitled to appear at the inquiry and who duly did so, the opportunity to make further comments on the case following the court's decision. The action taken by the Secretary of State will depend upon the defect that caused the original decision to be quashed. An unintelligible decision letter can be corrected by the issue of an intelligible decision letter; an oversight in the drafting of a condition can be cured merely by the making of the necessary correction of the condition, and the misreading or misinterpretation of an Inspector's decision will need to be cured by inviting the parties concerned to make further representations before the Secretary of State proceeds to make a fresh decision. A failure to allow the parties to comment on new matters of fact taken into account after the close of the inquiry or to ask for the inquiry to be reopened, can be cured by giving them that opportunity or by reopening the inquiry. In *Kingswood DC v Secretary of State for the Environment* [1988] JPL 248, it was held that following the quashing of a decision, the Secretary of State was obliged to deal with the matter *de novo* with a clean sheet, and that he had to have regard to the development plan and to any other material considerations, and thus to any further material considerations arising after the date of the original decision. **19.112**

L. JUDICIAL REVIEW

19.113 An appeal to the High Court under s 288 of the 1990 Act will normally follow upon a refusal by a local planning authority to grant planning permission for development or to grant it subject to conditions; a subsequent appeal being made to the Secretary of State against the authority's decision; and then the determination of that appeal by the Secretary of State. As has been seen, the statutory review procedure provided for in s 288 is available only to a 'person aggrieved' by the decision of the Secretary of State and to the local planning authority concerned. As interpreted by the courts a 'person aggrieved' may include not only the applicant or appellant, but a third party such as a neighbour.

19.114 The ability of a third party to make a legal challenge under s 288 to the grant of planning permission for development is dependent therefore upon the applicant appealing in the first instance to the Secretary of State against the authority's decision. If the applicant should be happy with the local planning authority's decision on the application and therefore does not appeal to the Secretary of State, a s 288 appeal cannot be maintained.

19.115 Due to the unavailability of s 288 in those circumstances, any third party wishing to challenge as *ultra vires* the decision of a local planning authority to grant planning permission for development must generally use the alternative procedure known as 'judicial review' which is available under the provisions of s 31 of the Supreme Court Act 1981 and and Part 54 of the Civil Procedure Rules. Under these rules an 'application for judicial review' has become a 'claim for judicial review' and it follows that an applicant is now known as a claimant. New terminology has also been introduced for some of the remedies which may be sought by judicial review. An order of mandamus; an order of prohibition; and an order of certiorari have become respectively a mandatory order; a prohibiting order; and a quashing order.

19.116 Unlike the procedure under s 288, the procedure for obtaining judicial review is in two stages. First, a claimant must make an application to the Administrative Court, which is a specialist part of the High Court, for permission to proceed with the claim. It would seem that the reason for this first stage is a recognition that public bodies are vulnerable to actions by busy bodies and meddlers and that some filter is necessary to prevent them being harassed by such people. Whereas in the past applications for judicial review were generally made without notice being served on any other party, the new claim for judicial review must now be served on the defendant and any person whom the claimant considers to be directly affected by the claim. This gives the defendant and those directly affected by the claim the opportunity to put before the Court summary grounds of defence before permission to proceed is given. As long as the applicant can show that he has an arguable case; that he has the necessary standing required to seek judicial review; and that he has acted promptly in doing so, permission to apply will normally be granted.

19.117 Another requirement is the introduction from 4 March 2002 of a pre-action protocol for judicial review. This requires a letter to be sent by the claimant to the defendant setting out the main facts and issues before the claim for permission to proceed with judicial review is formally lodged. The protocol requires that the defendant should send a letter of response to the claimant within 14 days. The procedure is to give a public authority the opportunity to act upon the claimant's concerns and so lead to a settlement.

M. THE REQUIREMENT OF STANDING

An claimant must have 'a sufficient interest in the matter to which the application relates'. This is a requirement of both s 31 of the Supreme Court Act 1981 and Part 54 of the Civil Procedure Rules 1998. It impacts not only on the application for permission stage, but also on the second stage when permission to proceed has been granted and the Court is considering the substantive merits of the application. The precise nature of the standing required to seek and obtain judicial review has given rise to much litigation. In *R v Inland Revenue Commissioners, ex p National Federation of Self-Employed and Small Businesses Ltd* [1982] AC 619, the House of Lords held that 'standing' was not just a preliminary issue to be determined only at the permission stage, but was also a substantial issue to be considered at the actual application stage as part of the merits of the case. In *R v Foreign Secretary, ex p World Development Movement Ltd)* [1995] 1 WLR 386, the Divisional Court applied the *Inland Revenue* case, holding that since standing went to 'jurisdiction', it was not to be treated merely as a preliminary issue, but had to be considered against the legal and factual context of the whole case, and that the merits of the challenge were the important, if not the dominant factor, in considering standing. According to the Court, factors to be considered included vindicating the rule of law, the importance of the issue raised, the likely absence of any other responsible challenger and the nature of the relief sought. The Court also considered as relevant to the case the prominent role of the applicants in giving advice, guidance and assistance on questions of overseas aid. **19.118**

Although neither of these cases involved planning issues, notable cases in this field where applicants have been held to have the necessary standing have included *Covent Garden Community Association Ltd v Greater London Council* [1981] JPL 183 (an incorporated body of local residents) and *R v Inspectorate of Pollution, ex p Greenpeace Ltd (No 2)* [1994] 4 All ER 329. In a more recent case, *R v Cotswold DC, ex p Barrington Parish Council* [1997] EGCS 66, the High Court held that despite the fact that the parish was situated some distance from the development site, the Parish Council had sufficient standing, as they were bona fide concerned about the increased through traffic which would go through the parish if redevelopment of the site went ahead. On the other hand, in *R v North Somerset DC and Pioneer Aggregates (UK) Ltd, ex p Garnett* [1997] JPL 1015, the High Court held that the applicants for judicial review had no standing when they lived three miles away from the development site, had no rights over the land, did not themselves object to the application for planning permission, had no commercial interest and had no statutory rights to be consulted on the application. **19.119**

N. THE NEED FOR EXPEDITION

In addition to having the necessary standing to bring a claim for judicial review, it is a requirement of Part 54 of the Civil Procedure Rules that an application for permission to proceed must be made 'promptly', and in 'any event not later than three months from the date when the grounds for the application first arose'. In addition. s 31 of the Supreme Court **19.120**

Act 1981 provides that the court may refuse to grant permission to proceed or any relief sought on the claim where there has been 'undue delay' in making it. The combined effect of these two provisions is that:

(a) the court should refuse leave if the application is not made promptly or within three months at the latest;
(b) if there is good reason for extending time, the appeal court may grant an extension; and
(c) even if the court considers there is good reason, it may still refuse leave if the granting of relief would be likely to cause substantial hardship or prejudice or be detrimental to good administration.

19.121 As regards (a) above however, it cannot be emphasised enough that the court may refuse to grant leave even where the claim is made within three months, if the claimant has not applied promptly. In a case dealing with a challenge to a planning permission *R v Exeter City Council, ex p J.L. Thomas and Co. Ltd* [1991] 1 QB 471, Simon Brown J (as he then was) said:

> I cannot sufficiently stress the crucial need in cases of this kind for applicants [claimants] to proceed with the greatest possible urgency, giving moreover to those affected the earliest possible warning of an intention to proceed.

19.122 Recently, the courts began to get concerned that whereas an applicant for statutory review of a planning decision given by the Secretary of State must take action in the courts within six weeks of the decision, the claimant for judicial review of a planning decision by a local planning authority will normally have three months in which to take appropriate action. Following the decision in *R v Ceredigion CC, ex p McKeown* [1998] 2 PLR 1, however, the normal period of bringing a claim for judicial review was aligned with that for statutory review. Accordingly by a process known as judicial legislation, a number of decisions of the High Court, some sustained on appeal by the Court of Appeal, held that the normal period for bringing a claim for judicial review should also be six weeks. The new practice was universally criticised, being eventually considered by the House of Lords in *R v Hammersmith and Fulham London Borough Council exp Burkett* [2002] JPL 1346. The case involved an application for judicial review made under old procedures, but one with the same time limits for commencing the action. The question to be considered was whether the time limit for commencing proceedings ran from the date of a resolution to grant planning permission or the grant of planning permission itself. Their Lordships held that time ran from the date of the grant for the reason that a mere resolution to great planning permission created no legal rights. With regard to the replacement of the three-month time limit by a six-week rule, their Lordships considered that the legislative three-month limit could not be contracted by a judicial policy decision. In addition, their Lordships considered it doubtful whether the obligation to apply 'promptly' was sufficiently certain to comply with the European Convention for the Protection of Human Rights and Fundamental Freedoms.

O. THE REMEDY

19.123 A claim for judicial review may be used to secure a mandatory order, a prohibiting order or a quashing order. It may also be used to secure an injunction or a declaration. The procedure is flexible, in that although the applicant must specify in his application for permission the particular remedy or remedies he seeks, the court may decide to grant some other remedy allowed for by the order if it considers it more appropriate to do so. Judicial review it must be emphasised is not an 'appeal' from a decision of a public authority, but a review of the manner in which the decision is made. It deals with the legality or validity of the decision, not as an appeal to the Secretary of State, on whether the decision is right or wrong. For that reason, the court cannot substitute its own decision for that being challenged.

P. THE ROLE OF THE OMBUDSMAN

The administration of government services, whether carried out by central or local government, may sometimes lead to complaints by citizens which the courts are either unable to deal with because no legal rights of the citizen have been infringed, or because where they have been, the courts are ill-equipped to provide an adequate remedy. As a result, Parliament has set up two Ombudsman systems to help the citizen. First, the Parliamentary Commissioner Act 1967 established the Parliamentary Commissioner for Administration (colloquially known as the Parliamentary Ombudsman) to receive and investigate complaints against Central Government Departments. Secondly, the Local Government Act 1974 established two Commissions for Local Administration, one for England and one for Wales, the membership of which consists of Local Commissioners (colloquially known as Local Government Ombudsmen) to receive and investigate complaints against local government. **19.124**

Although a number of important differences exist in the way in which the Parliamentary and Local Government Ombudsmen operate, their jurisdictional remit (though held in relation to different tiers of government activity) is the same, namely to investigate complaints by members of the public who claim to have 'suffered injustice in consequence of maladministration'. In addition, the maladministration must have occurred in connection with the exercise of the 'administrative functions' of the Department of authority concerned. **19.125**

Neither the Parliamentary Commissioner Act 1967 nor the Local Government Act 1974 attempted to define the meaning of the word 'maladministration', though in the debate in the House of Commons during the passage through Parliament of the Parliamentary Commission Act 1967, the Lord President of the Council defined it as covering 'bias, neglect, inattention, delay, incompetence, inaptitude, arbitrariness and so on'. It has been said that the greatest part of that ten-point catalogue is the 'and so on'. In *R v Local Commissioner for Administration, ex p Bradford MCC* [1979] QB 287, Lord Denning MR described the term as 'open-ended'. In truth, the catalogue has proved to be the working basis upon which the Ombudsmen proceed. **19.126**

Two important limits in the jurisdiction of the Parliamentary and Local Government Ombudsman must also be mentioned. First, both Ombudsmen are prohibited from questioning the merits of any decision taken without maladministration in the exercise of a discretion vested in the Department or in the authority, as the case may be. This means that a member of the public cannot complain to the Ombudsman merely because he considers the body concerned should have reached a different decision to the one it did reach. **19.127**

Maladministration must always be present, therefore, before the Ombudsman can issue an adverse report. Secondly, both Ombudsmen are prohibited from investigating cases where the person aggrieved has or had a remedy in any court of law, or a right of appeal, reference or review before any tribunal.

19.128 This provision is an attempt to devise demarcation lines, particularly between the remit of the courts and the remit of the Ombudsmen. It is not, however, a rigid demarcation line, since a proviso in both the Parliamentary Commissioner Act 1967 and the Local Government Act 1974 allows the Ombudsman to investigate a complaint if satisfied that in the particular circumstances it is not unreasonable to expect the complainant not to pursue his legal remedies or rights of appeal.

19.129 In two substantial ways the Parliamentary and the Local Government Ombudsman schemes differ. First, access to the Parliamentary Ombudsman can only be obtained via a Member of the House of Commons, whereas access by members of the public to the Local Government Ombudsman is direct. Secondly, whereas the Parliamentary Ombudsman is invariably successful when he finds maladministration and injustice in persuading the Central Government Department concerned to provide the remedy he has sought for the injustice suffered by the complainant, in some six per cent of cases where the Local Government Ombudsman has sought a remedy from the authority for injustice suffered by the complainant, the authority concerned has declined to provide it.

19.130 In *R v Commissioner for Local Administration, ex p Liverpool CC* [2001] 1 All ER 462, Henry LJ indicated that the circumstances where it might be appropriate for the Ombudsman to exercise discretion to investigate where judicial review might be available were where, having regard to the weaknesses of the coercive fact-finding potential of judicial review it would be difficult, if not impossible, for the complainants to obtain the necessary evidence in judicial review proceedings; where the complainants are unlikely to have the means to pursue a remedy through the courts; and where the Ombudsman's investigation and report can provide a just remedy when judicial review may fail to do so.

19.131 The statistics show that complaints of injustice suffered through maladministration made against the Secretary of State are rare. This is not the position, however, with regard to complaints made to the Local Government Ombudsmen against local authorities exercising their planning functions. The Annual Report of the Commission for Local Administration in England for 2003/04 shows that 18,892 complaints were received by the Commission during the year, of which 30 per cent related to planning or highway matters.

19.132 Among a selection of remedies obtained by Local Government Ombudsmen for complainants over the past few years have been the following:

(a) Failure to inform a purchaser that planning permission had been granted for an extension to neighbouring property — £7,800 for reduction in market value; £878 agents' fees; and £250 for time and trouble.

(b) Failure to deal with noise nuisance; complainant forced to take own legal action — £2,000 for having to endure nuisance; £13,000 and contribution to complainants legal costs.

(c) Failure to check accuracy of plans submitted with planning application — £2,000 plus reimbursement of professional fees.

(d) Giving inconsistent advice about whether or not land was within the green belt — £2,937 in respect of surveyors' fees and £250 for time and trouble.

(e) Advising neighbours incorrectly that planning permission for corner extension not required — £2,500 for loss of value and £800 costs.

(f) Failure to ensure developer complied with a planning condition requiring foul/surface water drainage — £8,067 for replacement kiln and £8,220 for reinstating building.

(g) Failure to confirm a compulsory purchase order preventing service by owner of business premises of blight notice — £6,500 for delay and uncertainty plus £250 for time and trouble.

(h) Failure to inform and consult on pedestrianisation proposal — £38,729, being half the costs incurred by the complainants in connection with the public local inquiry.

(i) Failure to properly appreciate the height of a proposed roller-coaster to be erected at a leisure park to the detriment of residents living nearby — £5,000 to each complainant being the loss in value of the complaints' homes.

(j) Not adequately dealing with complaints regarding the continuing development of a nearby industrial estate which had polluted a watercourse and affected the complainant's farming activities — £26,926 to cover a number of separate categories of harm identified by the Ombudsman.

(k) Failure to deal properly with an application for planning permission for two neighbouring sites in that the authority failed to advertise proposed development affecting the setting of a listed building, failed to notify English Heritage and failed to advertise the application as a departure from the provisions of the development plan — £40,000 to the owner of one site in return for his entering into a s 106 agreement not to implement the planning permission and £35,000 each to two other complainants.

(l) Incorrect advice given to complainant that planning permission required for the erection of a dwellinghouse — £3,000.

(m) The redesignation of land by the authority from community to retail use and an invitation to tender for a lease advertised. Complainant company awarded lease but application for planning permission subsequently refused. Compensation of £14,937 awarded, being half the company's costs associated with preparing planning application.

(n) Giving a prospective purchaser incorrect advice that planning permission was not needed to operate a hot food takeway shop, leading the complainant to incur extra costs in obtaining planning permission (on appeal) after purchase — £5,000.

(o) Failure to assess properly the merits of an amended application for the erection of a detached garage, resulting in the depreciation of a neighbour's property — £18,000.

(p) Granting planning permission having formed an incorrect view of the nature of the proposed development, resulting in the diminution of value of a neighbour's property — £10,000.

(q) Taking into account irrelevant considerations in granting planning permission for a forestry contractor's yard; not applying s 54A, ignoring the previous decision of the Inspector following an appeal against an earlier refusal — £10,000, being the loss in value of the complainant's home.

(r) Amended plans accepted after grant of planning permission for conversion of farm buildings when new application should have been sought — £2,500, being reduction in value of complainant's house.

(s) Failure to enforce condition relating to screening of complainant's property — £2,000, being consequent devaluation of his property.

(t) Grant of permission for supermarket without understanding the significance of the access and service arrangements — £7,500 to each of two complainants following adverse effects on their property/businesses.

(u) Approval of detail for large dwelling given contrary to provisions of development plan — £15,000 to complainant for depreciation in value of his property.

(v) Misleading advice as to right to restore farmhouse. Subsequent enforcement action and farmhouse had to be demolished — £70,686 to cover demolition and other costs.

(w) A local planning authority gave conflicting decisions as to whether development had commenced within the period of five years required by a condition in the grant of planning permission. Authority later issued lawful development certificate accepting that it had — £17,692 to cover complainants' financial losses (fees for legal advice, LDC application fee and interest lost because sale of land delayed).

(x) Council approved application for permission to extend an industrial estate into open countryside in the mistaken belief that the site was 'brownfield' or previously developed land — £5000 paid to local amenity society that made the complaint.

(y) Misleading advice given to Council by officers over planning status of land, leading to the grant of planning permission and loss in value of a neighbour's property — £25,000 being the loss suffered by the neighbour as a result.

(z) Failure to consider on a reserved matters planning application, the impact of a block of flats on a neighbour's cottage — £37,500 being the loss in value of the cottage.

(a_2) Failure of Council to secure the payment of a deposit from a developer to ensure that links to a private road were brought up to an adequate standard — £16,250.

(b_2) Failure to deal with an application to erect a mobile telephone mast within the statutory timescale, resulting in planning permission being given by default — £66,442 in total to four complainants in respect of the devaluation of their properties.

In the year 2003/04, remedies given resulted in a total of 22 'before and after' valuations where property had been devalued as a result of maladministration.

20

HUMAN RIGHTS

A. THE HUMAN RIGHTS ACT 1998

The substantive provisions of the Human Rights Act were brought into force on 2 October 2000. It incorporated into domestic law the provisions of the European Convention on Human Rights. The main features of the Act are: **20.01**

(a) So far as it is possible to do so, primary and subordinate legislation, whenever passed, must be read and given effect to in a way which is compatible with the Convention;
(b) Public authorities are forbidden to act in a way which is incompatible with Convention rights. If they should do so, 'the victim' of that act may proceed directly against the authority concerned, in the courts;
(c) Although the courts have not been given the power to strike down legislation which is incompatible with Convention rights, they may make a declaration of incompatibility. Any legislative provision declared by the courts to be incompatible with the Convention, however, does not necessarily make the decision unlawful. Although s 6(1) of the Act provides that it is unlawful for a public authority to act in such a way that is incompatible with a Convention right, the provision is disapplied in cases where the authority could not have acted differently. This means that a declaration of incompatibility does not affect the validity, continuing operation or enforcement of that provision in any particular case, nor is it binding upon the parties. Any declaration of incompatibility would of course be of great symbolic significance, which it would be impossible for the Government to ignore. Accordingly, the Act provides a 'fast track' procedure which enables the Secretary of State to amend statutes by way of statutory instrument.

The main Convention rights that are likely to be relevant to land use controls are set out in Art 1 of Protocol 1 and Arts 6 and 8 of the Convention. The following are the more important extracts from those Articles:

Article 1 of Protocol 1
Every natural or legal person is entitled to the peaceful enjoyment of his possessions except in the public interest.

Article 6(1) of the Convention

(1) In the determination of his civil rights and obligations or of any criminal charge against him, everyone is entitled to a fair and public hearing within a reasonable time by an independent and impartial tribunal established by law . . .

Article 8 of the Convention

(1) Everyone has the right to respect for his private and family life, his home and his correspondence.

(2) There shall be no interference by a public authority with the exercise of this right except such as is in accordance with the law and is necessary in a democratic society in the interests of national security, public safety or the economic well-being of the country, for the prevention of disorder or crime, for the protection of health or morals, or for the protection of the rights and freedoms of others.

20.02 Since 1966, it has been possible for individuals, after exhausting all domestic law remedies, to petition the European Court of Human Rights directly to complain that they have suffered from an infringement of their rights under the Convention. This will continue to be the case now that the 1998 Act has been brought into force.

20.03 In the past, the European Court of Human Rights has considered a number of complaints from individuals under this procedure. The following are three of the most important cases affecting land use decided by the European Court.

20.04 In *Bryan v United Kingdom* [1996] JPL 386 the applicant had been served with an enforcement notice and after exhausting all domestic remedies, unsuccessfully alleged a breach by the United Kingdom of Art 6(1) of the Convention in so far as he had not received in the determination of his civil rights 'a fair and public hearing . . . by an independent and impartial tribunal'. The Court held that although the review by an Inspector did not of itself satisfy the requirements of Art 6, the procedures and safeguards of judicial review available to him were sufficient compliance with the Convention.

20.05 In *Buckley v United Kingdom* [1996] JPL 1018, the applicant had been refused planning permission for the siting of a caravan on her own land. She alleged, *inter alia*, a breach of Art 8 of the Convention which protects a person's rights to respect for his home. It was held that Art 8 did not go so far as to allow an individual's preference as to his place of residence to override the general interest; and that since the regulatory framework within which the decision was made contained adequate procedural safeguards protecting the applicant's interest, there had been no violation of Art 8.

20.06 In *Chapman v United Kingdom* (2001) 33 EHRR 329 and other related cases, the European Court of Human Rights had to consider whether there had been a breach of Art 8 of the Convention as a result of action taken by the local planning authority, by way of injunctions and enforcement notices, to require the complainant to cease occupation of a caravan on her land. Although the Court held that the measures taken constituted an interference with her rights under Art 8(1), it also found the interference to have been 'in accordance with law' and that it pursued a legitimate aim of protecting 'the rights of others' through preservation of the environment. There had therefore been no breach of Art 8.

20.07 Given the views expressed by many commentators on the likelihood that some of the main principles of planning legislation would be found to be incompatible with the Convention, one could not be surprised at the flurry of litigation that followed the incorporation of the Convention into domestic law.

The most significant case (or rather collection of cases) gave rise to the landmark decision of the House of Lords in what has become known as the *Alconbury* decisions. Four applications had been made to the High Court for declarations that the planning process in each case was not compatible with Art 6(1) of the Convention. The *Alconbury* case itself involved an appeal against a refusal of planning permission recovered by the Secretary of State under ss 78 and 79 of the 1990 Act. Two of the other cases involved decisions by the Secretary of State to call in applications for planning permission under s 77 of the 1990 Act for determination by himself. The fourth case involved the proposed use by the Secretary of State of highway orders and related compulsory purchase orders in connection with a scheme to improve the A34/M4 road junction. In all four cases the Divisional Court of the Queen's Bench Division was prepared to grant the declarations of incompatibility sought. **20.08**

Appeals were pursued in three of the four cases. With the consent of the parties involved and the Divisional Court, the conjoined appeals were 'leapfrogged' to the House of Lords. The fourth case was not appealed since it did not raise any different issue. On 9 May 2001 the House of Lords in *R (on the application of Alconbury Developments Ltd) v Secretary of State for the Environment, Transport and the Regions; R (on the application of Holding & Barnes) v Secretary of State for the Environment, Transport and the Regions*; and *Secretary of State for the Environment, Transport and the Regions v Legal and General Society Ltd* [2001] 2 WLR 1389 unanimously allowed all three appeals from the Divisional Court's decision. **20.09**

The House of Lords agreed that the determination of administrative matters such as planning decisions involved the determination of 'civil rights and obligations' within the meaning of the Convention and that, in challenging them, people were entitled to the protection of Art 6. The Secretary of State had not claimed that in dealing with a called-in application or a recovered decision, he was acting as an independent tribunal and, for that reason, he could not be seen to be impartial. According to the House of Lords, the Divisional Court had erred in concluding that Art 6 prohibited the Secretary of State from being both a policy-maker and a decision-maker. The question for the courts was whether there was sufficient judicial control to ensure a determination by an independent and impartial tribunal subsequently. There was no requirement that this should constitute a rehearing by way of an appeal on the merits. What was required was that there should be a sufficient review of the legality of the decision and the procedures that were followed. None of the judgments of the European Court of Human Rights required that the courts should have 'full jurisdiction' to review policy or the overall merits of a planning decision. The European Court of Human Rights had recognised that planning decisions fell into a specialised area. As in the *Bryan* case, the European Court had recognised that in planning matters it was necessary to have regard to such matters as the subject matter of the decision appealed against, the way in which the decision was arrived at, and the content of the dispute, including the desired and actual grounds of appeal. In each of the cases there would be a public inquiry before an Inspector. The inquiry would be an occasion for the exploration of facts including the need for and desirability of the development. The inquiry would be regulated by rules to ensure fairness in the procedure, and there would be opportunities for judicial review after the eventual decision of the Secretary of State. Accordingly, in the cases before their Lordships, there had in **20.10** principle been no violation of Art 6 of the Convention. The scope of judicial review was sufficient to comply with the standards set by the European Court.

20.11 Although the basic features of the British planning process appear to have survived relatively unscathed by the incorporation of the Convention into domestic law, the clean bill of health given to it in the *Alconbury* judgment by the House of Lords does not necessarily mean that all aspects of the planning process are compatible with the Convention. Some aspects may yet be found to be in breach, so imposing on the Government an obligation to make appropriate changes. In addition, the incorporation of the Convention into British domestic law may have a peripheral influence on some of the ways in which planning decisions are made. It must be borne in mind, however, that under Art 8 planning authorities in exercising their powers are entitled to have regard to what 'is necessary in a democratic society in the interests of . . . the economic well-being of the country . . . the protection of health or morals . . . or for the protection of the rights and freedoms of others'. Likewise under Art 1 of Protocol 1 a person may not be deprived of his possessions 'except in . . . the general interest'. The decision-maker will frequently, therefore, be called upon to strike a balance between interference with a landowner's rights and the wider public issues such as harm to the environment. In this context, the European Court of Human Rights has accepted the principle that within that legitimate area of discretion given to the decision-maker, a 'margin of appreciation' should be allowed in a State's favour.

The application of the Act

20.12 The effect of these provisions is to strengthen the influence of proportionality as a factor to be taken into account by the decision maker. He will frequently have to strike a balance between landowners' rights and wider public concerns such as harm to the environment. In those cases the degree of interference must be proportionate to the harm. In the Court of Appeal in *David Lough v First Secretary of State* (Case No. C3/2004/0183) Pill L.J. spelt out the approach to be followed in considering Art. 8 and Art. 1 of the First Protocol:

> Recognition must be given to the fact that Article 8 and Article 1 of the First Protocol are part of the law of England and Wales. That being so, Article 8 should in my view normally be considered as an integral part of the decision maker's approach to material considerations and not, as happened in this case, in effect as a footnote. The different approaches will often, as in my judgment in the present case, produce the same answer but if true integration is to be achieved, the provisions of the Convention should inform the decision maker's approach to the entire issue. There will be cases where the jurisprudence under Article 8, and the standards it sets, will be an important factor in considering the legality of a planning decision or process.

He went on to say:

> The question whether the permission has 'an excessive or disproportionate effect on the interests of affected persons' is a question which has routinely been posed by decision makers both before and after the enactment of the 1998 Act. . . . He went on to say 'it is important to emphasise that the striking of a fair balance lies at the heart of proportionality'.

20.13 Yet cases challenging planning decisions continue to come before the courts. They include the following:

(a) In *R (on the application of Kathro) v Rhondda Cynon Taff CBC* [2002] PLCR 304, a distinction was made between the decision-making powers of a local planning authority and that of the Secretary of State. In that case it was acknowledged that where an authority (which is not an independent and impartial tribunal) has to determine a disputed issue of fact, the control exercised by the courts might not be sufficient to ensure compliance with Art 6.

(b) In *R (on the application of Vetterlein) v Hampshire CC and Hampshire Waste Services Ltd* [2002] PLCR 289, the claimants who were 'third parties', challenged the local planning authority's decision to grant planning permission for the construction of a waste incinerator. The court held that though it was appropriate in some circumstances to look beyond the claimants' front doorstep, there was no reasonable and convincing evidence that the claimants' quality of life was so directly affected by the incinerator as to engage Art 8. Furthermore, even if Art 6 entitled the claimants to a fair and public hearing, the opportunity given to the claimants to make detailed representations during the public consultation process and to address the committee had fulfilled that requirement.

(c) In *Lafarge Redland Aggregates Ltd v Scottish Ministers* [2001] SC 298, the Scottish Court of Session held that the failure of the Scottish Ministers to determine an application for planning permission made in 1991 for a 'super quarry' on the Isle of Harris was a breach of Art 6. The delay which had occurred after the application had been called in was described by the court as one of 'scandalous proportions'.

(d) In *South Bucks DC v Porter* [2003] UKHL 26, the House of Lords had to consider the implications of the Human Rights Act 1998 on the use of injunctions under the provisions of s 187B of the 1990 Act. The case (and other linked cases) concerned the use of injunctions against gypsies to secure their removal from land where there had been a breach of planning control. In spelling out the factors which needed to be considered, the House emphasised the duty under the Human Rights Act to act in accordance with the Convention. Proportionality required not only that the injunction be appropriate and necessary for the attainment of public interest objectives, but that it did not impose an excessive burden on the individual whose private interests were at stake. This case is considered more fully in Chapter 21 (Enforcement of Planning Control).

Article 6

Not unexpectedly, cases continue to be brought before the courts on human rights grounds particularly with regard to the decision of local planning authorities and third party rights. **20.14**

It would seem beyond doubt that in the case of the determination of planning applications, a local planning authority is not an independent and impartial tribunal for the purposes of art 6, in the same way as it was accepted in the *Alconbury* case that the Secretary of State was not. As with *Alconbury*, the question of whether Art 6 was engaged with regard to local planning authority decisions, will depend very much upon the authority's decision-making procedures and the extent to which any defects in them can be cured by the High Court's power of review. These procedures will often involve the rights of third parties. **20.15**

The following cases address this problem: **20.16**

In *R (Adlard) v the Secretary of State for Transport, Local Government and the Regions* [2002] JPL **20.17**

1379, the Court of Appeal had to consider a challenge to the Secretary of State's decision not to call in an application for planning permission for the redevelopment of Fulham Football Club. The local planning authority had previously resolved to grant planning permission, but in doing so, had not given objections to the development the opportunity to voice their objections at an oral hearing, The question for the Court to decide was whether that had been a breach of their rights under art 6. In considering that question the Court considered some earlier High Court decisions. Those were:

Friends Provident Life and Pensions Ltd. v the Secretary of State for Transport, Local Government and the Regions [2002] JPL 958. The claimants sought to challenge the local planning authority's grant of planning permission for a large shopping centre in Norwich. They argued that the Secretary of State's failure to call in the application was a breach of Art 6. The High Court considered that there was no reason why Art 6. should not extend to the administrative decision-making power, provided it directly affected their rights. On the facts however, the Court considered that the issues in dispute 'did not give rise to the type of investigation of fact which required the safeguards attaching to a public inquiry before an independent Inspector, which would then ensure that the determination of [the claimant's] civil rights was Art 6 compliant.

R (Cummins) v Camden London Borough Council [2001] EWHC Admin 116. Here, the High Court held that Art 6 was not engaged by the formulation and preparation of development plan policies.

R (Aggregate Industries UK Ltd.) v English Nature [2002] EWHC Admin 908. In this case the claimants had challenged the decision of a local planning authority to grant planning permission for the redevelopment of a leisure centre. It was claimed that the decision and the failure of the Secretary of State to call in the application for his own determination were in breach of their art 6 rights. The Court decided that a claim that an objectors' civil rights had been infringed had be to both significant and evidenced; and that the impact on 'view' was most unlikely to meet such a test.

20.18 In the Adlard case, the Court of Appeal, having considered the above four cases, went on to conclude that although in each case the objectives had been given limited opportunities to make their submissions, nothing in them suggested that oral hearings were necessary to satisfy Art 6. It also concluded that the statutory planning scheme as a whole was plainly compliant with Art 6. However, the Court would not rule out that an oral hearing might be necessary in an 'exceptional' case.

20.19 Other cases where the Courts have had to consider human rights issues include:

Boris Homes Ltd. v New Forest District Council [2002] EWHC Admin 483, where the High Court held that Art 6 did not apply to the local plan process because civil rights were not directly affected by that process.

R (Stewart) v Planning Appeals Commission (June 26, 2002 unrepaired), where the High Court of Northern Ireland held that the absence in law of compensation for planning restrictions was not incompatible with Convention rights.

Coal Mining Ltd. v Secretary of State for the Environment, Transport and the Regions [2002] JPL 1634, where the High Court held (*obiter*) that the claimant's rights under Art 6 had not been breached as the result of the excessive time taken by the Secretary of State (two and half years after receipt by him of the Inspector's report), to issue his decision letter. The decision was quashed however, for reasons other than Art 6 issues.

Perhaps a particular area of law where the Convention has had an albeit impact, indirectly, is in forcing the courts to consider the criteria used by local planning authorities in their use of injunctions to enforce planning control. This is dealt with in Chapter 21 (Enforcement of Planning Control). **20.20**

In the *David Lough* case, the Court of Appeal held that the diminution in the value of land did not *of itself* constitute a loss contemplated by Human Rights law, but that it might demonstrate the loss of privacy or amenity which would be a human rights issue. **20.21**

Lastly, one should note that before the Human Rights Act became law, the Government assessed the implications of the Act for the planning process and decided that no changes were required in order to avoid successful challenges under it. **20.22**

Post-Alconbury, that view has not been changed. In an Answer to a Parliamentary Question in the House of Commons on 15 October 2001, a Parliamentary Under-Secretary of State said, '[We] do not consider that there is any need on Human Rights Act grounds for changes to the appeals system generally or specifically in relation to third party objectors.'

21

ENFORCEMENT

A. INTRODUCTION

21.01 Under the Agricultural Land (Removal of Surface Soil) Act 1953 where the removal of surface soil from agricultural land constitutes development, it is an offence to do so without planning permission. Subject to that exception to develop land without planning permission is not a criminal offence. Nevertheless, there has to be a sanction to ensure that unauthorised development can be prevented. The sanction provided by the law is mainly imposed by the enforcement notice machinery contained in Part VII of the 1990 Act. Under this machinery, once an enforcement notice takes effect, the development which is unauthorised must cease or be removed. If it is not, then, and only then, is a criminal offence committed of failure to comply with the enforcement notice.

21.02 The law relating to enforcement notices has been strengthened over the years on numerous occasions, the most major being in 1991. Under the Planning and Compulsory Purchase Act 2004, however, the Crown will be made subject to enforcement action and a new 'temporary' stop notice procedure is to be introduced.

21.03 The provisions of Part I of the Planning and Compensation Act 1991 supplemented and amended the enforcement provisions contained in Part VII of the 1990 Act. The amendments, which strengthened and improved the enforcement of general planning control, were based on the recommendations in a report by Robert Carnwath QC, *Enforcing Planning Control*, published by the Department of the Environment in April 1989.

21.04 According to Baroness Blatch, Parliamentary Under-Secretary of State at the Department of the Environment, in introducing the Planning and Compensation Bill in the House of Lords in November 1990, the report showed that there was a small minority of people who were determined contraveners of planning regulations. Acknowledging this, Baroness Blatch said:

> it is those people who bring the system into disrepute; and it is their damaging and unwelcome activities . . . which the enforcement amendments are intended to deter or, failing that, to remedy through increased penalties; new methods of enforcing planning conditions; and improved powers of local authority officers to enter private land for enforcement purposes.

21.05 Part I of the 1991 Act supplemented the provisions of the 1990 Act by providing a new procedure for local planning authorities to obtain information relating to suspected breaches of planning control (planning contravention notices); for enforcing planning conditions (breach of condition notices); and for obtaining injunctions to restrain breaches of planning control (planning injunctions). The remainder of Part I of the 1991 Act amended the 1990 Act to alter the time-limits on the taking of enforcement action; to provide for greater flexibility in the drafting and service of enforcement notices; to revise the power of the Secretary of State on appeal; to extend the power of a local planning authority to execute works required by an enforcement notice; to increase the penalties for non-compliance with an enforcement notice; to revise the provisions relating to stop notices; to provide for a new certificate of lawful use or development; and to give authorities greater rights of entry to property for enforcement purposes.

21.06 Despite the changes made to the enforcement provisions by the 1991 Act, concern is still expressed with regard to those who disregard planning legislation. In the consultation paper, 'Delivering a Fundamental Change', published in December 2001, the Government accepted that 'Effective action needs to be taken against those who try wilfully to avoid planning controls . . . Where planning regulations are broken, there is a perception — often accurate — that they are not being sufficiently enforced'. Accordingly, the Government has introduced a 'temporary' stop notice procedure in the latest legislation.

B. PLANNING CONTRAVENTION NOTICES

In deciding whether or not to serve an enforcement notice, the local planning authority must, as far as possible, be sure of its facts. Accordingly, s 324 of the 1990 Act gives power to local planning authorities to enter land, subject to at least 24 hours notice of intention to do so, for the purposes of surveying it in connection with the service of notices, including enforcement notices. In addition, s 330 enables a local planning authority to demand information from the occupier of land as to his interest. The Carnwath report recommended that there should be a new optional statutory procedure, not only to enable authorities to obtain information, but to secure co-operation from an owner without recourse to enforcement action. This was done by the Planning and Compensation Act 1991, which inserted ss 171C and 171D into the 1990 Act providing for the service of planning contravention notices. Under s 171C(l), where it appears to the local planning authority that there may have been a breach of planning control in respect of any land, the authority may serve a notice to that effect (called a 'planning contravention notice') on any person who is the owner or occupier of the land or has any other interest in it, or who is carrying out operations on the land or using it for any purpose. Where a notice is served, s 171C(2) provides that the notice may require the recipient to give such information as may be specified in the notice about any operations being carried out on the land, any use of the land and any other activities being carried out on it, and any matter relating to conditions or limitations subject to which any planning permission has been granted in respect of the land. In addition, s 171C(3) provides that, without prejudice to the generality of s 171C(2), the notice may require the recipient, so far as he is able to do so, to state whether or not the land is being used for any purpose specified in the notice, or whether any operations or activities specified in the notice are being or have been carried out on the land; to state when any use, operations or activities began; to give the names and addresses of any persons known to him to use or have used the land for any purpose or to be carrying out or have carried out any operations or activities on the land; to give any information in his possession as to any planning permission for any use or operations or any reason for planning permission not being required for any use or operations; to state the nature of his interest (if any) in the land and the name and address of any other person known to him to have an interest in the land. 21.07

Under s 171C(5), a planning contravention notice must inform the recipient of the likely consequences of his failure to respond to the notice and, in particular, that enforcement action may be taken. In addition, the recipient must also be informed that in the event of enforcement action being taken, failure to respond to the notice may affect his entitlement to compensation in the event of a stop notice also being served. It should be noted that the service of a planning contravention notice in no way prejudices other action the planning 21.08

authority may wish to take in respect of a breach of planning control, including the service of a temporary stop notice. If a local planning authority is already in possession of all the information necessary, it may decide to take enforcement action without the earlier service of a planning contravention notice.

21.09 Sub-section (1) of s 171D provides that if any person fails to comply with any requirement of a planning contravention notice within a period of 21 days, he shall be guilty of a criminal offence. The section goes on to provide that if at any time after conviction that person continues to fail to comply with any requirement of the notice, he may be convicted of a second or subsequent offence, thereby ensuring that the requirement is eventually complied with. Under s 171D(3), it is a defence for a person charged with an offence to prove that he had a reasonable excuse for failing to comply with a requirement in the notice. In addition to the above, a person is guilty of an offence if the information he gives in response to a planning contravention notice is false or misleading in a material particular, or he recklessly makes a statement which is false or misleading in a material particular.

21.10 Under s 171C(4), a planning contravention notice may give notice of a time and place at which any offer which the recipient of the notice may wish to make to apply for planning permission, or to refrain from carrying out any operations or activities or to undertake remedial works, and any representations which he may wish to make about the notice, will be considered by the authority. The authority must give the recipient an opportunity to make any such offer or representations, in person, at a specified time and place.

21.11 It will be seen that the refusal of the person served with a planning contravention notice to make an offer (as opposed to providing the information required by the notice) is not a criminal offence. The recipient of the notice may well decline to do so without fear of any penalty. Hence, there must be considerable uncertainty as to the extent to which an offer would be made by that 'small minority of determined contraveners' mentioned by Baroness Blatch.

21.12 In the first case to consider this new provision, *R v Teignbridge DC, ex p Teignmouth Quay Co. Ltd* [1995] JPL 828, the procedure was described as 'intrusive and if properly served, the compliance was mandatory'. The court went on to grant judicial review to quash the notice, on the ground that the local planning authority's inquiries before service were not sufficient on their own to satisfy the minimal statutory requirements before which the notice could be served.

21.13 According to statistics published by the Department of the Environment, 4,629 planning contravention notices were issued by local planning authorities in the year ending 31 March 2004.

C. ADDITIONAL RIGHTS OF ENTRY ON PROPERTY

21.14 The rights of local planning authorities in the 1990 Act to enter on land did not distinguish between the power to enter land for the purposes of investigating a breach of planning control and other powers to enter land for planning purposes, such as in connection with development plan preparation; the consideration of applications for planning permission or the making, for example, of a revocation or modification order. It was often difficult, therefore, for a local planning authority to obtain the precise information needed in order to take formal and effective enforcement action. Mention has been made above of the powers now available to a local planning authority under the 1990 Act to obtain information by means of the 'planning contravention notice'. In addition, however, the 1991 Act introduced into the 1990 Act three new sections, 196A, 196B and 196C, in order to give local planning authorities more specific rights of entry on to land to be exercised where enforcement action is foreseen.

Sub-section (1) of s 196A provides that any person duly authorised in writing by a local planning authority may at any reasonable hour enter land to ascertain whether there is or has been any breach of planning control on land; to determine whether any of the powers conferred by the Act on a local planning authority should be exercised; to determine how any such power should be exercised; and to ascertain whether there has been compliance with any requirement arising from earlier enforcement action in relation to the land. The power of entry given by this sub-section is subject to the proviso that there must be reasonable grounds for entering the land for any of those purposes. In the case of any building used as a dwellinghouse, the section provides that admission to the building shall not be demanded 'as of right', unless 24 hours' notice of the intended entry has been given to the occupier of the building. It would appear that this 24 hours' notice is not necessary if the authority wish to enter upon land adjoining a dwellinghouse or on land within its curtilage. **21.15**

If entry in accordance with these provisions is refused, s 196B(1) provides that if it is shown to the satisfaction of a justice of the peace, on sworn information in writing, that there were reasonable grounds for entering any land for the purposes of ascertaining whether there has been a breach of planning control or for determining whether enforcement action should be taken, and that admission to the land has been refused, or a refusal is reasonably apprehended, or the case is one of urgency, the justice may issue a warrant authorising any person duly authorised in writing by the local planning authority to enter the land. It should be noted that the warrant authorises entry on to the land in question on one occasion only, and entry must be within one month from the date of issue of the warrant, and at a reasonable hour, unless the case is one of urgency. **21.16**

Section 196C of the 1990 Act contains provisions which are supplementary to ss 196A and 196B discussed above. All the provisions in s 196C replicate provisions previously found in the 1990 Act, being applicable to the exercise of rights of entry for a whole range of planning purposes. The section groups those supplementary provisions in one section to be exercised in connection with the enforcement of planning control. **21.17**

D. TEMPORARY STOP NOTICES

Section 52 of the Planning and Compulsory Purchase Act 2004 will add greatly to the powers for a local planning authority to deal with breaches of planning control which may have been disclosed, either by the service of a planning contravention notice, or otherwise. Section 52 when implemented fully will introduce four new sections 171E to 171H to the 1990 Act giving a local planning authority a wide new discretionary power to serve a **21.18** temporary stop notice to halt breaches of planning control for a period of up to 28 days. It will enable authorities to service the notice without waiting until an enforcement notice can be served. It will also prevent the intensification of a use or other form of development believed to be unlawful whilst further action is being considered. A temporary stop notice will have an immediate effect, though it may be withdrawn by the authority before the 28 days have expired. A second temporary stop notice may also be issued in respect of the same activity, but only if the authority has first taken some other enforcement action in relation to the breach of planning control constituted by the activity required to be stopped by the earlier notice. No reasons for the stop notice need be given, and there is no appeal.

21.19 It is provided that a temporary stop service cannot be issued to prohibit the use of a building as a dwelling house. In addition, the Secretary of State has the power by regulation to prescribe any other activity for which the temporary stop notice cannot be issued. Neither can the service prohibit the carrying out of any activity which has been carried out for at least four years, unless it is an activity consisting of or incidental to operational development, or the deposit of refuse or waste materials.

21.20 The new sections provide that the notice must be in writing; prohibit the carrying on of the activity; set out the reasons for issuing the notice; and be served on the person who the authority think is carrying on the activity, a person who is the occupier and a person who has an interest in the land.

21.21 A copy of the notice and statement of the effect of the notice must also be displayed by the authority on the land.

21.22 The provisions also make it an offence to contravene a temporary stop notice (which includes causing or permitting the contravention of a notice). It is punishable on summary conviction to a maximum fine of £20,000 or on conviction on indictment, a fine without limit. In determining a fine the court has to have regard to any financial benefit which has accrued to the person in consequence of the offence.

21.23 In certain cases the compensation may be payable by the local planning authority to the owner of an interest in the land to which the notice serves, where that person has suffered loss or damage directly attributable to the prohibition effected by the notice. The right to compensation is limited, however, to cases where the temporary stop notice is withdrawn by the authority, or the activity specified in the notice has been authorised by planning permission, a development order or a local development order, or a certificate of lawful use or development in respect of the activity is granted under Section 191 of the 1990 Act.

E. ENFORCEMENT NOTICES

Time-limits on enforcement action

21.24 Under sub-section (2) of s 171A of the 1990 Act, enforcement action may be taken by the issue of an enforcement notice or by the service of a breach of condition notice. Such enforcement action may only be taken in relation to a breach of planning control, defined in s 171A(1) as carrying out development without the required planning permission, or failing to comply with any condition subject to which planning permission has been granted.

The Planning and Compensation Act 1991 made important amendments to the 1990 Act with regard to the time-limits for the bringing of enforcement action by a local planning authority. Under the old law, where the breach of planning control was the carrying out without planning permission of operational development, no enforcement action could be taken after the end of a period of four years from the date the operations were completed. No change has been made in that provision, save that the period is now made to run for four years from the date on which the operations were substantially completed. A question may arise as to when an operation is *substantially* completed, particularly in the case of a dwellinghouse. In *Sage v Secretary of State for the Environment, Transport and the Regions and Maidstone BC* [2003] JPL 1299, the Court of Appeal had held that a dwellinghouse was not substantially completed if what still remained to be done amounted to development under s 55(1) of the 1990 Act. **21.25**

If that had remained the law, it would have meant that works which might still be needed to make the dwellinghouse fit for habitation, such as by the putting in of an internal staircase, would not prevent the building from being regarded as substantially completed. This is because of s.55(2) of the 1990 Act which provides that works for the maintenance, improvement or other alteration of a building which affect only the interior of the building or which do not materially affect its external appearance does not involve the development of land. **21.26**

The House of Lords however, thought otherwise. Lord Hobhouse, who gave the main speech, thought that any work carried out by way of completing an incomplete structure, would not be work for the maintenance, improvement or other alteration of the building. In short, his Lordship restricted the operation of s.55(2) to a building which had already been completed, not to one that remained uncompleted. According to Lord Hobhouse, one had to adopt a holistic approach to determine whether building works had been substantially completed. He observed that where an application for planning permission was made for a single operation, it was made in respect of the whole of that operation. The concept of a full planning permission required a detailed building of a certain character; if an operation was not carried out both externally and internally fully in accordance with the planning permission then the whole operation was unlawful. **21.27**

In *First Secretary of State v Chelmsford Borough Council* [2003] EWHC 2800 (Admin), the High Court applied *Saga* in holding that the bringing on to land of two static caravans and their bolting together did not amount to a substantial completion of the development and was therefore unauthorised. The holistic approach required by Lord Hobhouse in *Saga* meant that substantial completion had not occurred until after the subsequent application of cladding to the structure, which in itself would not have required planning permission. **21.28**

It should also be noted that under the previous law, no enforcement action could be taken in relation to a change of use of any building to use as a single dwellinghouse if the use has subsisted for more than four years. Again no change was made in 1991 to that provision. For the purposes of enforcement action, the Secretary of State has taken the view that in order to establish that a building has been used as a single dwellinghouse, it must be shown that for the four-year period ending with the taking of enforcement action, the building must comprise a self-contained independent unit of accommodation, containing all the facilities normally associated with a dwelling behind a single, lockable door. **21.29**

21.30 Where the contravening development involved some other change of use, however, there had been since 1964 no time-limit on the period within which an enforcement notice could be served. This has now been changed by the 1991 Act. Section 171B of the 1990 Act, now provides that in the case of any other breach of planning control (i.e., other than operational development or a change of use of any building to use as a single dwellinghouse), no enforcement action may be taken at the end of a period of ten years beginning with the date of the breach. A problem may arise if, during the ten-year period, there has been a time when the local planning authority had no legal power to enforce against the unauthorised change of use. This is considered further in section 22.171.

21.31 One further change was made to the time-limits for the bringing of enforcement action by the 1991 Act. Under the old law, where there had been a breach of a *condition* in a planning permission not involving a change of use to use as a single dwellinghouse, the condition could only be enforced on action taken within four years of the date of the breach. The effect of sub-section (3) of s 171B of the 1990 Act, is that the time-limit for enforcement action in such cases has raised from four years to ten years. The rationale of the four and ten-year periods of immunity is that, throughout the relevant period of unlawful use the local planning authority, although having the opportunity to take enforcement action, has failed to do so and consequently it would be unfair and/or could be regarded as unnecessary to permit enforcement.

21.32 A further important change should also be noted. Under the old law, where an enforcement notice had been issued and was subsequently held to have been defective, further enforcement action had to be taken before the period of immunity commenced. Now under s 171B(4)(b) if an enforcement notice is held to be defective, the authority is given a further four years from the taking of the previous enforcement action (or purported action) in which to issue another effective enforcement notice in respect of the same breach.

21.33 The purpose of this 'second bite' provision is to remove the protection given to developers whereby under the old law they were able to avoid enforcement action by establishing that a technical error had been made in the enforcement notice; and during the period they were doing so, the time for service was continuing to run and eventually expired, leaving it too late for another enforcement notice to be issued. In *Jarmain v Secretary of State for the Environment, Transport and the Regions* [2000] JPL 1063, it was held that it was not necessary for the actual breach of development control to be described in the same way in both enforcement notices. The sub-section could not be used to cover two different physical developments or two different changes of use, but it could be used to cover the same actual breach of development control, even though they were described in different ways. Accordingly, in the *Jarmain* case, the Court of Appeal dismissed an appeal from a decision of the High Court which had held that where the first enforcement notice had described incorrectly the breach of planning control as being the siting on land of a 'mobile home', the sub-section enabled the authority to issue a further enforcement notice which described the breach as the erection of 'a single storey building' on the land.

21.34 In *Fidler v First Secretary of State for the Environment and Reigate and Banstead Borough Council* [2004] JPL 630, it was said that where a second bite notice goes wider than the earlier notice, as for example by including land and uses outside that specified in the first notice, or does not describe more accurately that which had been wrongly described in the earlier notice, the later notice was more than a mere correction of a technicality. It thus fell outside the range of circumstances at which s.171B(4) was aimed.

F. ISSUE OF ENFORCEMENT NOTICES

Under s 172 of the 1990 Act, a local planning authority may *issue* an enforcement notice where it appears to them: **21.35**

(a) that there has been a breach of planning control; and
(b) that it is expedient to issue the notice, having regard to the provisions of the development plan and to any other material considerations.

The provision in para (b) above is, of course, to be read in conjunction with s 38(6) of the Planning and Compulsory Purchase Act 2004 (see Chapter 4), which gives the development plan a position of primacy over other material considerations where a determination has to be made under the planning Acts. Once issued, a copy of the enforcement notice is now required to be *served*. Sub-section (2) of s 172 provides that a copy shall be served: **21.36**

(a) on the owner and occupier of the land to which it relates, and
(b) on any other person having an interest in the land, being an interest which, in the opinion of the authority, is materially affected by the notice.

The term 'owner' in s 172(2) causes few problems. Section 336(1) of the 1990 Act defines an owner to mean: **21.37**

> . . . a person, other than a mortgagee not in possession, who, whether in his own right or as trustee for any other person, is entitled to receive the rack rent of the land or, where the land is not let at a rack rent, would be so entitled if it were so let.

The Act, however, does not define the term 'occupier'. The term has, therefore, given rise to some litigation, particularly over the question of whether caravan dwellers come within the term. In *Munnich v Godstone RDC* [1966] 1 WLR427, it was considered that they did not. In *Stevens v Bromley LBC* [1972] Ch 400, it was considered that they did. In a later case, *Scarborough BC v Adams* [1983] JPL 673, caravan dwellers were again held to be occupiers and entitled, therefore, to be served with a copy of the enforcement notice. In *Stevens*, it was held that the question of whether a caravan dweller was an occupier, was one of fact and degree in every case. There would be many cases where it would be difficult to decide on which side of the line it fell, but exclusive occupation and a degree of permanence were factors to be taken into account. Whether a person is an occupier and therefore has a right to be served with an enforcement notice may be critical, since s 174 of the 1990 Act allows a person who occupies the land to which a notice relates by virtue of a licence, a right of appeal to the Secretary of State against the notice. **21.38**

Where a person entitled to be served with a copy of an enforcement notice is not served, the position can be quite complicated. Before 1968, the position was that if an enforcement notice was challenged in the courts on the ground that a person required to be served with a notice had not been served, the court had no option but to quash the notice. This led to a practice known as 'shuffling of interests', whereby, after the local planning **21.39** authority had made inquiries about the nature of a person's interest in land prior to the service on him of the enforcement notice, that person transferred his interest to a friend or relative, so that when the notice was eventually served it was served on a person who was not the owner of an interest in the land, and was not served on the person who had now become the owner. Similar transfers sometimes took place between associated 'one-man' companies.

21.40 To meet this difficulty, the 1968 Act introduced a number of new provisions into the law. One, which is now found in s 176(5) of the 1990 Act, provides that where it would otherwise be a ground for determining an appeal in favour of the appellant that a person required to be served with a copy of the enforcement notice was not served, the Secretary of State may disregard that fact if neither the appellant nor that person has been substantially prejudiced by the failure to serve him.

21.41 This may meet the case of a transfer made between spouses prior to service of a copy of the enforcement notice. But it is not likely to meet the case of an innocent purchaser who may know nothing of the notice and is unable, therefore, to appeal to the Secretary of State before the notice has taken effect. Accordingly, the 1968 Act made a further change in the law which is now contained in s 285 of the 1990 Act. Normally, the validity of an enforcement notice cannot be questioned in the courts on any of the grounds on which a person may bring an appeal against it to the Secretary of State (see below). Since one of the grounds of appeal to the Secretary of State is that copies of the enforcement notice were not served on those required to be served by the Act, this provision would, by itself, mean that a person not served would be unable to question the legality of the notice if he were subsequently prosecuted under s 179(6) to (8) of the Act for a failure to comply with the notice.

21.42 Accordingly s 285 provides that the embargo on questioning the validity of an enforcement notice shall not apply to proceedings brought under s 179(6) to (8) of the 1990 Act against a person who:

(a) has held an interest in the land since before the enforcement notice was issued . . .;
(b) did not have a copy of the enforcement notice served on him . . .; and
(c) satisfies the court—
  (i) that he did not know and could not reasonably have been expected to know that the enforcement notice had been issued; and
  (ii) that his interests have been substantially prejudiced by the failure to serve him with a copy of it.

21.43 Despite those elaborate provisions, however, it may still be possible for a person to be bound by an enforcement notice of which he has no notice. The saving provisions of s 285 do not anticipate that a local planning authority might choose not to prosecute under s 179(6) to (8) but to exercise its powers under s 178(1) to enter the land and to carry out the work which is required to be done by the enforcement notice. In *R v Greenwich LBC, ex p Patel* (1985) 51 P & CR 282, the applicant sought by way of judicial review an order of prohibition against the local planning authority prohibiting them from entering his land and demolishing a shed which had been erected on the land by his wife without the grant of planning permission. The enforcement notice had been served on the applicant's wife as the person 'owning the land'. It was in fact owned by the applicant. There had been no appeal against the notice to the Secretary of State. Earlier, it appears, the applicant's wife had been refused planning permission to erect the shed on the land which she had stated she owned; and an appeal against the refusal had been dismissed by the Secretary of State. The applicant claimed he first knew of the notice when his wife received a letter from the local planning authority informing her of their intention to enter the land and demolish the shed.

In withholding the relief applied for, the Court of Appeal refused to hold that the failure to serve the enforcement notice in accordance with what is now s 172(2) rendered it a nullity. According to the Court of Appeal, Parliament has expressly provided machinery to deal with circumstances where an enforcement notice has not been served on a person who should have been served. In doing so, it felt able to distinguish the Scottish case of *McDaid v Clydebank District Council* [1984] JPL 579, where the Court of Session had seemingly held to the contrary. In that case, however, the local planning authority had erred in that they had been aware of the identity of the owner but had still failed to serve him. In the *Patel* case, the Court of Appeal found that there had been no deliberate disregard of the statutory requirement by the local planning authority; nor had they failed to show due diligence. Furthermore, there was no reason to suppose that the applicant had suffered any real prejudice. **21.44**

The Scottish case shows that despite the changes made in 1968, there may still be situations where the failure to serve an enforcement notice in accordance with the provisions of s 172(2) will render the notice a nullity. For that to happen, however, it appears that not only must the owner or occupier have been prejudiced by the failure to serve the notice on him, but there must also have been some malfeasance on the part of the authority. **21.45**

Sub-section (3) of s 172 of the 1990 Act also provides a strict time-limit for service of copies of the enforcement notice. According to the sub-section, the service of the notice shall take place: **21.46**

(a) not more than 28 days after its date of issue; and
(b) not less than 28 days before the date specified in it as the date on which it is to take effect.

The importance of this provision is that s 173(8) of the 1990 Act provides that any enforcement notice must specify the date on which it is to come into effect; after which date no appeal will lie to the Secretary of State. **21.47**

Two key dates, therefore, are the date when the enforcement notice is issued (i.e., made by the authority) and the specified date in the notice as the date on which it is to come into effect. The effect of s 172(3) is to ensure that within that time period all copies of an enforcement notice that have to be served are served within 28 days of the date of its issue, and that any recipient of a copy of such an enforcement notice has it in his possession for at least 28 days before it comes into effect. The effect can be shown thus: **21.48**

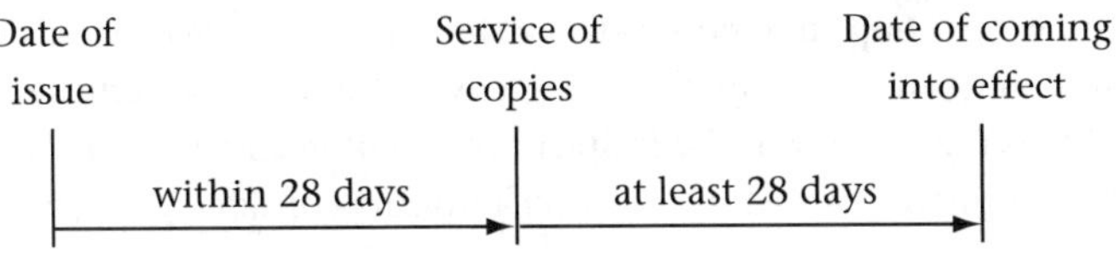

21.49 The purpose of the first period is to overcome a problem that sometimes used to arise when an enforcement notice was served on different persons on different days. In *Bambury v Hounslow London Borough Council* [1966] 2 QB 204, enforcement notices were served on three occupiers of land on 22 August 1964. Each notice required the unauthorised development to be discontinued within 28 days from the date on which the notice took effect. All stated that the notice should take effect on the expiration of 28 clear days after service of the notice.

21.50 Then on 8 September 1964 a further enforcement notice in similar terms was served on the owner. On appeal to the High Court the enforcement notices were quashed. The occupiers successfully contended that there could not be two dates for the coming into force of the same enforcement notice. If there were two separate dates, there were in effect two separate enforcement notices, neither of which had been served as required by the law on both the owners *and* occupiers of the land to which they related.

21.51 Under the 1990 Act provisions, the procedure is commenced not when the enforcement notice is served by the authority, but when it is *issued* by them; and it enables the authority to serve *copies* of the notice, on persons required to be served, on any number of different dates, so long as all persons are served within the time span set out in s 172(3).

21.52 The purpose of the second period is to give the recipient of the notice a minimum period of 28 days in which to decide whether or not to appeal against the notice. If he decides not to appeal, the notice takes effect on the date stated. If, however, he decides to appeal against the notice to the Secretary of State, s 175(4) provides that subject to any order made under s 289(4A) (of which see 18.7.2), the enforcement notice shall be of no effect pending the final determination or withdrawal of the appeal.

G. CONTENT OF ENFORCEMENT NOTICES

21.53 Section 173(1) of the 1990 Act provides that an enforcement notice shall state:

(a) the matters which appear to the local planning authority to constitute the breach of planning control; and
(b) the paragraph of s 171A(1) within which, in the opinion of the local planning authority, the breach falls.

21.54 Following the judgment in *Copeland Borough Council v Secretary of State for the Environment* [1976] JPL 304, where a building had been erected otherwise than in accordance with approved plans, an enforcement notice may be served alleging that the building as a whole had been built without planning permission.

21.55 The 1990 Act originally provided that an enforcement notice should 'specify' the matters alleged to constitute the breach. By requiring the notice now to 'state' these matters, the drafters of the 1991 Act hope that notices will be less likely to be challenged as being a nullity because the breach has not been specified correctly. In addition, the effect of sub-section (2) of the new s 173 is that as long as the recipient of an enforcement notice understands from the notice what the matters are which the local authority consider to be a breach of planning control, the notice is not to be regarded as defective on the ground that it did not state the breach with sufficient clarity or particularity.

It seems from the decision in *Westminster City Council v Secretary of State for the Environment and Aboro* [1983] JPL 602 that it is not necessary to specify in an enforcement notice the use from which it is alleged there has been a material change of use, though it is usual to do so. Furthermore, in *McCarthy v Secretary of State for the Environment, Transport and the Regions* [1999] JPL 993, the High Court held that an enforcement notice could lawfully be served in relation to part of a planning unit, provided the question of the materiality of the change of use was considered by reference to the whole of the planning unit. **21.56**

Having stated the breach of planning control, sub-sections (3) and (4) of section 173 then requires the notice to specify the steps which the authority require to be taken, or the activities which the authority require to cease, in order to achieve, wholly or partly, any of the following purposes: **21.57**

(a) remedying the breach by making any development comply with the terms (including conditions and limitations) of any planning permission granted in respect of the land, by discontinuing any use of land or by restoring the land to its condition before the breach took place; or
(b) remedying any injury to amenity which has been caused by the breach.

Sub-section (5) provides the following examples of what an enforcement notice may require:

(a) the alteration or removal of any building or works;
(b) the carrying out of any building or other operation;
(c) any activity on the land not to be carried on except to the extent specified in the notice;
(d) the contour of a deposit of refuse or waste materials on land to be modified by altering the gradient or gradients of its sides.

In addition, where an enforcement notice is issued in respect of a breach of planning control consisting of demolition of a building, the notice may require the construction of a 'replacement building', as similar as possible to the demolished building. **21.58**

By virtue of s 173(11), if the notice could have required any buildings or works to be removed or any activity to cease, but does not do so, or requires the construction of a replacement building, and the notice is complied with, planning permission is deemed to be granted for the buildings, works, activity or replacement building. Following the decision in *Lipsen v Secretary of State for the Environment* [1976] P & CR 95, it is long established that an enforcement notice cannot require a former use to be revived. **21.59**

This is a very important provision where there has been a breach of planning control and the local planning authority decides to 'under-enforce'. If the notice has been complied with, planning permission is granted for that development which has not been enforced against. The section does not grant planning permission for development not enforced against in the notice, but is limited to producing the effect of a grant of permission for that development. Hence, as held in *Sparkes v Secretary of State for the Environment, Transport and the Regions* [2000] PLCR 279, the provision does not allow conditions to be imposed on that unenforced development. **21.60**

21.61 In *Murfitt v Secretary of State for the Environment* [1980] JPL 598 and *Somark Travel v Secretary of State for the Environment* [1987] JPL 630, the principle was established that an enforcement notice can properly require the undoing or removal of any incidental operational development where it forms an integral part of the development enforced against. This is so even though the operational development may by itself not constitute a breach of planning control. So that, for example, where hard-standings and sheds are an integral part of an unauthorised use, an enforcement notice can require them to be removed as part of the cessation of that unauthorised use. The principle also applies to operational development which by itself is immune from enforcement action by virtue of the four-year rule or development which has been carried out as permitted development.

21.62 Having stated what has to be done to remedy the breach, the notice must also specify the period at the end of which the steps required to be taken must be taken or any activities required to cease must cease. In this connection, s 173(9) provides that a notice may specify different periods for the taking of different steps or activities.

21.63 An enforcement notice must specify such additional matters as may be prescribed, and regulations may require every copy of an enforcement notice to be accompanied by an explanatory note giving information about rights of appeal. Indeed, Regulation 4 of the Town and Country Planning (Enforcement Notices and Appeals) Regulations 2002 requires that the explanatory note should contain a copy of ss 171A to 177 of the 1990 Act, or a summary including information as to the right of appeal and of the recipient's duty to give his grounds of appeal. In addition, the regulations require the local planning authority to specify details of all policies and proposals in the development plan relevant to the decision to issue the notice; the fee payable for any deemed application for planning permission; and a requirement for the Secretary of State to notify the appellant and the local planning authority when he considers he has received all the documents required to enable him to entertain the appeal.

21.64 The new provisions in the 1990 Act relating to the steps which the recipient of the notice must take to remedy the breach were redrafted by the 1991 Act in order to give local planning authorities greater flexibility in the choice of those steps including, if the authority wish, the power to 'under-enforce'.

21.65 It should also be noted that local planning authorities are now given the power to withdraw an enforcement notice issued by them, or waive or relax any requirement of an enforcement notice, including, in particular, power to extend the time specified in the notice for compliance with it (s 173A(1)). When using this power, however, the authority must give notice of its exercise to every person served with a copy of the enforcement notice.

21.66 Where an enforcement notice is withdrawn, the local planning authority may issue another, and that other may be more onerous than the notice which was withdrawn (*Manchester City Council v McLoughlin* [1999] JPL B110).

21.67 According to statistics published by the Department of the Environment, 4,600 enforcement notices were issued by local planning authorities in the year ending 31 March 2004.

H. APPEALS AGAINST ENFORCEMENT NOTICES

Section 174(1) of the 1990 Act provides that: **21.68**

> A person having an interest in the land to which an enforcement notice relates or a relevant occupier may appeal to the Secretary of State against the notice, whether or not a copy of it has been served on him.

It should be noticed that the persons entitled to appeal under s 174(1) are not coterminous with the persons who are required to be served with a copy of the notice under s 172(2). The right of appeal to the Secretary of State is restricted to those having an interest in the land and relevant occupiers. A 'relevant occupier' is a person who: **21.69**

(a) on the date on which the enforcement notice is issued, occupies the land to which the notice relates by virtue of a licence, and
(b) continues so to occupy the land when the appeal is brought.

It would seem that the term relevant occupier would include a person entitled to a right of way over the land.

An appeal must be made by notice in writing to the Secretary of State before the specified date (i.e., the date specified in the notice as the date on which it is to take effect). Failure to appeal by that date may be fatal for any person wishing to do so, since, as was confirmed by the Court of Appeal in *Howard v Secretary of State for the Environment* [1975] QB 235, the Secretary of State has no jurisdiction to extend that date. After that date if no appeal has been made the enforcement notice will come into effect and must be complied with, unless that is, the notice is a nullity. **21.70**

Section 174(2) provides that an appeal may be brought on any of the following grounds: **21.71**

(a) that, in respect of any breach of planning control which may be constituted by the matters stated in the notice, planning permission ought to be granted or, as the case may be, the condition or limitation concerned ought to be discharged;
(b) that those matters have not occurred;
(c) that those matters (if they occurred) do not constitute a breach of planning control;
(d) that, at the date when the notice was issued, no enforcement action could be taken in respect of any breach of planning control which may be constituted by those matters;
(e) that copies of the enforcement notice were not served as required by section 172;
(f) that the steps required by the notice to be taken, or the activities required by the notice to cease, exceed what is necessary to remedy any breach of planning control which may be constituted by those matters or, as the case may be, to remedy any injury to amenity which has been caused by any such breach;
(g) that any period specified in the notice in accordance with section 173(9) falls short of what should reasonably be allowed.

It will be seen that ground (a) relates to the merits of the development, grounds (b) to (e) to question of law or fact or mixed question of law and fact and grounds (f) and (g) to remedial measures required to be taken by the notice. **21.72**

The real purpose of setting out the grounds of appeal in s 174(2) is not merely to list the **21.73** likeliest grounds on which an appeal will be brought. Its significance lies in the restrictive provisions of s 285(1) of the 1990 Act. That sub-section provides:

> Subject to the provisions of this section, the validity of an enforcement notice shall not, except by way of an appeal under Part VII, be questioned in any proceedings whatsoever on any of the grounds on which such an appeal may be brought.

21.74 The effect of this provision is to prevent the validity of the notice being challenged on any of the grounds specified in s 174(2) except by way of appeal to the Secretary of State. It prevents a person from questioning the validity of the notice on those grounds by way of proceedings for judicial review or (save for the one exception previously mentioned) in proceedings brought against that person for a failure to comply with the enforcement notice. The provision, however, does not prevent a person from questioning the validity of the notice by judicial review or by way of defence to a prosecution for failure to comply with the notice on grounds not specified in s 174(2). A person is not precluded, therefore, from challenging the legality of an enforcement notice other than by way of appeal, if he can show the notice to be a nullity. In *MacKay v Secretary of State for the Environment* [1996] JPL 761 it was held that for an enforcement notice to be a nullity, the notice has to be defective on its face. This would occur, for example, if a person could show that the notice failed to specify the date on which it was to take effect; failed adequately to state the matters alleged to constitute the breach; failed to identify the land affected; failed to specify the steps required to be taken to remedy the breach as occurred in *Tandridge DC v Verrechia* [2000] PLCR 1; or failed to state a compliance period. For an example of this latter deficiency, see [2000] JPL 549 where an Inspector treated six enforcement notices as nullities where no period for compliance had been stated.

21.75 Likewise, in *R (Lynes and Lynes) v West Berkshire District Council* [2003] JPL 1137, the High Court granted a declaration that an enforcement notice (and an associated stop notice) were nullities where the enforcement notice had stated that it was to take effect 'immediately', since this failed to specify the 'period for compliance' required by s.179(3).

21.76 In order to avoid the Secretary of State being unable to consider an appeal against an enforcement notice because, perhaps due to postal delays, the notice of appeal was not received before the date on which the enforcement notice was expressed to take effect, s 174(3) provides that an appeal shall be made either by giving written notice to the Secretary of State before the date specified in the notice as the date on which it is to take effect, or by sending such notices to him in a properly addressed and prepaid letter posted to him at such time that, in the ordinary course of post, it would be delivered to him before that date.

21.77 As a general principle of law, a person given a right of appeal on certain specified grounds (as with enforcement notice appeals) is the person who has to make good those grounds and on whom the onus rests. In *Nelsovil v Minister of Housing and Local Government* [1962] 1 WLR 404, it was held that where an appeal against an enforcement notice is made the burden of proof is on the appellant.

Appeal procedure

21.78 As already stated, an appeal must be made by notice in writing to the Secretary of State, before the date specified in the notice as the date on which it is to take effect. In order to determine the appeal properly, however, the Secretary of State needs to know the grounds upon which a person is appealing against the notice, as well as the facts upon which the appeal is based. He will also need to know the reason why the authority served the notice in the first place. Prior to the Local Government and Planning (Amendment) Act 1981, it was difficult for the Secretary of State to move to a speedy determination of the appeal if the parties concerned failed to provide this information, and in the absence of a power to make regulations requiring this to be done, his only course was to determine the appeal without that information. The 1981 Amendment Act resolved much of this difficulty by reformulating the obligation on the appellant to specify his grounds of appeal and to give the Secretary of State the power to make regulations with regard to enforcement notice appeals.

Section 174(4) and (5) of the 1971 Act now provides: **21.79**

(4) A person who gives notice under sub-section (3) shall submit to the Secretary of State, either when giving the notice or within the prescribed time, a statement in writing—
   (a) specifying the grounds on which he is appealing against the enforcement notice; and
   (b) giving such further information as may be prescribed.

(5) If, where more than one ground is specified in that statement, the appellant does not give information required under sub-section (4)(b) in relation to each of those grounds within the prescribed time, the Secretary of State may determine the appeal without considering any ground as to which the appellant has failed to give such information within that time.

Under s 175(1) of the 1990 Act the Secretary of State may by regulations prescribe the procedure which is to be followed on appeals under section 174 and, in particular, but without prejudice to the generality of this sub-section, may—

(a) require the local planning authority to submit, within such time as may be prescribed, a statement indicating the submissions which they propose to put forward on the appeal;
(b) specify the matters to be included in such a statement;
(c) require the authority or the appellant to give such notice of such an appeal as may be prescribed;
(d) require the authority to send to the Secretary of State, within such period from the date of the bringing of the appeal as may be prescribed, a copy of the enforcement notice and a list of the persons served with copies of it.

Under these provisions the Secretary of State has made the Town and Country Planning (Enforcement Notices and Appeals) Regulations 2002, SI 2682. These regulations require the appellant to specify (in addition to his grounds of appeal) the facts upon which the appeal is based. He must do this within 14 days of being required to do so. In practice, if the appellant has not supplied this information within one week of the end of the 14-day period, the First Secretary of State sends a warning letter to the appellant setting out the powers of the Secretary of State at the end of that period. Section 176(3) provides that the Secretary of State: **21.80**

(a) may dismiss an appeal if the appellant fails to comply with section 174(4) within the prescribed time; and
(b) may allow an appeal and quash the enforcement notice if the local planning authority

fail to comply with any requirement of regulations made by virtue of paragraph (a), (b) or (d) of section 175(1) within the prescribed period.

Furthermore, s 174(5) provides that:

> if where more than one ground is specified in that statement, the appellant does not give information required under sub-section (4)(b) in relation to each of those grounds within the prescribed time, the Secretary of State may determine the appeal without considering any ground as to which the appellant has failed to give such information within that time.

21.81 Under these provisions the local planning authority can also be required to provide information relevant to the appeal, and if they fail to do so, the Secretary of State is empowered to allow the appeal and quash the notice.

21.82 It will be seen that enforcement notice machinery contains a rigorous timetable within which each particular stage must be completed. In particular, the recipient of the notice has to ensure:

(a) that if he wishes to appeal he does so before the enforcement notice takes effect;
(b) that if he does appeal he specifies his grounds and the facts upon which each ground of appeal is based and in any event within 14 days of being required to do so;
(c) that in the event of the enforcement notice taking effect he takes, within the period or periods stated in the notice, the steps required by the notice to be taken to remedy the breach of planning control.

For its part, the local planning authority have to ensure:

(a) that copies of the notice are served on those required to be served within 28 days of issue by the authority;
(b) that each recipient is in possession of a copy of the notice for at least 28 days before it takes effect; and
(c) that if an appeal is made against the notice, they provide the Secretary of State, within the period prescribed for doing so, with the information required to be provided under the regulations.

21.83 Under s 175(3), the Secretary of State is required, if either the appellant or the local planning authority so desire, to give to each of them an opportunity of appearing before, and being heard by, a person appointed by the Secretary of State for the purpose. This may be done by a public local inquiry, although it is open to both parties to agree that the matter shall be dealt with by way of written representation procedure or hearing. Where an inquiry is held the procedure is governed by the Town and Country Planning (Enforcement) (Inquiries Procedure) (England) Rules 2002.

21.84 It has been estimated that evidence is given on oath in about half the cases involving appeals based on grounds (c), (d) or (e) of s 174(2).

21.85 Section 177 of the 1990 Act provides that on determination of an appeal under s 174, the Secretary of State may:

(a) grant planning permission in respect of the matters stated in the enforcement notice as constituting a breach of planning control, whether in relation to the whole or any part of those matters or in relation to the whole or any part of the land to which the notice relates;

(b) discharge any condition or limitation subject to which planning permission was granted;

(c) determine whether, on the date on which the appeal was made, any existing use of the land was lawful, any operations which had been carried out in, on, over or under the land were lawful or any matter constituting a failure to comply with any condition or limitation subject to which planning permission was granted was lawful and, if so, issue a certificate under s 191.

Indeed, s 177(5) provides that where an appeal against an enforcement notice is made, the appellant shall be deemed to have made an application for planning permission in respect of the matters stated in the enforcement notice as constituting a breach of planning control. Accordingly, the Secretary of State has power to grant planning permission, even though no appeal has been made on ground (a) of s.174(2), that planning permission ought to be granted for the matter alleged to be a breach of planning control. Under the section and the appropriate regulations, the planning application fee must be paid at the time written notice of appeal is given to the Secretary of State or within such period as is specified by the Secretary of State. If the appropriate fee is not paid, the deemed application, or the appeal to the extent to which it is based on ground (a) of s 174(2) will lapse. This latter provision is intended to overcome the problem where in the past the Secretary of State could quash the enforcement notice on the ground that planning permission for the contravening development should be granted, but was unable to grant planning permission because no planning application fee had been paid. That in effect left the planning status of the land in 'limbo'; without any planning permission existing for the development which had taken place, and enforcement powers being no longer available. 21.86

A further limitation on the power of the Secretary of State to grant planning permission under s 177 in respect of any matter stated in the enforcement notice to constitute a breach of planning control, is that the 'deemed' application related to development for which environmental assessment is required, the Secretary of State is precluded from granting planning permission unless an environmental statement has been submitted. 21.87

The power to vary

As the statistics show, many enforcement notices, although upheld by the Secretary of State, are varied by him on appeal. Power to do this is given by s 176(1) of the 1990 Act, which provides that on an appeal under s 174 the Secretary of State may: 21.88

(a) correct any defect, error or misdescription in the enforcement notice; or

(b) vary the terms of the enforcement notice.

if he is satisfied that the correction or variation will not cause injustice to the appellant or the local planning authority.

It seems that the power given to the Secretary of State under para (a) above allows him to alter the substance of an enforcement notice in order to enable him to give effect to the determination of one of the statutory grounds of appeal. The power given to him under para (b) above 21.89

allows him to give effect to its substance by overcoming a defect in form and thus failing on a technicality.

21.90 The powers of the Secretary of State under this provision are limited. An enforcement notice must tell the recipient clearly what he has done wrong and what he must do to remedy it. If it fails to do this, the notice is a nullity and beyond correction. The best known consideration of the scope of this power was by Lord Denning MR in *Miller-Mead v Minister of Housing and Local Government* [1963] 2 QB 196 where he said, at p. 221:

> The Minister has power . . . to correct any informality, defect or error in the enforcement notice if he is satisfied that the informality, defect or error is not a material one. This seems to me to be wider than the 'slip rule'. I think that it gives the Minister a power to amend, which is similar to the power of the court to amend an indictment. He can correct errors so long as, having regard to the merits of the case, the correction can be made without injustice. No informality, defect or error is a material one unless it is such as to produce injustice. Applied to misrecitals, it means this: if the misrecital goes to the substance of the matter, then the notice may be quashed. But if the misrecital does not go to the substance of the matter and can be amended without injustice, it should be amended rather than that the notice should be quashed or declared a nullity. In this way the legislature has disposed of the proposition that there must be a 'strict and rigid adherence to formalities'.

21.91 The statutory provisions considered by Lord Denning have been significantly reformulated in s 176(1) to reflect the construction placed by him on the earlier statutory provisions, and also to restrict the power of correction or variation to cases where this can be done without injustice to the authority as well as to the appellant. The power is often used to delete from an enforcement notice land falling outside the planning unit, to alter the steps required to remedy the breach, and to extend the time for compliance with the notice. It cannot be used, however, to turn a nullity into a valid enforcement notice.

21.92 The difficulties of expressing to the recipient of the notice in clear terms what must be done to remedy the breach is best seen in *Kaur v Secretary of State for the Environment* [1990] JPL 814. In that case the notice had required, *inter alia*, the removal of a mansard roof. On appeal, the Inspector considered the wording could have been clearer and amended it to require the reinstatement of a pitched roof the design of which was required to be 'first agreed with the local planning authority'. Sir Frank Layfield QC, sitting as a deputy High Court judge, held that the notice did not thus tell the recipient with reasonable certainty what steps had to be taken to remedy the breach. In that case the unacceptable clause was the requirement that the reinstatement be agreed with the local planning authority. It is possible, however, for an Inspector dealing with an appeal to vary such a requirement and introduce certainty in place of uncertainty about what needs to be done, as, for example, requiring reinstatement to conform as nearly as possible with a specified photograph.

21.93 The terms of an enforcement notice (and thus the power to vary), cannot require action to be taken beyond that of remedying the breach. It cannot be used to bring to an end an existing lawful use. In *Mansi v Elstree DC* (1964) 15 P & CR 153 the Divisional Court remitted to the Minister for variation a notice which required the discontinuance of sales of goods from premises, where it was clear that there was an established use for retail sales of produce from a garden nursery, and this use would have been lost if the notice in its original form had been upheld. A more recent example of the application of the *Mansi* principle can be seen in the case of *John Kennelly Sales Ltd v Secretary of State for the Environment* [1994] 1 PLR 10.

It also seems that an enforcement notice cannot prevent the subsequent implementation of development permitted by the General Permitted Development Order. This is because s 181(2) provides: **21.94**

> . . . any provision of an enforcement notice requiring a use of land to be discontinued shall operate as a requirement that it shall be discontinued permanently, to the extent that it is in contravention of Part III; and accordingly the resumption of that use at any time after it has been discontinued in compliance with the enforcement notice shall to that extent be in contravention of the enforcement notice.

Development permitted by the General Permitted Development Order is not in contravention of Part III of the 1990 Act. Accordingly, it cannot be required to be discontinued as part of an enforcement notice. In *Duguid v Secretary of State for the Environment, Transport and the Regions* [2001] JPL 323, the Court of Appeal upheld a decision of the High Court which had given pre-eminence to s 181(2) over other provisions in the Act which might suggest that an enforcement notice can require such development to be discontinued.

Problems may arise in protecting existing use rights from the effect of an enforcement notice. The approach to that problem has been set out by Duncan Ouseley QC, at that time sitting as a Deputy Judge in *Kinnersley Engineering Ltd v Secretary of State for the Environment, Transport and the Regions* [2001] JPL 1082 in the following way: **21.95**

> Given that existing use rights are to be protected, the question of whether it is necessary to spell those out in the enforcement notice depends on how obvious it is that the enforcement notice can and will be construed so as to protect them, in the context of a criminal prosecution. It needs to be remembered that subsequent landowners are also bound by the notice, and concern over its interpretation may affect dealings with them.
>
> In my judgment, the key issue is whether it is obvious that the existing use rights [as found by the Inspector] would be protected.

In *R (Reid) v Secretary of State for Transport, Local Government and the Regions* [2002] EWHC 2174 Sullivan J followed the same approach.

Where the Secretary of State determines to allow the appeal he may quash the enforcement notice. He may also give any directions necessary to give effect to his determination on the appeal. **21.96**

From the decision of the Secretary of State on appeal against an enforcement notice, the appellant or the local planning authority or any other person having an interest in the land may, according as rules of court provide (under s 289 of the 1990 Act) appeal to the High Court against the decision on a point of law or require the Secretary of State to state and sign a case for the opinion of the High Court. **21.97**

Because appellants have sometimes used the litigation process to delay or frustrate the implementation of an enforcement notice by submitting unmeritorious appeals, the Planning and Compensation Act 1991 introduced sub-section (6) into s 289 of the 1990 Act. The sub-section introduced an entirely new 'leave' requirement, by providing that 'No proceedings in the High Court shall be brought . . . except with the leave of that court and no appeal to the Court of Appeal shall be so brought except with the leave of the Court of Appeal or of the High Court.' This provision applies equally to a local planning authority, as it does to the recipient of an enforcement notice. Under the Rules of the Supreme Court, this action must **21.98** be taken within 28 days of the Secretary of State's decision (unless the period is extended by the Court for good reason). The 28-day period for appealing to the High Court under s.289 against a decision on an enforcement notice appeal should not be confused (which it often is) with the six-week period for appealing under s.288.

21.99 Section 175(4) provides that where an appeal is brought under s 174, the enforcement notice shall be of no effect pending the final determination or withdrawal of the appeal. In *London Parachuting Ltd v Secretary of State for the Environment* (1985) 52 P & CR 376, it was held that this meant final determination of the appeal by the Secretary of State. Once this determination had been made, the enforcement notice, if upheld, was required to be obeyed. In *R v Kuxhaus* [1988] QB 631, however, the court disapproved of that decision, holding (with reluctance) that where an appeal was made to the court, this had the effect of further suspending the operation of the enforcement notice until the court had finally determined the matter. This decision meant, therefore, that it was possible to frustrate the effect of an enforcement notice for a considerable length of time by pursuing an appeal to the Secretary of State, then beyond that to the courts. At that stage, it was not uncommon for the appellant then to withdraw the appeal.

21.100 To deal with this problem, the Planning and Compensation Act 1991 inserted sub-section (4A) into s 289 of the 1990 Act (the section which deals with appeals to the High Court against enforcement notices). The effect of the sub-section is that where an appeal is made to the courts against the decision of the Secretary of State in relation to an enforcement notice, the High Court or Court of Appeal may order that the notice shall have such effect or have effect to such extent as may be specified in the order, pending the final determination of the proceedings and any rehearing and determination by the Secretary of State. This provision will thus allow the courts, in dealing with the enforcement notice appeal, to decide whether, pending the determination of the appeal, the appellant should be made to comply with the enforcement notice and, if so, to what extent, or whether the notice should continue to be of no effect.

21.101 Although in determining an appeal against an enforcement notice, the Secretary of State has power to quash an enforcement notice, the powers of the court in dealing with an appeal are limited to remitting the matter to the Secretary of State with the opinion of the court for his rehearing and redetermination. There is no power available to the court, therefore, to quash or set aside an enforcement notice.

21.102 It appears that a decision made by the Secretary of State to allow an appeal against an enforcement notice on any of the grounds mentioned in (c) to (e) in s 174 of the 1990 Act is capable of giving rise to an estoppel *per rem judicatam* or to 'issue estoppel'. In *Thrasyvoulou v Secretary of State for the Environment* [1990] 2 AC 273, a number of enforcement notices alleging breaches of planning control had been issued in 1981. On appeal, an Inspector had decided that no material change of use had taken place. Following a second batch of enforcement notices issued in 1985, an Inspector hearing the appeals decided that he was not bound by the decision reached by the earlier Inspector in relation to the 1981 notices. The House of Lords held that there was an important distinction between an issue raised by an appeal against an enforcement notice on ground (a) of what is now s 174(2) of the 1990 Act, where the question is whether planning permission should be granted, and the issues raised by grounds (b) to (e). In the former case the public have a right to attend an inquiry and be heard as objectors, whereas in the latter case they have no *locus standi* as objectors, although they may be heard as witnesses of fact. Their Lordships thought that Parliament must have intended the determination of any issue arising under what are now grounds (c) to (e) of s 174(2) in favour of an appellant to be conclusive. Any such determination gives rise to an estoppel *per rem judicatam*. Such 'cause of action' estoppel will arise whenever the determination of the ground decided in favour of the appellant on an appeal against one enforcement notice can be relied on in an appeal against a second enforcement notice which is in the same terms and is directed against the same alleged development as the first.

In related proceedings (*Oliver v Havering LBC*) the House ruled that where on one enforcement notice appeal an Inspector had ruled that land was immune from enforcement proceedings (because the use had been established before 1964), a second Inspector on a subsequent enforcement notice appeal was bound by issue estoppel to accept the ruling. **21.103**

In *Porter v Secretary of State for Transport* [1996] 3 All ER 693 it was said that for issue estoppel to arise the four criteria that had to be established were: **21.104**

(a) The issue in question must have been decided by a court or tribunal of competent jurisdiction.
(b) The issue must be one which arises between parties who are parties to the decision.
(c) The issue must have been decided finally and must be of a type to which an issue estoppel can apply.
(d) The issue in respect of which the estoppel is said to operate must be the same as that previously decided.

The *Thrasyvoulou* principle was again applied by the Court of Appeal in *Hammond v Secretary of State for the Environment and Maldon DC* [1997] JPL 724. **21.105**

I. STOP NOTICES

At one time one of the difficulties with the enforcement of planning control was that a person could begin to develop without planning permission and, when an enforcement notice was served, use delaying mechanisms (including the right of appeal) to postpone its operation whilst at the same time continuing with the development. The effects of this were twofold. First, where the development involved the erection of a building, the Secretary of State, in determining the appeal, might be less likely to require the demolition of a building which had been completed than one in the early stages of erection; secondly, the adverse environmental effects of the unauthorised development could continue for a longer period than necessary if the enforcement notice were finally to take effect. **21.106**

The statutory provisions relating to stop notices are now contained in s 183 of the 1990 Act. Sub-section (1) of that section provides: **21.107**

> (1) Where the local planning authority consider it expedient that any relevant activity should cease before the expiry of the period for compliance with an enforcement notice, they may, when they serve a copy of the enforcement notice or afterwards, serve a notice (in this Act referred to as a 'stop notice') prohibiting the carrying out of that activity on the land to which the enforcement notice relates, or any part of that land specified in the stop notice.

Sub-section (2) of s 183 defines 'relevant activity' to mean any activity specified in the enforcement notice as an activity which the local planning authority require to cease and any activity carried out as part of that activity or associated with that activity. This provision makes it clear that a stop notice may be directed not merely to an activity specified in an enforcement notice as an activity the authority require should cease, but also to any use of land which is ancillary to its main use.

21.108 It should be noted that a stop notice may now be served on a person at the same time as the person is served with an enforcement notice, thus reversing the decision in *R v Southwark LBC, ex p Murdoch* (1990) 155 JP 163, that a local planning authority had no power to serve an enforcement notice and stop notice simultaneously.

21.109 A stop notice cannot, however, be served where the enforcement notice has taken effect, presumably because thereafter, the failure to comply with the enforcement notice is itself a criminal offence. The stop notice is given teeth by virtue of s 187(1) of the 1990 Act which provides for a criminal sanction if any person contravenes, or causes or permits the contravention of, a stop notice; and he may thereafter be convicted of a second or subsequent offence under the section. The Planning and Compensation Act 1991 amended the penalties for contravening a stop notice by raising the maximum fine from £2,000 to £20,000 on summary conviction. The 1991 Act amendment also requires the court in imposing a fine to have regard to any financial benefit which has accrued or is likely to accrue to the wrongdoer in consequence of the offence.

21.110 Cases have arisen where the imposition of criminal penalties has not prevented an activity being continued in breach of a stop notice. Accordingly, in November 1996, the Government proposed a change in the law to give local planning authorities the power to take physical steps to ensure compliance with a stop notice, such as preventing access to the site by any person in pursuance of the activity prohibited by the notice (by, for example, placing a barrier across the site entrance), and to enter land and confiscate any equipment or material being used by a person in pursuance of a prohibited activity. The new powers, however, when they are eventually introduced, will be linked to the prosecution of a stop notice offence under s 187 of the 1990 Act and will be available only where a person has been convicted of an offence and the court has made an order authorising the authority to take those steps.

21.111 Under s 183(6) the stop notice may be served by the local planning authority on any person who appears to them to have an interest in the land or to be engaged in any activity prohibited by the notice.

21.112 Section 183(4) of the 1990 Act provides that a stop notice shall not prohibit the use of any building as a dwellinghouse. Prior to the 1991 Act, this exclusion applied also to the use of land as the site for a caravan occupied by any person as his main residence. Because of the potential harm to local amenities caused by unauthorised residential caravan sites, the 1991 Act removed the prohibition against service with regard to caravans.

21.113 In addition, s 183(5) prohibits the use of a stop notice to prohibit the carrying out of any activity if that activity has been carried out (whether continuously or not) for a period of more than four years ending with the service of the notice. Prior to the 1991 Act, a stop notice could not be used to prohibit the carrying out of any activity on land begun more than 12 months earlier unless it was, or was incidental to, building, engineering, mining or other operations or the deposit of refuse or waste materials. Although the 1991 Act extended the limitation period for service of a stop notice from 12 months to four years, it has maintained the right of a local planning authority to serve a stop notice within that (now) extended period, for activities amounting to operational development or the deposit of refuse or waste, or activities incidental thereto. The general extension of the time limit from 12 months to four years reflects more, however, the fact that a use of land may at first be seen to be non-objectionable, but may become otherwise because of intensification.

According to statistics published by the Department of the Environment, 168 stop notices were issued by local planning authorities in the year ending 31 March 2004. **21.114**

Service of stop notices

A stop notice must refer to the enforcement notice to which it relates and have a copy of that notice annexed to it. It must also specify the date on which it will take effect. Before the Planning and Compensation Act 1991, the date on which a stop notice was specified to take effect was not to be earlier than three and not later than 28 days from the date of service. The purpose of giving three days' grace before the stop notice took effect was to cushion those affected from losses incurred by having to bring work to an immediate standstill. It was believed, however, that some activities, such as the depositing of waste, mineral extraction etc., could be sufficiently damaging to require them to be stopped immediately. Accordingly the 1991 Act amended the 1990 Act by substituting a provision to allow a stop notice to specify an earlier date than three days for its coming into effect, if the authority consider there are special reasons for so doing and a statement of those reasons is served with the stop notice. A stop notice will cease to have effect where the enforcement notice to which it relates is withdrawn or quashed, or the period for compliance with the enforcement notice has expired, or the local planning authority withdraw it. **21.115**

Compensation for loss due to stop notices

Local planning authorities have often claimed they are deterred from serving stop notices because of the risk they run of having to pay compensation to the person on whom the notice is served, if he is successful in an appeal to the Secretary of State against the related enforcement notice. In fact the liability to pay compensation is much restricted, compensation only being payable if the enforcement notice is quashed on grounds other than that planning permission ought to be granted for the development to which the notice relates; or where the authority decide to withdraw the stop notice; or it is varied on appeal so that the matter alleged to constitute a breach of planning control is no longer included in the notice. **21.116**

Section 18b(2) of the Act provides that when a stop notice is first served, a person who has an interest in or who occupies the land to which the notice relates shall be entitled to compensation in respect of any loss or damage directly attributable to the prohibition contained in the notice. In *International Traders Ferry Ltd v Adur (ADUR) District Council* [2004] EWCA Civ 288, it was held that the interest referred to in the subsection was a legal or equitable interest. As regards to whether an occupier qualified under this provision, the court approach was to **21.117** follow that laid down in *Stevens v Bromley London Borough Council* (22.36) with regard to a person's entitlement to be served with an enforcement notice.

21.118 Despite attempts to explain the statutory provisions in earlier Circulars, local planning authorities remained confused by the provisions relating to compensation. Accordingly, the Planning and Compensation Act 1991 amended the 1990 Act by substituting a new subsection (5) of s 186 to clarify the circumstances in which compensation is not to be payable where a stop notice ceases to have effect. It is now provided that no compensation is payable in respect of any prohibition in a stop notice of any activity which, at any time when the notice is in force, constitutes or contributes to a breach of planning control. In addition, it should be noted that under various other statutory provisions (e.g., planning contravention notices in s 171C of the 1990 Act; or the power to require information about interests in land under s 330 of the 1990 Act), a person may be required to provide a local planning authority with relevant information. If that person fails to provide that information, or otherwise fails to co-operate with the local planning authority when responding to the notice, no compensation is payable in respect of any loss or damage which could otherwise have been avoided. The justification for this provision is that the local authority should not be liable if insufficient information has been given to them to enable them to decide whether to take enforcement action, and if they do so, to draft the notice with complete precision.

21.119 The philosophy behind the compensation provisions is that no compensation should be payable merely because the landowner and the local planning authority have taken a different view on whether or not planning permission for development should be granted. The correct procedure for the landowner is to submit an application for planning permission to the local planning authority and on refusal to appeal to the Secretary of State. If he develops first, is served with an enforcement notice and related stop notice, and then the enforcement notice is quashed solely on the ground that planning permission for the development should be granted, no compensation for loss due to the stop notice is payable. The owner is the victim of his own actions. Compensation becomes payable, therefore, where for some reason other than the merits of the development proposed, the local planning authority has in the view of the Secretary of State made a mistake.

21.120 Mention has already been made of the case of *Malvern Hills DC v Secretary of State for the Environment* (1983) 46 P & CR 58, where compensation had to be paid for loss caused by service of a misconceived stop notice. Another example occurred in *Sample (Warkworth) Ltd v Alnwick DC* (1984) 48 P & CR 474. Here, an enforcement notice was quashed on the ground that there had been no breach of planning control. The award made (of £3,122) included rent for temporary accommodation, the cost of idle time of workmen and for additional work necessary to rectify deterioration caused by delay in completing the development.

Execution of works required by enforcement notices

21.121 Under s 178 of the 1990 Act as originally enacted, if any steps which an enforcement notice required to be taken *other* than the discontinuance of a use of land had not been taken, the local planning authority were entitled to enter the land and take those steps and recover from the owner of the land any expenses reasonably incurred in doing so. It was felt that the inability of authorities to use this power to secure the discontinuance of a use was a serious obstacle to their efforts to secure the cessation of illegal uses of land. Hence, the Planning and Compensation Act 1991 strengthened s 178 of the 1990 Act by removing that disability. Under the current provision, a local planning authority can enter land where *any steps* which an enforcement notice required to be taken have not been taken within the period for doing so and recover the expenses of so doing from the owner of the land.

Note that it may sometimes happen that the owner is prevented from taking the steps required to be taken by the notice because some other person (such as a tenant) has an interest in the land. In such cases, s 178(4) allows the owner to apply to the magistrates' court for an order under the Public Health Act 1936 that that other person should permit those steps to be taken. **21.122**

Offence where enforcement notice not complied with

Under s 179 of the 1990 Act, where, at any time after the end of the period for compliance with an enforcement notice, any step required by the notice to be taken has not been taken, or any activity required by the notice to cease is being carried on, the person who is then the owner of the land is in breach of the notice and guilty of an offence. **21.123**

Prior to the Planning and Compensation Act 1991, the person guilty of the offence of non-compliance with the notice was the person who was the owner of the land in respect of which the enforcement notice had been served. Where the person responsible for non-compliance was a subsequent owner, the original owner was entitled to have the subsequent owner brought before the court in any prosecution. Under a new s 179, it is now the owner of the land at any time after the end of the period for compliance with the notice who has primary responsibility for securing compliance with the notice. The section recognises, however, that the owner of the land may not be responsible for the failure to comply with an enforcement notice if, for example, another person (such as a tenant) occupies the land and is responsible for non-compliance.The section provides too that a person who occupies the land or has an interest in it (other than the owner) must not carry out any activity on it which is required by the notice to cease. If he should do so, the section makes this a criminal offence. It is also made clear that when an owner of land is in breach of an enforcement notice he shall be guilty of an offence, and he may be guilty of a second or subsequent offence if he continues in breach. **21.124**

The section provides that where a person charged with non-compliance with an enforcement notice has not been served with a copy of it, and the notice is not contained in the statutory register of enforcement and stop notices kept under s 188 of the 1990 Act, it shall be a defence for him to show that he was not aware of the existence of the notice. **21.125**

The maximum penalty that a magistrates' court may impose on a person guilty of non-compliance with an enforcement notice was increased under the Planning and Compensation Act 1991 from £2,000 to £20,000. In addition, however, in determining the amount of any fine to be imposed on a convicted person, the court (whether the offence was tried summarily or on indictment), must now have regard to any financial benefit which has accrued or is likely to accrue to that person in consequence of the offence. **21.126**

It is not uncommon, once an enforcement has come into effect, for an occupier of land to proceed to lodge an application for planning permission for the contravening development **21.127** which is the subject of the enforcement notice. Then, on prosecution for failure to comply with the notice, the occupier will ask for the criminal proceedings to be adjourned pending determination of the application for planning permission and/or any subsequent appeal. Magistrates have been advised not to adjourn such proceedings save in wholly exceptional circumstances. In *R v Beaconsfield Magistrates, ex p South Buckinghamshire DC* (1993) 157 JP 1073, Staughton LJ said:

> As a general rule, magistrates should . . . proceed to hear and determine the guilt or innocence of the defendant, notwithstanding that a planning application has recently been presented. If the defendant has a defence or claims to have a defence, it should be tried and determined whether he is guilty or not. If he does not have a defence and does not claim to have one, he should be convicted . . . other than in exceptional cases . . . where the fate of the planning application is expected to be determined shortly, the magistrates should also deal with sentence in such cases and not adjourn them. They can, of course, take into account in considering the severity or lenience of any penalty the fact that a planning application is pending. . . .
>
> I do not think that the magistrates are absolutely deprived of all discretion in such a case where compassionate circumstances exist. Section 179(5) of the Town and Country Planning Act 1990 provides that if after a person has been convicted he does not as soon as practicable do everything in his power to secure compliance with the enforcement notice, he should be guilty of a further offence. Thus a conviction has the effect that the defendant, besides being guilty of failing to comply with the notice in the first place, becomes liable to a fine of up to £200 for each day after that. The magistrates were entitled to consider the effect that the sub-section would have on Mrs K and Mrs S. They had outstanding planning applications which had not yet finally been determined. If they were convicted and did not thereafter comply with the previous enforcement notices they were liable to a daily fine. Bearing in mind the particular circumstances of the ladies, their age, means, state of health and the substantial period of time when the local authority had taken no action consequent on the breach of the enforcement notices, the justices were entitled to take a very unusual course in the wholly exceptional circumstances of the case.

If a person is prosecuted for failure to comply with an enforcement notice, he cannot, at that stage, challenge the earlier decision to issue the enforcement notice on the ground that the decision to do so was *ultra vires*. In *R v Wicks* [1997] 2 All ER 801, the defendant had been prosecuted for failure to comply with a notice. He had appealed to the Secretary of State against the notice, but unsuccessfully. He has not taken the opportunity to raise any questions about the validity of the notice on his appeal to the Secretary of State, or by way of judicial review. The House of Lords held he was not now entitled to raise in a criminal prosecution the question of whether the notice was *ultra vires* on the grounds of bad faith, perversity and irrelevant considerations. It is otherwise, however, in a prosecution for failure to comply with a breach of condition notice (see 21.144).

Once an enforcement notice, always an enforcement notice

21.128 Even though an enforcement notice may have been complied with, it continues to have effect as against any subsequent unauthorised development covered by the notice. Section 181(1) of the Act provides that:

> Compliance with an enforcement notice, whether in respect of—
>
> (a) the completion, removal or alteration of any buildings, or works;

(b) the discontinuance of any use of land; or
(c) any other requirements contained in the notice,

shall not discharge the notice.

This provision ensures that once a person has taken the steps required to be taken by the notice, the enforcement notice will continue to bite if the unauthorised development is recommenced. So too, a breach of condition notice is not discharged by compliance with its terms. **21.129**

The only limitation on this rule is that provided by s 180 of the 1990 Act, which provides that where after the service of a copy of an enforcement notice or a breach of condition notice, planning permission is granted for any development carried out before the grant of that permission, the notice shall cease to have effect in so far as it is inconsistent with that permission. **21.130**

The rule applies equally to a temporary planning permission as to a planning permission not so time limited. In *Cresswell v Pearson* [1997] JPL 860 the High Court held that where by virtue of s 180 an enforcement notice ceased to have effect because of the later grant of planning permission for a limited period, the enforcement notice did not revive at the end of that period. The Court held that the proviso in s 180(1) that the enforcement notice 'shall cease to have effect' was clear and that there was no question of the notice going into suspended animation for the duration of the permission. In these circumstances, however, the local planning authority would be able to issue a further enforcement notice if the breach of planning control continued beyond the limited period for which the permission was granted. **21.131**

J. BREACH OF CONDITION NOTICES

Under s 171A of the 1990 Act, failure to comply with any condition or limitation subject to which planning permission has been granted constitutes a breach of planning control. Accordingly, an enforcement notice may be served specifying the steps to be taken to remedy the breach. **21.132**

In 1989, evidence was given to the review of enforcement procedure conducted by Robert Carnwath QC that the enforcement notice procedure was insufficiently flexible to secure the enforcement of conditions. The view was expressed that '. . . enforcement action was very rarely an efficient means of dealing with breaches of conditions relating to the period of construction of a project on such things as noise or working hours, since a stop notice would be too drastic in most cases and enforcement is too slow and unsure'. It was thought that there was a need for a summary remedy which would enable conditions to be enforced without enabling the merits to be reopened through the full panoply of an enforcement notice appeal. **21.133**

Accordingly, the Planning and Compensation Act 1991 introduced a new s 187A into the 1990 Act to give local planning authorities a new procedure for the summary enforcement of a breach of a condition or a limitation subject to which a planning permission has been **21.134** granted. The procedure provides local planning authorities with an additional and independent method of dealing with breaches of a condition or limitation as an alternative to the service of an enforcement notice under s 171A or obtaining an injunction from the courts, in order to secure compliance with a condition.

21.135 The new s 187A applies where planning permission for the carrying out of any development of land has been granted subject to conditions; and any of the conditions are not complied with. In such cases sub-sections (1) and (2) of s 187A empower a local planning authority to serve a notice (called a breach of condition notice) on any person who is carrying out or has carried out the development, or any person having control of the land, requiring him to secure compliance with such of the conditions as are specified in the notice. The notice, which the authority have power to withdraw, must specify the steps which the authority consider ought to be taken, or the activities which the authority consider ought to cease, to secure compliance with conditions specified in the notice. In this context, the word 'conditions' is expressed to include limitations.

21.136 In *Nourish v Adamson* [1998] JPL 859, it was held that where it could be shown that a person was, at the relevant time, the owner of the land, the burden of proof then lay on that person to show that although he was the owner, he did not have the control which one would normally expect an owner to have, namely the ability to secure compliance with the notice.

21.137 Under s 187A(7), the breach of condition notice must specify the period allowed by the authority for compliance with it, which must be not less than 28 days from the date of service of the notice, or that period as extended by any further breach of condition notice served by the authority on that person.

21.138 Then, if at the end of that period any of the conditions specified in the notice are not complied with and the steps specified in the notice have not been taken, or the activities specified have not ceased, the recipient of the notice will be in breach and be guilty of an offence. Furthermore, if at any time after conviction the recipient of the notice continues to be in breach of the notice, he may be convicted of a second or subsequent offence, thereby ensuring that eventually he ceases to be in breach.

21.139 There have been a number of recent cases resulting from prosecutions for non-compliance with a breach of condition notice.

21.140 In *East Hampshire DC v SLV Building Products Ltd* [1996], the company successfully argued before magistrates that they had not been in breach of a condition in a planning permission which had restricted use of 'working machinery' to specified hours, by using a 'forklift truck' on the site outside those hours. In an appeal by the Council by way of case stated, the High Court upheld the Justice's findings.

21.141 In *John [and Joseph] Davenport v Hammersmith & Fulham LBC* [1999] JPL 1122 the appellants had been convicted by magistrates of a failure to comply with a breach of condition notice. The condition had been imposed on a grant of planning permission for the retention of two buildings in connection with the use of land for motor vehicle repairs. The condition provided that 'No vehicles which have been left with or are in the control of the applicant shall be stored or parked in Tasso Road'. The notice had been served on John Davenport as being 'a person having control of the land'. On appeal, by way of case stated, the High Court quashed his conviction, holding that the condition did not regulate the use of the land subject to the planning permission, but the use of Tasso Road, over which he had no control.

It should be noted that no right of appeal to the Secretary of State is provided where this new procedure is used. This is because the merits of the condition are not in issue. If the recipient does not comply with the notice, a criminal prosecution in the magistrates' court for being in breach of the notice should follow. The local planning authority will, of course, have to prove all the elements in the offence, though s 187A(11) recognises a defence that the recipient took all reasonable measures to secure compliance with the conditions specified in the notice; or if he was served with the notice as the person having control of the land, that he no longer had control. **21.142**

Judicial review may be sought, however, if in issuing a breach of condition notice the local planning authority has acted outside its statutory powers. In *R v Ealing LBC, ex p Zainuddin* [1995] JPL 925, the High Court quashed a breach of condition notice relating to the attendance of 1,500 people at a ceremony to lay a foundation stone for a mosque, which had been issued on the basis that the event was in breach of the conditions in a grant of planning permission that 'no religious or ceremonial gatherings or acts of worship shall take place within the site except within the building'. The High Court held that there had been no breach of the condition where the meeting of devotees had taken place at a time when only the frame of the building existed. The condition should of course have provided that no gatherings should take place within the building before it was completed. **21.143**

In *R v Wicks* [1997] 2 All ER 801, the House of Lords held that it was not open to the recipient of an enforcement notice to challenge the validity of the notice in criminal proceedings taken against him for non-compliance with the notice. It would seem that different considerations apply where the proceedings relate to non-compliance with a breach of condition notice. In *Alfonso Dilieto v Ealing LBC* [1998] PLCR 212, the Divisional Court of the Queen's Bench Division held that in a prosecution for the non-compliance with a breach of condition notice, magistrates had jurisdiction to consider the validity of the notice where a challenge to it had been based on the ground that since the contravention of the condition had been begun more than 10 years previously, the breach of condition notice had been issued out of time. Dilieto had been convicted by the Ealing Justices for failure to comply with a breach of condition notice. On appeal against conviction by way of case stated, the Council had argued that following the decision in *Wicks*, the magistrates could decide whether the notice was a nullity in the sense of its being invalid on its face, but could not decide whether it was invalid on the ground raised by the appellant. The Council claimed that in order to challenge the breach of condition notice, the appellant should have moved to have the notice quashed by way of judicial review. In the Divisional Court however, Sullivan J refused to accept that the approach of the House of Lords in *Wicks* as regards enforcement notices was equally applicable in the case of breach of condition notices. One of the reasons he gave for taking that view was that whereas s 174 contains elaborate provisions for enabling a person to appeal to the Secretary of State against an enforcement notice, there were no equivalent provisions with regard to breach of condition notices. He also pointed to the likelihood that Parliament could not have intended a person wishing to show the breach of condition notice had been served more than ten years after the breach of the condition to have no right of appeal whatsoever. To hold otherwise he thought, would **21.144** enable a planning authority unsure of whether enforcement would be out of time to sidestep the issue by serving a breach of condition notice.

21.145 The decision in *Dilieto*, whilst clearly to be welcome, leaves unclear what other points of law can now be raised before magistrates as a defence to a prosecution for failure to comply with a breach of condition notice. Sullivan J in the *Dilieto* case thought that allegations that a breach of condition notice had been served in bad faith, or for improper purposes, or on the basis of irrelevant considerations, were matters better suited to judicial review rather than to magistrates' courts. However, on the same day as judgment was given in the *Dilieto* case, the House of Lords gave judgment in *Boddington v British Transport Police* [1999] 2 AC 143 in which, in a case which was not concerned with planning issues, their Lordships appeared to draw a lesser demarcation line than that drawn in *Dilieto* between the grounds of challenge that could or could not be taken in magistrates' court proceedings. In particular, the Lord Chancellor, Lord Irvine of Lairg, referring to the charges of inconsistencies in magistrates having to deal with difficult points of administrative law, thought that magistrates should not be underestimated and that 'the practical risks of inconsistency are probably exaggerated'. It thus remains to be seen how far magistrates' courts will be able to deal with the whole range of legal challenges that can be made where invalidity is alleged on a prosecution for noncompliance with a breach of condition notice.

21.146 According to statistics published by the Department of the Environment, 1,068 breach of condition notices were served by local planning authorities in the year ending 31 March 2004.

K. INJUNCTIONS

21.147 From the early days of planning control, injunctions have occasionally been used by local planning authorities as an aid to enforcement. One of the earliest cases in this area was *Attorney-General v Bastow* [1957] 1 QB 514, where the Attorney-General, at the relation of the local planning authority, obtained an injunction restraining the defendant from using land or causing or permitting it to be used as a caravan site contrary to the terms of an enforcement notice. The defendant had continuously disregarded the notice and been prosecuted and convicted on a number of occasions for that offence.

21.148 A year later, in *Attorney-General v Smith* [1958] 2 QB 173, the Attorney-General, again at the relation of the local planning authority, was granted an injunction restraining the defendant from using or causing or permitting to be used as a caravan site, any land within the boundaries of the authority without the prior grant of planning permission. The evidence was that the defendant, by moving caravans from one unauthorised site to another, was using the machinery of the Planning Act not for the purpose of making genuine applications for planning permission, but for the purpose of delay in order to evade the provisions of the Act for as long as possible. The need for local authorities to obtain the fiat of the Attorney-General in order to to pursue such cases is now no longer needed. S 222 of the Local Government Act 1972 provides:

> Where a local authority consider it expedient for the promotion or protection of the interests of

> the inhabitants of their area . . . they may prosecute or defend or appear in any legal proceedings and, in the case of civil proceedings, may institute them in their own name.

This power was used on a number of occasions. Reference has previously been made to the case of *Bedfordshire CC v Central Electricity Generating Board* [1985] JPL 43. Another case, where a local planning authority obtained an injunction to restrain a contravening use against which enforcement notice proceedings had been taken, was *Westminster City Council v Jones* [1981] JPL 750. In this case, the local authority acted to prevent the operation of an amusement arcade causing nuisance and disturbance in a residential area. The defendant had known when he took a lease of premises that he needed planning permission for the new use but he had elected to proceed before he had got the permission or before he took adequate steps to ascertain the authority's attitude. The authority had served both an enforcement notice and a stop notice on the defendant; and a summons for failure to comply with the latter was shortly due to be heard. Rather than wait just under one month for the criminal proceedings to be heard, however, the court was prepared to grant the injunction asked for. **21.149**

In certain cases it was shown possible to obtain an injunction to restrain a threatened or actual breach of planning control even before an enforcement notice or stop notice was served. This was achieved in *Southwark LBC v M.L. Frow* [1989] JPL 645 where property had originally been used by members of the same family as two informal flats. Minor and superficial building works had taken place and the property was being prepared for occupation as nine bedsit flats. The owner was contacted and told that a planning application was required, but that it was likely that such an application would be refused. Additionally, he was informed that enforcement action was being considered and that the units should not be occupied. **21.150**

It needed to be established whether a material change of use had occurred, and whether enforcement and stop notices could be served. However, the use as bedsits was dependent upon occupation and thus the authority could not serve the notices as no change of use had yet occurred. As the premises began to become occupied, it became imperative that further occupation be prevented, although allowing the existing tenants to remain. It was the authority's opinion that full occupation of the building as bedsits was undesirable due to the effect of adjoining neighbours, the extremely poor quality of the accommodation itself and possible traffic implications in an already heavily parked and trafficked area. **21.151**

As the use, usefulness and legality of using enforcement notices and stop notices were in doubt, and as the warnings and advice to the owner were being ignored, an injunction was sought and obtained. **21.152**

The report *Enforcing Planning Control* in 1989 considered that injunctions had proved a useful back-up to the statutory system in difficult cases. In the view of Robert Carnwath QC there were doubts about the circumstances in which the remedy was available, particularly the extent to which it was available to restrain an actual or threatened breach of planning control *before* it had become a criminal offence following service of an enforcement notice or stop notice. **21.153**

The review recommended that an authority should be able to apply for an injunction in respect of any breach or threatened breach of planning control, whether or not an **21.154** enforcement notice or stop notice has been served. Such a remedy could be used in urgent cases where there was a serious threat to amenity and time was of the essence; or as a back-up for other remedies where they had failed to secure the termination of a breach. Accordingly, the Planning and Compensation Act 1991 introduces s 187B into the 1990 Act, to give local planning authorities an express right in planning law to obtain from the High Court or a county court an injunction. The section provides that where the authority '. . . consider it necessary or expedient for any actual or apprehended breach of planning control to be restrained by injunction, they may apply to the court for an injunction, whether or not they have exercised or are proposing to exercise any of their other powers under this Part'. The authority does not have to pursue other means of enforcement, including criminal prosecution under s 179 or 187A of the 1990 Act, before seeking injunctive relief under s 187B.

21.155 The use of the power to seek an injunction to remedy a breach or threatened breach of planning control under the statutory powers has been considered by the Court of Appeal in two decisions given on the same day. In *Croydon LBC v Gladden* [1994] JPL 723, it was held that the power enabled the court to issue a mandatory injunction requiring an occupier to remove a replica Spitfire aeroplane from the garden of a dwellinghouse. In *Runnymede DC v Harwood* [1994] JPL 724 the court granted an injunction which sought to restrain an occupier from using his land for the storage of motor vehicles contrary to the requirements of an enforcement notice. If the court were to have withheld injunctive relief it would have given temporary planning permission for the continuance of an activity for which the local planning authority had consistently refused permission. It was held that s 187B of the 1990 Act was much wider than the power previously available to a local planning authority. It was no longer necessary to show that criminal penalties were not enough to deter the defendant from infringing planning law. So an injunction might be sought, for example, in order to prevent the occupation of dwellinghouses where the developer has not complied with a condition in the grant of planning permission that an access road to the dwellings be provided before the dwellings are occupied. Furthermore, in *Connors v Reigate and Banstead BC* [2000] JPL 1178, it was said that there was no necessity for an authority to show either that there was a nuisance or a risk of irreparable harm. Its function was to uphold planning procedures and to ensure that those who wished to develop land should not pre-empt the statutory procedures which Parliament has laid down.

21.156 The scope of an injunction may be particularly useful where there are difficulties in ascertaining precisely who has the power to remedy the breach. In *Hillingdon LBC v Guinea Enterprises Ltd (and 15 others)* [1997] JPL B11, the court granted an injunction to restrain unauthorised aggregate reprocessing on land in the green belt. The injunction was sought in the following wide terms:

> The defendants (save for the trustees and the neighbours), any person controlling administering, financing, holding shares in or otherwise subscribing to or connected with the defendant companies or the servants or agents of such persons and any successor in title to any interest in the land be restrained from conducting whether by themselves, with others, or through any company tipping crushing or exporting waste etc. on the land or on any other land designated as Green Belt in the Borough and that all plant be removed from the land.

21.157 In *South Cambridgeshire District Council v Persons Unknown* (Times Law Reports, 11 November

2004), the Court of Appeal agreed that an injunction could be granted to restrain persons unknown from perpetrating identified breaches of planning control at an identified site.

In *Kettering Borough Council v Perkins* [1999] JPL 166, the court accepted that although there is a general rule that injunctions should be as precise as possible, it is not an absolute rule, and since the statutory scheme to control land use does not always admit of absolute precision, injunctions under s 187B may be granted in extensive terms. Indeed, in *Wealdon District Council v Nelson James Krushandal* [1999] JPL 174 the Court of Appeal dismissed an appeal against the granting of an injunction which prohibited the stationing of a mobile home on any land in the area of the District Council. **21.158**

An important decision by the House of Lords in *Kirklees MBC v Wickes Building Supplies Ltd* [1993] AC 227, that an injunction granted to enforce the law did not need to be supported by an undertaking in damages, further encourages the use of this provision. **21.159**

As a result of the Human Rights Act 1998, the use of injunctions to control breaches of planning law has been considered and clarified by the House of Lords. In the landmark case of *South Bucks District Council v Porter* [2003] JPL 1412, the House of Lords set out the cornerstone of the court's powers to grant an injunction under s.187B of the 1990 Act. The House had to consider a number of related cases concerning gypsies, who had challenged the grant of injunctions made against them by the High Court which required them to cease the use of land in the Green Belt for the stationing of caravans. In dismissing an appeal by the Council from the decision of the Court of Appeal to remit the matter back to the High Court for reconsideration, the House of Lords set out the principles governing the grant of an injunction. These principles have been subsequently summarised in the following propositions: **21.160**

(a) The court has a discretion as to whether an injunction should be granted. This discretion should be exercised with due regard to the purpose for which it was conferred, here to restrain actual threatened breaches of planning control. This is an original and discretionary, not a supervisory jurisdiction. The power exists mainly to permit abuses to be curbed and urgent solutions provided where these are called for.
(b) The court need not examine matters of planning policy or judgment that are the exclusive preserve of the authorities administering the planning regime.
(c) Nevertheless the court is not obliged to grant relief because a planning authority considered it necessary or expedient to restrain a planning breach.
(d) The court should have regard to all the circumstances, including the personal circumstances of the family, and the availability of other suitable accommodation. In this context, I accept that particular attention should be given to the position of members of the gypsy community, their needs and their lifestyle, together with any shortage of pitches or appropriate sites in the relevant area. Genuine absence of appropriate alternative accommodation makes the interference potentially more serious and, depending on other factors, may require greater justification.
(e) Having regard to section 6 of the Human Rights Act 1998 and Article 8 of the European Convention on Human Rights and Fundamental Freedoms, the court should only grant an injunction where it is just and proportionate to do so.

With regard to the last of these propositions, Lord Scott observed:

> The hardship likely to be caused to a Defendant by the grant of an injunction to enforce the public law will always, in my opinion, be relevant to the court's decision whether or not to grant

the injunction. In many, perhaps most, cases the hardship prayed in aid by the Defendant will be of insufficient weight to counterbalance a continued and persistent disobedience to the law. There is a strong general public interest that planning control should be observed and, if not observed enforced. But each case must depend upon its own circumstances.

21.161 Statistics show that in the year to 31 March 2004, 83 injunctions were granted to local planning authorities by the High Court or County Court. Eleven applications were unsuccessful.

L. REVERSION TO EARLIER USE

21.162 When an enforcement notice has taken effect, a question may arise as to what use the land can henceforth be put. Section 57(4) of the 1990 Act provides that where an enforcement notice has been issued in respect of any development of land, planning permission is not required for the use of that land for the purpose for which it could lawfully have been used if that development had not been carried out. In other words, where an enforcement notice takes effect, a landowner may revert to the use for which it could have been used immediately before the use complained of in the enforcement notice, provided that the use was lawful (see *Young v Secretary of State for the Environment* [1983] JPL 677).

M. CERTIFICATES OF LAWFULNESS OF EXISTING USE OR DEVELOPMENT (CLEUDs) AND CERTIFICATES OF LAWFULNESS OF PROPOSED USE OR DEVELOPMENT (CLOPUDs)

21.163 The report by Robert Carnwath QC, *Enforcing Planning Control*, recommended that a new single procedure be introduced to replace the former 'established use' certificate provisions in ss 191 to 196 of the 1990 Act and the provisions in s 64 of the 1990 Act that enabled a local planning authority to determine whether a proposal to carry out operations on land or make any change in the use of land was development and, if so, whether an application for planning permission in respect of the development was required. The Planning and Compensation Act 1991, however, established not one but two new procedures. First, a procedure to enable anyone who wishes to do so to apply to the local planning authority to determine whether *existing* operational development on land or an *existing* use of land, or any other matter constituting a failure to comply with any condition or limitation subject to which planning permission has been granted, was lawful, and, if so, to be granted a certificate to that effect. Secondly a procedure to enable anyone who wishes to ascertain whether any *proposed* operational development or use of land would be lawful, to apply similarly to the local planning authority for a determination of this question, and, if it would be, to obtain an appropriate certificate to that effect. As with the old s 64 procedure, neither of the two procedures gives a local planning authority power to answer a general question as to what use or operational development would be lawful for an owner to carry out on his land.

21.164 Furthermore, the local planning authority is not entitled to consider the planning merits of any application.

Certificate of lawfulness of existing use or development (CLEUD)

The main purpose of this certificate procedure is to simplify and modernise the old provisions in the 1990 Act which enabled the owner of land to obtain from the local planning authority a certificate of established use which granted him immunity from the subsequent enforcement action. That procedure originated in the Town and Country Planning Act 1968 when it was decided to change the rule that any development that had taken place more than four years previously should be immune from enforcement action, to a rule which limited that immunity to development of an operational nature and a change of use of any building to use as a single dwellinghouse. Furthermore, the 1968 Act provided that any other change of use was not to acquire immunity from enforcement action by the passage of time. Thereafter, enforcement action could be taken at any time. The changes made to the law by the 1968 Act created many problems. The position was that any change of use made on or before 31 December 1963 without a grant of planning permission continued to be immune from enforcement notice procedure, whereas a change of use made on or after 1 January 1964 could, apart from the one exception mentioned above, never acquire that immunity. Although immediately after 1968 it may not have been too difficult to prove the precise date on which a change had actually taken place, the difficulty of doing so was bound to increase with the passage of time and the frequency with which property is bought and sold. Hence the 1968 Act introduced a procedure for an owner to obtain an 'established use' certificate. The certificate was a procedural innovation designed to assist a vendor to sell his property with the aid of something like a guarantee that no enforcement notice would be served in respect of the use stated in the certificate. **21.165**

Unfortunately, many owners of land did not apply, preferring to wait until the land was sold or doubts were raised about the lawfulness of the existing use. By 1991, as 1964 became more remote, it became progressively more difficult to operate the established use certificate procedure satisfactorily. Reliable evidence as to the state of affairs in 1964 was difficult to obtain, with the result that many applications for such certificates, which had to be decided on the basis of a 'balance of probabilities', were considered to be unsatisfactory. The decision to phase out the established use certificate procedure was linked, of course, to the change in the law made by the 1991 Act relating to the period when immunity from enforcement action was acquired. **21.166**

The 1991 Act amended the 1990 Act by substituting new ss 191 to 194. Sub-section (1) of s 191 provides that if any person wishes to ascertain whether any existing use of buildings or other land is lawful; any operations which have been carried out in, on, over or under land are lawful; or any other matter constituting a failure to comply with any condition or limitation subject to which planning permission has been granted is lawful; he may apply to the local planning authority specifying the land and describing the use, operations or other matter. **21.167**

Sub-sections (2) and (3) of s 191 specify the circumstances in which development or the failure to comply with a condition is to be regarded as lawful. Under s 191(2), operations are lawful at any time if no enforcement action may then be taken in respect of them (whether because they did not involve development or require planning permission or because the time for enforcement action had expired or for any other reason) and they do not constitute a contravention of any of the requirements of any enforcement notice then in force. **21.168**

21.169 Under s 191(3) any matter constituting a failure to comply with any condition or limitation subject to which planning permission has been granted, is lawful at any time if the time for taking enforcement action in respect of the failure has then expired and it does not constitute a contravention of any of the requirements of any enforcement notice or breach of condition notice then in force.

21.170 Sub-section (4) of s 191 provides that if, on an application under this section, the local planning authority are provided with information satisfying them of the lawfulness at the time of the application of the use, operations or other matter described in the application, or that description as modified by the local planning authority or a description substituted by them, they must issue a certificate to that effect; and in any other case they must refuse the application.

21.171 The onus of proving the lawfulness of an existing use or development appears to rest with the applicant. The courts have held in *Gabbitas v Secretary of State for the Environment* [1985] JPL 630 that the relevant test of the evidence on such matters is 'the balance of probability'. Moreover, the courts have held that the applicant's own evidence does not need to be corroborated by 'independent' evidence in order to be accepted. If the local planning authority have no evidence of their own, or from others, to contradict or otherwise make the applicant's version of events less than probable, there is no good reason to refuse the application, provided the applicant's evidence alone is sufficiently precise and unambiguous to justify the grant of a certificate 'on the balance of probability'. This principle applies equally to enforcement notices where the ground of appeal is made under s 174(2)(d).

21.172 It should be noted that, as with the old certificates of established use, the local planning authority have no discretion as to whether or not to issue a certificate. It should be emphasised that the issue of a certificate under these provisions neither creates nor removes rights. It is merely a declaration, binding upon the authority, that certain existing rights attach to a given property. If the applicant can satisfy the local planning authority of the lawfulness of development carried out, he will be entitled to be issued with the certificate. Once issued, s 191(6) provides that the lawfulness of any use, operations or other matter for which a certificate is in force shall be conclusively presumed. It will not, therefore, be possible for the authority to take enforcement action against any use, operations or other matter specified in the certificate. Thus in order to ensure that a high degree of precision is achieved in describing the particular lawful use or development specified in the certificate, s 191(5) provides for a certificate to specify the land to which it relates, describe the uses, operations or other matter in question (including, if appropriate, the relevant Use Class), give the reasons for determining the use, operations or other matter to be lawful, and specify the date of the application for the certificate.

21.173 Many problems seem to have been caused by the certificate of lawful use or development procedure, although for the most part they have involved the application to particular cases of general planning law principles. However, in *Panton and Farmer v Secretary of State for the Environment, Transport and the Regions and Vale of White Horse DC* [1999] JPL 461, guidance was given by the High Court on the approach a decision-maker should follow in considering an application. This was first, to ask and answer the question, 'When did the material change of use specified in the application occur?' To be lawful, this would need to be before 1 July

1948, by 31 December 1963, or at a date at least 10 years prior to the current application. Secondly, if the material change of use took place prior to those dates, has the use specified in the application been lost by operation of law in one of the three possible ways, namely by abandonment, the formation of a new planning unit, or by way of a material change of use, be it by way of implementation of a further planning permission or otherwise? Thirdly, if he is satisfied that the description of the use specified in the application does not properly describe the nature of the use which resulted from the material change of use, the decision-maker must modify/substitute each description so as properly to describe the nature of the material change of use which occurred. The *Panton* decision was considered by the Court of Appeal in *Secretary of State for the Environment, Transport and the Regions v Thurrock BC* [2002] EWCA Civ 226. The case involved a challenge to an Inspector's decision to allow an appeal against an enforcement notice served by the Borough Council on the ground that service of the enforcement notice was time barred. It was unclear, however, if the Inspector had considered whether the change of use had been carried on for the whole 10 year period ending with the date of the enforcement notice. The Court of Appeal considered that the Inspector had wrongly interpreted *Panton* in thinking that if the use enforced against had first commenced before the ten year period, it could only be held to be unlawful if the use had been abandoned during that period.

In the *Thurrock* case, the Court of Appeal considered that the rationale of immunity from enforcement was that throughout the whole of the ten-year period of unlawful use the local planning authority, although having the power to take enforcement action, had failed to do so. So, if at any time during the relevant period the authority would not have been able to take enforcement proceedings in respect of the breach (because for example, the unlawful use had temporarily ceased), then any such period could not count towards the ten-year period which gives rise to the immunity. **21.174**

The effect of the decision in the *Thurrock* case therefore, is to require a far more stringent test of immunity than had previously been thought following the decision in *Panton and Farmer*. In particular, the decision means that if an unlawful use ceases and is then recommenced, the ten-year period required for immunity begins on the act of the recommencement. For an unlawful use to obtain immunity from enforcement it has to be exercised continually and without significant interruption for the whole of the ten-year period. **21.175**

The *Thurrock* test, if applied literally, would mean that any period of dormancy occurring during the relevant period would be enough to defeat any claim of immunity from enforcement proceedings. It will, therefore, be of interest to see to what extent a minimal interruption in an unlawful use during the claim period is held to be within the *Thurrock* principle. A short period of inactivity may be regarded as part of a continuing use; a longer period not. What constitutes a short period for these purposes must be a question of fact and degree for the decision-maker in every case. In *Thurrock* the Court of Appeal considered a factory's weekend break or a closure for the summer holidays would not be sufficient to constitute a break in the ten-year period. No doubt, further judicial guidance on this issue can be expected. **21.176**

The decision in *Thurrock* indicates that it is wrong to assume that a material change of use is a once and for all event. Now, in order to have a ten-year period of immunity, an owner must demonstrate that the use has been carried on continuously throughout the ten-year period, **21.177** during which the local planning authority could reasonably if it had so wished, have taken enforcement proceedings.

21.178 Mention should be made that in contrast with the statutory provisions for CLOPUDs, where a certificate once issued may be revoked by a local planning authority, there is no provision which would allow a CLEUD to be revoked. However, it should be possible for an authority to rescind a certificate and replace it with another when there has been an obvious mistake. In some cases (as where a person has acted upon the faith of a certificate rescinded by the authority) it might be appropriate to seek the intervention of the Court.

21.179 Lastly, it was held in *R v Epping Forest BC, ex p Philcox* [2000] PLCR 57 that if a certificate of lawful use or development is issued in respect of a limited area of land, it is within a local planning authority's power to subsequently issue another certificate covering a larger area of land than that covered by the earlier certificate.

Conversion of existing established use certificates

21.180 Following the repeal of the provisions which enabled a landowner to apply for an established use certificate and its replacement by the certificate of lawfulness of existing use or development, the Planning and Compensation Act 1991 provided that an order may provide for established use certificates to have effect as certificates of lawfulness of existing use or development, in such circumstances and to such extent as may be specified in the order. No such order was ever made. The position, therefore, is that an established use certificate retains its former effect and value, so that it continues to remain conclusive as respects any matters stated in it for the purpose of an appeal against an enforcement notice issued after the date specified in the certificate. As in the past, of course, the use described in the certificate may no longer be immune from enforcement action if, since the date of the certificate, there has been in respect of the land some subsequent unlawful material change of use or the established use has been abandoned. Whilst there is no compulsion on an owner of an established use certificate to convert it by application into a certificate of lawfulness of existing use or development, the former may be used in support of an application for the latter. The application, however, must be made in the same form as any other application for a certificate of lawfulness of existing use or development. Before issuing the certificate, however, the local planning authority may need to be satisfied that the 'established use' cited in the certificate has continued to subsist, and may decide in issuing the certificate of existing use or development to describe the use more precisely than that stated in the (old) established use certificate.

Certificate of lawfulness of proposed use or development (CLOPUD)

21.181 Although this certificate is authorised by Part VII of the 1990 Act, it has little to do with enforcement, except in so far as a certificate under s 192 may prevent enforcement action from being taken. Reference has been made to this certificate in Chapter 9.

N. PROPOSALS FOR CHANGE

In 2003 the Government issued a consultation paper inviting views on a number of aspects of the planning enforcement regime and setting out a number of options for improving the system. 21.182

The consultation paper examined the three fundamental principles that underpin the planning enforcement system — that the use of enforcement powers is discretionary, that developing without planning consent is not a criminal offence, and that planning permission may be sought retrospectively. It also looked at the range of powers available to local authorities and the rights of appeal. 21.183

Among the range of possible changes to the detailed powers and procedures are a power to require the submission of a retrospective planning application; to require a fee to be paid if permission is not sought for unauthorised development; the right for local authorities to decline to consider planning applications where an enforcement notice has already been issued in respect of the same development; and a requirement for developers to self-certify that an approved development accords with the permission granted. 21.184

The consultation paper also raised the possibility of abolishing in part the rule under which unauthorised development acquires lawfulness through the passage of time and thereby becomes immune from enforcement action. The paper suggested a number of good practice changes that might improve the speed and effectiveness of enforcement. They include the timing of enforcement notices where retrospective permission has been refused, skill sharing and joint working between local authorities, sharing legal representation, and grouping cases together to take to court. 21.185

The Government hope to have announced the results of the consultation paper by the end of 2004, but have not yet done so. 21.186

22

LISTED BUILDINGS AND CONSERVATION AREAS

Prior to 24 August 1990, the law relating to listed buildings and conservation areas was contained substantially in the Town and Country Planning Act 1971. Under the measures **22.01** taken to consolidate the law relating to town and country planning in 1990, it was decided to consolidate those statutory provisions relating to listed buildings and conservation areas into their own statute. The provisions are now to be found in the Planning (Listed Buildings and Conservation Areas) Act 1990.

A. LISTED BUILDINGS

22.02 Listed building control is a special form of control applicable to buildings of special architectural or historic interest. This special form of control, which is additional to that exercised over the development of land, is intended to prevent the unrestricted demolition, alteration or extension of a listed building without the express consent of the local planning authority or the Secretary of State. The control does not depend upon whether the proposed activity constitutes development under s 55 of the Town and Country Planning Act 1990. It extends to any works for the demolition of a listed building, or for its alteration or extension in any manner likely to affect its character as a building of special architectural or historic interest.

22.03 It may not always be clear whether works to a listed building constitute the demolition or alteration of a building. Whether work amounts to demolition or alteration of a listed building has to be considered in the context of the whole of the listed building. Following the decision of the House of Lords in *Schimizu (UK) Ltd v Westminster City Council* [1997] JPL 523, partial demolition will generally be regarded as an alteration rather than demolition. In that case the Lands Tribunal (who were dealing with an issue of compensation arising from the refusal of listed building consent) were held to have correctly decided that the removal of internal chimney breasts on five floors of a listed building constituted not works of demolition but an alteration to the building.

22.04 Despite the decision in *Schimizu*, problems can still arise where part only of a listed building is to be demolished. Para 15A of PPG 15 indicates that the substantive demolition of a listed building, or any significant part of it, should be treated similarly to total demolition of the building. As pointed out in *Sullivan v Warwick District Council and Wilson Bowden Developments Ltd and English Heritage* [2003] JPL 1545, in deciding whether the demolition of part of a listed building was significant, it was necessary to look not merely at the physical scale of the demolition, but also the quality of that part of the building to be demolished and its contribution to the character of the listed building as a whole.

22.05 The appropriate classification of works to a listed building as demolition or alteration, may impact upon whether notice needs to be given to the Royal Commission on Historic Monuments (which is required before a listed building can be demolished) and whether an application for listed building consent for works to the listed building is needed, and if it is whether notice needs to be given to specified amenity bodies. It also has implications for work done to non-listed buildings within conservation areas (see 22.120).

22.06 It should be emphasised that whilst the demolition (or in some cases partial demolition) is subject to listed building control, works for the alteration or extension of a listed building is subject to listed building control only if the work affects the character of the building as a listed building. In a Ministerial decision in 1972 the Secretary of State decided that the painting in yellow of the front door of a dwelling in the historic Georgian Royal Crescent in Bath amounted to unauthorised work altering the character of a listed building and was subject, therefore, to listed building control. But in *Windsor and Maidenhead RBC v Secretary of State for the Environment* [1988] JPL 410, the Secretary of State had taken the opposite view in finding that painting the Georgian stucco of a listed building in black, was not an alteration and was therefore outside listed building control. The High Court, however, held that having regard to the meaning of the word 'alteration' in ordinary language, and having regard to the relevant statutory provisions, repainting was capable of being an alteration. It also held that the critical question was whether repainting in any particular case affected the character of the building as one of special architectural or historic interest, and that was a matter for the Secretary of State to decide. It seems, therefore, that simple cleaning work to a listed building would not normally require listed building consent. This is probably true also of repainting unless the repainting were of a different colour and so affected its character as a building of special architectural or historic interest. In a Ministerial decision in 1989, it was held that the removal of the original-type glass forming the top glazed panels showing the word 'Telephone' in maroon on a white background on a number of listed telephone kiosks in Cheltenham, and their replacement with panels showing the word 'Phonecard' in white on a green background, affected their character as buildings of special architectural or historical importance.

Paragraph 3.12 of PPG15, in referring to alterations (and extensions) to listed buildings, suggests that in judging their effect, it is essential to assess the elements that make up the 'special interest' of the building in question. **22.07**

The law relating to listed building control is found in the Planning (Listed Buildings and Conservation Areas) Act 1990 (LBCA Act 1990) and the Planning (Listed Buildings and Conservation Areas) Regulations 1990, SI 1990/1519. **22.08**

Under s 1 of the LBCA Act 1990, the Secretary of State for Culture, Media and Sport is required to compile lists of buildings of special architectural or historic interest or approve, with or without modifications, such lists compiled by the Historic Buildings and Monuments Commission for England (known generally as English Heritage) or by other persons or bodies of persons. Furthermore, s 1(4) provides that before compiling, approving or amending any list, the Secretary of State shall consult with the Commission in relation to buildings situated in England and with such other persons or bodies of persons as appear to him appropriate as having special knowledge of, or interest in, buildings of special architectural or historic interest. **22.09**

The main criteria which the Secretary of State considers as appropriate in selecting which buildings to include in the statutory lists are contained in PPG15 Planning and the Historic Environment. The criteria are: **22.10**

— architectural interest: the lists are meant to include all buildings which are of importance to the nation for the interest of their architectural design, decoration and craftsmanship; also important examples of particular building types and techniques (e.g., buildings displaying technological innovation or virtuosity) and significant plan forms;
— historic interest: this includes buildings which illustrate important aspects of the nation's social, economic, cultural or military history;

— close historical association: with nationally important people or events;
— group value, especially where buildings comprise an important architectural or historic unity or a fine example of planning (e.g., squares, terraces or model villages).

22.11 The PPG then indicates that the application of these criteria will lead to the following buildings being listed:

— All buildings built before 1700 which survive in anything like their original condition.
— Most buildings built between 1700 and 1840, though some selection is necessary.
— Between 1840 and 1914, only buildings of definite quality and character including the best examples of particular building types.
— After 1914, only selected buildings.
— Between thirty and ten years old, only buildings which are of outstanding quality and under threat.
— Buildings less than ten years old are not listed.

Examples of selected buildings built after 1914 include Jodrell Bank Radio Telescope, Coventry Cathedral, the Runcorn-Widnes Transporter Bridge, Cripps Hall at the University of Nottingham, and in London the Royal National Theatre, Centre Point, Alexandra Palace, the Whitehall Theatre, Millbank Tower and New Zealand House.

22.12 It should be noted that economic factors cannot be taken into account in deciding whether or not to list a building. In March 1997 the Government confirmed its view that the rule was a sound one. Such matters as the cost of maintenance of a listed building or the cost of repairs to it, or whether the building should be allowed to be converted to a more economic use are, however, matters to be taken into account as material considerations in considering applications for listed building consent.

22.13 Buildings are classified in grades to show their relative importance. The grades are:

Grade I. These are buildings of outstanding architectural or historic interest (only about 2 per cent of listed buildings in England are in this grade).
Grade II.* These are particularly important buildings of more than special interest, but not in the outstanding class (probably some 4 per cent of listed buildings).
Grade II. These are buildings of special interest, but are not sufficiently important to be counted among the elite (about 94 per cent).

22.14 The significance of grading is that the more important the grade the more difficult it may be to obtain listed building consent to carry out work to the building, and the availability of obtaining financial assistance for repairs.

22.15 Section 1(3) of the LBCA Act 1990 provides that:

> In considering whether to include a building in a list compiled or approved under this section, the Secretary of State may take into account not only the building itself but also—
>
> (a) any respect in which its exterior contributes to the architectural or historic interest of any group of buildings of which it forms part; and
> (b) the desirability of preserving, on the ground of its architectural or historical interest, any feature of the building consisting of a man-made object or structure fixed to the building or forming part of the land and comprised within the curtilage of the building.

In other words, although an individual building may not in itself be worthy of listing in its own right, it becomes worthy and may be listed if in its setting it contributes to the architectural or historic interest of a group of buildings of which it is just one. **22.16**

There are about 376,000 entries in the statutory lists in England, but since list entries sometimes include more than one building, over 500,000 individual buildings are protected as listed buildings. About 9,000 are classified as Grade I and 19,000 buildings are classified as Grade II*. Domestic buildings account for 38 per cent of all buildings, with agricultural buildings accounting for just over 12 per cent. **22.17**

Occasionally listed buildings have their status withdrawn because either they have lost their qualifying features through alteration, fire, etc., their architectural or historic merits prove to have been misjudged, or they have been listed in error. In 1988 for example, a building at Sea Palling, Norfolk, was added to the lists as a 16th century house. It had in fact been built in the preceding five years. The roof had come from an old barn; lintels and doors from a demolition site; and the bressummers over the inglenook fireplaces from a scrapyard. For authenticity, the owner had built in settlement. It was subsequently claimed that the building deserved to be listed on grounds of its rarity and eccentricity if not antiquity! In addition, a building may be deleted from a list following demolition, with or without listed building consent. **22.18**

Needless to say, it is very rare for consent to be granted for the total demolition of a Grade I listed building. With regard to the other grades, figures show that in 1997/98, consent for the total demolition of a Grade II* listed building was given in only two cases; and total demolition of a Grade II (unstarred) listed building in 56 cases. In 1997, a total of 327 buildings were removed from the list during the year, that figure including those removed following the grant of consent for their demolition. **22.19**

There is no statutory provision requiring consultation with either the local planning authority or the owner or occupier of a building before it is added to a statutory list. However, following concern at the lack of any formal procedures for the public to be made aware that a building was being considered for listing, the Secretary of State announced in March 1995 that there would be public consultation on recommendations for listing made as a result of English Heritage's thematic studies of post-war and other building types. In August 1995, the Secretary of State announced that the consultation procedure would be extended to proposals to spot-list individual post-war buildings. Once a building is listed, the Department writes to the owner. This is in the nature of an early warning, because local planning authorities are required formally to notify owners and occupiers that a building has been included in a statutory list as soon as they receive notification of that fact from the Department. Authorities must also register the buildings as a local land charge. No formal machinery exists at this stage for an owner or occupier to challenge the inclusion of a building in a list. **22.20**

There is, however, an informal mechanism to challenge the listing of a building. If an owner or occupier makes representations to the Department, the matter is referred to a different Inspector from the one who made the original recommendation. A second opinion is obtained, and the Department may in the light of that second opinion decide that the building should not be listed after all. In 1992, this informal procedure was used in 141 cases. About half were successful, resulting in the removal of the buildings from the list. **22.21**

22.22 Some buildings that are listed under s 1 of the LBCA Act 1990 are also protected as a sheduled monument under the provisions of s 1 of the Ancient Monuments and Archaeological Areas Act 1979 (see Chapter 23). By virtue of s 61 of the LBCA Act 1990, however, most of the listed building control provisions of that Act are disapplied to buildings that are also scheduled monuments.

B. WHAT CAN BE LISTED

22.23 Under s 1(5) of the LBCA Act 1990, a listed building means a building which for the time being is included in a list compiled or approved by the Secretary of State under the section. It will be recalled that under s 336(1) of the 1990 Act, a building 'includes any structure or erection, and any part of a building, as so defined, but does not include plant or machinery comprised in a building'.

22.24 Section 91(1) of the LBCA Act 1990 provides also that except in so far as the context otherwise requires, the word 'building' in the Act shall have the same meaning as given to it in the Town and Country Planning Act 1990. The effect of these two provisions (as was recognised by the House of Lords in *Schimizu (UK) Ltd v Westminster City Council* [1997] JPL 523) is that it gives the Secretary of State the power not only to list a building, but to list part of a building; so that where a part is listed, the part becomes the listed building. Section 1(5) of the LBCA Act 1990 amplifies that definition by providing that the following shall be treated as part of a building:

(a) any object or structure fixed to the building;
(b) any object or structure within the curtilage of a building which, although not fixed to the building, forms part of the land and has done so since before 1 July 1948.

22.25 The effect of paragraph(a) is to enable control to be applied to both internal and external features of a building which are part of its historic fabric or of architectural interest, such as wall panelling, chimney-pieces and wrought-iron balconies.

22.26 The effect of paragraph (b) is to exclude from control any free-standing buildings erected within the curtilage of a listed building after 1 July 1948, unless, of course, the building has been listed in its own right.

22.27 A problem may arise with regard to paragraph (a) as to precisely what is covered by the term 'object or structure fixed to the building'. The problem was considered by the House of Lords in *Debenhams plc v Westminster City Council* [1987] AC 396. There, the respondents owned a hereditament comprising two separate buildings on opposite sides of a street but joined by a footbridge over and a tunnel under the street. One of the buildings (the Regent Street building) was listed in its own right. The other building (the Kingly Street building) was not listed. A dispute arose as to whether the respondents could claim listed building exemption from rates under the General Rate Act 1967 for the period the hereditament had been unoccupied. The magistrate had held that the respondents were not entitled to the listed building exemption because the Kingly Street building was not a listed building. The respondents contended that the whole hereditament was listed because the Kingly Street building was a 'structure fixed to a [listed] building'. The House of Lords, in supporting the magistrate's view that the respondents were not entitled to the exemption, held that the term 'structure fixed to a [listed] building', only encompassed a structure which was ancillary and subordinate to the listed building itself and which was either fixed to the main building or within its curtilage, as, for example, the stable block of a listed mansion house or the steading of a listed farmhouse. The fact that one building was subordinate to another for the commercial purposes of the occupier or that a completely distinct building was connected to a listed building to which it was not subordinate, did not make the building a structure fixed to a listed building.

The *Debenhams* decision was followed in a later case, *Watts v Secretary of State for the Environment* [1991] JPL 719, where a successful challenge was made to the decision of the Secretary of State to dismiss an appeal against a listed building enforcement notice in respect of the demolition of part of a garden wall in order to provide a vehicle access. The question for the High Court to consider was whether the wall was subject to listed building control as being a 'structure fixed to a [listed] building' within the meaning of what is now s 1(5)(a) of the LBCA Act 1990. The facts were that in 1985, the adjacent Bix Manor House and adjoining barn had been specifically listed, but other buildings within the curtilage of the manor house and the garden wall were not specifically referred to. At the date of the listing, the section of the wall now demolished had formed part of the curtilage of an adjacent property separate from the Manor in terms of both ownership and physical occupation. In quashing the decision of the Secretary of State and remitting the matter to him for further consideration, the court held that although historically and physically the wall had been associated with Bix Manor, at the time of listing, the part of the wall demolished was ancillary to another separate (unlisted) building and not a structure ancillary to Bix Manor. The structure was not, therefore, subject to listed building control. In *Secretary of State for the Environment, Transport and the Regions v Skerritts of Nottingham* [2000] JPL 789, the Court of Appeal told that a stable block standing in the grounds of a hotel fell within the curtilage of the hotel and was accordingly listed. **22.28**

It would seem that in determining whether a structure is within the curtilage of a listed building, one should take into account the physical layout of the listed building and the structure; evidence of common ownership both past and present; and their use or function past or present. In addition, it is necessary to consider the 'principal and ancillary' test formulated in the *Debenhams* case and the extent to which the structure has some degree of functional subordination to the building. **22.29**

The significance of the 'list description' was considered by the House of Lords in *City of Edinburgh Council v Secretary of State for Scotland* [1997] 3 PLR 71. It would seen that every part of a listed building is in law equally 'listed', so that listing may protect the interior of a building as much as its exterior, regardless of any special architectural or historic interest which any particular part may have. It is, of course, common for the Secretary of State to provide a description of each building listed. That description, however, does no more in law than provide an aid to its identification, and any features not noted in the description are also part of the listing. **22.30**

It should also be noted that in *Richardson Development Ltd v Birmingham City Council* [1999] JPL 1001 it was held that s 1(5)(a) allows a structure fixed to the land to be treated as part of the listed building, even though the structure was erected after the date of listing. However, **22.31** it would, of course, be subject to the principle enunciated in the *Debenhams* case, that it should be both fixed to the listed building and be ancillary to it.

22.32 A further difficulty concerns the extent to which control may be exercised over 'objects' fixed to a listed building. In 1989 the Secretary of State announced that in the light of legal advice, the statue of the *Three Graces*, believed to have been carved by Canova in 1817, which for many years had stood in a temple in Woburn Abbey, was subject to listed building control as being an 'object' fixed to a listed building. He had decided, however, not to take listed building enforcement action to secure its return to the temple.

22.33 Then in 1990, he announced that in the light of further information he had received, the better view was that the *Three Graces* was not part of the listed building and therefore not subject to listed building control ([1991] JPL 401). The Secretary of State's view was that the test to be applied was (as Lord Mackay had stated in the *Debenhams* case) the same test as applied at common law to decide whether an article was a fixture.

22.34 It appeared that the statue was installed in the *tempietto* in 1819 and remained there until 1872, when it was removed for exhibition at the Royal Academy. It was returned to Woburn Abbey in 1973 and remained installed in the *tempietto* until 1985. In that year it was sold and removed from Woburn Abbey. In his decision the Secretary of State said that the common law test, although easily stated, was not so easily applied. As regards the degree of annexation, the Secretary of State found it not to be great. The plinth on which the statue had stood had not been fastened to the floor in such a way as to make removal of the statue, which was free-standing, particularly difficult.

22.35 As regards the purpose of annexation, the Secretary of State said he now took the view, on further consideration, even accepting that the *tempietto* was specifically built or modified to house the statue, that this did not of itself mean that the statue became part of the building. According to the Secretary of State, he considered that even if the degree of annexation, looked at in isolation, could have been sufficient to satisfy the relevant test (which he doubted), the purpose of annexation in this case was not such as to make the statue part of the building. He thought that if the position was judged objectively, and without regard to the way in which the owners had regarded and treated the statue, it seemed that the object or purpose of installing the statue in the *tempietto* was not to dedicate it to the land or to incorporate it into the land, but to show off the statue. That, he felt, was consistent with the treatment of the *Three Graces* by the 'owners' of the land and the statue, and by the Revenue authorities, on the deaths of the 11th and 12th Dukes, when such owners chose to treat the statue as a chattel and not as a fixture. Accordingly, the Secretary of State decided that the weight of the arguments brought the scales firmly down against the *Three Graces* being a fixture at the time of listing in 1961. Free from the restrictions which would otherwise have prevented the statue being sold had it been regarded as part of the listed building, it was subsequently sold for £7.6m to the Victoria and Albert Museum and the National Gallery of Scotland who share its display.

22.36 It will be seen that in coming to the decision he eventually reached, the Secretary of State applied a two-fold test: first, the degree to which the object is attached or annexed to the building and secondly, the purpose of annexation. Clearly the first test must be satisfied for the second to need to be considered.

Then a little later [1991] JPL 1101, the Secretary of State decided that an 18th-century sundial, which had rested on a listed terrace but without being fixed to it, had not become part of the land and was not subject, therefore, to listed building control. **22.37**

The question of how far works of art can be regarded as objects fixed to a listed building, however, continues to cause difficulty. A few years ago, in a Ministerial decision, [1995] JPL 241, an Inspector quashed enforcement notices served byWestminster City Council requiring the return and reinstatement in a listed building in New Bond Street, London W1 of a bronze sculpture by Henry Moore; a painting, *Spirit of Architecture*, by Ben Nicholson; a heraldic clock by Christopher Ironside; and an iron sculpture by Geoffrey Clarke entitled *The Complexities of Man*. The Inspector found that all four works were commissioned to be enjoyed in their own right and to be part of a fitting-out scheme by the tenant of the building, Time-Life, on going into occupation. He concluded, therefore, that all the works of Art enforced against were chattels and not fixtures under the common law relating to fixtures. Hence they were not fixed to the listed building and were not part of it. The decision was in fact subsequently quashed by the High Court with the consent of both parties. This arose because the Inspector had incorrectly considered the question of whether the items were fixtures at the date on which the building was listed, rather than the date the objects were placed in the building. Subsequently, following a further inquiry, the Secretary of State decided to uphold the enforcement notices which had required the works of Art to be returned to the building [1999] JPL 292. **22.38**

In another Ministerial decision at [1995] JPL 256, issued just two months earlier, the Secretary of State for Wales had accepted his Inspector's recommendation in upholding enforcement notices served by the Montgomeryshire District Council, which required the return to Leighton Hall, Welshpool, of three ormolu bronze chandeliers and a carillon clock which had been removed from the Hall without listed building consent. In *Kennedy v Secretary of State for Wales* [1996] 1 PLR 97, the High Court refused to quash the Secretary of State's decision holding that the definition of a fixture was the same for listed building legislation as it was for any other area of law. On the question of whether a chattel or an article was a fixture, a clear test had to be applied, namely the degree to which it was annexed to the building and then, if it is found to be annexed, the purpose for which it was put there. Following the decision, the dealer to whom the clock had been sold refused to return it to Leighton Hall, but after the County Council obtained an interim injunction requiring compliance with the enforcement notice, he duly did so. **22.39**

A reminder of the way in which listed building control can impact upon the content of a listed building can be seen in a recent Ministerial decision [1999] JPL 1145, where the Secretary of State upheld enforcement action taken by Harborough District Council to secure the reinstatement in Noseley Hall, Noseley, Leicestershire, a Grade II* listed building, of seven paintings in the style of the Italian painter, Pannini. In dealing with the degree to which the paintings could be said to be annexed to the Hall, the Secretary of State accepted the Inspector's conclusions that 'the fixing of the seven Panninis with mirror plates and screws and the similar fixing, or the possible embedding of the large Pannini into the mantel plaster, provided a sufficient degree of connection [to the building] to meet the first test'. **22.40**

The Secretary of State also accepted the Inspector's conclusions with regard to the second test, namely the purpose of annexation. The Inspector found that that purpose had been to **22.41** enhance the 'beauty of the study by the careful matching of pictures with the interior architecture'. Accordingly, the Panninis were integrated into the internal décor of the study in the early 18th century and thereby became part of the building. They were therefore to be regarded as fixtures and as such had to be regarded as part of the listed building.

22.42 At the listed building enforcement notice appeal the owners also sought listed building consent to the removal of the seven Panninis, in the event of the Secretary of State finding that they were indeed objects fixed to a listed building. This application was, perhaps not surprisingly, refused.

22.43 A further enforcement notice served by the District Council with regard to two 18th-century paintings of a Galloway Mare entitled 'Ring Tail', was quashed by the Secretary of State on the recommendation of his Inspector, on the ground that whilst the use of several plates and supporting blocks provided a sufficient degree of annexation to pass the first test, they failed the purpose test in that the paintings had not been installed 'for the purposes of creating a beautiful room as a whole' and lacked any symbiotic relationship with the interior of the hall.

C. THE PROTECTION

22.44 The special control over listed buildings is secured in the main by a criminal sanction. Section 7 of the LBCA Act 1990 provides that subject to the following provisions of the Act, no person shall execute or cause to be executed any works for the demolition of a listed building or for its alteration or extension in any manner which would affect its character as a building of special architectural or historic interest, unless the works are authorised. Section 9 provides that if a person contravenes s 7 he shall be guilty of an offence. It is a defence to the prosecution, however, to prove all the following matters:

(a) that works to the building were urgently necessary in the interests of safety or health or for the preservation of the building;
(b) that it was not practicable to secure safety or health or, as the case may be, to preserve the building by works of repair or works for affording temporary support and shelter;
(c) that the works carried out were limited to the minimum measures immediately necessary; and
(d) that notice in writing justifying in detail the carrying out of the works was given to the local planning authority as soon as reasonably practicable.

22.45 Following changes introduced by the Planning and Compensation Act 1991, the maximum fine on summary conviction for executing, or causing to be executed, without listed building consent, any works for the demolition of a listed building or for its alteration or extension in a manner affecting its character as a building of special architectural or historic interest, or for the failure to comply with any conditions attached to listed building consent to carry out works to a listed building, has been increased from £2,000 to £20,000. In determining the amount of any fine however, the court is required to have regard to any financial benefit which has accrued or appears likely to accrue to the wrongdoer in consequence of the offence. This extends a requirement previously applicable only where a person was convicted on indictment. In addition, the maximum term of imprisonment on conviction on indictment has been increased from six months to two years.

There is no doubt that the courts are using the enhanced powers now available to them. In a Welsh case in 1998 the owners of a listed building (Grade II) had pleaded guilty to the partial demolition of the building one day after it had been listed. In fining the owners £200,000, based on the likely profit to them of redeveloping the site, the judge described the owner's conduct as a 'cynical commercial act'. In anther case, magistrates fined a development company £10,000 for gutting a 19th-century house (listed Grade II) and for removing all period features, in order to convert the building into bed-sits. The offences were described as being 'serious and flagrant'. **22.46**

The offence is an offence of strict liability, so that the prosecution do not have to prove that the defendant was aware that the building was a listed building in order to establish criminal liability. A consequence of this is that the intent or state of mind or motives of a person are irrelevant to the issue of guilt. In other words, it is an offence in which there is technically speaking no *mens rea*. However a person's intention, state of mind, motives and knowledge may be relevant to the punishment, if not to the issue of innocence or guilt (*R v Wells Street Metropolitan Stipendiary Magistrate, ex p Westminster City Council* [1986] 1 WLR 1046). **22.47**

D. BUILDINGS IN ECCLESIASTICAL USE AND MONUMENTS

It has been estimated that nearly 15,000 listed buildings are in religious use, 13,000 of them churches of the Church of England. Of the buildings listed Grade I, well over a third are Anglican parish churches. **22.48**

Section 60(1) and (2) of the LBCA Act 1990, however, provides that ecclesiastical buildings which are for the time being used for ecclesiastical purposes are not subject to ss 3, 4, 7 to 9, 47, 54 and 59 of the Act. These relate to listed building control, including building preservation notices, restrictions on works of demolition, alteration or extension, compulsory acquisition of buildings in need of repair, urgent preservation works by a local authority, English Heritage and the Secretary of State, and offences in relation to intentional damage. Section 75 of the Act provides that ecclesiastical buildings which are for the time being used for ecclesiastical purposes are not subject to s 74 of the Act which relates to the control of demolition of buildings in a conservation area. These exemptions are commonly collectively referred to as the 'ecclesiastical exemption'. **22.49**

It follows that although ecclesiastical buildings can be listed under s 1 of the LBCA Act 1990, no criminal offence can be committed under s 9 for unauthorised works for the demolition, alteration or extension of an ecclesiastical building which is for the time being used for ecclesiastical purposes or would be so used but for the works. Some limited control over unauthorised work to ecclesiastical buildings, however, has been recognised following the decision of the House of Lords in *Attorney-General v Howard United Reform Church Trustees, Bedford* [1976] AC 363. In that case their Lordships decided that the exemption does not apply to the total demolition of a church, as it would then be impossible for the building to be used any longer for ecclesiastical purposes. Following this ruling, therefore, works for the **22.50** total demolition of a church are not authorised and the appropriate consent must be obtained.

22.51 In 1984, following general concern over what is known as the 'ecclesiastical exemption', the Department of the Environment issued a consultation paper inviting comments on whether the exemption should be maintained. Following consideration of the responses to the paper, it was decided in general to retain the exemption. The Housing and Planning Act 1986, however, introduced a new provision to give the Secretary of State power to make orders for restricting or excluding the operation of s 60(1) to (3) in relation to ecclesiastical buildings in particular cases. These provisions are now contained in s 60(5) and (6) of the LBCA Act 1990.

22.52 Further consultation papers on the scope of the ecclesiastical exemption then followed in March 1989 and February 1992. Finally, in July 1 1994, the Government announced that as from October 1 1994 it would use its powers to bring religious bodies within the normal secular controls over both internal and external works to their listed buildings, except for those bodies who have an approved control system of their own which conforms with a Government Code of Practice. Those bodies which have approved control systems such as the Church of England, the Church in Wales, the Roman Catholic Church, the Methodist Church and the Baptist Union of Great Britain, the Baptist Union of Wales and the United Reformed Church continue, therefore, to benefit from exemption from listed building control. After October 1 1994, however, all other religious bodies were made subject to normal listed building and conservation controls.

22.53 The relevant subordinate legislation giving effect to the above, the Ecclesiastical Exemption (Listed Buildings and Conservation Areas) Order 1994, SI 1994/1771, did, however, somewhat reduce the scope of the exemption. Under the Order, the exemption applies only to buildings whose primary use is as a place of worship, and to objects or structures attached to their exterior or within their curtilage to the extent that they are not listed in their own right. It is also provided that special arrangements apply to cathedrals of the Church of England. In that case the exemption covers not only the cathedral itself and buildings, but objects or structures which are located within an area designated by the Secretary of State after consultation with the Cathedrals Fabric Commission for England and which fall within a Precinct indicated by the Commission under the Care of Cathedrals Measure 1990. The special arrangements also covers places of worship elsewhere within the precinct and tombstones elsewhere within the precinct which are not listed in their own right. The Government has announced that a further review of the ecclesiastical exemption regime is to take place during the lifetime of the present Parliament.

E. LISTED BUILDING CONSENT

22.54 Listing is not intended to 'mothball' a building or to ensure it is retained 'in aspic'. The philosophy behind listed building control is that as far as possible a listed building should be retained in use, and that where changes to it are necessary to enable it to be used, those changes should, as far as possible, respect and retain the quality and characteristics of the building.

Under s 8 of the LBCA Act 1990, works for the alteration of a listed building are authorised if: **22.55**

(a) written consent for their execution has been granted by the local planning authority or the Secretary of State; and
(b) they are executed in accordance with the terms of the consent and of any conditions attached to it.

The section also provides that:

> Works for the demolition of a listed building are authorised if—
>
> (a) such consent has been granted for their execution;
> (b) notice of the proposal to execute the works has been given to the Royal Commission;
> (c) after such notice has been given either—
> (i) for a period of at least one month following the grant of such consent, and before the commencement of the works, reasonable access to the building has been made available to members or officers of the Royal Commission for the purpose of recording it; or
> (ii) the Secretary of the Royal Commission, or another officer of theirs with authority to act on their behalf for the purposes of this section, has stated in writing that they have completed their recording of the building or that they do not wish to record it; and
> (d) the works are executed in accordance with the terms of the consent and of any conditions attached to it.

It will be seen that works for the demolition, alteration or extension of a listed building can **22.56** only be authorised by a specific grant of listed building consent. This is so even though the works do not constitute development, as in the case of works for the maintenance, improvement or other alteration of a building which affect only the interior of the building or which do not materially affect its external appearance. It will often happen, however, that before development or redevelopment can take place, both listed building consent and planning permission will be required. In such cases, both may be applied for at the same time. Sometimes, however, an applicant will wish to establish the planning position first before applying later for listed building consent. Whichever method is adopted, the local planning authority is required, in considering whether to grant planning permission for development or listed building consent for any works, to have special regard to the desirability of preserving the building or its setting or any features of special architectural or historic interest which the building possesses (s 66(1) and s 16(2) of the LBCA Act 1990).

Where redevelopment of land requires the demolition of a listed building, the submission of **22.57** an application for consent to demolition prior to the making of an application for planning permission for the redevelopment must be almost unknown, since the absence of any development proposals for a replacement building could be a material consideration in determining the application for listed building consent.

Procedure for obtaining listed building consent

The procedure for obtaining listed building consent is set out in s 10 of the LBCA Act 1990 **22.58** and in the Planning (Listed Buildings and Conservation Areas) Regulations 1990, SI 1990/1519. Application must be made to the local planning authority on a form obtainable from the authority, and must be accompanied by sufficient particulars to identify the building to which it relates, including a plan; such other plans and drawings necessary to describe the proposed works; and such other particulars as may be required by the authority. It is not possible for an owner to make an application for 'outline' listed building consent; he is required to give sufficient details to enable the impact of the works on the building to be assessed at this one stage. The degree of detail required to be submitted is primarily a matter for the local planning authority. If insufficient detail had been provided, the authority may either refuse the application for that reason or treat the application as invalid for failure to comply with the section. However, under s 17(2) of the LBCA Act 1990, the local planning authority may still decide to grant listed building consent on the information in its possession but subject to a condition reserving specified details of the proposed works for their subsequent approval.

22.59 Section 10(3) allows the Secretary of State to specify consultation requirements in respect of both listed building and conservation area consents. This power has now been strengthened by the Planning and Compulsory Purchase Act 2004 by allowing the Secretary of State to impose a duty on consultees to respond, within a fixed period, which mirror the requirement now imposed on consultees to planning applications.

22.60 Under s 19 of the LBCA Act 1990 there is a procedure for varying or discharging conditions which have previously been attached to a listed building consent. The section, however, gives the right to apply for variation or discharge of the conditions to any 'person interested in a listed building'. It seems that the purpose of this restriction is to prevent 'third parties' seeking an alteration to the earlier consent, where they would have no responsibility for carrying out the work if the conditions were to be varied or discharged.

22.61 The application form must be accompanied by certificates similar to those required by the General Development Procedure Order in relation to applications for planning permission made by persons other than the owner of the land to which the application relates. In addition, the regulations require local planning authorities to publish in a local newspaper circulating in the locality a notice regarding the application, display a site notice on or near the land to which the application relates and take into account any representations received as a result before determining the application.

22.62 Under s 15(5) of the LBCA Act 1990, the Secretary of State has power to direct local planning authorities to notify specified persons of any applications for listed building consent and the decision taken by the authority on them. Extensive use has been made of this power. Directions given in Circular 01/01 require all applications for consent for works for the demolition of a listed building, or for works for the alteration of a listed building which comprise or include the demolition of any part of the building and decisions taken thereon to be notified to the Ancient Monuments Society, the Council for British Archaeology, the Georgian Group, the Society for the Protection of Ancient Buildings, the Victorian Society and English Heritage. In relation to applications for listed building consent outside the Greater London area, the directions require the local planning authority to notify English Heritage and subsequently the Secretary of State, of all applications affecting Grade I or II* listed buildings, and those affecting Grade II (unstarred) buildings which involve the demolition of the principal building, the demolition of a principal external wall of the principal building, or the demolition of all or a substantial part of the interior of the principal building. Within the Greater London area, local planning authorities are required to notify English Heritage of all applications for works to Grade I and Grade II* listed buildings; all applications for works to Grade II unstarred railway and underground stations; theatres, cinemas, bridges across the Thames; as well as many other works; and works to listed buildings owned by a local planning authority, where the application is not made by the authority.

The obligation of the local planning authority to comply with these directions, does not affect the provisions in s 13 of the LBCA Act 1990 under which a local planning authority is required to notify the Secretary of State of any application for listed building consent which they propose to grant. The purpose of the provision is to enable the Secretary of State to call in any applications for listed building consent for his own determination. The Secretary of State, however, is empowered under s 15 of the LBCA Act 1990 to direct that notification to him shall not apply to a specified application. He also has power to withdraw that exemption from notification in individual cases. Slightly different notification arrangements apply within Greater London. **22.63**

Circular 01/01 contains a direction absolving local planning authorities from the obligation under s 13 to notify the Secretary of State of certain applications for listed building consent which they are proposing to grant. The absolution from the need to notify reflects the growing number of applications that are made as the number of listed buildings increases, and the fact that many of the applications relate to minor works to Grade II (unstarred) listed buildings. **22.64**

The absolution extends, therefore, to applications for listed building consent to carry out works for the demolition, alteration or extension of a Grade II (unstarred) listed building outside the Greater London area, unless the application proposes the carrying out of works for the demolition of a principal building or works for alteration of a principal building which comprise or include the demolition of a principal external wall of the principal building; or the demolition of all or a substantial part of the interior of the principal building. **22.65**

Determination of applications

Unless the Secretary of State has exercised the right to call in the application for his own determination, the local planning authority are free to determine it after having considered any representations received. As with applications for planning permission, there is a right of appeal to the Secretary of State if the application is not determined within eight weeks (s 20(2) of the LBCA Act 1990). As previously stated, s 16(2) of the LBCA Act 1990 provides that, in considering whether to grant listed building consent, the local planning authority must have special regard to the desirability of preserving the building or its setting or any features of special architectural or historic interest which it possesses. Furthermore, in deciding whether or not to grant listed building consent, it appears now to be an undisputed proposition that the quality of any replacement buildings may be a material consideration to be taken into account (see the speech by Lord Bridge of Harwich in *Save Britain's Heritage v Number 1 Poultry Ltd* [1991] 1 WLR 153). Likewise in *Richmond-upon-Thames LBC v Secretary of State for the Environment* (1978) 37 P & CR 151 and in *Kent CC v Secretary of State for the Environment* [1995] JPL 610, it was held that the nature or appearance of a replacement building is a material consideration in determining whether consent should be given for the **22.66** demolition of a building (in the *Richmond* case of an unlisted building within a conservation area).

Conditions

22.67 Section 16(1) of the LBCA Act 1990 provides that listed building consent may be granted subject to conditions. Section 17(1) provides that without prejudice to this general power, listed building consent may be granted subject to conditions with respect to:

(a) the preservation of particular features of the building, either as part of it or after severance therefrom;
(b) the making good, after the works are completed, of any damage caused to the building by the works; and
(c) the reconstruction of the building or any part of it following the execution of any works, with the use of original materials so far as practicable and with such alterations of the interior of the building as may be specified in the conditions.

In addition, s 17(3) provides that

> listed building consent for the demolition of a listed building may be granted subject to a condition that the building shall not be demolished before
>
> (a) a contract for the carrying out of works of redevelopment of the site has been made; and
> (b) planning permission has been granted for the redevelopment for which the contract provides.

The purpose of this condition is to ensure that a listed building is not demolished prematurely before redevelopment is ready to take place. It should also be noted that (as with planning permission) listed building consent enures for the benefit of the land. Section 16(3), however, allows the authority to impose a condition limiting the consent to a specified person or persons.

22.68 There is no power to grant a temporary listed building consent, but as with the grant of planning permission, listed building consents must include time-limits. Section 18(1) of the LBCA Act 1990 provides that every listed building consent shall be granted subject to a condition that the work to which it relates must be begun not later than the expiration of (a) three years beginning with the date on which the consent is granted; or (b) such other period (whether shorter or longer), being a period which the authority considers appropriate having regard to any material considerations. By sub-section (2), if the authority fail to grant consent subject to such a condition, the consent is deemed to be granted subject to the three-year time period. Under changes made in 2003 to the Listed Buildings Regulations, where a local planning authority grants listed building or conservation area consent where conditions have been attached, it must provide a summary of the reasons for granting the consent.

Listed building consent for work already executed

22.69 As in the case of general planning control under Part III of the 1990 Act which allows, by virtue of s 73A, a retrospective application to be made for planning permission to retain buildings or works or continue the use of land, s 8(3) of the LBCA Act 1990 enables a retrospective application to be made for listed building consent after work to a listed building has taken place. Such applications must be made in the same way as any other application for listed building consent. It should be noted, however, that the work is only authorised from the actual date the consent is given, so that a prosecution for executing or causing to be executed works for the demolition of a listed building or for its alteration or extension in a way which would affect its character can still be taken.

Appeals

Where a local planning authority refuse to grant listed building consent or grant consent subject to conditions, the applicant may appeal to the Secretary of State within a period of six months. **22.70**

The appeal procedures correspond closely with those for ordinary planning appeals under s 78 of the 1990 Act.

It should be noted that the appeal procedure provides an owner with one of the few opportunities he has to object formally to the listing. Under s 21(3) of the LBCA Act 1990, among the grounds on which an appeal may be brought is the ground that the building concerned is not of special architectural or historic interest and ought to be removed from any list compiled or approved by the Secretary of State. In determining the appeal, the Secretary of State may, if he thinks fit, remove the building from the list. **22.71**

F. LISTED BUILDING ENFORCEMENT NOTICES

As well as taking criminal proceedings for unauthorised works to a listed building, a local planning authority may, under s 38 of the LBCA Act 1990, issue a 'listed building enforcement notice'. Because of the existence of the criminal offence, there is no necessity for the related stop notice procedure as exists with general planning control. It should be noted that whereas criminal liability under the Act is imposed on any person who executes or causes to be executed work to a listed building which is unauthorised, enforcement action can be taken under s.38 irrespective of whoever carried out the works. This could include therefore a particular owner. Since there is no limitation period for the serving of a listed building enforcement notice, the sins of a previous owner may well be visited upon the present owner (see *Brown v First Secretary of State* [2003] JPL 1536. **22.72**

As well as specifying the alleged contravention, a listed building enforcement notice must require such steps as may be specified in the notice to be taken within such period as may be specified in the notice: **22.73**

(a) for restoring the building to its former state; or
(b) if the authority consider that such restoration would not be reasonably practicable or would be undesirable, for executing such further works specified in the notice as they consider necessary to alleviate the effect of the works which were carried out without listed building consent; or

(c) for bringing the building to the state in which it would have been if the terms and conditions of any listed building consent which has been granted for the works had been complied with.

22.74 It seems that a listed building enforcement notice can be served in respect of a listed building which has been demolished, so long as a substantial part of it is available for rebuilding. In *R v Leominster DC, ex p Antique Country Buildings Ltd* [1988] JPL 554 a 'cruck barn', a Grade II listed building with a timber frame which had been erected before 1620, was dismantled without listed building consent having been obtained. Some 70 to 80 per cent of the barn's timbers had been sold by the owner in a condition which rendered them suitable for re-erection elsewhere. The intention of the purchasers had been to export the timbers to the United States, where they would there be reassembled. On the question of whether a local planning authority had power to serve a listed building enforcement notice requiring the cruck barn to be re-erected on its original site notwithstanding that the building had been demolished, the High Court held that where the components of a building were substantially extant, its restoration was possible and could lawfully be required by the local planning authority.

22.75 Such action would not be an option, however, if a listed building were demolished and, like Humpty Dumpty, it was not possible to put its parts together again. If a listed building were accidentally demolished, as has occurred when a motor vehicle demolished a listed telephone kiosk ([1990] JPL 444), enforcement action would not be available to the local planning authority. In this particular case, the accident had totally destroyed the kiosk, which was lost forever.

22.76 The *Leominster* case also established that a listed building enforcement notice could be served on the owners of the disassembled parts of the listed building, though the ownership of 70 to 80 per cent of the component parts was thought to be a necessary threshold for this to be possible.

22.77 As with the enforcement procedure for general planning control, there is a right of appeal against the notice to the Secretary of State. The appeal procedures are similar. Two important differences, however, should be mentioned. First, there is no four-year limitation period for the issuing of a listed building enforcement notice similar to that which exists for operational development in general planning control. Secondly, the grounds of appeal to the Secretary of State can include the ground 'that the building is not of special architectural or historic interest'.

22.78 Section 25 of the Planning and Compensation Act 1991 made various amendments to the LBCA Act 1990. As far as possible, the amendments mirror amendments made by the 1991 Act in the field of the enforcement of general planning control. The main amendments were as follows:

(a) The power of a local planning authority to withdraw a listed building enforcement notice before it has taken effect was extended to include a power to withdraw a notice after it has taken effect.

(b) In order to prevent appeals against listed building enforcement notices being invalidated due to postal delays, it was provided that an appeal may be validly made if sent to the Secretary of State in a properly addressed and prepaid letter posted to him at such time that, in the ordinary course of post, it would be delivered to him before the date specified in the notice as the date on which it is to take effect.

(c) Section 39(3) of the LBCA Act 1990 provides that 'where . . . an appeal is brought the listed building enforcement notice shall . . . be of no effect pending the final determination or withdrawal of the appeal'. In *R v Kuxhaus* [1988] QB 631 (a decision on the related s 175(4) of the 1990 Act) the Court of Appeal held that the words 'final determination' meant that the enforcement notice was suspended not only up to the time the decision of the Secretary of State had been given on appeal, but until any appeal from his decision to the courts had been decided. This meant that an owner could delay having to comply with the enforcement notice by appealing to the Secretary of State and then to the courts before withdrawing his appeal to the courts at the last moment. In that way, the owner was able to use the procedure to continue to use his land in contravention of planning control for a longer period than would otherwise have been the case.

In order to prevent unnecessary appeals from decisions of the Secretary of State to the High Court, many of which are withdrawn before trial, the 1991 Act made two changes to s 65 of the LBCA Act 1990. First, a new sub-section (3A) provides that: **22.79**

> in proceedings brought by virtue of this section, the High Court or, as the case may be, the Court of Appeal may . . . order that the listed building enforcement notice shall have such effect, or have effect to such extent as may be specified in the order, pending the final determination of those proceedings and any rehearing and determination by the Secretary of State.

The effect of this provision means that a listed building enforcement notice may not necessarily be suspended by the taking of legal proceedings. Under s 65(3A), the court is given the power to decide the effect of the enforcement notice during the period before it comes to a final judgment on the appeal. **22.80**

(d) Schedule 3 to the 1991 Act made a further change to s 65 of the LBCA Act 1990, by substituting within it a new sub-section (5). The new sub-section provides that:

> No proceedings in the High Court shall be brought by virtue of this section except with the leave of the court and no appeal to the Court of Appeal shall be so brought except with the leave of the Court of Appeal or of the High Court.

This provision in relation to listed building enforcement notices, replicates a similar provision introduced by the 1991 Act in relation to the enforcement of general planning control.

(e) On an appeal against a listed building enforcement notice, the Secretary of State has power to correct any 'misdescription' in the notice, so long as he is satisfied that the correction or variation will not cause injustice to the appellant or the local planning authority. Before 1991, his power to correct a notice on appeal was limited to the correction of any 'informality, defect or error in the notice'.

(f) Where the steps required to be taken by a listed building enforcement notice have not been taken, it is provided that the person who is the current owner of the land is the person in breach of the notice. This, of course, may not be the same person as the owner on whom the notice was served.

(g) Where an owner of land has not taken the steps required to be taken by the listed building enforcement notice within the prescribed time, he is guilty of an offence. If at any time after conviction he still does not take those steps, he may be guilty of a second or subsequent offence.

(h) As previously mentioned, the maximum penalty for failure to comply with a listed building enforcement notice was increased on summary conviction from £2,000 to £20,000. In addition, however, in determining the amount of any fine, the court is required to have regard to any financial benefit which has accrued or appears likely to accrue to the wrongdoer in consequence of his offence.

(i) A local planning authority has express power to apply to the court for an injunction where it considers it necessary or expedient to restrain any actual or apprehended breach of listed building control. The power is available whether or not the authority has exercised or is proposing to exercise any of its other powers under the LBCA Act 1990.

22.81 Furthermore, where the rules of court so provide, an injunction may be issued against persons whose identity is unknown.

(j) Under s 88 of the LBCA Act 1990, the various authorities are given power to enter land at any reasonable time for certain specified purposes connected with listed building control. These purposes include ascertaining whether a breach of listed building control has taken place and whether a listed building is being maintained in a proper state of repair. The 1991 Act provided an opportunity to bring together in one section of the LBCA Act 1990 all the statutory provisions authorising 'rights of entry' to land in relation to listed building control. However, the 1991 Act, by adding a new s 88A to the LBCA Act 1990, also strengthened the power of the authorities to obtain information needed for a proper discharge of their listed building control functions. The section now allows a local planning authority, the Secretary of State or, in Greater London, the Historic Buildings and Monuments Commission for England, to enter on land for any of the purposes set out in s 88 of the 1990 Act under the warrant of a magistrate without prior notice. The applicant for a warrant must show to the satisfaction of the magistrate that there are reasonable grounds for entering the land for any of the purposes set out in s 88, and that admission to the land has been refused (or refusal is reasonably apprehended), or the case is one of urgency.

G. LISTED BUILDING PURCHASE NOTICES

22.82 If listed building consent has been refused or granted subject to conditions, an owner of land may serve on the council of the district or London borough in which the land is situated a notice, called a listed building purchase notice, requiring the council to purchase his interest in the land. In order to do so, however, he must be able to show that the land has become 'incapable of reasonably beneficial use'. The statutory provisions, which are contained in ss 32 to 37 of the LBCA Act 1990 are similar to the provisions in Part VI of the 1990 Act which enable the owner of an interest in land to serve a purchase notice where an application for planning permission to develop land is refused or granted subject to conditions.

H. CERTIFICATES OF IMMUNITY

At one time, one of the difficulties that occurred with listed building control was that a landowner might apply for and obtain planning permission for the redevelopment of land on which there stood a building of some architectural or historic interest, but one not protected by inclusion in the lists. The planning permission obtained was often an outline permission, which left the landowner with the obligation to obtain approval of reserved matters before the redevelopment could actually be commenced. Then, before approval of reserved matters had been obtained, the building would be added to a list compiled or approved by the Secretary of State. Since this would generally mean the redevelopment could not then take place, or at best could not take place in the way originally envisaged, the landowner might have spent a considerable sum of money in preparing the plans, etc. needed for detailed approval which would then be wasted. **22.83**

To meet this difficulty s 6 of the LBCA Act 1990 provides that where an application has been made for planning permission for any development involving the alteration, extension or demolition of a building, or planning permission has been granted for such development, any person may apply to the Secretary of State for a certificate stating that he does not intend to list the building. **22.84**

Once a certificate is issued, the building cannot be listed for a period of five years or be the subject of a building preservation notice made by the local planning authority during that period (22.102). If a certificate should not be granted, the building will almost certainly be added to the list. Although the law does not require that step to be taken, a failure to add it to the list at the same time as the decision is taken not to issue a certificate, might well lead to the building's immediate demolition. **22.85**

A recent use of the certificate procedure occurred in 1992, when the Secretary of State issued a certificate in relation to buildings in the South Bank Centre, including the Hayward Gallery, the Queen Elizabeth Hall, the Purcell Room and associated walkways. **22.86**

I. LISTED BUILDINGS IN NEED OF REPAIR

Under s 54 of the LBCA Act 1990, local authorities have power to execute any works which appear to them to be urgently necessary for the preservation of listed buildings in their area. Before doing so, they must give the owner of the building not less than seven days' notice in writing of their intention to do so. Such a notice can also be served in respect of the unused part of a partly occupied listed building, and the works executed may consist of or include works for providing temporary support (such as scaffolding or props) for the building. **22.87**

Under s 55 of the LBCA Act 1990, a local authority may recover the expenses incurred by them in carrying out such work. In such cases, the authority is required to give notice to the owner, who can make representations to the Secretary of State that 'some or all of the works were unnecessary for the preservation of the building'. The Secretary of State may then determine to what extent the representations are justified and, in consequence, the amount **22.88** the authority can require the owner to pay. Representations may also be made on the ground that the amount sought to be recovered is unreasonable or would cause hardship, or that in the case of works for affording temporary support or shelter, the temporary arrangements have continued for an unreasonable length of time. In *R v Secretary of State for Wales, ex p City and County of Swansea* [1999] JPL 524, it was held that, subject to those statutory defences, a defaulting owner is liable to pay the cost of work that was necessary to preserve20the building, provided that the local planning authority reasonably thought that the work was urgently necessary.

22.89 These provisions do not apply to ecclesiastical buildings or to scheduled monuments. The arrangements are subject to some modification in the case of listed buildings in Greater London, where the Historic Buildings and Monuments Commission for England has a similar power.

Compulsory purchase of listed buildings in need of repair

22.90 Under s 47 of the LBCA Act 1990, the Secretary of State may authorise a local authority (or English Heritage in Greater London) to acquire compulsorily any listed building (other than an ecclesiastical building or ancient monument) where it appears to him that reasonable steps are not being taken for the building's proper preservation.

22.91 A condition precedent to the exercise of this power is the service on the owner of the building of a 'repairs notice' under s 48, specifying the works which the authority consider reasonably necessary for the proper preservation of the building and explaining that if the works required by the notice are not carried out compulsory purchase proceedings may be taken.

22.92 In *Robbins v Secretary of State for the Environment* [1989] 1 WLR 201, the House of Lords rejected the argument that a repairs notice could only require the carrying out of works that were necessary for the proper preservation of a building as it subsisted at the date on which the notice was served. It was there held that the notice could require the owner to restore the building to the condition it was in at the date the building was listed, though not before it was listed.

22.93 Should the notice contain any items which are invalid because they require works to be done which are not for preservation, the notice remains valid and the invalid items may simply be disregarded. There is no right of appeal against the repairs notice. If the owner complies with it the authority need do no more. If, however, after two months from the date of service of the notice, reasonable steps have not been taken for properly preserving the building, the authority may commence compulsory purchase proceedings. If the authority proceed to do so, two special points should be noted. First, the compulsory purchase has to be authorised by the Secretary of State, who may not do so unless satisfied that it is expedient to make provision for the preservation of the building and to authorise its compulsory acquisition for that purpose. Hence, in objecting to the compulsory purchase order, the owner may claim that the building is not of special architectural or historic interest and should not be preserved, or that the work specified in the repairs notice is unnecessary for the preservation of the building. Secondly, any person having an interest in the land may apply within 28 days of service of notice of the order to a magistrates' court for an order staying further proceedings on the compulsory purchase order; and if the court is satisfied that reasonable steps have been taken for properly preserving the building, the court must order a stay.

The Secretary of State may also use the powers available under s 48 to local planning authorities. In 1992, the Secretary of State served a repairs notice on the owners of the former St Ann's Hotel in The Crescent, Buxton, a Grade I listed Georgian building. Following dissatisfaction with the lack of any significant progress being made to repair the building, and in order to halt any further deterioration through neglect and indecision, the Secretary of State later used his powers under s 48 of the LBCA Act 1990 to serve a compulsory purchase order on the owner. The building was subsequently purchased, however, by the local planning authority. With the help of funding from the National Lottery, the County Council and the District Council, the external part of the buildings in the Crescent have now been fully restored. It is hoped that work to the principle rooms will be carried out when further funding is available and that the buildings will then be put to some public use. Again, in June 2002, the Secretary of State used his powers under s 48 and commenced compulsory purchase proceedings for Apethorpe Hall, a Grade I listed county manor house in the village of Apethorpe, Northamptonshire. The proceedings followed the service of a repairs notice on the owner which was not complied with. **22.94**

Some light on the use of listed building repair notices has been shed by a published report [1992] JPL 609. The report, based on a survey of local planning authorities in England, shows that over a six-year period between 1984 and 1990, local planning authorities authorised the issue of 287 listed building repair notices. That step alone led the owners of 125 buildings affected either to commence repairs to the building or to sell it on for others to do so. Of the 162 repair notices that were actually served by local planning authorities, repairs were started by the original owner in 87 cases, though in 14 of the cases the repair work did not begin until the compulsory purchase order inquiry stage had been reached. **22.95**

Compensation

Where a listed building is compulsorily acquired as part of the normal process of land acquisition for public purposes, compensation is assessed on the normal market value basis. By s 49 of the LBCA Act 1990, for the purposes of assessing compensation for the compulsory acquisition of a listed building, it is to be assumed that listed building consent would be granted for any works for the alteration or extension of the building. No assumption may be made, however, that listed building consent would have been granted for works of the demolition of the building, apart from any works for the purposes of the limited development of any class specified in Sch 3 to the 1990 Act. It will, of course, still be possible for an owner to claim that, but for the acquisition, listed building consent would have been granted for the demolition of the building and planning permission granted for redevelopment of the land. **22.96**

Where a listed building in need of repair is acquired in order to preserve it, and it can be shown that the building was deliberately allowed to fall into disrepair for the purposes of justifying its demolition and the development or redevelopment of the site or adjoining site, the local authority may acquire the building at a substantially lower price. In order for this to happen, s 50 of the LBCA Act 1990 requires the compulsory purchase order to contain an **22.97** application for a 'direction for minimum compensation', and the Secretary of State must include such a direction in the order when confirmed by him. Where a direction for minimum compensation is made, compensation for the acquisition is to be assessed on the basis that it is to be assumed that, but for the acquisition, listed building consent would *not* be granted for any works for the demolition, alteration or extension of the building other than works necessary for restoring it to and maintaining it in a proper state of repair; and that planning permission would *not* be granted for any development or redevelopment of the site.

22.98 The owner of an interest in the land subject to a direction for minimum compensation may appeal to the Secretary of State against the direction at the time he appeals against the compulsory purchase order. Alternatively, he may apply to the magistrates' court for an order that the direction be not included in the order on the ground that the building has not been deliberately allowed to fall into disrepair for the purposes of justifying demolition and the development or redevelopment of the site.

22.99 In the report referred to in the previous section, it is disclosed that there has been a final decision about minimum compensation by the Secretary of State in only six cases. He confirmed the order for minimum compensation in three cases. In three cases the Secretary of State rejected the order for minimum compensation but this did not affect the case for acquisition; and in these cases the order was in any event confirmed by the Secretary of State.

22.100 Two further minimum compensation cases were taken to the magistrates' court. In one, the magistrates rejected the claim for minimum compensation although the owner had previously been refused listed building consent to demolish. The compulsory purchase order was one of those already cited which were subsequently confirmed by the Secretary of State. In another case, the authority was successful in convincing the magistrates that a direction for minimum compensation should be included in the compulsory purchase order but the Secretary of State ultimately rejected the compulsory purchase order entirely. In five cases the issue was never resolved because the owner's action obviated the need to pursue compulsory purchase; the other cases remained ongoing.

22.101 More recently, in December 1994, the Secretary of State confirmed a compulsory purchase order for the acquisition of a Grade II listed building in Alton, Hampshire ([1995] JPL 641). The order, which contained a direction for minimum compensation, followed service by the local planning authority of two 'urgent works notices' under s 54 of the 1990 Act, then a repair notice under s 48 of the Act. The owner had earlier applied to the magistrates' court to have the direction for minimum compensation removed but this had been refused. The Secretary of State took the view that he could only differ from the finding of the court if the owner had been able to produce evidence not then available.

J. BUILDING PRESERVATION NOTICES

22.102 If it appears to a local planning authority that a building in their area, which is not a listed building, is of special architectural or historic interest and it is in danger of demolition or of alteration in such a way as to affect its character as a building of such interest, they may, under s 3 of the LBCA Act 1990, serve on the owner and occupier a 'building preservation notice', stating that the building appears to them to be of special architectural or historic interest and that they have requested the Secretary of State to consider adding it to a statutory list. The notice must also explain its effect. A building preservation notice cannot be served if a certificate of immunity is in operation.

The effect of the notice is to apply to the building most of the provisions of the Act relating to listed buildings, so that it becomes a criminal offence to execute or cause to be executed works for the demolition of the building or for its alteration or extension in a manner which would affect its character as a listed building without listed building consent. **22.103**

A building preservation notice remains in effect for six months from the date of its service (though it may be renewed), unless it has previously lapsed through the inclusion of the building in a statutory list, or the earlier notification by the Secretary of State to the authority that he does not intend to so include it. If the Secretary of State gives notice that he does not intend to include the building in a list compiled or approved by him, no further building preservation notice may be served within the following 12 months. **22.104**

Once the notice has lapsed, all proceedings arising from the application of listed building control will also lapse, save for any criminal liability under ss 9 (execution of works to a listed building without consent) or 43 (penalties for non-compliance with a listed building enforcement notice). **22.105**

A fetter on the exercise by the local planning authority of their power to issue a building preservation notice, is that under s 29 of the LBCA Act 1990 compensation must be paid for any loss or damage which is directly attributable to the effect of the notice if the building is not subsequently listed by the Secretary of State. The compensation may include any sum for which the applicant has become liable in respect of any breach of contract caused by the requirement of the notice. **22.106**

Building preservation notices should be distinguished from what is known as 'spot listing'. This occurs when an approach is made to the Secretary of State by a local authority (or other body or person), without any service of a building preservation notice, to have a building added to the statutory lists. It is claimed that the listing process, which may take months or years when done as part of a general or thematic survey of buildings of architectural or historic interest, can be completed within 24 hours by the spot-listing method. Statistics show that of 3,574 buildings added to the statutory lists in 1990 (no later figures are currently available), 1,330 (37.2 per cent) were added as a result of spot listing, whereas only 49 (1.3 per cent) were added following service of a building preservation notice. In evidence given by English Heritage to the Committee of Public Accounts of the House of Commons in November 1992, it was disclosed that over 2,500 requests for spot listing were made each year, and that in 50 per cent of cases recommendations for listing were made. In the year 2001/02 681 buildings were added to the statutory lists as a result of spot listing. **22.107**

Buildings threatened by development proposals

Public concern for the preservation of buildings has led to increasing problems when proposals are made for the development of land which includes a building which is not **22.108** protected by listing. An application for planning permission may generate considerable public pressure for the preservation of existing buildings on the land, which, if achieved, would prevent the development proposed going ahead. Faced with an application for planning permission which generates such pressure, the local planning authority may decide to serve a building preservation notice. As stated, however, if the building is not subsequently listed, the local planning authority will be liable to pay compensation for any loss or damage suffered. If, on the other hand, the building is then listed, the application for planning permission may merely have served the purpose of alerting people's attention to the need to preserve the buildings on the site, with unfortunate results for the applicant.

22.109 It must be recognised that the act of listing may well diminish the landowner's prospects of developing or redeveloping the site and the possible loss of its value for that purpose. In *Amalgamated Investment & Property Co. Ltd v John Walker & Sons Ltd* [1976] JPL 308, the parties had entered an agreement for the sale and purchase of a disused warehouse. The purchase price of £1,700,000 reflected the potential of the site for redevelopment. On the day after contracts were exchanged, the Secretary of State added the building to the statutory list. As a result, the market value of the property (with no redevelopment potential) was no more than £200,000. The purchasers thereupon sought rescission of the contract on the ground of common mistake, claiming that the parties believed at the time of the contract that the property was capable of development, or alternatively, that the listing had frustrated the purposes of the contract so that it was void and of no effect and ought not to be enforced. Dismissing the application, the Court of Appeal held that loss must lie where it fell; that the only mistake made was one relating to the expectations of the parties and that a risk of listing was inherent in the ownership of all buildings. Although this case was concerned with which of the two parties should bear the loss, it illustrates the loss that any owner may suffer as the result of a building being listed.

22.110 In these circumstances, it is not surprising that an owner wishing to redevelop land on which stands a non-listed building, may decide first to demolish the building, and then to apply for planning permission for redevelopment. In this connection, although the definition of development now includes the demolition of buildings, the demolition of any building other than a dwellinghouse is excluded by virtue of s 55(2)(g) of the 1990 Act; and in relation to dwellinghouses, demolition of most is permitted development under the General Permitted Development Order. It should however be noted, that demolition of a building in a conservation area requires 'conservation area consent.'

22.111 The effect of listing on the value of an owner's interest in land, helps to explain why penalties for contravention of listed building control may reflect the benefit obtained by the wrongdoer and why the law contains provisions relating to the payment of minimum compensation where listed buildings in need of repair are compulsorily acquired in order to secure their preservation.

Historic parks and gardens

22.112 Since 1984 certain parks and gardens of special historic interest in England have been identified by English Heritage through its Register of Parks and Gardens. The main purpose of the Register is to identify and draw attention to the best historic parks and gardens which constitute an important part of the cultural heritage of England.

Like listed buildings, sites on the Register are listed in three grades, namely those of exceptional historic interest (Grade I); those of great historic interest (Grade II*); and those of special historic interest (Grade II). 22.113

Unfortunately, however, unlike listed buildings, sites on the Register have no special statutory protection, so that there are no additional powers available to control development and work done to them beyond normal planning powers. 22.114

However, Art 10(1), para (6), of the GDPO requires local planning authorities to consult English Heritage before granting planning permission for development affecting Grade I or II* historic parks and gardens on their Register. 22.115

Historic battlefields

Since 1991 English Heritage has started to compile a Register of Historic Battlefields, selection being based on the political significance of the engagement, its military historical significance or its biographical significance. As with historic parks and gardens, no special statutory protection is given to sites on the Register although, as with historic parks and gardens, the fact that they are on the Register should be a material consideration in determining applications for planning permission which affect them. 22.116

World Heritage Sites

There is no special control exercised over World Heritage Sites as such. Inclusion in the World Heritage List is essentially honorific and leaves the existing rights and obligations of owners, occupiers and planning authorities unaffected. A prerequisite for World Heritage Site status is, however, the existence of effective legal protection and the establishment or firm prospect of management plans to ensure a site's conservation and preservation. In the United Kingdom, legal protection is achieved through listing and scheduling and their associated controls, by the establishment of conservation areas, and by the outstanding international importance of the site being taken into account as a material consideration by local planning authorities. 22.117

There are 24 World Heritage Sites in the United Kingdom including dependent territories: 19 cultural heritage sites and 5 natural heritage sites. The cultural heritage sites are: Ironbridge Gorge; Stonehenge, Avebury and associated sites; Durham Castle and Cathedral; Studley Royal Park and Fountains Abbey; Castles and Town Walls of King Edward in Gwynedd; Blenheim Palace; City of Bath; Hadrian's Wall; Westminster Palace, Westminster Abbey and St Margaret's Church; Tower of London; Canterbury Cathedral, St Augustine's Abbey and St Martin's Church; Edinburgh Old and New Towns; Maritime Greenwich; Heart of Neolithic Orkney; the Historic Town of St George, Bermuda and related fortifications; Blaenavon Industry Landscape; the Derwent Valley Mills; Saltaire and New Lanark. The natural heritage sites are: Giant's Causeway; St Kilda; Henderson Island, Pitcairn Group; Gough Island Wildlife Reserve, St Helena Group and Dorset and East Devon Coast. 22.118

K. CONSERVATION AREAS

22.119 Under s 69 of the LBCA Act 1990, every local planning authority must from time to time determine which parts of their area are areas of special architectural or historic interest the character or appearance of which it is desirable to preserve or enhance, and shall designate those areas as conservation areas. It would appear that in deciding to designate such an area, a local planning authority can consider as one entity the whole of an area which gives rise to special architectural or historic interest and that not every part of that area need have in it something of special architectural or historic interest. In *R v Canterbury City Council, ex p Halford* [1992] 2 PLR 137, the High Court held it could only interfere with a decision to designate if there had been an infringement of the *Wednesbury* principles.

22.120 Designation of a conservation area by a local planning authority gives the authority considerable additional powers over the development and use of land in the area. In *R v Surrey CC, ex p Oakimber Ltd* [1995] EGCS 120 it was held that the authority had a broad discretion to determine which parts of their area were of special architectural or historic interest with a character or appearance which should be preserved or enhanced. In rejecting a challenge to the designation of land at Brooklands, Surrey, the High Court held that there was no obligation on the local planning authority to look at each piece of land in a proposed consultation area in isolation. The authority were entitled to consider, as an entity, the whole of an area which gave rise to special architectural or historic interest.

22.121 Land in a conservation area may not be included in a simplified planning zone (s 87(1) of the 1990 Act).

22.122 It will be seen that whilst listing procedures focus upon the protection of individual buildings, designation of conservation areas focusses upon conservation policies for particular areas. The designation of a conservation area has the following particular consequences:

(a) Under s 71 of the LBCA Act 1990, the local planning authority must from time to time formulate and publish proposals for the preservation and enhancement of such areas.
(b) Under s 72 of the LBCA Act 1990, in the exercise with respect to any buildings or other land in a conservation area of any powers under any of the provisions of the Planning Acts or Part I of the Historic Buildings and Ancient Monuments Act 1953, 'special attention should be paid to the desirability of preserving or enhancing the character or appearance of that area'.

22.123 This provision is derived from s 277(8) of the Town and Country Planning Act 1971. Its scope was first considered by the courts in *Steinberg v Secretary of State for the Environment* (1988) 58 P & CR 453, where the main issue for decision was whether the Inspector, in allowing an appeal against the decision of the local planning authority to refuse planning permission to erect a two-storey house in a conservation area, had correctly applied s 277(8) of the Town and Country Planning Act 1971. In his decision letter the Inspector had said that from his observations of the site and its surroundings and from representations received, he considered the main issue to be decided was whether the proposal would constitute overdevelopment of the site and whether the proposed development would harm the character of the conservation area. In quashing the decision, the High Court held that the Inspector had misdirected himself on a point of law. The duty imposed by s 277(8) was 'to pay special attention to the desirability of preserving or enhancing the character or appearance of the conservation area'. The Court held that there was a world of difference between what the Inspector had defined for himself — whether the proposed development would 'harm' the character of the conservation area — and the need to pay special attention to the desirability of preserving or enhancing the character or appearance of the area. Harm was one thing, preservation or enhancement another. The concept of avoiding harm was essentially negative, the underlying purpose of s 277(8) essentially positive.

The *Steinberg* decision was later considered by the High Court in *Unex Dumpton Ltd v Secretary of State for the Environment* [1990] JPL 344. According to the Court, the duty under s 277(8) did not relieve the Secretary of State or his Inspector of the need to consider whether harm would be caused by proposed development in a conservation area or if so, whether the benefits of the proposed development would outweigh that harm. Important though the provisions of s 277(8) were, they were only one of the material considerations that had to be taken into account and only required that 'special attention' be paid to the matters set out in s 277(8). **22.124**

The *Steinberg* decision was also considered by the Court of Appeal in *Ward v Secretary of State for the Environment* [1990] JPL 347. There, the Court held, *inter alia*, that by failing properly to consider whether proposed development in a conservation area would preserve or enhance the area, the Inspector had fallen short of the statutory requirement imposed by s 277(8). Although the Court of Appeal appeared to endorse the *Steinberg* principle, its application continued to give rise to difficulties. It seems that the positive duty imposed by s 277(8) is a material consideration in determining planning applications. It is, however, merely one material consideration, though one given a certain pre-eminence by the section. It may be, for example, that the decision-maker, having paid special attention to the desirability of preserving or enhancing the character or appearance of the conservation area, may decide nevertheless that the application should be refused because of insuperable highway objections. **22.125**

This approach was confirmed when the meaning of the provision was further considered by the House of Lords in *South Lakeland DC v Secretary of State for the Environment* [1992] 2 AC 141. There, their Lordships had to consider a decision by an Inspector to allow an appeal against a refusal of outline planning permission for the erection of a new vicarage on a site within a conservation area. The Inspector had allowed the appeal and granted planning permission for the development on the ground that, provided the proposed vicarage did not cause harm 'to the character of the conservation area', it would not damage the appearance of the village. The local planning authority then successfully applied to quash the Inspector's decision on the ground that he had failed to discharge the duty imposed on him by s 277(8) of the Town and Country Planning Act 1971 to pay special attention to the desirability of 'preserving or enhancing' the character or appearance of the conservation area. **22.126**

The Secretary of State appealed to the Court of Appeal which reversed the decision of the High Court on the ground that the Inspector had indeed discharged his duty under s 277(8) by his finding that, since the character and appearance of the conservation area would not be harmed by the development, the area's character and appearance would remain preserved. The planning authority appealed to the House of Lords. **22.127**

22.128 In his speech dismissing the appeal, Lord Bridge of Harwich approved the interpretation placed upon the provision by Mann LJ, in the Court of Appeal below, in which he said:

> In seeking to resolve the issue I start with the obvious. First, that which is desirable is the preservation or enhancement of the character or appearance of the conservation area. Second, the statute does not in terms require that a development must perform a preserving or enhancing function. Such a requirement would have been a stringent one which many an inoffensive proposal would have been inherently incapable of satisfying. I turn to the words. Neither 'preserving' nor 'enhancing' is used in any meaning other than its ordinary English meaning. The court is not here concerned with enhancement, but the ordinary meaning of 'preserve' as a transitive verb is 'to keep safe from harm or injury; to keep in safety, save, take care of, guard': *Oxford English Dictionary*, 2nd ed. (1989), vol. 12, p. 404. In my judgment character or appearance can be said to be preserved where they are not harmed. Cases may be envisaged where development would itself make a positive contribution to preservation of character or appearance. A work of reinstatement might be such. The parsonages board never advocated the new vicarage on that basis. It was not a basis which the Inspector was invited to address but importantly he did not have to address it because the statute does not require him so to do. The statutorily desirable object of preserving the character or appearance of an area is achieved either by a positive contribution to preservation or by development which leaves character or appearance unharmed, that is to say, preserved.

22.129 After agreeing with the construction placed upon the provision by Mann LJ Lord Bridge concluded:

> We may, I think, take judicial notice of the extensive areas, both urban and rural, which have been designated as conservation areas. It is entirely right that in any such area a much stricter control over development than elsewhere should be exercised with the object of preserving or, where possible, enhancing the qualities in the character or appearance of the area which underlie its designation as a conservation area under s 277. But where a particular development will not have any adverse effect on the character or appearance of the area and is otherwise unobjectionable on planning grounds, one may ask rhetorically what possible planning reason there can be for refusing to allow it. All building development must involve change and if the objective of s 277(8) were to inhibit any building development in a conservation area which was not either a development by way of reinstatement or restoration on the one hand ('positive preservation') or a development which positively enhanced the character or appearance of the area on the other hand, it would surely have been expressed in very different language from that which the draftsman has used.

22.130 It is now settled law that preserving the charater or appearance of a conservation area can be achieved not only by a positive contribution to preservation, but also by development which leaves the character or appearance of the area unharmed.

22.131 Lastly, the wording of s 72 also suggests that where an application is being made for the demolition of an unlisted building in a conservation area (see (h) below), the local planning authority must consider details of the replacement development (if any) or the treatment of the land, before it can discharge its duty under the section. In fact, it is not uncommon for an authority in granting conservation area consent for demolition, to tie the demolition to redevelopment of the site. This is in order to prevent the site lying vacant and detracting from the character and appearance of the area. The wording of the condition will be such as to ensure that demolition does not take place until a contract for the carrying out of works of redevelopment has been entered into and planning permission received for the redevelopment for which the contract provides.

(c) Under s 73 of the LBCA Act 1990, the local planning authority must give publicity to any applications for planning permission where the development would, in the opinion of the authority, affect the character or appearance of a conservation area. Under s 67 of the LBCA Act 1990, local planning authorities must send a copy of any notice published in accordance with this provision to English Heritage. The Secretary of State has power, after consultation with the Commission, to make a direction modifying the requirement. The effect of a direction (contained in Circular 01/01 as regards advice on the handling of heritage sites) is to restrict, *inter alia*, the requirement of notification to the Commission to development of a site of more than 1,000 square metres or the construction of any building more than 20 metres in height above ground level.

(d) Under the provisions of Art 4 of the General Permitted Development Order, directions are often made in relation to specified classes of development in conservation areas, thus restricting permitted development rights under the order in those areas.

(e) Land in a conservation area is within the definition of Art 1(5) land in the General Development Order. The significance of this is that the permitted development in such areas is not as wide as development which is permitted by the order in respect of non-Art 1(5) land.

(f) Under the provisions of s 211 of the 1990 Act, a person proposing to cut down, top or lop a tree in a conservation area (other than a tree already protected by a tree preservation order) is required to give six weeks' prior notification to the local planning authority of his intention to do so. The purpose of this provision is to enable the authority to make a tree preservation order if it considers it necessary to do so. Under Part III of the Town and Country Planning (Trees) Regulations 1999, however, s 211 is not to apply to trees which are dying, dead or dangerous; to work necessary to prevent or abate a nuisance; work in accordance with a felling licence or a forestry dedication or approved plan of operations; work in compliance with a statutory obligation; or work to a tree whose diameter does not exceed 75 millimetres. If, however, the cutting down or uprooting of a tree is for the sole purpose of improving the growth of other trees, the exemption applies to trees not exceeding 100 millimetres. The diameter of a tree for these purposes is to be ascertained by measurement, over the bark of the tree, at a point 1.5 metres above the natural ground level. A special rule applies to multiple-stemmed trees if they are to qualify as small trees under this exception.

(g) Under the Town and Country Planning (Control of Advertisements) Regulations 1992, SI 1992/666, the local planning authority may submit to the Secretary of State for his approval an order designating the whole or part of a conservation area as an area of special control of advertisements (see Chapter 22). In such cases stricter control is exercised over the display of advertisements.

(h) Under s 74 of the LBCA Act 1990, the *demolition* of buildings in conservation areas is controlled by applying, with modifications, many of the provisions relating to the control of listed buildings found in Part I of the LBCA Act 1990. Anyone seeking to demolish a building to which these provisions apply must first obtain 'conservation area consent' to do so from the local planning authority. Conservation area consent is not needed for the demolition of a listed building (which, of course, requires listed building consent) an ancient monument or an ecclesiastical building. In addition the Secretary of State may direct that the section shall not apply to descriptions of buildings specified in the direction. A direction in Circular 01/01 provides that (in addition to other buildings mentioned in that direction which are also exempt) the section shall not apply (*inter alia*) to:

(i) any building with a total cubic content not exceeding 115 cubic metres;

(ii) any gate, wall, fence or railing erected before 1 July 1948 which is less than 1 metre high where abutting on a highway, waterway or public open space, or less than 2 metres high in any other case;

(iii) any building erected since 1 January 1914 and used or last used for the purposes of agriculture or forestry.

22.132 As indicated, conservation area consent is required for the demolition of an unlisted building in a conservation area. Prior to *Schimizu (UK) Ltd v Westminster City Council* [1997] JPL 523, it was considered that consent was needed for both the total and partial demolition of such a building. However, following the decision of the House of Lords in the *Schimizu* case, consent is now only required for the total or substantial demolition of an unlisted building in a conservation area and not for works of alteration such as work for the removal of chimneys, extensions or porches attached to an unlisted building.

22.133 In general, the procedure for applying for conservation area consent for the demolition of a building in a conservation area is similar to that for applying for listed building consent. It should be noted, however, that there is no certificate of immunity procedure as exists with listed buildings. But a person may be prosecuted for breach of the provisions and the local authority may take listed building enforcement proceedings.

22.134 It has been estimated that there are around 8,750 conservation areas designated in England, containing 4 per cent of the nation's building stock.

L. PROPOSALS FOR CHANGE

22.135 In July 2003, the Department of Culture, Media and Sport published a consultation paper 'Protecting our Historic Environment; making the system work better'. The paper sought views on proposals for updating and improving historic environment control. Among the changes to be considered were the following:

(a) the bringing together of the different regimes for protecting the historic environment with a List of Historic Sites and Buildings of England. The list would include listed buildings, ancient monuments, certain conservation areas and World Heritage Sites.

(b) giving English Heritage the statutory responsibility for maintaining the list, subject to a number of safeguards.

(c) giving consideration when a building is listed, as to whether the site or building is one which should be recorded rather than listed.

(d) giving consideration as to whether the present gradings of buildings listed be retained; and whether Grade II buildings be moved to 'local lists' or of delegating Grade II listing to local authorities.

(e) showing in the list entry on a map, exactly what areas and structures are covered by the listing.

(f) the provision of a 'statement of significance' in the list entry, showing the reasons for the listing and indicating the works for which consent would be required.

(g) the provision of a statement of reasons for any decision not to list.

(h) supplying owners with a more comprehensive information pack explaining what listing means.

(i) the provision of a new right of appeal, but limited to challenging whether the designating authority had reached its decision correctly by applying the statutory process and criteria and any publishing policy guidance.

(j) requiring owners, local authorities, amenity societies, parish councils and the public to be informed and consulted when a proposal to list is being considered and to provide protection during consideration of listing as if the building were listed.

(k) giving new entrants to the list freedom from control when they enter into a management agreement with English Heritage or, in some cases, the local authority.

(l) requiring regional spatial strategies to set out policies for the region; the issuance of guidance to make clear what policies district and unitary authorities should develop for the protection and enhancement of their historic environment as part of their local development framework and sustainable framework.

As yet, none of these proposals have been carried forward.

23

ANCIENT MONUMENTS AND AREAS OF ARCHAEOLOGICAL IMPORTANCE

Statutory protection of ancient monuments has existed since 1882. Today the protection is secured in varying degrees by the Ancient Monuments and Archaeological Areas Act 1979 (the 1979 Act). Section 61(7) of the 1979 Act defines a 'monument' as meaning: **23.01**

(a) any building, structure or work, whether above or below the surface of the land, and any cave or excavation;
(b) any site comprising the remains of any such building, structure or work or of any cave or excavation; and
(c) any site comprising, or comprising the remains of, any vehicle, vessel, aircraft or other moveable structure or part thereof which neither constitutes nor forms part of any work which is a monument within paragraph (a) above;

and any machinery attached to a monument shall be regarded as part of the monument if it could not be detached without being dismantled.

A. SCHEDULED MONUMENTS

The degree of protection given to a monument under the 1979 Act depends upon whether it is classified as a 'scheduled monument' or as an 'ancient monument'. Under the Act the Secretary of State is required to compile and maintain a 'schedule of monuments'; hence a scheduled monument is defined in terms of inclusion within that schedule. A monument can only be included in the schedule where it appears to the Secretary of State to be of national importance. An 'ancient monument', on the other hand, is defined in wider terms than a scheduled monument and means any scheduled monument and 'any other monument which in the opinion of the Secretary of State is of public interest by reason of the historic, architectural, traditional, artistic or archaeological interest attached to it.' **23.02**

23.03 The Act gives the greatest degree of protection to monuments which are scheduled monuments. Under s 2 of the Act, a criminal offence is committed where a person executes or causes or permits to be executed prescribed works to a scheduled monument without first having obtained 'scheduled monument consent' for the works. The works referred to in the section include demolition, destruction or damage to a scheduled monument, removing or repairing a scheduled monument or any part of it, altering or adding to it, or flooding or tipping operations on land in, on, or under which there is a scheduled monument. Scheduled monument consent may be granted subject to conditions.

23.04 Under s 3 of the 1979 Act, the Secretary of State may make an order granting scheduled monument consent for the execution of works of any class or description specified in the order. The order currently in force is the Ancient Monuments (Class Consents) Order 1994, SI 1994/1381. As with the General Permitted Development Order in relation to the development of land, this order removes the need for an express application to be made for scheduled monument consent where the work involved is of a minor nature.

23.05 Section 5(1) of the 1979 Act provides that where any works are urgently necessary for the preservation of a scheduled monument, the Secretary of State may enter the site and carry out these works, but at his own expense.

23.06 At present there are about 17,500 entries in the schedule of monuments in England, representing about 23,000 individual monuments subject to protection. These include ecclesiastical ruins, megalithic monuments, crosses and inscribed stones, as well as famous sites such as Stonehenge, the Tower of London and Hadrian's Wall. The Historic Buildings and Monuments Commission for England (known as English Heritage), has embarked on a resurvey programme, which is expected to result eventually in significant additional numbers (perhaps 50,000) being given protection by the Secretary of State as scheduled monuments.

23.07 One difficulty with the provisions relating to the scheduling mechanism is that the definition of the term 'monument' presupposes some definable and identifiable entity. It is difficult, therefore, to schedule 'general urban debris' from an earlier age which may be spread over a large area. For that reason, few monuments have been scheduled in urban areas.

B. ANCIENT MONUMENTS

23.08 The 1979 Act also contains powers for the protection of 'ancient' monuments. As previously indicated, the term 'ancient monument' includes all scheduled monuments, but is not restricted merely to that category.

23.09 Under the Act, the Secretary of State is given power to acquire compulsorily any ancient monument for the purpose of securing its preservation. In addition, he is given power to acquire an ancient monument by agreement or by gift.

23.10 As an alternative to acquisition of an ancient monument, the Secretary of State may by s 12 of the 1979 Act be constituted its guardian. Guardianship provides a means whereby the Secretary of State can assume responsibility for maintaining an ancient monument where the owner or occupier is unable or unwilling to do so, but without disturbing the existing ownership of the monument. Where an ancient monument is taken into guardianship, a duty is placed on the guardian to maintain the monument, for which purpose he is given control and management powers. An obligation is also placed on the guardian to permit public access to the monuments under his guardianship.

C. AREAS OF ARCHAEOLOGICAL IMPORTANCE

In addition to the powers relating to scheduled and ancient monuments, s 33 of the 1979 Act provides for the designation by the Secretary of State of what are called 'areas of archaeological importance.' Areas designated so far are the historic centres of Canterbury, Chester, Exeter, Hereford and York. Designation, however, does not protect the site from damage or destruction. Its purpose is merely to allow time for a site which is threatened by development proposals to be excavated and recorded. Under s 35 of the Act, it is a criminal offence for any person to carry out or cause or permit to be carried out on the designated land any operation involving disturbance of the ground, flooding or tipping, without first having served a notice of that operation (called an 'operations notice') on the local authority in whose area the land is situated. The notice must be served at least six weeks before the operation is due to commence. After receiving an operations notice, the local authority or other investigating authority (such as a University Archaeological Unit) may enter and inspect the site, observe any operations and carry out excavations. An authority can only carry out excavations, however, if within four weeks of service of the operations notice, it has itself given notice of its intention to carry out excavations. In such a case, the authority is given four months and two weeks from the end of the six week period to carry out the excavation, during which period no operation involving disturbance of the ground, etc. (i.e. development) can be carried out. Thus under these provisions, development can be delayed for a maximum period of six months. **23.11**

Although more relevant to the field of movable artefacts, s 42(4) of the 1979 Act also contains a provision making it a criminal offence for a person to use a metal detector in a protected place without consent. A protected place means any place which is either the site of a scheduled monument or any monument in the ownership or guardianship of the Secretary of State or situated in an area of archaeological importance. **23.12**

D. PROTECTION UNDER PLANNING LEGISLATION

Ancient monuments and sites of archaeological interest may also be protected under town and country planning legislation. Development plans may contain policies for the protection of ancient monuments and sites of archaeological interest and the effect of development on a scheduled monument may be a material consideration to be taken into account in determining applications for planning permission. **23.13**

According to a Planning and Policy Guidance Note 'Archaeology and Planning', PPG16, issued by the Department of the Environment in November 1990, detailed development **23.14** plans (i.e., local plans and unitary development plans) should include policies for the protection, enhancement and preservation of sites of archaeological interest and their settings. According to this guidance, archaeological remains identified and scheduled as being of national importance should normally be earmarked in development plans for preservation. The guidance goes on to state that the desirability of preserving an ancient monument and its setting is a material consideration in determining planning applications whether the monument is scheduled or unscheduled. (See *Hoveringham Gravels Ltd v Secretary of State for the Environment* [1975] QB 754.) Where the proposed development would affect a monument which is not a scheduled monument, the authority may impose a condition in a grant of planning permission placing an embargo on any development taking place until specified archaeological facilities have been provided. A model condition, which the Secretary of State has advised should be used in appropriate circumstances (Circular 11/95 Appendix A, para 54), provides that the developer shall afford access at all reasonable times to any archaeologist nominated by the local planning authority, and shall allow him to observe the excavations and record items of interest and finds. Whilst the model condition does not require the developer to pay for these facilities, if the condition imposed is that 'no construction work shall be carried out until an archaeological investigation has taken place to the satisfaction of the local planning authority', the condition effectively means that the developer will have to fund such excavation before he is able to proceed. (See [1990] JPL 87.)

23.15 In addition, PPG16 suggests (at para 30) that:

> In cases when planning authorities have decided that planning permission may be granted but wish to secure the provision of archaeological excavation and the subsequent recording of the remains, it is open to them to do so by the use of a negative condition, i.e. a condition prohibiting the carrying out of development until such time as works or other action, e.g. an excavation, have been carried out by a third party. In such cases the following model is suggested:
>
>> No development shall take place within the area indicated (this would be the area of archaeological interest) until the applicant . . . has secured the implementation of a programme of archaeological work in accordance with a written scheme of investigation which has been submitted by the applicant and approved in writing by the planning authority.

23.16 As an alternative to the imposition of conditions in the grant of planning permission, s 106 of the Town and Country Planning Act 1990 has enabled a person interested in land, by agreement or otherwise, to enter into an obligation for the purpose of restricting the development or use of land. It has not been uncommon under this provision for developers to provide not only archaeological facilities on the site, but also the funding of those facilities.

23.17 In addition to the statutory provisions protecting ancient monuments described above, it should be emphasised that voluntary co-operation between archaeologists and developers for the protection of ancient monuments and archaeological sites has become a well-established practice in the United Kingdom.

23.18 This co-operation has been formalised in a voluntary Code of Practice drawn up by the British Property Federation and the Standing Conference of Archaeological Unit Managers. Experience has shown that this voluntary co-operation is preferable when the objective sought is physical preservation — particularly where it concerns the preservation of buried remains *in situ*. Thus, where development of land is to be allowed, it may be possible to minimise damage to a monument by raising ground levels under the proposed new buildings, by using foundations which minimise any damage, or by sealing archaeological remains underneath the new buildings in order to secure their preservation for the future. Where preservation *in situ* is not possible, however, the only acceptable alternative may be archaeological excavation for the purposes of 'preservation by record'. Preservation by record is a general term used to describe the process of documentation by means of photographic record, written report and, where appropriate, the display of the important artefacts/remains which have been uncovered in the course of an excavation.

An example of this co-operation may be seen in the dispute over the remains of Rose **23.19** Theatre, in Southwark, London, where it is believed two of Shakespeare's plays received their first performance. The remains of the theatre were discovered in the course of preliminary works connected with redevelopment. Despite requests to do so, the Secretary of State refused to exercise his powers under the 1979 Act to make the site a scheduled monument, which had he done so, would have then required scheduled monument consent to be obtained before the redevelopment could proceed.

Under the existing law, compensation for loss of development value of land is not payable **23.20** where loss results from a site being made a scheduled monument. If, however, planning permission for development of land has been granted and the development is then frustrated because the site is subsequently scheduled, compensation for loss of development value becomes payable. In *R* v *Secretary of State for the Environment, ex p Rose Theatre Trust Co.* [1990] 1 QB 504, an action was brought challenging the decision of the Secretary of State not to make the site and remains of the theatre a scheduled monument. Dismissing an application for judicial review to quash the decision, the High Court held that the risk that compensation might be payable was a relevant factor for the Secretary of State to consider in coming to his decision. The Court also found that in deciding whether or not to exercise his powers, the Secretary of State was entitled to take into account the developer's desire to co-operate in preserving the remains. As a result of this co-operation, the developers agreed at a cost to them of over £10m, to redesign their proposed development in order to protect the site, to remove all piling from the area, to contain remains of the theatre footings and to provide sufficient headroom over the remains to allow for their future display. Following the development of the Rose Court building, which included those proposals, the Secretary of State decided to include the site of the remains in the schedule of ancient monuments.

In a consultation paper, '*Protecting Our Heritage*', issued by the Government in 1996, a num- **23.21** ber of possible amendments were proposed to the law relating to ancient monuments including a proposal to repeal the statutory provisions relating to Areas of Archaeological Importance. Other proposals were to:

(a) devolve the administration of schedule monument control to local authorities;
(b) impose a statutory duty on authorities to maintain site and monument records; and
(c) lift the requirement for schedule monument consent for work beneath Church of England places of worship.

These proposals have not yet been implemented.

24

MINERALS

A. INTRODUCTION

24.01 Because of the particular nature and effect of mineral working, special provisions have been considered necessary to control its environmental effects. Following the report of the Stevens Committee on Planning Control over Mineral Working in 1976, the Government decided to implement many of the report's recommendations, which it did in the Town and Country Planning (Minerals) Act 1981. The main features of that Act, which have now been incorporated in the 1990 Act, were as follows:

(a) It established 'mineral planning authorities' to be responsible for all planning control over mineral working, including the service of enforcement notices and stop notices. Since the winning and working of minerals is a 'county matter' under Sch 1 to the Town and Country Planning Act 1990, the mineral planning authority (MPA) will be the county planning authority except in respect of a site in a metropolitan district or London Borough or other unitary authority, when it will be the local planning authority (s 1(4) of the 1990 Act).
(b) It amplified the definition of development to bring within its scope activities relating to mineral working which may not previously have been regarded as being included within the definition (s 55 (4) of the 1990 Act).
(c) It provided that owners of 'mineral rights' should be notified of applications for planning permission for the mining and working of minerals in the same way as other owners are required to be notified (s 65 of the 1990 Act and General Development Procedure Order).
(d) It authorises the MPA, in a grant of planning permission for mineral working, to impose both 'restoration' and 'aftercare' conditions. A restoration condition secures that any or all of subsoil, topsoil and soil-making materials are replaced after the completion of the mineral working and the site contoured in an appropriate manner. An aftercare condition imposes an obligation to bring the land back to a required standard where the land is to be restored to agricultural, forestry or amenity use after the working has ceased (para 2, Sch 5 to the 1990 Act). An aftercare condition, which can only be used in

conjunction with a restoration condition, becomes operative after the restoration condition has been complied with. Aftercare may also be secured by the imposition of a condition in the planning permission requiring the subsequent approval by the MPA of an 'aftercare scheme'.

(e) It made every planning permission for mineral working subject to a time-limit upon its life. Where the MPA fail to impose a time-limit, a 60-year time-limit is deemed to be imposed. The 60-year time-limit is also made to apply to existing planning permission granted before 22 February 1982 and to run from that date (paras. 1–6 of Sch 5 to the 1990 Act). The reason for the imposition of a 60-year time limit on the life of a mineral planning permission was due to the need to avoid paying compensation to landowners for the imposition of a restriction on the life of the permission. It would seem from *Earthline Ltd v West Berkshire Council* [2003] JPL 715, that the power given by subsequent legislation to amend the conditions subject to which a mineral planning permission is subject, does not give the local planning authority the power to amend the condition relating to the life of the permission.

(f) It imposed a duty on the MPA to review every site in their area of current or former mineral working to determine whether they should revoke or modify a planning permission; order the discontinuance of a use or the alteration or removal of buildings; prohibit the resumption of mining and the working of minerals; or order the suspension of mineral working (s 105 of the 1990 Act). Section 105 of the 1990 Act has now been repealed; but has been replaced by the further provisions of s 96 of the Environment Act 1995 (see 24.15).

(g) It authorised the MPA to prohibit by order the resumption of mineral working which has not been carried on for at least two years and it appears to them that the resumption of such development is unlikely (paras. 3 and 4, Sch 9 to the 1990 Act). Any order made may impose requirements to alter or remove plant, etc. and restoration and aftercare conditions. Apart from Kent County Council, which by July 1993 had made nine prohibition orders under this provision, little use appears to have been made of the new power.

(h) It authorised the MPA to suspend by order the winning and working of minerals where the development has begun but has not been carried on for at least 12 months, and it appears that a resumption is likely. The order must specify a period during which specified steps must be taken for the protection of the environment (paras. 5 to 10, Sch 9 to the 1990 Act). The purpose of this provision is to secure the temporary restoration of the site before mineral working is resumed.

(i) Where a local planning authority revoke or modify planning permission, compensation becomes payable where any person has incurred expenditure in carrying out work rendered abortive by the revocation or modification or has otherwise sustained loss directly attributable to that restoration or modification. The Act authorises the Secretary of State to make regulations which in some circumstances will reduce the amount of compensation for which MPAs will be liable when revoking or modifying a planning permission for mineral working, or making a discontinuance order relating to such development or making a prohibition or suspension order under the Act (s 116 of the 1990 Act). The relevant regulations are now the Town and Country Planning (Compensation for Restrictions on Mineral Working and Mineral Waste Depositing) Regulations 1997.

The provisions in the 1981 Act for a review and updating of conditions did not work well in practice. MPAs were reluctant to risk incurring compensation liabilities, which were difficult to assess, in advance of using their order-making powers. The shortcomings of the 1981 Act were recognised in due course, when further fundamental legislation was enacted. 24.02

B. OLD MINING PERMISSIONS

Towards the end of 1990 concern also began to be expressed over old permissions for mineral working, granted before 1946 under a then legislative scheme known as interim development orders (IDOs). Under the Town and Country Planning Act 1947, permissions granted under IDOs before 22 July 1943 ceased to be effective on 1 July 1948. However, where consent for development had been granted on or after 22 July 1943, permission for that development (insofar as it had not been carried out before 1 July 1948) was deemed to be granted under the 1947 Act and no fresh application was needed. The existence of such permissions led to the following problems: 24.03

(a) Unlike planning permission granted after the 1947 Act came into force, there was no requirement that such permissions be registered. Hence, many people (including local planning authorities) were ignorant of the existence or the precise details of a permission.
(b) Because such permissions were not registered, long dormant workings could be reactivated without warning.
(c) The permissions were frequently indefinite in duration and were not subject to the type of conditions that are normally attached to present-day permissions aimed at protecting the environment, such as conditions relating to hours of work, noise, vibrations and dust emissions.
(d) The extension of existing works covered by these permissions could have a significant adverse impact on the environment and amenity.

To meet these problems, s 22 and Sch 2 of the Planning and Compensation Act 1991 introduced new procedures for dealing with permissions for the winning and working of minerals or the depositing of mineral waste originally granted under IDOs. They are referred to in the Act as 'old mining permissions'. The main effect of these provisions was that a landowner or mineral owner with planning permission for development consisting of the winning and working of minerals or involving the depositing of mineral waste authorised by interim development orders made after 21 July 1943 could, within six months of the new provisions being brought into operation, apply to the MPA to have the permission registered. If no application for registration of the permission was made by 25 March 1992, therefore, the permission ceased to have effect and no compensation was payable. Any dispute about the validity of the permission in respect of which the application to register was made, had to be determined by the Secretary of State. It is believed that 508 applications were made for the registration of interim development order permissions. Some decisions about the validity of the permission sought to be registered may yet still be outstanding. They have often involved the resolution of disputed issues of fact and, on occasions, where it could be shown that all parties have proceeded on the basis that there was in existence a planning 24.04

permission, the concept of the 'presumption of regularity', as propounded in *Calder Gravel Ltd v Kirklees MBC* (1989) 60 P & CR 322, has been applied.

24.05 The next stage was to settle suitable conditions. In *R v North Yorkshire County Council, ex p Brown* [1999] JPL 616, Lord Hoffman (at p. 619) set out precisely the procedure required by Sch 2 to the 1991 Act to be followed. He said:

> Once the application for registration had been granted, the owner of the land became entitled to apply to the mineral planning authority to determine the conditions to which the permission was to be subject: para 2(2). The application had to be made (subject to any agreed extension) within 12 months of the grant of registration or the determination of an appeal against its refusal: para 2(4)(b). If no application was made within such period, the permission ceased to have effect. The land owner was required in the first instance to propose his own conditions, but the mineral planning authority was entitled (subject to an appeal to the Secretary of State) to include 'any conditions which may be imposed on a grant of planning permission for development consisting of the winning and working of minerals or involving the depositing of mineral waste': para 2(1)(a). These words plainly confer a very wide discretion to impose conditions for the protection of the environment, subject of course to any policy guidance which may be given by the Secretary of State. In addition, the mineral planning authority was required to impose a condition that working should cease not later than 21 February 2042: para 2(1)(c).
>
> The schedule gave the mineral planning authority three months in which to determine the conditions. If it failed to do so, it was treated as if it had determined that the permission was to be subject to the conditions set out in the application: para 2(6)(b). Once the conditions had been finally determined, the conditions were required to be registered (para 3(2)) and the old permission had effect as if it had been granted subject to those conditions: section 22(2).
>
> In the period before the final determination of the conditions, section 22 distinguishes between what is sometimes called a 'dormant permission', where in the period of two years before 1 May 1991, no development had been carried out to any substantial extent on the land to which the permission related, and a permission by virtue of which extraction had been going on. In the case of a dormant permission, no extraction could take place until the conditions had been finally determined: section 22(3). In the case of an active permission, the owner could continue to operate as before, subject to having to comply with the conditions when they were determined or to cease operations if the permission lapsed on account of his failure to apply for their determination.

24.06 This distinction between dormant and active conditions, therefore, was intended to prevent the reactivation of dormant permissions without proper planning conditions; avoid applicants having to prepare and submit schemes of conditions too far in advance of their need to work the site; ensures that schemes that are prepared and submitted are appropriate to the circumstances pertaining at the time; and ensures that the workload for both applicants and MPAs is more evenly spread.

24.07 The purpose of these provisions was to ensure that eventually the extent and terms of old mining permissions is publicly known; that where old mining permissions are being implemented, conditions imposed on the permissions ensure that operational activity complies with modern standards; and that operations cannot be recommenced on sites which have recently been lying dormant without first proving the validity of an old mining permission and having conditions relating to operating and restoration aspects attached to it.

24.08 The provisions have given rise to much litigation. In the *North Yorkshire* case their Lordships held that EC Directive 85/337, The Assessment of the Effects of Certain Public and

Private Projects on the Environment, applied to the determination by the Council under s 22 of the 1991 Act of the conditions attached to an old mining permission, since that decision was the equivalent of a 'decision of the competent authority or authorities which entitles the development to proceed'. Accordingly, since the Council had not considered whether environmental assessment was required at that time, the Court of Appeal had been right to reverse the decision of the High Court and quash the determination of the conditions.

Two further cases should be mentioned. In *R v Peak District National Park Authority, ex p Blacklow Industries Ltd* [2000] JPL 290, the applicants applied for certiorari to quash a determination by the minerals planning authority in respect of an application made to the authority under Sch 13 Environment Act 1995 for the determination of conditions to which a 1952 planning permission was to be subject. The authority had determined the application in the absence of an environmental impact assessment. Days later the authority, in the light of the decision of the courts in the North Yorkshire County Council case, wrote to the applicants to say that it had made its determination without prejudice to its view that in the absence of an environmental impact assessment it had no jurisdiction to determine the application and its decision was therefore a nullity. Granting the order, the High Court held that since the determination was a public document, it was right that it should be made public that the determination was of no legal effect. **24.09**

In *R v Somerset CC, ex p Morris & Perry (Gurney Slade Quarry) Ltd* [2000] 2 PLCR 117, the County Council as the mineral planning authority for the area, had given the applicants notice of their determination of the conditions to which old planning permission was to be made subject, after the expiration of an extended period to which the applicant and authority had earlier agreed in writing. Accordingly, by virtue of Sch 2, para 2(6) of the 1991 Act, that had the effect of the authority being treated as having determined that the permission was to be subject to the conditions put forward by the applicants. Thus, due to non-compliance with the strict time limits or extensions agreed in writing, the conditions were significantly less stringent than environmental considerations might otherwise justify or require. **24.10**

It should be noted that under the Planning and Compulsory Purchase Act 2004, the Crown is to be entitled to register old mining permissions and to apply for the determination of new conditions to be attached to them. **24.11**

However, notwithstanding the measures taken in the Town and Country Planning (Minerals) Act 1981 and in the Planning and Compensation Act 1991 relating to old mineral permissions, concern continued to be expressed about the adequacy of planning controls over development involving mineral working. **24.12**

C. MINING PERMISSIONS GRANTED BETWEEN 1948 AND 1982

The changes to the law relating to mineral working made by the Town and Country Planning (Minerals) Act 1981 and by the Planning and Compensation Act 1991 in relation to old mining permissions (see 21.2), left unaffected those planning permissions for mineral working which had been granted between 1948 and 1982. **24.13**

24.14 By the early 1990s it had become clear that many of the provisions of the 1981 Act had not worked well. In March 1992 the Government issued a consultation paper which proposed a number of reforms, both for mineral planning permissions granted between 1948 and 1982 and for those granted after 1982. The overall aim of the proposals for the 1948–82 permissions was to establish a 'level playing field' for mineral operators regardless of the date of their permissions. As things were, holders of modern permissions and of 'reformed' IDO permissions granted between 1943 and 1948 were seen to be at a disadvantage compared to others.

24.15 The Government's proposals have now been given effect to by the Environment Act 1995, s 96 and Schs 13 and 14. These provide for an 'initial review' and updating of permissions granted between 1948 and 1982 and 'periodic reviews' of *all* mineral permissions thereafter. Permissions granted between 1948 and 1982 are known as 'old mineral planning permissions' to distinguish them from 'old mining permissions' referred to earlier. The provisions related to England, Wales and Scotland. The work was to be carried out in two stages.

24.16 Schedule 13 provided for an initial review and updating of mineral sites where the predominant planning permission for minerals development was granted after 30 June 1948 and before 22 February 1982 (one of the principal commencement dates of the Town and Country Planning (Minerals) Act 1981).

24.17 The scheme of the initial review was as follows:

- The Schedule makes a distinction between 'dormant' sites and 'active' sites. A dormant site is one where no substantial development has been carried out in the period beginning on 22 February 1982 and ending on 6 June 1995. No further mineral development can be carried out on dormant sites until a new scheme of conditions has been submitted to, and approved by the MPA.
- Active sites have to be reviewed in two successive phases, each of three years. A Phase I site is an active site where the minerals permission was granted after 30 June 1948 and before 1 April 1969. A Phase II site is a site where the mineral permission was granted after 31 March 1969 and before 22 February 1982.
- By 31 January 1996, every MPA had to prepare a list (known as the 'first' list) of all dormant and active Phase I and Phase II mineral sites in their area. MPAs were required to advertise that the list had been prepared, and to notify owners. If a site had been omitted from the list, landowners had to apply within three months for the inclusion of their land within the list, failing which the mineral permission ceased to have effect. In addition the list had to specify in respect of active Phase I sites the date by which an application for approval of new conditions had to be submitted to the MPA. If applications were not submitted by that date, then again the mineral permission ceased to have effect.
- By 31 October 1998, every MPA had to prepare a list (known as the 'second' list) of all active Phase II sites in their area. Preparation of this list meant in effect taking the first list of active Phase II sites, but incorporating in the second list specific dates for the submission by landowners of applications for approval of new conditions. As with the first list, a failure to do so meant the mineral permission ceasing to have any effect.
- No compensation is payable for loss suffered from the imposition of new conditions for a dormant site. For active sites, compensation is payable for loss suffered from the

imposition of new conditions, only if the new conditions restrict working rights and, in the opinion of the MPA, the effect of the more restrictive conditions would prejudice to an unreasonable degree the economic viability of the operation or the asset value of the site.

Schedule 13 then provides that the owner of any land or mineral which forms part of a dormant Phase I or II site may apply to the MPA to determine conditions to which the relevant planning permissions relating to the site are to be subject. The MPA must then proceed to determine the conditions to which the planning permission is to be subject. If the MPA do not do this within three months of the receiving the owner's application, the planning permission becomes subject to the conditions proposed by the owner. **24.18**

In the case of *R. v Oldham MBC and Pugmanor Properties Ltd, ex p. Foster* [2000] JPL 111, Keene J. described the duty of the MPA. The list it had to compile was a list of mineral sites, not a definitive list of relevant planning permissions. It only had to consider whether a relevant planning permission or permissions exist in respect of a given site, it need not identify those permissions in the list. Under the schedule, the MPA's duty was to determine conditions to which each relevant planning permission relating to the site is to be subject, as there may be more than one permission relating to the site. **24.19**

Schedule 14 provides for a subsequent and ongoing review by the MPA of all planning permissions for mineral development, including of course, old mining permission which would have been reviewed under the 1991 Act. The scheme of periodic reviews is that they should take place every 15 years from the date of either a previous review, or, if no revision has taken place, from the date of the latest mineral permission relating to the site. When the scheme is in operation, MPAs will be required to give owners 12 months' notice of the date by which an application for approval of new conditions must be submitted to them. If no such application is made by that date, the permission will cease to have effect. **24.20**

It should be noted that MPG14: The Environment Act 1995: Review of Mineral Planning Permissions, explains in great detail the requirements introduced by the Environment Act for the initial and periodic reviews of mineral planning permissions. **24.21**

The application of the Environment Act 1995 to mineral planning permissions has attracted some litigation. In *Dorset CC v Secretary of State for the Environment, Transport and the Regions and Rothchild Estates Ltd* [1999] JPL 633, the High Court refused an application by the MPA to quash a decision of the Secretary of State allowing an appeal by Rothchild Estates against the MPA's decision not to include their land in the 'first list' of mineral sites. The MPA had unsuccessfully argued that the development of part of the site for housing rendered the mineral permission incapable of implementation; and that since the permission was no longer valid it could not be registered. **24.22**

In *R v North Lincolnshire Council, ex p Horticulture and Garda Products Sales (Humberside) Ltd* [1998] Env LR 295, the applicants for judicial review had first learnt of the exclusion of their land from the first list of mineral sites after the three-month period for them to seek its inclusion had passed. The applicants had not been at fault; neither indeed had the North Lincolnshire Council who had inherited the list from the Humberside Metropolitan Borough Council under local government reorganisation, and who had omitted the site from the first list in breach of statutory duty. The North Lincolnshire Council considered that it **24.23** had no power to extend the three-month period or to otherwise remedy the omission from the first list and its consequences. The High Court held that it could only intervene if the MPA had acted unlawfully, and refused the application.

24.24 It should also be noted that although the *North Yorkshire* case referred to earlier in this chapter involved the legislation relating to pre-1948 mineral permissions contained in the Planning and Compensation Act 1991, the reasoning in the *North Yorkshire CC* case must apply equally to determinations of conditions attached to mineral permissions granted between 1948 and 1982 which are governed by Sch 13 of the Environment Act 1995 and to conditions attached to permissions subjected to periodic review under Sch 14. However, the Secretary of State was clearly concerned about the impact of the decision given by the Court of Appeal in that case and no doubt feared, rightly as it turned out, that the House of Lords would dismiss an appeal from the Court of Appeal's decision. In anticipation that this might happen, therefore, the Secretary of State announced that he was drafting on a contingent basis, regulations under s 2(2) of the European Communities Act 1972 to adopt the review procedures of both the 1991 and 1995 Acts to enable requirement of environmental impact assessment in appropriate cases. He duly did so, and amendments to the 1999 Regulations were made by SI 2000/2876, which came into force on 15 November 2000. The amendments provide that the Regulations now impact upon applications to determine the conditions to which a planning permission is to be subject, in the same way as they apply to applications for planning permission. The amendments also introduced into the main regulations a change in terminology. The Regulations use the word ROMP, which is clearly an acronym derived from 'Registration of Old Mining (or Mineral) Permissions'.

24.25 A ROMP may be a ROMP application or ROMP development. A ROMP application means an application to a MPA to determine the conditions to which a planning permission is to be subject under:

(a) para 2(2) of Sch 2 to the 1991 Act (registration of old mining conditions);
(b) para 9(1) of Sch 13 to the 1995 Act (review of old mineral planning permissions); or
(c) para 6(1) of Sch 14 to the 1995 Act (periodic review of mineral planning perinissions).

ROMP development is development, which is yet to be carried out, and which is authorised in a planning permission in respect of which a ROMP application has been or is to be made.

24.26 A number of other cases, some involving the application of environmental impact assessment on mineral permissions, are dealt with in Chapter 11. See generally, also recent cases of *R v Hammersmith and Fulham LBC, ex p CPRE; R v Durham CC and Sherburn Stone Company Limited, ex p Huddleston*; and *R v Rochdale MBC, ex p Tew.*

25

THE CONTROL OF OUTDOOR ADVERTISEMENTS

A. INTRODUCTION

The source of the power to control advertisements is found in ss 220 to 225 of the 1990 Act. Section 220 gives the Secretary of State power to make regulations for restricting or regulating the display of advertisements, so far as it appears to him to be expedient in the interests of amenity or public safety. The present regulations are the Town and Country Planning (Control of Advertisements) Regulations 1992, SI 1992/666. Guidance on advertisement control and advertising appeals procedure is given in Circulars 5/92 and 15/94. Planning Policy Guidance Note PPG19 gives advice on how advertising control should be exercised. **25.01**

The power to control advertisements can only be exercised in the interests of amenity or public safety. As the content of an advertisement can only be considered from these aspects, the control cannot be used as an instrument of censorship. Under the regulations, the local planning authority are required to exercise their powers only in the interests of amenity and public safety, taking account of any material factors and in particular: **25.02**

(a) in the case of amenity, of the general characteristics of the locality, including the presence of any feature of historic, architectural, cultural or similar interest, disregarding, if they think fit, any advertisements being displayed there;
(b) in the case of public safety—

(i) the safety of any person who may use any road, railway, waterway (including coastal waters), docks, harbour or airfield;

(ii) whether any display of advertisements is likely to obscure, or hinder the ready interpretation of, any road traffic sign, railway signal, or aid to navigation by water or air.

25.03 It needs to be emphasised that under Regulation 4, a local planning authority may exercise its powers only on this basis. There is no statutory requirement either in s 220 of the 1990 Act or in the regulations, that authorities should have regard to the provisions of the development plan when exercising advertising control powers. The result is that the provision found in s 70(2) of the 1990 Act, which requires a local planning authority to have regard to the development plan, so far as it is material to the application, does not apply to applications made under the advertisement regulations. It follows, therefore, that s 38(6) Planning and Compulsory Purchase Act 2004, which requires local planning authorities to determine applications in accordance with the plan unless material considerations indicate otherwise, also does not apply.

25.04 Many development plans do include policies relating to advertising control. As such, they can be regarded as a material consideration in so far as they are relevant to amenity and safety, but they cannot be given the weight that would be the case were s 38(6) to be applicable.

25.05 The position is not readily appreciated by local planning authorities. Accordingly in a consultation paper 'Outdoor Advertising Control' issued in July 1999, the Government proposed to amend Regulation 4 so as to make the development plan a consideration that an authority must take into account when exercising powers under the regulations. However, the application of s 38(6) to advertising control, though proposed by the Government, must wait for a legislative change.

25.06 Section 224 of the 1990 Act contains provisions relating to enforcement. Under the section, the regulations may make provision to enable the local planning authority to require the removal of any advertisement displayed in contravention of the regulations, or the discontinuance of the use for the display of advertisements of any site which is being so used in contravention of the regulations. In addition s 224(3) provides that if any person displays an advertisement in contravention of the regulations he shall be guilty of an offence and liable on summary conviction to a fine of such amount as may be prescribed, not exceeding level 4 on the standard scale and, in the case of a continuing offence, £40 for each day during which the offence continues after conviction.

25.07 In *Kingston upon Thames RBC v National Solus Sites Ltd* [1994] JPL 251, the Queen's Bench Divisional Court held that where different posters, each advertising goods, were displayed on an advertising hoarding on different sites without consent, each display constituted a single and separate offence under the Control of Advertisement Regulations. The decision greatly increases the maximum sentence a court may impose where an authority lays multiple informations in respect of each advertisement poster.

25.08 In addition to the powers given to local planning authorities under s 224 of the 1990 Act, s 225 empowers local planning authorities to remove or obliterate any placard or poster displayed in contravention of any regulations made under s 220. It should be noted, too, that Private Acts promoted by local authorities may vary or extend the powers available to authorities under s 225 of the Act as, for example, the London Local Authorities Act 1995 which, *inter alia*, gives the relevant local authorities power to require the occupier of premises to remove signs other than advertisements on the surface of any building, fence or other structure or erection. The same Act also amends sub-sections (3) to (5) of s 225 so as to require a person displaying a placard or poster in contravention of the regulations made under s 220 to remove it within two days.

The control of advertisements system under the 1990 Act covers a wide range of advertisements and signs. The last amendments to the definition of the word 'advertisement' in s 336(1) of the 1990 Act were made by s. 24 of the Planning and Compensation Act 1991. As amended, the definition (with the amendments in italics) now reads: **25.09**

> advertisement means any word, letter, model, sign, placard, board, notice, *awning, blind*, device or representation, whether illuminated or not, in the nature of, and employed wholly or partly for the purposes of, advertisement, announcement or direction, and (without prejudice to the previous provisions of this definition) includes any hoarding or similar structure used, *or designed*, or adapted for use, *and anything else principally used, or designed or adapted principally for use*, for the display of advertisements, and references to the display of advertisements shall be construed accordingly.

The purpose of each of the amendments was as follows: **25.10**

(a) *Awning, blind*. These words brought two additional methods of displaying advertisements within the statutory definition. Before this amendment was made, it was not clear whether awnings and blinds on which an advertisement was displayed, but held in place by metal supporting arms secured to the wall of a building, were to be treated solely as an outdoor advertisement or whether, independent of the provisions in the Act granting deemed planning permission for advertisements displayed in accordance with the Advertisement Regulations, planning permission was needed for any development that they might involve. The amendment means that awnings and blinds can now be treated solely as an outdoor advertisement.

(b) *Or designed*. The purpose of this amendment was to make it clear that the definition of 'advertisement' includes hoardings and similar structures (such as rotating poster-panels) designed for use for the display of advertisements, even though no actual display is presently taking place.

(c) *And anything else principally used or designed or adapted principally for use*. The purpose of this amendment was to extend the definition of 'advertisement' so that it includes objects such as gantries, pylons, or free-standing drums often found in shopping precincts.

So far there has been little litigation on the meaning of the word 'advertisement'. In two recent, linked cases, however, *Great Yarmouth BC v Secretary of State for the Environment* and *Newport BC v Secretary of State for Wales* [1997] JPL 650, spaceflower lighting equipment had been placed on the top of amusement centres. Although free-standing, the equipment could project a beam of light skywards to produce an image, generally a flower, on the base of any cloud cover. Its purpose was to announce the holding at the centre of certain leisure activities. The respective local planning authorities had invited the owners of the amusement arcades to apply for express consent to the display of an advertisement. On refusal of their **25.11** applications, the owners appealed to the Secretary of State, who declined to entertain the appeals on the ground that no advertisement was being displayed. In quashing the Secretary of State's decision to refuse to entertain the appeals, the High Court held that he had proceeded on the basis that an advertisement had to have a tangible or physical presence. That was not necessary in the case of 'a sign', the Deputy Judge calling in aid the biblical description of what appeared in the sky at the time of the nativity.

25.12 The cases highlighted the changing nature of advertisement technology and the possible difficulty of bringing some forms within the existing system of advertising control. The Government has proposed, therefore, that notwithstanding the judgment in the *Great Yarmouth* case, the definition of 'advertisement' be extended to make clear that the term includes lasers, search lights and beams of light. Furthermore, the greater use of illuminated lights incorporating moving parts and/or flashing lights has implications for road safety. Accordingly, the Government proposes to amend the regulations to ensure that before consent is granted for such advertisements, the local highway authority (or the Highways Agency for trunk roads) are to be consulted. Furthermore in deemed consent Classes where illumination is permitted, an extra condition should be imposed to prevent advertisements with moving parts on them/or flashing lights from being displayed.

Exclusions from control

25.13 Although all advertisements are subject to control, the degree of control over certain advertisements is substantially relaxed. For the purposes of the regulations, advertisement does not include anything employed wholly as a memorial or as a railway signal (Regulation 2(17)).

25.14 Under Regulation 3(2) of and Sch 2 to the regulations, no control is exercised by the regulations over the following advertisements:

Class A The display of a single advertisement on or consisting of a balloon not more than 60 metres above the ground on not more than 10 days in total in any calendar year.

Class B An advertisement displayed on enclosed land and not readily visible from outside or from any place to which the public has a right of access. (Because doubt exists as to whether shopping malls and shopping arcades come within the definition of 'enclosed land', the Government has proposed its intention to widen the definition so as to include them.)

Class C An advertisement displayed on or in a moving vehicle.

Class D An advertisement incorporated in the fabric of a building, other than a building used principally for the display of advertisements. It was this particular provision in earlier advertising regulations that allowed without the need for consent, the word 'OXO' to be incorporated within the fabric of the building on the south bank of the River Thames occupied by the manufacturers of that commodity. For many years, tourists were advised that one could obtain within the building, 'the cheapest square meal in London'.

Class E An advertisement displayed on an article for sale which is not illuminated and does not exceed 0.1 of a square metre in area.

Class F An advertisement related specifically to a pending Parliamentary, European Assembly or local government election.

Class G An advertisement displayed by Standing Orders of either House of Parliament or by any enactment.

Class H A traffic sign.

Class I The national flag of any country. (At present each flag must be displayed on a 'single vertical' flagstaff. This is considered unduly restrictive and the Government proposes to exempt flags from control, however flown from a flagstaff.)

Class J An advertisement displayed inside a building. (To be exempt from control the building in which the advertisement is displayed must be a building not used principally for the display of advertisements. Because such buildings have proved difficult to identify, the Government has proposed to delete this requirement.)

Reference should be made to each Class of the Schedule for other particular limitations from this exclusion from control. **25.15**

To benefit from the exclusions, however, advertisements in the above classes have also to comply with the conditions and limitations set out in the schedule, and to standard conditions set out in Sch 1. **25.16**

The scheme of control

Advertisements subject to control by the regulations fall into two main groups, namely, advertisements for which deemed consent is granted by the regulations and advertisements which require express consent from the local planning authority or the Secretary of State. **25.17**

B. DEEMED CONSENT

Under Regulation 6 and Part 1 of Sch 3, deemed consent is granted for the display of the following broad category of advertisements subject to stated conditions and limitations and the power of the local planning authority to serve a discontinuance notice: **25.18**

Class 1 Functional advertisement of local authorities, statutory undertakers and public transport undertakers. (The Government has proposed to extend this category by adding to it functional advertisements by Government Departments and Agencies; but also to limit the overall size of advertisements within the Class to 1.42 square metres in area.)

Class 2 Miscellaneous advertisements relating to the premises on which they are displayed (e.g., advertisements relating to professions, businesses or trades carried on in premises). (There is doubt as to whether 'Bed and Breakfast' establishments are included within this Class. The Government is considering whether to identify these establishments, specifically in Class 2C, or to include them in Class 5 along with hotels, inns, etc.)

Class 3 Miscellaneous temporary advertisements (e.g., advertisements relating to the sale or letting of premises).

Class 4 Illuminated advertisements on business premises. (The Government has proposed to ban the use of retroflective material which reflects light from vehicles' headlights back to drivers in Classes 4A and 4B. The Government has also proposed to remove the restriction in Condition 2 of Class 4A 'that in the case of a shop, no advertisement may be displayed except on a wall containing a shop window'.)

Class 5 Advertisements (other than illuminated advertisements) on business premises. (This Class permits illumination as an exception, for an advertisement which indicates that 'medical or similar services or supplies are available at the premises'. This exception is to be widened to include pharmaceutical services or supplies including dental surgeries, chiropractitioners, osteopaths and veterinary services available at the premises. In addition, the Government has proposed to limit the size of poster displays permitted under this Class to 1.42 square metres in area.)

Class 6 An advertisement on a forecourt of business premises. (The Government has proposed to revise this Class by specifying a maximum area for all signs on a forecourt of 4.6 square metres with no single sign to exceed 1.42 metres.)

Class 7 Flag advertisements.

Class 8 Advertisements on hoardings.

Class 9 Advertisements on highway structures. (The Government has proposed to change the reference to 'four-sheet' panel displays to 'six-sheet' to reflect a maximum size limit of 2.16 square metres.)

Class 10 Advertisements for neighbourhood watch and similar schemes. (The Government has proposed to extend this Class to include CCTV signs provided they bear no resemblance to traffic signs.)

Class 11 Directional advertisements.

Class 12 Advertisements inside buildings. (The Government has proposed to introduce a size limitation for advertisements in this Class of 0.75 metres high and 0.3 metres high within areas of special control.)

Class 13 Sites used for the display of advertisements on 1 April 1974. (Because confusion has arisen as to whether the deemed consent applies to the advertisement or to the site, the Government has proposed to make it clear that references to the display of advertisements shall be construed as references also to the use of the site. The Government also proposes to remove the need to show continuous use since 1 April 1974 and substitute a requirement to show use over a ten-year rolling period.)

Class 14 Advertisements displayed after expiry of express consent. (The Government has proposed to include a condition to make clear that the introduction of illumination represents a material change, thus excluding the advertisement displayed from this Class.)

25.19 The deemed consent granted for the display of the advertisements in the above classes, as well as being granted subject to any conditions and limitations stated in each class, is also subject to what are referred to as the standard conditions.

25.20 The standard conditions (set out in Sch 1 to the regulations) are:

1. Any advertisements displayed, and any site used for the display of advertisements, shall be maintained in a clean and tidy condition to the reasonable satisfaction of the local planning authority.
2. Any structure or hoarding erected or used principally for the purpose of displaying advertisements shall be maintained in a safe condition.

3. Where an advertisement is required under these Regulations to be removed, the removal shall be carried out to the reasonable satisfaction of the local planning authority.
4. No advertisement is to be displayed without the permission of the owner of the site or any other person with an interest in the site entitled to grant permission.
5. No advertisement shall be sited or displayed so as to obscure, or hinder the ready interpretation of, any road traffic sign, railway signal or aid to navigation by water or air, or so as otherwise to render hazardous the use of any highway, railway, waterway or aerodrome (civil or military).

The other conditions and limitations to which the deemed consent may be subject relate to such matters as size of the advertisement, size of characters or symbols on the advertisement, area and height of the advertisement and its position. **25.21**

The deemed consent to the display of the above classes of advertisements may be restricted in two ways. First, under Regulation 7, the Secretary of State, if satisfied upon a proposal made to him by the local planning authority that the display of advertisements of any class or description (other than Class 12 or 13) should not be undertaken in any particular area or in any particular case without express consent, may direct that the consent granted by the regulations for that class or description shall not apply in that area or case, for a specified period or indefinitely. **25.22**

In the early part of 1990, following representations made by Camden Borough Council and Westminster City Council, the Secretary of State issued directions with regard to estate agents' notice-boards in a number of conservation areas within Central London. Similar directions had previously been made in relation to advertisements in the Royal Borough of Kensington and Chelsea and in the City of Bath. The directions meant that before displaying 'for sale' or 'to let' notices in those areas, specific consent for the display needed to be obtained. **25.23**

Secondly, under Regulation 8, a local planning authority may serve a notice requiring the discontinuance of the display of an advertisement, or the use of a site for the display of an advertisement for which deemed consent is granted under the regulations, if they are satisfied that it is necessary to do so to remedy a substantial injury to the amenity of the locality or a danger to members of the public. The notice must be served on the advertiser and on the owner and occupier of the site on which the advertisement is displayed. There is a right of appeal against the notice to the Secretary of State. **25.24**

In *O'Brien v Croydon LBC* [1998] JPL 47 the High Court held that a local planning authority had to serve a discontinuance notice on the person whose specific interests were promoted by an advertisement, since that person was an 'advertiser' within Regulation 8. The Government considers that there are practical difficulties in a local planning authority having to serve a discontinuance notice on the person or company whose interests are promoted by the advertisement. Hence the Government is proposing to amend the regulations to make clear that the discontinuance notice need be served only on the owner of the site and/or the person placing the advertisement, but giving the authority discretion to serve the notice on the person or company whose interests are being served by the advertisement if it is felt necessary to do so. **25.25**

C. EXPRESS CONSENT

25.26 Unless an advertisement requiring consent has deemed consent for its display under Regulation 6, express consent is required. An application for express consent is made to the authority on whom it falls to determine them. The authority may then refuse consent, or grant consent, in whole or in part, subject to the standard conditions and to such additional conditions as they think fit. Regulation 13(5) provides that an express consent shall be subject to the condition that it expires at the end of a period of five years from the date of the consent, or such longer or shorter period as the authority may specify. The regulations give a right of appeal to the Secretary of State against a decision of the authority on an application for express consent.

25.27 The reason for having a fixed period of consent is that there can be no guarantee that whilst the effects of a particular advertisement display on amenity and public safety may be acceptable at the time express consent is granted, subsequent changes to the built environment may make the continued display of the advertisement unacceptable. To save the trouble of advertisers having to apply for express consent at the end of the five-year period, such advertisements are given the benefit of deemed consent for their continued display (Class 14). Similarly, because documentary evidence may not be available to show a grant of express consent for an advertisement on a site used for the display of advertisement before 1 April 1974, the same deemed consent provisions apply (Class 13).

25.28 Consequent upon the changes made to the 1990 Act by the Planning and Compensation Act 1991, the regulations now give to a local planning authority the same power to decline to determine an application for express consent to the display of an advertisement as they have to decline to determine an application for planning permission which is the same or substantially the same as one dismissed by the Secretary of State on appeal within the previous two years. In addition, the regulations now give to the Secretary of State the power to dismiss an application for express consent where there has been undue delay in the prosecution of an appeal, as is available with planning appeals.

25.29 In 2003/4 there were 1,378 appeals to the Secretary of State, of which 28 per cent were successful.

D. AREAS OF SPECIAL CONTROL (ASC)

25.30 Under s 221 of the 1990 Act, the advertisement regulations may make different provision with respect to different areas. In particular, the regulations may make special provision with respect to conservation areas, areas defined as experimental areas and areas defined as areas of special control.

25.31 An experimental area is an area prescribed for a period, for the purpose of assessing the effect on amenity or public safety of advertisements of a prescribed description.

25.32 As regards ASC, Regulations 18 and 19 provide more detailed provisions. The local planning authorities are required to advertise any proposal to designate or modify them and to consider any representations they receive. If they then decide to proceed, a formal ASC Order is submitted for the Secretary of State's consideration. He may decide to approve the submitted Order; to approve it with specified modifications; or not to approve it. If an Order is fully or partly approved, the local planning authority must advertise the approval and its effective date. There are special transitional provisions for advertisements already displayed on the date a new Order comes into force. Orders must be reviewed at least every five years, though non-compliance with that duty is not infrequent.

As regards such areas, designation as such has the following four main practical effects: **25.33**

(a) certain types of outdoor advertisement (mainly general advertising hoardings) may not be displayed at all;
(b) three Classes of advertisement normally benefitting from 'deemed consent' (Classes 4A, 4B and 8 in Sch 3) may only be displayed with the local planning authority's specific consent;
(c) stricter limitations on size, height of lettering and height above ground apply to certain other 'deemed consent' Classes; and
(d) in applying to display an outdoor advertisement for which the local planning authority's specific consent is needed, an applicant has to demonstrate a 'reasonable requirement' for the advertisement.

The purpose of requiring the Secretary of State's approval is to ensure that nationally applicable standards are applied in determining what areas are subject to this stricter control. It is believed that about 50 per cent of the area of England and Wales has been designated as areas of special control. **25.34**

In November 2000, following concern over the current operation of the ASC regime, the Government asked local planning authorities to undertake a review of ASC in their area in order to satisfy themselves that their extent remains appropriate and necessary. The legislative scope of the ASC regime is to remain unchanged. **25.35**

E. FLY-POSTING

There is no formal definition of 'fly-posting' in the 1990 Act or the Control of Advertisement Regulations 1992. It is, however, generally considered to apply to advertisements displayed on buildings and street furniture without the consent of the owner, contrary to the provisions of the regulations. It is often used indiscriminately to promote records, musical or other events and market products such as food, drink and clothing as well as business cards displayed in telephone boxes. Fly-posting is notoriously difficult to control, let alone eradicate. The reasons for this include: the time and resources necessary to identify who carried out the fly-posting, visiting the site, collecting evidence and revisiting the site to confirm whether the posters have been removed; the difficulties in prosecuting unincorporated organisations such as political groups; the low level of fines imposed and costs awarded; and the minimal deterrent effect of a successful prosecution. **25.36**

It would appear that the very nature of the problem prevents the planning system from obtaining more effective control over fly-posting. In December 1998, the Government **25.37** published an independent research report on the issue which recommended a number of changes to existing legislation and for a revised/updated guidance to local planning authorities in the form of a Good Practice Guide. In July 1999 the Government indicated that they would be pursuing the Good Practice Guide recommendation and would consider the adoption of an amendment to strengthen s 224(5) of the 1990 Act so that the test of liability is changed from the owner's 'knowledge or consent' to the display, to whether he 'took all reasonable precautions and exercised all due diligence to avoid the commission of an offence'.

25.38 Furthermore, the Government is considering an amendment to s 225 of the 1990 Act to allow local authorities to remove posters where they consider them to be illegal, thus bringing their powers into line with other forms of planning control. In addition, in May 2002 the Government announced that it considered that 'kiosk glass advertising' should benefit from deemed consent, but subject to conditions and limitations relating to geographical coverage, illumination and size. None of these changes have yet been made.

25.39 An attempt has been made however, to control the worst excesses of fly-posting. Section 43 of the Anti-social Behaviour Act 2003 provides for a local authority to issue a 'penalty notice' on any person the authority has reason to believe has committed a 'relevant offence' in the area of the authority. The Act makes the display of an advertisement in contravention of the Control of Advertisements Regulations one of the relevant offences. A proviso that may meet enforcement difficulties however, is that a penalty notice relating to fly-posting can only be given to a person if the authority believes that he personally affixed or placed the advertisement in position against or on the land.

F. DEVELOPMENT AND THE DISPLAY OF ADVERTISEMENTS

25.40 Where the display of advertisements in accordance with the regulations involves the development of land, s 222 of the 1990 Act provides that planning permission for that development shall be deemed to be granted and that no application shall be necessary for that development under Part III of the Act.

26

TREES AND HEDGEROWS

A. THE PROTECTION OF TREES

Cutting down a tree does not appear to be development within s 55 of the 1990 Act; hence it is not subject to general development control. The Act contains other provisions, however, to secure the preservation or planting of trees. Under s 197 of the 1990 Act, a duty is imposed on a local planning authority to ensure, whenever it is appropriate, that in granting planning permission for development adequate provision is made, by the imposition of conditions, for the preservation or planting of trees. In addition, the authority may make orders under s 198 of the 1990 Act in connection with a grant of such permission. **26.01**

Under s 198, if it appears to a local planning authority that it is expedient in the interests of amenity to make provision for the preservation of trees or woodlands in their area, they may for that purpose make a tree preservation order with respect to such trees, groups of trees, areas of trees or woodlands as may be specified in the order. In particular, the order may make provision for prohibiting the cutting down, topping, lopping, uprooting, wilful damage or wilful destruction of trees except with the consent of the local planning authority, and for securing the replanting of any part of a woodland area which is felled in the course of forestry operations permitted by or under the order. **26.02**

In 'Tree Preservation Orders: A Guide to the Law and Practice', issued by the Secretary of State, the view is taken that 'area classification' (the so-called 'area order') should only be used in emergencies, and then only as a temporary measure until the trees within the area can be assessed properly and re-classified with a view to its replacement with individual or group classification where appropriate. **26.03**

The Act does not contain a definition of the word 'tree'. According to Lord Denning MR in **26.04**

Kent CC v Batchelor (1976) 33 P & CR 185, a 'woodland' tree 'ought to be something over seven or eight inches in diameter'. Lord Denning's observations in the case, however, were *obiter*, and in a later case *Bullock v Secretary of State for the Environment and Malvern Hills DC* [1980] JPL 461, it was said that the word 'tree' should bear its ordinary meaning and that what is or is not a tree is not to be defined by any particular diameter. According to current policy guidance, the view is taken that a tree preservation order cannot apply to bushes, hedges or shrubs and that if a hedgerow is made subject to such an order, then only the 'trees' in the hedgerows will be protected.

26.05 A tree preservation order cannot prohibit the cutting down, uprooting, topping or lopping of trees which are dying or dead or have become dangerous (s 198(6)(a)), or where the cutting down, uprooting, topping or lopping is in compliance with any obligations imposed under an Act of Parliament, or is necessary for the prevention or abatement of a nuisance or which is necessary in order to carry out development for which full planning permission has been granted (s 198(6)(b)). Furthermore, the order cannot prohibit work carried out in compliance with a tree felling licence (ss 15 and 198 of the Forestry Act 1967), or a forestry dedication plan or operations or covenant approved by the Forestry Commission (s 200 of the 1990 Act) during open-cast coal mining (s 198).

26.06 Sections 206 to 210 of the 1990 Act provide for the enforcement of tree preservation orders. Under s 210, if any person, in contravention of a tree preservation order, cuts down, uproots or wilfully destroys a tree, or wilfully damages, tops or lops a tree in such a manner as to be likely to destroy it, he shall be guilty of an offence and may be fined on summary conviction to a fine not exceeding the statutory maximum or twice the value of the tree, whichever is the greater, or on conviction on indictment, to a fine which may reflect the financial benefit which has accrued or is likely to accrue to him in consequence of the offence. In *Maidstone BC v Mortimer* (1980) 43 P & CR 67, it was held that the offence is an absolute offence and that proof of knowledge by the accused of the existence of an order is not required. The penalties may indeed be heavy. In one case ([1991] JPL 101), a property company was fined £50,000 for breach of a tree preservation order and ordered to pay the local authority's costs in the sum of £2,250. Under s 206 of the 1990 Act, if any tree is removed, uprooted or destroyed in contravention of a tree preservation order the owner (unless the local planning authority dispense with the requirement) must plant another tree of appropriate size and species in the same place as soon as he reasonably can. In such cases, the tree preservation order will then apply to the replacement tree. Similarly, if a tree is cut down because it is dead, dying or dangerous, the landowner is under a duty to replace it.

26.07 If a landowner fails to comply with the requirements of s 206, s 207 provides that the local planning authority may serve a notice on the owner of the land, within four years of the failure, requiring him to plant a tree or trees of such a size as may be specified in the notice. Under s 208 there is a right of appeal against the notice to the Secretary of State. Once the notice has taken effect, the local authority may enter the land under s 209 of the 1990 Act and take the steps required by the notice.

26.08 Section 23 of the Planning and Compensation Act 1991 made a number of changes to the provisions of the 1990 Act which related to the preservation of trees, in order to reflect, as far as practicable, the amendments made by the 1991 Act to enforcement notice procedure generally. The main changes were as follows:

(a) Where an order has been made under s 206 of the 1990 Act requiring replacement of a tree, or conditions of a consent given under a tree preservation order require the replacement of a tree and the replacement has not been effected, any order made by the authority under s 207(1) to enforce that duty, is *required* to specify a period at the end of which the notice is to take effect. In addition, the amending legislation provides that the specified period is to be one not less than 28 days beginning with the date of service of the notice.
(b) Where a notice has been served under s 207 of the 1990 Act to require the replacement of a tree, the person on whom the notice is served may appeal against the notice on the additional ground that in all the circumstances, the duty to plant a replacement tree should be dispensed with.
(c) In order to prevent appeals against an order requiring the replacement of a tree being invalidated due to postal delays, it is provided that an appeal is validly made if sent to the Secretary of State in a properly addressed and prepaid letter posted to him at such time that, in the ordinary course of post, it would have been delivered to him before the end of the period specified (see (a) above) as the date on which the notice is to take effect.
(d) On appeal against an order requiring the replacement of a tree the Secretary of State has an additional power to correct any 'misdescription' in the notice, so long as he is satisfied that the correction or variation will not cause injustice to the appellant or the local planning authority. Previously, his power to do this on appeal was limited to the correction of any 'informality, defect or error' in the notice.
(e) As indicated, under s 209 of the 1990 Act, a local planning authority may enter land in order to plant trees required to be planted by a replacement order where the owner has not complied with that notice. Under an amendment made by the 1991 Act to that section it is a criminal offence for any person wilfully to obstruct a person acting in exercise of that power.
(f) The maximum penalty on summary conviction for a breach of a tree preservation order was increased from £2,000 to £20,000. In addition, the requirement that the court should have regard to any financial benefit which has accrued or appears likely to accrue to a person convicted on indictment of a breach of an order has been extended to include summary conviction.
(g) The 1991 Act inserted s 214A into the 1990 Act to give local planning authorities an express power to apply to the court for an injunction where they consider it necessary or desirable to restrain an actual or apprehended offence under s 210 (non-compliance with a tree preservation order) or s 211 (preservation of trees in conservation areas) of the 1990 Act.
(h) Magistrates now have the power to issue a warrant giving a person duly authorised by the local planning authority or Secretary of State the right to enter land where admission to the land has been refused or refusal is reasonably apprehended, or where the case is one of urgency. This power may be useful where necessary to enter land in the middle of the night to prevent a tree subject to a preservation order being felled.

A tree preservation order is required to be made in the form, or substantially in the form prescribed by the Town and Country Planning (Trees) Regulations 1999, SI 1999/1892. **26.09**

The regulations provide that an order shall specify the trees, groups of trees or woodlands to **26.10** which it relates and indicate their position by reference to a map. Where the order relates to a group of trees, the number of trees in the group must be specified. Once the authority has made the order, but before confirming it, a copy of the order must be served on the persons interested in the land affected, with a notice stating the reasons for making the order and a statement that objections or other representations may be made to the authority within 28 days. A copy of the order must also be made available for inspection, free of charge, at all reasonable hours, at the offices of the authority.

26.11 After having considered any objections or representations made in respect of the order, the authority may then confirm it, which they may do with or without modifications, with notice of confirmation being given to persons interested in the land affected by the order. Under the regulations, a 'person interested' in relation to land affected by an order, means every owner and occupier of the land and every other person whom the authority know to be entitled to fell any of the trees to which the order relates or to work by surface working any materials in or under the land. Furthermore, land affected by the order includes adjoining land.

26.12 The order will not take effect until confirmed by the authority, though under s 201 of the Act, the local planning authority may include in the order a direction that it shall take effect immediately, in which case it remains in force for a period of six months or until the order is confirmed, whichever is the earlier. There is so right of appeal to the Secretary of State against the making of the order. Once the order is confirmed, it cannot be questioned in any legal proceedings whatsoever, except by way of application made within six weeks to the High Court under s 288 of the 1990 Act.

26.13 Any order made can be varied or revoked by the local planning authority. The model order contains a procedure for obtaining the consent of the local planning authority to do work which would otherwise be prohibited by the order. The person seeking consent must make a written application to the authority identifying the tree or trees to which it relates, the work for which consent is sought and stating his reasons for making the application. The authority may then grant consent, either unconditionally or subject to conditions as the authority think fit, or refuse consent. In granting consent, the authority may require, by a direction given in writing, a replacement tree to be replanted. The direction may include requirements as to species, number of trees per hectare, the preparation of the land prior to planting and the erection of fencing necessary to protect newly planted trees.

26.14 The applicant may appeal to the Secretary of State against the refusal of the authority to grant consent, or their failure to make a determination within the prescribed eight-week period.

26.15 As previously mentioned, protection is also given to trees which are not subject to a tree preservation order but which are located in a conservation area. Special provisions apply to the Crown following the Planning and Compulsory Purchase Act 2004 which will make the Crown subject to the Planning Acts.

B. COMPENSATION

The present model form of tree preservation order provides that if a person has suffered loss or damage caused or incurred in consequence of the refusal of any consent required by an order, or by the grant of consent subject to conditions, compensation shall be payable by the authority. In order to claim compensation, the claim must be made within 12 months of the date of the authority's decision (or the Secretary of State's on appeal). Furthermore, no claim may be made if the loss or damage amounts to less than £500. In addition, the model form now provides that no compensation shall be payable in respect of any loss of development value or other diminution in the value of land resulting from the refusal of consent or conditional grant. The above provisions apply only to tree prevention orders made after 2 August 1999 when the Trees Regulations 1999 came into force. Tree preservation orders already in force on that date will continue to be regulated by the more restrictive Town and Country Planning (Tree Preservation Order) Regulations 1969, which are less restrictive as regards compensation than the 1999 Regulations which replaced them. **26.16**

C. PROPOSED CHANGES

In July 1994, the Government proposed the following amendments to the law which would require legislation. The changes have not been pursued: **26.17**

— a clarification of the present exemption given to trees causing a nuisance;
— the replacement of the present offence of 'wilful' destruction or damage to a protected tree by an offence based on 'recklessness';
— the creation of a new offence of 'failing' to comply with a tree replacement notice; and
— the repeal of the exemption allowing work to be carried out on a dying tree.

D. THE PROTECTION OF HEDGEROWS

The Regulations

In 1994 a report by the Institute of Terrestrial Ecology revealed that between 1990 and 1993, an annual average of 3,600 km of hedgerows in England and Wales were removed or destroyed. As a result, the Government took powers in s 97 of the Environment Act 1995 to enable it to protect important hedgerows, but left the detailed arrangements for doing so to be set out in regulations. This has now been done by the Hedgerows Regulations 1997, SI 1997/1160 which came into force on 1 June 1997. **26.18**

The regulations make no attempt to define the term 'hedgerow'. It should be noted however, that the *Oxford English Dictionary* defines a hedgerow as 'a row of bushes forming a hedge with the trees, etc. growing out of it'. **26.19**

It has been estimated that the regulations are at most likely to protect only about 20 per cent of existing hedgerows. One of the reasons for this is that protection afforded by the **26.20** regulations applies only to 'important' hedgerows, though in order to facilitate their protection the regulations apply to a far wider class of hedgerows.

26.21 By Regulation 3, the regulations are to apply to any hedgerow growing in, or adjacent to, any common land, protected land, or land used for agriculture, forestry or the breeding or keeping of horses, ponies and donkeys, if the hedgerow has a continuous length of 20 m or more, or meets another hedgerow at each end.

26.22 'Protected land' for this purpose means land managed as a nature reserve pursuant to s 21 of the National Parks and Access to the Countryside Act 1949 and land notified as an area of special scientific interest under s 28 of the Wildlife and Countryside Act 1981.

26.23 The regulations, however, do not apply to any hedgerow within the curtilage of, or making a boundary of the curtilage of, a dwellinghouse.

26.24 Before removing a hedgerow to which the regulations apply, the owner must first notify the local planning authority that he proposes to do so. The form of notice is set out in Sch 4 to the regulations and is called a 'hedgerow removal notice'.

26.25 The following activities may, however, proceed without *any* prior notification to the authority:

(a) removal to allow necessary or reasonable access, either in place of an existing opening of where none is available;
(b) removal to give assistance in emergencies;
(c) removal for national defence purposes;
(d) development authorised by planning permission; or for which planning permission is deemed to have been granted, except for most of the classes of development for which planning permission is granted under Art 3 of the General Permitted Development Order;
(e) work undertaken by drainage authorities and authorised by legislation for the purpose of flood defence or land drainage;
(f) work to prevent the spread of, or ensuring the eradication of, a plant or tree pest notifiable under plant health legislation;
(g) proper management practice such as normal trimming, coppicing and laying; and
(h) work carried out by the Secretary of State of his functions with respect to highways for which he is the highway authority.

26.26 Following the receipt of a hedgerow removal notice and after consulting with the parish council in England or any community council in Wales within whose area the hedgerow is situated, the local planning authority may give to the owner written notice that the hedgerow may be removed, or serve on the owner a notice called a 'hedgerow retention notice' indicating that the hedgerow may not be removed. If no hedgerow retention notice has been served by the authority within 42 days of the receipt by the authority of a hedgerow removal notice, the owner is free to proceed to carry out the work proposed in that notice.

26.27 It is a requirement of the regulations that unless a hedgerow retention notice has been served, the removal of a hedgerow must be carried out in accordance with the proposal specified in the hedgerow removal notice, and be completed within two years of the date that notice was served on the authority.

Limitation on control

Although notice of proposed removal of a hedgerow is required to be given for a wide class of hedgerow, Regulation 5(6) provides that a local planning authority: **26.28**

(a) shall not give a hedgerow retention notice in respect of a hedgerow which is not an 'important' hedgerow;
(b) shall give such a notice in respect of an 'important' hedgerow unless satisfied, having regard in particular to the reasons given for its proposed removal in the hedgerow removal notice, that there are circumstances which justify the hedgerow's removal.

The definition of an 'important' hedgerow is thus crucial to the authority's exercise of the power to prevent its removal. Regulation 4 states that a hedgerow is 'important' if it, or the hedgerow of which it is a stretch: **26.29**

(a) has existed for 30 years or more; and
(b) satisfies at least one of the criteria listed in Part II of Sch 1 to the Regulations.

The criteria listed in Part II of Sch 1 are too extensive to be quoted *in extenso* in this work, but they all relate to hedgerows which have some archaeological or historical significance or are important to wildlife or landscape qualities. **26.30**

The regulations also contain provisions which make contravention of a number of the regulations a criminal offence (Regulation 7); require replacement of any hedgerow removed in contravention of the regulations (Regulation 8); provide for appeals against hedgerow retention notices to the Secretary of State (Regulation 9); require the local planning authority to maintain records (Regulation 10); allow for enforcement by way of injunction (Regulation 11); and provide for rights of entry (Regulations 12 to 14). There are also further provisions for hedgerows owned by local planning authorities (Regulation 15) and on ecclesiastical property (Regulation 16). **26.31**

Control of high hedges

In the last few years, concern has been expressed over the way in which high hedges (often containing Leylandii) on private property can cause a nuisance to neighbouring properties. **26.32**

The problems will now be dealt with by the provisions of Part 8 of the Anti-Social Behaviour Act 2003. Under the Act, if it is not possible for people to settle their hedge dispute amicably, either of the parties can refer their dispute to the local authority. For this to be done: **26.33**

(a) the hedge in question must be formed wholly or predominantly of a line of two or more evergreen or semi-evergreen trees or shrubs; and
(b) must rise to a height of more than two metres above ground level.

In addition:

(c) the hedge must act, to some degree, as a barrier to light or access; and
(d) because of its height, adversely affect the complainant's reasonable enjoyment of their domestic property.

26.34 Domestic property is defined as a dwelling or garden or yard used or enjoyed wholly or mainly in connection with a dwelling.

26.35 In each case the authority (who may charge a fee to be paid by the complainant) must consider initially whether the complaint is justified. If they do so, they can decide the action that should be taken in order to remedy the adverse affect. This is done by the authority serving a 'nuisance notice'. The notice however, cannot require the hedge to be reduced to a height of less than two metres above ground level, or indeed, require it to be removed altogether.

26.36 Power is given to the authority to specify in the notice the 'initial action' which must be taken before the end of the compliance period; as well as any preventative action it is considered should be taken after the end of the compliance period where the hedge remains on the land.

26.37 The Act provides for a right of appeal by the owner or occupier of the land affected to appeal to the Secretary of State, which must be done within 28 days of issue of the remedial notice. The Secretary of State may then appoint a person to hear and determine the appeal on his behalf. He may on appeal quash the remedial notice, vary it or himself issue a notice where none was issued by the local authority.

26.38 If the hedge owner fails to comply with a remedial notice, he would be liable on conviction in the magistrate's court, to a level 3 fine (up to £1000). In addition, the local authority would have default powers to go in and do the required work and recover the cost of so doing from the hedge owner.

26.39 The Government has consulted on the regulations to be made before the provisions can be brought into effect. This was expected to be before the end of 2004, but has been delayed.

27

CONSERVATION OF NATURAL HABITATS

A further impact on town and country planning law by the country's membership of the European Community, has arisen from the need to implement the EC Council Directive on the Conservation of Natural Habitats and of Wild Fauna and Flora (92/43/EEC: the Habitats Directive). This has been done by the Conservation (Natural Habitats etc.) Regulations 1994, SI 1994/2716, made under the European Communities Act 1972, s 2. The Regulations comprise a total 'implementation package' which strengthens all existing legislation dealing with nature conservation. Part IV of the regulations, however, specifically amends the Town and Country Planning Act 1990, in so far as it affects applications for planning permission, development orders, grants of deemed planning permission, approvals for development and other consents and to ensure that any permission, approval, order or consent given under the Act is subject to the provisions of the Directive. **27.01**

The regulations will apply to sites that will be designated as Special Areas of Conservation (SACs) under the Habitats Directive and also to sites classified as Special Protection Areas (SPAs) under the EC Council Directive on the Conservation of Wild Birds (79/409/EEC: The Birds Directive). The Habitats Directive applies a common protection regime to SACs and SPAs, and they are referred to collectively in the regulations as 'European sites'. **27.02**

The regulations make four main amendments to planning legislation as follows: **27.03**

(a) They restrict the granting of planning permission for development likely to significantly affect a SPA designated under the Birds Directive or a SAC classified under the Habitats Directive.

Regulation 48(1) provides:

> A competent authority, before deciding to undertake, or give any consent, permission or other authorisation for, a plan or project which—
> (a) is likely to have a significant effect on a European site in Great Britain (either alone or in combination with other plans or projects), and
> (b) is not directly connected with or necessary to the management of the site,
> shall make an appropriate assessment of the implications for the site in view of the site's conservation objectives.

The regulation provides that for the purposes of the assessment, the competent authority shall consult the relevant nature conservation body and, if they consider it correct, take the opinion of the general public, by such steps as they consider appropriate.

27.04 The competent authority (normally the local planning authority or Secretary of State) may agree to the plan or project only after having ascertained that it will not adversely affect the integrity of the European site. Regulation 49, however, provides that:

> (1) If they are satisfied that, there being no alternative solutions, the plan or project must be carried out for imperative reasons of overriding public interest (which, subject to paragraph (2), may be of a social or economic nature), the competent authority may agree to the plan or project notwithstanding a negative assessment of the implications for the site.
>
> (2) Where the site concerned hosts a priority natural habitat type or a priority species, the reasons referred to in paragraph (1) must be either—
>
> (a) reasons relating to human health, public safety or beneficial consequences of primary importance to the environment, or
>
> (b) other reasons which in the opinion of the European Commission are imperative reasons of overriding public interest.

27.05 If the local planning authority intends to grant planning permission despite a negative assessment of the implications for a European site, the authority must first notify the Secretary of State, who thus may use his power to call in the application. The regulation is also made to apply to the grant of planning permission on an application under Part III of the 1990 Act, or an appeal under s 78, or where it follows from the service of the purchase notice, enforcement notice or discontinuance order.

27.06 (b) Regulation 55 requires the review of existing planning permissions which have not been fully implemented and which are likely significantly to affect a designated SPA or classified SAC; and if necessary, the taking of appropriate action.

27.07 The duty to review applies to any planning permission or deemed planning permission except that granted by development order or by virtue of the adoption of, or alterations to, a simplified planning zone scheme. Neither does the duty apply to a permission where the development has been completed, or which is granted for a limited period that has expired, or which was subject to a time condition relating to commencement and that time has elapsed without the development having begun.

27.08 Under Regulation 56, where the competent authority ascertain that the carrying out or continuation of the development would adversely affect the integrity of a European site, it must consider whether any adverse effects could be overcome by a planning obligation made under s 106 of the 1990 Act and, if so, invite those concerned to enter into such an obligation. If no such obligation is entered into, the competent authority must proceed to use its powers under the 1990 Act to either revoke or modify the planning permission or require the discontinuance of a use or the removal of buildings or works so as to overcome the adverse effects.

27.09 (c) They prevent the General Permitted Development Order granting permitted development rights which adversely affect the integrity of a SAP or SAC. Regulation 60 provides:

> (1) It shall be a condition of any planning permission granted by a general development order, whether made before or after the commencement of these Regulations, that development which—

(a) is likely to have a significant effect on a European site in Great Britain (either alone or in combination with other plans or projects), and

(b) is not directly connected with or necessary to the management of the site,

shall not be begun until the developer has received written notification of the approval of the local planning authority under Regulation 62.

(2) It shall be a condition of any planning permission granted by a general development order made before the commencement of these Regulations that development which—

(a) is likely to have a significant effect on a European site in Great Britain (either alone or in combination with other plans or projects), and

(b) is not directly connected with or necessary to the management of the site,

and which was begun but not completed before the commencement of these Regulations, shall not be continued until the developer has received written notification of the approval of the local planning authority under Regulation 62.

Regulation 61 provides for the opinion of the appropriate nature conservation body to be sought that the development is not likely to have the effect mentioned in Regulation 60(1)(a) or (2) above and that such opinion shall be conclusive of that question for the purpose of relying on the planning permission granted by the order. Alternatively, Regulation 62 provides that a person intending to carry out development in reliance on the permission granted by the order may apply in writing to the local planning authority for their approval (with the appropriate fee), which the authority must then consider after taking into account any representations made by the appropriate nature conservation body. **27.10**

(d) They prevent existing and future simplified planning zone schemes granting planning permission for development which is likely significantly to affect a SPA or SAC. Regulations 65 and 66 provide: **27.11**

Simplified planning zones

65. The adoption or approval of a simplified planning zone scheme after the commencement of these Regulations shall not have effect to grant planning permission for development which— **27.12**

(a) is likely to have a significant effect on a European site in Great Britain (either alone or in combination with other plans or projects), and

(b) is not directly connected with or necessary to the management of the site;

and every simplified planning zone scheme already in force shall cease to have effect to grant such permission, whether or not the development authorised by the permission has been begun.

Enterprise zones

66. An order designating an enterprise zone, or the approval of a modified scheme, if made or given after the commencement of these Regulations, shall not have effect to grant planning permission for development which— **27.13**

(a) is likely to have a significant effect on a European site in Great Britain (either alone or in combination with other plans or projects), and

(b) is not directly connected with or necessary to the management of the site;

and where the order or approval was made or given before that date, the permission granted by virtue of the taking effect of the order or the modifications shall, from that date, cease to have effect to grant planning permission for such development, whether or not the development authorised by the permission has been begun.

27.14 The status of a site as an SPA can have unusual consequences. In *R (Medway District Council and others) v Secretary of State for Transport, Local Government and the Regions* [2003] JPL 583, the Secretary of State in a consultation paper on airport development in the South East, had omitted to include Gatwick Airport as a possible site for expansion. This was because it had been agreed in 1979 that no second runway would be built there before 2019. The High Court held that it was irrational not to include Gatwick as a possible site for expansion since if Cliffe in Kent, the site of an SPA which was included as a possible site for airport expansion were to be chosen for the expansion, it would have significant adverse affects for the SPA. It was necessary to include Gatwick in the consultation paper because of the obligation to consider alternatives before giving any grant of planning permission where there would be adverse affects on the SPA.

28

REMEDIES FOR ADVERSE PLANNING DECISIONS

A. COMPENSATION FOR RESTRICTIONS ON DEVELOPMENT

The general principle of allowing compensation to owners who suffer loss through the exercise by a planning authority of its statutory powers to control development was recognised in early legislation. **28.01**

Thus the Housing, Town Planning etc. Acts of 1909 to 1925, gave a right to compensation, with certain exceptions, for any injurious affection to an owner's interest in land due to the making of a town planning scheme. The Town and Country Planning Act 1932 also gave a right to compensation for injurious affection to land due to the coming into operation of any provisions in a town planning scheme, or the doing of any work under it, which infringed or curtailed the owner's legal rights. **28.02**

These earlier Acts were concerned, however, with the effects of the coming into operation of a 'town planning scheme'. But when, under the Town and Country Planning Act 1947, the town planning scheme was replaced by the much more flexible 'development plan' and planning permission became obligatory for all forms of 'development', the right to compensation (if any) became related to the actual decision taken by the planning authority in any particular case and not to the provisions of the development plan. **28.03**

By 1990, the law provided for the payment of compensation for adverse planning decisions in two distinct situations. **28.04**

(a) planning decisions restricting development other than 'new development' (s 114 of the 1990 Act); and

(b) restrictions on new development where land has an 'unexpended balance of development value' (Part V of the 1990 Act).

28.05 In 1991, the Government decided, in s 31 of the Planning and Compensation Act 1991, to repeal the right to compensation in both cases.

28.06 As regards (a) above, the repeal was made retrospectively to apply to cases where the relevant application for planning permission was made on or after 16 November 1990. It was considered that the payment of compensation for restriction on development other than new development (often referred to as development within the 'existing use of land') was regarded as outdated and gave rise to abuse by stimulating applications for planning permission simply in order to obtain compensation for any refusal. According to the Government, the opportunities for developers to exploit the right to compensation under s 114 of the 1990 Act were a matter of concern, particularly in conservation areas in parts of central London where property prices were high. The purpose in making the repeal of s 114 retrospective to 16 November 1990 (the day following publication of the original 1991 Bill) was to prevent a flood of applications for planning permission being made in order to elicit payment of compensation before the law had been changed.

28.07 With regard to the repeal of the provisions for the payment of compensation for restrictions on new development, (b) above, the view taken by the Government was that the number of successful claims had become very small, whilst the cost of administrative work in examining potential claims and in recovering any compensation paid where planning permission was subsequently granted for development was no longer justified.

B. COMPENSATION FOR THE REVOCATION OR MODIFICATION OF PLANNING PERMISSIONS UNDER SECTION 97 OF THE 1990 ACT

28.08 Where an order revoking or modifying a planning permission has been made, s 107 of the 1990 Act provides for the payment of compensation by the local planning authority under the following heads:

(a) expenditure in carrying out work which is rendered abortive by the revocation or modification; or

(b) loss or damage otherwise sustained which is directly attributable tothe revocation or modification.

28.09 For the purposes of these provisions, any expenditure incurred in the preparation of plans for the purposes of any work, or upon other similar matters preparatory to it, are to be taken to be included in the expenditure incurred in carrying out that work. No compensation, however, can be paid for any work carried out before the grant of the permission which has been revoked or modified.

28.10 Compensation will include any depreciation in the value of an interest in the land. The measure of compensation will be the amount by which the value of the claimant's interest, with the benefit of the original planning permission, exceeded the value of that interest with the planning permission revoked or modified under the order. Values are based on the rules in s 5 of the Land Compensation Act 1961, so far as applicable, and it must be assumed that planning permission would be granted for development falling within paras. 1 and 2 of Sch 3 to the 1990 Act.

The Act also provides that where planning permission for the development of land has been granted by a development order and that permission is withdrawn, whether by the revocation or amendment of the order or by the issue of directions, and on a subsequent application for planning permission for that development the application is refused, or is granted subject to conditions (other than those previously imposed by the development order), the provisions of s 107 are to apply as if the planning permission granted by the development order had been expressly granted under the Act and then revoked or modified by an order under s 97 (s 108). **28.11**

Section 108 further provides, however, that where planning permission granted by development order is withdrawn by revocation or amendment of the order, compensation will only be payable if the subsequent application for planning permission is made within 12 months of the date on which the revocation or amendment became operative. **28.12**

The main purpose of this provision is to ensure that a right to compensation does not exist in perpetuity simply because a type of development was once permitted development under a development order. However, a one-year period of grace is allowed to provide compensation for a person who was in the process of undertaking a development for which permission under a development order was then withdrawn, and who may already have incurred expenditure in reliance on that permission. **28.13**

C. COMPENSATION FOR DISCONTINUANCE OF A USE OR THE ALTERATION OR REMOVAL OF BUILDINGS OR WORKS UNDER SECTION 102 OF THE 1990 ACT

Any person who suffers loss in consequence of such an order, either through depreciation in the value of his land, or by disturbance, or by expense incurred in complying with the order, is entitled, under s 115 of the 1990 Act, to compensation from the local planning authority, provided his claim is made within six months. **28.14**

Compensation for depreciation in the value of land will be assessed in accordance with the rules in s 5 of the Land Compensation Act 1961, subject to a reduction in respect of the value to the claimant of any timber, apparatus or other materials removed for the purpose of complying with the order. **28.15**

D. PURCHASE NOTICES

Sections 137 to 148 of the 1990 Act contain provisions enabling the owner of an interest in land affected by a planning decision or order to require the purchase of that interest. This has sometimes been described as a form of 'compulsory purchase in reverse', since it is the owner who initiates the proceedings leading to the acquisition of his interest. **28.16**

28.17 The Act provides that where, on an application for planning permission to develop any land, permission is refused or is granted subject to conditions, then if the owner of the land claims:

(a) that the land has become incapable of reasonably beneficial use in its existing state; and
(b) in a case where planning permission was granted subject to conditions or was modified by the imposition of conditions, that the land cannot be rendered capable of reasonably beneficial use by the carrying out of the permitted development in accordance with those conditions; and
(c) in any case, that the land cannot be rendered capable of reasonably beneficial use by the carrying out of any other development for which planning permission has been granted or for which the local planning authority or the Secretary of State has undertaken to grant planning permission,

he may, within 12 months from the date of the planning decision, serve on the council of the district or London borough in which the land is situated, a notice requiring that council to purchase his interest in the land.

28.18 There is no statutory definition of the term 'reasonably beneficial use' but, following the case of *R v Minister of Housing and Local Government, ex p Chichester RDC* [1960] WLR 587, it seems that the test is not whether the land is less valuable to the owner than if developed in accordance with the owner's wishes. Rather, the test is whether the use is reasonably beneficial to the owner in all the relevant circumstances of the particular site. Use by a prospective owner may be taken into account, but only where there is evidence to conclude that there is in fact a prospective purchaser for the land in question.

28.19 The Secretary of State's policy guidance, contained in Circular 13/83, Purchase Notices, at para 13, says:

> In considering what capacity for use the land has, relevant factors are the physical state of the land, its size, shape and surroundings, and the general pattern of land-uses in the area; a use of relatively low value may be regarded as reasonably beneficial if such a use is common for similar land in the vicinity . . . Profit may be a useful comparison in certain circumstances, but the absence of profit (however calculated) is not necessarily material: the concept of reasonably beneficial use is not synonymous with profit.

In *Colley v Canterbury City Council* [1992] JPL 925, the Court of Appeal expressed agreement with that approach.

28.20 For the purpose of determining what is a 'reasonably beneficial' use of the land, no account shall be taken of any prospective use of the land which would involve the carrying out of development other than any development specified in paras 1 or 2 of Sch 3 to the 1990 Act.

28.21 The council on whom a purchase notice is served shall, within three months of such service, serve a responding notice on the owner stating either:

(a) that the council are willing to comply with it; or
(b) that another local authority or statutory undertakers specified in the response notice have agreed to comply with it in their place; or
(c) that, for reasons specified the council are not willing to comply with the purchase notice and have not found any other local authority or statutory undertakers who will

agree to comply with it in their place, and that a copy of the purchase notice and of the response notice has therefore been sent to the Secretary of State.

In cases (a) and (b) above, the council on whom the purchase notice was served, or the other authority who have agreed to comply with it, as the case may be, will be deemed to be authorised to acquire the owner's interest in the land and to have served a notice to treat on him on the same date as the service of the response notice. **28.22**

In case (c) the council on whom the purchase notice is served must send a copy of it and their response notice to the Secretary of State together with their reasons for being unwilling to comply with it. **28.23**

Before confirming, or taking any other action, the Secretary of State must give notice of his proposed action to the person who served the notice, to the local authority on whom it was served, to the local planning authority and to any other local authority or statutory undertakers who might be substituted for the authority on whom the notice was served. He must also afford to any of these persons or authorities the opportunity of a hearing if they so require. **28.24**

After such hearing the Secretary of State may decide to take action available to him under the Act, other than that specified in his notice to the parties concerned. **28.25**

The following courses of action are open to the Secretary of State: **28.26**

(a) to confirm the purchase notice if satisfied that the land is in fact incapable of reasonably beneficial use;
(b) to confirm the notice, but to substitute some other authority or statutory undertakers for the authority on whom the notice is served;
(c) to refuse to confirm, on grounds that the necessary conditions are not fulfilled;
(d) instead of confirming the notice, to grant permission for the development in question, or to revoke or amend any conditions imposed;
(e) instead of confirming the notice, to direct that if a planning application is made, permission shall be given for some other form of development.

Where an owner of land which has a restricted use by virtue of a *previous* planning permission serves a purchase notice, the Secretary of State is not obliged to confirm the notice if he considers that the land ought to remain undeveloped in accordance with the previous planning permission or, as the case may be, remain or be preserved or laid out as amenity land in relation to the remainder of the larger area for which that previous planning permission was granted. **28.27**

This provision was introduced by the Town and Country Planning Act 1968 to reverse the effect of the decision in *Adams& Wade Ltd v Minister of Housing and Local Government* (1965) 18 P & CR 60. There, planning permission had been granted for the development of part of an area of land subject to a condition which required the remainder to be preserved as amenity land for the benefit of the part developed. Application was then made for permission to develop the amenity land, and when the application was refused the owner served a purchase notice claiming it to be incapable of reasonably beneficial use. The Minister's contention that, having had the benefit of the previous permission, the purchase order **28.28** procedure could not be used to avoid the burdens of that permission was rejected, and his decision not to confirm the notice held to be invalid.

28.29 The provision which gives the Secretary of State power to refuse to confirm a purchase notice served in respect of amenity land is now found in s 142 of the 1990 Act. The power extends beyond the situation found in the *Adams & Wade Ltd* case, since it is expressed to cover not only cases where the preservation of amenity land is an express condition of a previous planning permission, but also where the application for the previous permission contemplated that the part not comprised in the development should be treated in that way.

28.30 Purchase notices are rarely used. In 2000/01, only 14 purchase notices were referred to the Secretary of State, of which 11 were rejected and the remaining 3 were either invalid or withdrawn.

28.31 Any party aggrieved by the decision of the Secretary of State on a purchase notice may, within six weeks, make an application to the High Court on the grounds that either (a) the decision of the Secretary of State is not within the powers of the Act, or (b) the interests of the applicant have been substantially prejudiced by a failure to comply with any relevant requirements (ss 284 and 288).

28.32 The court has power to quash the Secretary of State's decision, in which case the purchase notice is treated as cancelled.

28.33 If, within nine months from the service of a purchase notice or six months from its transmission to the Secretary of State (whichever is the less), the Secretary of State has neither confirmed the notice, nor taken any other action, nor notified the owner that he does not propose to confirm, the notice is deemed to be confirmed at the end of that period.

28.34 Where a purchase notice is confirmed, or deemed to be confirmed, the effect is that the authority on whom it was served will be deemed to be authorised to acquire the owner's interest compulsorily and to have served a notice to treat either on such date as the Secretary of State may specify, if he confirms the notice, or otherwise at the expiration of the period referred to in the previous paragraph (s 143).

28.35 In the above cases (and also where a local authority confirms a purchase notice without reference to the Secretary of State) since notice to treat is deemed to have been served, the owner may, if necessary, take the requisite steps to secure the assessment of compensation and the acquisition of his interest in the land, as in any other compulsory purchase case.

28.36 The usual power to withdraw a notice to treat, under s 31 of the Land Compensation Act 1961, is not exercisable in these cases (s 143(8) of the 1990 Act).

28.37 Compensation for land acquired under a purchase notice will, in general, be assessed on the same basis as that of any other land compulsorily acquired.

28.38 Where, instead of confirming a purchase notice in respect of the whole or part of the land, the Secretary of State directs that planning permission should be given for some other form of development then, if the 'permitted development value' of the interest in the land (or part of it) is less than its 'schedule 3 value', the owner may claim compensation equal to the difference, estimated in accordance with the rules of s 5 of the Land Compensation Act 1961, so far as applicable. Any dispute about the compensation will be determined by the Lands Tribunal.

'Permitted development value' means the value of the owner's interest calculated on the assumption that planning permission would only be given in accordance with the Secretary of State's direction. 'Schedule 3 value' means open market value on the assumption that planning permission would only be given for the forms of development specified in paras. 1 and 2 of Sch 3 to the 1990 Act. **28.39**

A purchase notice is also available in the case of the revocation or modification of a planning permission under s 97 or the discontinuance of a use or removal etc. of buildings or works under s 102. **28.40**

APPENDIX 1

Town and Country Planning Act 1990, section 55

Meaning of 'Development'

(1) Subject to the following provisions of this section, in this Act, except where the context otherwise requires, 'development' means the carrying out of building, engineering, mining or other operations in, on, over or under land, or the making of any material change in the use of any buildings or other land.

(1A) For the purposes of this Act 'building operations' includes—

- (a) demolition of buildings;
- (b) rebuilding;
- (c) structural alterations of or additions to buildings; and
- (d) other operations normally undertaken by a person carrying on business as a builder.

(2) The following operations or uses of land shall not be taken for the purposes of this Act to involve development of the land—

- (a) the carrying out for the maintenance, improvement or other alteration of any building of works which—
  - (i) affect only the interior of the building, or
  - (ii) do not materially affect the external appearance of the building, and are not works for making good war damage or works begun after 5th December 1968 for the alteration of a building by providing additional space in it underground;
- (b) the carrying out on land within the boundaries of a road by a highway authority of any works required for the maintenance or improvement of the road but, in the case of any such works which are not exclusively for the maintenance of the road, not including any works which may have significant adverse effects on the environment;
- (c) the carrying out by a local authority or statutory undertakers of any works for the purpose of inspecting, repairing or renewing any sewers, mains, pipes, cables or other apparatus, including the breaking open of any street or other land for that purpose;
- (d) the use of any buildings or other land within the curtilage of a dwellinghouse for any purpose incidental to the enjoyment of the dwellinghouse as such;
- (e) the use of any land for the purposes of agriculture or forestry (including afforestation) and the use for any of those purposes of any building occupied together with land so used;
- (f) in the case of buildings or other land which are used for a purpose of any class specified in an order made by the Secretary of State under this section, the use of the buildings or other land or, subject to the provisions of the order, of any part of the buildings or the other land, for any other purpose of the same class.
- (g) the demolition of any description of building specified in a direction given by the Secretary of State to local planning authorities generally or to a particular local planning authority.

(2A) The Secretary of State may in a development order specify any circumstances or description of circumstances in which subsection (2) does not apply to operations mentioned in paragraph (a) of that subsection which have the effect of increasing the gross floor space of the building by such amount or percentage amount as is so specified.

(2B) The development order may make different provision for different purposes.

(3) For the avoidance of doubt it is hereby declared that for the purposes of this section—

(a) the use as two or more separate dwellinghouses of any building previously used as a single dwellinghouse involves a material change in the use of the building and of each part of it which is so used;

(b) the deposit of refuse or waste materials on land involves a material change in its use, notwithstanding that the land is comprised in a site already used for that purpose, if—

(i) the superficial area of the deposit is extended, or

(ii) the height of the deposit is extended and exceeds the level of the land adjoining the site.

(4) For the purposes of this Act mining operations include—

(a) the removal of material of any description—

(i) from a mineral-working deposit;

(ii) from a deposit of pulverised fuel ash or other furnace ash or clinker; or

(iii) from a deposit of iron, steel or other metallic slags; and

(b) the extraction of minerals from a disused railway embankment.

(4A) Where the placing or assembly of any tank in any part of any inland waters for the purpose of fish farming there would not, apart from this subsection, involve development of the land below, this Act shall have effect as if the tank resulted from carrying out engineering operations over that land; and in this subsection—

'fish farming' means the breeding, rearing or keeping of fish or shellfish (which includes any kind of crustacean and mollusc);

'inland waters' means waters which do not form part of the sea or of any creek, bay or estuary or of any river as far as the tide flows; and

'tank' includes any cage and any other structure for use in fish farming.

(5) Without prejudice to any regulations made under the provisions of this Act relating to the control of advertisements, the use for the display of advertisements of any external part of a building which is not normally used for that purpose shall be treated for the purposes of this section as involving a material change in the use of that part of the building.

APPENDIX 2

Town and Country Planning (Use Classes) Order 1987, SI 1987/764 (as amended)

[Dated 28 April 1987. Made by the Secretary of State for the Environment under ss. 22(2)(f) and 287(3) of the Town and Country Planning Act 1971; now ss. 55(2)(f) and 333(3) of the Town and Country Planning Act 1990.]

Citation and commencement

1. This Order may be cited as the Town and Country Planning (Use Classes) Order 1987 and shall come into force on 1st June 1987.

Interpretation

2. In this order, unless the context otherwise requires:—

'care' means personal care for people in need of such care by reason of old age, disablement, past or present dependence on alcohol or drugs or past or present mental disorder, and in class C2 also includes the personal care of children and medical care and treatment;

'day centre' means premises which are visited during the day for social or recreational purposes or for the purposes of rehabilitation or occupational training, at which care is also provided;

'industrial process' means a process for or incidental to any of the following purposes:—

(a) the making of any article or part of any article (including a ship or vessel, or a film, video or sound recording);

(b) the altering, repairing, maintaining, ornamenting, finishing, cleaning, washing, packing, canning, adapting for sale, breaking up or demolition of any article; or

(c) the getting, dressing or treatment of minerals;

in the course of any trade or business other than agriculture, and other than a use carried out in or adjacent to a mine or quarry;

'Schedule' means the Schedule to this Order;

'site' means the whole area of land within a single unit of occupation.

Use classes

3.—(1) Subject to the provisions of this Order, where a building or other land is used for a purpose of any class specified in the Schedule, the use of that building or that other land for any other purpose of the same class shall not be taken to involve development of the land.

(2) References in paragraph (1) to a building include references to land occupied with the building and used for the same purposes.

(3) A use which is included in and ordinarily incidental to any use in a class specified in the Schedule is not excluded from the use to which it is incidental merely because it is specified in the Schedule as a separate use.

(4) Where land on a single site or on adjacent sites used as parts of a single undertaking is used for purposes consisting of or including purposes falling within any two or more of classes B1 and B2

in the Schedule, those classes may be treated as a single class in considering the use of that land for the purposes of this Order, so long as the area used for a purpose falling either within class B2 is not substantially increased as a result.

[(5) Revoked by SI 1992, 1992/657.]

(6) No class specified in the Schedule includes use—

(a) as a theatre,

(b) as an amusement arcade or centre, or a fun-fair,

(c) as a launderette,

(d) for the sale of fuel for motor vehicles,

(e) for the sale or display for sale of motor vehicles,

(f) for a taxi business or business for the hire of motor vehicles,

(g) as a scrapyard, or a yard for the storage or distribution of minerals or the breaking of motor vehicles,

(h) for any work registrable under the Alkali, etc.,Works Regulation Act 1906,

(i) as a hostel

(j) as a waste disposal installation for the incineration, chemical treatment (as defined in Annex IIA to Directive 75/442/EEC under heading D9), or landfill of waste to which Directive 91/689/EEC applies,

(k) as a retail warehouse club being a retail club where goods are sold, or displayed for sale, only to persons who are members of that club,

(l) as a night-club.

[(7) Where a building or other land is situated in Wales, class B8 (storage or distribution) does not include use of that building or land for the storage of, or as a distribution centre for, radioactive material or radioactive waste.]

[(8) For the purpose of paragraph (7), radioactive material and radioactive waste have the meanings assigned to those terms in the Radioactive Substances Act 1993.]

Change of use of part of building or land

4. In the case of a building used for a purpose within class C3 (dwellinghouses) in the Schedule, the use as a separate dwellinghouse of any part of the building or of any land occupied with and used for the same purposes as the building is not, by virtue of this Order, to be taken as not amounting to development.

Revocation

5. The Town and Country Planning (Use Classes) Order 1972 and the Town and Country Planning (Use Classes) (Amendment) Order 1983 are hereby revoked.

SCHEDULE

PART A

Class A1. Shops

Use for all or any of the following purposes—

(a) for the retail sale of goods other than hot food,

(b) as a post office,

(c) for the sale of tickets or as a travel agency,

(d) for the sale of sandwiches or other cold food for consumption off the premises,

(e) for hairdressing,

(f) for the direction of funerals,

(g) for the display of goods for sale,
(h) for the hiring out of domestic or personal goods or articles,
(i) for the washing or cleaning of clothes or fabrics in the premises,
(j) for the reception of goods to be washed, cleaned or repaired,
(k) as an internet café; where the primary purpose of the premises is to provide facilities for enabling members of the public to access the internet,

where the sale, display or service is to visiting members of the public.

Class A2. Financial and professional services

Use for the provision of—

(a) financial services, or
(b) professional services (other than health or medical services), or
(c) any other services (including use as a betting office) which it is appropriate to provide in a shopping area,

where the services are provided principally to visiting members of the public.

Class A3. Restaurants and cafes

Use for the sale of food and drink for consumption on the premises.

Class A4. Drinking establishments

Use as a public house, wine-bar or other drinking establishment.

Class A5. Hot food takeaways

Use for the sale of hot food for consumption off the premises.

PART B

Class B1. Business

Use for all or any of the following purposes—

(a) as an office other than a use within class A2 (financial and professional services),
(b) for research and development of products or processes, or
(c) for any industrial process,

being a use which can be carried out in any residential area without detriment to the amenity of that area by reason of noise, vibration, smell, fumes, smoke, soot, ash, dust or grit.

Class B2. General industrial

Use for the carrying on of an industrial process other than one falling within class B1 above.

[Classes B3 to B7. Those classes, which were special industrial groups A, B, C, D and E respectively, have now been removed from the Order.]

Class B8. Storage or distribution

Use for storage or as a distribution centre.

PART C

Class C1. Hotels

Use as a hotel or as a boarding or guest-house where, in each case, no significant element of care is provided.

Class C2. Residential institutions

Use for the provision of residential accommodation and care to people in need of care (other than a use within class C3 (dwellinghouses)).
Use as a hospital or nursing home.
Use as a residential school, college or training centre.

Class C3. Dwelling-houses

Use as a dwellinghouse (whether or not as a sole or main residence)—

(a) by a single person or by people living together as a family, or
(b) by not more than six residents living together as a single household (including a household where care is provided for residents).

PART D

Class D1. Non-residential institutions

Any use not including a residential use—

(a) for the provision of any medical or health services except the use of premises attached to the residence of the consultant or practitioner,
(b) as a crèche, day nursery or day centre,
(c) for the provision of education,
(d) for the display of works of Art (otherwise than for sale or hire),
(e) as a museum,
(f) as a public library or public reading room,
(g) as a public hall or exhibition hall,
(h) for, or in connection with, public worship or religious instruction.

Class D2. Assembly and leisure

Use as—

(a) a cinema,
(b) a concert hall,
(c) a bingo hall or casino,
(d) a dance-hall,
(e) a swimming-bath, skating-rink, gymnasium or area for other indoor or outdoor sports or recreations, not involving motorised vehicles or firearms.

APPENDIX 3

Town and Country Planning (General Permitted Development) Order 1995, SI 1995/418 (as amended)

Brought into force: 3rd June 1995

ARTICLE

1. Citation, commencement and interpretation.
2. Application.
3. Permitted development.
4. Directions restricting permitted development.
5. Approval of Secretary of State for article 4(1) directions.
6. Notice and confirmation of article 4(2) directions.
7. Directions restricting permitted development under Class B of Part 22 or Class B of Part 23.
8. Directions.
9. Revocations.

SCHEDULE 1

PART

1. Article 1(4) land.
2. Article 1(5) land.
3. Article 1(6) land.

SCHEDULE 2 PERMITTED DEVELOPMENT

PART

1. Development within the curtilage of a dwellinghouse.
2. Minor operations.
3. Changes of use.
4. Temporary buildings and uses.
5. Caravan sites.
6. Agricultural buildings and operations.
7. Forestry buildings and operations.
8. Industrial and warehouse development.
9. Repairs to unadopted streets and private ways.
10. Repairs to services.
11. Development under local or private Acts or orders.
12. Development by local authorities.
13. Development by local highway authorities.
14. Development by drainage bodies.

15. Development by the Environment Agency.
16. Development by or on behalf of sewerage undertakers.
17. Development by statutory undertakers.
18. Aviation development.
19. Development ancillary to mining operations.
20. Coal mining development by the Coal Authority and licensed operators.
21. Waste tipping at a mine.
22. Mineral exploration.
23. Removal of material from mineral-working deposits.
24. Development by Electronic Communications Code Operators.
25. Other telecommunications development.
26. Development by the Historic Buildings and Monuments Commission for England.
27. Use by members of certain recreational organisations.
28. Development at amusement parks.
29. Driver information systems.
30. Toll road facilities.
31. Demolition of buildings.
32. Schools, colleges, universities and hospitals.
33. Closed circuit television cameras.

SCHEDULE 3 STATUTORY INSTRUMENTS REVOKED

1. Citation, commencement and interpretation

(1) This Order may be cited as the Town and Country Planning (General Permitted Development) Order 1995 and shall come into force on 3rd June 1995.

(2) In this Order, unless the context otherwise requires—

'the Act' means the Town and Country Planning Act 1990;

'the 1960 Act' means the Caravan Sites and Control of Development Act 1960;

'aerodrome' means an aerodrome as defined in article 106 of the Air Navigation Order 1989 (interpretation) which is—

(a) licensed under that Order,
(b) a Government aerodrome,
(c) one at which the manufacture, repair or maintenance of aircraft is carried out by a person carrying on business as a manufacturer or repairer of aircraft,
(d) one used by aircraft engaged in the public transport of passengers or cargo or in aerial work, or
(e) one identified to the Civil Aviation Authority before 1st March 1986 for inclusion in the UK Aerodrome Index,

and, for the purposes of this definition, the terms 'aerial work', 'Government aerodrome' and 'public transport' have the meanings given in article 106;

'aqueduct' does not include an underground conduit;

'area of outstanding natural beauty' means an area designated as such by an order made by the Countryside Agency, as respects England, or the Countryside Council for Wales, as respects Wales, under section 87 of the National Parks and Access to the Countryside Act 1949 (designation of areas of outstanding natural beauty) as confirmed by the Secretary of State;

'building'—

(a) includes any structure or erection and, except in Parts 24, 25 and 33, and Class A of Part 31, of Schedule 2, includes any part of a building, as defined in this article; and

(b) does not include plant or machinery and, in Schedule 2, except in Class B of Part 31 and Part 33, does not include any gate, fence, wall or other means of enclosure;

'caravan' has the same meaning as for the purposes of Part I of the 1960 Act (caravan sites);

'caravan site' means land on which a caravan is stationed for the purpose of human habitation and land which is used in conjunction with land on which a caravan is so stationed;

'classified road' means a highway or proposed highway which—

(a) is a classified road or a principal road by virtue of section 12(1) of the Highways Act 1980 (general provision as to principal and classified roads); or

(b) is classified by the Secretary of State for the purposes of any enactment by virtue of section 12(3) of that Act;

'cubic content' means the cubic content of a structure or building measured externally;

'dwellinghouse' does not include a building containing one or more flats, or a flat contained within such a building;

'electric communication' has the meaning given in Section 15 of the Electronic Communications Act 2000

'erection', in relation to buildings as defined in this article, includes extension, alteration, or re-erection;

'existing', in relation to any building or any plant or machinery or any use, means (except in the definition of 'original') existing immediately before the carrying out, in relation to that building, plant, machinery or use, of development described in this Order;

'flat' means a separate and self-contained set of premises constructed or adapted for use for the purpose of a dwelling and forming part of a building from some other part of which it is divided horizontally;

'floor space' means the total floor space in a building or buildings;

'industrial process' means a process for or incidental to any of the following purposes—

(a) the making of any article or part of any article (including a ship or vessel, or a film, video or sound recording);

(b) the altering, repairing, maintaining, ornamenting, finishing, cleaning, washing, packing, canning, adapting for sale, breaking up or demolition of any article; or

(c) the getting, dressing or treatment of minerals in the course of any trade or business other than agriculture, and other than a process carried out on land used as a mine or adjacent to and occupied together with a mine;

'land drainage' has the same meaning as in section 116 of the Land Drainage Act 1976 (interpretation);

'listed building' has the same meaning as in section 1 of the Planning (Listed Buildings and Conservation Areas) Act 1990 (listing of buildings of special architectural or historic interest);

'by local advertisement' means by publication of the notice in at least one newspaper circulating in the locality in which the area or, as the case may be, the whole or relevant part of the conservation area to which the direction relates is situated;

'machinery' includes any structure or erection in the nature of machinery;

'microwave' means that part of the radio spectrum above 1,000 MHz;

'microwave antenna' means a satellite antenna or a terrestrial microwave antenna;

'mine' means any site on which mining operations are carried out;

'mining operations' means the winning and working of minerals in, on or under land, whether by surface or underground working;

'notifiable pipe-line' means a pipe-line, as defined in section 65 of the Pipe-lines Act 1962 (meaning of pipe-line), which contains or is intended to contain a hazardous substance, as defined in regulation 2(1) of the Notification Regulations (interpretation), except—

(a) a pipe-line the construction of which has been authorised under section 1 of the Pipe-lines Act 1962 (cross-country pipe-lines not to be constructed without the Minister's authority); or

(b) a pipe-line which contains or is intended to contain no hazardous substance other than—

(i) a flammable gas (as specified in item 1 of Part II of Schedule 1 to the Notification Regulations (classes of hazardous substances not specifically named in Part I)) at a pressure of less than 8 bars absolute; or

(ii) a liquid or mixture of liquids, as specified in item 4 of Part II of that Schedule;

'Notification Regulations' means the Notification of Installations Handling Hazardous Substances Regulations 1982;

'original' means, in relation to a building existing on 1st July 1948, as existing on that date and, in relation to a building built on or after 1st July 1948, as so built;

'plant' includes any structure or erection in the nature of plant;

'private way' means a highway not maintainable at the public expense and any other way other than a highway;

'proposed highway' has the same meaning as in section 329 of the Highways Act 1980 (further provision as to interpretation);

'public service vehicle' means a public service vehicle within the meaning of section 1 of the Public Passenger Vehicles Act 1981 (definition of public service vehicles) or a tramcar or trolley vehicle within the meaning of section 192(1) of the Road Traffic Act 1988 (general interpretation);

'satellite antenna' means apparatus designed for transmitting microwave radio energy to satellites or receiving it from them, and includes any mountings or brackets attached to such apparatus;

'scheduled monument' has the same meaning as in section 1(11) of the Ancient Monuments and Archaeological Areas Act 1979 (schedule of monuments);

'by site display' means by the posting of the notice by firm affixture to some object, sited and displayed in such a way as to be easily visible and legible by members of the public;

'site of archaeological interest' means land which is included in the schedule of monuments compiled by the Secretary of State under section 1 of the Ancient Monuments and Archaeological Areas Act 1979 (schedule of monuments), or is within an area of land which is designated as an area of archaeological importance under section 33 of that Act (designation of areas of archaeological importance), or which is within a site registered in any record adopted by resolution by a county council in England by a local planning authority or by a local planning authority in Wales and known in England as the County Sites and Monuments Record and in Wales as the Sites and Monuments Record for the local planning authority area;

'site of special scientific interest' means land to which section 28(1) of the Wildlife and Countryside Act 1981 (areas of special scientific interest) applies;

'statutory undertaker' includes, in addition to any person mentioned in section 262(1) of the Act (meaning of statutory undertakers), a universal service provider (within the meaning of the Postal Services Act 2000) in connection with the provision of a universal postal service (within the meaning of that Act), the Civil Aviation Authority, the Environment Agency, any water undertaker, any public gas transporter, and any licence holder within the meaning of section 64(1) of the Electricity Act 1989 (interpretation etc. of Part 1;

'terrestrial microwave antenna' means apparatus designed for transmitting or receiving terrestrial microwave radio energy between two fixed points;

'trunk road' means a highway or proposed highway which is a trunk road by virtue of section 10(1) or 19 of the Highways Act 1980 (general provisions as to trunk roads, and certain special roads and other highways to become trunk roads) or any other enactment or any instrument made under any enactment;

'the Use Classes Order' means the Town and Country Planning (Use Classes) Order 1987.

(3) Unless the context otherwise requires, any reference in this Order to the height of a building or of plant or machinery shall be construed as a reference to its height when measured from ground level; and for the purposes of this paragraph 'ground level' means the level of the surface of the ground immediately adjacent to the building or plant or machinery in question or, where the level of the surface of the ground on which it is situated or is to be situated is not uniform, the level of the highest part of the surface of the ground adjacent to it.

(4) Revoked.

(5) The land referred to elsewhere in this Order as article 1(5) land is the land described in Part 2 of Schedule 1 to this Order (National Parks, areas of outstanding natural beauty and conservation areas etc.).

(6) The land referred to elsewhere in this Order as article 1(6) land is the land described in Part 3 of Schedule 1 to this Order (National Parks and adjoining land and the Broads).

(7) Paragraphs (8) to (12) apply where an electronic communication is used by a person for the purpose of fulfilling any requirement in this Order or in any Schedule to this Order to give or send any statement, notice or other document to any other person ('the recipient').

(8) The requirement shall be taken to be fulfilled where the notice or other document transmitted by means of the electronic communication is—

(a) capable of being accessed by the recipient,

(b) legible in all material respects, and

(c) sufficiently permanent to be used for subsequent reference.

(9) In paragraph (8), 'legible in all material respects' means that the information contained in the notice or document is available to the recipient to no lesser extent than it would be if sent or given by means of a document in printed form.

(10) Where the electronic communication is received by the recipient outside the recipient's business hours, it shall be taken to have been received on the next working day; and for this purpose 'working day' means a day which is not a Saturday, Sunday, Bank Holiday or other public holiday.

(11) A requirement in this Order or in any Schedule to this Order that any document should be in writing is fulfilled where that document meets the criteria in paragraph (8), and 'written' and cognate expressions are to be construed accordingly.

(12) References in this Order or in any Schedule to this Order to plans, drawings, notices or other documents, or to copies of such documents, include references to such documents or copies of them in electronic form.'

2. Application

(1) This Order applies to all land in England and Wales, but where land is the subject of a special development order, whether made before or after the commencement of this Order, this Order shall apply to that land only to such extent and subject to such modifications as may be specified in the special development order.

(2) Nothing in this Order shall apply to any permission which is deemed to be granted under section 222 of the Act (planning permission not needed for advertisements complying with regulations).

3. Permitted development

(1) Subject to the provisions of this Order and regulations 60 to 63 of the Conservation (Natural Habitats, &c.) Regulations 1994 (general development orders), planning permission is hereby granted for the classes of development described as permitted development in Schedule 2.

(2) Any permission granted by paragraph (1) is subject to any relevant exception, limitation or condition specified in Schedule 2.

(3) References in the following provisions of this Order to permission granted by Schedule 2 or by

any Part, Class or paragraph of that Schedule are references to the permission granted by this article in relation to development described in that Schedule or that provision of that Schedule.

(4) Nothing in this Order permits development contrary to any condition imposed by any planning permission granted or deemed to be granted under Part III of the Act otherwise than by this Order.

(5) The permission granted by Schedule 2 shall not apply if—

(a) in the case of permission granted in connection with an existing building, the building operations involved in the construction of that building are unlawful;

(b) in the case of permission granted in connection with an existing use, that use is unlawful.

(6) The permission granted by Schedule 2 shall not, except in relation to development permitted by Parts 9, 11, 13 or 30, authorise any development which requires or involves the formation, laying out or material widening of a means of access to an existing highway which is a trunk road or classified road, or creates an obstruction to the view of persons using any highway used by vehicular traffic, so as to be likely to cause danger to such persons.

(7) Any development falling within Part 11 of Schedule 2 authorised by an Act or order subject to the grant of any consent or approval shall not be treated for the purposes of this Order as authorised unless and until that consent or approval is obtained, except where the Act was passed or the order made after 1st July 1948 and it contains provision to the contrary.

(8) Schedule 2 does not grant permission for the laying or construction of a notifiable pipe-line, except in the case of the laying or construction of a notifiable pipe-line by a public gas transporter in accordance with Class F of Part 17 of that Schedule.

(9) Except as provided in Part 31, Schedule 2 does not permit any development which requires or involves the demolition of a building, but in this paragraph 'building' does not include part of a building.

(10) Subject to paragraph (12), Schedule 1 development or Schedule 2 development within the meaning of the Town and Country Planning (Environmental Impact Assessment) (England and Wales) Regulations 1999 ('the EIA Regulations') is not permitted by this Order unless:

(a) the local planning authority has adopted a screening opinion under regulation 5 of those Regulations that the development is not EIA development;

(b) the Secretary of State has made a screening direction under regulation 4(7) or 6(4) of those Regulations that the development is not EIA development; or

(c) the Secretary of State has given a direction under regulation 4(4) of those Regulations that the development is exempted from the application of those Regulations.

(11) Where:

(a) the local planning authority has adopted a screening opinion pursuant to regulation 5 of the EIA Regulations that development is EIA development and the Secretary of State has in relation to that development neither made a screening direction to the contrary under regulation 4(7) or 6(4) of those Regulations nor directed under regulation 4(4) of those Regulations that the development is exempted from the application of those Regulations; or

(b) the Secretary of State has directed that development is EIA development, that development shall be treated, for the purposes of paragraph (10), as development which is not permitted by this Order.

(12) Paragraph (10) does not apply to—

(a) [Revoked by SI 1999/293.];

(b) development which consists of the carrying out by a drainage body within the meaning of the Land Drainage Act 1991 of improvement works within the meaning of the Land Drainage Improvement Works (Assessment of Environmental Effects) Regulations 1988;

(c) [Revoked by SI 1999/293.];

(d) development for which permission is granted by Part 7, Class D of Part 8, Part 11, Class B of Part 12, Class F(a) of Part 17, Class A or Class B of Part 20 or Class B of Part 21 of Schedule 2;

(e) development for which permission is granted by Class C or Class D of Part 20, Class A of Part 21 or Class B of Part 22 of Schedule 2 where the land in, on or under which the development is to be carried out is—

(i) in the case of Class C or Class D of Part 20, on the same authorised site,

(ii) in the case of Class A of Part 21, on the same premises or, as the case may be, the same ancillary mining land,

(iii) in the case of Class B of Part 22, on the same land or, as the case may be, on land adjoining that land,

as that in, on or under which development of any description permitted by the same Class has been carried out before 14th March 1999;

(f) the completion of any development begun before 14th March 1999.

(13) Where a person uses electronic communications for making any application required to be made under any of Parts 6, 7, 22, 23, 24, 30 or 31 of Schedule 2, that person shall be taken to have agreed—

(a) to the use of electronic communications for all purposes relating to his application which are capable of being effected using such communications;

(b) that his address for the purpose of such communications is the address incorporated into, or otherwise logically associated with, his application; and

(c) that his deemed agreement under this paragraph shall subsist until he gives notice in writing that he wishes to revoke the agreement (and such revocation shall be final and shall take effect on a date specified by him but not less than seven days after the date on which the notice is given).

4. Directions restricting permitted development

(1) If the Secretary of State or the appropriate local planning authority is satisfied that it is expedient that development described in any Part, Class or paragraph in Schedule 2, other than Class B of Part 22 or Class B of Part 23, should not be carried out unless permission is granted for it on an application, he or they may give a direction under this paragraph that the permission granted by article 3 shall not apply to—

(a) all or any development of the Part, Class or paragraph in question in an area specified in the direction; or

(b) any particular development, failing within that Part, Class or paragraph, which is specified in the direction,

and the direction shall specify that it is made under this paragraph.

(2) If the appropriate local planning authority is satisfied that it is expedient that any particular development described in paragraph (5) below should not be carried out within the whole or any part of a conservation area unless permission is granted for it on an application, they may give a direction under this paragraph that the permission granted by article 3 shall not apply to all or any particular development of the Class in question within the whole or any part of the conservation area, and the direction shall specify the development and conservation area or part of that area to which it relates and that it is made under this paragraph.

(3) A direction under paragraph (1) or (2) shall not affect the carrying out of—

(a) development permitted by Part II authorised by an Act passed after 1st July 1948 or by an order requiring the approval of both Houses of Parliament approved after that date;

(b) any development in an emergency; or

(c) any development mentioned in Part 24, unless the direction specifically so provides.

(4) A direction given or having effect as if given under this article shall not, unless the direction

so provides, affect the carrying out by a statutory undertaker of the following descriptions of development—

(a) the maintenance of bridges, buildings and railway stations;

(b) the alteration and maintenance of railway track, and the provision and maintenance of track equipment, including signal boxes, signalling apparatus and other appliances and works required in connection with the movement of traffic by rail;

(c) the maintenance of docks, harbours, quays, wharves, canals and towing paths;

(d) the provision and maintenance of mechanical apparatus or appliances (including signalling equipment) required for the purposes of shipping or in connection with the embarking, disembarking, loading, discharging or transport of passengers, livestock or goods at a dock, quay, harbour, bank, wharf or basin;

(e) any development required in connection with the improvement, maintenance or repair of watercourses or drainage works;

(f) the maintenance of buildings, runways, taxiways or aprons at an aerodrome;

(g) the provision, alteration and maintenance of equipment, apparatus and works at an aerodrome, required in connection with the movement of traffic by air (other than buildings, the construction, erection, reconstruction or alteration of which is permitted by Class A of Part 18 of Schedule 2).

(5) The development referred to in paragraph (2) is development described in—

(a) Class A of Part 1 of Schedule 2, consisting of the enlargement, improvement or other alteration of a dwellinghouse, where any part of the enlargement, improvement or alteration would front a relevant location;

(b) Class C of Part 1 of that Schedule, where the alteration would be to a roof slope which fronts a relevant location;

(c) Class D of Part 1 of that Schedule, where the external door in question fronts a relevant location;

(d) Class E of Part 1 of that Schedule, where the building or enclosure, swimming or other pool to be provided would front a relevant location, or where the part of the building or enclosure maintained, improved or altered would front a relevant location;

(e) Class F of Part 1 of that Schedule, where the hard surface would front a relevant location;

(f) Class H of Part 1 of that Schedule, where the part of the building or other structure on which the satellite antenna is to be installed, altered or replaced fronts a relevant location;

(g) Part 1 of that Schedule, consisting of the erection, alteration or removal of a chimney on a dwellinghouse or on a building within the curtilage of a dwellinghouse;

(h) Class A of Part 2 of that Schedule, where the gate, fence, wall or other means of enclosure would be within the curtilage of a dwellinghouse and would front a relevant location;

(i) Class C of Part 2 of that Schedule, consisting of the painting of the exterior of any part, which fronts a relevant location, of—

(i) a dwellinghouse; or

(ii) any building or enclosure within the curtilage of a dwellinghouse;

(j) Class B of Part 31 of that Schedule, where the gate, fence, wall or other means of enclosure is within the curtilage of a dwellinghouse and fronts a relevant location.

(6) In this article and in articles 5 and 6—

'appropriate local planning authority' means—

(a) in relation to a conservation area in a non-metropolitan county in England, the county planning authority or the district planning authority; and

(b) in relation to any other area, the local planning authority whose function it would be to determine an application for planning permission for the development to which the direction relates or is proposed to relate;

'relevant location' means a highway, waterway or open space.

5. Approval of Secretary of State for article 4(1) directions

(1) Except in the cases specified in paragraphs (3) and (4), a direction by a local planning authority under article 4(1) requires the approval of the Secretary of State, who may approve the direction with or without modifications.

(2) On making a direction under article 4(1) or submitting such a direction to the Secretary of State for approval—

(a) a county planning authority shall give notice of it to any district planning authority in whose district the area to which the direction relates is situated; and

(b) except in metropolitan districts, a district planning authority shall give notice of it to the county planning authority, if any.

(3) Unless it affects the carrying out of development by a statutory undertaker as provided by article 4(4), the approval of the Secretary of State is not required for a direction which relates to—

(a) a listed building;

(b) a building which is notified to the authority by the Secretary of State as a building of architectural or historic interest; or

(c) development within the curtilage of a listed building,

and does not relate to land of any other description.

(4) Subject to paragraph (6), the approval of the Secretary of State is not required for a direction made under article 4(1) relating only to development permitted by any of Parts 1 to 4 or Part 31 of Schedule 2, if the relevant authority consider the development would be prejudicial to the proper planning of their area or constitute a threat to the amenities of their area.

(5) A direction not requiring the Secretary of State's approval by virtue of paragraph (4) shall, unless disallowed or approved by the Secretary of State, expire at the end of six months from the date on which it was made.

(6) Paragraph (4) does not apply to a second or subsequent direction relating to the same development or to development of the same Class or any of the same Classes, in the same area or any part of that area as that to which the first direction relates or related.

(7) The local planning authority shall send a copy of any direction made by them to which paragraph (4) applies to the Secretary of State not later than the date on which notice of that direction is given in accordance with paragraph (10) or (12).

(8) The Secretary of State may give notice to the local planning authority that he has disallowed any such direction and the direction shall then cease to have effect.

(9) The local planning authority shall as soon as reasonably practicable give notice that a direction has been disallowed in the same manner as notice of the direction was given.

(10) Subject to paragraph (12), notice of any direction made under article 4(1) shall be served by the appropriate local planning authority on the owner and occupier of every part of the land within the area to which the direction relates as soon as practicable after the direction has been made or, where the direction is required to be approved by the Secretary of State, as soon as practicable after it has been so approved; and a direction shall come into force in respect of any part of the land within the area to which the direction relates on the date on which notice is so served on the occupier of that part, or, if there is no occupier, on the owner.

(11) If a direction to which paragraph (4) applies is approved by the Secretary of State within the period of six months referred to in paragraph (5), then (unless paragraph (12) applies) the authority who made the direction shall, as soon as practicable, serve notice of that approval on the owner and occupier of every part of the land within the area to which the direction relates; and where the Secretary of State has approved the direction with modifications the notice shall indicate the effect of the modifications.

(12) Where in the case of a direction under article 4(1)(a) an authority consider that individual service in accordance with paragraph (10) or (11) is impracticable for the reasons set out in paragraph (14) they shall publish a notice of the direction, or of the approval, by local advertisement.

(13) A notice published pursuant to paragraph (12) shall contain a statement of the effect of the direction and of any modification made to it by the Secretary of State, and shall name a place or places where a copy of the direction, and of a map defining the area to which it relates, may be seen at all reasonable hours.

(14) The reasons referred to in paragraph (12) are that the number of owners and occupiers within the area to which the direction relates makes individual service impracticable, or that it is difficult to identify or locate one or more of them.

(15) Where notice of a direction has been published in accordance with paragraph (12), the direction shall come into force on the date on which the notice is first published.

(16) A local planning authority may, by making a subsequent direction and without the approval of the Secretary of State, cancel any direction made by them under article 4(1), and the Secretary of State may make a direction cancelling any direction under article 4(1) made by the local planning authority.

(17) Paragraphs (10) and (12) to (15) shall apply to any direction made under paragraph (16).

6. Notice and confirmation of article 4(2) directions

(1) Notice of any direction made under article 4(2) shall, as soon as practicable after the direction has been made, be given by the appropriate local planning authority—

(a) by local advertisement; and

(b) subject to paragraphs (4) and (5), by serving the notice on the owner and occupier of every dwellinghouse within the whole or the relevant part of the conservation area to which the direction relates.

(2) The notice referred to in paragraph (1) shall—

(a) include a description of the development and the conservation area or part of that area to which the direction relates, and a statement of the effect of the direction;

(b) specify that the direction is made under article 4(2) of this Order;

(c) name a place where a copy of the direction, and a copy of the map defining the conservation area or part of that area to which it relates, may be seen at all reasonable hours; and

(d) specify a period of at least 21 days, stating the date on which that period begins, within which any representations concerning the direction may be made to the local planning authority.

(3) The direction shall come into force in respect of any part of the land within the conservation area or part of that area to which it relates—

(a) on the date on which the notice is served on the occupier of that part of the land or, if there is no occupier, on the owner; or

(b) if paragraph (4) or (5) applies, on the date on which the notice is first published in accordance with paragraph (1)(a).

(4) The local planning authority need not serve notice on an owner or occupier in accordance with paragraph (1)(b) where they consider that individual service on that owner or occupier is impracticable because it is difficult to identify or locate him.

(5) The local planning authority need not serve any notice in accordance with paragraph (1)(b) where they consider that the number of owners or occupiers within the conservation area or part of that area to which the direction relates makes individual service impracticable.

(6) On making a direction under article 4(2)

(a) a county planning authority shall give notice of it to any district planning authority in whose district the conservation area or part of that area to which the direction relates is situated; and

(b) except in metropolitan districts, a district planning authority shall give notice of it to the county planning authority, if any.

(7) A direction under article 4(2) shall expire at the end of six months from the date on which it was

made unless confirmed by the appropriate local planning authority in accordance with paragraphs (8) and (9) before the end of that six month period.

(8) In deciding whether to confirm a direction made under article 4(2), the local planning authority shall take into account any representations received during the period specified in the notice referred to in paragraph (2)(d).

(9) The local planning authority shall not confirm the direction until a period of at least 28 days has elapsed following the latest date on which any notice relating to the direction was served or published.

(10) The appropriate local planning authority shall as soon as practicable give notice that a direction has been confirmed in the same manner as in paragraphs (1)(a) and (b) above.

7. Directions restricting permitted development under Class B of Part 22 or Class B of Part 23

(1) If, on receipt of a notification from any person that he proposes to carry out development within Class B of Part 22 or Class B of Part 23 of Schedule 2, a mineral planning authority are satisfied as mentioned in paragraph (2) below, they may, within a period of 21 days beginning with the receipt of the notification, direct that the permission granted by article 3 of this Order shall not apply to the development, or to such part of the development as is specified in the direction.

(2) The mineral planning authority may make a direction under this article if they are satisfied that it is expedient that the development, or any part of it, should not be carried out unless permission for it is granted on an application because—

(a) the land on which the development is to be carried out is within—

(i) a National Park,

(ii) an area of outstanding natural beauty,

(iii) a site of archaeological interest, and the operation to be carried out is not one described in the Schedule to the Areas of Archaeological Importance (Notification of Operations) (Exemption) Order 1984 (exempt operations),

(iv) a site of special scientific interest, or

(v) the Broads;

(b) the development, either taken by itself or taken in conjunction with other development which is already being carried out in the area or in respect of which notification has been given in pursuance of the provisions of Class B of Part 22 or Class B of Part 23, would cause serious detriment to the amenity of the area in which it is to be carried out or would adversely affect the setting of a building shown as Grade I in the list of buildings of special architectural or historic interest compiled by the Secretary of State under section 1 of the Planning (Listed Buildings and Conservation Areas) Act 1990 (listing of buildings of special architectural or historic interest);

(c) the development would constitute a serious nuisance to the inhabitants of a nearby residential building, hospital or school; or

(d) the development would endanger aircraft using a nearby aerodrome.

(3) A direction made under this article shall contain a statement as to the day on which (if it is not disallowed under paragraph (5) below) it will come into force, which shall be 29 days from the date on which notice of it is sent to the Secretary of State in accordance with paragraph (4) below.

(4) As soon as is reasonably practicable a copy of a direction under this article shall be sent by the mineral planning authority to the Secretary of State and to the person who gave notice of the proposal to carry out development.

(5) The Secretary of State may, at any time within a period of 28 days beginning with the date on which the direction is made, disallow the direction; and immediately upon receipt of notice in writing from the Secretary of State that he has disallowed the direction, the mineral planning

authority shall give notice in writing to the person who gave notice of the proposal that he is authorised to proceed with the development.

8. Directions

Any power conferred by this Order to give a direction includes power to cancel or vary the direction by a subsequent direction.

9. Revocations

The statutory instruments specified in column 1 of Schedule 3 are hereby revoked to the extent specified in column 3.

SCHEDULE 1 PART 1: ARTICLE 1(4) LAND

[Revoked by SI 1999/1661.]

PART 2: ARTICLE 1(5) LAND

Land within—

(a) a National Park;

(b) an area of outstanding natural beauty;

(c) an area designated as a conservation area under section 69 of the Planning (Listed Buildings and Conservation Areas) Act 1990 (designation of conservation areas);

(d) an area specified by the Secretary of State and the Minister of Agriculture, Fisheries and Food for the purposes of section 41(3) of the Wildlife and Countryside Act 1981 (enhancement and protection of the natural beauty and amenity of the countryside);

(e) the Broads.

PART 3: ARTICLE 1(6) LAND

Land within a National Park or within the following areas—

(a) In England, the Broads or land outside the boundaries of a National Park, which is within the parishes listed below—

in the district of Allerdale—

Blindcrake, Bothel and Threapland, Bridekirk, Brigham, Broughton, Broughton Moor, Camerton, Crosscanonby, Dean, Dearham, Gilcrux, Great Clifton, Greysouthen, Little Clifton, Loweswater, Oughterside and Allerby, Papcastle, Plumbland, Seaton, Winscales;

in the borough of Copeland—

Arlecdon and Frizington, Cleator Moor, Distington, Drigg and Carleton, Egremont, Gosforth, Haile, Irton with Santon, Lamplugh, Lowca, Lowside Quarter, Millom, Millom Without, Moresby, Parton, Ponsonby, St Bees, St Bridget's Beckermet, St John's Beckermet, Seascale, Weddicar;

in the district of Eden—

Ainstable, Asby, Bandleyside, Bolton, Brough, Brough Sowerby, Brougham, Castle Sowerby, Catterlen, Clifton, Cliburn, Crackenthorpe, Crosby Garrett, Crosby Ravensworth, Culgaith, Dacre, Dufton, Glassonby, Great Salkeld, Great Strickland, Greystoke, Hartley, Hesket, Hillbeck, Hunsonby, Hutton, Kaber, Kings Meaburn, Kirkby Stephen, Kirby Thore, Kirkoswald, Langwathby, Lazonby, Little Strickland, Long Marton, Lowther, Mallerstang, Milburn,

Morland, Mungrisdale, Murton, Musgrave, Nateby, Newbiggin, Newby, Orton, Ousby, Ravenstonedale, Shap, Skelton, Sleagill, Sockbridge and Tirril, Soulby, Stainmore, Tebay, Temple Sowerby, Thrimby, Waitby, Warcop, Wharton, Winton, Yanwath and Eamont Bridge;

in the borough of High Peak—

Chapel-en-le-Frith, Charlesworth, Chinley Buxworth and Brownside, Chisworth, Green Fairfield, Hartington Upper Quarter, Hayfield, King Sterndale, Tintwistle, Wormhill;

in the district of South Lakeland—

Aldingham, Angerton, Arnside, Barbon, Beetham, Blawith and Subberthwaite, Broughton West, Burton, Casterton, Docker, Egton-with-Newland, Fawcett Forest, Firbank, Grayrigg, Helsington, Heversham, Hincaster, Holme, Hutton Roof, Killington, Kirkby Ireleth, Kirkby Lonsdale, Lambrigg, Levens, Lower Allithwaite, Lower Holker, Lowick, Lupton, Mansergh, Mansriggs, Middleton, Milnthorpe, Natland, New Hutton, Old Hutton and Holmescales, Osmotherley, Pennington, Preston Patrick, Preston Richard, Scalthwaiterigg, Sedgwick, Skelsmergh, Stainton, Strickland Ketel, Strickland Roger, Urswick, Whinfell, Whitwell and Selside;

in the district of West Derbyshire—

Aldwark, Birchover, Stanton; and

(b) In Wales, land outside the boundaries of a National Park which is—

(i) within the communities listed below—

in the borough of Aberconwy and Colwyn—

Caerhun, Dolgarrog;

in the county of Caernarfonshire and Merionethshire—

Arthog, Betws Garmon, Bontnewydd, Corris, Llanberis, Llanddeiniolen, Llandwrog, Llanfrothen, Llanllyfni, Llanwnda, Penrhyndeudraeth, Waunfawr; or

(ii) within the specified parts of the communities listed below—

in the county borough of Aberconwy and Colwyn—

those parts of the following communities which were on 31st March 1974 within the former rural district of Nant Conway—

Conwy, Henryd, Llanddoged and Maenan, and Llanrwst;

that part of the community of Llangwm which was on 31st March 1974 within the former rural district of Penllyn;

in the county of Caernarfonshire and Merionethshire:

those parts of the following communities which were on 31st March 1974 within the former rural district of Gwyrfai—

Caernarfon, Clynnog, Dolbenmaen, Llandygai, Llanaelhaearn, Llanrug, Pentir, Y Felinheli;

that part of the community of Talsarnau which was on 31st March 1974 within the former rural district of Deudraeth;

that part of the community of Barmouth which was on 31st March 1974 within the former rural district of Dolgellau;

that part of the community of Llandderfel which was on 31st March 1974 within the former rural district of Penllyn;

in the county of Denbighshire, that part of the community of Llandrillo which was on 31st March 1974 within the former rural district of Penllyn.

ARTICLE 3 **SCHEDULE 2** PART 1: DEVELOPMENT WITHIN THE CURTILAGE OF A DWELLINGHOUSE

Class A

Permitted development **A. The enlargement, improvement or other alteration of a dwellinghouse.**

Development not permitted

A.1 Development is not permitted by Class A if—

(a) the cubic content of the resulting building would exceed the cubic content of the original dwellinghouse—

(i) in the case of a terrace house or in the case of a dwellinghouse on article 1(5) land, by more than 50 cubic metres or 10%, whichever is the greater,

(ii) in any other case, by more than 70 cubic metres or 15%, whichever is the greater,

(iii) in any case, by more than 115 cubic metres;

(b) the part of the building enlarged, improved or altered would exceed in height the highest part of the roof of the original dwellinghouse;

(c) the part of the building enlarged, improved or altered would be nearer to any highway which bounds the curtilage of the dwellinghouse than—

(i) the part of the original dwellinghouse nearest to that highway, or

(ii) any point 20 metres from that highway,

whichever is nearer to the highway;

(d) in the case of development other than the insertion, enlargement, improvement or other alteration of a window in an existing wall of a dwellinghouse, the part of the building enlarged, improved or altered would be within 2 metres of the boundary of the curtilage of the dwellinghouse and would exceed 4 metres in height;

(e) the total area of ground covered by buildings within the curtilage (other than the original dwellinghouse) would exceed 50% of the total area of the curtilage (excluding the ground area of the original dwellinghouse);

(f) it would consist of or include the installation, alteration or replacement of a satellite antenna;

(g) it would consist of or include the erection of a building within the curtilage of a listed building; or

(h) it would consist of or include an alteration to any part of the roof

A.2 In the case of a dwelling house on any article 1(5) land, development is not permitted by Class A if it would consist of or include the cladding of any part of the exterior with stone, artificial stone, timber, plastic or tiles.

Interpretation of Class A

A.3 For the purposes of Class A—

(a) the erection within the curtilage of a dwellinghouse of any building with a cubic content greater than 10 cubic metres shall be treated as the enlargement of the dwellinghouse for all purposes (including calculating cubic content) where—

(i) the dwellinghouse is on article 1(5) land, or

(ii) in any other case, any part of that building would be within 5 metres of any part of the dwellinghouse;

(b) where any part of the dwellinghouse would be within 5 metres of an existing building within the same curtilage, that building shall be treated as forming part of the resulting building for the purpose of calculating the cubic content.

Class B

Permitted development **B. The enlargement of a dwellinghouse consisting of an addition or alteration to its roof.**

Development not permitted

B.1 Development is not permitted by Class B if—

(a) any part of the dwellinghouse would, as a result of the works, exceed the height of the highest part of the existing roof;

(b) any part of the dwellinghouse would, as a result of the works, extend beyond the plane of any existing roof slope which fronts any highway;

(c) it would increase the cubic content of the dwellinghouse by more than 40 cubic metres, in the case of a terrace house, or 50 cubic metres in any other case;

(d) the cubic content of the resulting building would exceed the cubic content of the original dwellinghouse—

(i) in the case of a terrace house by more than 50 cubic metres or 10%, whichever is the greater,

(ii) in any other case, by more than 70 cubic metres or 15%, whichever is the greater, or

(iii) in any case, by more than 115 cubic metres; or

(e) the dwellinghouse is on article 1(5) land.

Class C

Permitted development **C. Any other alteration to the roof of a dwellinghouse.**

Development not permitted

C.1 Development is not permitted by Class C if it would result in a material alteration to the shape of the dwellinghouse.

Class D

Permitted development **D. The erection or construction of a porch outside any external door of a dwellinghouse.**

Development not permitted

D.1 Development is not permitted by Class D if—

(a) the ground area (measured externally) of the structure would exceed 3 square metres;

(b) any part of the structure would be more than 3 metres above ground level; or

(c) any part of the structure would be within 2 metres of any boundary of the curtilage of the dwellinghouse with a highway.

Class E

Permitted development **E. The provision within the curtilage of a dwellinghouse of any building or enclosure, swimming or other pool required for a purpose incidental to the enjoyment of the dwellinghouse as such, or the maintenance, improvement or other alteration of such a building or enclosure.**

Development not permitted

E.1 Development is not permitted by Class E if—

(a) it relates to a dwelling or a satellite antenna;

(b) any part of the building or enclosure to be constructed or provided would be nearer to any highway which bounds the curtilage than—

(i) the part of the original dwellinghouse nearest to that highway, or

(ii) any point 20 metres from that highway,

whichever is nearer to the highway;

(c) where the building to be constructed or provided would have a cubic content greater than 10 cubic metres, any part of it would be within 5 metres of any part of the dwellinghouse;

(d) the height of that building or enclosure would exceed—

(i) 4 metres, in the case of a building with a ridged roof, or

(ii) 3 metres, in any other case;

(e) the total area of ground covered by buildings or enclosures within the curtilage (other than the original dwellinghouse) would exceed 50% of the total area of the curtilage (excluding the ground area of the original dwellinghouse); or

(f) in the case of any article 1(5) land or land within the curtilage of a listed building, it would consist of the provision, alteration or improvement of a building with a cubic content greater than 10 cubic metres.

Interpretation of Class E

E.2 For the purposes of Class E—

'purpose incidental to the enjoyment of the dwellinghouse as such' includes the keeping of poultry, bees, pet animals, birds or other livestock for the domestic needs or personal enjoyment of the occupants of the dwellinghouse.

Class F

Permitted development

F. The provision within the curtilage of a dwellinghouse of a hard surface for any purpose incidental to the enjoyment of the dwellinghouse as such.

Class G

Permitted development

G. The erection or provision within the curtilage of a dwellinghouse of a container for the storage of oil for domestic heating.

Development not permitted

G.1 Development is not permitted by Class G if—

(a) the capacity of the container would exceed 3,500 litres;

(b) any part of the container would be more than 3 metres above ground level; or

(c) any part of the container would be nearer to any highway which bounds the curtilage than—

(i) the part of the original building nearest to that highway, or

(ii) any point 20 metres from that highway,

whichever is nearer to the highway.

Class H

Permitted development

H. The installation, alteration or replacement of a satellite antenna on a dwellinghouse or within the curtilage of a dwellinghouse.

Development not permitted

H.1 Development is not permitted by Class H if—

(a) the size of the antenna (excluding any projecting feed element, reinforcing rim, mountings and brackets) when measured in any dimension would exceed—

(i) 45 centimetres in the case of an antenna to be installed on a chimney;

(ii) 90 centimetres in the case of an antenna to be installed other than on a chimney;

(b) the highest part of an antenna to be installed on a roof or a chimney would, when installed, exceed in height—

(i) in the case of an antenna to be installed on a roof, the highest part of the roof;

(ii) in the case of an antenna to be installed on a chimney, the highest part of the chimney;

(c) there is any other satellite antenna on the dwellinghouse or within its curtilage;

(d) in the case of article 1(5) land, it would consist of the installation of an antenna—

(i) on a chimney;

(ii) on a building which exceeds 15 metres in height;

(iii) on a wall or roof slope which fronts a highway;

(iv) in the Broads, on a wall or roof slope which fronts a waterway.

Conditions

H.2 Development is permitted by Class H subject to the following conditions—

(a) an antenna installed on a building shall, so far as practicable, be sited so as to minimise its effect on the external appearance of the building;

(b) an antenna no longer needed for the reception or transmission of microwave radio energy shall be removed as soon as reasonably practicable.

Interpretation of Part 1

1. For the purposes of Part 1—

'resulting building' means the dwellinghouse as enlarged, improved or altered, taking into account any enlargement, improvement or alteration to the original dwellinghouse, whether permitted by this Part or not; and

'terrace house' means a dwellinghouse situated in a row of three or more dwellinghouses used or designed for use as single dwellings, where—

(a) it shares a party wall with, or has a main wall adjoining the main wall of, the dwellinghouse on either side; or

(b) if it is at the end of a row, it shares a party wall with or has a main wall adjoining the main wall of a dwellinghouse which fulfils the requirements of sub-paragraph (a) above.

PART 2: MINOR OPERATIONS

Class A

Permitted development

A. The erection, construction, maintenance, improvement or alteration of a gate, fence, wall or other means of enclosure.

Development not permitted

A.1 Development is not permitted by Class A if—

(a) the height of any gate, fence, wall or means of enclosure erected or constructed adjacent to a highway used by vehicular traffic would, after the carrying out of the development, exceed one metre above ground level;

(b) the height of any other gate, fence, wall or means of enclosure erected or constructed would exceed two metres above ground level;

(c) the height of any gate, fence, wall or other means of enclosure maintained, improved or altered would, as a result of the development, exceed its former height or the height referred to in sub-paragraph (a) or (b) as the height appropriate to it if erected or constructed, whichever is the greater; or

(d) it would involve development within the curtilage of, or to a gate, fence, wall or other means of enclosure surrounding, a listed building.

Class B

Permitted development

B. The formation, laying out and construction of a means of access to a highway which is not a trunk road or a classified road, where that access is required in connection with development permitted by any Class in this Schedule (other than by Class A of this Part).

Class C

Permitted development **C. The painting of the exterior of any building or work.**

Development not permitted C.1 Development is not permitted by Class C where the painting is for the purpose of advertisement, announcement or direction.

Interpretation of Class C C.2 In Class C, 'painting' includes any application of colour.

PART 3: CHANGES OF USE

Class A

Permitted development **A. Development consisting of a change of use of a building to a use falling within Class A1 (shops) of the Schedule to the Use Classes Order from a use falling within Class A3 (restaurants and cafes), A4 (drinking establishments) or A5 (hot food takeaways) of the Schedule.**

Class AA

Permitted development **AA. Development consisting of a change of use of a building to a use falling within Class A3 (restaurants and cafes) of the Schedule to the Use Classes Order from a use falling within Class A4 (drinking establishments) or Class A5 (hot food takeaways) of that Schedule.**

Class B

Permitted development **B. Development consisting of a change of the use of a building—**

(a) to a use for any purpose falling within Class B1 (business) of the Schedule to the Use Classes Order from any use failing within Class B2 (general industrial) or B8 (storage and distribution) of that Schedule;

(b) to a use for any purpose failing within Class B8 (storage and distribution) of that Schedule from any use falling within Class B1 (business) or B2 (general industrial).

Development not permitted Development is not permitted by Class B where the change is to or from a use failing within Class B8 of that Schedule, if the change of use relates to more than 235 square metres of floor space in the building.

Class C

Permitted development **C. Development consisting of a change of use to a use falling within Class A2 (financial and professional services) of the Schedule to the Use Classes Order from a use falling within Class A3 (restaurants and cafes), Class A4 (drinking establishments) or Class A5 (hot food takeaways).**

Class D

Permitted development **D. Development consisting of a change of use of any premises with a display window at ground floor level to a use falling within Class A1 (shops) of the Schedule to the Use Classes Order from a use falling within Class A2 (financial and professional services) of that Schedule.**

Class E

Permitted development **E. Development consisting of a change of the use of a building or other land from a use permitted by planning permission granted on an application, to another use which that permission would have specifically authorised when it was granted.**

Development not permitted

E.1 Development is not permitted by Class E if—
(a) the application for planning permission referred to was made before the 5th December 1988;
(b) it would be carried out more than 10 years after the grant of planning permission; or
(c) it would result in the breach of any condition, limitation or specification contained in that planning permission in relation to the use in question.

Class F

Permitted development **F. Development consisting of a change of the use of a building—**

(a) to a mixed use for any purpose within Class A1 (shops) of the Schedule to the Use Classes Order and as a single flat, from a use for any purpose within Class A1 of that Schedule;

(b) to a mixed use for any purpose within Clan A2 (financial and professional services) of the Schedule to the Use Classes Order and as a single flat, from a use for any purpose within Class A2 of that Schedule;

(c) where that building has a display window at ground floor level, to a mixed use for any purpose within Class A1 (shops) of the Schedule to the Use Classes Order and as a single flat, from a use for any purpose within Class A2 (financial and professional services) of that Schedule.

Conditions

F.1 Development permitted by Class F is subject to the following conditions—
(a) some or all of the parts of the building used for any purposes within Class A1 or Class A2, as the case may be, of the Schedule to the Use Classes Order shall be situated on a floor below the part of the building used as a single flat;
(b) where the development consists of a change of use of any building with a display window at ground floor level, the ground floor shall not be used in whole or in part as the single flat;
(c) the single flat shall not be used otherwise than as a dwelling (whether or not as a sole or main residence)—
(i) by a single person or by people living together as a family, or
(ii) by not more than six residents living together as a single household (including a household where care is provided for residents).

Interpretation of Class F

F.2 For the purposes of Class F—
'care' means personal care for people in need of such care by reason of old age, disablement, past or present dependence on alcohol or drugs or past or present mental disorder.

Class G

Permitted development **G. Development consisting of a change of the use of a building—**

(a) to a use for any purpose within Class A1 (shops) of the Schedule to the Use Classes Order from a mixed use for any purpose within Class A1 of that Schedule and as a single flat;

(b) to a use for any purpose within Class A2 (financial and professional services) of the Schedule to the Use Classes Order from a mixed use for any purpose within Class A2 of that Schedule and as a single flat;

(c) where that building has a display window at ground floor level, to a use for any purpose within Class A1 (shops) of the Schedule to the Use Classes Order from a mixed use for any purpose within Class A2 (financial and professional services) of that Schedule and as a single flat.

Development not permitted

G.1 Development is not permitted by Class G unless the part of the building used as a single flat was immediately prior to being so used used for any purpose within Class A1 or Class A2 of the Schedule to the Use Classes Order.

PART 4: TEMPORARY BUILDINGS AND USES

Class A

Permitted development

A. The provision on land of buildings, moveable structures, works, plant or machinery required temporarily in connection with and for the duration of operations being or to be carried out on, in, under or over that land or on land adjoining that land.

Development not permitted

A.1 Development is not permitted by Class A if—

(a) the operations referred to are mining operations, or

(b) planning permission is required for those operations but is not granted or deemed to be granted.

Conditions

A.2 Development is permitted by Class A subject to the conditions that, when the operations have been carried out—

(a) any building, structure, works, plant or machinery permitted by Class A shall be removed, and

(b) any adjoining land on which development permitted by Class A has been carried out shall, as soon as reasonably practicable, be reinstated to its condition before that development was carried out.

Class B

Permitted development

B. The use of any land for any purpose for not more than 28 days in total in any calendar year, of which not more than 14 days in total may be for the purposes referred to in paragraph B.2, and the provision on the land of any moveable structure for the purposes of the permitted use.

Development not permitted

B.1 Development is not permitted by Class B if—

(a) the land in question is a building or is within the curtilage of a building,

(b) the use of the land is for a caravan site,

(c) the land is, or is within, a site of special scientific interest and the use of the land is for—

(i) a purpose referred to in paragraph B.2(b) or other motor sports;

(ii) clay pigeon shooting; or

(iii) any war game,

or

(d) the use of the land is for the display of an advertisement.

Interpretation of Class B

B.2 The purposes mentioned in Class B above are—

(a) the holding of a market;

(b) motor car and motorcycle racing including trials of speed, and practising for these activities.

B.3 In Class B, 'war game' means an enacted, mock or imaginary battle conducted with weapons which are designed not to injure (including smoke bombs, or guns or grenades which fire or spray paint or are otherwise used to mark other participants), but excludes military activities or training exercises organised by or with the authority of the Secretary of State for Defence.

PART 5: CARAVAN SITES

Class A

Permitted development	**A. The use of land, other than a building, as a caravan site in the circumstances referred to in paragraph A.2.**
Condition	A.1 Development is permitted by Class A subject to the condition that the use shall be discontinued when the circumstances specified in paragraph A.2 cease to exist, and all caravans on the site shall be removed as soon as reasonably practicable.
Interpretation of Class A	A.2 The circumstances mentioned in Class A are those specified in paragraphs 2 to 10 of Schedule 1 to the 1960 Act (cases where a caravan site licence is not required), but in relation to those mentioned in paragraph 10 do not include use for winter quarters.

Class B

Permitted development	**B. Development required by the conditions of a site licence for the time being in force under the 1960 Act.**

PART 6: AGRICULTURAL BUILDINGS AND OPERATIONS

Class A

Permitted development

Development on units of 5 hectares or more

A. The carrying out on agricultural land comprised in an agricultural unit of 5 hectares or more in area of—

(a) works for the erection, extension or alteration of a building; or

(b) any excavation or engineering operations,

which are reasonably necessary for the purposes of agriculture within that unit.

Development not permitted

A.1 Development is not permitted by Class A if—

(a) the development would be carried out on a separate parcel of land forming part of the unit which is less than 1 hectare in area;

(b) it would consist of, or include, the erection, extension or alteration of a dwelling;

(c) it would involve the provision of a building, structure or works not designed for agricultural purposes;

(d) the ground area which would be covered by—

(i) any works or structure (other than a fence) for accommodating livestock or any plant or machinery arising from engineering operations; or

(ii) any building erected or extended or altered by virtue of Class A,

would exceed 465 square metres, calculated as described in paragraph D.2 below;

(e) the height of any part of any building, structure or works within 3 kilometres of the perimeter of an aerodrome would exceed 3 metres;
(f) the height of any part of any building, structure or works not within 3 kilometres of the perimeter of an aerodrome would exceed 12 metres;
(g) any part of the development would be within 25 metres of a metalled part of a trunk road or classified road;
(h) it would consist of, or include, the erection or construction of, or the carrying out of any works to, a building, structure or an excavation used or to be used for the accommodation of livestock or for the storage of slurry or sewage sludge where the building, structure or excavation is, or would be, within 400 metres of the curtilage of a protected building; or
 (i) it would involve excavations or engineering operations on or over article 1(6) land which are connected with fish farming.

Conditions

A.2(1) Development is permitted by Class A subject to the following conditions—
(a) where development is carried out within 400 metres of the curtilage of a protected building, any building, structure, excavation or works resulting from the development shall not be used for the accommodation of livestock except in the circumstances described in paragraph D.3 below or for the storage of slurry or sewage sludge;
(b) where the development involves—
 (i) the extraction of any mineral from the land (including removal from any disused railway embankment); or
 (ii) the removal of any mineral from a mineral-working deposit,
 the mineral shall not be moved off the unit;
(c) waste materials shall not be brought on to the land from elsewhere for deposit except for use in works described in Class A(a) or in the provision of a hard surface and any materials so brought shall be incorporated forthwith into the building or works in question.

(2) Subject to paragraph (3), development consisting of—
(a) the erection, extension or alteration of a building;
(b) the formation or alteration of a private way;
(c) the carrying out of excavations or the deposit of waste material (where the relevant area, as defined in paragraph D.4 below, exceeds 0.5 hectare); or
(d) the placing or assembly of a tank in any waters, is permitted by Class A subject to the following conditions–
 (i) the developer shall, before beginning the development, apply to the local planning authority for a determination as to whether the prior approval of the authority will be required to the siting, design and external appearance of the building, the siting and means of construction of the private way, the siting of the excavation or deposit or the siting and appearance of the tank, as the case may be;
 (ii) the application shall be accompanied by a written description of the proposed development and of the materials to be used and a plan indicating the site together with any fee required to be paid;
 (iii) the development shall not be begun before the occurrence of one of the following—
  (aa) the receipt by the applicant from the local planning authority of a written notice of their determination that such prior approval is not required;
  (bb) where the local planning authority give the applicant notice

within 28 days following the date of receiving his application of their determination that such prior approval is required, the giving of such approval; or

(cc) the expiry of 28 days following the date on which the application was received by the local planning authority without the local planning authority making any determination as to whether such approval is required or notifying the applicant of their determination;

(iv) (aa) where the local planning authority give the applicant notice that such prior approval is required the applicant shall display a site notice by site display on or near the land on which the proposed development is to be carried out, leaving the notice in position for not less than 21 days in the period of 28 days from the date on which the local planning authority gave the notice to the applicant;

(bb) where the site notice is, without any fault or intention of the applicant, removed, obscured or defaced before the period of 21 days referred to in sub-paragraph (aa) has elapsed, he shall be treated as having complied with the requirements of that sub-paragraph if he has taken reasonable steps for protection of the notice and, if need be, its replacement;

(v) the development shall, except to the extent that the local planning authority otherwise agree in writing, be carried out—

(aa) where prior approval is required, in accordance with the details approved;

(bb) where prior approval is not required, in accordance with the details submitted with the application; and

(vi) the development shall be carried out—

(aa) where approval has been given by the local planning authority, within a period of five years from the date on which approval was given;

(bb) in any other case, within a period of five years from the date on which the local planning authority were given the information referred to in sub-paragraph (d)(ii).

(3) The conditions in paragraph (2) do not apply to the extension or alteration of a building if the building is not on article 1(6) land except in the case of a significant extension or a significant alteration.

(4) Development consisting of the significant extension or the significant alteration of a building may only be carried out once by virtue of Class A(a).

(5) Where development consists of works for the erection, significant extension or significant alteration of a building and

(a) the use of the building or extension for the purposes of agriculture within the unit permanently ceases within ten years from the date on which the development was substantially completed; and

(b) planning permission has not been granted on an application, or has not been deemed to be granted under Part III of the Act, for development for purposes other than agriculture, within three years from the date on which the use of the building or extension for the purposes of agriculture within the unit permanently ceased,

then, unless the local planning authority have otherwise agreed in writing, the building or, in the case of development consisting on an extension, the extension, shall be removed from the land and the land shall, so far as is practicable, be restored to its condition before the development took place, or to such condition as may have been agreed in writing between the local planning authority and the developer.

(6) Where an appeal has been made, under the Act, in relation to an application for development described in paragraph 5(b), within the period described in that pargraph, that period shall be extended until the appeal is finally determined or withdrawn.

(7) Where development is permitted by Class A(a), the developer shall notify the local planning authority, in writing and within 7 days, of the date on which the development was substantially completed.

Class B

Permitted development — **Development on units of less than 5 hectares**

B. The carrying out on agricultural land comprised in an agricultural unit of not less than 0.4 but less than 5 hectares in area of development consisting of—

(a) the extension or alteration of an agricultural building;

(b) the installation of additional or replacement plant or machinery;

(c) the provision, rearrangement or replacement of a sewer, main, pipe, cable or other apparatus;

(d) the provision, rearrangement or replacement of a private way;

(e) the provision of a hard surface;

(f) the deposit of waste; or

(g) the carrying out of any of the following operations in connection with fish farming, namely, repairing ponds and raceways; the installation of grading machinery, aeration equipment or flow meters and any associated channel; the dredging of ponds; and the replacement of tanks and nets, where the development is reasonably necessary for the purposes of agriculture within the unit.

Development not permitted

B.1 Development is not permitted by Class B if—

(a) the development would be carried out on a separate parcel of land forming part of the unit which is less than 0.4 hectare in area;

(b) the external appearance of the premises would be materially affected;

(c) any part of the development would be within 25 metres of a metalled part of a trunk road or classified road;

(d) it would consist of, or involve, the carrying out of any works to a building or structure used or to be used for the accommodation of livestock or the storage of slurry or sewage sludge where the building or structure is within 400 metres of the curtilage of a protected building; or

(e) it would relate to fish farming and would involve the placing or assembly of a tank on land or in any waters or the construction of a pond in which fish may be kept or an increase (otherwise than by the removal of silt) in the size of any tank or pond in which fish may be kept.

B.2 Development is not permitted by Class B(a) if—

(a) the height of any building would be increased;

(b) the cubic content of the original building would be increased by more than 10%;

(c) any part of any new building would be more than 30 metres from the original building;

(d) the development would involve the extension, alteration or provision of a dwelling;

(e) any part of the development would be carried out within 5 metres of any boundary of the unit; or

(f) the ground area of any building extended by virtue of Class B(a) would exceed 465 square metres.

B.3 Development is not permitted by Class B(b) if—

(a) the height of any additional plant or machinery within 3 kilometres of the perimeter of an aerodrome would exceed 3 metres;

(b) the height of any additional plant or machinery not within 3 kilometres of the perimeter of an aerodrome would exceed 12 metres;

(c) the height of any replacement plant or machinery would exceed that of the plant or machinery being replaced; or

(d) the area to be covered by the development would exceed 465 square metres calculated as described in paragraph D.2 below.

B.4 Development is not permitted by Class B(e) if the area to be covered by the development would exceed 465 square metres calculated as described in paragraph D.2 below.

Conditions

B.5 Development permitted by Class B and carried out within 400 metres of the curtilage of a protected building is subject to the condition that any building which is extended or altered, or any works resulting from the development, shall not be used for the accommodation of livestock except in the circumstances described in paragraph D.3 below or for the storage of slurry or sewage sludge.

B.6 Development consisting of the extension or alteration of a building situated on article 1(6) land or the provision, rearrangement or replacement of a private way on such land is permitted subject to—

(a) the condition that the developer shall, before beginning the development, apply to the local planning authority for a determination as to whether the prior approval of the authority will be required to the siting, design and external appearance of the building as extended or altered or the siting and means of construction of the private way; and

(b) the conditions set out in paragraphs A.2(2)(ii) to (vi) above.

B.7 Development is permitted by Class B(f) subject to the following conditions—

(a) that waste materials are not brought on to the land from elsewhere for deposit unless they are for use in works described in Class B(a), (d) or (e) and are incorporated forthwith into the building or works in question; and

(b) that the height of the surface of the land will not be materially increased by the deposit.

B.8 Development is permitted by Class B(a) subject to the following conditions—

(a) Where development consists of works for the significant extension or significant alteration of a building and

(i) the use of the building or extension for the purposes of agriculture within the unit permanently ceases within ten years from the date on which the development was substantially completed; and

(ii) planning permission has not been granted on an application, or has not been deemed to be granted under Part III of the Act, for development for purposes other than agriculture, within three years from the date on which the use of the building or extension for the purposes of agriculture within the unit permanently ceased,

then, unless the local planning authority have otherwise agreed in writing, the extension, in the case of development consisting of an extension, shall be removed from the land and the land shall, so far as is practicable, be restored to its condition before the development took place, or to such condition as may have been agreed in writing between the local planning authority and the developer.

(b) Where an appeal has been made, under the Act, in relation to an application for development described in paragraph B.8(a)(ii), within the period described in that paragraph, that period shall be extended until the appeal is finally determined or withdrawn.

(c) The developer shall notify the local planning authority in writing and within 7 days, of the date on which the development was substantially completed.

Class C

Permitted development — **Mineral working for agricultural purposes**

C. The winning and working on land held or occupied with land used for the purposes of agriculture of any minerals reasonably necessary for agricultural purposes within the agricultural unit of which it forms part.

Development not permitted — C.1 Development is not permitted by Class C if any excavation would be made within 25 metres of a metalled part of a trunk road or classified road.

Condition — C.2 Development is permitted by Class C subject to the condition that no mineral extracted during the course of the operation shall be moved to any place outside the land from which it was extracted, except to land which is held or occupied with that land and is used for the purposes of agriculture.

Interpretation of Part 6 — D.1 For the purposes of Part 6—

'agricultural land' means land which, before development permitted by this Part is carried out, is land in use for agriculture and which is so used for the purposes of a trade or business, and excludes any dwellinghouse or garden;

'agricultural unit' means agricultural land which is occupied as a unit for the purposes of agriculture, including—

(a) any dwelling or other building on that land occupied for the purpose of farming the land by the person who occupies the unit, or

(b) any dwelling on that land occupied by a farmworker;

'building' does not include anything resulting from engineering operations;

'fish farming' means the breeding, rearing or keeping of fish or shellfish (which includes any kind of crustacean and mollusc);

'livestock' includes fish or shellfish which are farmed;

'protected building' means any permanent building which is normally occupied by people or would be so occupied, if it were in use for purposes for which it is apt; but does not include—

(i) a building within the agricultural unit; or

(ii) a dwelling or other building on another agricultural unit which is used for or in connection with agriculture;

'significant extension' and 'significant alteration' mean any extension or alteration of the building where the cubic content of the original building would be exceeded by more than 10% or the height of the building as extended or altered would exceed the height of the original building;

'slurry' means animal faeces and urine (whether or not water has been added for handling); and

'tank' includes any cage and any other structure for use in fish farming.

D.2 For the purposes of Part 6—

(a) an area calculated as described in this paragraph comprises the ground area which would be covered by the proposed development, together with the ground area of any building (other than a dwelling), or any structure, works, plant, machinery, ponds or tanks within the same unit which are being provided or have been provided within the preceding two years and any part of which would be within 90 metres of the proposed development;

(b) 400 metres is to be measured along the ground.

D.3 The circumstances referred to in paragraphs A.2(1)(a) and B.5 are—

(a) that no other suitable building or structure, 400 metres or more from the curtilage of a protected building, is available to accommodate the livestock; and

(b) (i) that the need to accommodate the livestock arises from—

(aa) quarantine requirements; or

(bb) an emergency due to another building or structure in which the livestock could otherwise be accommodated being unavailable because it has been damaged or destroyed by fire, flood or storm;

or

(ii) in the case of animals normally kept out of doors, they require temporary accommodation in a building or other structure—

(aa) because they are sick or giving birth or newly born; or

(bb) to provide shelter against extreme weather conditions.

D.4 For the purposes of paragraph A.2(2)(c), the relevant area is the area of the proposed excavation or the area on which it is proposed to deposit waste together with the aggregate of the areas of all other excavations within the unit which have not been filled and of all other parts of the unit on or under which waste has been deposited and has not been removed.

D.5 In paragraph A.2(2)(iv), 'site notice'meansa notice containing—

(a) the name of the applicant,

(b) the address or location of the proposed development,

(c) a description of the proposed development and of the materials to be used,

(d) a statement that the prior approval of the authority will be required to the siting, design and external appearance of the building, the siting and means of construction of the private way, the siting of the excavation or deposit or the siting and appearance of the tank, as the case may be,

(e) the name and address of the local planning authority, and which is signed and dated by or on behalf of the applicant.

D.6 For the purposes of Class B—

(a) the erection of any additional building within the curtilage of another building is to be treated as the extension of that building and the additional building is not to be treated as an original building;

(b) where two or more original buildings are within the same curtilage and are used for the same undertaking they are to be treated as a single original building in making any measurement in connection with the extension or alteration of either of them.

D.7 In Class C, 'the purposes of agriculture' includes fertilising land used for the purposes of agriculture and the maintenance, improvement or alteration of any buildings, structures or works occupied or used for such purposes on land so used.

PART 7: FORESTRY BUILDINGS AND OPERATIONS

Class A

Permitted development

A. The carrying out on land used for the purposes of forestry, including afforestation, of development reasonably necessary for those purposes consisting of—

(a) works for the erection, extension or alteration of a building;

(b) the formation, alteration or maintenance of private ways;

(c) operations on that land, or on land held or occupied with that land, to obtain the materials required for the formation, alteration or maintenance of such ways;

(d) other operations (not including engineering or mining operations).

Development not permitted

A.1 Development is not permitted by Class A if—

(a) it would consist of or include the provision or alteration of a dwelling;

(b) the height of any building or works within 3 kilometres of the perimeter of an aerodrome would exceed 3 metres in height; or

(c) any part of the development would be within 25 metres of the metalled portion of a trunk road or classified road.

A.2(1) Subject to paragraph (3), development consisting of the erection of a building or the extension or alteration of a building or the formation or alteration of a private way is permitted by Class A subject to the following conditions—

(a) the developer shall, before beginning the development, apply to the local planning authority for a determination as to whether the prior approval of the authority will be required to the siting, design and external appearance of the building or, as the case may be, the siting and means of construction of the private way;

(b) the application shall be accompanied by a written description of the proposed development, the materials to be used and a plan indicating the site together with any fee required to be paid;

(c) the development shall not be begun before the occurrence of one of the following—

(i) the receipt by the applicant from the local planning authority of a written notice of their determination that such prior approval is not required;

(ii) where the local planning authority give the applicant notice within 28 days following the date of receiving his application of their determination that such prior approval is required, the giving of such approval;

(iii) the expiry of 28 days following the date on which the application was received by the local planning authority without the local planning authority making any determination as to whether such approval is required or notifying the applicant of their determination;

(d) (i) where the local planning authority give the applicant notice that such prior approval is required the applicant shall display a site notice by site display on or near the land on which the proposed development is to be carried out, leaving the notice in position for not less than 21 days in the period of 28 days from the date on which the local planning authority gave the notice to the applicant;

(ii) where the site notice is, without any fault or intention of the applicant, removed, obscured or defaced before the period of 21 days referred to in sub-paragraph (i) has elapsed, he shall be treated as having complied with the requirements of that sub-paragraph if he has taken reasonable steps for protection of the notice and, if need be, its replacement;

(e) the development shall, except to the extent that the local planning authority otherwise agree in writing, be carried out—

(i) where prior approval is required, in accordance with the details approved;

(ii) where prior approval is not required, in accordance with the details submitted with the application;

(f) the development shall be carried out—

(i) where approval has been given by the local planning authority, within a period of five years from the date on which approval was given,

(ii) in any other case, within a period of five years from the date on which the local planning authority were given the information referred to in sub-paragraph (b).

(2) In the case of development consisting of the significant extension or the significant alteration of the building such development may be carried out only once.

(3) Paragraph (1) does not preclude the extension or alteration of a building if the building is not on article 1(6) land except in the case of a significant extension or a significant alteration.

Interpretation of class A

A.3 For the purposes of Class A—

'significant extension' and 'significant alteration' mean any extension or alteration of the building where the cubic content of the original building would be exceeded by more than 10% or the height of the building as extended or altered would exceed the height of the original building; and

'site notice' means a notice containing—

(a) the name of the applicant,

(b) the address or location of the proposed development,

(c) a description of the proposed development and of the materials to be used,

(d) a statement that the prior approval of the authority will be required to the siting, design and external appearance of the building or, as the case may be, the siting and means of construction of the private way,

and (e) the name and address of the local planning authority, and which is signed and dated by or on behalf of the applicant.

PART 8: INDUSTRIAL AND WAREHOUSE DEVELOPMENT

Class A

Permitted development — **A. The extension or alteration of an industrial building or a warehouse.**

Development not permitted

A.1 Development is not permitted by Class A if—

(a) the building as extended or altered is to be used for purposes other than those of the undertaking concerned;

(b) the building is to be used for a purpose other than—

(i) in the case of an industrial building, the carrying out of an industrial process or the provision of employee facilities;

(ii) in the case of a warehouse, storage or distribution or the provision of employee facilities;

(c) the height of the building as extended or altered would exceed the height of the original building;

(d) the cubic content of the original building would be exceeded by more than—

(i) 10%, in respect of developmentonany article 1(5) land, or

(ii) 25%, in any other case;

(e) the floor space of the original building would be exceeded by more than—

(i) 500 square metres in respect of development on any article 1(5) land, or

(ii) 1,000 square metres in any other case;

(f) the external appearance of the premises of the undertaking concerned would be materially affected;

(g) any part of the development would be carried out within 5 metres of any boundary of the curtilage of the premises; or

(h) the development would lead to a reduction in the space available for the parking or turning of vehicles.

Conditions

A.2 Development is permitted by Class A subject to the conditions that any building extended or altered—

(a) shall only be used—

(i) in the case of an industrial building, for the carrying out of an industrial process for the purposes of the undertaking or the provision of employee facilities;

(ii) in the case of a warehouse, for storage or distribution for the purposes of the undertaking or the provision of employee facilities;

(b) shall not be used to provide employee facilities between 7.00 p.m. and 6.30 a.m. for employees other than those present at the premises of the undertaking for the purpose of their employment;

(c) shall not be used to provide employee facilities if a notifiable quantity of a hazardous substance is present at the premises of the undertaking.

Interpretation of Class A

A.3 For the purposes of Class A—

(a) the erection of any additional building within the curtilage of another building (whether by virtue of Class A or otherwise) and used in connection with it is to be treated as the extension of that building, and the additional building is not to be treated as an original building;

(b) where two or more original buildings are within the same curtilage and are used for the same undertaking, they are to be treated as a single original building in making any measurement;

(c) 'employee facilities' means social, care or recreational facilities provided for employees of the undertaking, including creche facilities provided for the children of such employees.

Class B

Permitted development **B. Development carried out on industrial land for the purposes of an industrial process consisting of—**

(a) the installation of additional or replacement plant or machinery,

(b) the provision, rearrangement or replacement of a sewer, main, pipe, cable or other apparatus, or

(c) the provision, rearrangement or replacement of a private way, private railway, siding or conveyor.

Development not permitted B.1 Development described in Class B(a) is not permitted if—

(a) it would materially affect the external appearance of the premises of the undertaking concerned, or

(b) any plant or machinery would exceed a height of 15 metres above ground level or the height of anything replaced, whichever is the greater.

Interpretation of Class B B.2 In Class B, 'industrial land' means land used for the carrying out of an industrial process, including land used for the purposes of an industrial undertaking as a dock, harbour or quay, but does not include land in or adjacent to and occupied together with a mine.

Class C

Permitted development **C. The provision of a hard surface within the curtilage of an industrial building or warehouse to be used for the purpose of the undertaking concerned.**

Class D

Permitted development **D. The deposit of waste material resulting from an industrial process on any land comprised in a site which was used for that purpose on 1st July 1948 whether or not the superficial area or the height of the deposit is extended as a result.**

Development not permitted D.1 Development is not permitted by Class D if—

(a) the waste material is or includes material resulting from the winning and working of minerals, or

(b) the use on 1st July 1948 was for the deposit of material resulting from the winning and working of minerals.

Interpretation of Part 8 E. For the purposes of Part 8, in Classes A and C—

'industrial building' means a building used for the carrying out of an industrial process and includes a building used for the carrying out of such a process on land used as a dock, harbour or quay for the purposes of an industrial undertaking but does not include a building on land in or adjacent to and occupied together with a mine; and

'warehouse' means a building used for any purpose within Class B8 (storage or distribution) of the Schedule to the Use Classes Order but does not include a building on land in or adjacent to and occupied together with a mine.

PART 9: REPAIRS TO UNADOPTED STREETS AND PRIVATE WAYS

Class A

Permitted development **A. The carrying out on land within the boundaries of an unadopted street or private way of works required for the maintenance or improvement of the street or way.**

Interpretation of Class A A.1 For the purposes of Class A—

'unadopted street' means a street not being a highway maintainable at the public expense within the meaning of the Highways Act 1980.

PART 10: REPAIRS TO SERVICES

Class A

Permitted development **The carrying out of any works for the purposes of inspecting, repairing or renewing any sewer, main, pipe, cable or other apparatus, including breaking open any land for that purpose.**

PART 11: DEVELOPMENT UNDER LOCAL OR PRIVATE ACTS OR ORDERS

Class A

Permitted development **A. Development authorised by—**

(a) a local or private Act of Parliament,

(b) an order approved by both Houses of Parliament, or

(c) an order under section 14 or 16 of the Harbours Act 1964 (orders for securing harbour efficiency etc., and orders conferring powers for improvement, construction etc. of harbours)

which designates specifically the nature of the development authorised and the land upon which it may be carried out.

Condition A.1 Development is not permitted by Class A if it consists of or includes—

(a) the erection, construction, alteration or extension of any building, bridge, aqueduct, pier or dam, or

(b) the formation, laying out or alteration of a means of access to any highway used by vehicular traffic,

unless the prior approval of the appropriate authority to the detailed plans and specifications is first obtained.

Prior approvals A.2 The prior approval referred to in paragraph A.1 is not to be refused by the appropriate authority nor are conditions to be imposed unless they are satisfied that—

(a) the development (other than the provision of or works carried out to a dam) ought to be and could reasonably be carried out elsewhere on the land; or

(b) the design or exteral appearance of any building, bridge, aqueduct, pier or dam would injure the amenity of the neighbourhood and is reasonably capable of modification to avoid such injury.

Interpretation of Class A A.3 In Class A, 'appropriate authority' means—

(a) in Greater London or a metropolitan county, the local planning authority,

(b) in a National Park in England, outside a metropolitan county, the county planning authority,
(c) in any other case in England, the district planning authority,
(d) in Wales, the local planning authority.

PART 12: DEVELOPMENT BY LOCAL AUTHORITIES

Class A

Permitted development

A. The erection or construction and the maintenance, improvement or other alteration by a local authority or by an urban development corporation of—

(a) any small ancillary building, works or equipment on land belonging to or maintained by them required for the purposes of any function exercised by them on that land otherwise than as statutory undertakers;

(b) lamp standards, information kiosks, passenger shelters, public shelters and seats, telephone boxes, fire alarms, public drinking fountains, horse troughs, refuse bins or baskets, barriers for the control of people waiting to enter public service vehicles, and similar structures or works required in connection with the operation of any public service administered by them.

Interpretation of Class A

A.1 For the purposes of Class A—

'urban development corporation' has the same meaning as in Part XVI of the Local Government, Planning and Land Act 1980 (urban development).

A.2 The reference in Class A to any small ancillary building, works or equipment is a reference to any ancillary building, works or equipment not exceeding 4 metres in height or 200 cubic metres in capacity.

Class B

Permitted development

B. The deposit by a local authority of waste material on any land comprised in a site which was used for that purpose on 1st July 1948 whether or not the superficial area or the height of the deposit is extended as a result.

Development not permitted

B.1 Development is not permitted by Class B if the waste material is or includes material resulting from the winning and working of minerals.

Interpretation of Part 12

C.1 For the purposes of Part 12—

local authority' includes a parish or community council.

PART 13: DEVELOPMENT BY LOCAL HIGHWAY AUTHORITIES

Class A

Permitted development

A. The carrying out by a local highway authority—

(a) on land within the boundaries of a road, of any works required for the maintenance or improvement of the road, where such works involve development by virtue of section 55(2)(b) of the Act; or

(b) on land outside but adjoining the boundary of an existing highway of works required for or incidental to the maintenance or improvement of the highway.

PART 14: DEVELOPMENT BY DRAINAGE BODIES

Class A

Permitted development

A. Development by a drainage body in, on or under any watercourse or land drainage works and required in connection with the improvement, maintenance or repair of that watercourse or those works.

Interpretation of Class A

A.1 For the purposes of Class A—

'drainage body' has the same meaning as in section 72(1) of the Land Drainage Act 1991 (interpretation) other than the National Rivers Authority.

PART 15: DEVELOPMENT BY THE ENVIRONMENT AGENCY

Class A

Permitted development

A. Development by the Environment Agency, for the purposes of their functions, consisting of—

(a) development not above ground level required in connection with conserving, redistributing or augmenting water resources,

(b) development in, on or under any watercourse or land drainage works and required in connection with the improvement, maintenanceor repair of that watercourse or those works,

(c) the provision of a building, plant, machinery or apparatus in, on, over or under land for the purpose of survey or investigation,

(d) the maintenance, improvement or repair of works for measuring the flow in any watercourse or channel,

(e) any works authorised by or required in connection with an order made under section 73 of the Water Resources Act 1991 (power to make ordinary and emergency drought orders),

(f) any other development in, on, over or under their operational land, other than the provision of a building but including the extension or alteration of a building.

Development not permitted

A.1 Development is not permitted by Class A if—

(a) in the case of any Class A(a) development, it would include the construction of a reservoir,

(b) in the case of any Class A(f) development, it would consist of or include the extension or alteration of a building so that—

(i) its design or external appearance would be materially affected,

(ii) the height of the original building would be exceeded, or the cubic content of the original building would be exceeded by more than 25%, or

(iii) the floor space of the original building would be exceeded by more than 1,000 square metres,

or

(c) in the case of any Class A(f) development, it would consist of the installation or erection of any plant or machinery exceeding 15 metres in height or the height of anything it replaces, whichever is the greater.

Condition — A.2 Development is permitted by Class A(c) subject to the condition that, on completion of the survey or investigation, or at the expiration of six months from the commencement of the development concerned, whichever is the sooner, all such operations shall cease and all such buildings, plant, machinery and apparatus shall be removed and the land restored as soon as reasonably practicable to its former condition (or to any other condition which may be agreed with the local planning authority).

PART 16: DEVELOPMENT BY OR ON BEHALF OF SEWERAGE UNDERTAKERS

Class A

Permitted development

A. Development by or on behalf of a sewerage undertaker consisting of—

(a) development not above ground level required in connection with the provision, improvement, maintenance or repair of a sewer, outfall pipe, sludge main or associated apparatus;

(b) the provision of a building, plant, machinery or apparatus in, on, over or under land for the purpose of survey or investigation;

(c) the maintenance, improvement or repair of works for measuring the flow in any watercourse or channel;

(d) any works authorised by or required in connection with an order made under section 73 of the Water Resources Act 1991 (power to make ordinary and emergency drought orders);

(e) any other development in, on, over or under their operational land, other than the provision of a building but including the extension or alteration of a building.

Development not permitted — A.1 Development is not permitted by Class A(e) if—

(a) it would consist of or include the extension or alteration of a building so that—

(i) its design or external appearance would be materially affected;

(ii) the height of the original building would be exceeded, or the cubic content of the original building would be exceeded, by more than 25%; or

(iii) the floor space of the original building would be exceeded by more than 1,000 square metres;

or

(b) it would consist of the installation or erection of any plant or machinery exceeding 15 metres in height or the height of anything it replaces, whichever is the greater.

Condition — A.2 Development is permitted by Class A(b) subject to the condition that, on completion of the survey or investigation, or at the expiration of 6 months from the commencement of the development concerned, whichever is the sooner, all such operations shall cease and all such buildings, plant, machinery and apparatus shall be removed and the land restored as soon as reasonably practicable to its former condition (or to any other condition which may be agreed with the local planning authority).

Interpretation of Class A

A.3 For the purposes of Class A—

'associated apparatus', in relation to any sewer, main or pipe, means pumps, machinery or apparatus associated with the relevant sewer, main or pipe;

'sludge main' means a pipe or system of pipes (together with any pumps or other machinery or apparatus associated with it) for the conveyance of the residue of water or sewage treated in a water or sewage treatment works as the case may be, including final effluent or the products of the dewatering or incineration of such residue, or partly for any of those purposes and partly for the conveyance of trade effluent or its residue.

PART 17: DEVELOPMENT BY STATUTORY UNDERTAKERS

Class A

Permitted development

Railway or light railway undertakings

A. Development by railway undertakers on their operational land, required in connection with the movement of traffic by rail.

Development not permitted

A.1 Development is not permitted by Class A if it consists of or includes—

(a) the construction of a railway,

(b) the construction or erection of a hotel, railway station or bridge, or

(c) the construction or erection otherwise than wholly within a railway station of—

(i) an office, residential or educational building, or a building used for an industrial process, or

(ii) a car park, shop, restaurant, garage, petrol filling station or other building or structure provided under transport legislation.

Interpretation of Class A

A.2 For the purposes of Class A, references to the construction or erection of any building or structure include references to the reconstruction or alteration of a building or structure where its design or external appearance would be materially affected.

Class B

Permitted development

Dock, pier, harbour, water transport, canal or inland navigation undertakings

B. Development on operational land by statutory undertakers or their lessees in respect of dock, pier, harbour, water transport, or canal or inland navigation undertakings, required—

(a) for the purposes of shipping, or

(b) in connection with the embarking, disembarking, loading, discharging or transport of passengers, livestock or goods at a dock, pier or harbour, or with the movement of traffic by canal or inland navigation or by any railway forming part of the undertaking.

Development not permitted

B.1 Development is not permitted by Class B if it consists of or includes—

(a) the construction or erection of a hotel, or of a bridge or other building not required in connection with the handling of traffic,

(b) the construction or erection otherwise than wholly within the limits of a dock, pier or harbour of—

(i) an educational building, or

(ii) a car park, shop, restaurant, garage, petrol filling station or other building provided under transport legislation.

Interpretation of Class B

B.2 For the purposes of Class B, references to the construction or erection of any building or structure include references to the reconstruction or alteration of a building or structure where its design or external appearance would be materially affected, and the reference to operational land includes land designated by an order made under section 14 or 16 of the Harbours Act 1964 (orders for securing harbour efficiency etc., and orders conferring powers for improvement, construction etc. of harbours), and which has come into force, whether or not the order was subject to the provisions of the Statutory Orders (Special Procedure) Act 1945.

Class C

Permitted development

Works to inland waterways

C. The improvement, maintenance or repair of an inland waterway (other than a commercial waterway or cruising waterway) to which section 104 of the Transport Act 1968 (classification of the Board's waterways) applies, and the repair or maintenance of a culvert, weir, lock, aqueduct, sluice, reservoir, let-off valve or other work used in connection with the control and operation of such a waterway.

Class D

Permitted development

Dredgings

D. The use of any land by statutory undertakers in respect of dock, pier, harbour, water transport, canal or inland navigation undertakings for the spreading of any dredged material.

Class E

Permitted development

Water or hydraulic power undertakings

E. Development for the purposes of their undertaking by statutory undertakers for the supply of water or hydraulic power consisting of—

(a) development not above ground level required in connection with the supply of water or for conserving, redistributing or augmenting water resources, or for the conveyance of water treatment sludge,

(b) development in, on or under any watercourse and required in connection with the improvement or maintenance of that watercourse,

(c) the provision of a building, plant, machinery or apparatus in, on, over or under land for the purpose of survey or investigation,

(d) the maintenance, improvement or repair of works for measuring the flow in any watercourse or channel,

(e) the installation in a water distribution system of a booster station, valve house, meter or switch-gear house,

(f) any works authorised by or required in connection with an order made under section 73 of the Water Resources Act 1991 (power to make ordinary and emergency drought orders),

(g) any other development in, on, over or under operational land other than the provision of a building but including the extension or alteration of a building.

Development not permitted

E.1 Development is not permitted by Class E if—

(a) in the case of any Class E(a) development, it would include the construction of a reservoir,

(b) in the case of any Class E(e) development involving the installation of a station or house exceeding 29 cubic metres in capacity, that installation is carried out at or above ground level or under a highway used by vehicular traffic,

(c) in the case of any Class E(g) development, it would consist of or include the extension or alteration of a building so that—

(i) its design or external appearance would be materially affected;

(ii) the height of the original building would be exceeded, or the cubic content of the original building would be exceeded by more than 25%, or

(iii) the floor space of the original building would be exceeded by more than 1,000 square metres, or

(d) in the case of any Class E(g) development, it would consist of the installation or erection of any plant or machinery exceeding 15 metres in height or the height of anything it replaces, whichever is the greater.

Condition

E.2 Development is permitted by Class E(c) subject to the condition that, on completion of the survey or investigation, or at the expiration of six months from the commencement of the development, whichever is the sooner, all such operations shall cease and all such buildings, plant, machinery and apparatus shall be removed and the land restored as soon as reasonably practicable to its former condition (or to any other condition which may be agreed with the local planning authority).

Class F

Permitted development

Public gas transporters

F. Development by a public gas supplier required for the purposes of its undertaking consisting of—

(a) the laying underground of mains, pipes or other apparatus;

(b) the installation in a gas distribution system of apparatus for measuring, recording, controlling or varying the pressure, flow or volume of gas, and structures for housing such apparatus;

(c) the construction in any storage area or protective area specified in an order made under section 4 of the Gas Act 1965 (storage authorisation orders), of boreholes, and the erection or construction in any such area of any plant or machinery required in connection with the construction of such boreholes;

(d) the placing and storage on land of pipes and other apparatus to be included in a main or pipe which is being or is about to be laid or constructed in pursuance of planning permission granted or deemed to be granted under Part III of the Act (control over development);

(e) the erection on operational land of the public gas transporter of a building solely for the protection of plant or machinery;

(f) any other development carried out in, on, over or under the operational land of the public gas transporter.

Development not permitted

F.1 Development is not permitted by Class F if—

(a) in the case of any Class F(b) development involving the installation of a structure for housing apparatus exceeding 29 cubic metres in capacity, that installation would be carried out at or above ground level, or under a highway used by vehicular traffic,

(b) in the case of any Class F(c) development—

(i) the borehole is shown in an order approved by the Secretary of State for Trade and Industry for the purpose of section 4(6) of the Gas Act 1965; or

(ii) any plant or machinery would exceed 6 metres in height, or

(c) in the case of any Class F(e) development, the building would exceed 15 metres in height, or

(d) in the case of any Class F(f) development—

(i) it would consist of or include the erection of a building, or the reconstruction or alteration of a building where its design or external appearance would be materially affected;

(ii) it would involve the installation of plant or machinery exceeding 15 metres in height, or capable without the carrying out of additional works of being extended to a height exceeding 15 metres; or

(iii) it would consist of or include the replacement of any plant or machinery, by plant or machinery exceeding 15 metres in height or exceeding the height of the plant or machinery replaced, whichever is the greater.

Conditions

F.2 Development is permitted by Class F subject to the following conditions—

(a) in the case of any Class F(a) development, not less than eight weeks before the beginning of operations to lay a notifiable pipe-line, the public gas transporter shall give notice in writing to the local planning authority of its intention to carry out that development, identifying the land under which the pipe-line is to be laid,

(b) in the case of any Class F(d) development, on completion of the laying or construction of the main or pipe, or at the expiry of a period of nine months from the beginning of the development, whichever is the sooner, any pipes or other apparatus still stored on the land shall be removed and the land restored as soon as reasonably practicable to its condition before the development took place (or to any other condition which may be agreed with the local planning authority),

(c) in the case of any Class F(e) development, approval of the details of the design and external appearance of the building shall be obtained, before the development is begun, from—

(i) in Greater London or a metropolitan county, the local planning authority,

(ii) in a National Park in England, outside a metropolitan county, the county planning authority,

(iii) in any other case in England, the district planning authority,

(iv) in Wales, the local planning authority.

Class G

Permitted development

Electricity undertakings

G. Development by statutory undertakers for the generation, transmission or supply of electricity for the purposes of their undertaking consisting of—

(a) the installation or replacement in, on, over or under land of an electric line and the construction of shafts and tunnels and the installation or replacement of feeder or service pillars or transforming or switching stations or chambers reasonably necessary in connection with an electric line;

(b) the installation or replacement of any telecommunications line which connects any part of an electric line to any electrical plant or building, and the installation or replacement of any support for any such line;

(c) the sinking of boreholes to ascertain the nature of the subsoil and the installation of any plant or machinery reasonably necessary in connection with such boreholes;

(d) the extension or alteration of buildings on operational land;

(e) the erection on operational land of the undertaking or a building solely for the protection of plant or machinery;

(f) any other development carried out in, on, over or under the operational land of the undertaking.

Development not permitted

G.1 Development is not permitted by Class G if—

(a) in the case of any Class G(a) development—

(i) it would consist of or include the installation or replacement of an electric line to which section 37(1) of the Electricity Act 1989 (consent required for overhead lines) applies; or

(ii) it would consist of or include the installation or replacement at or above ground level or under a highway used by vehicular traffic, of a chamber for housing apparatus and the chamber would exceed 29 cubic metres in capacity;

(b) in the case of any Class G(b) development—

(i) the development would take place in a National Park, an area of outstanding natural beauty, or a site of special scientific interest;

(ii) the height of any support would exceed 15 metres; or

(iii) the telecommunications line would exceed 1,000 metres in length;

(c) in the case of any Class G(d) development—

(i) the height of the original building would be exceeded;

(ii) the cubic content of the original building would be exceeded by more than 25% or, in the case of any building on article 1(5) land, by more than 10%, or

(iii) the floor space of the original building would be exceeded by more than 1,000 square metres or, in the case of any building on article 1(5) land, by more than 500 square metres;

(d) in the case of any Class G(e) development, the building would exceed 15 metres in height, or

(e) in the case of any Class G(f) development, it would consist of or include—

(i) the erection of a building, or the reconstruction or alteration of a building where its design or external appearance would be materially affected, or

(ii) the installation or erection by way of addition or replacement of any plant or machinery exceeding 15 metres in height or the height of any plant or machinery replaced, whichever is the greater.

Conditions

G.2 Development is permitted by Class G subject to the following conditions—

(a) in the case of any Class G(a) development consisting of or including the replacement of an existing electric line, compliance with any conditions contained in a planning permission relating to the height, design or position of the existing electric line which are capable of being applied to the replacement line;

(b) in the case of any Class G(a) development consisting of or including the installation of a temporary electric line providing a diversion for an existing electric line, on the ending of the diversion or at the end of a period of six months from the completion of the installation (whichever is the sooner) the temporary electric line shall be removed and the land on which any operations have been carried out to install that line shall be restored as soon as reasonably practicable to its condition before the installation took place;

(c) in the case of any Class G(c) development, on the completion of that development, or at the end of a period of six months from the beginning of that development (whichever is the sooner) any plant or machinery installed shall be removed and the land shall be restored as soon as reasonably practicable to its condition before the development took place;

(d) in the case of any Class G(e) development, approval of details of the design and external appearance of the buildings shall be obtained, before development is begun, from—

(i) in Greater London or a metropolitan county, the local planning authority,

(ii) in a National Park in England, outside a metropolitan county, the county planning authority,

(iii) in any other case in England, the district planning authority,

(iv) in Wales, the local planning authority.

Interpretation of Class G

G.3 For the purposes of Class G(a), 'electric line' has the meaning assigned to that term by section 64(1) of the Electricity Act 1989 (interpretation etc. of Part 1).

G.4 For the purposes of Class G(b), 'electrical plant' has the meaning assigned to that term by the said section 64(1) and 'electronic communications line' means a wire or cable (including its casing or coating) which forms part of a telecommunication apparatus within the meaning assigned to that term by paragraph 1 of Schedule 2 to the Telecommunications Act 1984 (the electronic communications code).

G.5 For the purposes of Class G(d), (e) and (0, the land of the holder of a licence under section 6(2) of the Electricity Act 1989 (licences authorising supply etc.) shall be treated as operational land if it would be operational land within section 263 of the Act (meaning of 'operational land') if such licence holders were statutory undertakers for the purpose of that section.

Class H

Permitted development

Tramway or road transport undertakings

H. Development required for the purposes of the carrying on of any tramway or road transport undertaking consisting of—

(a) the installation of posts, overhead wires, underground cables, feeder pillars or transformer boxes in, on, over or adjacent to a highway for the purpose of supplying current to public service vehicles;

(b) the installation of tramway tracks, and conduits, drains and pipes in connection with such tracks for the working of tramways;

(c) the installation of telephone cables and apparatus, huts, stop posts and signs required in connection with the operation of public service vehicles;

(d) the erection or construction and the maintenance, improvement or other alteration of passenger shelters and barriers for the control of people waiting to enter public service vehicles;

(e) any other development on operational land of the undertaking.

Development not permitted

H.1 Development is not permitted by Class H if it would consist of—

(a) in the case of any Class H(a) development, the installation of a structure exceeding 17 cubic metres in capacity,

(b) in the case of any Class H(e) development—

(i) the erection of a building or the reconstruction or alteration of a building where its design or external appearance would be materially affected,

(ii) the installation or erection by way of addition or replacement of any plant or machinery which would exceed 15 metres in height or the height of any plant or machinery it replaces, whichever is the greater,

(iii) development, not wholly within a bus or tramway station, in pursuance of powers contained in transport legislation.

Class I

Permitted development

Lighthouse undertakings

I. Development required for the purposes of the functions of a general or local lighthouse authority under the Merchant Shipping Act 1894 and any other statutory provision made with respect to a local lighthouse authority, or in the exercise by a local lighthouse authority of rights, powers or duties acquired by usage prior to the 1894 Act.

Development not permitted

I.1 Development is not permitted by Class I if it consists of or includes the erection of offices, or the reconstruction or alteration of offices where their design or external appearance would be materially affected.

Class J

Permitted development

Universal Service Providers

J. Development required for the purposes of a universal service provider (within the meaning of the Postal Services Act 2000) in connection with the provision of a universal postal service (within the meaning of that Act) consisting of—

(a) the installation of posting boxes or self-service machines,

(b) any other development carried out in, on, over or under the operational land of the undertaking.

Development not permitted

J.1 Development is not permitted by Class J if—

(a) it would consist of or include the erection of a building, or the reconstruction or alteration of a building where its design or external appearance would be materially affected, or

(b) it would consist of or include the installation or erection by way of addition or replacement of any plant or machinery which would exceed 15 metres in height or the height of any existing plant or machinery, whichever is the greater.

Interpretation of Part 17

K. For the purposes of Part 17—

'transport legislation' means section 14(1)(d) of the Transport Act 1962 (supplemental provisions relating to the Board's powers) or section 10(1)(x) of the Transport Act 1968 (general powers of Passenger Transport Executive).

PART 18: AVIATION DEVELOPMENT

Class A

Permitted development

Development at an airport

A. The carrying out on operational land by a relevant airport operator or its agent of development (including the erection or alteration of an operational building) in connection with the provision of services and facilities at a relevant airport.

Development not permitted

A.1 Development is not permitted by Class A if it would consist of or include—

(a) the construction or extension of a runway;

(b) the construction of a passenger terminal the floor space of which would exceed 500 square metres;

(c) the extension or alteration of a passenger terminal, where the floor space of the building as existing at 5th December 1988 or, if built after that date, of the building as built, would be exceeded by more than 15%;

(d) the erection of a building other than an operational building;

(e) the alteration or reconstruction of a building other than an operational building, where its design or external appearance would be materially affected.

Condition

A.2 Development is permitted by Class A subject to the condition that the relevant airport operator consults the local planning authority before carrying out any development, unless that development falls within the description in paragraph A.4.

Interpretation of Class A

A.3 For the purposes of paragraph A.1, floor space shall be calculated by external measurement and without taking account of the floor space in any pier or satellite.

A.4 Development falls within this paragraph if—

(a) it is urgently required for the efficient running of the airport, and

(b) it consists of the carrying out of works, or the erection or construction of a structure or of an ancillary building, or the placing on land of equipment, and the works, structure, building, or equipment do not exceed 4 metres in height or 200 cubic metres in capacity.

Class B

Permitted development

Air traffic services development at an airport

B. The carrying out on operational land within the perimeter of a relevant airport by a relevant airport operator or its agent of development in connection with the provision of air traffic services at an airport

Class C

Permitted development

Air traffic services development near an airport

C. The carrying out on operational land outside but within 8 kilometres of the perimeter of a relevant airport, by a relevant airport operator or its

agent, of development in connection with the provision of air traffic services.

Development not permitted

[C.1 Development is not permitted by Class C if—

(a) any building erected would be used for a purpose other than housing equipment used in connection with the provision of air traffic services.]

(b) any building erected would exceed a height of 4 metres; or

(c) it would consist of the installation or erection of any radar or radio mast antenna or other apparatus which would exceed 15 metres in height, or where an existing mast, antenna or apparatus is replaced, the height of that mast, antenna or apparatus, if greater

Class D

Permitted development

Development by an air traffic services licence holder within an airport

D. The carrying out by [an air traffic services licence holder] or its agents, within the perimeter of an airport of development in connection with the provision of air traffic control services.

Class E

Permitted development

Development by an air traffic services licence holder on operational land

E. The carrying out on operational land of an air traffic services licence holder by that licence holder or its agents of development in connection within the provision of air traffic control services.

Development not permitted

E.1 Development is not permitted by Class E if—

(a) any building erected would be used for a purpose other than housing equipment used in connection with the provision of air traffic services;

(b) any building erected would exceed a height of 4 metres; or

(c) it would consist of the installation or erection of any radar or radio mast antenna or other apparatus which would exceed 15 metres in height, or where an existing mast, antenna or apparatus is replaced, the height of that mast, antenna or apparatus, if greater

Class F

Permitted development

Development by an air traffic services licence holder in an emergency

F. The use of land by or on behalf of an air traffic services licence holder in an emergency to station moveable apparatus replacing unserviceable apparatus.

Condition

F.1 Development is permitted by Class F subject to the condition that on or before the expiry of a period of six months beginning with the date on which the use began, the use shall cease, and any apparatus shall be removed, and the land shall be restored to its condition before the development took place, or to any other condition as may be agreed in writing between the local planning authority and the developer.

Class G

Permitted development

Development by an air traffic services licence holder involving moveable structures etc.

G. The use of land by or on behalf of an air traffic services licence holder to provide services and facilities in connection with the provision of air traffic services and the erection or placing of moveable structures on the land for the purpose of that use.

Condition G.1 Development is permitted by Class G subject to the condition that, on or before the expiry of the period of six months beginning with the date on which the use began, the use shall cease, and any structure shall be removed, and the land shall be restored to its condition before the development took place, or to any other condition as may be agreed in writing between the local planning authority and the developer.

Class H

Permitted development

Development by the Civil Aviation Authority for surveys etc.

H. The use of land by or on behalf of the Civil Aviation Authority for the stationing and operation of apparatus in connection with the carrying out of surveys or investigations.

Condition H.1 Development is permitted by Class H subject to the condition that on or before the expiry of the period of six months beginning with the date on which the use began, the use shall cease, and any apparatus shall be removed, and the land shall be restored to its condition before the development took place, or to any other condition as may be agreed in writing between the local planning authority and the developer.

Class I

Permitted development

Use of airport buildings managed by relevant airport operators

I. The use of buildings within the perimeter of an airport managed by a relevant airport operator for purposes connected with air transport services or other flying activities at that airport.

Interpretation of Part 18

J. For the purposes of Part 18—

'air traffic services' has the same meaning as in section 98 of the Transport Act 2000 (air traffic services);'

'air traffic licence holder' means a person who holds a licence under Chapter 1 of Part 1 of the Transport Act 2000;'

'operational building' means a building, other than a hotel, required in connection with the movement or maintenance of aircraft, or with the embarking, disembarking, loading, discharge or transport of passengers, livestock or goods at a relevant airport; 'relevant airport' means an airport to which Part V of the Airports Act 1986 (status of certain airports as statutory undertakers etc.) applies; and

'relevant airport operator' means a relevant airport operator within the meaning of section 57 of the Airports Act 1986 (scope of Part V).

PART 19: DEVELOPMENT ANCILLARY TO MINING OPERATIONS

Class A

Permitted development

A. The carrying out of operations for the erection, extension, installation, rearrangement, replacement, repair or other alteration of any—

(a) plant or machinery,

(b) buildings,

(c) private ways or private railways or sidings, or

(d) sewers, mains, pipes, cables or other similar apparatus, on land used as a mine.

Development not permitted

A.1 Development is not permitted by Class A—

(a) in relation to land at an underground mine—

(i) on land which is not an approved site; or

(ii) on land to which the description in paragraph D.1(b) applies, unless a plan of that land was deposited with the mineral planning authority before 5th June 1989;

(b) if the principal purpose of the development would be any purpose other than—

(i) purposes in connection with the winning and working of minerals at that mine or of minerals brought to the surface at that mine; or

(ii) the treatment, storage or removal from the mine of such minerals or waste materials derived from them;

(c) if the external appearance of the mine would be materially affected;

(d) if the height of any building, plant or machinery which is not in an excavation would exceed—

(i) 15 metres above ground level; or

(ii) the height of the building, plant or machinery, if any, which is being rearranged, replaced or repaired or otherwise altered, whichever is the greater;

(e) if the height of any building, plant or machinery in an excavation would exceed—

(i) 15 metres above the excavated ground level; or

(ii) 15 metres above the lowest point of the unexcavated ground immediately adjacent to the excavation; or

(iii) the height of the building, plant or machinery, if any, which is being rearranged, replaced or repaired or otherwise altered, whichever is the greatest;

(f) if any building erected (other than a replacement building) would have a floor space exceeding 1,000 square metres; or

(g) if the cubic content of any replaced, extended or altered building would exceed by more than 25% the cubic content of the building replaced, extended or altered or the floor space would exceed by more than 1,000 square metres the floor space of that building.

Condition

A.2 Development is permitted by Class A subject to the condition that before the end of the period of 24 months from the date when the mining operations have permanently ceased, or any longer period which the mineral planning authority agree in writing—

(a) all buildings, plant and machinery permitted by Class A shall be removed from the land unless the mineral planning authority have otherwise agreed in writing; and

(b) the land shall be restored, so far as is practicable, to its condition before the development took place, or restored to such condition as may have been agreed in writing between the mineral planning authority and the developer.

Class B

Permitted development

B. The carrying out, on land used as a mine or on ancillary mining land, with the prior approval of the mineral planning authority, of operations for the erection, installation, extension, rearrangement, replacement, repair or other alteration of any—

(a) plant or machinery,
(b) buildings, or
(c) structures or erections.

Development not permitted

B.1 Development is not peremitted by Class B—
(a) in relation to land at an underground mine—
(i) on land which is not an approved site; or
(ii) on land to which the description in paragraph D.1(b) applies, unless a plan of that land was deposited with the mineral planning authority before 5th June 1989;
or
(b) if the principal purpose of the development would be any purpose other than—
(i) purposes in connection with the operation of the mine,
(ii) the treatment, preparation for sale, consumption or utilization of minerals won or brought to the surface at that mine, or
(iii) the storage or removal from the mine of such minerals, their products or waste materials derived from them.

B.2 The prior approval referred to in Class B shall not be refused or granted subject to conditions unless the authority are satisfied that it is expedient to do so because—
(a) the proposed development would injure the amenity of the neighbourhood and modifications can reasonably be made or conditions reasonably imposed in order to avoid or reduce that injury, or
(b) the proposed development ought to be, and could reasonably be, sited elsewhere.

Condition

B.3 Development is permitted by Class B subject to the condition that before the end of the period of 24 months from the date when the mining operations have permanently ceased, or any longer period which the mineral planning authority agree in writing—
(a) all buildings, plant, machinery, structures and erections permitted by Class B shall be removed from the land unless the mineral planning authority have otherwise agreed in writing; and
(b) the land shall be restored, so far as is practicable, to its condition before the development took place or restored to such condition as may have been agreed in writing between the mineral planning authority and the developer.

Class C

Permitted development

C. The carrying out with the prior approval of the mineral planning authority of development required for the maintenance or safety of a mine or a disused mine or for the purposes of ensuring the safety of the surface of the land at or adjacent to a mine or a disused mine.

Development not permitted

C.1 Development is not permitted by Class C if it is carried out by the Coal Authority or any licensed operator within the meaning of section 65 of the Coal Industry Act 1994 (interpretation).

Prior approvals

C.2(1) The prior approval of the mineral planning authority to development permitted by Class C is not required if—
(a) the external appearance of the mine or disused mine at or adjacent to which the development is to be carried out would not be materially affected;

(b) no building, plant, machinery, structure or erection—

(i) would exceed a height of 15 metres above ground level, or

(ii) where any building, plant, machinery, structure or erection is rearranged, replaced or repaired, would exceed a height of 15 metres above ground level or the height of what was rearranged, replaced or repaired, whichever is the greater,

and

(c) the development consists of the extension, alteration or replacement of an existing building, within the limits set out in paragraph (3).

(2) The approval referred to in Class C shall not be refused or granted subject to conditions unless the authority are satisfied that it is expedient to do so because—

(a) the proposed development would injure the amenity of the neighbourhood and modifications could reasonably be made or conditions reasonably imposed in order to avoid or reduce that injury, or

(b) the proposed development ought to be, and could reasonably be, sited elsewhere.

(3) The limits referred to in paragraph C.2(1)(c) are—

(a) that the cubic content of the building as extended, altered or replaced does not exceed that of the existing building by more than 25%, and

(b) that the floor space of the building as extended, altered or replaced does not exceed that of the existing building by more than 1,000 square metres.

Interpretation of Part 19

D.1 An area of land is an approved site for the purposes of Part 19 if—

(a) it is identified in a grant of planning permission or any instrument by virtue of which planning pemission is deemed to be granted, as land which may be used for development described in this Part; or

(b) in any other case, it is land immediately adjoining an active access to an underground mine which, on 5th December 1988, was in use for the purposes of that mine, in connection with the purposes described in paragraph A.1(b)(i) or (ii) or paragraph B.1 (b)(i) to (iii) above.

D.2 For the purposes of Part 19—

'active access' means a surface access to underground workings which is in normal and regular use for the transportation of minerals, materials, spoil or men;

'ancillary mining land' means land adjacent to and occupied together with a mine at which the winning and working of minerals is carried out in pursuance of planning permission granted or deemed to be granted under Part III of the Act (control over development);

'minerals' does not include any coal other than coal won or worked during the course of operations which are carried on exclusively for the purpose of exploring for coal or confined to the digging or carrying away of coal that it is necessary to dig or carry away in the course of activities carried on for purposes which do not include the getting of coal or any product of coal;

'the prior approval of the mineral planning authority' means prior written approval of that authority of detailed proposals for the siting, design and external appearance of the building, plant or machinery proposed to be erected, installed, extended or altered;

'underground mine' is a mine at which minerals are worked principally by underground methods.

PART 20: COAL MINING DEVELOPMENT BY THE COAL AUTHORITY AND LICENSED OPERATORS

Class A

Permitted development **A. Development by a licensee of the Coal Authority, in a mine started before 1st July 1948, consisting of—**

(a) the winning and working underground of coal or coal-related minerals in a designated seam area; or

(b) the carrying out of development underground which is required in order to gain access to and work coal or coal-related minerals in a designated seam area.

Conditions A.1 Development is permitted by Class A subject to the following conditions—

(a) subject to sub-paragraph (b)—

(i) except in a case where there is an approved restoration scheme or mining operations have permanently ceased, the developer shall, before 31st December 1995 or before any later date which the mineral planning authority may agree in writing, apply to the mineral planning authority for approval of a restoration scheme;

(ii) where there is an approved restoration scheme, reinstatement, restoration and aftercare shall be carried out in accordance with that scheme;

(iii) if an approved restoration scheme does not specify the periods within which reinstatement, restoration or aftercare should be carried out, it shall be subject to conditions that—

(aa) reinstatement or restoration, if any, shall be carried out before the end of the period of 24 months from either the date when the mining operations have permanently ceased or the date when any application for approval of a restoration scheme under sub-paragraph (a)(i) has been finally determined, whichever is later, and

(bb) aftercare, if any, in respect of any part of a site, shall be carried out throughout the period of five years from either the date when any reinstatement or restoration in respect of that part is completed or the date when any application for approval of a restoration scheme under sub-paragraph (a)(i) has been finally determined, whichever is later;

(iv) where there is no approved restoration scheme—

(aa) all buildings, plant, machinery, structures and erections used at any time for or in connection with any previous coal-mining operations at that mine shall be removed from any land which is an authorised site unless the mineral planning authority have otherwise agreed in writing, and

(bb) that land shall, so far as practicable, be restored to its condition before any previous coal-mining operations at that mine took place or to such condition as may have been agreed in writing between the mineral planning authority and the developer, before the end of the period specified in sub-paragraph (v);

(v) the period referred to in sub-paragraph (iv) is—

(aa) the period of 24 months from the date when the mining operations have permanently ceased or, if an application for approval of a restoration scheme has been made under sub-paragraph (a)(i) before that date, 24 months from the date when that application has been finally determined, whichever is later, or

(bb) any longer period which the mineral planning authority have agreed in writing;

(vi) for the purposes of sub-paragraph (a), an application for approval of a restoration scheme has been finally determined when the following conditions have been met—

(aa) any proceedings on the application, including any proceeding on or in consequence of an application under section 288 of the Act (proceedings for questioning the validity of certain orders, decisions and directions), have been determined, and

(bb) any time for appealing under section 78 (right to appeal against planning decisions and failure to take such decisions), or applying or further applying under section 288, of the Act (where there is a right to do so) has expired;

(b) sub-paragraph (a) shall not apply to land in respect of which there is an extant planning permission which—

(i) has been granted on an application under Part III of the Act, and

(ii) has been implemented.

Interpretation of Class A

A.2 For the purposes of Class A—

'a licensee of the Coal Authority' means any person who is for the time being authorised by a licence under Part II of the Coal Industry Act 1994 to carry on coal-mining operations to which section 25 of that Act (coal-mining operations to be licensed) applies;

'approved restoration scheme' means a restoration scheme which is approved when an application made under paragraph A.1(a)(i) is finally determined, as approved (with or without conditions), or as subsequently varied with the written approval of the mineral planning authority (with or without conditions);

'coal-related minerals' means minerals other than coal which are, or may be, won and worked by coal-mining operations;

'designated seam area' means land identified, in accordance with paragraph (a) of the definition of 'seam plan', in a seam plan which was deposited with the mineral planning authority before 30th September 1993;

'previous coal-mining operations' has the same meaning as in section 54(3) of the Coal Industry Act 1994 (obligations to restore land affected by coal-mining operations) and references in Class A to the use of anything in connection with any such operations shall include references to its use for or in connection with activities carried on in association with, or for purposes connected with, the carrying on of those operations;

'restoration scheme' means a scheme which makes provision for the reinstatement, restoration or aftercare (or a combination of these) of any land which is an authorised site and has been used at any time for or in connection with any previous coal-mining operations at that mine; and 'seam plan' means a plan or plans on a scale of not less than 1 to 25,000 showing—

(a) land comprising the maximum extent of the coal seam or seams that could have been worked from shafts or drifts existing at a mine at 13th November 1992, without further development on an authorised site other than development permitted by Class B of Part 20 of Schedule 2 to the Town and Country Planning General Development Order 1988, as originally enacted;

(b) any active access used in connection with the land referred to in paragraph (a) of this definition;

(c) the National Grid lines and reference numbers shown on Ordnance Survey maps;

(d) a typical stratigraphic column showing the approximate depths of the coal seam referred to in paragraph (a) of this definition.

Class B

Permitted development

B. Development by a licensee of the British Coal Corporation, in a mine started before 1st July 1948, consisting of—

(a) the winning and working underground of coal or coal-related minerals in a designated seam area; or

(b) the carrying out of development underground which is required in order to gain access to and work coal or coal-related minerals in a designated seam area.

Interpretation of Class B

B.1 For the purposes of Class B—

'designated seam area' has the same meaning as in paragraph A.2 above;

'coal-related minerals' means minerals other than coal which can only be economically worked in association with the working of coal or which can only be economically brought to the surface by the use of a mine of coal; and

'a licensee of the British Coal Corporation' means any person who is for the time being authorised by virtue of section 25(3) of the Coal Industry Act 1994 (coal-mining operations to be licensed) to carry on coal-mining operations to which section 25 of that Act applies.

Class C

Permitted development

C. Any development required for the purposes of a mine which is carried out on an authorised site at that mine by a licensed operator, in connection with coal-mining operations.

Development not permitted

C.1 Development is not permitted by Class C if—

(a) the external appearance of the mine would be materially affected;

(b) any building, plant or machinery, structure or erection or any deposit of minerals or waste—

(i) would exceed a height of 15 metres above ground level, or

(ii) where a building, plant or machinery would be rearranged, replaced or repaired, the resulting development would exceed a height of 15 metres above ground level or the height of what was rearranged, replaced or repaired, whichever is the greater;

(c) any building erected (other than a replacement building) would have a floor space exceeding 1,000 square metres;

(d) the cubic content of any replaced, extended or altered building would exceed by more than 25% the cubic content of the building replaced, extended or altered or the floor space would exceed by more than 1,000 square metres, the floor space of that building;

(e) it would be for the purpose of creating a new surface access to underground workings or of improving an existing access (which is not an active access) to underground workings; or

(f) it would be carried out on land to which the description in paragraph F.2(1)(b) applies, and a plan of that land had not been deposited with the mineral planning authority before 5th June 1989.

Conditions

C.2 Development is permitted by Class C subject to the condition that before the end of the period of 24 months from the date when the mining operations have permanently ceased, or any longer period which the mineral planning authority agree in writing—

(a) all buildings, plant, machinery, structures and erections and deposits of minerals or waste permitted by Class C shall be removed from the land unless the mineral planning authority have otherwise agreed in writing; and

(b) the land shall, so far as is practicable, be restored to its condition before the development took place or to such condition as may have been agreed in writing between the mineral planning authority and the developer.

Class D

Permitted development

D. Any development required for the purposes of a mine which is carried out on an authorised site at that mine by a licensed operator in connection with coal-mining operations and with the prior approval of the mineral planning authority.

Development not permitted

D.1 Development is not permitted by Class D if—

(a) it would be for the purpose of creating a new surface access or improving an existing access (which is not an active access) to underground workings; or

(b) it would be carried out on land to which the description in paragraph F.2(1)(b) applies, and a plan of that land had not been deposited with the mineral planning authority before 5th June 1989.

Condition

D.2 Development is permitted by Class D subject to the condition that before the end of the period of 24 months from the date when the mining operations have permanently ceased, or any longer period which the mineral planning authority agree in writing—

(a) all buildings, plant, machinery, structures and erections and deposits of minerals or waste pemiitted by Class D shall be removed from the land, unless the mineral planning authority have otherwise agreed in writing; and

(b) the land shall, so far as is practicable, be restored to its condition before the development took place or to such condition as may have been agreed in writing between the mineral planning authority and the developer.

Interpretation of Class D

D.3 The prior approval referred to in Class D shall not be refused or granted subject to conditions unless the authority are satisfied that it is expedient to do so because—

(a) the proposed development would injure the amenity of the neighbourhood and modifications could reasonably be made or conditions reasonably imposed in order to avoid or reduce that injury, or

(b) the proposed development ought to be, and could reasonably be, sited elsewhere.

Class E

Permitted development **E. The carrying out by the Coal Authority or a licensed operator, with the prior approval of the mineral planning authority, of development required for the maintenance or safety of a mine or a disused mine or for the purposes of ensuring the safety of the surface of the land at or adjacent to a mine or a disused mine.**

Prior approvals

E.1(1) The prior approval of the mineral planning authority to development permitted by Class E is not required if—

(a) the external appearance of the mine or disused mine at or adjacent to which the development is to be carried out would not be materially affected;

(b) no building, plant or machinery, structure or erection—

(i) would exceed a height of 15 metres above ground level, or

(ii) where any building, plant, machinery, structure or erection is rearranged, replaced or repaired, would exceed a height of 15 metres above ground level or the height of what was rearranged, replaced or repaired, whichever is the greater, and

(c) the development consists of the extension, alteration or replacement of an existing building, within the limits set out in paragraph (3).

(2) The approval referred to in Class E shall not be refused or granted subject to conditions unless the authority are satisfied that it is expedient to do so because—

(a) the proposed development would injure the amenity of the neighbourhood and modifications could reasonably be made or conditions reasonably imposed in order to avoid or reduce that injury, or

(b) the proposed development ought to be, and could reasonably be, sited elsewhere.

(3) The limits referred to in paragraph E.1(1)(c) are—

(a) that the cubic content of the building as extended, altered or replaced does not exceed that of the existing building by more than 25%, and

(b) that the floor space of the building as extended, altered or replaced does not exceed that of the existing building by more than 1,000 square metres.

Interpretation of Part 20

F.1 For the purposes of Part 20—

'active access' means a surface access to underground workings which is in normal and regular use for the transportation of coal, materials, spoil or men;

'coal-mining operations' has the same meaning as in section 65 of the Coal Industry Act 1994 (interpretation) and references to any development or use in connection with coal-mining operations shall include references to development or use for or in connection with activities carried on in association with, or for purposes connected with, the carrying on of those operations;

'licensed operator' has the same meaning as in section 65 of the Coal Industry Act 1994;

'normal and regular use' means use other than intermittent visits to inspect and maintain the fabric of the mine or any plant or machinery; and

'prior approval of the mineral planning authority' means prior written approval of that authority of detailed proposals for the siting, design and external appearance of the proposed building, plant or machinery, structure or erection as erected, installed, extended or altered.

F.2(1) Subject to sub-paragraph (2), land is an authorised site for the purposes of Part 20 if—

(a) it is identified in a grant of planning permission or any instrument by virtue of which planning permission is deemed to be granted as land which may be used for development described in this Part; or

(b) in any other case, it is land immediately adjoining an active access which, on 5th December 1988, was in use for the purposes of that mine in connection with coal-mining operations.

(2) For the purposes of sub-paragraph (1), land is not to be regarded as in use in connection with coal-mining operations if—

(a) it is used for the permanent deposit of waste derived from the winning and working of minerals; or

(b) there is on, over or under it a railway, conveyor, aerial ropeway, roadway, overhead power line or pipe-line which is not itself surrounded by other land used for those purposes.

PART 21: WASTE TIPPING AT A MINE

Class A

Permitted development

A. The deposit, on premises used as a mine or on ancillary mining land already used for the purpose, of waste derived from the winning and working of minerals at that mine or from minerals brought to the surface at that mine, or from the treatment or the preparation for sale, consumption or utilization of minerals from the mine.

Development not permitted

A.1 Development is not permitted by Class A if—

(a) in the case of waste deposited in an excavation, waste would be deposited at a height above the level of the land adjoining the excavation unless that is provided for in a waste management scheme or a relevant scheme;

(b) in any other case, the superficial area or height of the deposit (measured as at 21st October 1988) would be increased by more than 10%, unless such an increase is provided for in a waste management scheme or in a relevant scheme.

Conditions

A.2 Development is permitted by Class A subject to the following conditions—

(a) except in a case where a relevant scheme or a waste management scheme has already been approved by the mineral planning authority, the developer shall, if the mineral planning authority so require, within three months or such longer period as the authority may specify, submit a waste management scheme for that authority's approval;

(b) where a waste management scheme or a relevant scheme has been approved, the depositing of waste and all other activities in relation to that deposit shall be carried out in accordance with the scheme as approved.

Interpretation of Class A

A.3 For the purposes of Class A—

'ancillary mining land' means land adjacent to and occupied together with a mine at which the winning and working of minerals is carried out in pursuance of planning permission granted or deemed to be granted under Part III of the Act (control over development); and

'waste management scheme' means a scheme required by the mineral planning authority to be submitted for their approval in accordance with the condition in paragraph A.2(a) which makes provision for—

(a) the manner in which the depositing of waste (other than waste deposited on a site for use for filling any mineral excavation in the mine or on ancillary mining land in order to comply with the terms of any planning permission granted on an application or deemed to be granted under Part III of the Act) is to be carried out after the date of the approval of that scheme;

(b) where appropriate, the stripping and storage of the subsoil and topsoil;

(c) the restoration and aftercare of the site.

Class B

Permitted development **B. The deposit on land comprised in a site used for the deposit of waste materials or refuse on 1st July 1948 of waste resulting from coal-mining operations.**

Development not permitted — B.1 Development is not permitted by Class B unless it is in accordance with a relevant scheme approved by the mineral planning authority before 5th December 1988.

Interpretation of Class B — B.2 For the purposes of Class B—

'coal-mining operations' has the same meaning as in section 65 of the Coal Industry Act 1994 (interpretation).

Interpretation of Part 21 — C. For the purposes of Part 21—

'relevant scheme' means a scheme, other than a waste management scheme, requiring approval by the mineral planning authority in accordance with a condition or limitation on any planning permission granted or deemed to be granted under Part III of the Act (control over development), for making provision for the manner in which the deposit of waste is to be carried out and for the carrying out of other activities in relation to that deposit.

PART 22: MINERAL EXPLORATION

Class A

Permitted Development **A. Development on any land during a period not exceeding 28 consecutive days consisting of—**

(a) the drilling of boreholes;

(b) the carrying out of seismic surveys; or

(c) the making of other excavations,

for the purpose of mineral exploration, and the provision or assembly on that land or adjoining land of any structure required in connection with any of those operations.

Development not permitted — A.1 Development is not permitted by Class A if—

(a) it consists of the drilling of boreholes for petroleum exploration;

(b) any operation would be carried out within 50 metres of any part of an occupied residential building or a building occupied as a hospital or school;

(c) any operation would be carried out within a National Park, an area of outstanding natural beauty, a site of archaeological interest or a site of special scientific interest;

(d) any explosive charge of more than 1 kilogram would be used;

(e) any excavation referred to in paragraph A(c) would exceed 10 metres in depth or 12 square metres in surface area;

(f) in the case described in paragraph A(c) more than 10 excavations would, as a result, be made within any area of 1 hectare within the land during any period of 24 months; or

(g) any structure assembled or provided would exceed 12 metres in height, or, where the structure would be within 3 kilometres of the perimeter of an aerodrome, 3 metres in height.

Conditions

A.2 Development is permitted by Class A subject to the following conditions—

(a) no operations shall be carried out between 6.00 p.m. and 7.00 a.m.;

(b) no trees on the land shall be removed, felled, lopped or topped and no other thing shall be done on the land likely to harm or damage any trees, unless the mineral planning authority have so agreed in writing;

(c) before any excavation (other than a borehole) is made, any topsoil and any subsoil shall be separately removed from the land to be excavated and stored separately from other excavated material and from each other;

(d) within a period of 28 days from the cessation of operations unless the mineral planning authority have agreed otherwise in writing—

(i) any structure permitted by Class A and any waste material arising from other development so permitted shall be removed from the land,

(ii) any borehole shall be adequately sealed,

(iii) any other excavation shall be filled with material from the site,

(iv) the surface of the land on which any operations have been carried out shall be levelled and any topsoil replaced as the uppermost layer, and

(v) the land shall, so far as is practicable, be restored to its condition before the development took place, including the carrying out of any necessary seeding and replanting.

Class B

Permitted development

B. Development on any land consisting of—

(a) the drilling of boreholes;

(b) the carrying out of seismic surveys; or

(c) the making of other excavations,

for the purposes of mineral exploration, and the provision or assembly on that land or on adjoining land of any structure required in connection with any of those operations.

Development not permitted

B.1 Development is not permitted by Class B if—

(a) it consists of the drilling of boreholes for petroleum exploration;

(b) the developer has not previously notified the mineral planning authority in writing of his intention to carry out the development (specifying the nature and location of the development);

(c) the relevant period has not elapsed;

(d) any explosive charge of more than 2 kilograms would be used;

(e) any excavation referred to in paragraph B(c) would exceed 10 metres in depth or 12 square metres in surface area; or

(f) any structure assembled or provided would exceed 12 metres in height.

Conditions

B.2 Development is permitted by Class B subject to the following conditions—

(a) the development shall be carried out in accordance with the details in the notification referred to in paragraph B.1(b), unless the mineral planning authority have otherwise agreed in writing;

(b) no trees on the land shall be removed, felled, lopped or topped and no other thing shall be done on the land likely to harm or damage any trees, unless specified in detail in the notification referred to in paragraph B.1(b) or the mineral planning authority have otherwise agreed in writing;

(c) before any excavation other than a borehole is made, any topsoil and any subsoil shall be separately removed from the land to be excavated and stored separately from other excavated material and from each other;

(d) within a period of 28 days from operations ceasing, unless the mineral planning authority have agreed otherwise in writing—

(i) any structure permitted by Class B and any waste material arising from other development so permitted shall be removed from the land,

(ii) any borehole shall be adequately sealed,

(iii) any other excavation shall be filled with material from the site,

(iv) the surface of the land shall be levelled and any topsoil replaced as the uppermost layer, and

(v) the land shall, so far as is practicable, be restored to its condition before the development took place, including the carrying out of any necessary seeding and replanting,

and

(e) the development shall cease no later than a date six months after the elapse of the relevant period, unless the mineral planning authority have otherwise agreed in writing.

Interpretation of Class B

B.3 For the purposes of Class B—

'relevant period' means the period elapsing—

(a) where a direction is not issued under article 7, 28 days after the notification referred to in paragraph B.1(b) or, if earlier, on the date on which the mineral planning authority notify the developer in writing that they will not issue such a direction, or

(b) where a direction is issued under article 7, 28 days from the date on which notice of that decision is sent to the Secretary of State, or, if earlier, the date on which the mineral planning authority notify the developer that the Secretary of State has disallowed the direction.

Interpretation of Part 22

C. For the purposes of Part 22—

'mineral exploration' means ascertaining the presence, extent or quality of any deposit of a mineral with a view to exploiting that mineral; and

'structure' includes a building, plant or machinery.

PART 23: REMOVAL OF MATERIAL FROM MINERAL-WORKING DEPOSITS

Class A

Permitted development

A. The removal of material of any description from a stockpile.

Class B

Permitted Development

B. The removal of material of any description from a mineral-working deposit other than a stockpile.

Development not permitted

B.1 Development is not permitted by Class B if—

(a) the developer has not previously notified the mineral planning authority in writing of his intention to carry out the development and supplied them with the appropriate details;

(b) the deposit covers a ground area exceeding 2 hectares, unless the deposit contains no mineral or other material which was deposited on the land more than 5 years before the development; or

(c) the deposit derives from the carrying out of any operations permitted under Part 6 of this Schedule or any Class in a previous development order which it replaces.

Conditions B.2 Development is permitted by Class B subject to the following conditions—

(a) it shall be carried out in accordance with the details given in the notice sent to the mineral planning authority referred to in paragraph B.1(a) above, unless that authority have agreed otherwise in writing;

(b) if the mineral planning authority so require, the developer shall within a period of three months from the date of the requirement (or such other longer period as that authority may provide) submit to them for approval a scheme providing for the restoration and aftercare of the site;

(c) where such a scheme is required, the site shall be restored and aftercare shall be carried out in accordance with the provisions of the approved scheme;

(d) development shall not be commenced until the relevant period has elapsed.

Interpretation of Class B B.3 For the purposes of Class B—

'appropriate details' means the nature of the development, the exact location of the mineral-working deposit from which the material would be removed, the proposed means of vehicular access to the site at which the development is to be carried out, and the earliest date at which any mineral presently contained in the deposit was deposited on the land; and

'relevant period' means the period elapsing—

(a) where a direction is not issued under article 7, 28 days after the notification referred to in paragraph B.1(a) or, if earlier, on the date on which the mineral planning authority notify the developer in writing that they will not issue such a direction; or

(b) where a direction is issued under article 7, 28 days from the date on which notice of that direction is sent to the Secretary of State, or, if earlier, the date on which the mineral planning authority notify the developer that the Secretary of State has disallowed the direction.

Interpretation of Part 23 C. For the purposes of Part 23—

'stockpile' means a mineral-working deposit consisting primarily of minerals which have been deposited for the purposes of their processing or sale.

PART 24: DEVELOPMENT BY ELECTRONIC COMMUNICATIONS CODE OPERATORS

(This Part of the Order does not apply to Wales, which has a different version)

Class A

Permitted development **A. Development by or on behalf of an electric communications code operator for the purpose of the operator's electronic communications network in, on, over or under land controlled by that operator or in accordance with the electronic communications code, consisting of—**

(a) the installation, alteration or replacement of any electronic communications apparatus,

(b) the use of land in an emergency for a period not exceeding six months to station and operate moveable electronic communications apparatus required for the replacement of unserviceable electronic communications apparatus including the provision of moveable structures on the land for the purposes of that use, or

(c) development ancillary to radio equipment housing.

Development not permitted

A.1 Development is not permitted by Class A(a) if—

(a) in the case of the installation of apparatus (other than on a building or other structure) the apparatus, excluding any antenna, would exceed a height of 15 metres above ground level;

(b) in the case of the alteration or replacement of apparatus already installed (other than on a building or other structure), the apparatus, excluding any antenna, would when altered or replaced exceed the height of the existing apparatus or a height of 15 metres above ground level, whichever is the greater;

(c) in the case of the installation, alteration or replacement of apparatus on a building or other structure, the height of the apparatus (taken by itself) would exceed—

(i) 15 metres, where it is installed, or is to be installed, on a building or other structure which is 30 metres or more in height; or

(ii) 10 metres in any other case;

(d) in the case of the installation, alteration or replacement of apparatus on a building or other structure, the highest part of the apparatus when installed, altered or replaced would exceed the height of the highest part of the building or structure by more than—

(i) 10 metres, in the case of a building or structure which is 30 metres or more in height;

(ii) 8 metres, in the case of a building or structure which is more than 15 metres but less than 30 metres in height;

(iii) 6 metres in any other case;

(e) in the case of the installation, alteration or replacement of apparatus (other than an antenna) on a mast, the height of the mast would, when the apparatus was installed, altered or replaced, exceed any relevant height limit specified in respect of apparatus in paragraphs A.1(a), (b), (c) and (d), and for the purposes of applying the limit specified in sub-paragraph (c), the words '(taken by itself)' shall be omitted;

(f) in the case of the installation, alteration or replacement of any apparatus other than—

(i) a mast,

(ii) an antenna,

(iii) a public call box,

(iv) any apparatus which does not project above the level of the surface of the ground, or

(v) radio equipment housing,

the ground or base area of the structure would exceed 1.5 square metres;

(g) in the case of the installation, alteration or replacement of an antenna on a building or structure (other than a mast) which is less than 15 metres in height; on a mast located on such a building or structure; or, where the antenna is to be located below a height of 15 metres above ground level, on a building or structure (other than a mast) which is 15 metres or more in height—

(i) the antenna is to be located on a wall or roof slope facing a highway which is within 20 metres of the building or structure on which the antenna is to be located;

(ii) in the case of dish antennas, the size of any dish would exceed 0.9 metres or the aggregate size of all of the dishes on the building, structure or mast would exceed 1.5 metres, when measured in any dimension;

(iii) in the case of antennas other than dish antennas, the development (other than the installation, alteration or replacement of one small antenna) would result in the presence on the building or structure of more than two antenna systems; or

(iv) the building or structure is a listed building or a scheduled monument;

(h) in the case of the installation, alteration or replacement of an antenna on a building or structure (other than a mast) which is 15 metres or more in height, or on a mast located on such a building or structure, where the antenna is located at a height of 15 metres or above, measured from ground level—

(i) in the case of dish antennas, the size of any dish would exceed 1.3 metres or the aggregate size of all of the dishes on the building, structure or mast would exceed 3.5 metres, when measured in any dimension;

(ii) in the case of antenna systems other than dish antennas, the development (other than the installation, alteration or replacement of a maximum of two small antennas) would result in the presence on the building or structure of more than three antenna systems; or

(iii) the building or structure is a listed building or a scheduled monument;

(i) in the case of development (other than the installation, alteration or replacement of one small antenna on a dwellinghouse or within the curtilage of a dwellinghouse) of any article 1(5) land or of any land which is, or is within, a site of special scientific interest, it would consist of—

(i) the installation or alteration of an antenna or of any apparatus which includes or is intended for the support of such an antenna; or

(ii) the replacement of such an antenna or such apparatus by an antenna or apparatus which differs from that which is being replaced, unless the development is carried out in an emergency;

(j) it would consist of the installation, alteration or replacement of system apparatus within the meaning of section 8(6) of the Road Traffic (Driver Licensing and Information Systems) Act 1989 (definitions of driver information systems etc.);

(k) in the case of the installation of a mast, on a building or structure which is less than 15 metres in height, such a mast would be within 20 metres of a highway;

(l) in the case of the installation, alteration or replacement of radio equipment housing—

(i) the development is not ancillary to the use of any other electronic communications apparatus;

(ii) the development would exceed 90 cubic metres or, if located on the roof of a building, the development would exceed 30 cubic metres;

(iii) on any article 1(5) land, or on any land which is, or is within, a site of special scientific interest, the development would exceed 2.5 cubic metres, unless the development is carried out in an emergency;

(m) in the case of the installation, alteration or replacement on a dwellinghouse or within the curtilage of a dwellinghouse of any telecommunications apparatus, that apparatus—

(i) is not a small antenna;

(ii) being a small antenna, would result in the presence on that dwellinghouse or within the curtilage of that dwellinghouse of more than one such antenna; or

(iii) being a small antenna, is to be located on a roof or on a chimney so that the highest part of the antenna would exceed in height the highest part of that roof or chimney respectively;

(n) in the case of the installation, alteration or replacement on article 1(5) land of a small antenna on a dwellinghouse or within the curtilage of a dwellinghouse, the antenna is to be located—

(i) on a chimney;

(ii) on a building which exceeds 15 metres in height;

(iii) on a wall or roof slope which fronts a highway; or

(iv) in the Broads, on a wall or roof slope which fronts a waterway;

(o) in the case of the installation, alteration or replacement of a small antenna on a building which is not a dwellinghouse or within the curtilage of a dwellinghouse—

(i) the building is on article 1(5) land;

(ii) the building is less than 15 metres in height, and the development would result in the presence on that building of more than one such antenna; or

(iii) the building is 15 metres or more in height, and the development would result in the presence on that building of more than two such antennas.

Conditions

A.2(1) Class A(a) and Class A(c) development is permitted subject to the condition that any antenna or supporting apparatus, radio equipment housing or development ancillary to radio equipment housing constructed, installed, altered or replaced on a building in accordance with that permission shall, so far as is practicable, be sited so as to minimise its effect on the external appearance of the building.

(2) Class A(a) and Class A(c) development is permitted subject to the condition that any apparatus or structure provided in accordance with that permission shall be removed from the land, building or structure on which it is situated—

(a) if such development was carried out in an emergency on any article 1(5) land or on any land which is, or is within, a site of special scientific interest, at the expiry of the relevant period, or

(b) in any other case, as soon as reasonably practicable after it is no longer required for electronic communications purposes,

and such land, building or structure shall be restored to its condition before the development took place, or to any other condition as may be agreed in writing between the local planning authority and the developer.

(3) Class A(b) development is permitted subject to the condition that any apparatus or structure provided in accordance with that permission shall at the expiry of the relevant period be removed from the land and the land restored to its condition before the development took place.

(4) Class A development—

(a) on article 1(5) land or land which is, or is within, a site of special scientific interest, or

(b) on any other land and consisting of the construction, installation, alteration or replacement of a mast; or of an antenna on a building or structure (other than a mast) where the antenna (including any supporting structure) would exceed the height of the building or structure at the point where it is installed or to be installed by 4 metres or more; or of a public call box; or of radio equipment housing with a volume in excess of 2.5 cubic metres or of development ancillary to radio equipment housing—

is permitted subject, except in a case of emergency, to the conditions set out in A.3.

A.3(1) The developer shall give notice of the proposed development to any person (other than the developer) who is an owner of the land to which the development relates, or a tenant, before making the application required by paragraph (3)—

(a) by serving a developer's notice on every such person whose name and address is known to him; and

(b) where he has taken reasonable steps to ascertain the names and addresses of every such person, but has been unable to do so, by local advertisement.

(2) Where the proposed development consists of the installation of a mast within 3 kilometres of the perimeter of an aerodrome, the developer shall notify the Civil Aviation Authority, the Secretary of State for Defence or the aerodrome operator, as appropriate, before making the application required by paragraph (3).

(3) Before beginning the development, the developer shall apply to the local planning authority for a determination as to whether the prior approval of the authority will be required to the siting and appearance of the development.

(4) The application shall be accompanied—

(a) by a written description of the proposed development and a plan indicating its proposed location together with any fee required to be paid;

(b) where paragraph (1) applies, by evidence that the requirements of paragraph (1) have been satisfied; and

(c) where paragraph (2) applies, by evidence that the Civil Aviation Authority, the Secretary of State for Defence or the aerodrome operator, as the case may be, has been notified of the proposal.

(5) Subject to paragraphs (7)(c) and (d), upon receipt of the application under paragraph (4) the local planning authority shall—

(a) for development which, in their opinion, falls within a category set out in the table of article 10 of the Procedure Order, consult the authority or person mentioned in relation to that category, except where—

(i) the local planning authority are the authority so mentioned; or

(ii) the authority or person so mentioned has advised the local planning authority that they do not wish to be consulted, and shall give the consultees at least 14 days within which to comment;

(b) in the case of development which does not accord with the provisions of the development plan in force in the area in which the land to which the application relates is situated or which would affect a right of way to which Part III of the Wildlife and Countryside Act 1981(a) (public rights of way) applies, shall give notice of the proposed development, in the appropriate form set out in Schedule 3 to the Procedure Order—

(aa) by site display in at least one place on or near the land to which the application relates for not less than 21 days, and

(bb) by local advertisement;

(c) in the case of development which does not fall within paragraph (b) but which involves development carried out on a site having an area of 1 hectare or more, shall give notice of the proposed development, in the appropriate form set out in Schedule 3 to the Procedure Order—

(i) (aa) by site display in at least one place on or near the land to which the application relates for not less than 21 days, or

(bb) by serving notice on any adjoining owner or occupier, and

(ii) by local advertisement;

(d) in the case of development which does not fall within (b) or (c), shall give notice of the proposed development, in the appropriate form set out in Schedule 3 to the Procedure Order—

(i) by site display in at least one place on or near the land to which the application relates for not less than 21 days, or

(ii) by serving the notice on any adjoining owner or occupier.

(6) The local planning authority shall take into account any representations made to them as a result of consultations or notices given under A.3, when determining the application made under paragraph (3).

(7) The development shall not be begun before the occurrence of one of the following—

(a) the receipt by the applicant from the local planning authority of a written notice of their determination that such prior approval is not required;

(b) where the local planning authority gives the applicant written notice that such prior approval is required, the giving of that approval to the applicant, in writing, within a period of 56 days beginning with the date on which they received his application;

(c) where the local planning authority gives the applicant written notice that such prior approval is required, the expiry of a period of 56 days beginning with the date on which the local planning authority received his application without the local planning authority notifying the applicant, in writing, that such approval is given or refused; or

(d) the expiry of a period of 56 days beginning with the date on which the local planning authority received the application without the local planning authority notifying the applicant, in writing, of their determination as to whether such prior approval is required.

(8) The development shall, except to the extent that the local planning authority otherwise agree in writing, be carried out—

(a) where prior approval has been given as mentioned in paragraph (7)(b) in accordance with the details approved;

(b) in any other case, in accordance with the details submitted with the application.

(9) The development shall be begun—

(a) where prior approval has been given as mentioned in paragraph (7)(b), not later than the expiration of five years beginning with the date on which the approval was given;

(b) in any other case, not later than the expiration of five years beginning with the date on which the local planning authority were given the information referred to in paragraph (4).

(10) In a case of emergency, development is permitted by Class A subject to the condition that the operator shall give written notice to the local planning authority of such development as soon as possible after the emergency begins.

Interpretation of Class A

A.4 For the purposes of Class A—

'aerodrome operator' means the person for the time being having the management of an aerodrome or, in relation to a particular aerodrome, the management of that aerodrome;

'antenna system' means a set of antennas installed on a building or structure and operated by a single telecommunications code system operator in accordance with his licence;

'development ancillary to radio equipment housing' means the construction, installation, alteration or replacement of structures, equipment or means of access which are ancillary to and reasonably required for the purposes of the radio equipment housing;

'developer's notice' means a notice signed and dated by or on behalf of the developer and containing—

(i) the name of the developer;

(ii) the address or location of the proposed development;

(iii) a description of the proposed development (including its siting and appearance and the height of any mast);

(iv) a statement that the developer will apply to the local planning authority for a determination as to whether the prior approval of the authority will be required to the siting and appearance of the development;

(v) the name and address of the local planning authority to whom the application will be made;

(vi) a statement that the application shall be available for public inspection at the offices of the local planning authority during usual office hours;

(vii) a statement that any person who wishes to make representations about the siting and appearance of the proposed development may do so in writing to the local planning authority;

(viii) the date by which any such representations should be received by the local planning authority, being a date not less than 14 days from the date of the notice; and

(ix) the address to which such representations should be made.

'land controlled by the operator' means land occupied by the operator in right of a freehold interest or a leasehold interest under a lease granted for a term of not less than 10 years;

'local advertisement' means by publication of the notice in a newspaper circulating in the locality in which the land to which the application relates is situated;

'mast' means a radio mast or a radio tower;

'owner' means any person who is the estate owner in respect of the fee simple, or who is entitled to a tenancy granted or extended for a term of years certain of which not less than seven years remain unexpired;

'Procedure Order' means the Town and Country Planning (General Development Procedure) Order 1995;

'relevant period' means a period which expires—

(i) six months from the commencement of the construction, installation, alteration or replacement of any apparatus or structure permitted by Class A(a) or Class A(c) or from the commencement of the use permitted by Class A(b), as the case may be, or

(ii) when the need for such apparatus, structure or use ceases,

whichever occurs first;

'site display' means by the posting of the notice by firm affixture to some object, sited and displayed in such a way as to be easily visible and legible by members of the public;

'small antenna' means an antenna which—

(i) is for use in connection with a telephone system operating on a point to fixed multi-point basis;

(ii) does not exceed 50 centimetres in any linear measurement; and

(iii) does not, in two-dimensional profile, have an area exceeding 1,591 square centimetres,

and any calculation for the purposes of (ii) and (iii) shall exclude any feed element, reinforcing rim mountings and brackets;

'tenant' means the tenant of an agricultural holding any part of which is comprised in the land to which the application relates.

PART 25: OTHER TELECOMMUNICATIONS DEVELOPMENT

Class A

Permitted development

A. The installation, alteration or replacement on any building or other stucture of a height of 15 metres or more of a microwave antenna and any structure intended for the support of a microwave antenna.

Development

A.1 Development is not permitted by Class A if—

(a) the building is a dwellinghouse or the building or other structure is within the curtilage of a dwellinghouse;

(b) it would consist of development of a kind described in paragraph A of Part 24;

(c) the development would result in the presence on the building or structure of more than two microwave antennas;

(d) in the case of a satellite antenna, the size of the antenna, including its supporting structure but excluding any projecting feed element, would exceed 90 centimetres;

(e) in the case of a terrestrial microwave antenna—

(i) the size of the antenna, when measured in any dimension but excluding any projecting feed element, would exceed 1.3 metres; and

(ii) the highest part of the antenna or its supporting structure would be more than 3 metres higher than the highest part of the building or structure on which it is installed or is to be installed;

(f) it is on article 1(5) land; or

(g) it would consist of the installation, alteration or replacement of system apparatus within the meaning of section 8(6) of the Road Traffic (Driver Licensing and Information Systems) Act 1989 (definitions of driver information systems etc.).

Conditions

A.2 Development is permitted by Class A subject to the following conditions—

(a) the antenna shall, so far as is practicable, be sited so as to minimise its effect on the external appearance of the building or structure on which it is installed;

(b) an antenna no longer needed for the reception or transmission of microwave radio energy shall be removed from the building or structure as soon as reasonably practicable.

Class B

Permitted development

B. The installation, alteration or replacement on any building or other structure of a height of less than 15 metres of a satellite antenna.

Development not permitted

B.1 Development is not permitted by Class B if—

(a) the building is a dwellinghouse or the building or other structure is within the curtilage of a dwellinghouse;

(b) it would consist of development of a kind described in paragraph A of Part 24;

(c) it would consist of the installation, alteration or replacement of system apparatus within the meaning of section 8(6) of the Road Traffic (Driver Licensing and Information Systems) Act 1989 (definitions of driver information systems etc.);

(d) the size of the antenna (excluding any projecting feed element, reinforcing rim, mountings or brackets) when measured in any dimension would exceed 90 centimetres.

(e) the highest part of an antenna to be installed on a roof would, when installed, exceed in height the highest part of the roof,

(f) there is any other satellite antenna on the building or other structure on which the antenna is to be installed;

(g) it would consist of the installation of an antenna on a chimney;

(h) it would consist of the installation of an antenna on a wall or roof slope which fronts a highway;

(i) in the Broads, it would consist of the installation of an antenna on a wall or roof slope which fronts a waterway.

Condition

B.2 Development is permitted by Class B subject to the following conditions—

(a) the antenna shall, so far as is practicable, be sited so as to minimise its effect on the external appearance of the building or structure on which it is installed;

(b) an antenna no longer needed for the reception or transmission of microwave radio energy shall be removed from the building or structure as soon as reasonably practicable.

PART 26: DEVELOPMENT BY THE HISTORIC BUILDINGS AND MONUMENTS COMMISSION FOR ENGLAND

Class A

Permitted development

A. Development by or on behalf of the Historic Buildings and Monuments Commission for England, consisting of—

(a) the maintenance, repair or restoration of any building or monument;

(b) the erection of screens, fences or covers designed or intended to protect or safeguard any building or monument; or

(c) the carrying out of works to stabilise ground conditions by any cliff, watercourse or the coastline;

where such works are required for the purposes of securing the preservation of any building or monument.

Development not permitted

A.1 Development is not permitted by Class A(a) if the works involve the extension of the building or monument.

Condition

A.2 Except for development also falling within Class A(a), Class A(b) development is permitted subject to the condition that any structure erected in accordance with that permission shall be removed at the expiry of a period of six months (or such longer period as the local planning authority may agree in writing) from the date on which work to erect the structure was begun.

Interpretation of Class A

A.3 For the purposes of Class A—

'building or monument' means any building or monument in the guardianship of the Historic Buildings and Monuments Commission for England or owned, controlled or managed by them.

PART 27: USE BY MEMBERS OF CERTAIN RECREATIONAL ORGANISATIONS

Class A

Permitted development

A. The use of land by members of a recreational organisation for the purposes of recreation or instruction, and the erection or placing of tents on the land for the purposes of the use.

Development not permitted

A.1 Development is not permitted by Class A if the land is a building or is within the curtilage of a dwellinghouse.

Interpretation of Class A

A.2 For the purposes of Class A—

'recreational organisation' means an organisation holding a certificate of exemption under section 269 of the Public Health Act 1936 (power of local authority to control use of moveable dwellings).

PART 28: DEVELOPMENT AT AMUSEMENT PARKS

Class A

Permitted development

A. Development on land used as an amusement park consisting of—

(a) the erection of booths or stalls or the installation of plant or machinery to be used for or in connection with the entertainment of the public within the amusement park; or

(b) the extension, alteration or replacement of any existing booths or stalls, plant or machinery so used.

Development not permitted

A.1 Development is not permitted by Class A if—

(a) the plant or machinery would—

(i) if the land or pier is within 3 kilometres of the perimeter of an aerodrome, exceed a height of 25 metres or the height of the highest existing structure (whichever is the lesser), or

(ii) in any other case, exceed a height of 25 metres;

(b) in the case of an extension to an existing building or structure, that building or structure would as a result exceed 5 metres above ground level or the height of the roof of the existing building or structure, whichever is the greater, or

(c) in any other case, the height of the building or structure erected, extended, altered or replaced would exceed 5 metres above ground level.

Interpretation of Class A

A.2 For the purposes of Class A—

'amusement park' means an enclosed area of open land, or any part of a seaside pier, which is principally used (other than by way of a temporary use) as a funfair or otherwise for the purposes of providing public entertainment by means of mechanical amusements and side-shows; but, where part only of an enclosed area is commonly so used as a funfair or for such public entertainment, only the part so used shall be regarded as an amusement park; and 'booths or stalls' includes buildings or structures similar to booths or stalls.

PART 29: DRIVER INFORMATION SYSTEMS

Class A

Permitted development

A. The installation, alteration or replacement of system apparatus by or on behalf of a driver information system operator.

Development

A.1 Development is not permitted by Class A if—

(a) in the case of the installation, alteration or replacement of system apparatus other than on a building or other structure—

(i) the ground or base area of the system apparatus would exceed 1.5 square metres; or

(ii) the system apparatus would exceed a height of 15 metres above ground level;

(b) in the case of the installation, alteration or replacement of system apparatus on a building or other structure—

(i) the highest part of the apparatus when installed, altered, or replaced would exceed in height the highest part of the building or structure by more than 3 metres; or

(ii) the development would result in the presence on the building or structure of more than two microwave antennas.

Conditions

A.2 Development is permitted by Class A subject to the following conditions—

(a) any system apparatus shall, so far as practicable, be sited so as to minimise its effect on the external appearance of any building or other structure on which it is installed;

(b) any system apparatus which is no longer needed for a driver information system shall be removed as soon as reasonably practicable.

Interpretation of Class A

A.3 For the purposes of Class A—

'driver information system operator' means a person granted an operator's

licence under section 10 of the Road Traffic (Driver Licensing and Information Systems) Act 1989 (operators' licences); and
'system apparatus' has the meaning assigned to that term by section 8(6) of that Act (definitions of driver information systems etc.).

PART 30: TOLL ROAD FACILITIES

Class A

Permitted development

A. Development consisting of—

(a) the setting up and the maintenance, improvement or other alteration of facilities for the collection of tolls;

(b) the provision of a hard surface to be used for the parking of vehicles in connection with the use of such facilities.

Development not permitted

A.1 Development is not permitted by Class A if—

(a) it is not located within 100 metres (measured along the ground) of the boundary of a toll road;

(b) the height of any building or structure would exceed—

(i) 7.5 metres excluding any rooftop structure; or

(ii) 10 metres including any rooftop structure;

(c) the aggregate area of the floor space at or above ground level of any building or group of buildings within a toll collection area, excluding the floor space of any toll collection booth, would exceed 1,500 square metres.

Conditions

A.2 In the case of any article 1(5) land, development is permitted by Class A subject to the following conditions—

(a) the developer shall, before beginning the development, apply to the local planning authority for a determination as to whether the prior approval of the authority will be required to the siting, design and external appearance of the facilities for the collection of tolls;

(b) the application shall be accompanied by a written description, together with plans and elevations, of the proposed development and any fee required to be paid;

(c) the development shall not be begun before the occurrence of one of the following—

(i) the receipt by the applicant from the local planning authority of a written notice of their determination that such prior approval is not required;

(ii) where the local planning authority give the applicant notice within 28 days following the date of receiving his application of their determination that such prior approval is required, the giving of such approval; or

(iii) the expiry of 28 days following the date on which the application was received by the local planning authority without the local planning authority making any determination as to whether such approval is required or notifying the applicant of their determination;

(d) the development shall, except to the extent that the local planning authority otherwise agree in writing, be carried out—

(i) where prior approval is required, in accordance with the details approved;

(ii) where prior approval is not required, in accordance with the details submitted with the application;

and

(e) the development shall be carried out—

(i) where approval has been given by the local planning authority, within a period of five years from the date on which the approval was given;

(ii) in any other case, within a period of five years from the date on which the local planning authority were given the information referred to in sub-paragraph (b).

Interpretation of Class A

A.3 For the purposes of Class A—

'facilities for the collection of tolls' means such buildings, structures, or other facilities as are reasonably required for the purpose of or in connection with the collection of tolls in pursuance of a toll order;

'ground level' means the level of the surface of the ground immediately adjacent to the building or group of buildings in question or, where the level of the surface of the ground on which it is situated or is to be situated is not uniform, the level of the highest part of the surface of the ground adjacent to it;

'rooftop structure' means any apparatus or structure which is reasonably required to be located on and attached to the roof, being an apparatus or structure which is—

(a) so located for the provision of heating, ventilation, air conditioning, water, gas or electricity;

(b) lift machinery; or

(c) reasonably required for safety purposes;

'toll' means a toll which may be charged pursuant to a toll order;

'toll collection area' means an area of land where tolls are collected in pursuance of a toll order, and includes any facilities for the collection of tolls;

'toll collection booth' means any building or structure designed or adapted for the purpose of collecting tolls in pursuance of a toll order;

'toll order' has the same meaning as in Part I of the New Roads and Street Works Act 1991 (new roads in England and Wales); and

'toll road' means a road which is the subject of a toll order.

PART 31: DEMOLITION OF BUILDINGS

Class A

Permitted development

A. Any building operation consisting of the demolition of a building.

Development not permitted

A.1 Development is not permitted by Class A where—

(a) the building has been rendered unsafe or otherwise uninhabitable by the action or inaction of any person having an interest in the land on which the building stands; and

(b) it is practicable to secure safety or health by works of repair or works for affording temporary support.

Conditions

A.2 Development is permitted by Class A subject to the following conditions—

(a) where demolition is urgently necessary in the interests of safety or health and the measures immediately necessary in such interests are the demolition of the building the developer shall, as soon as reasonably practicable, give the local planning authority a written justification of the demolition;

(b) where the demolition does not fall within sub-paragraph (a) and is not excluded demolition—

(i) the developer shall, before beginning the development, apply to the local planning authority for a determination as to whether the prior approval of the authority will be required to the method of demolition and any proposed restoration of the site;

(ii) the application shall be accompanied by a written description of the proposed development, a statement that a notice has been posted in accordance with sub-paragraph (iii) and any fee required to be paid;

(iii) subject to sub-paragraph (iv), the applicant shall display a site notice by site display on or near the land on which the building to be demolished is sited and shall leave the notice in place for not less than 21 days in the period of 28 days beginning with the date on which the application was submitted to the local planning authority;

(iv) where the site notice is, without any fault or intention of the applicant, removed, obscured or defaced before the period of 21 days referred to in sub-paragraph (iii) has elapsed, he shall be treated as having complied with the requirements of that sub-paragraph if he has taken reasonable steps for protection of the notice and, if need be, its replacement;

(v) the development shall not be begun before the occurrence of one of the following—

(aa) the receipt by the applicant from the local planning authority of a written notice of their determination that such prior approval is not required;

(bb) where the local planning authority give the applicant notice within 28 days following the date of receiving his application of their determination that such prior approval is required, the giving of such approval; or

(cc) the expiry of 28 days following the date on which the application was received by the local planning authority without the local planning authority making any determination as to whether such approval is required or notifying the applicant of their determination;

(vi) the development shall, except to the extent that the local planning authority otherwise agree in writing, be carried out—

(aa) where prior approval is required, in accordance with the details approved;

(bb) where prior approval is not required, in accordance with the details submitted with the application;

and

(vii) the development shall be carried out

(aa) where approval has been given by the local planning authority, within a period of five years from the date on which approval was given;

(bb) in any other case, within a period of five years from the date on which the local planning authority were given the information referred to in sub-paragraph (ii).

Interpretation of Class A

A.3 For the purposes of Class A—

'excluded demolition' means demolition—

(a) on land which is the subject of a planning permission, for the redevelopment of the land, granted on an application or deemed to be granted under Part III of the Act (control over development),

(b) required or permitted to be carried out by or under any enactment, or

(c) required to be carried out by virtue of a relevant obligation;

'relevant obligation' means—

(a) an obligation arising under an agreement made under section 106 of the Act, as originally enacted (agreements regulating development or use of land);

(b) a planning obligation entered into under section 106 of the Act, as substituted by section 12 of the Planning and Compensation Act 1991 (planning obligations), or under section 299A of the Act (Crown planning obligations);

(c) an obligation arising under or under an agreement made under any provision corresponding to section 106 of the Act, as originally enacted or as substituted by the Planning and Compensation Act 1991, or to section 299A of the Act; and

'site notice' means a notice containing—

(a) the name of the applicant,

(b) a description, including the address, of the building or buildings which it is proposed be demolished,

(c) a statement that the applicant has applied to the local planning authority for a determination as to whether the prior approval of the authority will be required to the method of demolition and any proposed restoration of the site,

(d) the date on which the applicant proposes to carry out the demolition, and

(e) the name and address of the local planning authority, and which is signed and dated by or on behalf of the applicant.

Class B

Permitted development

B. Any building operation consisting of the demolition of the whole or any part of any gate, fence, wall or other means of enclosure.

PART 32: SCHOOLS, COLLEGES, UNIVERSITIES AND HOSPITALS

Class A

Permitted development

The erection on the site of any school, college, university or hospital of any building required for use as part of, or for a purpose incidental to the use of, the school, college, university or hospital as such, as the case may be.

Development not permittted

A.1 Development is not permitted by Class A—

(a) unless—

(i) in the case of school, college or university buildings, the predominant use of the existing buildings on the site is for the provision of education, or

(ii) in the case of hospital buildings, the predominant use of the existing buildings on the site is for the provision of any medical or health services;

(b) where the cumulative total floor space of any buildings erected on a particular site (other than the original school, college, university or hospital buildings) would exceed 10% of the total floor space of the original school, college, university or hospital buildings on that site;

(c) where the cumulative total cubic content of buildings erected on a particular site (other than the original school, college, university or hospital buildings) would exceed 250 cubic metres;

(d) where any part of a building erected would be within 20 metres of the boundary of the site;

(e) where, as a result of the development, any land, used as a playing field immediately before the development took place, could no longer be so used.

Condition

A.2 Development is permitted by Class A subject to the condition that, in the case of any article 1(5) land, any materials used shall be of a similar appearance to those used for the original school, college, university or hospital buildings.

Interpretation of Class A

A.3 For the purposes of Class A—

'cumulative total floor space' or 'cumulative total cubic content', as the case may be, of buildings erected, includes the total floor space or total cubic content of any existing buildings previously erected at any time under Class A; and

'original school, college, university or hospital buildings' means any school, college, university or hospital buildings, as the case may be, other than any buildings erected at any time under Class A.

PART 33: CLOSED CIRCUIT TELEVISION CAMERAS

Class A

Permitted development

A. The installation, alteration or replacement on a building of a closed circuit television camera to be used for security purposes.

Development not permitted

A.1 Development is not permitted by Class A if—

(a) the building on which the camera would be installed, altered or replaced is a listed building or a scheduled monument;

(b) the dimensions of the camera including its housing exceed 75 centimetres by 25 centimetres by 25 centimetres;

(c) any part of the camera would, when installed, altered or replaced, be less than 250 centimetres above ground level;

(d) any part of the camera would, when installed, altered or replaced, protrude from the surface of the building by more than one metre when measured from the surface of the building;

(e) any part of the camera would, when installed, altered or replaced, be in contact with the surface of the building at a point which is more than one metre from any other point of contact;

(f) any part of the camera would be less than 10 metres from any part of another camera installed on a building;

(g) the development would result in the presence of more than four cameras on the same side of the building; or

(h) the development would result in the presence of more than 16 cameras on the building.

Conditions

A.2 Development is permitted by Class A subject to the following conditions—

(a) the camera shall, so far as practicable, be sited so as to minimise its effect on the external appearance of the building on which it is situated;

(b) the camera shall be removed as soon as reasonably practicable after it is no longer required for security purposes.

Interpretation of Class A

A.3 For the purposes of Class A—

'camera', except in paragraph A.1(b), includes its housing, pan and tilt mechanism, infra red illuminator, receiver, mountings and brackets; and

'ground level' means the level of the surface of the ground immediately adjacent to the building or, where the level of the surface of the ground is not uniform, the level of the highest part of the surface of the ground adjacent to it.

ARTICLE 9 **SCHEDULE 3** STATUTORY INSTRUMENTS REVOKED

[omitted]

APPENDIX 4

Town and Country Planning (General Development Procedure) Order 1995, SI 1995/419

Brought into force: 3rd June 1995

1. Citation, commencement and interpretation

(1) This Order may be cited as the Town and Country Planning (General Development Procedure) Order 1995 and shall come into force on 3rd June 1995.

(2) In this Order, unless the context otherwise requires—

'the Act' means the Town and Country Planning Act 1990;

'building' includes any structure or erection, and any part of a building, as defined in this article, but does not include plant or machinery or any structure in the nature of plant or machinery;

'dwellinghouse' does not include a building containing one or more flats, or a flat contained within such a building;

'electronic development' has the meaning given in section 15(1), of the Electronic Communications Act 2000

'EIA development', 'environmental information' and 'environmental statement' have the same meanings respectively as in regulation 2 of the Town and Country Planning (Environmental Impact Assessment) (England and Wales) Regulations 1999;

'erection', in relation to buildings as defined in this article, includes extension, alteration, or re-erection;

'flat' means a separate and self-contained set of premises constructed or adapted for use for the purpose of a dwelling and forming part of a building from some other part of which it is divided horizontally;

'floor space' means the total floor space in a building or buildings;

'landscaping' means the treatment of land (other than buildings) being the site or part of the site in respect of which an outline planning permission is granted, for the purpose of enhancing or protecting the amenities of the site and the area in which it is situated and includes screening by fences, walls or other means, the planting of trees, hedges, shrubs or grass, the formation of banks, terraces or other earthworks, the laying out of gardens or courts, and the provision of other amenity features;

'by local advertisement' means—

(a) publication of the notice in a newspaper circulating in the locality in which the land to which the application relates is situated; and

(b) where the local planning authority maintain a website for the purpose of advertisement of applications, by publication of the notice on the website;

'mining operations' means the winning and working of minerals in, on or under land, whether by surface or underground working;

'outline planning permission' means a planning permission for the erection of a building, which is granted subject to a condition requiring the subsequent approval of the local planning authority with respect to one or more reserved matters;

'planning obligation' means an obligation entered into by agreement or otherwise by any person interested in land pursuant to section 106 of the Act;

'proposed highway' has the same meaning as in section 329 of the Highways Act 1980 (further provision as to interpretation);

'1988 Regulations' means the Town and Country Planning (Applications) Regulations 1988;

'reserved matters' in relation to an outline planning permission, or an application for such permission, means any of the following matters in respect of which details have not been given in the application, namely—

(a) siting,

(b) design,

(c) external appearance,

(d) means of access,

(e) the landscaping of the site;

'section 278 agreement' means an agreement entered into pursunt to section 278 of the Highways Act 1980;

'by site display' means by the posting of the notice by firm affixture to some object, sited and displayed in such a way as to be easily visible and legible by members of the public;

'special road' means a highway or proposed highway which is a special road in accordance with section 16 of the Highways Act 1980 (general provisions as to special roads);

'trunk road' means a highway or proposed highway which is a trunk road by virtue of sections 10(1) or 19 of the Highways Act 1980 (general provisions as to trunk roads, and certain special roads and other highways to become trunk roads) or any other enactment or any instrument made under any enactment.

(3) In this Order and in relation to the use of electronic communications or electronic storage for any purpose of this Order which is capable of being carried out electronically—

(a) the expression 'address' includes any number or address used for the purpose of such communications or storage, except that where this Order imposes any obligation on any person to provide a name and address to any other person, the obligation shall not be fulfilled unless the person on whom it is imposed provides a postal address;

(b) references to documents, maps, plans, drawings, certificates or other documents or to copies of such things, include references to such documents or copies of them in electronic form.

(4) Paragraphs (5) to (8) apply where an electronic communication is used by a person for the following purposes—

(a) fulfilling any requirement in this Order to give or send any application, notice or other document to any other person; or

(b) lodging an application, certificate or other document under article 20(3) with an authority mentioned in that article:

and in those paragraphs, 'the recipient' means the person mentioned in sub-paragraph (a) of this paragraph, or the authority mentioned in sub-paragraph (b), as the case may be.

(5) The requirement shall not be taken to be fulfilled, or (as the case may be) the application or other document shall not be taken to have been lodged, unless the document transmitted by the electronic communication is—

(a) capable of being accessed by the recipient,

(b) legible in all material respects, and

(c) sufficiently permanent to be used for subsequent reference.

(6) In paragraph (5), 'legible in all material respects' means that the information contained in the notice or document is available to the recipient to no lesser extent than it would be if sent or given by means of a document in printed form.

(7) Where the electronic communication is received by the recipient outside the recipient's business hours, it shall be taken to have been received on the next working day; and for this purpose 'working day' means a day which is not a Saturday, Sunday, Bank Holiday or other public holiday.

(8) A requirement in this Order that any application, notice or other document should be in writing is fulfilled where the document meets the criteria in paragraph (5), and 'written' and cognate expressions are to be construed accordingly.

2. Application

(1) This Order applies to all land in England and Wales, but where land is the subject of a special development order, whether made before or after the commencement of this Order, this Order shall apply to that land only to such extent and subject to such modifications as may be specified in the special development order.

(2) Nothing in this Order shall apply to any permission which is deemed to be granted under section 222 of the Act (planning permission not needed for advertisements complying with regulations).

3. Applications for outline planning permission

(1) Where an application is made to the local planning authority for outline planning permission, the authority may grant permission subject to a condition specifying reserved matters for the authority's subsequent approval.

(2) Where the authority who are to determine an application for outline planning permission are of the opinion that, in the circumstances of the case, the application ought not to be considered separately from all or any of the reserved matters, they shall within the period of one month beginning with the receipt of the application notify the applicant that they are unable to determine it unless further details are submitted, specifying the further details they require.

4. Applications for approval of reserved matters

An application for approval of reserved matters—

(a) shall be made in writing to the local planning authority and shall give sufficient information to enable the authority to identify the outline planning permission in respect of which it is made;

(b) shall include such particulars, and be accompanied by such plans and drawings, as are necessary to deal with the matters reserved in the outline planning permission; and

(c) except where the authority indicate that a lesser number is required or where the application is made using electronic communications, shall be accompanied by three copies of the application and the plans and drawings submitted with it.

4A. Applications in respect of Crown land

An application for planning permission made by virtue of section 299(2) of the Act shall be accompanied by—

(a) a statement that the application is made, by virtue of section 299(2) of the Act, in respect of Crown land; and

(b) where the application is made by a person authorised in writing by the appropriate authority, a copy of that authorisation.

5. General provisions relating to applications

(1) Any application made under regulation 3 of the 1988 Regulations (applications for planning permission) or article 4 above, shall be made—

- (a) where the application relates to land in Greater London or a metropolitan county or to land inWales, to the local planning authority;
- (b) where the application relates to land in England which is neither in Greater London nor a metropolitan county and—

(i) that land is in a National Park, or

(ii) the application relates to a county matter,

to the county planning authority;

(c) in any other case, to the district planning authority.

(2) When the local planning authority with whom an application has to be lodged receive—

(a) in the case of an application made under paragraph (1) of regulation 3 of the 1988 Regulations, the form of application required by that paragraph, together with the certificate or other documents required by article 7;

(b) in the case of an application made under regulation 3(3) of the 1988 Regulations, sufficient information to enable the authority to identify the previous grant of planning permission, together with the certificate or other documents required by article 7;

(c) in the case of an application made under article 4 above, the documents and information required by that article,

and the fee, if any, required to be paid in respect of the application, the authority shall as soon as is reasonably practicable, send to the applicant an acknowledgement of the application in the terms (or substantially in the terms) set out in Part 1 of Schedule 1 hereto.

(3) Where an application is made to a county planning authority in accordance with paragraph (1), that authority shall, as soon as practicable, send a copy of the application and of any accompanying plans and drawings to the district planning authority, if any.

(4) Where, after sending an acknowledgement as required by paragraph (2) of this article, the local planning authority consider that the application is invalid by reason of a failure to comply with the requirements of regulation 3 of the 1988 Regulations or article 4 above or any other statutory requirement, they shall as soon as reasonably practicable notify the applicant that his application is invalid.

(5) In this article, 'county matter' has the meaning given to that expression in paragraph 1(1) of Schedule 1 to the Act (local planning authorities — distribution of functions).

(5A) Omitted (as affecting Wales).

6. Notice of applications for planning permission

(1) Subject to paragraph (2), an applicant for planning permission shall give requisite notice of the application to any person (other than the applicant) who on the prescribed date is an owner of the land to which the application relates, or a tenant,—

(a) by serving the notice on every such person whose name and address is known to him; and

(b) where he has taken reasonable steps to ascertain the names and addresses of every such person, but has been unable to do so, by local advertisement after the prescribed date.

(2) In the case of an application for planning permission for development consisting of the winning and working of minerals by underground operations, instead of giving notice in the manner provided for by paragraph (1), the applicant shall give requisite notice of the application to any person (other than the applicant) who on the prescribed date is an owner of any of the land to which the application relates, or a tenant,—

(a) by serving the notice on every such person whom the applicant knows to be such a person and whose name and address is known to him;

(b) by local advertisement after the prescribed date; and

(c) by site display in at least one place in every parish or community within which there is situated any part of the land to which the application relates, leaving the notice in position for not less than seven days in the period of 21 days immediately preceding the making of the application to the local planning authority.

(3) The notice required by paragraph (2)(c) shall (in addition to any other matters required to be contained in it) name a place within the area of the local planning authority to whom the

application is made where a copy of the application for planning permission, and of all plans and other documents submitted with it, will be open to inspection by the public at all reasonable hours during such period as may be specified in the notice.

[(3A) Where a local planning authority maintain a website for the purpose of advertisement of applications for planning permission, the notice required by paragraph (2)(c) shall (in addition to any other matters required to be contained in it) state the address of the website where a copy of the application, and of all plans and other documents submitted with it, will be open to inspection by the public at all reasonable hours during such period as may be specified in the notice, and the place on the website where such documents may be accessed, and how they may be accessed.]

(4) Where the notice is, without any fault or intention of the applicant, removed, obscured or defaced before the period of seven days referred to in paragraph (2)(c) has elapsed, he shall be treated as having complied with the requirements of that paragraph if he has taken reasonable steps for protection of the notice and, if need be, its replacement.

(5) (a) The date prescribed for the purposes of section 65(2) of the Act (notice etc. of applications for planning permission), and the 'prescribed date' for the purposes of this article, is the day 21 days before the date of the application;

(b) The applications prescribed for the purposes of paragraph (c) of the definition of 'owner' in section 65(8) of the Act are minerals applications, and the minerals prescribed for the purposes of that paragraph are any minerals other than oil, gas, coal, gold or silver.

(6) In this article—

'minerals applications' mean applications for planning permission for development consisting of the winning and working of minerals;

'requisite notice' means notice in the appropriate form set out in Part 1 of Schedule 2 to this Order or in a form substantially to the like effect, but shall not include notice served using electronic communications; and

'tenant' means the tenant of an agricultural holding any part of which is comprised in the land to which an application relates.

(7) For the purposes of this article and the certificates required by article 7, where an application for planning permission is made by virtue of section 299(2) of the Act, the applicant shall be treated as an owner of the land and no account shall be taken of any Crown interest or Duchy interest in the land or in any mineral in the land.

7. Certificates in relation to notice of applications for planning permission

(1) Where an application for planning permission is made, the applicant shall certify, in the appropriate form prescribed in Part 2 of Schedule 2 to this Order or in a form substantially to the like effect, that the requirements of article 6 have been satisfied.

(2) If an applicant has cause to rely on paragraph (4) of article 6, the certificate must state the relevant circumstances.

8. Publicity for applications for planning permission

(1) An application for planning permission shall be publicised by the local planning authority to which the application is made in the manner prescribed by this article.

(2) In the case of a planning application for planning permission within the designated area for development—

(a) which is the subject of an EIA application accompanied by an environmental statement, the application shall be publicised in the manner specified in paragraph (3);

(b) which does not accord with the provisions of the development plan in force in the area in which the land to which the application relates is situated, shall be publicised in the manner specified in paragraph (3A);

(c) which would affect a right of way to which Part III of the Wildlife and Countryside Act 1981 (public rights of way) applies the application shall be publicised in the manner specified in paragraph (3A).

(3) An application falling within paragraph (2) (a) shall be publicised by the local planning authority giving requisite notice—

(a) by site display in at least one place on or near the land to which the application relates for not less than 21 days, and

(b) by local advertisement.

(3A) An application falling within paragraph (2)(b) or (2)(c) shall be publicised by the local planning authority giving requisite notice—

(a) by site display in at least one place on or near the land to which the application relates for not less than 21 days; and

(b) where the local planning authority maintains a website for the purpose of advertisement of applications, by publication of the notice on the website.

(4) In the case of an application for planning permission to which paragraph (2) does not apply, if the application is for major development the application shall be publicised by the local planning authority—

(a) by giving requisite notice by site display in at least one place on or near the land to which the application relates for not less than 21 days; or

(b) by serving the notice on any adjoining owner or occupier, and where the local planning authority maintains a website for the purpose of advertisement of applications, shall also be published on that website.

(5) In the case of an application to which neither paragraph (2) nor paragraph (4) applies, the application shall be publicised by the local planning authority giving requisite notice—

(a) by site display in at least one place on or near the land to which the application relates for not less than 21 days; or

(b) by serving the notice on any adjoining owner or occupier.

(6) Where the notice is, without any fault or intention of the local planning authority, removed, obscured or defaced before the period of 21 days referred to in paragraph (3)(a), (4)(a)(i) or (5)(a) has elapsed, the authority shall be treated as having complied with the requirements of the relevant paragraph if they have taken reasonable steps for protection of the notice and, if need be, its replacement.

(7) In this article—

'adjoining owner or occupier' means any owner or occupier of any land adjoining the land to which the application relates;

'EIA application' has the meaning given in regulation 2 of the Town and Country Planning (Environmental Impact Assessment) (England and Wales) Regulations 1999; 'environmental statement' means a statement which the applicant refers to as an environmental statement for the purposes of those Regulations;

'major development' means development involving any one or more of the following—

(a) the winning and working of minerals or the use of land for mineralworking deposits;

(b) waste development;

(c) the provision of dwellinghouses where—

(i) the number of dwellinghouses to be provided is 10 or more; or

(ii) the development is to be carried out on a site having an area of 0.5 hectare or more and it is not known whether the development falls within paragraph (c)(i);

(d) the provision of a building or buildings where the floor space to be created by the development is 1,000 square metres or more; or

(e) development carried out on a site having an area of 1 hectare or more;

'requisite notice' means notice in the appropriate form set out in Schedule 3 to this Order or in a form substantially to the like effect;

'waste development' means any operational development designed to be used wholly or mainly for the purpose of, or a material change of use to, treating, storing, processing or disposing of refuse or waste materials.

9. Applications for planning permission referred to the Secretary of State and appeals to the Secretary of State

(1) Articles 6 and 7 apply to any appeal to the Secretary of State under section 78 of the Act (right to appeal against planning decisions and failure to take such decisions) as they apply to applications for planning permission.

(2) Subject to paragraph (3), if the local planning authority have failed to satisfy the requirements of article 8 in respect of an application for planning permission at the time the application is referred to the Secretary of State under section 77 of the Act (reference of applications to Secretary of State), or any appeal to the Secretary of State is made under section 78 of the Act, article 8 shall continue to apply, as if such referral or appeal to the Secretary of State had not been made.

(3) Where paragraph (2) applies, when the local planning authority have satisfied the requirements of article 8, they shall inform the Secretary of State that they have done so.

10. Consultations before the grant of permission

(1) Before granting planning permission for development which, in their opinion, falls within a category set out in the table below, a local planning authority shall consult the authority or person mentioned in relation to that category, except where—

- (i) the local planning authority are the authority so mentioned;
- (ii) the local planning authority are required to consult the authority so mentioned under articles 11 or 12;
- (iii) the authority or person so mentioned has advised the local planning authority that they do not wish to be consulted; or
- (iv) the development is subject to any standing advice provided by the authority or person so mentioned to the local planning authority in relation to the category of development.'.

(1A) The exception in article 10(1)(iii) shall not apply where, in the opinion of the local planning authority, development falls within paragraph (zb) of the table below.

(1B) The exception in article 10(iv) shall not apply where—

- (a) the development is an EIA development; or
- (b) the standing advice was issued more that two years before the date of the application for planning permission for the development and the guidance has not been amended or confirmed as being extant by the authority or person within that period

TABLE

Para	*Description of Development*	*Consultee*
(a)	Development likely to affect land in Greater London or in a metropolitan county or, in relation to Wales, land in the area of another local planning authority	The local planning authority concerned
(b)	Development likely to affect land in a non-metropolitan county in England, other than land in a National Park	The district planning authority concerned
(c)	Development likely to affect land in a National Park in England	The county planning authority concerned

(d)	Development within an area which has been notified to the local planning authority by the Health and Safety Executive for the purpose of this provision because of the presence within the vicinity of toxic, highly reactive, explosive or inflammable substances and which involves the provision of— (i) residential accommodation; (ii) more than 250 square metres of retail floor space; (iii) more than 500 square metres of office floor space; or (iv) more than 750 square metres of floor space to be used for an industrial process, or which is otherwise likely to result in a material increase in the number of persons working within or visiting the notified area	The Health and Safety Executive
(e)	Development likely to result in a material increase in the volume or a material change in the character of traffic— (i) entering or leaving a trunk road; or	In England, the Secretary of State for Transport, Local Government and the Regions and, in Wales, the National Assembly for Wales
	(ii) using a level crossing over a railway	The operator of the network which includes or consists of the railway in question, and in England, the Secretary of State for Transport, Local Government and the Regions and, in Wales, the National Assembly for Wales
(f)	Development likely to result in a material increase in the volume or a material change in the character of traffic entering or leaving a classified road or proposed highway	The local highway authority concerned
(g)	Development likely to prejudice the improvement or construction of a classified road or proposed highway	The local highway authority concerned
(h)	Development involving— (i) the formation, laying out or alteration of any means of access to a highway (other than a trunk road); or	The local highway authority concerned
	(ii) the construction of a highway or private means of access to premises affording access to a road in relation to which a toll order is in force	The local highway autority concerned, and in the case of a road subject to a concession, the concessionare
(i)	Development which consists of or includes the laying out or construction of a new street	The local highway authority

(j)	Development which involves the provision of a building or pipe-line in an area of coal working notified by the Coal Authority to the local planning authority	The Coal Authority
(k)	Development involving or including mining operations	The Environment Agency
(l)	Development within three kilometres of Windsor Castle, Windsor Great Park, or Windsor Home Park, or within 800 metres of any other royal palace or park, which might affect the amenities (including security) of that palace or park	The Secretary of State for National Heritage
(m)	Development of land in Greater London involving the demolition, in whole or part, or the material alteration of a listed building	The Historic Buildings and Monuments Commission for England
(n)	Development likely to affect the site of a scheduled monument	In England, the Historic Buildings and Monuments Commission for England and, in Wales, the National Assembly for Wales
(o)	Development likely to affect any garden or park of special historic interest which is registered in accordance with section 8C of the Historic Buildings and Ancient Monuments Act 1953 (register of gardens) and which is classified as Grade I or Grade II*.	The Historic Buildings and Monuments Commission for England
(p)	Development involving the carrying out of works or operations in the bed of or on the banks of a river or stream	The Environment Agency
(q)	Development for the purpose of refining or storing mineral oils and their derivatives	The Environment Agency
(r)	Development involving the use of land for the deposit of refuse or waste	The Environment Agency
(s)	Development relating to the retention, treatment or disposal of sewage, trade-waste, slurry or sludge (other than the laying of sewers, the construction of pumphouses in a line of sewers, the construction of septic tanks and cesspools serving single dwellinghouses or single caravans or single buildings in which not more than ten people will normally reside, work or congregate, and works ancillary thereto)	The Environment Agency
(t)	Development relating to the use of land as a cemetery	The Environment Agency
(u)	Development— (i) in or likely to affect a site of special scientific interest of which notification has been given, or has effect as if given, to the local planning authority by the Nature Conservancy Council for England or the Countryside Council for Wales, in accordance with section 28 of the Wildlife and Countryside Act 1981 (areas of special scientific interest); or	The Council which gave, or is to be regarded as having given, the notice

	(ii) within an area which has been notified to the local planning authority by the Nature Conservancy Council for England or the Countryside Council for Wales, and which is within two kilometres of a site of special scientific interest of which notification has been given or has effect as if given as aforesaid	
(v)	Development involving any land on which there is a theatre	The Theatres Trust
(w)	Development which is not for agricultural purposes and is not in accordance with the provisions of a development plan and involves— (i) the loss of not less than 20 hectares of grades 1, 2 or 3a agricultural land which is for the time being used (or was last used) for agricultural purposes; or (ii) the loss of less than 20 hectares of grades 1, 2 or 3a agricultural land which is for the time being used (or was last used) for agricultural purposes, in circumstances in which the development is likely to lead to a further loss of agricultural land amounting cumulatively to 20 hectares or more	In England, the Minister of Agriculture, Fisheries and Food and, in Wales, the National Assembly for Wales
(x)	Development within 250 metres of land which— (i) is or has, at any time in the 30 years before the relevant application, been used for the deposit of refuse or waste; and (ii) has been notified to the local planning authority by the waste regulation authority for the purposes of this provision	The waste regulation authority concerned
(y)	Development for the purposes of fish farming	The Environment Agency
(z)	Development which— (i) is likely to prejudice the use, or lead to the loss of use, of land being used as a playing field; or (ii) is on land which has been: (aa) used as a playing field at any time in the 5 years before the making of the relevant application and which remains undeveloped; or (bb) allocated for use as a playing field in a development plan or in proposals for such a plan or its alteration or replacement; or (iii) involves the replacement of the grass surface of a playing pitch on a playing field with an artificial, man-made or composite surface.	In England, the Sports Council for England; in Wales, the Sports Council for Wales
(za)	Development likely to affect (i) any inland waterway (whether natural or artificial) or reservoir owned or managed by the British Waterways Board; or (ii) any canal feeder channel, watercourse, let off or culvert, which is within an area which has been notified for the purposes of this provision to the local planning authority by the British Waterways Board.	The British Waterways Board

(zb) Development— (i) involving the siting of new establishments; or (ii) consisting of modifications to existing establishments which could have significant repercussions on major-accident hazards; or (iii) including transport links, locations frequented by the public and residential areas in the vicinity of existing establishments, where the siting or development is such as to increase the risk or consequences of a major accident.	The Health and Safety Executive and the Environmental Agency, and, where it appears to the local planning authority that an area of particular natural sensitivity or interest may be affected, in England, the Nature Conservancy Council for England, or in Wales, the Countryside Council for Wales.
(zc) Development which— (i) involves or is likely to affect the provision of an existing or proposed strategic infrastructure project of which notification has been given to the local planning authority and which is likely to have a significant impact upon a policy in the Regional Development Agency's Strategy; or (ii) is within an area of which notification has been given to the local planning authority for the purpose of this provision and is likely to affect the implementation of a strategic regional investment or employment policy in the Regional Development Agency's Strategy"	The Regional Development Agency which gave the notice

(2) In the above table—

(a) in paragraph (d)(iv), 'industrial process' means a process for or incidental to any of the following purposes—

(i) the making of any article or part of any article (including a ship or vessel, or a film, video or sound recording);

(ii) the altering, repairing, maintaining, ornamenting, finishing, cleaning, washing, packing, canning, adapting for sale, breaking up or demolition of any article; or

(iii) the getting, dressing or treatment of minerals in the course of any trade or business other than agriculture, and other than a process carried out on land use as a mine or adjacent to and occupied together with a mine (and in this sub-paragraph, 'mine' means any site on which mining operations are carried out),

(b) in paragraph (e)(ii), 'network' and 'operator' have the same meaning as in Part I of the Railways Act 1993 (the provision of railway services);

(c) in paragraphs (f) and (g), 'classified road' means a highway or proposed highway which—

(i) is a classified road or a principal road by virtue of section 12(1) of the Highways Act 1980 (general provision as to principal and classified roads); or

(ii) is classified for the purposes of any enactment by the Secretary of State by virtue of section 12(3) of that Act;

(d) in paragraph (h), 'concessionaire', 'road subject to a concession' and 'toll order' have the same meaning as in Part I of the New Roads and Street Works Act 1991 (new roads in England and Wales);

(e) in paragraph (i), 'street' has the same meaning as in section 48(1) of the New Roads and Street Works Act 1991 (streets, street works and undertakers), and 'new street' includes a continuation of an existing street;

(f) in paragraph (m), 'listed building' has the same meaning as in section 1 of the Planning (Listed Buildings and Conservation Areas) Act 1990 (listing of buildings of special architectural or historic interest);

(g) in paragraph (n), 'scheduled monument' has the same meaning as in section 1(11) of the Ancient Monuments and Archaeological Areas Act 1979 (schedule of monuments);

(h) in paragraph (s), 'slurry' means animal faeces and urine (whether or not water has been added for handling), and 'caravan' has the same meaning as for the purposes of Part I of the Caravan Sites and Control of Development Act 1960 (caravan sites);

(i) in paragraph (u), 'site of special scientific interest' means land to which section 28(1) of the Wildlife and Countryside Act 1981 (areas of special scientific interest) applies;

(j) in paragraph (v), 'theatre' has the same meaning as in section 5 of the Theatres Trust Act 1976 (interpretation);

(k) in paragraph (x), 'waste regulation authority' has the same meaning as in section 30(1) of the Environmental Protection Act 1990 (authorities for purposes of Part II);

(l) in paragraph (z)—

   (i) 'playing field' means the whole of a site which encompasses at least one playing pitch;

   (ii) 'playing pitch' means a delineated area which, together with any run-off area, is of 0.4 hectares or more, and which is used for association football, American football, rugby, cricket, hockey, lacrosse, rounders, baseball, softball, Australian football, Gaelic football, shinty, hurling, polo or cycle polo; and

(m) the expressions used in paragraph (zb), have the same meaning as in Council Directive 96/82/EC on the control of major accident hazards involving dangerous substances.

(n) in paragraph (zc) 'Regional Development Agency' has the same meaning as in section 41 of the Regional Development Agencies Act 1998(a) and 'Regional Development Agency's Strategy' is a strategy formulated and kept under review under section 7 and section 7A of that Act

(3) The Secretary of State may give directions to a local planning authority requiring that authority to consult any person or body named in the directions, in any case or class of case specified in the directions.

(4) Where, by or under this article, a local planning authority are required to consult any person or body ('the consultee') before granting planning permission—

   (a) they shall, unless an applicant has served a copy of an application for planning permission on the consultee, give notice of the application to the consultee; and

   (b) they shall not determine the application until at least 14 days after the date on which notice is given under paragraph (a) or, if earlier, 14 days after the date of service of a copy of the application on the consultee by the applicant.

(5) The local planning authority shall, in determining the application, take into account any representations received from a consultee.

11. Consultation with county planning authority

Where a district planning authority are required by paragraph 7 of Schedule 1 to the Act (local planning authorities — distribution of functions) to consult the county planning authority before determining an application for planning permission, they shall not determine the application until the expiry of at least 14 days after the date of the notice given to the county planning authority in accordance with sub-paragraph (6)(b) of that paragraph.

12. Applications relating to county matters

(1) A county planning authority shall, before determining—

   (a) an application for planning permission under Part III of the Act (control over development);

(b) an application for a certificate of lawful use or development under section 191 or 192 of the Act (certificates of lawfulness of existing or proposed use or development); or

(c) an application for approval of reserved matters,

give the district planning authority, if any, for the area in which the relevant land lies a period of at least 14 days, from the date of receipt of the application by the district authority, within which to make recommendations about the manner in which the application shall be determined; and shall take any such recommendations into account.

(2) A county planning authority shall—

(a) on determining an application of a kind mentioned in paragraph (1), as soon as reasonably practicable notify the district planning authority, if any, of the terms of their decision; or

(b) if any such application is referred to the Secretary of State, inform the district planning authority, if any, of the date when it was so referred and, when notified to them, of the terms of the decision.

13. Notice to parish and community councils

(1) Where the council of a parish or community are given information in relation to an application pursuant to paragraph 8(1) of Schedule 1 to the Act (local planning authorities — distribution of functions) or the council of a community are given information in relation to paragraph 2 of Schedule 1A to the Act (distribution of local planning authority functions: Wales), they shall, as soon as practicable, notify the local planning authority who are determining the application whether they propose to make any representations about the manner in which the application should be determined, and shall make any representations to that authority within 14 days of the notification to them of the application.

(2) A local planning authority shall not determine any application in respect of which a parish or community are required to be given information before—

(a) the council of the parish or community inform them that they do not propose to make any representations;

(b) representations are made by that council; or

(c) the period of 14 days mentioned in paragraph (1) has elapsed,

whichever shall first occur; and in determining the application the authority shall take into account any representations received from the council of the parish or community.

(3) The district planning authority (or, in a metropolitan county or Wales, the local planning authority) shall notify the council of the parish or community of the terms of the decision on any such application or, where the application is referred to the Secretary of State, of the date when it was so referred and, when notified to them, of the terms of his decision.

14. Directions by the Secretary of State

(1) The Secretary of State may give directions restricting the grant of permission by a local planning authority, either indefinitely or during such a period as may be specified in the directions, in respect of any development or in respect of development of any class so specified.

(2) The Secretary of State may give directions that development which is both of a description set out in Column 1 of the table in Schedule 2 to the Town and Country Planning (Environmental Impact Assessment) (England and Wales) Regulations 1999, and of a class described in the direction is EIA development for the purposes of those Regulations.

(3) A local planning authority shall deal with applications for planning permission for development to which a direction given under this article applies in such manner as to give effect to the direction.

15. Special provisions as to permission for development affecting certain existing and proposed highways

(1) Where an application is made to a local planning authority for planning permission for development which consists of or includes—

(a) the formation, laying out or alteration of any access to or from any part of a trunk road which is either a special road or, if not a special road, a road subject to a speed limit exceeding 40 miles per hour; or

(b) any development of land within 67 metres (or such other distance as may be specified in a direction given by the Secretary of State under this article) from the middle of—

(i) any highway (other than a trunk road) which the Secretary of State has provided, or is authorised to provide, in pursuance of an order under Part II of the Highways Act 1980 (trunk roads, classified roads, metropolitan roads, special roads) and which has not for the time being been transferred to any other highway authority;

(ii) any highway which he proposes to improve under Part V of that Act (improvement of highways) and in respect of which notice has been given to the local planning authority;

(iii) any highway to which he proposes to carry out improvements in pursuance of an order under Part II of that Act; or

(iv) any highway which he proposes to construct, the route of which is shown on the development plan or in respect of which he has given notice in writing to the relevant local planning authority together with maps or plans sufficient to identify the route of the highway,

the local planning authority shall notify the Secretary of State by sending him a copy of the application and any accompanying plans and drawings.

(2) An application referred to in paragraph (1) above shall not be determined unless—

(a) the local planning authority receive a direction given under article 14 of this Order (and in accordance with the terms of that direction);

(b) they receive notification by or on behalf of the Secretary of State that he does not propose to give any such direction in respect of the development to which the application relates; or

(c) a period of 28 days (or such longer period as may be agreed in writing between the local planning authority and the Secretary of State) from the date when notification was given to the Secretary of State has elapsed without receipt of such a direction.

(3) The Secretary of State may, in respect of any case or any class or description of cases, give a direction specifying a different distance for the purposes of paragraph 1(b) above.

16. Notification of mineral applications

(1) Where notice has been given for the purposes of this article to a mineral planning authority as respects land which is in their area and specified in the notice—

(a) by the Coal Authority that the land contains coal;

(b) by the Secretary of State for Trade and Industry that it contains gas or oil; or

(c) by the Crown Estates Commissioners that it contains silver or gold,

the mineral planning authority shall not determine any application for planning permission to win and work any mineral on that land, without first notifying the body or person who gave the notice that an application has been made.

(2) In this article, 'coal' means coal other than that—

(a) won or worked during the course of operations which are carried on exclusively for the purpose of exploring for coal; or

(b) which it is necessary to dig or carry away in the course of activities carried on for purposes which do not include the getting of coal or any product of coal.

17. Development not in accordance with the development plan

A local planning authority may in such cases and subject to such conditions as may be prescribed by directions given by the Secretary of State under this Order grant permission for development which does not accord with the provisions of the development plan in force in the area in which the land to which the application relates is situated.

18. Notice of reference of applications to the Secretary of State

On referring any application to the Secretary of State under section 77 of the Act (reference of applications to Secretary of State) pursuant to a direction in that behalf, a local planning authority shall serve on the applicant a notice—

(a) setting out the terms of the direction and any reasons given by the Secretary of State for issuing it;

(b) stating that the application has been referred to the Secretary of State; and

(c) containing a statement that the Secretary of State will, if the applicant so desires, afford to him an opportunity of appearing before and being heard by a person appointed by the Secretary of State for the purpose, and that the decision of the Secretary of State on the application will be final.

19. Representations to be taken into account

(1) A local planning authority shall, in determining an application for planning permission, take into account any representations made, where any notice of the application has been—

(a) given by site display under article 6 or 8, within 21 days beginning with the date when the notice was first displayed by site display;

(b) served on—

(i) an owner of the land or a tenant of an agricultural holding under article 6, or

(ii) an adjoining owner or occupier under article 8,

within 21 days beginning with the date when the notice was served on that person, provided that the representations are made by any person who satisfies them that he is such an owner, tenant or occupier; or

(c) given by local advertisement under article 6 or 8, within 14 days beginning with the date on which the notice was published,

and the representations and periods in this article are representations and periods prescribed for the purposes of section 71(2)(a) of the Act (consultations in connection with determinations under section 70).

(2) A local planning authority shall give notice of their decision to every person who has made representations which they were required to take into account in accordance with paragraph (1)(b)(i), and such notice is notice prescribed for the purposes of section 71(2)(b) of the Act.

(3) Paragraphs (1) and (2) of this article apply to applications referred to the Secretary of State under section 77 of the Act (reference of applications to Secretary of State) and paragraphs (1)(b) and (2) apply to appeals to the Secretary of State made under section 78 of the Act (right to appeal against planning decisions and failure to take such decisions), as if the references to—

(a) a local planning authority were to the Secretary of State, and

(b) determining an application for planning permission were to determining such application or appeal, as the case may be.

20. Time periods for decision

(1) Subject to paragraph (5), where a valid application under article 4 or regulation 3 of the 1988 Regulations (applications for planning permission) has been received by a local planning

authority, they shall within the period specified in paragraph (2) give the applicant notice of their decision or determination or notice that the application has been referred to the Secretary of State.

(2) The period specified in this paragraph is—

(a) a period of eight weeks beginning with the date when the application was received by a local planning authority;

(b) except where the applicant has already given notice of appeal to the Secretary of State, such extended period as may be agreed in writing between the applicant and the local planning authority by whom the application falls to be determined; or

(c) where a fee due in respect of an application has been paid by a cheque which is subsequently dishonoured, the appropriate period specified in (a) or (b) above calculated without regard to any time between the date when the authority sent the applicant written notice of the dishonouring of the cheque and the date when the authority are satisfied that they have received the full amount of the fee.

(3) For the purposes of this article, the date when the application was received shall be taken to be the date when each of the following events has occurred—

(a) the application form or application in writing has been lodged with the authority mentioned in article 5(1);

(b) any certificate or documents required by the Act or this Order has been lodged with that authority; and

(c) any fee required to be paid in respect of the application has been paid to that authority and, for this purpose, lodging a cheque for the amount of a fee is to be taken as payment.

(4) A local planning authority shall provide such information about applications made under article 4 or regulation 3 of the 1988 Regulations (including information as to the manner in which any such application has been dealt with) as the Secretary of State may by direction require; and any such direction may include provision as to the persons to be informed and the manner in which the information is to be provided.

(5) Subject to paragraph (6), a local planning authority shall not determine an application for planning permission, where any notice of the application has been—

(a) given by site display under article 6 or 8, before the end of the period of 21 days beginning with the date when the notice was first displayed by site display;

(b) served on—

(i) an owner of the land or a tenant of an agricultural holding under article 6, or

(ii) an adjoining owner or occupier under article 8

before the end of the period of 21 days beginning with the date when the notice was served on that person;

(c) given by local advertisement under article 6 or 8, before the end of the period of 14 days beginning with the date on which the notice was published,

and the periods in this paragraph are periods prescribed for the purposes of section 71(1) of the Act (consultations in connection with determinations under section 70).

(6) Where, under paragraph (5), more than one of the prescribed periods applies, the local planning authority shall not determine the application before the end of the later or latest of such periods.

21. Applications made under planning condition

Where an application has been made to a local planning authority for any consent, agreement or approval required by a condition or limitation attached to a grant of planning permission (other than an application for approval of reserved matters or an application for approval under Part 24 of Schedule 2 to the Town and Country Planning (General Permitted Development) Order 1995 (development by telecommunications code system operators)) the authority shall give notice to the applicant of their decision on the application within a period of eight weeks from the date when the application was received by the authority, or such longer period as may be agreed by the applicant and the authority in writing.

22. Written notice of decision or determination relating to a planning application

(1) When the local planning authority give notice of a decision or determination on an application for planning permission or for approval of reserved matters and—

(a) planning permission is granted, the notice shall include a summary of their reasons for the grant and a summary of the policies and proposals in the development plan which are relevant to the decision;

(b) planning permission is granted subject to conditions, the notice shall:—

(i) include a summary of their reasons for the grant together with a summary of the policies and proposals in the development plan which are relevant to the decision to grant permission; and

(ii) shall state clearly and precisely their full reasons for each condition imposed, specifying all policies and proposals in the development plan which are relevant to the decision;

(c) planning permission is refused, the notice shall state clearly and precisely their full reasons for the refusal, specifying all policies and proposals in the development plan which are relevant to the decision; and

(d) where the Secretary of State has given a direction restricting the grant of planning permission for the development for which application is made or where he or a Government Department has expressed the view that the permission should not be granted (either wholly or in part) or should be granted subject to conditions, the notice shall give details of the direction or of the view expressed,

and in the case of notification required by sub-paragraph (b) (c) or (d) the notice shall be accompanied by a notification in the terms (or substantially in the terms) set out in Part 2 of Schedule 1 to this Order.

(2) Where—

(a) the applicant for planning permission has submitted an environmental statement; and

(b) the local planning authority have decided (having taken environmental information into consideration) to grant permission (whether unconditionally or subject to conditions),

the notice given to the applicant in accordance with article 20(1) shall include a statement that environmental information has been taken into consideration by the authority.

23. Appeals

(1) An applicant who wishes to appeal to the Secretary of State under section 78 of the Act (right to appeal against planning decisions and failure to take such decisions) shall give notice of appeal to the Secretary of State by—

(a) serving on him, within the time limit specified in paragraph (2), a form obtained from him, together with such of the documents specified in paragraph (3) as are relevant to the appeal; and

(b) serving on the local planning authority a copy of the form mentioned in paragraph (a), as soon as reasonably practicable, together with a copy of any relevant documents mentioned in paragraph (3)(e).

(2) The time limit mentioned in paragraph (1) is three months from—

(a) the date of the notice of the decision or determination giving rise to the appeal;

(b) the expiry of the period specified in article 20 or, as the case may be, article 21; or

(c) In a case in which the authority have served a notice on the applicant in accordance with article 3(2) that they require further information, and he has not provided the information, the date of service of that notice,

or such longer period as the Secretary of State may, at any time, allow.

(3) The documents mentioned in paragraph (1) are—

(a) the application made to the local planning authority which has occasioned the appeal;

(b) all plans, drawings and documents sent to the authority in connection with the application;

(c) all correspondence with the authority relating to the application;

(d) any certificate provided to the authority under article 7;

(e) any other plans, documents or drawings relating to the application which were not sent to the authority;

(f) the notice of the decision or determination, if any;

(g) if the appeal relates to an application for approval of certain matters in accordance with a condition on a planning permission, the application for that permission, the plans submitted with that application and the planning permission granted.

(4) The Secretary of State may refuse to accept a notice of appeal from an applicant if the documents required under paragraphs (1) and (3) are not served on him within the time limit specified in paragraph (2).

[(5) The Secretary of State may provide, or arrange for the provision of, a website for use for such purposes as he thinks fit which—

(a) relate to appeals under section 78 of the Act and this article, and

(b) are capable of being carried out electronically.

[(6) Where a person gives notice of appeal to the Secretary of State using electronic communications, the person shall be taken to have agreed—

(a) to the use of such communications for all purposes relating to his appeal which are capable of being carried out electronically,

(b) that his address for the purpose of such communications is the address incorporated into, or otherwise logically associated with, his notice of appeal, and

(c) that his deemed agreement under this paragraph shall subsist until he gives notice in accordance with article 27A that he wishes to revoke the agreement.]

24. Certificate of lawful use or development

(1) An application for a certificate under section 191(1) or 192(1) of the Act (certificates of lawfulness of existing or proposed use or development) shall be in writing and shall, in addition to specifying the land and describing the use, operations or other matter in question in accordance with those sections, include the following information—

(a) the paragraph of section 191(1) or, as the case may be, section 192(1), under which the application is made;

(b) in the case of an application under section 191(1), the date on which the use, operations or other matter began or, in the case of operations carried out without planning permission, the date on which the operations were substantially completed;

(c) in the case of an application under section 191(1)(a), the name of any use class specified in an order under section 55(2)(f) of the Act (meaning of 'development') which the applicant considers applicable to the use existing at the date of the application;

(d) in the case of an application under section 191(1)(c), sufficient details of the planning permission to enable it to be identified;

(e) in the case of an application under section 192(1)(a), the use of the land at the date of the application (or, when the land is not in use at that date, the purpose for which it was last used) and the name of any use class specified in an order under section 55(2)(f) of the Act which the applicant considers applicable to the proposed use;

(f) the applicant's reasons, if any, for regarding the use, operations or other matter described in the application as lawful; and

(g) such other information as the applicant considers to be relevant to the application.

(2) An application to which paragraph (1) applies shall be accompanied by—

(a) a plan identifying the land to which the application relates;

(b) such evidence verifying the information included in the application as the applicant can provide; and

(c) a statement setting out the applicant's interest in the land, the name and address of any other person known to the applicant to have an interest in the land and whether any such other person has been notified of the application.

(2A) Where, by virtue of section 299(2) of the Act, an application for a certificate under section 192(1) of the Act is made in respect of Crown land, it shall, in addition to the documents required by paragraph (2), be accompanied by—

(a) a statement that the application is made, by virtue of section 299(2) of the Act, in respect of Crown land; and

(b) where the application is made by a person authorised in writing by the appropriate authority, a copy of that authorisation.

(3) Where such an application specifies two or more uses, operations or other matters, the plan which accompanies the application shall indicate to which part of the land each such use, operation or matter relates.

(4) Articles 5(1) and 20(4) shall apply to an application for a certificate to which paragraph (1) applies as they apply to an application for planning permission.

(5) When the local planning authority receive an application to which paragraph (1) applies and any fee required to be paid in respect of the application, they shall, as soon as reasonably practicable, send to the applicant an acknowledgement of the application in the terms (or substantially in the terms) set out in Part 1 of Schedule 1.

(6) Where, after sending an acknowledgement as required by paragraph (5), the local planning authority consider that the application is invalid by reason of the failure to comply with the preceding paragraphs of this article or any other statutory requirement, they shall, as soon as practicable, notify the applicant that his application is invalid.

(7) The local planning authority may by notice in writing require the applicant to provide such further information as may be specified to enable them to deal with the application.

(8) The local planning authority shall give the applicant written notice of their decision within a period of eight weeks beginning with the date of receipt by the authority of the application and any fee required to be paid in respect of the application or, except where the applicant has already given notice of appeal to the Secretary of State, within such extended period as may be agreed upon in writing between the applicant and the authority.

(9) For the purpose of calculating the appropriate period specified in paragraph (8), where any fee required has been paid by a cheque which is subsequently dishonoured, the time between the date when the authority send the applicant written notice of the dishonouring of the cheque and the date when the authority receive the full amount of the fee shall not be taken into account.

(10) Where an application is refused, in whole or in part (including a case in which the authority modify the description of the use, operations or other matter in the application or substitute an alternative description for that description), the notice of decision shall state clearly and precisely the authority's full reasons for their decision and shall include a statement to the effect that if the applicant is aggrieved by the decision he may appeal to the Secretary of State under section 195 of the Act (appeals against refusal or failure to give decision on application).

(11) A certificate under section 191 or 192 of the Act shall be in the form set out in Schedule 4, or in a form substantially to the like effect.

(12) Where a local planning authority propose to revoke a certificate issued under section 191 or 192 of the Act in accordance with section 193(7) of the Act (certificates under sections 191 and 192:

supplementary provisions), they shall, before they revoke the certificate, give notice of that proposal to—

(a) the owner of the land affected;
(b) the occupier of the land affected;
(c) any other person who will in their opinion be affected by the revocation; and
(d) in the case of a certificate issued by the Secretary of State under section 195 of the Act, the Secretary of State.

(13) A notice issued under paragraph (12) shall invite the person on whom the notice is served to make representations on the proposal to the authority within 14 days of service of the notice and the authority shall not revoke the certificate until all such periods allowed for making representations have expired.

(14) An authority shall give written notice of any revocation under section 193(7) of the Act to every person on whom notice of the proposed revocation was served under paragraph (12).

25. Register of applications

(1) In this article and in article 26, 'the local planning register authority' means—

(a) in Greater London or a metropolitan county in Wales, the local planning authority (and references to the area of the local planning register authority are, in this case, to the area of the local planning authority);
(b) in relation to land in a National Park (except in a metropolitan county in Wales), the county planning authority (and references to the area of the local planning register authority are, in this case, to the area of the county planning authority within a National Park);
(c) in relation to any other land, the district planning authority (and references to the area of the local planning register authority are, in this case, to the area of the district planning authority, other than any part of their area failing within a National Park).

(2) Each local planning register authority shall keep, in two parts, a register of every application for planning permission relating to their area.

(3) Part I of the register shall contain in respect of each such application and any application for approval of reserved matters made in respect of an outline planning permission granted on such an application, made or sent to the local planning register authority and not finally disposed of—

(a) a copy (which may be photographic or in electronic form) of the application together with any accompanying plans and drawings;
(b) a copy (which may be photographic or in electronic form) of any planning obligation or section 278 agreement proposed or entered into in connection with the application;
(c) a copy (which may be photographic or in electronic form) of any other planning obligation or section 278 agreement entered into in respect of the land the subject of the application which the applicant considers relevant; and
(d) particulars of any modification to any planning obligation or section 278 agreement included in Part I of the register in accordance with sub-paragraphs (b) and and (c) above.

(4) Part II of the register shall contain, in respect of every application for planning permission relating to the local planning register authority's area—

(a) a copy (which may be photographic or in electronic form) of the application and of plans and drawings submitted in relation thereto;
(b) particulars of any direction given under the Act or this Order in respect of the application;
(c) the decision, if any, of the local planning authority in respect of the application, including details of any conditions subject to which permission was granted, the date of such decision and the name of the local planning authority;
(d) the reference number, the date and effect of any decision of the Secretary of State in respect

of the application, whether on appeal or on a reference under section 77 of the Act (reference of applications to Secretary of State);

(e) the date of any subsequent approval (whether approval of reserved matters or any other approval required) given in relation to the application.

(f) a copy (which may be photographic or in electronic form) of any planning obligation or section 278 agreement entered into in connection with any decision of the local planning authority or the Secretary of State in respect of the application;

(g) a copy (which may be photographic or in electronic form) of any other planning obligation or section 278 agreement taken into account by the local planning authority or the Secretary of State when making the decision; and

(h) particulars of any modification to or discharge of any planning obligation or section 278 agreement included in Part II of the register in accordance with sub-paragraphs (f) and (g) above and paragraph (5) below.

(5) Where, on any appeal to the Secretary of State under section 174 of the Act (appeal against enforcement notices), the appellant is deemed to have made an application for planning permission and the Secretary of State has granted permission, the local planning register authority shall, on receipt of notification of the Secretary of State's decision, enter into Part II of the register referred to in paragraph (2) particulars of the development concerned, the land on which it was carried out, and the date and effect of the Secretary of State's decision together with a copy (which may be photographic or in electronic form) or—

(a) any planning obligation or section 278 agreement entered into in connection with the decision; and

(b) any other planning obligation or section 278 agreement taken into account by the Secretary of State when making the decision.

(6) The register kept by the local planning register authority shall also contain the following information in respect of every application for a certificate under section 191 or 192 of the Act (certificates of lawfulness of existing or proposed use or development) relating to the authority's area—

(a) the name and address of the applicant;

(b) the date of the application;

(c) the address or location of the land to which the application relates;

(d) the description of the use, operations or other matter included in the application;

(e) the decision, if any, of the local planning authority in respect of the application and the date of such decision; and

(f) the reference number, date and effect of any decision of the Secretary of State on an appeal in respect of the application.

(7) The register shall contain the following information about simplified planning zone schemes in the area of the authority—

(a) brief particulars of any action taken by the authority or the Secretary of State in accordance with section 83 of or Schedule 7 to the Act (making of simplified planning zone schemes etc.) to establish or approve any simplified planning zone scheme, including the date of adoption or approval, the date on which the scheme or alteration becomes operative and the date on which it ceases to be operative;

(b) a copy of any simplified planning zone scheme, or alteration to an existing scheme, including any diagrams, illustrations, descriptive matter or any other prescribed material which has been made available for inspection under Schedule 7 to the Act;

(c) an index map showing the boundary of any operative or proposed simplified planning zone schemes, including alterations to existing schemes where appropriate, together with a reference to the entries in the register under sub-paragraph (a) and (b) above.

(8) To enable any person to trace any entry in the register, every register shall include an index

together with a separate index of applications for development involving mining operations or the creation of mineral working deposits.

(9) Every entry in the register shall be made within 14 days of the receipt of an application, or of the giving or making of the relevant direction, decision or approval as the case may be.

(10) The register shall either be kept at the principal office of the local planning register authority or that part of the register which relates to land in part of that authority's area shall be kept at a place within or convenient to that part.

(11) For the purposes of paragraph (3) of this article, an application shall not be treated as finally disposed of unless—

(a) it has been decided by the authority (or the appropriate period allowed under article 20(2) of this Order has expired without their giving a decision) and the period of three months specified in article 23 of this Order has expired without any appeal having been made to the Secretary of State;

(b) if it has been referred to the Secretary of State under section 77 of the Act. (reference of applications to Secretary of State) or an appeal has been made to the Secretary of State under section 78 of the Act (right to appeal against planning decisions and failure to take such decisions), the Secretary of State has issued his decision and the period of six weeks specified in section 288 of the Act (proceedings for questioning the validity of certain orders, decisions and directions) has expired without any application having been made to the High Court under that section;

(c) an application has been made to the High Court under section 288 of the Act and the matter has been finally determined, either by final dismissal of the application by a court or by the quashing of the Secretary of State's decision and the issue of a fresh decision (without a further application under the said section 288); or

(d) it has been withdrawn before being decided by the authority or the Secretary of State, as the case may be, or an appeal has been withdrawn before the Secretary of State has issued his decision.

(12) Where the register kept by a local planning register authority under this article is kept using electronic storage, the authority may make the register available for inspection by the public on a website maintained by the authority for that purpose.

26. Register of enforcement and stop notices

(1) Subject to paragraph (2) of this article, the register under section 188 of the Act (register of enforcement and stop notices) shall contain the following information with respect to every enforcement notice issued in relation to land in the area of the authority maintaining the register—

(a) the address of the land to which the notice relates or a plan by reference to which its situation can be ascertained;

(b) the name of the issuing authority;

(c) the date of issue of the notice;

(d) the date of service of copies of the notice;

(e) a statement or summary of the breach of planning control alleged and the requirements of the notice, including the period within which any required steps are to be taken;

(f) the date specified in the notice as the date on which it is to take effect;

(g) information on any postponement of the date specified as the date on which the notice will take effect by reason of section 175(4) of the Act (appeals: supplementary provisions) and the date of the final determination or withdrawal of any appeal;

(h) the date of service and, if applicable, of withdrawal of any stop notice referring to the enforcement notice, together with a statement or summary of the activity prohibited by any such stop notice;

(i) the date, if any, on which the local planning authority are satisfied that steps required by the notice for a purpose mentioned in section 173(4)(b) of the Act (remedying any injury to amenity) have been taken.

(2) That register shall also contain the following information with respect to every breach of condition notice served in relation to land in the area of the authority maintaining the register—

(a) the address of the land to which the notice relates or a plan by reference to which its situation can be ascertained;

(b) the name of the serving authority;

(c) the date of service of the notice;

(d) details of the relevant planning permission sufficient to enable it to be identified;

(e) a statement or summary of the condition which has not been complied with and the requirements of the notice, including the period allowed for compliance.

(3) All entries relating to an enforcement notice, stop notice or breach of condition notice shall be removed from the register if—

(a) in the case of an enforcement notice or stop notice, the relevant enforcement notice is quashed by the Secretary of State;

(b) in the case of a breach of condition notice, the notice is quashed by a court;

(c) in any case, the relevant notice is withdrawn.

(4) Every register shall include an index for enabling a person to trace any entry in the register by reference to the address of the land to which the notice relates.

(5) Where a county planning authority issue an enforcement notice or serve a stop notice or a breach of condition notice, they shall supply the information specified in paragraph (1) or (2) of this article, as the case may be, in relation to the notice to the district planning authority in whose area the land to which the notice relates is situated and shall inform that authority if the notice is withdrawn or the relevant enforcement notice or breach of condition notice is quashed.

(6) The information prescribed in paragraphs (1) and (2) of this article shall be entered in the register as soon as practicable and in any event within 14 days of the occurrence to which it relates, and information shall be so supplied under paragraph (5) that entries may be made within the said period of 14 days.

(7) The register shall either be kept at the principal office of the local planning register authority or that part of the register which relates to land in part of that authority's area shall be kept at a place within or convenient to that part.

27. Directions

Any power conferred by this Order to give a direction includes power to cancel or vary the direction by a subsequent direction.

27A. Withdrawal of consent to use of electronic communications

Where a person is no longer willing to accept the use of electronic communications for any purpose of this Order which is capable of being carried out electronically, he shall give notice in writing—

(a) withdrawing any address notified to the Secretary of State or to a local planning authority for that purpose, or

(b) revoking any agreement entered into or deemed to have been entered into with the Secretary of State or with a local planning authority for that purpose,

and such withdrawal or revocation shall be final and shall take effect on a date specified by the person in the notice but not less than seven days after the date on which the notice is given.

28. Revocations, transitionals and savings

(1) Subject to paragraphs (2) to (5) of this article, the statutory instruments specified in Schedule 5 are revoked to the extent not already revoked.

(2) Where an area of coal working has been notified to the local planning authority for the purposes of paragraph (i) of the table in article 18 of the Town and Country Planning General Development Order 1988 (consultations before the grant of permission) before the date of the coming into force of this Order, such notification shall be treated as if it had been made for the purposes of paragraph (j) of the table in article 10 of this Order by the Coal Authority on or after that date; and, in relation to a particular application for planning permission made before 31st October 1994, the local planning authority are not required to consult the Coal Authority if they have already consulted the British Coal Corporation.

(3) Any notice given for the purposes of article 13 of the Town and Country Planning General Development Order 1988 (notification of mineral applications) before the date of the coming into force of this Order, shall be treated as if it had been given for the purposes of article 16 of this Order by the Coal Authority on or after that date; and, in relation to a particular application for planning permission made before 31st October 1994, the mineral planning authority are not required to notify the Coal Authority, before determining the application, if they have already notified the British Coal Corporation that that application has been made.

(4) The relevant provisions of the Town and Country Planning General Development Order 1988, in the form in which they were in force immediately before 27th July 1992, shall continue to apply with respect to applications made under section 64 of the Act (applications to determine whether planning permission required) before 27th July 1992.

(5) The relevant provisions of the Town and Country Planning General Development Order 1988, in the form in which they were in force immediately before 27th July 1992, shall continue to apply with respect to applications for established use certificates made under section 192 of the Act (applications for established use certificates), as originally enacted, before 27th July 1992.

SCHEDULE 1 Articles 5, 22 and 24

PART 1: TOWN AND COUNTRY PLANNING ACT 1990

Letter to be sent by a local planning authority when they receive an application for planning permission or for a certificate of lawful use or development.

Thank you for your application dated ....

which I received on ....

I am still examining your application form and the accompanying plans and documents to see whether they comply with the law.*

If I find that your application is invalid because it does not comply with the statutory requirements then I shall write to you again as soon as I can.*

If, by (*insert date at end of period of eight weeks beginning with the date when the application was received*) .

- you have not been told that your application is invalid; or
- you have not been told that your fee cheque has been dishonoured; or
- you have not been given a decision in writing; or
- you have not agreed in writing to extend the period in which the decision may be given, then you can appeal to the Secretary of State for the Environment/Wales* under section 78/ section 195* of the Town and Country Planning Act 1990. You should appeal within six months and you must use a form which you can get from the Planning Inspectorate at Tollgate House, Houlton Street, Bristol BS2 9DJ/Cathays Park, Cardiff CF1 3NQ*.

This does not apply if your application has already been referred to the Secretary of State for the Environment/Wales*.

*Delete where inappropriate

PART 2: TOWN AND COUNTRY PLANNING ACT 1990

Notification to be sent to an applicant when a local planning authority refuse planning permission or grant it subject to conditions (*To be endorsed on notices of decision*)

Appeals to the Secretary of State

- If you are aggrieved by the decision of your local planning authority to refuse permission for the proposed development or to grant it subject to conditions, then you can appeal to the First Secretary of State National Assembly for Wales* under section 78 of the Town and Country Planning Act 1990.
- If you want to appeal, then you must do so within three months of the date of this notice, using a form which you can get from the Planning Inspectorate at Customer Support Unit, Room 3/15 Eagle Wing, Temple Quay House, 2 The Square, Temple Quay, Bristol BS1 6PN/Cathays Park, Cardiff, CF1 3NQ*.
- The Secretary of State can allow a longer period for giving notice of an appeal, but he will not normally be prepared to use this power unless there are special circumstances which excuse the delay in giving notice of appeal.
- The Secretary of State need not consider an appeal if it seems to him that the local planning authority could not have granted planning permission for the proposed development or could not have granted it without the conditions they imposed, having regard to the statutory requirements, to the provisions of any development order and to any directions given under a development order.
- In practice, the Secretary of State does not refuse to consider appeals solely because the local planning authority based their decision on a direction given by him.

Purchase Notices

- If either the local planning authority or the First Secretary of State National Assembly for Wales* refuses permission to develop land or grants it subject to conditions, the owner may claim that he can neither put the land to a reasonably beneficial use in its existing state nor render the land capable of a reasonably beneficial use by the carrying out of any development which has been or would be permitted.
- In these circumstances, the owner may serve a purchase notice on the Council (District Council, London Borough Council or Common Council of the City of London in county or County Borough in Wales) in whose area the land is situated. This notice will require the Council to purchase his interest in the land in accordance with the provisions of Part VI of the Town and Country Planning Act 1990.

*Delete where inappropriate.

SCHEDULE 2 Articles 6, 7 and 9

PART 1: TOWN AND COUNTRY PLANNING (GENERAL DEVELOPMENT PROCEDURE) ORDER 1995

NOTICE UNDER ARTICLE 6 OF APPLICATION FOR PLANNING PERMISSION

(to be published in a newspaper or to be served on an owner or a tenant**)*

Proposed development at *(a)* . . . .

I give notice that *(b)* . . . .

is applying to the *(c)*. . . . . Council

for planning permission to *(d)*. . . . .

Any owner* of the land or tenant** who wishes to make representations about this application should write to the Council at *(e)*. . . . .

by *(f)*. . . . .

* 'owner' means a person having a freehold interest or a leasehold interest the unexpired term of which is not less than seven years, or, in the case of development consisting of the winning or working of minerals, a person entitled to an interest in a mineral in the land (other than oil, gas, coal, gold or silver).

** 'tenant' means a tenant of an agricultural holding any part of which is comprised in the land.

Signed . . . .

†On behalf of . . . .

Date . . . .

Statement of owners' rights

The grant of planning permission does not affect owners' rights to retain or dispose of their property, unless there is some provision to the contrary in an agreement or in a lease.

Statement of agricultural tenants' rights

The grant of planning permission for non-agricultural development may affect agricultural tenants' security of tenure.

†delete where inappropriate

Insert:

(a) address or location of the proposed development

(b) applicant's name

(c) name of Council

(d) description of the proposed development

(e) address of the Council

(f) date giving a period of 21 days beginning with the date of service, or 14 days beginning with the date of publication, of the notice (as the case may be)

TOWN AND COUNTRY PLANNING (GENERAL DEVELOPMENT PROCEDURE) ORDER 1995

NOTICE UNDER ARTICLE 6 OF APPLICATION FOR PLANNING PERMISSION

(to be posted in the case of an application for planning permission for development consisting of the winning and working of minerals by underground operations (in addition to the service or publication of any other requisite notices in this Schedule))

Proposed development at *(a)* . . . .
I give notice that *(b)* . . . .
is applying to the *(c)*. . . . . Council
for planning permission to *(d)*. . . . .
Members of the public may inspect copies of:

- the application
- the plans
- and other documents submitted with it

at *(e)* . . . .
during all reasonable hours until *(f)* . . . .
Anyone who wishes to make representations about this application should write to the Council at *(g)*
. . . . by *(f)* . . . .

Signed . . . .
†On behalf of . . . .
Date. . . . .

†Delete where inappropriate

Insert:

(a) address or location of the proposed development
(b) applicant's name
(c) name of Council
(d) description of the proposed development
(e) address at which the application may be inspected (the applicant is responsible for making the application available for inspection within the area of the local planning authority)
(f) date giving a period of 21 days, beginning with the date when the notice is posted
(g) address of Council

TOWN AND COUNTRY PLANNING (GENERAL DEVELOPMENT PROCEDURE) ORDER 1995

NOTICE UNDER ARTICLES 6 AND 9(1) OF APPEAL

(to be published in a newspaper or to be served on an owner or a tenant**)*. . . . .

Proposed development at *(a)* . . . .

I give notice that *(b)* . . . .

having applied to the *(c)* . . . . Council

to *(d)*. . . . .

is appealing to the Secretary of State for the Environment/Secretary of State for Wales†

against the decision of the Council†

on the failure of the Council to give notice of a decision†

Any owner* of the land or tenant** who wishes to make representations about this appeal should write to the First Secretary of State/National Assembly for Wales† at Customer Support Unit, Room 3/15 Eagle Wing, Temple Quay House, 2 The Square, Temple Quay, Bristol BS1 6PN/Cathays Park, Cardiff, CF1 3NQ, by *(e)* . . . .

* 'owner' means a person having a freehold interest or a leasehold interest the unexpired term of which is not less than seven years, or, in the case of development consisting of the winning or working of minerals, a person entitled to an interest in a mineral in the land (other than oil, gas, coal, gold or silver).

** 'tenant' means a tenant of an agricultural holding any part of which is comprised in the land.

Signed . . . .

†On behalf of . . . .

Date. . . . .

Statement of owners' rights

The grant of planning permission does not affect owners' rights to retain or dispose of their property, unless there is some provision to the contrary in an agreement or in a lease.

Statement of agricultural tenants' rights

The grant of planning permission for non-agricultural development may affect agricultural tenants' security of tenure.

†delete where inappropriate

Insert:

(a) address or location of the proposed development

(b) applicant's name

(c) name of Council

(d) description of the proposed development

(e) date giving a period of 21 days beginning with the date of service, or 14 days beginning with the date of publication, of the notice (as the case may be)

TOWN AND COUNTRY PLANNING (GENERAL DEVELOPMENT PROCEDURE) ORDER 1995

NOTICE UNDER ARTICLES 6 AND 9(1) OF APPEAL

(to be posted in the case of an application for planning permission for development consisting of the winning and working of minerals by underground operations (in addition to the service or publication of any other requisite notices in this Schedule))

Proposed development at *(a)* . . . .
I give notice that *(b)* . . . .
having applied to the *(c)* . . . . Council
to *(d)*. . . . .
is appealing to the Secretary of State for the Environment/Secretary of State for Wales*
against the decision of the Council*
on the failure of the Council to give notice of a decision*

Members of the public may inspect copies of:

- the application
- the plans
- and other documents submitted with it

at *(e)* . . . . during all reasonable hours until *(f)* . . . .

Anyone who wishes to make representations about this appeal should write to the First Secretary of State/National Assembly for Wales* at Customer Support Unit, Room 3/15 Eagle Wing, Temple Quay House, 2 The Square, Temple Quay, Bristol BS1 6PN/Cathays Park, Cardiff, CF1 3NQ by *(f)* . . . .

Signed . . . .
*On behalf of . . . .
Date. . . . .

*delete where inappropriate

Insert:

(a) address or location of the proposed development
(b) applicant's name
(c) name of Council
(d) description of the proposed development
(e) address of Council
(f) date giving a period of 21 days, beginning with the date when the notice is posted

PART 2: TOWN AND COUNTRY PLANNING (GENERAL DEVELOPMENT PROCEDURE) ORDER 1995

CERTIFICATE UNDER ARTICLE 7

Certificate A*(a)*
I certify that:

on the day 21 days before the date of the accompanying application/appeal* nobody, except the applicant/appellant*, was the owner*(b)* of any part of the land to which the application/appeal* relates.

Signed . . . .
*On behalf of . . . .
Date. . . . .

*delete where inappropriate

(a) This Certificate is for use with applications and appeals for planning permission (articles 7 and 9(1) of the Order). One of Certificates A, B, C or D (or the appropriate certificate in the case of certain minerals applications) must be completed, together with the Agricultural Holdings Certificate.

(b) 'owner' means a person having a freehold interest or a leasehold interest the unexpired term of which is not less than seven years, or, in the case of development consisting of the winning and working of minerals, a person entitled to an interest in a mineral in the land (other than oil, gas, coal, gold or silver).

TOWN AND COUNTRY PLANNING (GENERAL DEVELOPMENT PROCEDURE) ORDER 1995

CERTIFICATE UNDER ARTICLE 7

Certificate B*(a)*

I certify that:

I have/The applicant has/The appellant has* given the requisite notice to everyone else who, on the day 21 days before the date of the accompanying application/appeal*, was the owner*(b)* of any part of the land to which the application/appeal* relates, as listed below.

Owner's *(b)* name	Address at which notice was served	Date on which notice was served

Signed . . . .
*On behalf of . . . .
Date. . . . .

*delete where inappropriate

(a) This Certificate is for use with applications and appeals for planning permission (articles 7 and 9(1) of the Order). One of Certificates A, B, C or D (or the appropriate certificate in the case of certain minerals applications) must be completed, together with the Agricultural Holdings Certificate.

(b) 'owner' means a person having a freehold interest or a leasehold interest the unexpired term of which is not less than seven years, or, in the case of development consisting of the winning and working of minerals, a person entitted to an interest in a mineral in the land (other than oil, gas, coal, gold or silver).

TOWN AND COUNTRY PLANNING (GENERAL DEVELOPMENT PROCEDURE) ORDER 1995

CERTIFICATE UNDER ARTICLE 7

Certificate C*(a)*

I certify that:

- I/The applicant/The appellant* cannot issue a Certificate A or B in respect of the accompanying application/appeal*.
- I have/The applicant has/The appellant has* given the requisite notice to the persons specified below, being persons who on the day 21 days before the date of the application/ appeal*, were owners*(b)* of any part of the land to which the application/appeal* relates.

Owner's*(b)* name	Address at which notice was served	Date on which notice was served

- I have/The applicant has/The appellant has* taken all reasonable steps open to me/him/her* to find out the names and addresses of the other owners*(b)* of the land, or of a part of it, but have/has* been unable to do so. These steps were as follows:
  (c) ....
  ....
- Notice of the application/appeal*, as attached to this Certificate, has been published in the *(d)* ....
  on *(e)* ....

Signed ....
*On behalf of ....
Date......................................

*delete where inappropriate

(a) This Certificate is for use with applications and appeals for planning permission (articles 7 and 9(1) of the Order). One of Certificates A, B, C or D (or the appropriate certificate in the case of certain minerals applications) must be completed, together with the Agricultural Holdings Certificate.

(b) 'owner' means a person having a freehold interest or a leasehold interest the unexpired term of which is not less than seven years, or, in the case of development consisting of the winning and working of minerals, a person entitled to an interest in a mineral in the land (other than oil, gas, coal, gold or silver).

Insert:

(c) description of steps taken

(d) name of newspaper circulating in the area where the land is situated

(e) date of publication (which must be not earlier than the day 21 days before the date of the application or appeal)

TOWN AND COUNTRY PLANNING (GENERAL DEVELOPMENT PROCEDURE) ORDER 1995

CERTIFICATE UNDER ARTICLE 7

Certificate D(a)
I certify that:

- I/The applicant/The appellant* cannot issue a Certificate A in respect of the accompanying application/appeal*.
- I/The applicant/The appellant* have/has* taken all reasonable steps open to me/him/her* to find out the names and addresses of everyone else who, on the day 21 days before the date of the application/appeal*, was the owner*(b)* of any part of the land to which the application/appeal* relates, but have/has* been unable to do so.
  These steps were as follows:
  (c) . . . .

  . . . .
- Notice of the application/appeal*, as attached to this certificate, has been published in the *(d)* . . . .
  on *(e)* . . . .

Signed . . . .
*On behalf of . . . .
Date. . . . .

*delete where inappropriate

(a) This Certificate is for use with applications and appeals for planning permission (articles 7 and 9(1) of the Order). One of Certificates A, B, C or D (or the appropriate certificate in the case of certain minerals applications) must be completed, together with the Agricultural Holdings Certificate.

(b) 'owner' means a person having a freehold interest or a leasehold interest the unexpired term of which is not less than seven years, or, in the case of development consisting of the winning and working of minerals, a person entitled to an interest in a mineral in the land (other than oil, gas, coal, gold or silver).

Insert:
(c) description of steps taken
(d) name of newspaper circulating in the area where the land is situated
(e) date of publication (which must be not earlier than the day 21 days before the date of the application or appeal)

TOWN AND COUNTRY PLANNING (GENERAL DEVELOPMENT PROCEDURE) ORDER 1995

CERTIFICATE UNDER ARTICLE 7

Agricultural Holdings Certificate *(a)*

Whichever is appropriate of the following alternatives must form part of Certificates A, B, C or D. If the applicant is the sole agricultural tenant he or she must delete the first alternative and insert 'not applicable' as the information required by the second alternative.

• None of the land to which the application/appeal relates is, or is part of, an agricultural holding.

or

• I have/The applicant has/The appellant has given the requisite notice to every person other than my/him/her* self who, on the day 21 days before the date of the application/ appeal*, was a tenant of an agricultural holding on all or part of the land to which the application/appeal* relates, as follows:

Tenant's name	Address at which notice was served	Date on which notice was served

Signed.......................................

*On behalf of ....

Date...

*delete where inappropriate

(a) This Certificate is for use with applications and appeals for planning permission (articles 7 and 9(1) of the Order). One of Certificates A, B, C or D (or the appropriate certificate in the case of certain minerals applications) must be completed together with the Agricultural Holdings Certificate.

TOWN AND COUNTRY PLANNING (GENERAL DEVELOPMENT PROCEDURE) ORDER 1995

CERTIFICATE UNDER ARTICLE 7

(for use with applications and appeals for planning permission for development consisting of the winning and working of minerals by underground operations)

I certify that:

- I have/The applicant has/The appellant has* given the requisite notice to the persons specified below being persons who, on the day 21 days before the date of the accompanying application/ appeal, were owners*(a)* of any part of the land to which the application/appeal relates.

Owner's *(a)* name	Address at which notice was served	Date on which notice was served

- There is no person (other than me/the applicant/the appellant*) who, on the day 21 days before the date of the accompanying application/appeal*, was the owner*(a)* of any part of the land to which this application/appeal* relates, whom I/the applicant/ the appellant* know/s* to be such a person and whose name and address is known to me/the applicant/the appellant* but to whom I have/the applicant/the appellant has* not given the requisite notice.
- I have/The applicant/The appellant has* posted the requisite notice, sited and displayed in such a way as to be easily visible and legible by members of the public, in at least one place in every parish or community within which there is situated any part of the land to which the accompanying application/appeal* relates, as listed below.

Parish/Community	Location of notice	Date posted

- Save as specified below* this/these* notice/s* was/were* left in position for not less than seven days in the period of 21 days immediately preceding the making of the application/ appeal*.

• The following notice/s was/were*, however, left in position for less than seven days in the period of not more than 21 days immediately preceding the making of the application/appeal*.

Parish/Community	Location of notice	Date posted

This happened because it/they* was/were* removed/obscured/defaced* before seven days had passed during the period of 21 days mentioned above. This was not my/the applicant's/ the appellant's* fault or intent.

I/The applicant/The appellant* took the following steps to protect and replace the notice:

(b) ....

....

- Notice of the application/appeal*, as attached to this certificate, has been published in the

(c) ....

on *(d)* ....

Agricultural Holdings Certificate

Whichever is appropriate of the following alternatives must form part of this certificate. If the applicant is the sole agricultural tenant he or she must delete the first alternative and insert 'not applicable' as the information required by the second alternative.

- None of the land to which the application/appeal* relates is, or is part of, an agricultural holding.

or

- I have/The applicant has/The appellant has* given the requisite notice to every person other than my/him/her* self who, on the day 21 days before the date of the application/ appeal*, was a tenant of an agricultural holding on all or part of the land to which the application/appeal* relates, as follows:

Tenant's name	Address at which notice was served	Date on which notice was served

Signed.......................................
*On behalf of...............................
Date...

*delete where inappropriate

(a) 'owner' means a person having a freehold interest or a leasehold interest the unexpired term of which is not less than seven years or a person entitled to an interest in a mineral in the land (other than oil, gas, coal, gold or silver).

Insert:

(b) description of steps taken

(c) name of newspaper circulating in the area where the land is situated

(d) date of publication (which must be not earlier than the day 21 days before the date of the application or appeal)

ARTICLE 8 **SCHEDULE 3**

TOWN AND COUNTRY PLANNING (GENERAL DEVELOPMENT PROCEDURE) ORDER 1995

NOTICE UNDER ARTICLE 8

(to be published in a newspaper, displayed on or near the site, or served on owners and/or occupiers of adjoining land)

Proposed development at *(a)* . . . .
I give notice that *(b)* . . . .
is applying to the *(c)*. . . . . Council
for planning permission to *(d)*. . . . .
The proposed development does not accord with the provisions of the development plan in force in the area in which the land to which the application relates is situated* Members of the public may inspect copies of:

- the application
- the plans
- and other documents submitted with it

at *(e)* . . . . during
all reasonable hours until *(f)* . . . .
Anyone who wishes to make representations about this application should write to the Council at
(g) . . . .
. . . . by *(f)* . . . .

Signed . . . .
. . . .
(Council's authorised officer)
On behalf of. . . . . Council
Date. . . . .

*delete where inappropriate

Insert:

(a) address or location of the proposed development
(b) applicant's name
(c) name of Council
(d) description of the proposed development
(e) address at which the application may be inspected
(f) date giving a period of 21 days, beginning with the date when the notice is first displayed on or near the site or served on an owner and/or occupier of adjoining land, or a period of 14 days, beginning with the date when the notice is published in a newspaper (as the case may be)
(g) address of Council

NOTICE OF APPLICATION FOR PLANNING PERMISSION

TOWN AND COUNTRY PLANNING (GENERAL DEVELOPMENT PROCEDURE) ORDER 1995

NOTICE UNDER ARTICLE 8 OF APPLICATION FOR PLANNING PERMISSION ACCOMPANIED BY AN ENVIRONMENTAL STATEMENT

(to be published in a newspaper and displayed on or near the site)

Proposed development at *(a)*. . . . .

I give notice that *(b)* . . . .

is applying to the *(c)*. . . . . Council

for planning permission to *(d)*. . . . .

and that the application is accompanied by an environmental statement

The proposed development does not accord with the provisions of the development plan in force in the area in which the land to which the application relates is situated*

Members of the public may inspect copies of:

- the application
- the plans
- the environmental statement
- and other documents submitted with the application

at *(e)*. . . . . during

all reasonable hours until *(f)* . . . .

Members of the public may obtain copies of the environmental statement from *(g)* . . . .

. . . .

so long as stocks last, at a charge of *(h)*. . . . .

Anyone who wishes to make representations about this application should write to the Council at *(i)* . . . .

. . . . by *(f)* . . . .

Signed. . . . .

. . . .

(Council's authorised officer)

On behalf of. . . . . Council

Date. . . . .

*delete where inappropriate

Insert:

(a) address or location of the proposed development
(b) applicant's name
(c) name of Council
(d) description of the proposed development
(e) address at which the application may be inspected
(f) date giving a period of 21 days, beginning with the date when the notice is first displayed on or near the site, or a period of 14 days, beginning with the date when the notice is published in a newspaper (as the case may be)
(g) address from where copies of the environmental statement may be obtained (whether or not the same as *(e)*)
(h) amount of charge, if any
(i) address of Council

SCHEDULE 4 **Article 24**

TOWN AND COUNTRY PLANNING ACT 1990: SECTIONS 191 AND 192 (AS AMENDED BY SECTION 10 OF THE PLANNING AND COMPENSATION ACT 1991)

TOWN AND COUNTRY PLANNING (GENERAL DEVELOPMENT PROCEDURE) ORDER 1995: ARTICLE 24

CERTIFICATE OF LAWFUL USE OR DEVELOPMENT

The *(a)* . . . . Council
hereby certify that on *(b)* . . . . the use*/operations*/matter* described in the First Schedule to this certificate in respect of the land specified in the Second Schedule to this certificate and edged*/hatched*/ coloured* *(c)* . . . . on the plan attached to this certificate, was*/were*/would have been* lawful within the meaning of section 191 of the Town and Country Planning Act 1990 (as amended), for the following reason(s):

. . . .

. . . .

Signed . . . . (Council's authorised officer)
On behalf of *(a)*. . . . . Council
Date . . . .
First Schedule
(d)
Second Schedule
(e)

Notes

1 This certificate is issued solely for the purpose of section 191*/192* of the Town and Country Planning Act 1990 (as amended).

2 It certifies that the use*/operations*/matter* specified in the First Schedule taking place on the land described in the Second Schedule was*/were*/would have been* lawful, on the specified date and, thus, was not*/were not*/would not have been* liable to enforcement action under section 172 of the 1990 Act on that date.

3 This certificate applies only to the extent of the use*/operations*/matter* described in the First Schedule and to the land specified in the Second Schedule and identified on the attached plan. Any use*/operations*/matter* which is*/are* materially different from that*/those* described or which relate/s* to other land may render the owner or occupier liable to enforcement action.

*4 The effect of the certificate is also qualified by the proviso in section 192(4) of the 1990 Act, as amended, which states that the lawfulness of a described use or operation is only conclusively presumed where there has been no material change, before the use is instituted or the operations begun, in any of the matters relevant to determining such lawfulness.

*delete where inappropriate

Insert:
(a) name of Council
(b) date of application to the Council
(c) colour used on the plan
(d) full description of use, operations or other matter, if necessary, by reference to details in the application or submitted plans, including a reference to the use class, if any, specified in an order under section 55(2)(f) of the 1990 Act, within which the certificated use falls
(e) address or location of the site

APPENDIX 5

The metrication of planning law

From October 1, 1995, metric units became the primary system of measurement for the conduct of public business in the United Kingdom. This is the effect of the Unit of Measurement Regulations 1995 (S.I. 1995/1804), which implements EEC Council Directive 80/181 (as amended by Council Directive 85/1 and 89/617). The Directive provides for the phasing out of the use of imperial measurements and requires Member States to adopt metric units as the primary system of measurement for 'economic, public health, public safety and administrative purposes'.

The Regulations impact particularly on:

(i) primary and secondary legislation, including private and local Act and byelaws;
(ii) documents (including documents having legal effect), such as court orders, consents, authorisations, circulars and guidance notes;
(iii) invitations to tender and contracts, including for public purchasing.

With certain exceptions, the use of imperial measurements after October 1, 1995, render liable to legal challenge, expressions of quantity in *future* legislation and documentation, etc. on the ground of inconsistency with the Units of Measurement Directive. Exceptions to this, where imperial units of measurement remain available for primary use *after* October 1, 1995, include the use of 'mile, yard, foot and inch for road traffic signs and for related distance and speed measurement', and 'acre' for land registration.

After October 1, 1995, public sector organisations can continue to use imperial units, but only as supplementary indications of quantity. Fortunately, metric measurements are already used in the new General Permitted Development Order and the General Development Procedure Order.

Where references to imperial units are contained in legislation and documents made before October 1, 1995, and having legal effect after that date, the Regulations provide for the conversion of the imperial quantities to metric.

Applications for planning permission submitted after 30 September, 1995, therefore, should refer to metric units. Where an application is submitted in imperial units, the local planning authority may either ask the applicant to resubmit in metric units or grant planning permission for the metric equivalent.

For the benefit of readers the following is an extract from the conversion table given in the above Regulations:

Relevant imperial unit	*Corresponding metric unit*	*Metric equivalent*
	Length	
inch	centimetre	2.54 centimeters
hand	metre	0.1016 meters
foot	metre	0.3048 meters
yard	metre	0.9144 meters
fathom	metre	1.8288 meters
chain	metre	20.1168 meters
furlong	kilometre	0.201168 kilometers
mile	kilometre	1.609344 kilometers
nautical mile (UK)	metre	1852 meters
	Area	
square inch	square centimetre	6.4516 square centimetres
square foot	square metre	0.09290304 square metres
square yard	square metre	0.83612736 square metres
rood	square metre	1011.7141056 square metres
acre	square metre	4046.8564224 square metres
square mile	square kilometre	2.589988110336 square kilometres

INDEX